Forensic Science

Forensic Science

Volume 3

Napoleon's death—Y chromosome analysis
Appendixes
Indexes

Edited by

Ayn Embar-Seddon
Capella University

Allan D. Pass
National Behavioral Science Consultants

Salem Press, Inc.
Pasadena, California   Hackensack, New Jersey

Editorial Director: Christina J. Moose

Development Editor: R. Kent Rasmussen   *Layout:* Mary Overell

Project Editor: Judy Selhorst   *Graphics and Design:* James Hutson

Acquisitions Editor: Mark Rehn   *Photo Editor:* Cynthia Breslin Beres

Production Editor: Joyce I. Buchea   *Editorial Assistant:* Dana Garey

Cover photo: ©iStockphoto.com/Stefan Klein

Library of Congress Cataloging-in-Publication Data

Forensic science / edited by Ayn Embar-Seddon, Allan D. Pass.
    p. cm.
Includes bibliographical references and index.
    ISBN 978-1-58765-423-7 (set : alk. paper) — ISBN 978-1-58765-424-4 (vol. 1 : alk. paper) — ISBN 978-1-58765-425-1 (vol. 2 : alk. paper) — ISBN 978-1-58765-426-8 (vol. 3 : alk. paper) 1. Forensic sciences. I. Embar-Seddon, Ayn. II. Pass, Allan D.

HV8073.F5837 2009
363.25—dc22

2008030674

Contents

Contents

Complete List of Contents

Volume 1

Volume 2

Volume 3

Napoleon's death

Date: May 5, 1821

The Event: After the French emperor Napoleon I was defeated by the British at the Battle of Waterloo in 1815, he was exiled to the remote island of Saint Helena, a British possession in the South Atlantic. He arrived on the island on October 17, 1815, and died there after less than six years of captivity at the age of fifty-one under circumstances that are still debated.

Significance: The question of whether Napoleon I died from natural causes or from criminal action, as some allege, has been an ongoing source of controversy among historians. Forensic science has played a small role in the examination of the available evidence in this case.

Physical as well as psychosomatic reasons could account for Napoleon I's deteriorating health condition some two years after the exiled former French emperor arrived to live on the desolate island of Saint Helena. Napoleon's father died from pyloric (lower stomach) cancer, so genetics may also have played a role. It is true, however, that more than one person may have had reasons to want the former emperor out of the way; this fact has lent credence to theories that Napoleon's cause of death may have been poisoning.

Sickness

By 1817, Napoleon was intermittently complaining of a number of physical problems, including a pain in his stomach, discomfort in his spleen or kidneys, frequent heavy sweating, nausea and vomiting, and weariness. The several British doctors who examined him, as well as the French-Corsican physician Napoleon's family eventually sent to care for him, Francesco Antommarchi, variously diagnosed chronic hepatitis, stomach cancer, an ulcerated stomach lining, and other ailments. The doctors subjected the often unwilling patient to such standard remedies of the time as emetics and bleeding.

Some of the physicians who were more astute than others suggested that Napoleon's lack of physical exercise and isolation were contributory causes; they encouraged Napoleon's predilection for horse riding and gardening. Indeed, when Napoleon felt well enough to engage in these activities, he became more energized. His seeming remission would then end, however, or he would become too depressed to want to engage in any activities and would instead spend long hours dozing or sleeping. He took part in socializing with the members of his dwindling entourage only intermittently.

By all accounts, Napoleon was very sensitive to his surroundings—his remoteness from family, Saint Helena's unhealthy climate, his rat-infested residence at Longwood House, and especially the demeaning attitude of his captors. The British governor of Saint Helena, Sir Hudson Lowe, insisted on calling him "General Bonaparte" instead of "Emperor," adding to Napoleon's unhappiness. In addition, the governor ordered that a British officer check on Napoleon daily to make sure he did not escape, despite the large British garrison and strong naval presence around the island that made flight practically impossible. Perhaps the most depressing for Napoleon was the hopelessness of his situation—that he would never be allowed to return to where he belonged.

Death

For political reasons, the British governor refused to accept any diagnosis of Napoleon's condition that would suggest that the former emperor had been mistreated in any way or even that he was adversely affected by the island's inclement climate. By 1821, however, Napoleon's condition had clearly deteriorated significantly. Dr. Antommarchi as well as the approximately half dozen British doctors who had examined the prisoner (or, because of Napoleon's refusal, had conferred with others who had seen him) eventually agreed with Napoleon's own prediction, voiced in December, 1820, that there was "no more oil in the lamp."

The end came in May, 1821. Napoleon had been confined to bed for some days, existing mainly on arrowroot and gentian, occasionally taking a sip of flavored water or a spoonful of wine mixed with water, and dozing much of the time. His mind began to wander, and he finally became delirious, repeating certain inarticulate words that have been variously interpreted. He died at 5:49 P.M. on the afternoon of May 5, surrounded by several members of his much-diminished entourage.

Autopsy

The autopsy was performed by Antommarchi, presumably because he was more experienced in postmortems than the six British physicians who attended the process (only five signed the autopsy report because the sixth was considered too junior in rank). The doctors agreed that the pylorus was surrounded by tumors and that Napoleon's ulcers were conceivably cancerous and had eaten into the stomach, but they disagreed on the condition of the liver—that is, on whether or not chronic hepatitis was also present. The doctors did not consider the possibility that physician error in Napoleon's treatment could have led to his death. Napoleon had been treated with large doses of almond-flavored calomel, a mercurial chloride used as a purgative, and this could have been a contributing factor in his death, especially if he also ingested arsenic in whatever form. Saint Helena's British governor favored an autopsy report that prioritized cancer as the leading cause of death.

The theory that Napoleon died from arsenic poisoning surfaced much later, when samples of his hair, which had been deeded to some of his

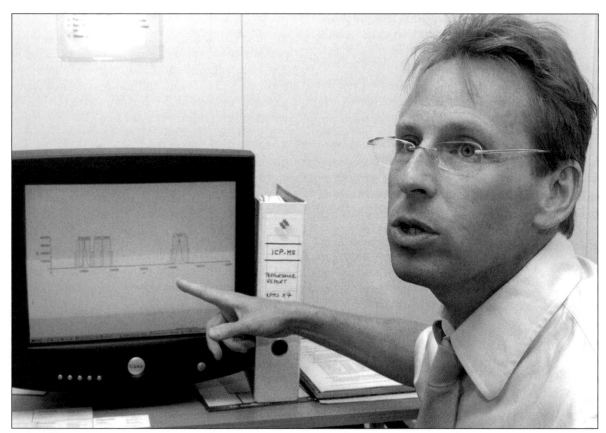

A toxicologist at France's University of Strasbourg shows on a computer the high levels of arsenic found in a sample of the hair of French emperor Napoleon I. This evidence gives weight to the theory that Napoleon was poisoned. *(AP/Wide World Photos)*

entourage and family members, were examined microscopically and found to contain excessively high levels of arsenic (a substance readily available at Longwood House, where it was used to keep the large rat population under control). In addition, when Napoleon's body was moved from Saint Helena to Paris, France, in 1840, it was found to be in nearly perfect condition even though it had not been embalmed; this preservation and the fact that the body was also hairless both pointed to arsenic poisoning.

The leading suspect for administering the poison to Napoleon in small doses over time was the former emperor's chief chamberlain, Count Charles-Tristan de Montholon. Montholon had some connection with the count of Artois, later France's King Charles X, who may have feared a comeback and second coup d'état by the former leader. Montholon was also a major beneficiary of Napoleon's will; thus, if Napoleon's intention to leave the count two million francs was clear at an early date, Montholon had a financial interest in Napoleon's early demise. Another theory, however, is that Montholon did administer the poison to Napoleon in small doses, mixed with the former emperor's wine, to which he had access, but his intent was not to kill his benefactor; rather, he wanted to induce sufficient ill health for Napoleon to be allowed to return to his kin in Europe.

Given that Napoleon I's legend as a leader who has had few equals in the history of the world is well established, the French government has not been concerned with debates regarding his possible cause of death. Although it is possible that the techniques of modern forensic science could shed light on this issue, French authorities have shown little inclination to allow researchers to open the former emperor's coffin to subject his body to the tests that would be necessary to gather new evidence.

Peter B. Heller

Further Reading

Asprey, Robert. *The Reign of Napoleon Bonaparte*. New York: Basic Books, 2001. Pinpoints Napoleon's terminal illness as beginning on March 17, 1821.

Hibbert, Christopher. *Napoleon: His Wives and Women*. New York: W. W. Norton, 2002. Suggests that the arsenic found in Napoleon's body may have originated from a coloring in wallpaper containing copper arsenite and widely used at that time.

Johnson, Paul. *Napoleon*. New York: Viking Penguin, 2002. Brief biography is noncommittal about the cause of Napoleon's death.

McLynn, Frank. *Napoleon: A Biography*. 1997. Reprint. New York: Arcade, 2002. Comprehensive work on the emperor's life includes discussion of the politicization of Napoleon's autopsy report.

Weider, Ben, and Sten Forshufvud. *Assassination at St. Helena Revisited*. Rev. ed. New York: John Wiley & Sons, 1995. Interesting work by the two most persistent supporters of the thesis that Napoleon was deliberately murdered, with small doses of arsenic, by the one who stood to gain most from the crime, Charles de Montholon.

See also: Ancient criminal cases and mysteries; Arsenic; Autopsies; Beethoven's death; Decomposition of bodies; Document examination; Food poisoning; Hair analysis; Mummification; Taylor exhumation.

Narcotics

Definition: Substances with a stuporous effect, used in low doses to relieve moderate to severe pain, suppress coughing, and control diarrhea.

Significance: Although narcotics have many legal uses, these drugs are also widely abused. Law-enforcement agencies devote many of their resources to the investigation of crimes associated with the illegal manufacture, sale, and use of narcotics.

The word "narcotic" is derived from the Greek word *narkitos*, which means numbing. Narcotics are efficient pain reducers and cough suppressants. Short-term effects of narcotics include drowsiness, dry mouth, nausea, vomiting, and sweating. The narcotic drug class includes both opiates (drugs that are derived from opium) and opioids (manufactured drugs that produce the same effects as opiates). Opiate narcotics include codeine, oxycodone, and dihydrocodeine. Examples of opioid narcotics include meperidine (brand name Demerol), dextropropoxyphene (Darvon), and fentanyl.

Opium has been used for medicinal purposes for more than nine thousand years. The active substance in opium, called morphine, was first isolated in 1803. During the nineteenth century, opium and morphine preparations were considered "wonder drugs." They provided relief from diarrhea caused by two of the major killers of that era: cholera and dysentery. In 1874, heroin was synthesized from morphine for the first time. It quickly became a major ingredient in many tonics and medicines. In the United States, the Harrison Narcotic Drug Act went into effect in 1914; this law regulated the manufacturing and distribution of heroin and other drugs.

The opium poppy plant is the source of all opium, and opium is the source of all opiate drugs (morphine, heroin, codeine, and others). Although opium poppies grow wild in many areas of the world, most illicit cultivation of these plants occurs in Mexico, South America, and the areas known as the Golden Crescent (Pakistan, Afghanistan, and Iran) and the Golden Triangle (Myanmar, Laos, and Thailand). The roots of the opium poppy produce opium, most of which accumulates in the seed pod. Opium farmers make cuts on the seed pods so that the milky opium bleeds out. Once this opium resin hardens, it can be collected. A typical opium farm can yield nine to twenty pounds of opium per acre.

Most heroin users inject the drug, but it can also be smoked or snorted. Drug users who inject heroin risk becoming infected with hepatitis C or the human immunodeficiency virus (HIV) if they share needles or other drug paraphernalia. Many other narcotics, such as codeine and oxycodone, are available in pill form. Some narcotics, such as fentanyl, are administered through patches that are placed on the skin.

Megan N. Bottegal

Further Reading

Hicks, John. *Drug Addiction: "No Way I'm an Addict."* Brookfield, Conn.: Millbrook Press, 1997.

Laci, Miklos. *Illegal Drugs: America's Anguish.* Detroit: Thomson/Gale, 2004.

Sonder, Ben. *All About Heroin.* New York: Franklin Watts, 2002.

See also: Canine substance detection; Controlled Substances Act of 1970; Drug abuse and dependence; Drug classification; Drug Enforcement Administration, U.S.; Drug paraphernalia; Harrison Narcotic Drug Act of 1914; Opioids; Psychotropic drugs.

National Church Arson Task Force

Date: Formed in June, 1996

Identification: Federal organization established to coordinate federal, state, and local law-enforcement agencies in response to a dramatic increase in arson cases involving churches attended by African Americans.

Significance: The coordination of church arson investigations among law-enforcement agencies made investigations of church arson cases more efficient.

President Bill Clinton called for the forming of the National Church Arson Task Force (NCATF) in June, 1996. The agency was created within the Bureau of Alcohol, Tobacco, Firearms and Explosives under the umbrella of the U.S. Department of Justice. Congress assisted the president's efforts by passing the Church Arson Prevention Act of 1996. This act gave prosecutors more power to prosecute church arson cases and increased penalties for the crime, which included fines, prison sentences, and the death penalty. The act also made the collection of hate crime data part of the federal government's Uniform Crime Reports, a move that improved the tracking of bias-motivated crimes.

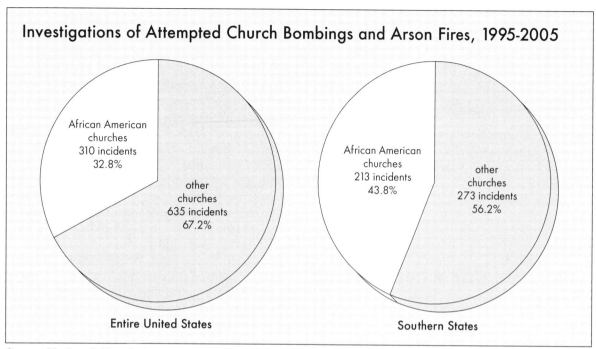

Source: National Church Arson Task Force, 2008. "Churches" include all houses of worship.

During the 1990's, the number of arson attacks targeting African American churches increased, particularly in the South. Arson has traditionally been a difficult crime to track and prosecute. Before the creation of the NCATF, it was difficult for law-enforcement agencies to assess the full scope of the church arson cases because records were not well kept. Arson fires are sometimes mislabeled as accidents, and the motivations behind arson cases can be unclear. Hate crime data were not examined separately.

With the creation of the NCATF, improved collection and tracking of church arson data revealed that church arson is not confined to churches with primarily African American congregations; churches attended by other ethnic and racial groups are also targeted. Also, many perpetrators are not motivated by hate or racism to burn or bomb churches. Some perpetrators are motivated by revenge or simply by the love of setting fires. NCATF statistics have shown that more than 90 percent of perpetrators of church arson nationwide are male, more than 80 percent are white, and more than 50 percent are between the ages of fourteen and twenty-four. Moreover, only about half of all

churches targeted by arsonists have been attended predominantly by African Americans.

The task force has at its disposal specially trained agents, chemists, and laboratories and uses computer technology to analyze information and determine whether church fires are arson cases. During its first year, the NCATF investigated 429 church burnings. Its arrest rate was 35 percent—more than double the national arrest rate for arson. The NCATF was also actively involved in prevention efforts through the Federal Emergency Management Agency (FEMA), which established a clearinghouse for telephone inquiries and distributed arson prevention packets. The task force has also assisted in developing grassroots arson prevention programs.

Ayn Embar-Seddon and Allan D. Pass

Further Reading

Blackstock, Terri. *Trial by Fire*. Grand Rapids, Mich.: Zondervan, 2000.

Johnson, Sandra E. *Standing on Holy Ground: A Triumph over Hate Crime in the Deep South*. Columbia: University of South Carolina Press, 2005.

National Church Arson Task Force. *First Year Report for the President*. Washington, D.C.: U.S. Department of the Treasury, 1996.
_____. *Second Year Report for the President*. Washington, D.C.: U.S. Department of the Treasury, 1998.

See also: Accelerants; Arson; Blast seat; Bomb damage assessment; Bureau of Alcohol, Tobacco, Firearms and Explosives; Burn pattern analysis; Fire debris.

National Crime Information Center

Date: Established in January, 1967
Identification: Central U.S. database for crime-related information, maintained by the Federal Bureau of Investigation and available electronically to local, state, and federal law-enforcement agencies.
Significance: The National Crime Information Center provides law-enforcement agencies, both in the United States and abroad, with ready access to information on crimes, criminals, and crime victims, thus aiding in investigations of many different kinds, from searches for dangerous fugitives to the location of missing persons and property.

In 1965, officials with the Federal Bureau of Investigation (FBI) became concerned about steadily increasing crime rates across the United States and realized that, to address the problem, law-enforcement agencies across the nation needed to be able to collect and share information regarding crimes and criminals. The FBI created an advisory board to develop standards of operation for a new center that would be tasked with information sharing among law-enforcement agencies. The board was made up of FBI statisticians, who created and disseminated the agency's annual Uniform Crime

Reports, and members of the International Association of Chiefs of Police. The FBI next approached the U.S. Commerce Department for assistance in procuring an appropriate telecommunications system that would be capable of warehousing and sharing information electronically at high speeds.

Two years later, in January of 1967, the National Crime Information Center (NCIC) began operations when high-speed computers went online at fifteen state and metropolitan-area police departments throughout the United States. These fifteen terminals were directly connected to a central computer housed in the FBI's Criminal Justice Information Services Division, located near Clarksburg, West Virginia. The new system allowed information sharing—between participating police departments and the FBI as well as among the police departments—to take place at unprecedented speeds. By the end of 1971, all fifty U.S. states and the District of Columbia were connected directly to the NCIC. Eventually, more than eighty thousand law-enforcement and criminal justice agencies in the United States and abroad gained secure access to the database. An advisory council of law-enforcement officials from all levels and department sizes functions to ensure that the database is meeting the needs of its many users.

Contents of the Database

When the NCIC initially went online, the database housed ninety-five thousand records in five separate file categories. These five original categories were wanted persons (divided into state fugitives and federal fugitives), stolen autos, stolen license plates, stolen guns, and other identifiable stolen articles. NCIC records were entered directly into the system by the law-enforcement agencies that had jurisdiction to investigate the crimes reported. With this safeguard, all NCIC users knew that the records were valid, as only the investigative agencies that posted the information could update or eventually clear the posted data. This procedure still remains in effect.

Since its inception, the NCIC has been expanded and updated significantly. By 2008, a total of eighteen file categories contained more than ten million records. Additionally, nearly twenty-five million criminal history records had been stored on the Interstate Identification Index, which is available through the NCIC. Among the most notable additions to the database since it began operations are the Missing Persons File, which helps law-enforcement agencies locate noncriminal missing adults and children; the U.S. Secret Service Protective File, which consists of information on individuals who pose a direct threat to the president of the United States; the Interstate Identification Index, which allows law-enforcement officers quick access to criminal history information, especially during traffic stops; the Violent Gang/Terrorist File, which contains information on criminal gangs and terrorist organizations; and the Convicted Sex Offender Registry.

Uses and Successes

Local law-enforcement agencies use the NCIC frequently to get information quickly about persons with whom officers come into contact during routine activities. For example, when a police officer makes a routine traffic stop, the officer radios the police dispatcher and provides information on both the driver and the vehicle, including license plate number and state driver's license information. The dispatcher enters this information first in a search of the state database to see whether the person stopped by the officer is wanted or missing in that particular state. If this search results in no hits, the dispatcher runs a federal check against the NCIC. If this search of the national database also returns no hits, it can be concluded that the

person has not been in trouble with law enforcement or is not listed as a missing person in the United States.

This use of the NCIC has proven to be effective, at the least, in safeguarding the lives of patrol officers who may be dealing with potentially violent offenders during routine traffic stops. The success of this procedure has led some police departments to install computers in patrol cars so that officers can search state and federal databases directly, without taking the extra step of contacting dispatchers.

Overall, the NCIC has contributed substantially to improved law-enforcement services, from the apprehension of wanted suspects to

NCIC 2000

In 1999, the FBI enhanced the National Crime Information Center with NCIC 2000, which gave the system additional capabilities, including in the following areas:

- **Enhanced name search:** Uses the New York State Identification and Intelligence System (NYSIIS), which returns phonetically similar names (for example, Marko, Marco, or Knowles, Nowles) and derivatives of names (such as William, Willie, Bill).
- **Fingerprint searches:** Stores and searches the right index fingerprint. Search inquiries compare a print to all fingerprint data on file (wanted persons and missing persons).
- **Probation/parole:** The Convicted Persons or Supervised Release File contains records of subjects under supervised release.
- **Information linking:** Connects two or more records so that an inquiry on one retrieves the others.
- **Mug shots:** Allows for the entry of one mug shot per person record. One fingerprint, one signature, and up to ten other identifying images (scars, marks, tattoos) may also be entered.
- **Convicted Sex Offender Registry:** Contains records of individuals who are convicted sexual offenders or violent sexual predators.
- **SENTRY File:** Contains an index of individuals incarcerated in the federal prison system. Responses provide descriptive information and locations of the prisons.
- **Delayed inquiry:** Checks every record entered or modified against the inquiry log, and the entering and inquiring agency receives a response if any other agency has inquired on the subject in the past five days.

the location of missing persons and stolen cars. Two of the most notable criminal suspects who have been apprehended with the help of information contained in the database are James Earl Ray, who was arrested in 1968 for the assassination of the Reverend Martin Luther King, Jr., and Timothy McVeigh, key figure in the 1995 bombing of the Alfred P. Murrah Federal Building in Oklahoma City.

Paul M. Klenowski

Further Reading

Kessler, Ronald. *The Bureau: The Secret History of the FBI*. New York: St. Martin's Press, 2002. Offers a historical portrait of the agency and discusses its significance in efforts to combat crime in the United States.

_____. *The FBI: Inside the World's Most Powerful Law Enforcement Agency*. New York: Pocket Books, 1993. Provides a unique look into the investigative history of the FBI and its use of technology in solving crimes.

O'Hara, Charles E., and Gregory L. O'Hara. *Fundamentals of Criminal Investigation*. 7th ed. Springfield, Ill.: Charles C Thomas, 2003. Presents a detailed overview of the criminal investigative process, including the impacts of the uses of computer technology.

Pattavina, April, ed. *Information Technology and the Criminal Justice System*. Thousand Oaks, Calif.: Sage, 2005. Offers a comprehensive look at how technology has enhanced law-enforcement agencies' ability to catch criminals.

Theoharis, Athan G., with Tony G. Poveda, Susan Rosenfeld, and Richard Gid Power. *The FBI: A Comprehensive Reference Guide*. Phoenix, Ariz.: Oryx Press, 1999. Provides a detailed look at the FBI and its evolution over time.

See also: CODIS; DNA database controversies; Federal Bureau of Investigation; Federal Bureau of Investigation Laboratory; Integrated Automated Fingerprint Identification System; Integrated Ballistics Identification System; Interpol; National DNA Index System.

National DNA Index System

Date: Established in 1998

Identification: Computerized system for storing DNA profiles, maintained and operated by the Federal Bureau of Investigation and supported by the Combined DNA Index System, that permits state and local law-enforcement agencies to collaborate in identifying missing persons and matching DNA profiles of suspected offenders to unsolved crimes.

Significance: Technological advances in DNA analysis and computerized comparison of DNA profiles have created a powerful crime-solving tool at the national level. The National DNA Index System enables law-enforcement agencies to identify violent criminal offenders and match them to unsolved crimes across state lines, and it also possesses the power to exonerate the wrongfully convicted. The National DNA Index System allows law-enforcement agencies across the United States to communicate about and collaborate in criminal investigations at a level never before possible.

The National DNA Index System (NDIS) is an electronic resource of DNA profiles designed to aid in criminal investigations as well as searches for missing persons at the national level. Established in response to the Violent Crime Control and Law Enforcement Act of 1994 and operated by the Federal Bureau of Investigation (FBI), NDIS represents the highest level in the Combined DNA Index System (CODIS) hierarchy. CODIS, which began as a pilot project in 1990, represents a database of DNA profiles collected by law-enforcement agencies across the United States. CODIS is a computerized DNA profile processing system that provides law-enforcement agencies with the ability to search electronically for DNA profile matches. The CODIS hierarchy includes support at the national (NDIS), state (State DNA Index System, or SDIS), and local (Local

DNA Index System, or LDIS) levels. DNA profiles from the state and local levels constitute NDIS.

The primary purpose of NDIS is to assist in criminal investigations across state and local levels by providing an electronic database containing DNA profiles from participating laboratories across states. NDIS offers law-enforcement agencies in different states the opportunity to search for possible matches between suspected or convicted criminals and DNA profiles obtained from the scenes of unsolved crimes. This index system also enables the identification of serial offenders.

The federal DNA Identification Act of 1994 requires NDIS to record five DNA profile categories: DNA samples from individuals convicted of crimes, DNA samples recovered from crime scenes, DNA samples from unidentified human remains, DNA samples from relatives of missing persons, and reference samples from missing persons. Relatives of missing persons may contribute DNA samples to NDIS voluntarily; convicted offenders are given no notice or control over the collection and use of their DNA samples. In respect to criminal investigations, DNA samples from individuals convicted of crimes and DNA samples recovered from crime scenes are separated into two primary indexes, the offender index and the forensic index.

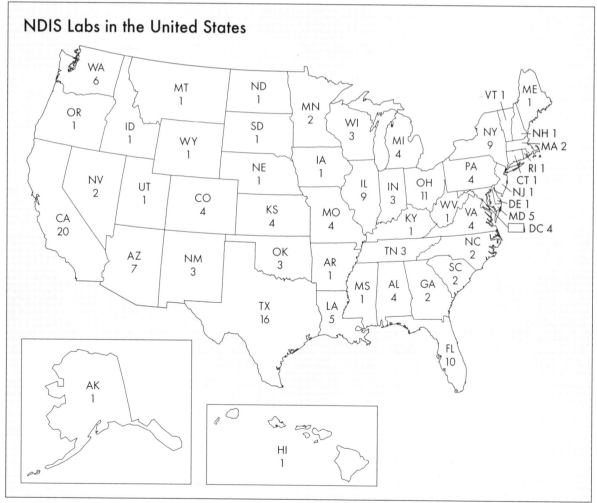

Source: Federal Bureau of Investigation, 2008.

Through NDIS, law-enforcement agencies can identify missing individuals, match offenders to previously unsolved crimes, and make connections between separate crime scenes.

To prevent personal identification from DNA profiles, no personal information is provided in NDIS, and only authorized personnel have access to identifying information. Each DNA profile in NDIS is connected only with the following information: identification of the particular laboratory or agency that submitted the profile, the name of the staff member associated with the DNA analysis, and an identification number for the specimen.

All fifty U.S. states contribute DNA profiles to NDIS, but the collection of DNA samples varies across states. As a result, some states submit more DNA profiles than do other states. The number of profiles submitted is not related to the level of crime in a state; rather, it is related to state laws that specify what types of offenders are required to submit DNA samples. For example, some states require submission of DNA samples in connection with only a small number of serious offenses, whereas other states permit law-enforcement agencies wide latitude in collecting DNA samples from suspects and convicted offenders. Some state laws permit the collection of samples from all persons arrested, whether or not they are ultimately convicted.

Erin J. Farley

Further Reading

Butler, John M. *Forensic DNA Typing: Biology, Technology, and Genetics of STR Markers.* 2d ed. Burlington, Mass.: Elsevier Academic Press, 2005.

Lazer, David, ed. *DNA and the Criminal Justice System: The Technology of Justice.* Cambridge, Mass.: MIT Press, 2004.

Lee, Henry C., and Frank Tirnady. *Blood Evidence: How DNA Is Revolutionizing the Way We Solve Crimes.* Cambridge, Mass.: Perseus, 2003.

See also: CODIS; DNA analysis; DNA database controversies; DNA fingerprinting; DNA isolation methods; DNA profiling; DNA recognition instruments; DNA sequencing; DNA typing; Federal Bureau of Investigation; Federal Bureau of Investigation Laboratory; Mass graves; National Crime Information Center; Postconviction DNA analysis; Short tandem repeat analysis.

National Institute of Justice

Date: Established in 1969

Identification: U.S. government agency responsible for researching crimes and investigation techniques as well as training state and local law-enforcement personnel in the most advanced investigative methods.

Significance: The National Institute of Justice has led the way in the development of improved techniques for law-enforcement investigation, including DNA analysis, biometric identification, and compilation of criminal records in electronic databases. The agency's establishment represented the first attempt by the U.S. government to conduct research into crime control and to spread that information to state and local law enforcement.

A dramatic increase in crime during the 1960's and the inability of state and local governments to deal with it goaded the U.S. Congress into passing the Omnibus Crime Control and Safe Streets Act of 1968. The law toughened criminal penalties and weakened restrictions on police investigation and interrogation. It also jump-started federal involvement in local crime control as Congress created a new agency within the Department of Justice. The National Institute of Justice (NIJ) became the research arm of the department; its mission was to analyze methods of controlling crime and of improving investigation and prosecution. Formed in 1969, the NIJ was unusual in that it was headed by a political appointee rather than by a member of the permanent government bureaucracy.

The NIJ is divided into the Office of Science and Technology and the Office of Research and Evaluation. The Office of Science and Technology provides training and research on the most advanced scientific techniques for law enforcement. Under the Office of Research and Evaluation, research divisions develop and direct evaluations in the areas of crime control and prevention, violence and victimization, and justice systems. This office also oversees an international research center.

The NIJ and Forensic Science

In response to the increasing scientific complexity of police investigations, the NIJ provides training to local and state law-enforcement agencies and prosecutors in the collection, interpretation, and presentation of scientific evidence such as DNA (deoxyribonucleic acid)

analysis, biometric readings, and fingerprint analysis. The NIJ's Office of Science and Technology collaborated with other federal agencies to create a set of nationally recognized standards for DNA identification, and the agency trains law-enforcement personnel to use those standards when collecting and analyzing evidence.

The NIJ is part of the U.S. government's continuing efforts to update and improve the use of DNA analysis in criminal investigations. The agency joined with others as part of President George W. Bush's DNA Initiative, launched in 2003, to ensure that the newest and best technology is available to local law-enforcement agencies. The DNA project has also continued the work of a previous commission in studying how DNA testing might be used to free persons who have been convicted of crimes they did not commit.

In addition, the NIJ funds competitions within the private sector aimed at producing the best law-enforcement tools, including technologies in areas such as biometric identification systems, including voice matching, iris identification, and facial recognition. Among NIJ-funded studies on the test issues for biometrics was one concerning the most effective identification technology for keeping track of prisoners. The researchers concluded that iris recognition and fingerprint identification were more effective than simple facial identification. Another study tested the use of biometric iris identification as a security measure in a New Jersey school.

After the terrorist attacks on the World Trade Center and the Pentagon on September 11, 2001, the NIJ be-

---

The NIJ and Forensic Science

On its Web site, the National Institute of Justice describes the ways in which it supports advancements in forensic science.

Forensic science has greatly benefited from breakthroughs in broader areas of science and technology that make it possible for scientists to analyze evidence more quickly using ever smaller sample sizes that may be of poor quality.

The National Institute of Justice provides funding to:

- Develop tools and technologies.
- Better understand the impact of forensic science.
- Provide technology assistance to forensic laboratories.
- Enhance laboratory capabilities and capacity.

Tools and technologies. Demand exceeds capacity at most crime laboratories. NIJ develops innovative tools and technologies that will save time and money. These research and development projects provide:

- Faster, more reliable and widely applicable, less costly, and less labor-intensive tools for identifying, collecting, preserving, and analyzing crime scene evidence.
- Tools that provide more information about the source of evidence and circumstances surrounding the crime.

Understanding the impact of forensic science. NIJ has initiated several evaluations to assess the impact of forensic science on the criminal justice system—for example, training of first responders, perceptions of jurors, case processing.

Technology assistance and training. Through the Forensic Resource Network and the Forensic Science Technology Center of Excellence, NIJ provides assistance with quality assurance, evaluation, and implementation of new technologies and has developed several interactive training and field guidance documents.

Enhancing laboratories. NIJ provides funding to help laboratories streamline their operations, recruit qualified staff, and process more cases faster, with greater accuracy.

came involved in research concerning the use of DNA to identify victims of the disaster. The agency identified new methods of collecting DNA in mass-casualty incidents and also developed new methods for keeping track of thousands of DNA samples while ensuring fast and accurate matches. As a result of this work, the NIJ produced a handbook for use by law-enforcement agencies in the event of another mass-casualty terrorist attack.

The NIJ is also involved in research on computer crimes. The agency maintains a national software reference library that local and state law-enforcement agencies can use to investigate computer crime. This collaborative effort relies heavily on software donated by private firms and by other federal agencies such as the Federal Bureau of Investigation. Through the NIJ, law-enforcement agencies can access software that can enable them to trace attempts to hack computers as well as software that can help them to review the files on seized computers.

Making Law Enforcement More Scientific

The NIJ collaborates with other federal agencies and with state and local police departments to improve the technological and scientific capabilities of law enforcement. One of its first efforts was a movement to computerize all police records across the United States during the 1970's and 1980's so that record keeping would be more efficient and local, state, and federal police agencies would be able to share information on crimes and suspects. The NIJ provided both technological support and training for local police in the use of the new computerized system.

Also in the agency's early years, NIJ researchers emphasized victim studies, trying to understand how victims of crime are psychologically affected. The findings of these studies eventually led to legislation on victims' rights and the introduction of such procedures as the solicitation of victim impact statements in death penalty cases.

The NIJ collaborates with other federal agencies in efforts to find the best equipment for use by law-enforcement personnel, from body armor to traffic radar devices. The agency has conducted mock prison riots as training exercises

for correctional officers, providing them with realistic experiences in using the latest technologies for handling rioting prisoners.

Since its founding, the NIJ has studied many other innovations in law-enforcement procedures and technologies, examining everything from private prisons to devices that allow police to "see" through walls. The NIJ also studies the impacts of the criminal justice mandates passed by Congress and state legislatures. For example, the 1994 Crime Act introduced community policing to limit crime and drug courts to handle the exploding number of drug cases. The NIJ studied and reported on the effectiveness of these techniques, documenting successes and failures and making suggestions for improvement.

Developing, testing, and disseminating improvements in technology for law enforcement constitute only part of the NIJ's duties. The agency is also involved in training law-enforcement personnel through both online seminars and on-site programs. The NIJ offers training to personnel at all levels of the criminal justice system, including police, judges, lawyers, and forensic scientists. One area of emphasis in NIJ training encompasses the collection, preservation, analysis, and presentation of DNA evidence.

Douglas Clouatre

Further Reading

Cohn, Jeffery. "Keeping an Eye on School Security" *NIJ Journal* 254 (July, 2006). Reports on an NIJ study that examined the use of iris identification technology as a security measure in a New Jersey elementary school.

Connors, Edward, Thomas Lundregan, Neal Miller, and Tom McEwan. *Convicted by Juries, Exonerated by Science: Case Studies in the Use of DNA Evidence to Establish Innocence After Trial*. Washington, D.C.: National Institute of Justice, 1996. NIJ research report discusses a study initiated to identify and review cases in which convicted persons were released from prison as a result of posttrial DNA testing of evidence.

Miles, Christopher, and Jeffery Cohn. "Tracking Prisoners in Jail with Biometrics." *NIJ Journal* 253 (January, 2006). Describes an

NIJ-sponsored study that used fingerprint and iris analysis to track prisoners in a U.S. Navy brig and discusses how such technology could be used for other purposes, including security at public buildings.

National Institute of Justice. *The Future of Forensic DNA Testing: Predictions of the Research and Development Working Group.* Honolulu: University Press of the Pacific, 2005. Discusses advances in DNA collecting and testing as well as likely future uses of DNA analysis in law enforcement.

_____. *Investigative Uses of Technology: Devices, Tools, and Techniques.* Washington, D.C.: Author, 2007. Special report discusses techniques and resources for investigating technology-related crime.

See also: American Society of Crime Laboratory Directors; Biometric eye scanners; Biometric identification systems; Crime laboratories; DNA analysis; DNA recognition instruments; Federal Bureau of Investigation; Forensic Science Service; International Association of Forensic Sciences; Trace and transfer evidence.

The investigator in charge of the National Transportation Safety Board's investigation of the May, 1996, crash of ValuJet Flight 592 in Florida looks over some of the pieces of the airplane's wreckage collected at a hangar at a Miami airport a few days after the crash. *(AP/Wide World Photos)*

National Transportation Safety Board

Date: Established on April 1, 1967

Identification: U.S. government agency responsible for investigating major transportation accidents involving motor vehicles, trains, airplanes, and ships.

Significance: Investigators for the National Transportation Safety Board use forensic science techniques to examine the causes of transportation accidents and make recommendations aimed at improving safety based on their findings.

The National Transportation Safety Board (NTSB) was created within the U.S. Department of Transportation in 1967 by President Lyndon B. Johnson. Initially, the NTSB was a political organization and thus susceptible to political manipulation, but in 1974 it was granted independent agency status. This meant that board members could not be removed by the president and that both the Republican and Democratic parties could nominate members to ensure partisan balance on the board.

One of the smallest agencies within the federal government, the NTSB is responsible for investigating accidents and incidents involving most major forms of transportation. Although the work of the NTSB is perhaps most strongly associated with airplane crashes, the board is also responsible for the investigation of pipeline, railroad, and ship accidents as well as some accidents involving motor vehicles. Pipeline ruptures and accidents involving vehicles carrying hazardous waste fall under NTSB control, as do train derailments and collisions and any incidents causing injury or death to railroad employees. Marine accidents (such as ships running aground or sinking) and other incidents (such as fires) involving commercial cargo ships or passenger cruise ships also come under NTSB scrutiny. The highway accidents investigated by the NTSB are usually those involving multiple vehicles or large passenger vehicles, such as interstate buses. The board also examines accidents caused by failures in road construction and engineering.

Making Air Flight Safer

The NTSB focuses on finding the causes of the accidents it investigates and making recommendations to prevent future accidents. The NTSB categorizes the causes of accidents as resulting from mechanical failure, human error, or a mix of both. When NTSB investigators find mechanical failure as a cause of an airplane crash, this prompts NTSB recommendations to manufacturers that are intended to solve the problem and prevent future accidents.

Carrying out NTSB recommendations following a finding of human error in an airplane crash can require coordination among the NTSB, the airline, and the Federal Aviation Administration (FAA). For example, the crash of ValuJet Flight 592 in the Florida Everglades in 1996 was attributed to a fire in the plane's cargo hold caused by chemical oxygen generators. Following the NTSB investigation, the NTSB and FAA created new guidelines for airline cargo, including a requirement for active fire suppression devices, to prevent any other occurrence of the same kind of disaster.

NTSB and Forensic Science

Unlike most law-enforcement investigators, NTSB investigators have access to "eyewitness" evidence in almost every air crash. The flight data recorder, popularly known as the black box, provides evidence of a plane's mechanical functions before and during a crash, including any malfunctioning. The voice data recorder allows investigators to hear all conversations among the flight crew and between the crew and airport tower personnel. Both recorders are designed to survive crashes. The information provided by the recorders provides NTSB investigators with clues as to where they should look to explain the disaster. From there, they can examine parts of the plane that malfunctioned or interview members of the crew or tower personnel to find out what went wrong.

The ability of NTSB investigators to piece together what occurred immediately before and during an air disaster has put the NTSB in the forefront of forensic science. In the case of the explosion and crash of Trans World Airline (TWA) Flight 800 in the Atlantic Ocean in 1996, for example, NTSB investigators literally rebuilt the plane from recovered pieces and traced back what may have malfunctioned and led to the explosion. This effort required minute examination of every part of the plane, but the investigators eventually determined that the likely cause of the explosion and resulting crash was faulty wiring near a center fuel tank.

An NTSB Investigation

The National Transportation Safety Board provides this description of how the agency undertakes a major investigation.

When the Board is notified of a major accident, it launches a "Go Team," which varies in size depending on the severity of the accident and the complexity of the issues involved. The team may consist of experts in as many as 14 different specialties, coordinated by the investigator-in-charge. Each expert manages a group of other specialists from government agencies and industry in collecting the facts and determining the conditions and circumstances surrounding the accident. The investigative groups formed vary, depending on the nature of the accident, and may look into areas such as structures, systems, powerplants, human performance, fire and explosion, meteorology, radar data, event recorders, and witness statements, among others. After an investigation is completed, a detailed narrative report is prepared that analyzes the investigative record and identifies the probable cause of the accident.

Another crash, that of Air Midwest Flight 5481 soon after takeoff from Charlotte, North Carolina, in 2003, was attributed by the NTSB to plane maintenance problems but also to FAA regulations concerning passengers and their luggage. By not updating these regulations, the FAA had allowed the plane to fly with excessive weight that was unbalanced as the plane took off, leading to the crash. In this case, the NTSB conducted a more conventional forensic investigation, using simulations and eyewitness reports to determine how the weight had shifted within the plane during takeoff.

In investigating airplane manufacturing or design problems, the NTSB works with aircraft companies and examines how particular airplanes are constructed. Investigators also seek out information on any mechanical problems that have been noted with particular types of airplanes and records on the maintenance of the aircraft in question. After Alaska Airlines Flight 261 crashed into the Pacific Ocean in January, 2000, the NTSB investigated the possibility of both human and mechanical errors. Investigators concluded from their examination of mechanical aspects of the plane as well as maintenance records that the airline and the FAA were lax in their procedures and allowed some routine maintenance to be delayed beyond recommended times.

Douglas Clouatre

Further Reading

Adair, Bill. *The Mystery of Flight 427: Inside a Crash Investigation.* Washington, D.C.: Smithsonian Institution Press, 2002. Presents an in-depth examination of a single crash investigation, delineating the work of the many groups that participated in reaching a conclusion and placing blame.

Bibel, George. *Beyond the Black Box: The Forensics of Airline Crashes.* Baltimore: The Johns Hopkins University Press, 2007. Describes in detail how NTSB investigators discover the causes of airplane crashes, including pilot error and mechanical malfunctions.

Cobb, Roger W., and David M. Primo. *The Plane Truth: Airline Crashes, the Media, and Transportation Policy.* Washington, D.C.: Brookings Institution, 2003. Discusses the NTSB and its investigations of plane crashes in the late 1990's. Addresses how outside influences, such as the news media, airlines and their unions, and aircraft manufacturers, have affected the conclusions reached by the agency.

Faith, Nicholas. *Black Box: The Air-Crash Detectives—Why Air Safety Is No Accident.* Osceola, Wis.: Motorbooks International, 1997. Provides information on how aircraft accident investigations are conducted and how the U.S. government uses the results of such investigations to improve air safety.

Krause, Shari Stamford. *Aircraft Safety: Accident Investigations, Analyses, and Applications.* 2d ed. New York: McGraw-Hill, 2003. Analyzes the causes of a number of specific airplane crashes, including human error, weather, and mechanical failure.

Lebow, Cynthia C., et al. *Safety in the Skies: Personnel and Parties in NTSB Aviation Accident Investigations.* Santa Monica, Calif.: RAND, 1999. Presents a synopsis of the challenges faced by the NTSB, discusses the agency's successes and failures in investigations, and offers a series of recommendations for maintaining and improving the agency.

Schiavo, Mary, with Sabra Chartrand. *Flying Blind, Flying Safe.* New York: Avon Books, 1997. Overview of the U.S. government regulatory system and the airline industry by the former inspector general of the Department of Transportation is critical of flight safety measures and the various agencies responsible for protecting the flying public.

See also: Accident investigation and reconstruction; Airport security; *Challenger* and *Columbia* accident investigations; Federal Bureau of Investigation; Flight data recorders; Sobriety testing; ValuJet Flight 592 crash investigation.

NDIS. *See* National DNA Index System

Nerve agents

Definition: Chemical weapons, usually liquid or gas, that incapacitate or kill by poisoning the nervous system.

Significance: Given the deadly nature of nerve agents and the possibility that such substances could be used in terrorist attacks, law-enforcement personnel must be familiar with the various types of nerve agents, decontamination procedures, and treatments for exposure.

The earliest use of poison gases as weapons took place during World War I; the agents used were vesicants, or blister-causing agents, such as chlorine gas, phosgene gas, and mustard gas. These injured by inflicting chemical burns on the lungs (and, in the case of mustard gas, on the skin and eyes as well). The gases had to be deployed in massive quantities (six hundred tons was a common amount), inflicted a low death rate, and soon dispersed, and gas masks provided sufficient protection to potential targets. Nerve agents, in contrast, are extremely toxic and can contaminate an area for days or weeks; protection of targets requires full body coverings in addition to masks.

Nerve agents function like modern organophosphate insecticides: They attack the nervous system. They inhibit the process by which cholinesterase neutralizes the neurotransmitter acetylcholine, thus clearing the nerve to transmit another signal. Acetylcholine then builds up in the nerves, causing the nervous system to malfunction; the nerves essentially transmit a continuous signal, causing the muscular system to lock up. The first symptoms—a feeling of tightness in the chest, dimming vision, and headache—may appear within seconds of exposure. Unconsciousness, coma, and death from respiratory paralysis follow within minutes or at most within a few hours. Survivors may suffer lasting impairment to their nervous systems.

G-Agents

Nerve gases are commonly divided into the three categories defined by the North Atlantic Treaty Organization (NATO): G-agents, V-agents, and Novichok agents. The first of these, the G-agents, were reportedly so named because they were German inventions. GA, or tabun, was discovered in 1936 by the German scientist Gerhard Schrader, who was researching insecticides. This agent is extremely toxic compared with the World War I vesicants and, unlike them, it is not simply a gas. At room temperature it takes the form of a liquid that evaporates slowly (albeit more rapidly than its successor G-agents). It is colorless and has only a faint odor, described as fruity.

Although its primary lethal mechanism is inhalation, liquid tabun will penetrate the skin; exposure to a single droplet can kill. When tabun is delivered by an artillery round or missile warhead, a large area is splattered with droplets, lethal in themselves, the vapors from which contaminate the air for an extended period of time. Because the droplets can kill through skin contact, a gas mask is insufficient protection; the body must be fully covered. Ordinary clothing, however, can make tabun even more dangerous, as it can trap droplets and hold them in contact with the skin.

Tabun's fumes are five times as dense as air, so they do not easily disperse into the atmosphere. Dangerous concentrations can thus remain for long periods in low-lying areas, including trenches and dugouts. Decontamination of areas contaminated with G-agents generally takes the form of rinsing the affected areas down with chlorine bleach. With tabun, however, this results in the release of toxic cyanogen chloride gas.

The second G-agent, known as GB or sarin, was invented by a German team in 1938. It is about twice as deadly as tabun (lethal skin dose for a human is less than a milligram) and so toxic that even its vapor can kill through skin exposure. Sarin evaporates more slowly than tabun, and thus its droplets can contaminate an area for a longer period.

Sarin has an unusual feature: It can be delivered as a binary agent, in the form of two or three harmless chemicals that, when mixed, convert into sarin. This makes sarin relatively safe to store, and it can be used in artillery shells, missile warheads, and bombs that are not dangerous until they are on the way to their targets.

Another G-agent, GD, or soman, was discovered by German scientist Richard Kuhn in 1944. GD, more deadly than sarin, can also be used as a binary agent. It is slower to evaporate than its predecessors and thus is a more persistent area contaminant. In its pure form it is colorless and has only a faint odor. In impure forms it can have a brown coloration and an odor resembling that of camphor.

GF, or cyclosarin, was invented in 1949. It is more persistent than its predecessors, evaporating at a speed about one-twentieth that of water and one-seventieth that of sarin. It is colorless and has a faint odor variously described as similar to peaches or shellac.

By the end of World War II, Germany had produced about twelve thousand tons of nerve agents. Although the Germans thus held a technological advantage over their enemies, they were reluctant to initiate chemical warfare for a simple reason: Most of their artillery, and much of their transport, was still horse-drawn, and efforts to design gas masks for horses had proven unsuccessful. The Allies' use of even World War I gases would have immobilized the Germans' artillery and stopped much of their resupply efforts.

V-Agents

The G-agents were succeeded in the years following World War II by the British-created V-agents, known as VE, VG, VM, and VX. Like the G-agents, these originated with researchers seeking to create insecticides (VG was briefly marketed for that purpose until it was withdrawn owing to its extreme toxicity).

Of these, VX was the only variant chosen for development as a war gas. VX was developed in Great Britain in the 1950's, and its secret was traded to the United States in exchange for information on construction of thermonuclear warheads. The Soviet Union reportedly developed its own version, known in the West as VR and in the Soviet Union as Substance 33, and produced more than fifteen thousand tons of it.

VX possesses all the characteristics that make nerve agents so deadly. It is viscous (its consistency has been likened to that of motor oil), so that it adheres to objects and persons. It can be delivered in binary form. It evaporates very slowly, at about one-fifteen-hundredth the rate of water. It is deadlier than its predecessors: A lethal skin dose is estimated at ten micrograms. When VX does evaporate, its fumes are nine times the density of air, so that it is not easily dispersed by wind.

Novichok Agents

For many years, VX represented the zenith of the development of nerve agents. That changed with Russia's development of Novichok (Russian for "newcomer") agents. Novichok agents take the form of a fine powder or dust that can evade modern chemical warfare protection equipment. These agents may be several times more potent than VX. Further, existing chemical agent detection systems may not detect Novichok agents, and antidotes may not function against them. The existence of these agents was revealed in 1992 by Russian chemists Lev Fedorov and Vil Mirzayanov, who were imprisoned after they went public.

Responses to Nerve Agent Attacks

Nerve agents are potent area-denial weapons. That is, an area that is attacked with the use of such weapons will be dangerous for unprotected humans for an extended period unless it is completely washed down with decontaminates (typically chlorine bleach, although steam and ammonia may be used in restricted areas). As the smallest missed droplet can kill, decontamination must be exceptionally thorough. Belowground areas must be flushed of any vapors.

Treatment of casualties is likewise complicated. First responders must themselves wear protective outfits. Unprotected personnel must not have contact with any exposed person until that person has been undressed, any known droplets of agent on the body have been neutralized, and the hair has been washed.

The earliest antidote used in response to exposure to nerve agents was atropine, which is itself a toxin. Atropine counters the effects of nerve agents by binding to nerve receptor sites and blocking excess acetylcholine. Biperiden, originally developed for use against Parkinson's

An operations supervisor stands between two one-thousand-gallon reactors where the nerve agent VX is chemically neutralized at the Newport Chemical Depot in Newport, Indiana. The Chemical Weapons Convention of 1993 requires signatory nations to destroy existing stockpiles of nerve agents. *(AP/Wide World Photos)*

disease, is also useful. Pralidoxime chloride (2-PAM chloride, known in the military simply as 2-PAM) offers a more direct and safe approach, in that it reactivates the acetylcholinesterase deactivated by the nerve agent. Treatment with 2-PAM must be begun more quickly than treatment with atropine, as 2-PAM takes effect more slowly. Military personnel are commonly issued kits containing self-injectors of atropine and 2-PAM if nerve agents are considered to be a risk. Diazepam can also be employed to counteract convulsions caused by nerve agents.

Employment of Nerve Agents

The deployment of nerve agents has been mercifully rare. During the Iran-Iraq War (1980-1988), Iraq used tabun, sarin, and cyclosarin against Iranian infantry and later used these agents to kill thousands of Kurds. In Japan, the Aum Shinrikyo religious cult used homemade sarin in a 1995 attack on the Tokyo subway system. Owing to the crude nature of the material used and a rather inept delivery system (leaky cans left in subway cars), casualties in that incident were held to twelve deaths and about five thousand hospitalizations.

The risk of future use may be curtailed by treaties. Early agreements such as the Geneva Protocol of 1925 forbade the use of poisonous gases, but not their manufacture and storage. More recently, the Chemical Weapons Convention of 1993, which entered into force in 1997, requires signatory nations to destroy existing stockpiles of nerve agents. In the United States, government efforts to destroy such stockpiles by breaking the substances down chemically and discharging the by-products into water have encountered objections from groups concerned with possible negative environmental impacts.

David T. Hardy

Further Reading

Croddy, Eric A., with Clarisa Perez-Armendariz and John Hart. *Chemical and Biological Warfare: A Comprehensive Survey for the Concerned Citizen*. New York: Copernicus Books, 2002. Addresses the uses of sarin and other nerve agents as weapons.

Ellison, D. Hank. *Handbook of Chemical and Biological Warfare Agents*. 2d ed. Boca Raton, Fla.: CRC Press, 2007. Excellent reference source for information on agents used in chemical and biological warfare, including nerve agents.

Hammond, James W. *Poison Gas: The Myths Versus Reality*. Westport, Conn.: Greenwood Press, 1999. Provides historical information on the original use of poison gas weapons and then discusses the cultural perceptions of chemical weapons and why those conceptions exist.

Hoenig, Steven L. *Compendium of Chemical Warfare Agents*. New York: Springer, 2007. Describes and discusses the use of various agents that may be employed in chemical warfare, including how they can be identified at scenes of release and in the laboratory.

U.S. Army Chemical School. *Potential Military Chemical/Biological Agents and Compounds*. Ft. Leonard Wood, Mo.: Author, 2005. Military field manual provides extensive information on all chemical agents, their deadliness, and recommended treatments for exposure.

See also: Blood agents; Chemical agents; Chemical warfare; Chemical Weapons Convention of 1993; Mustard gas; Nervous system; Poisons and antidotes; Sarin; Soman; Tabun.

Nervous system

Definition: Bodily system that coordinates muscle activity, monitors internal organs, receives and interprets input from sense organs, and initiates actions in response to stimuli.

Significance: Information regarding the working of the human nervous system can be an important part of forensic evidence in legal cases involving persons whose mental functions and responses may have been impaired by toxins, including drugs or alcohol.

The basic units of the nervous system are specialized cells called neurons that are able to conduct stimuli. Neurons may be divided into three types: sensory neurons, which conduct sensations into the central nervous system; motor neurons, which conduct stimuli from the central nervous system to effector organs and muscles; and association neurons, which communicate stimuli between adjacent neurons.

Neurons are the only cells in the human body that can conduct stimuli. They exist in an electrical-chemical state that is said to be charged or polarized. When stimulated, the charge on the neuron is momentarily reversed in a process called depolarization or action potential. The action potential (stimulus) is initiated at one end of the neuron, the dendrites, and continues to the other end, the axons, from which neurotransmitters are released into the synapse between the neuron and the next neuron, effector gland, muscle, or organ. Arrival of sufficient quantities of neurotransmitters at the dendrites on the next neuron causes that neuron to exhibit an action potential along its length. In this way the stimulus is transmitted from neuron to neuron or from neuron to muscle.

Three Nervous Systems in One

The human nervous system can be subdivided into the central nervous system, consisting of the brain and spinal cord; the peripheral nervous system, consisting of nerves that carry information to and from the central nervous system; and the autonomic nervous system, which monitors

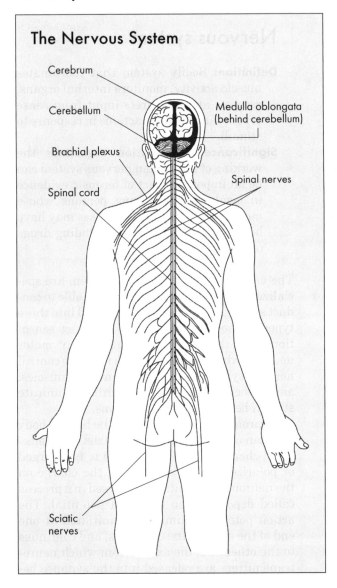

The Nervous System

- Cerebrum
- Cerebellum
- Medulla oblongata (behind cerebellum)
- Brachial plexus
- Spinal nerves
- Spinal cord
- Sciatic nerves

The autonomic nervous system monitors and maintains the body's internal state. These maintenance activities are performed primarily without conscious control. The autonomic nervous system comprises two subdivisions with opposing functions: the parasympathetic division and the sympathetic division. Generally, the sympathetic division of the autonomic nervous system works to mobilize body activity to meet emergencies, whereas the parasympathetic division is responsible for maintaining body homeostasis at other times.

The central nervous system—the brain and spinal cord—serves as the main processing center for the entire nervous system and controls all the workings of the body. The brain receives sensory input from the spinal cord as well as from its own nerves. Much of its computational power is used to process various sensory inputs and to initiate appropriate and coordinated motor outputs. The spinal cord conducts sensory information from the peripheral nervous system to the brain and also conducts motor information from the brain to various effectors. Nerve impulses reaching the spinal cord are transmitted to higher brain regions. Signals arising in the motor areas of the brain that control movement and other responses travel down the spinal cord to synapse with motor neurons that deliver the stimulus to an organ or muscle. The spinal cord is also the center for certain reflexes in concert with the peripheral nervous system.

The brain is the ultimate controller of all body activities, including physiology and behavior. The brain is subdivided into a number of distinctive components, each with a specific function. The cortex is where neural integration occurs. Responses involving muscle movement are coordinated with another part of the brain called the cerebellum. Central to the brain is the thalamus, which is the center for pain reception and also serves to relay important incoming stimuli to higher parts of the brain. The hypothalamus is responsible for monitoring and maintaining water and mineral balance and ap-

and maintains internal organs and their functions. The peripheral nervous system contains sensory receptors that respond to information from the external world and the individual's internal environment and sensory neurons that transfer this information to the central nervous system. It also contains motor neurons that carry information from the central nervous system to voluntary muscles, allowing movement. The peripheral nervous system regulates the activities of the body that are under conscious control. It controls all voluntary systems within the body, with the exception of reflex arcs.

petite. The hippocampus is involved in memory. The deepest part of the brain, the medulla, controls such vital activities as breathing and heart rate.

Forensic Toxicology and the Nervous System

As the nervous system is ultimately responsible for all behavior, physiological function, and reflexes, an analysis of the forensics of the nervous system can have far-reaching consequences and can raise concerns in a number of areas, including injury and sickness, especially as these may relate to accidents or deaths. Specialists in neuropsychiatry, psychopharmacology, and toxicology thus evaluate the nervous system for evidence in cases of traumatic brain injury, post-traumatic stress disorder, and similar disorders that may follow injury.

Forensic investigations regarding the nervous system generally focus on the types and concentrations of chemicals detected in neurological cells and tissue fluids that surround and protect the nervous system. Using techniques of toxicology, forensic analysts evaluate the possible role of toxins or drugs that may affect or impair the nervous system to determine whether any toxins present are related to the cause of death or bodily injury. Neuropsychologists are concerned with evaluating basic chemicals in the brain and nervous system to determine whether underlying or root causes of neurological or behavioral disorders may have contributed to the crime or accident being investigated.

Dwight G. Smith

Further Reading

DiMaio, Vincent J. M., and Suzanna E. Dana. *Handbook of Forensic Pathology*. 2d ed. Boca Raton, Fla.: CRC Press, 2007. Comprehensive volume illustrates core aspects of modern forensic pathology.

Doerr, Hans O., and Albert S. Carlin, eds. *Forensic Neuropsychology: Legal and Scientific Bases*. New York: Guilford Press, 1991. Provides information on the legal system for neuropsychologists who may become involved in that system through participation as expert witnesses.

Dolinak, David, Evan W. Matshes, and Emma O. Lew. *Forensic Pathology: Principles and Practice*. Burlington, Mass.: Elsevier Academic Press, 2005. Reference volume covers all aspects of forensic pathology. Includes more than eighteen hundred color photographs.

Haines, Duane E. *Fundamental Neuroscience*. 2d ed. New York: Churchill Livingstone, 2002. Offers a thorough compendium of information about the structure and function of the human nervous system.

Kolb, Bryan, and Ian Q. Whishaw. *An Introduction to Brain and Behavior*. 2d ed. New York: Worth, 2005. Correlates brain structure and functions with the behaviors controlled or modified by the brain. Exquisitely written and highly detailed.

See also: Antipsychotics; Barbiturates; Brainwave scanners; Halcion; Narcotics; Nerve agents; Sarin; Soman; Tabun; Truth serum.

Neuroleptic drugs. *See* Antipsychotics

Nicholas II remains identification

Date: Began in July, 1991

The Event: After the collapse of the Soviet Union in 1991, the remains of nine bodies reported to be those of Czar Nicholas II, members of his family, and retainers were found north of the city of Yekaterinburg, Russia. The family and others had been executed in 1918 by Bolshevik revolutionaries. The Russians gave the bodies a state funeral, but they also took samples from the bodies, which they sent to researchers at the Forensic Science Service laboratory in England and Carnegie Mellon University in the United States for positive identification. Peter Gill of the Forensic Science Service was the lead researcher on the project.

Significance: The positive identification of the body of the last Romanov ruler of Russia had substantial political and emotional meaning for Russian history. There had long been some mystery about the location of the body, and claims that some members of the royal family had escaped death had circulated during the course of the twentieth century. Forensic science was able to establish with certainty that the remains were those of the imperial family.

At the beginning of the Russian Revolution in early 1917, Czar Nicholas II of the Romanov dynasty was forced to abdicate his throne. Nicholas, his wife, Alexandra, and their children (four daughters and a son) were held under guard. After the Bolsheviks seized control of the government at the end of the year, civil war broke out in Russia, and the Bolsheviks moved their royal captives to the distant town of Yekaterinburg.

Vladimir Ilich Lenin, the new head of the Russian government, and other revolutionary leaders were afraid that the royal family would become a rallying point for the White Russian armies fighting against the Bolsheviks. On the morning of July 17, 1918, a group of Bolshevik soldiers herded the royal family as well as the family's physician and three servants into a basement and shot and killed them all.

In 1991, when the Russian government first unearthed the bodies thought to belong to Nich-

Alexei Nikitin, chief of a group of Russian scientists who examined the exhumed bones of the last Russian czar, Nicholas II, his family, their physician, and three servants, lays out the vertebrae of one of the servants in a forensics laboratory in Yekaterinburg in January, 1998. In the foreground are the skulls of the deposed czar and czarina; Nicholas's skull is on the right. *(AP/Wide World Photos)*

olas II and his family members, investigators attempted to establish their identities by generating computer images of the reconstructed skulls and then superimposing these images on photographs of the imperial family. Although the results, as well as the location of the remains, made it seem likely that the last czar had been found, this technique could not establish identification with a high degree of confidence. In addition, only nine bodies were found in the grave; the bodies of two of those executed had not yet been located.

The English and American researchers to whom the Russians sent samples from the bodies used both nuclear DNA (deoxyribonucleic acid) and mitochondrial DNA in their investigations. They began by extracting DNA from the nuclei of cells in bones. Using genetic fingerprinting, they were able to determine the sexes of the persons represented by the remains and to establish that five of the skeletons were from members of the same family.

For more positive identification, they then turned to mitochondrial DNA, which is transmitted only through mothers with almost no change over the course of generations. In particular, the D-loop portion of mitochondrial DNA tends to mutate little over the course of thousands of years. Members of European royal families who shared the maternal ancestry of Nicholas II donated blood samples, and the analysis established a probability of more than 98 percent that the last czar and his family had been located.

In 2007, Russian archaeologists announced that they believed they had found the remains of the two missing children of the imperial family, the Crown Prince Alexei and the Grand Duchess Maria, near the site where Nicholas, Alexandra, and the other three daughters were

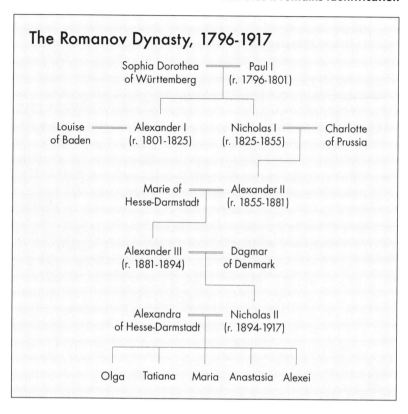

The Romanov Dynasty, 1796-1917

found. In early 2008, Russian forensic scientists who had performed analyses using teeth, bones, and other fragments from the remains noted that preliminary tests indicated a high degree of probability that the bodies were those of the Romanov children.

Carl L. Bankston III

Further Reading

King, Greg, and Penny Wilson. *The Fate of the Romanovs.* Hoboken, N.J.: John Wiley & Sons, 2003.

Klier, John, and Helen Mingay. *Quest for Anastasia: Solving the Mystery of the Lost Romanovs.* Secaucus, N.J.: Carol, 1997.

Warth, Robert D. *Nicholas II: The Life and Reign of Russia's Last Monarch.* Westport, Conn.: Praeger, 1997.

See also: Anastasia remains identification; Anthropometry; DNA analysis; DNA fingerprinting; Forensic anthropology; Louis XVII remains identification; Mitochondrial DNA analysis and typing; Skeletal analysis.

Night vision devices

Definition: Devices designed to allow operators to see in low light conditions without shining visible lights.

Significance: Using night vision devices, law-enforcement personnel can conduct surveillance at night or in dark indoor spaces without those who are being watched knowing that they are under surveillance. Such devices also benefit police in that they effectively remove the cover of darkness often used to hide criminal activities.

Night vision devices were first developed for military use during World War II, but they were not used extensively until the Vietnam War. Like many other military technologies, night vision equipment eventually found its way into civilian uses, including law enforcement.

Night vision equipment falls into two different technology categories: image intensification and thermal imaging. Image-intensification systems use low levels of visual light or infrared light just beyond the visual range. The heart of this kind of system is an image-intensifier tube. When light enters the tube, it strikes a material that releases electrons. The electrons are then accelerated down the tube, where they run into atoms releasing other electrons in a cascade effect, amplifying the effect of the initial light. The electrons then strike a phosphor screen, causing it to glow. Typically, a green phosphor screen is used because the human eye can differentiate many different levels of green light intensity. Image-intensifier tube technology has improved since it was introduced; light amplification has been increased from a factor of one thousand or less to a factor of more than fifty thousand.

Different types of night vision devices are often classified according to when they were developed and the types of technology they use. Early devices, or Generation 1 devices, amplified light by only a factor of one thousand or so and often required powerful infrared illuminators to light the targets. Generation 2 devices could operate under only moonlight, whereas Generation 3 devices can often operate using only bright starlight. No image-intensification system can operate in complete darkness, however, so many night vision devices come with small infrared illuminators for use when the ambient light level is too low. Most police departments in the United States are equipped with Generation 3 night vision devices.

A separate type of night vision technology uses thermal imaging. In these devices, thermal imaging cameras detect long wavelength infrared radiation. All living creatures give off thermal radiation. The warmer an object is, the more radiation it emits and the shorter the wavelength of the most intense radiation. Be-

A U.S. Air Force pilot tests panoramic night vision goggles. *(U.S. Air Force)*

cause thermal imaging night vision systems use light emitted by objects, they can operate in total darkness. Fire departments sometimes use such systems to find people in smoke-filled rooms or to find smoldering hot spots after a fire has been brought under control. However, thermal imaging systems are far more expensive than image-intensification night vision devices, so they are less frequently used by police departments.

Raymond D. Benge, Jr.

Further Reading

Clemens, Candace. "From Starlight to Streetlight." *Law Enforcement Technology* 34 (May, 2007): 26-35.

Peterson, Julie K. *Understanding Surveillance Technologies: Spy Devices, Their Origins, and Applications.* Boca Raton, Fla.: CRC Press, 2001.

See also: Closed-circuit television surveillance; Electronic bugs; Facial recognition technology; Forensic photography; Imaging; Infrared detection devices; Satellite surveillance technology.

9/11. *See* September 11, 2001, victim identification

Nipah virus

Definition: RNA virus of the henipavirus group in the family Paramyxoviridae that causes disease characterized by fever and severe influenza-like symptoms with high mortality in animals and humans.

Significance: Nipah virus is an emerging pathogen of increasing occurrence in deaths of humans and domestic animals. The U.S. Centers for Disease Control and Prevention classifies Nipah virus as a Category C agent, the lowest of three categories of possible bioterrorism agents.

Nipah virus was first discovered in 1998 when domestic pigs in Malaysia experienced an outbreak of disease initiated by fruit-eating bats. Subsequent outbreaks occurred in India and Bangladesh. Outbreaks of the closely related Hendra virus, another henipavirus also spread by fruit bats, have occurred in horses in Australia. All these outbreaks were characterized by transmission from animals to humans, with high mortality. Regions of the world where fruit bats (also called flying foxes) are found include much of South Asia from Madagascar to Australia. These regions can be anticipated as sites of natural outbreaks of Nipah virus and Hendra virus, especially wherever domestic animals are raised in proximity to fruit bats.

Nipah virus is identified by its epidemiology, pathology with high mortality, and laboratory tests on blood and tissue of victims. It can be detected by serological tests that identify antibodies to viral proteins in blood. The virus has also been isolated from patients and grown in cells in culture, then further identified by antibody reactions to surface proteins of the virus and through its ultrastructure as seen in the electron microscope. Nipah virus RNA (ribonucleic acid) is detectable by the reverse transcriptase-polymerase chain reaction (RT-PCR) method. Forensic labs should retain blood and tissue samples from suspected victims of the virus for future tests and should take care to preserve the chain of evidence.

In animals, the symptoms of Nipah virus are mainly respiratory; in humans, symptoms are both respiratory and neurological. In humans symptoms begin as fever and headache, progressing to nausea, vomiting, weakness, coughing, and ultimately to respiratory distress and possibly very high fever and encephalitis. No effective treatment has yet been developed beyond supportive care. The mortality rate for humans who contract Nipah virus is often more than 50 percent. Vaccines have been developed that show promise; tests with hamsters and cats indicate that they offer significant protection from the disease.

Transmission of Nipah virus from fruit bats to animals most likely takes place through exposure to bat saliva, urine, or feces. Transmission to humans is likely from saliva and respiratory exudates in aerosols, with the further possibility of human-to-human transmission.

Outbreaks of Nipah virus infection outside the regions of fruit bat territory may be expected to have different causes, such as exposure to infected meat or to animals shipped from affected regions. One outbreak in humans took place because workers in a Singapore slaughterhouse were exposed to infected pigs from neighboring Malaysia in 1999. Potential exists for other episodes to take place outside the regions where Nipah virus occurs naturally, such as through transmission from travelers exposed during stays in fruit bat territory, through accidents in clinical or research laboratories, or through bioterrorist attacks.

R. L. Bernstein

Further Reading

Anderson, Burt, Herman Freedman, and Mauro Bendinelli, eds. *Microorganisms and Bioterrorism*. New York: Springer, 2006.

Flint, S. J., L. W. Enquist, V. R. Racaniello, and A. M. Skalka. *Principles of Virology: Molecular Biology, Pathogenesis, and Control of Animal Viruses*. 2d ed. Washington, D.C.: ASM Press, 2004.

Hsu, V. P., et al. "Nipah Virus Encephalitis Reemergence, Bangladesh." *Emerging Infectious Diseases* 10 (December, 2004): 2082-2087.

See also: Antibiotics; Biological terrorism; Biotoxins; Centers for Disease Control and Prevention; Ebola virus; Hantavirus; Hemorrhagic fevers; Smallpox.

Nuclear detection devices

Definition: Instruments used to detect nuclear radiation and to measure its properties.

Significance: Forensic science can aid law-enforcement authorities in the detection of radioactive materials and in establishing the levels of danger such materials present so that appropriate warnings can be disseminated. Given ongoing threats of international terrorism, nuclear detection devices are important tools for locating lost or stolen radioactive materials that might otherwise be used as weapons in some form.

Atomic nuclei emit two types of radiation: ionizing and nonionizing. Alpha particles (two protons and two neutrons bound together, making a helium-4 nucleus), beta particles (high-energy electrons or positrons), and gamma rays (streams of high-energy photons) are ionizing radiation. Each of these particles can knock electrons away from their parent atoms, leaving them ionized. Geiger counters detect such freed electrons, as do detectors made from the semiconductors germanium and silicon.

When electrons recombine with the positive ions, they emit flashes of light (scintillations). A scintillation detector might consist of a large, transparent crystal of sodium iodide that is shielded from outside light and optically coupled to a phototube. The phototube detects and amplifies the scintillation, and then it converts the light flash into an electrical signal. The larger the crystal, the weaker the source that can be detected. Cylindrical crystals 7.6 centimeters (3 inches) in diameter, with associated electronics, can be mounted on a helicopter that then flies low to detect radioactive sources on the ground. Larger detectors can be made from scintillator plastic such as polyvinyl toluene (PVT).

Neutrons are nonionizing radiation, so they must be made to interact with something like helium 3 in such a way that ionizing radiation will be produced. Neutrons are emitted by heavy elements that spontaneously fission, such as plutonium and uranium. Customs agents at points of entry into the United States use portals—two columns, 2 to 4 meters (about 6 to 13 feet) high—containing helium-3 neutron detectors and PVT gamma detectors. People, cars, trucks with shipping containers, and trains pass through such portals, which can detect radioactive isotopes and plutonium, but not highly enriched uranium (HEU). A small number of detector portals are available that can examine targets with X rays or neutron beams;

these can detect HEU. As it is generally thought that terrorists would find it easier to build bombs from HEU than from plutonium, it is particularly important that law-enforcement agencies be able to detect smuggled HEU.

Some detectors, including sodium iodide, germanium, and silicon, can measure the energy of gamma rays. The energy patterns are different for different atoms, so scientists can use the patterns as fingerprints to determine which isotopes are present. Germanium detectors have much finer energy resolution than do sodium iodides, but they must be held at very low temperatures (77 Kelvins, or −321 degrees Fahrenheit). A promising new detector material introduced during the early 1990's, cadmium zinc tellurium (CdZnTe), is a room-temperature superconductor. Improved detector portals will have energy-determining capability and will be able to determine which isotopes are present. A powerful new imaging gamma-ray camera that is under development should be able to spot a weak radioactive source up to 100 meters (328 feet) away.

Charles W. Rogers

Further Reading

Ahmed, Syed Naeem. *Physics and Engineering of Radiation Detection*. San Diego, Calif.: Academic Press, 2007.

Kleinknecht, Konrad. *Detectors for Particle Radiation*. 2d ed. New York: Cambridge University Press, 2001.

Saha, Gopal B. "Instruments for Radiation Detection and Measurement." In *Fundamentals of Nuclear Pharmacy*. 5th ed. New York: Springer, 2004.

See also: Environmental Measurements Laboratory; Nuclear spectroscopy; Radiation damage to tissues; Silkwood/Kerr-McGee case; Spectroscopy.

A detective with the New York City Police Department Counterterrorism Unit uses a radiation-detection device to inspect a truck at a checkpoint near the Holland Tunnel in June, 2007. (AP/Wide World Photos)

Nuclear spectroscopy

Definition: Technique for identifying tiny quantities of elements by detecting, recording, and graphically displaying the intensity and energy of their decaying gamma-ray emissions.

Significance: The most sensitive type of spectroscopy, nuclear spectroscopy is a valuable and frequently employed tool in forensic science because it can be used to identify and measure minute amounts of substances that may be undetectable through other techniques.

Nuclear spectroscopy is based on analysis of radiation emitted by unstable atomic nuclei in elements. Gamma decay occurs when unstable atomic nuclei give off excess energy through a spontaneous electromagnetic process. Gamma rays resemble X rays except they come from the nuclei of elements, instead of electrons, and they generally have higher energy than X rays.

Nuclear spectroscopy equipment displays a gamma ray's detection and energy by placing a dot on a monitor screen. If another gamma ray with the same energy is detected, a second dot is placed above the first. Eventually, the monitor displays a graphical image resembling a mountain range on which the vertical height of a peak represents the intensity of gamma rays of that energy and the horizontal position represents the energies of the gamma rays. This graphical mountain range is the gamma-ray spectrum. The positions and relative peak heights differ among different isotopes, and the plotted spectra can be used to identify the isotopes emitting the radiation. Each element has a fixed number of protons in its nucleus; isotopes of the same element all have identical numbers of protons but different numbers of neutrons. The magic of nuclear spectroscopy is that it is more sensitive than almost all other methods of detection. It can detect the presence of an isotope even if it is only a few parts per billion.

If an analyzed sample is not already radioactive, it may be made so through placement in a nuclear reactor, where neutron bombardment can make isotopes in the sample material radioactive. This technique was used in the so-called Beltway Sniper case in late 2002, when ten people were shot to death in the Washington, D.C., area. After several bullet fragments found by investigators underwent neutron activation, nuclear spectroscopy showed that bullets used at different sniping sites probably came from the same source. Eventually, John Allen Muhammad and Lee Boyd Malvo were convicted of the murders.

Another notable example of the application of nuclear spectroscopy to a murder case occurred in Russia. On November 1, 2006, Alexander Litvinenko, a former Russian spy who had been critical of Russian president Vladimir Putin, was poisoned with the radioactive metal polonium 210 in London, England. He died three weeks later from the damage done to his internal organs by alpha radiation. A simple Geiger-counter examination would show that he had ingested some kind of radioactive material and find traces of it in places where he had been. However, the amount necessary to kill Litvinenko—a tiny fraction of a milligram— was too small to be identified by any method other than nuclear spectroscopy. Nuclear spectroscopy was used not only to identify the polonium 210 but also to determine the impurities in the sample taken from Litvinenko's body. The sample was found to be unique to a particular nuclear reactor in Russia. However, Russia denied Britain's request to extradite Andrei Lugovoi, the chief suspect in Litvinenko's murder.

Charles W. Rogers

Further Reading

De Graaf, Robin A. *In Vivo NMR Spectroscopy: Principles and Techniques*. 2d ed. Hoboken, N.J.: John Wiley & Sons, 2007.

Ferguson, Charles D., and William C. Potter. *The Four Faces of Nuclear Terrorism*. New York: Routledge, 2005.

O'Hara, Charles E., and Gregory L. O'Hara. *Fundamentals of Criminal Investigation*. 7th ed. Springfield, Ill.: Charles C Thomas, 2003.

See also: Assassination; Environmental Measurements Laboratory; Nuclear detection devices; Radiation damage to tissues; Spectroscopy.

Number theory. *See* Cryptology and number theory

Oblique lighting analysis

Definition: Technique used in examining evidence that involves lighting an object from different angles to enhance the visibility of its surface features.

Significance: Forensic scientists often use the nondestructive imaging technique of oblique lighting analysis in examining many kinds of trace evidence. By viewing evidence samples under indirect angles of lighting, they may be able to detect faint and latent images on them. This technique can be particularly useful in the examination of documents, fingerprints, footprints, and other types of impression evidence.

In oblique lighting analysis, also known as sidelight examination, the light source shone on an object is adjusted so that the light strikes the surface of the object being examined at a very low angle, which can enhance the visibility of features on the object's surface. Forensic scientists use oblique lighting to enhance contrast when they are examining questioned documents and many types of impression evidence. When using oblique lighting analysis, the investigator must determine the best angle and shadowing effect to produce the greatest contrast in impression.

In forensic science, one of the main uses of oblique lighting is in the examination of questioned documents. Optical examination using different light sources and lighting conditions, including oblique lighting, is a critical nondestructive first step in examining this type of evidence. Oblique lighting enhances image contrast and provides many clues about a document. An original document may be written on with enough force that handwriting impressions are transferred to any sheet of paper beneath it, resulting in indented writing. Tracing is a widely used method to forge signatures on documents and also results in indented impressions. Such impressions are not readily visible when examined using normal light, but they become apparent when illuminated with oblique lighting.

When light strikes the surface of a document at a very low angle, the result is a grazing illumination, with different amounts of light reflected from shadowed and nonshadowed areas of the document. Shining light at a shallow oblique angle causes the surface of a document to appear three-dimensional, which allows the impressions to be more easily viewed. The enhanced image that results is helpful for detecting many features of the document, such as the presence of indented writing, signs of erasure, imprinting, and other impressions.

Oblique lighting can also be used to analyze other types of impression evidence, such as fingerprints and footwear impressions. Shoe prints, for example, often leave residues on surfaces such as flooring, paper, glass, and plastic. Such latent footwear impressions are difficult to see under standard lighting conditions, but they may be detected and enhanced through the use of oblique lighting. Light shone at a low angle across the surface of interest will reflect off the residues and make the prints easier to see.

C. J. Walsh

Further Reading

Blackledge, Robert D., ed. *Forensic Analysis on the Cutting Edge: New Methods for Trace Evidence Analysis.* Hoboken, N.J.: John Wiley & Sons, 2007.

Ellen, David. *Scientific Examination of Documents: Methods and Techniques.* 3d ed. Boca Raton, Fla.: CRC Press, 2006.

Houck, Max M., and Jay A. Siegel. *Fundamentals of Forensic Science.* Burlington, Mass.: Elsevier Academic Press, 2006.

James, Stuart H., and Jon J. Nordby, eds. *Forensic Science: An Introduction to Scientific and Investigative Techniques.* 2d ed. Boca Raton, Fla.: CRC Press, 2005.

Koppenhaver, Katherine M. *Forensic Document Examination: Principles and Practice.* Totowa, N.J.: Humana Press, 2007.

See also: Crime scene investigation; Document examination; Forensic photography; Imaging; Lindbergh baby kidnapping; Locard's exchange principle; Microspectrophotometry; Physical evidence; Questioned document analysis; Trace and transfer evidence; Writing instrument analysis.

Oklahoma City bombing

Date: April 19, 1995

The Event: The explosion of a bomb next to the Alfred P. Murrah Federal Building killed 168 people, injured more than 600 others, and launched a massive rescue effort.

Significance: Signaling a dramatic rise in the scale of domestic terrorism, the Oklahoma City bombing prompted one of the largest criminal investigations in U.S. history and prompted new legislation to fight terrorism.

Shortly after 9:00 A.M. on April 19, 1995, a bomb inside a rented van parked on the street next to the Alfred P. Murrah Federal Building in Oklahoma City exploded. Its blast struck the northern face of the office building, leaving one-third of the structure in ruins and much of downtown Oklahoma City devastated. The entire front of the nine-story building collapsed under the force of the blast, and the concussion was felt more than fifty miles away.

According to forensic engineers who reconstructed the blast, the federal office building collapsed easily because of its design. The engineers determined which of the building's support columns failed first and the approximate force with which the blast hit those columns. The blast was estimated to have been equivalent to that of about two tons of TNT. It damaged more than three hundred buildings, overturned nearby cars, and started numerous fires. About 5 percent of the bombing's death toll was caused by flying pieces of window glass alone.

The truck carrying the bomb was later determined to have contained about forty-eight hundred pounds of an explosive mixture of common ammonium nitrate fertilizer and diesel oil, packed into about twenty plastic drums. The mixture was the same compound that Arab terrorists had used in the bombing of the World Trade Center in New York, on February 26, 1993. The mode of delivery was also the same—a parked rental vehicle.

The Investigation

Similarities between the Oklahoma City and World Trade Center bombings made Arab terrorists prime suspects at first. This suspicion was reinforced by the fact that Oklahoma, a major oil-producing state, had strong ties to world oil markets and was well known to Middle Easterners. Early leads in the Oklahoma City investigation also developed in a fashion similar to those that led to the arrest of the Arabs responsible for the World Trade Center bombing. The vehicle carrying the explosives was quickly identified and tracked to the agency that had rented it.

Only one day after the blast, the Federal Bureau of Investigation (FBI) released composite sketches of two men who had rented the van; both were white Americans. Armed with these sketches, FBI agents acted quickly in what would develop into one of the most massive criminal investigations in U.S. history. Eventually, tens of thousands of persons were interviewed and millions of pieces of evidence were collected. One of the suspects identified by the composite drawings was eventually cleared of involvement in the bombing, but the second suspect, Timothy McVeigh, was soon arrested and charged.

As authorities reconstructed events, they determined that the planning of the attack had begun as early as the previous December, when McVeigh and an Army buddy, Michael Fortier, cased the federal building in Oklahoma City. Afterward, the two men raised the money needed to buy the fertilizer used in their bomb by selling firearms at gun shows. Meanwhile, Terry Lynn Nichols, another of McVeigh's Army buddies, apparently helped McVeigh make the bomb.

McVeigh was eventually convicted on eleven federal charges and was sentenced to death on

June 13, 1997; he was executed on June 11, 2001. Terry Nichols was convicted of manslaughter and of conspiracy to use a weapon of mass destruction but was found innocent on the count of actually using the weapon. He was sentenced to life in prison on June 4, 1998. In 2004, an Oklahoma state court found Nichols guilty on 160 counts of murder, but he was spared the death sentence because of a deadlocked jury. In a plea bargain, Fortier testified against both McVeigh and Nichols at their trials, and in 1998 he was sentenced to twelve years in prison and a fine of $200,000 for failing to alert authorities to the impending attack. He served only part of his sentence, however; he was released from prison in January, 2006.

Aftermath

As the Oklahoma City bombing investigation proceeded, there arose a national call for action against domestic and foreign terrorist threats. The bombing demonstrated the vulnerability to terrorism of an open society such as that of the United States. Both citizens and foreign visitors could travel freely throughout the United States and easily obtain the materials needed to make devastating bombs. Within weeks after the bombing, all federal buildings in major U.S. cities were fitted with prefabricated Jersey barriers to prevent similar attacks. Additionally, the federal government ruled that all new government buildings had to be constructed of stronger materials, with truck-resistant barriers, and set back from the street. The U.S. Congress then enacted a number of measures to prevent acts of terrorism, including the Antiterrorism and Effective Death Penalty Act of 1996.

Sheryl L. Van Horne

On the day after the Oklahoma City bombing, an FBI agent examines debris that the blast blew more than a block from the site of the explosion, the Alfred P. Murrah Federal Building. *(AP/Wide World Photos)*

Further Reading

Brownell, Richard. *The Oklahoma City Bombing*. San Diego, Calif.: Lucent Books, 2007. Discusses the collection of evidence at the bombing site and the forensic techniques used to examine the evidence.

Hansen, Jon. *Oklahoma Rescue*. New York: Ballantine, 1995. Illustrated memoir of an assistant fire chief who was one of Oklahoma's City's pivotal rescue workers.

Hinman, Eve E., and David J. Hammond. *Lessons from the Oklahoma City Bombing: Defensive Design Techniques*. Washington, D.C.: American Society of Civil Engineers, 1996. Brief work addresses the physical characteristics of the Murrah Building that contributed to its becoming a target of a terrorist attack.

Kight, Marsha, comp. *Forever Changed: Remembering Oklahoma City, April 19, 1995*. Amherst, N.Y.: Prometheus Books, 1998. Collection of essays includes testimony of survivors of the bombing and recollections of friends and family members of those who died. Kight lost her twenty-three-year-old daughter in the bombing.

Linenthal, Edward T. *The Unfinished Bombing: Oklahoma City in American Memory*. New York: Oxford University Press, 2001. Examines the psychological impact on Americans of terrorist bombings and the effect of the Oklahoma City tragedy on the relatives of its victims.

Roleff, Tamara L., ed. *The Oklahoma City Bombing*. Detroit: Thomson/Gale, 2004. Collection of speeches, court documents, and interviews with eyewitnesses presents information on the planning, implementation, and aftereffects of the bombing.

Serrano, Richard A. *One of Ours: Timothy McVeigh and the Oklahoma City Bombing*. New York: W. W. Norton, 1998. Journalist's account focuses on McVeigh's background and role in the bombing.

See also: Blast seat; Bomb damage assessment; Bombings; Bureau of Alcohol, Tobacco, Firearms and Explosives; Driving injuries; Federal Bureau of Investigation; First responders; Improvised explosive devices; Structural analysis; Unabomber case; World Trade Center bombing.

McVeigh States His Reasons

The following is excerpted from a letter that Timothy McVeigh wrote to several media figures and news outlets on April 27, 2001, less than seven weeks before he was executed for his role in the bombing of the Alfred P. Murrah Federal Building.

I chose to bomb a federal building because such an action served more purposes than other options. Foremost, the bombing was a retaliatory strike; a counter attack, for the cumulative raids (and subsequent violence and damage) that federal agents had participated in over the preceding years (including, but not limited to, Waco). From the formation of such units as the FBI's "Hostage Rescue" and other assault teams amongst federal agencies during the '80's; culminating in the Waco incident, federal actions grew increasingly militaristic and violent, to the point where at Waco, our government—like the Chinese—was deploying tanks against its own citizens.

Knowledge of these multiple and ever-more aggressive raids across the country constituted an identifiable pattern of conduct within and by the federal government and amongst its various agencies. For all intents and purposes, federal agents had become "soldiers" . . . and they were escalating their behavior. Therefore, this bombing was also meant as a pre-emptive (or pro-active) strike against these forces and their command and control centers within the federal building. When an aggressor force continually launches attacks from a particular base of operation, it is sound military strategy to take the fight to the enemy.

Bombing the Murrah Federal Building was morally and strategically equivalent to the U.S. hitting a government building in Serbia, Iraq, or other nations. . . . From this perspective, what occurred in Oklahoma City was no different than what Americans rain on the heads of others all the time, and subsequently, my mindset was and is one of clinical detachment.

Opioids

Definition: Natural substances derived from opium poppies and synthetic and semisynthetic substances that have properties similar to those derived from opium, generally used for pain relief in medical settings and also as drugs of abuse.

Significance: Opioids are important medicinal drugs for the management of pain, but they are also substances of abuse. Even when opioids are prescribed, users can develop problems such as drug dependence. Because of the addictive nature of opioids, these substances are widely bought and sold illegally.

"Opiate" is the term used to refer to naturally occurring compounds derived from the opium poppy, such as codeine, morphine, and opium. In contrast, "opioid" is a broader, more inclusive term used to describe both naturally occurring and synthetic or semisynthetic opiates. Examples of the latter include heroin, hydromorphone, and oxycodone.

Uses and Effects

Opioids are generally considered narcotics, both in name and legally. Functionally, narcotics are drugs that numb the senses, promote sleep, and elicit stupor. Clinically they are prescribed for analgesia—that is, to reduce pain. The ability of opioids to reduce pain is pronounced, so for individuals who need to manage chronic pain, these drugs can be of significant help. For individuals with careers that may expose them to chronic pain, such as athletes, opioids may also be akin to performance-enhancing drugs, such as steroids and stimulants. Similarly,

for soldiers on the battlefield opioids may be a godsend, but if misused, these substances may be a source of danger to fellow soldiers and others. Given the potential dangers of these drugs, the forensic issues around opioids extend to the identification and regulation of their appropriate use in certain professional arenas, such as is achieved through drug testing.

In addition to analgesia, opioids may induce other changes, including initial warm flushing of the skin, a rush of feelings in the abdomen, and changes in mood. Other effects include constipation (as these drugs slow peristaltic muscle movement in the colon), decrease in rate of respiration, drowsiness, and euphoria. Opioids are also known to cause depression of the central nervous system and the heart (such as in overdoses).

Common routes of administration for these drugs are oral (ingested as pills), nasal (through snorting), inhalation (through smoking), and injection. Individuals may also take these drugs in other ways, such as subdermally and anally, but these are less common. Perhaps the greatest complications associated with these drugs are those that come with injection use among individuals using street drugs. For users who do

Opium poppies. (© iStockphoto.com/Stephanie Horrocks)

not have access to clean means of injection, shared or improperly cleaned needles can lead to problems such as abscesses and the contraction of flesh-eating diseases, hepatitis C, and human immunodeficiency virus (HIV), which causes acquired immunodeficiency syndrome (AIDS). Other problems may result from overdose (using more of the drug than the body can tolerate) and from the use of drugs that are mixed with other substances that may not be good for the body (such as contaminants or materials used to dilute or artificially extend the perceived quantity of the drug).

Scope of Heroin Use

A 2005 research report from the National Institute on Drug Abuse (NIDA) provides this information on heroin use in the United States.

According to the 2003 National Survey on Drug Use and Health, which may actually underestimate illicit opiate (heroin) use, an estimated 3.7 million people had used heroin at some time in their lives, and over 119,000 of them reported using it within the month preceding the survey. An estimated 314,000 Americans used heroin in the past year, and the group that represented the highest number of those users were twenty-six or older. The survey reported that, from 1995 through 2002, the annual number of new heroin users ranged from 121,000 to 164,000. During this period, most new users were age eighteen or older (on average, 75 percent) and most were male. In 2003, 57.4 percent of past-year heroin users were classified with dependence on or abuse of heroin, and an estimated 281,000 persons received treatment for heroin abuse.

According to the Monitoring the Future survey, NIDA's nationwide annual survey of drug use among the nation's eighth-, tenth-, and twelfth-graders, heroin use remained stable from 2003 to 2004. Lifetime heroin use measured 1.6 percent among eighth-graders and 1.5 percent among tenth- and twelfth-graders.

The Drug Abuse Warning Network, which collects data on drug-related hospital emergency department (ED) episodes from twenty-one metropolitan areas, reported that in 2002, heroin-related ED episodes numbered 93,519.

Substance Abuse, Dependence, and Criminal Behavior

Opioids may cause the conditions of substance abuse and substance dependence. As defined in the *Diagnostic and Statistical Manual of Mental Disorders*, fourth edition, text revision (*DSM-IV-TR*), substance abuse is use of a substance to such a degree that it leads to repeated problems at work, home, or school; repeated legal problems; repeated use of the substance in dangerous situations; or repeated interpersonal problems related to the consequences of the substance use. In contrast, substance dependence is characterized by the following: the need to use more of the drug to get the same effect or getting less effect from the same amount of the drug (tolerance); the experience of symptoms when the user ceases or significantly cuts back on use of the drug (withdrawal); use of the drug more often or in greater quantities than intended; unsuccessful attempts to quit or persistent desire to quit; significant time spent obtaining, using, or recovering from the drug; reduction of other meaningful activities in order to use the drug; and the causing or exacerbation of other psychological or physical problems. These symptoms are significant and speak to the motivation that users of illicit or even prescribed opioids may feel to secure their drug supplies, whatever the means or consequences.

Those who use street opioids may also experience malnutrition and pronounced weight loss because the drugs tend to be so powerful that users fail to pay attention to hunger or to be motivated enough to eat. Often, chronic users of opioids ignore all other activities except what they need to do to obtain and use the drugs. In some cases, they engage in criminal behavior to secure the drugs. This may range from dealing drugs, so that they can maintain access to an adequate supply, to theft and other crimes (including prostitution) that can provide them with resources to buy drugs.

Opioid dependency can also occur among persons who begin using the drugs under their doctors' care. Sometimes such users will work very hard to build up networks of doctors and other outlets where they can gain access to the drugs. Some may spend entire days going from doctor to doctor to procure the supplies of drugs they need. This may lead them to commit fraud and misrepresentation to doctors, prescription forgery, and theft and other crimes to secure the drugs. In some cases, prescribing doctors may be involved in significant violations of the law related to drug diversion.

Dangers and the Drug Trade

When opioid-dependent users cannot get enough of their preferred drugs, they frequently mix these substances with alcohol, other prescription or illicit drugs, and even herbal remedies and over-the-counter drugs. This practice can be very dangerous, as mixing opioids with barbiturates, alcohol, and other drugs that act as depressants on the body can cause synergistic effects that can detrimentally affect the body's basic ability to function. Synergistic effects make the impact of the drugs together greater than the impact any of the drugs would have individually. With opioids, this can often lead to respiratory distress or cardiac distress. These reactions may be magnified in persons whose health is compromised by other problems.

Given the broad medical value of opioids and the abuse potential of these substances, it is no surprise that a significant black market exists for their manufacture, distribution, and sale. The illicit trade in opioids ranges from the manufacture of illegal, unregulated supplies in small clandestine laboratories to the large-scale manufacture of look-alike drugs (some of which may fall into the hands of non-substance-abusing consumers), to the theft or diversion of legal drug supplies from their intended points of distribution. The legal and illegal uses of opioids thus pose significant challenges for government authorities, who must balance the protection of appropriate medical uses of these substances against the need to address drug-related crimes such as theft, prostitution, forgery, fraud, assault, and murder.

Nancy A. Piotrowski

Further Reading

Harris, Nancy, ed. *The History of Drugs: Opiates*. Farmington Hills, Mich.: Greenhaven Press, 2005. Provides a historical perspective on opioids, including how they have been used and the political and social issues they have stirred over time.

Julien, Robert M. *A Primer of Drug Action: A Comprehensive Guide to the Actions, Uses, and Side Effects of Psychoactive Drugs*. 10th ed. New York: Worth, 2005. Reliable, long-standing text presents information regarding how these drugs affect individuals at various stages of the life span, from youth to old age.

Moraes, Debra, and Francis Moraes. *The Little Book of Opium*. Oakland, Calif.: Ronin, 2003. Easy-to-read book provides a hodgepodge of information about myths and facts related to opium, its history, chemistry, and effects.

Robbins, David. *Heavy Traffic: Thirty Years of Headlines and Major Ops from the Case Files of the DEA*. New York: Chamberlain Bros., 2005. Chronicles the varied activities of the U.S. Drug Enforcement Administration.

Strain, Eric C., and Maxine L. Stitzer. *The Treatment of Opioid Dependence*. 2d ed. Baltimore: The Johns Hopkins University Press, 2005. Presents a well-informed perspective on how to treat opioid dependence. Suitable for a broad audience, including students, family members of opioid-dependent drug users, and practitioners.

Weil, Andrew, and Winifred Rosen. *From Chocolate to Morphine: Everything You Need to Know About Mind-Altering Drugs*. Rev. ed. Boston: Houghton Mifflin, 2004. Presents a down-to-earth discussion of drugs that affect the mind. Easy to read.

See also: Antianxiety agents; Barbiturates; *Diagnostic and Statistical Manual of Mental Disorders*; Drug abuse and dependence; Drug classification; Illicit substances; Narcotics; Performance-enhancing drugs; Psychotropic drugs.

Oral autopsy

Definition: Examination of the mouth and teeth of a deceased person, usually for the purpose of establishing the person's identity.

Significance: In cases of multiple deaths in disasters such as hurricanes or airplane crashes, oral autopsies are important for establishing the identities of the deceased. This procedure is also used in individual cases when bodies are so decomposed or badly burned that little remains except bones and teeth.

Comparison of the dental characteristics of a deceased person with antemortem (before death) dental records of a known person is an accepted method of identification when it is not possible for investigators to rely on other methods, such as identification by a person familiar with the deceased, fingerprinting, or DNA (deoxyribonucleic acid) analysis. Oral autopsies serve as the primary means of identification in three general kinds of situations: when a body is burned beyond recognition, when a body is severely decomposed or skeletonized, and when multiple bodies must be identified following mass disasters in which people died violently.

Dentists trained in forensic pathology perform oral autopsies. This field is also called forensic odontology. In the United States, the American Board of Forensic Odontology has established guidelines to standardize the procedures of the oral autopsy and to ensure that oral autopsies yield the maximum possible amount of information and properly preserved evidence.

Procedure

The oral autopsy is usually performed after any standard autopsy procedures have been completed, because the oral autopsy destroys facial tissue. The first steps in an oral autopsy are visual examination, photographing, and X-raying of the exterior jaw and mouth area. Next, the mouth is opened. In some cases, the forensic dentist can open the mouth manu-

ally, but in many cases, rigor mortis, carbonization (burning), or fragmentation of the body makes it necessary to gain access to the oral cavity by dissection. The jaw may be broken with a mallet and chisel or cut with pruning shears or a bone saw, or the dentist may expose the interior of the mouth by dissecting away the facial muscles. Interior photographs and X rays are then taken.

The forensic dentist next makes a dental chart, using a numbering system to record the presence or absence of each of the thirty-two teeth an adult usually has; the dentist notes whether each tooth is a primary (baby) tooth or a permanent tooth. For each tooth, any unusual features (such as chips) and dental work (such as fillings and crowns) are noted. The presence of dental prostheses (such as bridges) or orthodontic appliances (such as braces) is also recorded. If the body is not badly damaged, the dentist also records information about the soft tissue of the mouth. The dental chart is supplemented with a narrative record of what the dentist sees. Depending on the condition of the body, the dentist may also make a permanent cast of the teeth using a material called dental stone.

From the condition of the teeth, it is possible to estimate the age of the deceased. The types of materials used in crowns and fillings and the styles of such dental work provide clues to the country or region where the deceased lived when the dental work was done and may possibly also indicate socioeconomic status. This gives law-enforcement investigators some guidance regarding the best places to look for antemortem dental records for the individual. In the United States, investigators might seek dental records from a number of sources, including personal dentists, dental schools and clinics, dental insurance companies, the National Crime Information Center (a database maintained by the Federal Bureau of Investigation), and the Military Personnel Records Center.

After antemortem records are found for the person suspected to be the deceased, the forensic dentist compares the information gathered in the oral autopsy with the dental work detailed in the antemortem records. Based on this comparison, the records are declared a positive match, a possible match, or a definite nonmatch to the deceased, or the dentist states that too little information is available on which to base a conclusion.

It may be weeks or months following the oral autopsy before dental records are found for comparison. For this reason, the forensic dentist must make excellent notes and casts, because the body may no longer be available for examination by the time antemortem dental records are in hand.

Possible Complications

The teeth tend to withstand burning and trauma better than many other parts of the body. Nevertheless, some situations can complicate identification by oral autopsy. When a body is burned beyond recognition (carbonized), the teeth may remain intact but become very fragile. In addition, before the dentist can complete a dental chart and cast, the teeth must be cleaned with an enzyme solution, which is likely to make them even more fragile.

In mass disasters such as airplane crashes and bombings, the bodies of victims are apt to be fragmented. During the oral autopsy, the dentist may have to work with incomplete or misleading information. For example, if the jaw is splintered at the time of death, teeth may be missing that were present during life. The forensic team must collect all body fragments and determine to which set of remains each fragment belongs if complete dental records are to be made for individual victims.

Another kind of complication can arise because multiple systems are used worldwide to number teeth. When forensic dentists in the United States are working with dental records from other countries, they must be familiar with those countries' numbering and nomenclature systems to make valid comparisons.

Sometimes antemortem dental records are simply unavailable, and sometimes those that do exist are incomplete or indecipherable. One advantage of an oral autopsy is that dental casts and notes can be stored easily and do not decompose. They remain readily available should a possible match in dental records turn up years later.

Martiscia Davidson

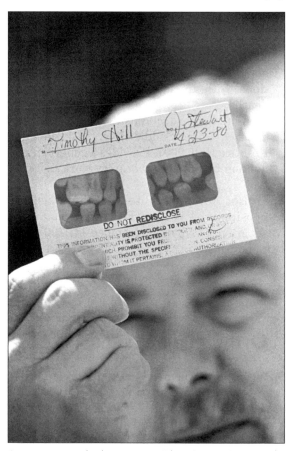

An associate medical examiner in Fulton County, Georgia, displays a set of dental X rays used to help identify the body of a child as that of a thirteen-year-old boy who had gone missing a few weeks earlier. The boy was one of the victims in what became known as the Atlanta child murders. *(AP/Wide World Photos)*

Further Reading

Bowers, C. Michael. *Forensic Dental Evidence: An Investigator's Handbook*. San Diego, Calif.: Elsevier Academic Press, 2004. Outlines the basics of forensic dentistry for law-enforcement personnel and others who must handle and understand dental evidence but who are not dentists.

Fairgrieve, Scott I. *Forensic Cremation: Recovery and Analysis*. Boca Raton, Fla.: CRC Press, 2008. Examines the effects of fire on human tissue, paying special attention to the use of DNA and dental remains as means of reconstructing crimes and making identifications.

Redsicker, David R., and John J. O'Connor. *Practical Fire and Arson Investigation.* 2d ed. Boca Raton, Fla.: CRC Press, 1997. Thoroughly covers all aspects of fire investigations, with an emphasis on fires that cause deaths.

Saferstein, Richard. *Forensic Science: An Introduction.* Upper Saddle River, N.J.: Pearson Prentice Hall, 2007. Provides a general introduction to forensic laboratory work.

See also: Autopsies; Bite-mark analysis; Decomposition of bodies; Forensic odontology; Mass graves; Saliva; September 11, 2001, victim identification.

Orthotolidine

Definition: Chemical used in presumptive tests for blood at crime scenes.

Significance: A positive reaction to orthotolidine of a stain found at a crime scene suggests that the stain is probably blood; such information can facilitate an initial reconstruction of a crime and prompt follow-up.

In the presence of heme iron and hydrogen peroxide, orthotolidine, clear in the reduced state, is converted to an oxidized state, which is blue. Because heme iron is present in hemoglobin, the protein that carries oxygen in red blood cells, a positive test can indicate the presence of blood. Such a test does not distinguish between human blood and animal blood, however; further testing is necessary to make that distinction and, if the blood is human, to determine whose blood it is. In addition, constituents of some plants, such as potatoes and horseradish, as well as oxidizing agents found in some cleansers, can catalyze the reaction. Accordingly, an orthotolidine test is only presumptive for blood; a positive result must be confirmed by laboratory tests.

Typically, a forensic investigator performs the test by moistening a cotton swab with deionized water and rubbing the swab on the suspect stain, adding a drop of orthotolidine solution to the swab, waiting thirty seconds, and then adding a drop of 3 percent hydrogen peroxide to the swab. A positive reaction will turn the swab an intense blue color within fifteen seconds. Often, a swab taken near the stain of interest is used as a control. If the swab turns pinkish before the hydrogen peroxide is added, the test is invalid. To ensure that the reagents have not deteriorated before use, the investigator validates the test using a known blood standard.

First introduced in 1912, orthotolidine, also known as o-tolidine, became almost as widely used as benzidine for testing suspected blood. It has a high sensitivity and is quite specific. It is less carcinogenic than benzidine but more so than phenolphthalein (also used for testing suspected blood), and it poses some risk to users. This risk has been minimized with the introduction of a product marketed as Hemastix: orthotolidine-impregnated sticks designed for use by medical professionals who need to identify the presence of blood in urine. Hemastix can also be used at crime scenes: A drop of deionized water is placed on the stain to be tested, and that drop is transferred to the stick. A resulting blue color suggests the presence of blood. Aside from the convenience this product offers, it allows the investigator to avoid direct contact with orthotolidine. However, whereas the standard orthotolidine test does not interfere with subsequent blood typing and DNA typing, the results of one study suggest that samples collected using Hemastix may interfere with some automated DNA testing procedures.

James L. Robinson

Further Reading

Geberth, Vernon J. *Practical Homicide Investigation: Tactics, Procedures, and Forensic Techniques.* 4th ed. Boca Raton, Fla.: CRC Press, 2006.

Lee, Henry C., Timothy Palmbach, and Marilyn T. Miller. *Henry Lee's Crime Scene Handbook.* San Diego, Calif.: Academic Press, 2001.

Nickell, Joe, and John F. Fischer. *Crime Science: Methods of Forensic Detection.* Lexington: University Press of Kentucky, 1999.

See also: Benzidine; DNA typing; Luminol; Phenolphthalein; Presumptive tests for blood; Reagents; Serology.

Osteology and skeletal radiology

Definition: Subdiscipline of physical anthropology specializing in the scientific study of bone and bony anatomy.

Significance: When remains are discovered that are decomposed, skeletonized, or otherwise unrecognizable, osteology and radiology are used to determine whether the remains are human and how many individuals are represented. Osteological examination may further enable identification of the person or persons and the possible manner of death.

Bone is connective tissue that comprises both organic (living bone cells) and inorganic (mineral) components. Bones provide support for the body's locomotion and other movement, protection of the vital organs, and regulation of bodily substances (such as calcium). Osteologists study the growth, development, morphology, and functions of bone, as well as the pathologies that affect it, in order to understand the human skeletal system.

Origins of the Field

In 1897, George A. Dorsey became the first anthropologist to apply a knowledge of osteology toward expert testimony in a criminal trial—the infamous Luetgert sausage factory trial in Chicago. Dorsey testified that he had identified four small fragments of human bone (believed to be the bones of the wife of factory owner Adolph Luetgert) found in a sausage vat in Luetgert's factory. Luetgert was convicted of the murder of his wife and sentenced to prison, where he died shortly thereafter.

Forensic anthropologist Wilton Marion Krogman illustrated the importance of osteology to law enforcement in his seminal 1939 work "A Guide to the Identification of Human Skeletal Material," which appeared in the *FBI Law Enforcement Bulletin*. World War II, the Korean War, and the Vietnam War saw the regular application of osteology toward the identification and repatriation of the remains of U.S. soldiers. In the twenty-first century, forensic anthropologists routinely use osteology and radiology in the identification of decomposed or unrecognizable human remains and the interpretation of the events preceding, surrounding, and postdating deaths in situations involving both individual and multiple fatalities.

Identifying Human Bones

The first question in a forensic investigation of decomposed, skeletonized, or otherwise unrecognizable animal remains is whether the remains are human. Osteologists answer this question by applying their detailed knowledge of human bony fragments. Such an assessment can often be made visually through comparison of the remains with known human ones in terms of size, shape, density, and significant bony features. Radiographic and microscopic comparisons may be needed, focusing on bone density, trabecular (spongy) bone patterns, and microscopic structures of human versus animal bone.

After remains are confirmed as human, osteologists assess the number of individuals represented by the remains. This can be accomplished through a variety of methods, one of which is the principle known as the minimum number of individuals (MNI), a conservative estimate of the smallest number of persons the remains could represent. MNI is assessed through the documentation of duplication of bony elements (for example, the presence of two right femurs, or thighbones, equals the presence of at least two individuals) as well as differences in age, sex, ancestry, stature, size, shape, coloration, and overall morphology of the bony fragments.

Individuating Remains

The primary applications of osteology and skeletal radiology to forensic science are toward individuation of human remains and reconstruction of perimortem events—that is, the events around the time of death. Individuation is ac-

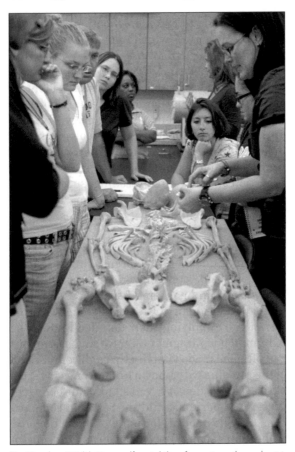

Dr. Heather Walsh-Haney (far right), a forensic anthropologist, teaches a class in human osteology at Florida Gulf Coast University in August, 2007. *(Ronna Gradus/MCT/Landov)*

complished in a variety of ways, the most basic of which is determination of a biological profile for the remains. Such a profile, which is derived from detailed analysis of the recovered remains, comprises the individual's age at death, sex, ancestry, and stature. For example, age at death for a child may be determined through analysis of the growth of long bones and dental eruption, whereas for an adult the osteologist may consider dental wear and degeneration of significant bony regions (such as pubic symphysis) and joints (osteoarthritis). Sex of the remains is established through consideration of the morphology and metrics of major long bones, pelvis, and cranium, if present, and stature is mathematically derived from the maximum length of a long bone. Ancestry is suggested by morphological and metric features of the mid and lower face.

Tentative identification may be based on a comparison of the biological profile of a set of remains with the biological profile of a missing individual or potential victim. A more confident (in some cases, positive) identification can be derived from a comparison of unique antemortem (before death) anomalies and pathologies observed on the remains to those from a suspected identity. These might include prior healed fractures, unique anomalies, or identifying pathological conditions.

Discovery of such anomalies and pathologies is often accelerated through the use of forensic radiology—that is, the application of radiological imaging to a legal context. This can involve traditional radiology (X rays), computed tomography (CT or CAT scans), or magnetic resonance imaging (MRI). One of the most common methods of obtaining positive identifications of remains involves antemortem and postmortem comparisons of radiographic images of teeth; forensic odontologists focus on patterns of missing and filled teeth as well as unique dental traits in applying this method.

In the absence of dental comparisons, frontal sinus patterns can be used. Frontal sinus patterns are believed to be similar to human fingerprints in that each person's sinus "print" is unique. Radiographic comparisons of antemortem and postmortem frontal sinus morphology—including area size, bilateral symmetry, and superior margin outline—have been admissible in court cases to confirm identification. Comparisons of other sinuses (of the maxilla, ethmoid, sphenoid, and mastoid process) have also been used.

Remains may also be identified based on the exact placement of orthopedic and other surgical devices (such as surgical plates, screws, rods); in addition, such devices sometimes carry identifying serial numbers. The presence of pathological (disease) states (such as osteoporosis or osteoarthritis) can be helpful for identification in terms of their level of severity and location within the body, if medically documented. Morphology of trabecular bone patterns within the postcranium has also been used in identification. Trabecular bone is found in the ends of long bones and is characterized by a complex crisscross pattern that may be unique for every individual. Finally, comparisons of multiple and unique concordant bony anomalies (such as an extra rib) may offer supportive evidence for a positive identification.

Interpreting Trauma at Time of Death

A second important application of forensic osteology and skeletal radiology is the interpretation of perimortem trauma. Evidence for blunt force, sharp force, and gunshot wound trauma is often (but not always) visible in characteristic signatures on bone. Such signatures include gunshot entrance and exit defects, impact fractures, radiating and concentric fractures, and cut marks. Osteologists can assess the number of traumatic events (such as gunshot, blunt force, or sharp force wounds), the directionality and trajectories of the events, and sometimes the sequence of impacts (if multiple), often with the help of forensic radiology. These interpretations can be applied toward assessment of the individual's manner of death.

Osteologists must be cautious when interpreting and comparing antemortem and postmortem radiographs to avoid possible sources of error. For example, the body positions of postmortem radiographs must match those from antemortem sources. Other technical difficulties may arise from the level of detail captured in the radiographs as well as the level of skill of the technician in reading them. Bone remodeling over many years may eliminate many potentially concordant details (for example, evidence of healed fractures may fade over several decades and may not be visible on radiographs). Finally, locating antemortem radiographs may be difficult—without comparative antemortem radiographs of appropriate bony regions, a positive identification based on forensic osteology and radiology may not be possible.

Donna C. Boyd

Further Reading

Bass, William M. *Human Osteology: A Laboratory and Field Manual.* 5th ed. Columbia: Missouri Archaeological Society, 2005. Classic guide to human osteology discusses bone identification and completion of a biological profile for skeletonized remains.

Brogdon, B. G., ed. *Forensic Radiology.* Boca Raton, Fla.: CRC Press, 1998. Focuses on the interpretation of radiographic images in courts of law and the applications of radiology in forensic science.

Klepinger, Linda L. *Fundamentals of Forensic Anthropology.* Hoboken, N.J.: John Wiley & Sons, 2006. Introduces methods of estimating age, sex, ancestry, and stature based on skeletal remains and discusses skeletal markers of activity and life history.

Komar, Debra A., and Jane E. Buikstra. *Forensic Anthropology: Contemporary Theory and Practice.* New York: Oxford University Press, 2008. Basic forensic anthropology text includes a section on personal identification through radiological as well as other means.

Matshes, Evan, et al. *Human Osteology and Skeletal Radiology: An Atlas and Guide.* Boca Raton, Fla.: CRC Press, 2005. User-friendly volume intended as a field guide presents comparative images of bones in photographic and radiographic form and addresses the differences among adult, juvenile, and fetal bones.

Schwartz, Jeffrey H. *Skeleton Keys: An Introduction to Human Skeletal Morphology, Development, and Analysis.* 2d ed. New York: Oxford University Press, 2007. Osteology text focuses on human development and individual variation.

White, Tim D., and Pieter A. Folkens. *The Human Bone Manual.* Burlington, Mass.: Elsevier Academic Press, 2005. Handy and portable osteology manual provides detailed photographs of human bony anatomy. Designed for use in the field by anthropologists, forensic scientists, and researchers.

_____. *Human Osteology.* 2d ed. San Diego, Calif.: Academic Press, 2000. Textbook presents detailed discussion of human bony anatomy accompanied by hundreds of high-quality photographs.

See also: Anthropometry; Body farms; Forensic anthropology; Forensic archaeology; Forensic pathology; Forensic sculpture; Imaging; Sex determination of remains; Sinus prints; Skeletal analysis.

P

Paint

Definition: Substance that is spread over surfaces and dries to leave a thin decorative or protective coating.

Significance: Paint is present on a multitude of surfaces in many environments. If a painted surface is damaged during the commission of a crime, paint may be transferred from that surface onto the victim, the offender, or other persons or objects present. Forensic scientists most commonly encounter paint evidence in motor vehicle hit-and-run cases and in burglary cases.

The quantity of paint that is transferred in any particular incident in which a painted surface is damaged depends on the force of contact, the area of contact, and the paint's characteristics, such as its softness and state of deterioration. In hit-and-run cases, where a vehicle has struck a person or another vehicle, a large amount of paint may be transferred, especially if a number of the striking vehicle's panels have been damaged. In contrast, only a small amount of paint is likely to be transferred to a tool when it is used to pry open a window during a burglary.

Composition and Types

Different kinds of paint consist of mixtures of a number of different chemical compounds. Paint can broadly be described as being composed of pigment, binder (also called vehicle or resin), solvent, and other additives. The pigment imparts the color and opacity (hiding power) to the paint. The binder, usually a polymeric compound, provides the medium to spread the pigment across surfaces. The solvent, which may be either organic or water-based, is designed to evaporate after the paint has been applied to the surface, leaving the dried paint film. A range of additives can be included in the formulation of paints, depending on the paints' intended uses; these can include plasticizers, driers, and mildew-resistant agents.

Most of the work of forensic scientists in relation to paint evidence involves the comparison of either automotive paint or architectural paint, although other types of specialized paint, such as marine paint or art paint, are sometimes encountered. When an automobile is manufactured, its finishing system usually consists of four layers of paint, called the original manufacturer's paint. First, the electrocoat primer layer is applied directly to the metal of the car body to provide corrosion resistance. This layer is usually black or gray. The primer layer is then applied. The purpose of this layer is to provide a smooth surface for the base-coat application. The base-coat layer imparts the color and appearance to the final product and provides resistance to environmental conditions, such as weather and ultraviolet radiation. The base coat may contain additives to affect the final look of the paint; for example, aluminum flakes give a metallic finish, and mica pigments coated with metal oxide produce interference colors. Finally, a clear-coat layer is applied to protect the base-coat layer and add a glossy appearance to the paint.

In contrast to automotive paint, architectural paint is not applied in any set sequence of paint layers. The choices of paints used on building interiors and exteriors are usually made by individuals and may include varying numbers of base- and top-coat layers. The walls of older buildings may be coated with large numbers of paint layers, reflecting the many times they have been repainted.

Depending on the cost and availability of individual components, paint manufacturers may alter the ingredients they add to their products at different times while still ensuring that the paint meets strict quality-control requirements. Such differences in batch formulation can provide forensic scientists with additional points of discrimination as they make paint comparisons.

Comparison of Paint Samples

The first step in the forensic examination of any paint evidence is a visual comparison between the paint sample recovered from the crime scene and a control sample. This comparison, often aided by a microscope, involves analysis of the color and texture of each layer of paint. Inspection of the sequence of paint layers present is extremely important for evaluating the evidential significance of any match.

For automotive paints, the examiner should be able to establish whether the paint is the original manufacturer's paint or whether additional layers of paint have subsequently been added. The presence of additional paint layers means that the sample of paint, and therefore the vehicle from which it came, is likely to be distinguishable from other vehicles of the same model made by the same manufacturer.

For architectural paints, an assessment of the commonness of the color and type of paint present is required. Thousands of different paint colors are available, and new colors are continually being marketed as fashions change. No set number of paint layers must be matched between samples for the examiner to determine a conclusive match, but matches that include the presence of uncommon paint colors or large numbers of corresponding layers are considered to be of higher evidential value.

The comparison of the visual appearance of paint samples can be complicated if the recovered sample is present only as a paint smear. Smears are frequently encountered on the clothing of hit-and-run victims and on tools used to pry open painted windows or doors during the commission of burglaries. The color of a paint smear may be altered slightly because of the influence of the substrate color or because a number of different paint layers have been crushed together.

If two samples of paint cannot be differentiated after a visual examination, the examiner's next step is to compare the chemical compositions of the paint layers. As most paints contain mixtures of organic and inorganic compounds, the instrumental techniques used must be able to detect the full range of compounds present. In addition, each layer should be analyzed separately, if possible. For some techniques, this means that the examiner must section the paint, either by hand or using a microtome.

Pyrolysis gas chromatography (PyGC) is frequently used to compare the organic compounds present in the paint layers. This technique is particularly suited to the analysis of polymers, as the heat present in the pyrolyzer decomposes the polymer into smaller oligomers that are able to be chromatographed. Fourier transform infrared (FTIR) spectroscopy can also be used to compare the major organic compounds present and some of the inorganic compounds present (such as titanium dioxide).

The examiner may use a variety of techniques to compare the inorganic compounds present in each paint layer, such as X-ray fluorescence (XRF) and scanning electron microscopy with energy-dispersive spectroscopy (SEM-EDS). SEM-EDS has the added advantage of allowing a visual examination of each layer at a very high magnification. This can reveal the presence of additives such as aluminum flakes.

The PDQ Database

The Forensic Laboratory Services of the Royal Canadian Mounted Police maintains one of the world's largest databases of information on the colors and chemical compositions of the paints used by automobile manufacturers, the International Forensic Automotive Paint Data Query (PDQ) database. By using the PDQ, law-enforcement agencies can identify the makes and models of many vehicles from samples of their paint; often, even the assembly plant in which a vehicle was made can be determined.

Through collaborative efforts involving automakers and law-enforcement agencies in Canada and around the world, the PDQ has accumulated a library of more than fifty thousand layers of paint. Samples of paint included in the database come from forensic laboratories as well as from automobile manufacturers. In return for contributing sixty new samples of automotive paint to expand the database each year, accredited users receive a copy of the PDQ. Users include law-enforcement agencies in the United States, the European Union, Australia, New Zealand, Japan, and Singapore.

A forensic scientist for the Michigan State Police testifies about the similarity between paint samples collected from the defendant's shoes and paint samples collected from the suspected scene of a murder in a 2006 trial. *(AP/Wide World Photos)*

Evaluation of Paint Evidence

If the paint layers present in the recovered and control samples cannot be distinguished by their physical appearance and chemical composition, the next step is the assessment of the evidential value of these findings. This is usually a subjective exercise based on the experience of the analyst, who takes into consideration the number of corresponding paint layers and the commonness of the types of paint present. For automotive paint, it is important to establish whether the paint layers are the original manufacturer's paint or whether additional layers of paint have been added.

The finding of a number of corresponding paint layers usually provides strong evidence to link the two samples of paint. For cases involving the collision of two vehicles, the finding of two-way paint transfer can provide very strong evidence, and in some cases a conclusive finding

may be made. A conclusive match can also be reported when the analyst considers that the combination of corresponding paint layers is unique and therefore no alternative sources are possible.

Forensic scientists are also sometimes asked to identify the makes and models of automobiles from paint layers present in samples recovered from crime scenes. Such requests are commonly made to provide investigative evidence on the specific kinds of vehicles that were present at the scenes, whether hit-and-run or other kinds of crime scenes. To make such identifications, the scientists consult databases containing extensive information on the paints used by automobile manufacturers, such as the International Forensic Automotive Paint Data Query (PDQ) database established by the Forensic Laboratory Services of the Royal Canadian Mounted Police.

Sally A. Coulson

Further Reading

Caddy, Brian, ed. *Forensic Examination of Glass and Paint: Analysis and Interpretation*. New York: Taylor & Francis, 2001. Detailed text provides thorough discussion of all aspects of forensic paint examination.

Challinor, John. "Paint Examination." In *Expert Evidence*, edited by Ian Freckelton and Hugh Selby. North Ryde, N.S.W.: Lawbook, 1993. Presents an overview discussion of paint evidence and comparative techniques. Intended for members of the legal community.

Houck, Max M., and Jay A. Siegel. *Fundamentals of Forensic Science*. Burlington, Mass.: Elsevier Academic Press, 2006. Good general textbook includes a section on paint examination and analysis.

Inman, Keith, and Norah Rudin. *Principles and Practice of Criminalistics: The Profession of Forensic Science*. Boca Raton, Fla.: CRC Press, 2001. Discusses the interpretation of various kinds of forensic evidence, including paint evidence.

Saferstein, Richard. *Criminalistics: An Introduction to Forensic Science*. 9th ed. Upper Saddle River, N.J.: Pearson Prentice Hall, 2007. Standard textbook includes discussion of the general points of forensic paint examination. Presents examples of cases in which paint evidence was used.

See also: Arsenic; Art forgery; Chromatography; Fourier transform infrared spectrophotometer; Gas chromatography; Hit-and-run vehicle offenses; Lead; Mass spectrometry; Micro-Fourier transform infrared spectrometry; Microspectrophotometry; Spectroscopy.

Paper

Definition: Flexible sheets of compressed wood pulp, or similar substrates made of other materials, used chiefly for written and printed documents but also for disposable containers.

Significance: Paper figures most commonly as evidence in civil forgery cases. Many of the tools that forensic scientists use to analyze inks and toners can also be applied to the paper on which these substances appear. Questioned document analysts focus more attention on ink and handwriting than on paper, because the writing itself usually provides more definitive clues than the substrate. Analysis of paper, however, can be crucial to proving forgery or the authenticity of works of art and historical documents. In addition, fragments of paper found at crime scenes may provide evidence that can link suspects to crimes.

A piece of paper, independent of any writing or printing that may appear on it, conveys a wealth of information. By examining it closely, an expert can often tell where and when it was manufactured. Telltale signs of its subsequent history—how it was stored and whether it was treated in any way—may be discernible as well. Forensic scientists may also be able to match paper fragments that have been torn or cut from larger original pieces to those original pieces in a process known as fracture matching.

Differing Characteristics

Paper manufacture originated in the Orient and was imported into Europe in the late Middle Ages. Paper is basically a felt made of plant fibers, compressed to form a thin, tough sheet. Certain characteristics imparted by the paper-making process are visible in the finished product. These include the species of plant from which the fibers were derived, the chemical and mechanical means used to extract and treat the fibers to make them suitable for papermaking, bleaching agents and dyes, density, surface texture imparted by rollers, watermarks, fillers, and substances used for coating.

The older the paper, the more likely the species of plant used in its manufacture is to be diagnostic. In the twenty-first century, wood chips used in pulping are shipped all over the world. In contrast to new paper from large international conglomerates, which varies little in its species composition, recycled paper can be highly diagnostic, because the species mix changes so much from batch to batch.

Because visible surface features of documents can be photocopied, many firms and government agencies print their most sensitive documents on security paper that is manufactured for specific purposes. Such paper incorporates fibers, watermarks, invisible reactive inks, and other features that forgers and counterfeiters cannot reproduce without access to the original, tightly controlled paper stock.

Analysis Techniques

Document analysts use radiocarbon dating as well as the analysis of paper manufacturing techniques to determine the ages of old documents and drawings. Serious forgers of purportedly old documents attempt to avoid discovery by using antique paper. In initial authentication of the Vinland map, which was claimed to be a fifteenth century copy of a thirteenth century map proving Viking settlement in the New World, investigators concluded that the map was genuine because it was drawn on fifteenth century parchment. A supposed center fold, however, turned out to be a seam where two leaves were joined before the map itself was drawn. Through microscopic examination, fo-

rensic document examiners can readily determine whether folds or mechanical damage on a piece of paper occurred before or after the paper was written on. Something written after the paper was damaged raises suspicion of forgery.

The origins of the fibers used in paper can be determined through examination of the morphology of individual fibers with either transmitted light or scanning electron microscopy (SEM). Forensic scientists use the same spectrographic methods they apply to analyzing ink in analyzing paper. SEM produces a high-resolution image of surface features, and a laser scanning confocal microscope produces a three-dimensional image. As an adjunct to SEM, energy-dispersive spectroscopy (EDS; also known as energy-dispersive X-ray spectroscopy, or EDX) measures the X-ray emission spectra of compounds bombarded by electrons. An EDS reading indicates which atomic elements are present in a sample and in what proportions.

Infrared absorption spectrometry detects specific types of chemical bonds in organic molecules. This technique is useful for detecting coating agents on paper and for tracing plastics used in place of paper. Photographic papers of-

Paper and Forgery

One of the most skilled document forgers in modern history, Mark Hofmann was a disaffected Mormon who specialized in faking key documents in his church's history. A major reason for his success in fooling church officials, collectors, historians, and forensic experts was the care he took in producing his forgeries on paper manufactured during the periods in which his documents were supposedly written. He was also skilled in making inks that chemically matched those in authentic historical documents. Two decades after his criminal career ended, his forgeries were still giving headaches to scholars, archivists, and document collectors. Hofmann's downfall came after mounting financial difficulties moved him to launch a bombing campaign against his clients in Salt Lake City that led to his conviction for murder and a life sentence in Utah State Prison. Pictured here during his 1986 trial, he is seated in a wheelchair because he was severely injured by one of his own bombs.

(AP/Wide World Photos)

ten have distinctive chemical signatures and surface characteristics. Trace-element analysis using plasma mass spectrometry has been used to identify batches of recycled paper. Examination under ultraviolet light reveals erasures and stains, and raking (low-angle) light shows buckling and watermarks.

A discarded paper match found at an arson scene or at another kind of crime scene can be a valuable piece of evidence. If investigators identify a suspect and find in that person's possession the matchbook from which the discarded match came, the torn end of the match will correspond to the stub in the matchbook. Also, because paper matches are made from recycled cardboard, the lot number and its distribution pattern can be determined from the fiber content of the match. This information can provide investigators with a range of places the suspect might have been seen immediately prior to the commission of the crime.

Although paper analysis has entered into a number of high-profile historical criminal cases, notably in the analysis of the ransom notes in the 1932 kidnapping of Charles A. Lindbergh's infant son, the findings of paper analysis are rarely definitive. An exception is the hoax involving diaries purportedly written by Adolf Hitler, in which the handwriting, writing style, and supposed origin of the documents were plausible, but analysts determined that the paper itself could not have been manufactured before 1950.

Martha Sherwood

Further Reading

Conners, Terrance E., and Sujit Banerjee, eds. *Surface Analysis of Paper*. Boca Raton, Fla.: CRC Press, 1995. Technically oriented volume provides detailed information on paper surfaces. Intended mainly for use in quality-control applications in the paper industry.

Dines, Jess E. *Document Examiner Textbook*. Irvine, Calif.: Pantex International, 1998. Practical manual for forensic document examiners includes good coverage on watermarks.

Eckert, William G., ed. *Introduction to Forensic Sciences*. 2d ed. Boca Raton, Fla.: CRC Press, 1997. Text aimed at students considering ca-reers in forensic sciences offers useful tips on identifying types of paper.

Houck, Max M. *Forensic Science: Modern Methods of Solving Crime*. Westport, Conn.: Praeger, 2007. Highly readable volume provides a rigorous overview of many aspects of forensic science, with numerous examples. Includes brief coverage of document analysis.

Kaye, Brian H. *Science and the Detective. Selected Reading in Forensic Science*. New York: VCH, 1995. Presents clear descriptions of the manufacturing processes used in the paper industry and discusses how to detect the differences among types of paper.

Spencer, Ronald D. *The Expert Versus the Object: Judging Fakes and False Attributions in the Visual Arts*. New York: Oxford University Press, 2004. Describes scientific methods for the authentication of art, including radiocarbon dating and analysis of historic paper-making techniques.

White, Peter, ed. *Crime Scene to Court: The Essentials of Forensic Science*. 2d ed. Cambridge, England: Royal Society of Chemistry, 2004. Contains a lengthy discussion of questioned document analysis.

See also: Art forgery; Counterfeit-detection pens; Counterfeiting; Document examination; Energy-dispersive spectroscopy; Forgery; Fracture matching; Hitler diaries hoax; Lindbergh baby kidnapping; Questioned document analysis; Scanning electron microscopy; Writing instrument analysis.

Parasitology

Definition: Study of a class of debilitating organisms that feed on other organisms.

Significance: In some death investigations, parasites observed in corpses during autopsy may provide important information. Specific parasites have unique life histories and distribution patterns, and the presence of certain parasites can indicate when a corpse was subjected to particular conditions. This information may be useful to investigators in determining the sequence of events leading to the death. Forensic examination of parasites is also sometimes important in liability cases involving the contamination of food, water, medicines, or building systems such as air conditioning.

Parasitologists study the ecological and evolutionary adaptations and relationships between parasites and their host organisms, the impacts of parasites and hosts on each other, and the populations and distributions of parasites. Virtually every species of animal and plant hosts at least one variety of parasite that is specific to that species. Some parasites are affiliated with multiple host types during their life histories. The modern study of parasitology combines information from the disciplines of biology, ecology, biochemistry, cell and molecular biology, microbiology, and immunology.

Types and Impacts of Parasites

Parasitism occurs when one organism (the parasite) benefits from a relationship in which it feeds on another organism (the host) and, in so doing, harms that organism in some way. (A relationship between organisms that does not harm either is referred to as mutualistic rather than parasitic.) Parasites may use host organisms for refuge or as platforms for reproduction. Typically, parasites are much smaller in size than their hosts, and they are usually much more numerous as well.

Two basic types of parasites are endoparasites, which live inside the body (such as tapeworms, flukes, and amoeboid parasites of body fluids), and ectoparasites, which live on the skin or among hairs (such as fleas, ticks, and lice). A familiar example of a parasite-host relationship is the presence of fleas on a dog or cat. Fleas obtain food, a safe and sheltered living habitat in the animal's fur, and trans-

portation that allows them to infect other cats and dogs, thus increasing their distribution across a landscape. The impacts of parasites on their hosts include neurological, physical, and behavioral changes that collectively can diminish the ability of the hosts to survive and reproduce. Fleas, for example, can cause skin irritations, infections, and even life-threatening anemia in their animal hosts.

Human Parasitology

An important branch of medicine is devoted to the prevention and cure of diseases caused by parasites in humans. A wide range of organisms have parasitic relationships with humans; among the most common of these are bacteria, viruses, protozoans, and helminths (worms). In humans, parasite-induced diseases arise when parasites deprive the body of nutrients, destroy tissues, and release or create toxic wastes that disrupt the functioning of tissues, organs, and systems such as the nervous system.

Humans are often affected by protozoan (single-celled) parasites, amoebae, flukes, and helminths. An example of a pathogenic amoeba is *Entamoeba histolytica*, which causes amoebic dysentery and can penetrate the digestive wall and spread to other tissues of the body. This organism is introduced into the body most often

One of the most common ectoparasites that afflicts human beings is the tick, a biting insect that helps to spread hemorrhagic fevers and tularemia. (© iStockphoto.com/Eric Delmar)

Common Human Parasites

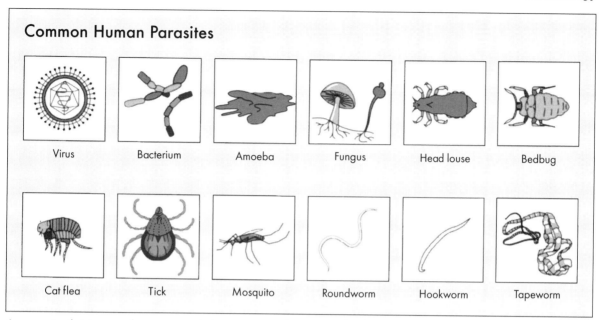

Virus   Bacterium   Amoeba   Fungus   Head louse   Bedbug

Cat flea   Tick   Mosquito   Roundworm   Hookworm   Tapeworm

Any organism that, temporarily or permanently, lives on or in another organism for the purpose of procuring food is considered a parasite; these parasites may cause infection in human hosts.

through drinking water that has been contaminated with fecal products. Infections of amoebic dysentery, which causes severe diarrhea and bleeding of the digestive tract, can result in death if untreated or treated too late.

Forensic Applications

In criminal cases involving deaths or illnesses, pathologists and other forensic scientists usually take complete inventories of both ectoparasites and endoparasites found on or in the bodies of the deceased or ill victims. They are especially concerned with identifying organisms that can cause death or may be factors leading to death. They also note the presence of any parasites that may provide clues regarding certain aspects of the life histories of the victims, such as health issues. An autopsy of someone who has died from parasitic infection reveals the causal parasites through their chemical traces or by-products and through their typical destructive pattern in tissues and organs.

When the body of a possible crime victim is discovered, forensic parasitology can sometimes provide law-enforcement investigators with important information concerning the circumstances, location, and time of death. By ex-

amining the body for parasites that can survive in and feed on dead hosts, a parasitologist may be able to determine, for example, whether or not the body was moved from the location where the person died. Also, when living parasites are found on a corpse, this is a strong indication that the individual died within a short period before the body was found.

Forensic scientists may also be involved in examining the relationship between outbreaks of illness caused by parasites and the likely sources of the parasites. Deaths and illnesses related to parasites are on the rise in the United States and in many other countries, in part owing to the ever-increasing mobility of the global population. International travelers may unintentionally transport parasites and their eggs or larvae on their clothing, shoes, or skin, and the introduction of parasites to new areas may not be detected immediately. When lawsuits arise as the result of parasitic infections caused by contaminated food, water, or other products or facilities, forensic parasitologists are called upon to identify and clarify the transmission modes of the parasites and the most likely sources of the contamination.

Dwight G. Smith

Further Reading

Ash, Lawrence R., and Thomas C. Orihel. *Atlas of Human Parasitology*. 5th ed. Chicago: American Society for Clinical Pathology Press, 2007. Useful reference work provides identification methods for the parasites seen most often in human beings in forensic science applications. Includes more than eight hundred color photographs of parasites.

Bogitsh, Burton J., Clint E. Carter, and Thomas N. Oeltmann. *Human Parasitology*. 3d ed. Burlington, Mass.: Elsevier Academic Press, 2005. Discusses the full range of parasites found in humans. Intended for students in the health professions.

Breeze, Roger G., Bruce Budowle, and Steven E. Schutzer, eds. *Microbial Forensics*. Burlington, Mass.: Elsevier Academic Press, 2005. Collection focuses on the relationship between forensic science and microbe physiology. Includes some discussion of parasites.

Mahon, Connie R., Donald C. Lehman, and George Manuselis, eds. *Textbook of Diagnostic Microbiology*. 3d ed. St. Louis: Saunders Elsevier, 2007. Well-illustrated, comprehensive volume covers all aspects of microbiology.

See also: Air and water purity; Antibiotics; Biological terrorism; Biological warfare diagnosis; Biological weapon identification; Bubonic plague; Centers for Disease Control and Prevention; Pathogen genomic sequencing; Pathogen transmission.

Parental alienation syndrome

Definition: Set of symptoms in which a child is obsessively preoccupied with unjustified or exaggerated deprecation or criticism of a parent (the target parent) owing to the influence of the favored parent (the alienating parent) combined with the child's own contributions.

Significance: Forensic psychiatrists and psychologists testifying as expert witnesses in child-custody cases sometimes discuss parental alienation syndrome. Attorneys seek to have such testimony admitted into evidence to establish that the alienating parent has created a psychological disorder in the child. Controversy exists about the scientific basis for parental alienation syndrome, however, because it is not a diagnostic syndrome recognized by the American Psychiatric Association's *Diagnostic and Statistical Manual of Mental Disorders*.

Richard A. Gardner, a child psychiatrist, coined the term "parental alienation syndrome" (PAS) in 1985 to describe a set of symptoms indicative of intense rejection of a parent by a child following parental divorce or separation. When a child's parents separate, the child may resist contact with one of the parents for a variety of normal reasons, including reasons having to do with the child's stage of development. The alienated child described by Gardner, however, persistently refuses and rejects contact with a parent because of unreasonable negative views and feelings toward that parent.

Gardner described the child exhibiting PAS as obsessed with hatred of the target parent. This hatred is irrational and stems from the influence of the alienating parent on the child's feelings toward the target parent. According to Gardner, the alienating parent is unable to tolerate separation from the child and so engages in a campaign to program the child to denigrate the target parent. In this way, the alienating parent uses the child to meet the alienating parent's own emotional needs. Gardner's account of PAS captured the attention of both mental health professionals and the legal community in the United States and stimulated research on the syndrome's conceptualization, identification, diagnosis, and treatment.

Conceptualization of PAS

Gardner posited three essential elements as necessary for a diagnosis of PAS. First is the child's denigration of the target parent, which is persistent and reaches the level of a campaign. This persistent denigration has a rehearsed quality, and it often includes phraseology not typically used by a child. Second, the denigration and rejection of the target parent are irrational, not reasonable responses to any behavior on the part of the target parent. Child abuse, child neglect, the child's witnessing of episodes of domestic violence, or other dysfunctional factors are not present. Third, the denigration is the result of the influence of the alienating parent as well as the self-created contributions by the child in support of the alienating parent's campaign to denigrate the target parent. The child contributes to the alienating parent's campaign because the child fears the loss of the love of the alienating parent. Hatred of the target parent often extends to include members of the target parent's extended family.

In presenting his conceptualization, Gardner wanted to distinguish PAS from situations in which a child prefers one parent but still maintains a relationship with the other parent. In addition, he distinguished situations in which a child resists spending time with a parent after divorce or separation but that resistance is short-lived; in such cases, the child is not alienated and is not under the influence of an alienating parent.

Legal and Therapeutic Interventions

A mental health clinician makes a diagnosis of PAS and may testify in court as an expert witness in a child-custody or visitation case. Gardner has recommended that any legal intervention in a given case should be based on whether a behavioral science expert has assessed the case as mild, moderate, or extreme parental alienation. In mild parental alienation cases, the alienating parent does not have any severe emotional problems. A court order for visitation is the only intervention necessary in such a case, because a clear court order will alleviate the child's guilt about contact with the target parent and should lower the conflict between the parents.

In moderate parental alienation cases, Gardner has recommended a combination of court orders for visitation and for therapy. Therapy is necessary because the alienating parent is giving verbal and nonverbal cues to the child, encouraging the child to denigrate the target parent. The goals of the therapy are to structure the visitation between the child and

the target parent by deprogramming the child and confronting the tactics of the alienating parent.

In severe parental alienation cases, a change in custody is likely to be necessary, because typically the alienating parent has severe psychopathology that is also affecting other aspects of his or her parenting. The vast majority of PAS cases that are seen in therapeutic settings fall within the category of moderate parental alienation.

Limitations

PAS is a controversial concept within the mental health and legal communities. Proponents of the concept claim that it helps attorneys and judges to understand and address a phenomenon long recognized by the mental health community. They assert that expert testimony on PAS can be useful to the court in that it can shed light on a child's refusal to see a parent and can help the court determine how much weight to give to the child's preferences regarding custody.

Critics charge that PAS lacks an adequate scientific foundation for recognition as a diagnostic syndrome and that, therefore, expert testimony regarding its diagnosis and treatment should be inadmissible. They point to the fact that little research exists concerning the scientific reliability of a diagnosis of PAS—that is, the degree to which different clinicians examining the same children reach a high rate of agreement on which children do or do not have the syndrome. Critics also emphasize the lack of empirical research substantiating whether PAS accurately describes a disturbance suffered by some children. The accurate description of such a disturbance requires empirical research to identify what kinds and how many symptoms are necessary for a diagnosis of PAS. This research should include the examination of the prevalence of PAS and its long-term effects on children. In addition, critics assert that the use of the medical designation "syndrome" may convey a legitimacy to testimony on PAS that is not warranted given the lack of empirical research. Further research is necessary to resolve these controversies.

Patricia E. Erickson

Further Reading

Gardner, Richard A. *The Parental Alienation Syndrome.* 2d ed. Creskill, N.J.: Creative Therapeutics, 1998. Presents a comprehensive discussion of PAS in the context of the American adversarial legal system.

Gardner, Richard A., Richard S. Sauber, and Demosthenes Lorandos, eds. *The International Handbook of Parental Alienation Syndrome: Conceptual, Clinical, and Legal Considerations.* Springfield, Ill.: Charles C Thomas, 2006. Collection of articles provides information useful for understanding research findings concerning PAS.

Warshak, Richard A. "Current Controversies Regarding Parental Alienation Syndrome." *American Journal of Forensic Psychology* 19 (2001): 29-59. Presents a clearly written discussion of the controversies that surround the use of the diagnosis of PAS in the courtroom.

See also: Borderline personality disorder; Child abuse; *Daubert v. Merrell Dow Pharmaceuticals*; Expert witnesses; False memories; Forensic psychiatry; Forensic psychology; Minnesota Multiphasic Personality Inventory; Paternity evidence.

Paternity evidence

Definition: Evidence used to determine whether a person is the father of a specific child.

Significance: Information on paternity can be important for a number of legal reasons, from issues of inheritance to cases involving rape. Most often, tests for paternity are conducted using DNA evidence. Forensic scientists compare the DNA of an alleged father to a child's DNA to determine whether there is evidence of paternity based on the fact that the man cannot be excluded as the father of the child.

Before forensic experts began to analyze DNA (deoxyribonucleic acid), the evidence used in paternity cases was far from conclusive. Courts in the United States applied a common-law "presumption of paternity" after a mother named a particular person as the father of her child. The alleged father might rebut the presumption by producing evidence such as sterility or impotence or evidence showing that he was not present in the same location as the mother at the time of conception. Because of the lack of definitive evidence, however, many cases of paternity fraud were perpetrated, as most U.S. states did not require mothers to disclose the names of all potential fathers of their children.

Although modern methods of examining DNA evidence may exclude a person as the fraternal parent of a child with almost 100 percent accuracy, scientists have not yet been able to use DNA to prove positively that a specific person is the father. In addition, paternity fraud still exists in those courts that are slow to accept some of the newer technologies used by forensic scientists to establish paternity. After paternity has been established, the person designated as the father may find it difficult to obtain rescission of the paternity court order, even if more sophisticated evidence is produced at a later date.

Reasons for Establishing Paternity

Establishing paternity serves several purposes. One of the largest demands for paternity testing relates to child support. The government wants to make sure that parents pay to support their children rather than have taxpayers fund child support through public assistance. In fact, U.S. law requires a woman to name possible fathers in order to obtain public assistance for her children.

Paternity must also be established before children and fathers are able to inherit from each other under state intestacy laws that require a biological relationship. Insurance companies and the government may also require a father-child determination before paying insurance or Social Security benefits. Children may want to know the identities of their biological fathers for personal, medical, and emotional reasons. Finally, it is important to identify fathers for purposes of prosecution in criminal paternity cases such as rape, sexual abuse of a child, and incest.

Blood and DNA Heredity Evidence

In some paternity cases, forensic serologists may still use blood typing. Using blood as the only evidence to establish paternity, however, has limitations, not the least of which is the amount of blood evidence needed to run such tests and the lack of genetic information generated from blood typing.

DNA provides better evidence of paternity, as it is unique and the hereditary factors found in DNA work well to exclude people as biological parents of a child. Half of a person's DNA is contributed by the mother and the other half by the father. By comparing the specific short tandem repeats (STRs) of a child's DNA to the DNA of possible parents of the child, forensic scientists are able to identify people who could not be the mother and father based on dissimilarities in their DNA (assuming a genetic mutation did not result in a false exclusion). To determine the most likely father, forensic scientists use probability calculations after finding consistent genetic patterns between the DNA of the alleged father and the child.

Sources of DNA Evidence

The most credible way to test for paternity is by comparing samples of DNA extracted from body fluids (such as saliva, semen, or blood) collected directly from the purported father and the child. Noninvasive buccal samples—collected by scraping the inside of the mouth with a foam applicator or cotton swab—may also be used; this method is especially useful for collecting DNA from infants. When an individual of interest is not available, scientists must collect DNA evidence from some other source that person has left behind. For example, paternity testing can be conducted with a small DNA sample obtained from a hair (with root intact) left in a hairbrush or from saliva on a toothbrush, envelope flap, or cigarette butt. The blood in the umbilical cord of a newborn or cells from a fetus also provide sufficient DNA for testing.

In some cases, the purported father or child is deceased, and DNA samples are collected during autopsy or from the body at the funeral home; if a case requires DNA from a body after burial, a court-ordered exhumation may take place so that a specimen can be collected. For

Larry Birkhead emerges from a court hearing in Nassau, Bahamas, in April, 2007. Citing expert testimony based on DNA evidence, the court ruled that Birkhead is the father of the infant daughter of former Playboy Playmate Anna Nicole Smith, a legal resident of the Bahamas who had died two months earlier. Smith died while in the midst of a prolonged lawsuit over the estate of her billionaire husband, an octogenarian who had died in 1995. As Smith's only surviving child, the daughter stood to inherit an immense fortune. After Smith died, Birkhead was one of several men who stepped forward to claim paternity of the daughter. (AP/Wide World Photos)

children, DNA exemplars may be available from dried blood samples stored on so-called Guthrie cards, which many U.S. states use to screen for genetic diseases at the time of birth. In criminal paternity cases involving fetuses aborted before full term, DNA from the fetuses can be compared with the DNA of the alleged fathers.

Carol A. Rolf

Further Reading

Buckleton, John, Christopher M. Triggs, and Simon J. Walsh, eds. *Forensic DNA Evidence Interpretation.* Boca Raton, Fla.: CRC Press, 2005. Provides good explanations regarding biology and DNA analysis, including the interpretation of DNA in paternity identification.

Butler, John M. *Forensic DNA Typing: Biology, Technology, and Genetics of STR Markers.* 2d ed. Burlington, Mass.: Elsevier Academic Press, 2005. Readable text includes discussion of the use of short random repeats in the genome, which provides useful evidence in determining paternity.

Coleman, Howard, and Eric Swenson. *DNA in the Courtroom: A Trial Watcher's Guide.* Seattle: GeneLex, 1994. Discusses in simple terms the comparison of DNA evidence for use in court trials.

Evett, Ian W., and Bruce S. Weir. *Interpreting DNA Evidence: Statistical Genetics for Forensic Scientists.* Sunderland, Mass: Sinauer Associates, 1998. Addresses the basics of the mathematical analysis of DNA evidence, including the determination of statistical probability in paternity cases.

Kobilinsky, Lawrence F., Thomas F. Liotti, and Jamel Oeser-Sweat. *DNA: Forensic and Legal Applications.* Hoboken, N.J.: Wiley-Interscience, 2005. Presents a comprehensive overview of the uses of DNA analysis in American legal proceedings, including paternity cases.

See also: DNA analysis; DNA database controversies; DNA fingerprinting; DNA isolation methods; DNA profiling; DNA sequencing; DNA typing; Jefferson paternity dispute; Parental alienation syndrome; Paternity testing; Polymerase chain reaction; Y chromosome analysis.

Paternity testing

Definition: Use of DNA profiling or examination of blood proteins to determine whether specific men are the biological fathers of particular children.

Significance: Forensic paternity testing may be used for a variety of reasons, including in legal cases regarding inheritance rights or child support. The ability to answer questions of paternity is also sometimes important in criminal cases involving pregnancies, such as rape and incest cases.

During the 1920's, paternity testing was done using the ABO blood group types. This test could exclude a man as the father of another person, but it could not prove that a man was the father. The ABO blood group types are caused by the particular modification of a specific red blood cell surface protein called H antigen. The A and B genes code for enzymes that put specific sugars on the H antigen, and the O gene does not modify the H antigen. The human blood types are A, B, AB, and O; A and B are codominant, and O is recessive. A person has two ABO blood group genes, one from each parent. Based on the father's and mother's blood types, the blood type of the offspring can be determined. If a man has AB blood, he cannot have children with blood type O; a man with blood type AB thus would be excluded as the father of a blood type O child. By the 1930's, paternity testing also began to take into account other red blood cell surface proteins, such as Rh, Kell, and Duffy blood groups.

During the 1970's, human leukocyte antigens (HLAs) were used for paternity testing as well as for typing for organ transplants. HLAs are abundant in white blood cells, are in all cells of the body except red blood cells, and are used by the immune system to detect foreign cells. Each person has a unique set of HLA proteins inherited from parents. The usefulness of HLA type to determine paternity depends on how unusual (rare) a man's HLA type is in the population. Also, related men may share the same HLAs and cannot be distinguished from each other by the HLA typing test.

DNA Tests for Paternity

During the 1980's, DNA (deoxyribonucleic acid) profiling was developed. DNA analysis can be used to determine paternity conclusively, but this procedure requires large amounts of intact DNA. English geneticist Alec Jeffreys and his colleagues studied minisatellites made of a DNA sequence that is tandemly (end-to-end) repeated hundreds of times. These are called restriction fragment length polymorphisms (RFLPs) or variable number of tandem repeats (VNTRs). Individuals vary in the numbers of tandem repeats of the DNA sequence in their genomes. To detect these RFLPs, analysts isolate DNA and

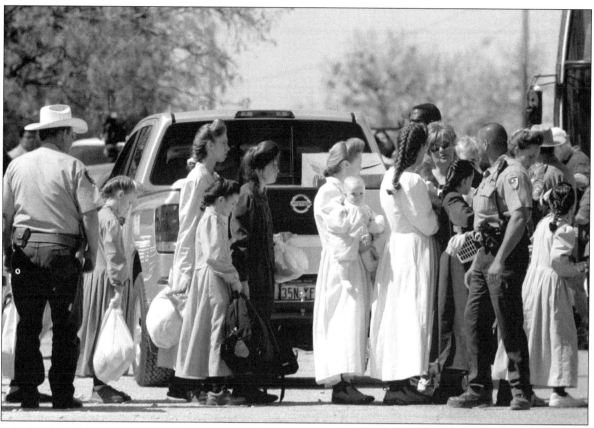

Members of the polygamist Fundamentalist Church of Jesus Christ of Latter-day Saints walk past sheriff's deputies on their way to submit DNA samples in Eldorado, Texas, in April, 2008. Texas authorities sought the samples in order to determine the familial relationships among the group's adult and child members after allegations of child abuse led the state to remove the children from the group's custody. *(AP/ Wide World Photos)*

add a restriction enzyme (which makes sequence-specific cuts in DNA) to make cuts outside the repeating sequence. Gel electrophoresis is used to separate the DNA based on size. The DNA fragments are transferred from the gel to a membrane called a Southern blot, and a single-stranded, labeled DNA probe that is complementary to the repeating sequence is hybridized with the DNA on the membrane. This labeled probe allows the VNTR regions to be detected among all the DNA in the genome. The size of the fragment detected varies depending on the number of tandem repeats the individual has. This is length polymorphism—length variation from individual to individual.

During the 1990's, polymerase chain reaction (PCR) became available to analyze DNA. Using sequence-specific primers, specific segments of DNA are amplified. Small quantities of a sample are readily amplified to give large amounts of DNA for analysis. The polymorphic sequences—those sequences that vary greatly from person to person—that are used for paternity testing include single nucleotide polymorphisms (SNPs) and short tandem repeats (STRs) that occur in the genome. In multiplex PCR, thirteen core loci that show large variability in the population are copied at the same time. Gel electrophoresis is used to separate the DNA fragments by size, and a DNA profile is created. In paternity testing, the DNA profile of the child is compared with the profiles of potential fathers. This analysis is rapid to perform and can determine paternity conclusively.

Susan J. Karcher

Further Reading

Brinkmann, B. "Is the Amelogenin Sex Test Valid?" *International Journal of Legal Medicine* 116, no. 2 (2001): 63. Brief article addresses the use of the amelogenin gene for sex determination.

Cho, Mildred K., and Pamela Sankar. "Forensic Genetics and Ethical, Legal, and Social Implications Beyond the Clinic." *Nature Genetics* 36 (2004): S8-S12. Discusses the ethical considerations related to DNA and genetic analysis.

Dawid, A. Philip, Julia Mortera, and Vincenzo L. Pascali. "Non-fatherhood or Mutation? A Probabilistic Approach to Parental Exclusion in Paternity Testing." *Forensic Science International* 124, no. 1 (2001): 55-61. Addresses the effects of mutations on paternity tests.

Fisher, Barry A. J. *Techniques of Crime Scene Investigation.* 7th ed. Boca Raton, Fla.: CRC Press, 2004. Provides a broad overview of many areas of forensics, including DNA and RFLP typing.

Kobilinsky, Lawrence F., Thomas F. Liotti, and Jamel Oeser-Sweat. *DNA: Forensic and Legal Applications.* Hoboken, N.J.: Wiley-Interscience, 2005. Presents a general overview of the uses of DNA analysis.

Petkovski, Elizabet, Christine Keyser-Tracqui, Rémi Hienne, and Bertrand Ludes. "SNPs and MALDI-TOF MS: Tools for DNA Typing in Forensic Paternity Testing and Anthropology." *Journal of Forensic Sciences* 50, no. 3 (2005): 535-541. Provides details regarding single nucleotide polymorphisms.

Ruitberg, Christian M., Dennis J. Reeder, and John M. Butler. "STRBase: A Short Tandem Repeat DNA Database for the Human Identity Testing Community." *Nucleic Acids Research* 29, no. 1 (2001): 320-322. Describes the database of short tandem repeats.

See also: Argentine disappeared children; CODIS; DNA database controversies; DNA profiling; Ethics of DNA analysis; Jefferson paternity dispute; Paternity evidence; Polymerase chain reaction; Semen and sperm.

Pathogen genomic sequencing

Definition: Techniques used to determine the linear order of monomers (small molecules such as nucleotides) that can be linked together to form polymers, mainly nucleic acids, found in the genomes of disease-causing microbes such as certain viruses, bacteria, and fungi.

Significance: Microbial forensics, the branch of forensic science that deals with microorganisms, extends the scope of epidemiology by going into greater detail to characterize pathogens for use as possible evidence in legal proceedings. The sequencing of pathogens is an especially important technique in forensic science as it pertains to increasingly dangerous global scourges of infectious emerging diseases.

Using a triad of techniques—polymerase chain reaction (PCR) and genomic sequencing followed by phylogenetic studies, which infer relationships among microbial strains—forensic scientists have the ability to determine the origin of a disease-causing agent, or pathogen, used in a biocrime and to determine who or what organization was responsible for its dissemination. In 2000, the human genome was characterized through sequencing techniques; this accomplishment revolutionized molecular biology. The comparatively small viral genomes of human immunodeficiency virus (HIV), hantaviruses, and *Haemophilus influenzae* have been elucidated through sequencing, as have the larger genomes of bacteria including *Mycobacterium tuberculosis* (TB) and its drug-resistant strains, *Yersinia pestis* (plague), *Mycobacterium leprae* (leprosy or Hansen's disease), *Salmonella typhi* (typhus), *Bacillus anthracis* (anthrax), and *Neisseria meningitidis* (meningitis). All of these pathogens are considered threats to global health.

The techniques used by forensic scientists in the collection, handling, shipping, and preservation of potential pathogens are different from those employed for nonpathogenic samples.

Forensic microbial analysis is based on a technique that identifies tandemly repeated sequences within the pathogen's genome. (Tandem repeats are repetitive sequences consisting of two or more nucleotides that serve as genetic markers and are frequently used to establish attribution—the source of a pathogen—in legal proceedings.)

After an unknown attacker sent letters containing *B. anthracis* to addresses in New York City, Washington, D.C., and Boca Raton, Florida, in the fall of 2001, careful preservation of initial and follow-up samples of the contents of the envelopes allowed forensic scientists to identify the Ames strain of *B. anthracis* as the specific pathogen used in the attacks. Before the entire genome was sequenced, the sample in question was compared with natural strains of *B. anthracis*; this comparison narrowed the possible source to a human-made strain of anthrax as opposed to one that might be found in nature. Further comparison to attribute the Ames strain to this biocrime was possible because the first strain, isolated from a victim in Florida (the index case), and the strains isolated from other victims as well as those found in anthrax spores recovered in the letters had previously been collected and preserved according to microbial forensic guidelines.

Specialized facilities, such as the J. Craig Venter Institute (JCVI), have been established to enable microbial forensic analysts to ascertain the entire genomic sequences of about five million bases of *B. anthracis* so as to identify polymorphisms (variations in DNA sequences) that serve as genomic signatures. In late 2007, the National Institute of Allergy and Infectious Diseases announced that twenty-eight hundred human and avian isolates had been completely sequenced and were publicly accessible.

Cynthia Racer

Further Reading

Binnewies, Tim T., et al. "Ten Years of Bacterial Genome Sequencing: Comparative-Genomics-Based Discoveries." *Functional and Integrative Genomics* 6 (July, 2006): 165-185.

Breeze, Roger G., Bruce Budowle, and Steven E. Schutzer, eds. *Microbial Forensics.* Burlington, Mass.: Elsevier Academic Press, 2005.

Budowle, Bruce, et al. "Genetic Analysis and Attribution of Forensic Evidence." *Critical Review of Microbiology* 31 (October, 2005): 233-254.

_____. "Quality Sample Collection, Handling, and Preservation for an Effective Microbial Forensics Program." *Applied and Environmental Microbiology* 72 (October, 2006): 6431-6438.

Cole, Leonard A. *The Anthrax Letters: A Medical Detective Story.* Washington, D.C.: Joseph Henry Press, 2003.

See also: Anthrax; Anthrax letter attacks; Biodetectors; Biological warfare diagnosis; Biological weapon identification; *Escherichia coli*; Parasitology; Pathogen transmission; Viral biology.

Pathogen transmission

Definition: Manner in which a disease-causing organism moves through the environment to infect plants or animals, including human beings.

Significance: Forensic scientists need to understand how microorganisms can inflict disease on humans directly or through contamination of food, water, animals, or plants. Their concerns include both how such pathogens affect the primary victims and whether and how the pathogens can be transmitted from primary victims to other healthy individuals.

Bacteria, protozoa, fungi, and viruses can all act as natural pathogens. Transmission occurs either directly, through contact with a host, or indirectly, through contact with a contaminated object (a fomite) or with a vehicle carrying the pathogen, such as air, water, or food. Living vectors, such as insects or animals, can also transmit various pathogens. Each pathogen has a specific way it gains entry to a host to cause disease and a specific manner by which it is released from the initial host to find a new host.

Criminals employing pathogens as weapons can use any of the natural transfer mechanisms to inflict damage or death, or they can artificially cause transfer, introducing pathogens or their parts (such as spores or toxins) by routes that the natural organisms would not or could not use. For example, consider the toxin produced by the bacterium *Clostridium botulinum*. This organism is normally found in the soil and infects improperly prepared foods. A malefactor, however, might affect a single individual by putting the bacterium in the target's food or injecting it into the person; alternatively, terrorists might contaminate a city's water supply with *C. botulinum*, potentially affecting millions of people.

Investigators working to solve cases involving pathogen transmission typically use techniques of epidemiology, the science of understanding how diseases behave in populations. These techniques include detecting organisms using their DNA (deoxyribonucleic acid)—that is, through genomic sequencing. The process starts with the examination of affected individuals, living or dead, to determine the organism that caused the disease by noting symptoms and taking samples from appropriate body locations. Investigators determine the manner in which the victims were infected by looking for the presence of the organism in the surrounding environment and identifying how the victims were exposed to the organism.

It is critical for investigators to understand how pathogens are transmitted, as they must determine not only the nature of specific crimes to individual victims but also the degree of danger to the rest of the healthy population. Of particular concern are organisms that cause life-threatening contagious diseases, such as smallpox, that can be transmitted from infected individuals to large numbers of other people. Containing human-to-human contagion in an unprotected population is much more difficult than dealing with the effects of an agent such as anthrax, which causes people and animals to become sick but is not transmitted directly from infected persons to others. This was illustrated in 2001, when envelopes with anthrax spores were sent through the mail to different cities in the United States. A few individuals were infected, but none of them (even those who contracted pulmonary anthrax) directly transmitted the pathogen to other people; the outbreaks thus remained small.

Steven A. Kuhl

A sales representative for a technology company shows off a kit for identifying biological agents that uses freeze-dried reagents to test for traces of pathogens such as anthrax. *(AP/Wide World Photos)*

Further Reading

Henderson, Donald A., and Thomas V. Inglesby. *Bioterrorism: Guidelines for Medical and Public Health Management.* Chicago: American Medical Association, 2002.

Loue, Sana. *Case Studies in Forensic Epidemiology.* New York: Springer, 2002.

Wheelis, Mark, Lajos Rózsa, and Malcolm Dando, eds. *Deadly Cultures: Biological Weapons Since 1945*. Cambridge, Mass.: Harvard University Press, 2006.

See also: Air and water purity; Anthrax; Anthrax letter attacks; Biodetectors; Biological terrorism; Biotoxins; Botulinum toxin; Bubonic plague; Ebola virus; Epidemiology; Hantavirus; Mad cow disease investigation; Parasitology; Pathogen genomic sequencing; Smallpox.

Pathology. *See* Forensic pathology

PCR. *See* Polymerase chain reaction

People v. Lee

Date: Ruling issued on May 8, 2001
Court: New York Court of Appeals
Significance: In the case of *People v. Lee*, the New York Court of Appeals held that the decision regarding whether or not to admit expert testimony at trial regarding the reliability of eyewitness identification is at the discretion of the trial court judge.

The court case *People v. Lee* focused on eyewitness testimony and the issue of whether the defense can introduce the testimony of expert witnesses during trial to raise doubt about a witness's reliability. The court exercised its discretion in determining that this testimony was not necessary to assist the jury in reaching a verdict. Key factors relating to the court's decision were the lack of any taint regarding the victim's out-of-court identification and the existence of corroborating evidence.

The case involved the theft of a motor vehicle at gunpoint, in a lighted area, where the defendant was about four feet from the victim. Two months after the theft, the defendant was arrested after committing a traffic violation; at that time, he was in possession of the victim's vehicle. About six months after the arrest, the police presented the victim with a photo array from which he identified the defendant. Ten days later, the victim also identified the defendant in a lineup.

During a pretrial hearing, the defendant sought to introduce at trial a psychology expert who would testify regarding factors that could influence perception, memory, and the accuracy of victims' identification of their assailants. The hearing court denied the defense motion to present this evidence at trial. After the trial began, the defendant renewed his request, and the request was again denied.

The New York Court of Appeals affirmed that it is up to the discretion of the trial judge whether this type of testimony is appropriate. The appellate court indicated that the trial court is in the best position to "weigh the request against other relevant factors, such as . . . the existence of corroborating evidence." The defendant had an opportunity to cross-examine the victim (witness) during the trial to question and to place before the jury any facts relevant to the identification of the defendant.

In two earlier cases, the New York Court of Appeals addressed issues relating to the admissibility of expert testimony regarding eyewitness identification. In *People v. Cronin* (1983), the court indicated that "it is for the trial court in the first instance to determine when jurors are able to draw conclusions from the evidence based on their day-to-day experience, their common observation and their knowledge, and when they would be benefited by the specialized knowledge of an expert witness." The decision in this case is consistent with the court's holding in *People v. Mooney* (1990); however, it was the dissent that stated that "the emerging trend today is to find expert psychological testimony on eyewitness identification sufficiently reliable to be admitted, and the vast majority of academic commentators have urged its acceptance."

In a later case, *People v. Young* (2006), the

court noted that several factors could affect an eyewitness's identification, such as race, stress, experience, opportunity to observe, and the weapon used during commission of the crime (often, crime victims focus more closely on the weapons used against them than on the persons committing the crimes). The appellate court acknowledged that an expert witness could provide information to jurors that they may not know but determined that the court appropriately exercised its discretion to exclude the testimony of an expert witness as requested by the defense. In this case, as in *People v. Lee*, in addition to the victim's identification of the defendant, corroborating evidence was presented to the jury for evaluation.

Keith G. Logan

Further Reading

Brewer, Neil, and Kipling D. Williams, eds. *Psychology and Law: An Empirical Perspective.* New York: Guilford Press, 2005.

Technical Working Group on Eyewitness Evidence. *Eyewitness Evidence: A Guide for Law Enforcement.* Washington, D.C.: National Institute of Justice, 1999.

Wells, Gary L., and Elizabeth F. Loftus. "Eyewitness Memory for People and Events." In *Forensic Psychology*, edited by Alan M. Goldstein. Vol. 11 in *Handbook of Psychology*, edited by Irving B. Weiner. Hoboken, N.J.: John Wiley & Sons, 2003.

See also: Cognitive interview techniques; Courts and forensic evidence; Expert witnesses; Eyewitness testimony; False memories; Trial consultants.

Performance-enhancing drugs

Definition: Substances taken by persons seeking to improve their athletic performance or their physical work capacity.

Significance: As the level of athletic competition continues to rise throughout the

world, athletes are always looking for ways to get a competitive edge. Superior nutrition and training programs are not enough for some athletes; many choose to use performance-enhancing drugs even though such substances are banned by sports federations and illegal unless prescribed for medical purposes. Law-enforcement agencies expend significant resources in efforts to address the illegal sale and use of such drugs.

Athletes' use of particular substances to improve their physical performance dates back to ancient Greece. Competitors in the ancient Olympics took stimulants such as strychnine, hashish, and extracts from cola plants, cacti, and fungi to improve their performance. Although the beneficial effects of these substances are questionable, many believe that their widespread use was one of the elements that led to the termination of the Olympic Games and other sporting competitions in about 400 C.E.

Competitive sports did not gain great popularity again until the time of the second phase of the Industrial Revolution, around 1850. With competition, the use of performance-enhancing drugs also returned. In particular, competitive swimmers, runners, and cyclists used caffeine, strychnine, codeine, cocaine, heroin, and nitroglycerin to stimulate their bodies to perform. Numerous athletes died from taking these drugs, but their deaths did deter many others from using such drugs. After World War II and throughout the Cold War period, the use of performance-enhancing drugs escalated, particularly the use of anabolic steroids.

Bodybuilding Supplements

The most widely known class of performance-enhancing drugs used since the 1930's is that of anabolic steroids (also known as anabolic-androgenic steroids). These are testosterone-like substances that augment male sex characteristics and the building of muscle. Anabolic steroids were first developed in Nazi Germany, where they were used to increase the aggressiveness of troops in battle.

Many studies have shown that anabolic steroids increase muscle mass and strength, which has made them popular among many different kinds of athletes, from football players to track-and-field athletes who participate in throwing events. Two strategies that athletes use to maximize strength and muscle mass with anabolic steroids are known as stacking and pyramiding. Stacking is the blending of different types of the drug in oral and injectable forms to maximize effect. Pyramiding is the continual increase in dosage over time to maximize benefit. Taking large doses of anabolic steroids comes with many dangerous side effects, however. Because the liver is responsible for breaking down and removing excess chemicals from the body, anabolic steroids can cause severe liver damage. These substances have also been linked to high blood pressure, adult-onset diabetes mellitus, increased blood clotting factors, and decreased high-density lipoproteins (good cholesterol) in the blood, all of which increase the risk of cardiovascular disease.

Another substance that has been reported to increase muscle mass and strength is human growth hormone (HGH). With the advances made in the field of genetic engineering during the 1980's, HGH became increasingly widely available and hit the black market, where athletes could get access to it. Research on the effects of HGH has been very limited, however, and any actual benefits of the substance for athletes have not been identified conclusively.

Two other substances that have been promoted as useful in increasing muscle mass and strength are dehydroepiandrosterone (DHEA) and androstenedione. Both are precursors to testosterone that are converted to testosterone by the body. Research has not found either substance to be effective for the enhancement of athletic abilities, and both decrease the high-density lipoproteins in the blood, which increases the risk of cardiovascular disease.

One supplement that has been shown to be effective in improving performance in high-intensity exercise is creatine. Research indicates that the ingestion of creatine in high doses helps the muscles to work harder and increases the body's ability to gain muscle and strength. Although creatine is not regulated by the U.S. Food and Drug Administration (FDA), it is banned by most sports federations. The long-

Marion Jones celebrates after winning a gold medal in the women's 100-meter run during the Summer Olympic Games in Sydney, Australia, in 2000. Later accused of having used steroids to enhance her Olympic performance, Jones finally admitted, in 2007, that she had done so. Shortly afterward, she returned all her Olympic medals. Convicted of lying to investigators, she was sentenced to a term in a federal prison in early 2008. *(AP/Wide World Photos)*

term side effects of this substance have not been clearly identified.

Stimulants

The primary stimulant substances used by athletes for much of recent history are amphetamines. Athletes take these drugs to decrease fatigue, increase alertness, and decrease reaction time. Most research has found, however, that these drugs do not improve athletes' quickness; rather, under influence of the drugs, the athletes only perceive themselves as being quicker. In addition, amphetamines offer only short-term reduction of fatigue; thus in using amphetamines athletes gain no real performance benefits while exposing themselves to

Operation Raw Deal

This excerpt from a U.S. Drug Enforcement Administration (DEA) press release, dated September 24, 2007, gives some idea of the scope of law-enforcement efforts to deal with the problem of trafficking in illegal performance-enhancing drugs.

DEA and federal law enforcement officials from the FDA's Office of Criminal Investigations and the U.S. Postal Inspection Service today announced the culmination of Operation Raw Deal, an international case targeting the global underground trade of anabolic steroids, human growth hormone (HGH) and insulin growth factor (IGF). . . . The investigation represents the largest steroid enforcement action in U.S. history and took place in conjunction with enforcement operations in nine countries worldwide. The Internal Revenue Service (IRS), Immigration and Customs Enforcement (ICE), Federal Bureau of Investigation (FBI), and the National Drug Intelligence Center (NDIC) also played key roles in the investigation.

143 federal search warrants were executed on targets nationwide, resulting in 124 arrests and the seizure of 56 steroid labs across the United States. In total, 11.4 million steroid dosage units were seized, as well as 242 kilograms of raw steroid powder of Chinese origin. As part of Operation Raw Deal, $6.5 million was also seized, as well as 25 vehicles, 3 boats, 27 pill presses, and 71 weapons.

. . . The nearly two-year-old operation . . . took place in conjunction with enforcement operations in Mexico, Canada, China, Belgium, Australia, Germany, Denmark, Sweden, and Thailand.

dangerous side effects: Amphetamines are highly addictive, and those who take them experience increased metabolism, loss of appetite, and weight loss.

Athletes also use two stimulants that are not regulated drugs: caffeine and ephedrine. Endurance athletes use caffeine to increase their bodies' use of fat for energy and to conserve carbohydrates for later stages of their competitive events. Research has found such use to be effective and to have limited side effects, which include increased urine output and blood vessel spasms. The sports federations have not banned caffeine, but most place limits on the amount allowed in a competing athlete's body. Ephedrine is a naturally occurring stimulant similar to amphetamines. Like amphetamines, it has not been shown to have performance-enhancing benefits, and it has similar side effects. Despite the fact that it is not regulated by the FDA,

ephedrine is banned by most sports federations.

Blood Doping

Many athletes in the past have improved their performance through blood doping—that is, by increasing the amount of red blood cells, which carry oxygen, in their blood. This increases the oxygen available to muscles and improves athletic performance in endurance events.

Historically, athletes who practiced blood doping would have several units of their own blood drawn and placed in storage six to eight weeks before competition. Their bodies would produce more red blood cells in the intervening time, and then, prior to the competition, the athletes would reinfuse their stored blood to increase their red blood cells. This process has generally been replaced by the use of the hormone erythropoietin, which causes the body to increase the production of red blood cells. All methods of blood doping are banned by sports federations.

Important Issues

A major concern related to performance-enhancing drugs is the lack of information available about them. New drugs and variations on older drugs are continually being developed, in large part because manufacturers and users are interested in staying ahead of the technology available to test athletes for the use of banned and illegal drugs. When new drugs or new forms of older drugs are developed, several years of research are required to determine if they are effective, what the proper dosages are, and what their side effects are, as well as to develop new tests to detect their use by athletes.

Typically, a new drug formulation is available for more than a year before awareness of it becomes widespread enough that research on the drug is undertaken. After the research begins, more than another year might elapse before scientists are able to determine whether the drug is effective at all, and many years might pass before the negative side effects of the drug can be identified. Developing an effective method of testing for a new drug can also take months or even years. Given this lengthy process, athletes who use performance-enhancing drugs have a wide window of opportunity for cheating.

Another serious concern raised by the use of performance-enhancing drugs is the effect of such substances on athletes' health. Many athletes, whether taking FDA-approved drugs or nontested substances, take very high doses. In fact, many take higher doses than what researchers can ethically test, and thus the true benefits and side effects of these substances are not known. Given that many of the known side effects have negative health implications, athletes who use illegal and banned substances to enhance their performance are not only breaking the rules but also risking serious health problems.

Bradley R. A. Wilson

Further Reading

Aretha, David. *Steroids and Other Performance-Enhancing Drugs*. Berkeley Heights, N.J.: Enslow, 2005. Focuses on the negative effects of steroid use. Presented in easy-to-read style.

Bahrke, Michael S., and Charles E. Yesalis, eds. *Performance-Enhancing Substances in Sport and Exercise*. Champaign, Ill.: Human Kinetics, 2002. Text includes information on the history of athletes' use and abuse of performance-enhancing drugs.

Haley, James, and Tamara Roleff. *Performance-Enhancing Drugs*. San Diego, Calif.: Greenhaven Press, 2003. Presents a wide range of opinions on performance-enhancing drugs. Includes good information on resources.

Monroe, Judy. *Steroids, Sports, and Body Image: The Risks of Performance-Enhancing Drugs*. Berkeley Heights, N.J.: Enslow, 2004. Provides an overview of steroid use and abuse by athletes. Aimed at young readers.

Yesalis, Charles E. *Anabolic Steroids in Sport and Exercise*. Champaign, Ill.: Human Kinetics, 2000. Takes a scientific approach in discussing the problems with performance-enhancing drugs in sports.

See also: Amphetamines; Anabolic Steroid Control Act of 2004; Athlete drug testing; Drug classification; Drug Enforcement Administration, U.S.; Mandatory drug testing; Stimulants.

Peruvian Ice Maiden

Date: Remains discovered on September 8, 1995

The Event: Archaeologists discovered the mummy of a fully clothed young adolescent girl frozen atop 20,700-foot Mount Ampato in Peru. Investigation revealed that the girl, who became known as the Peruvian Ice Maiden, was about fourteen years old when she died, probably as the result of a human sacrifice, about 550 years earlier.

Significance: At the time the remains were discovered, the Ice Maiden was the best-preserved mummy ever found. Although the body had not been intentionally mummified, the low temperatures and dry, thin air on the mountain had created a mummy. Because the remains were frozen rather than dried, the DNA in the body was well preserved.

Archaeologist Johan Reinhard climbed Mount Ampato, in the Andes of Peru, to get a better view of an active volcano nearby—Mount Nevado Sabancaya. The heat from the volcanic eruption, which had begun in 1990, had cleared some of the snowpack from nearby mountains, including Mount Ampato. As Reinhard and his associate Miguel Zarate neared the summit, they saw some feathers that turned out to be part of the clothing on the mummified remains of a child who had died atop the mountain more

The mummy known as the Peruvian Ice Maiden on display in Arequipa, Peru, in 1997. The mummy was later taken to Japan, raising concerns among Peruvian archaeologists that too much travel would damage the delicate body. *(AP/Wide World Photos)*

than five centuries earlier. The body's burial site had been disturbed by the snow melting caused by the nearby volcano. Reinhard and Zarate carried the eighty-pound mummy down the mountain on their backs at night, when the temperatures were lowest, to keep the frozen body from melting. It was then loaded onto the back of a mule for further transport, with sufficient padding between the mule and the frozen mummy to protect the mummy from the animal's body heat.

Importance of the Discovery

Also known as Momia Juanita (Mummy Juanita in Spanish) and the Lady of Ampato, the Ice Maiden was such a significant discovery that *Time* magazine called the event one of the ten greatest scientific discoveries of the year. In addition to the remarkable condition of the body, the burial site itself had never been

touched by looters, and the gold and silver statues found there provided archaeologists with information on traditional Inca religious rituals. Because the body was accompanied by many items believed to have been offerings to the gods, experts hypothesized that the girl had herself been a sacrificial offering. Two other children's bodies were later found near the site where the Ice Maiden's remains were found.

Amid criticism from a number of native Peruvian politicians, the mummy was temporarily moved to the United States in early 1996, where it was exhibited at the National Geographic Society headquarters in Washington, D.C. President Bill Clinton was one of those who viewed the body. In 1999, the mummy visited Japan, where it was viewed by thousands.

The Ice Maiden was the best-preserved mummy in the world until 1999, when another Reinhard-led expedition found three other frozen mummies on a mountain in Argentina. The Argentine mummies still had blood in their lungs and hearts—something that was not the case with the Ice Maiden.

The Forensic Investigation

Because the Ice Maiden's mitochondrial DNA (deoxyribonucleic acid) was well preserved, scientists were able to use genetic information provided by the Human Genome Project to learn that the girl had shared ancestry with the Ngöbe people of Panama, with old Taiwanese and Korean peoples, and with Native Americans. The mummification had also preserved the internal organs well enough that several biological tests were possible, with the result that new insights were gained into nutrition and health among the Inca during the fifteenth century. While the mummy was in the United States, it was taken to Johns Hopkins Hospital in Baltimore, Maryland, where a virtual autopsy was performed, and additional scientific tests were conducted in Peru. It was found that the Ice Maiden had a well-balanced diet, strong bones, and good teeth. In general, she was in excellent health. She died from blunt force trauma to her head.

The Ice Maiden is housed in a museum at the Universidad Católica de Santa María in the Andean city of Arequipa, Peru. In 2006, Peru's leading newspaper reported that the Ice Maiden was at risk from humidity, as dampness had gotten into the glass-enclosed refrigeration compartment where the mummy is stored. The temperature is kept at about −19 degrees Celsius (−2 degrees Fahrenheit). Peruvian authorities were informed that the mummy could deteriorate within five years unless the dampness problem could be solved. Changes in the mummy's skin color have been noted—a sign that storage conditions have not been optimal. Other, more recently discovered, frozen mummies are also kept at the same museum.

Dale L. Flesher

Further Reading

Bahn, Paul. *Written in Bones: How Human Remains Unlock the Secrets of the Dead*. Buffalo, N.Y.: Firefly Books, 2003. Provides information for general readers on various discoveries of mummies and old bones, including not only Incan bodies but also Ötzi the Iceman (also known as the Tyrolean Iceman), and the so-called bog bodies of Europe. Features many photographs.

Chamberlain, Andrew T., and Michael Parker Pearson. *Earthly Remains: The History and Science of Preserved Human Bodies*. New York: Oxford University Press, 2001. Readable and well-illustrated volume describes the ways in which bodies have been preserved over the years.

Cockburn, Aidan, Eve Cockburn, and Theodore A. Reyman, eds. *Mummies, Disease, and Ancient Cultures*. 2d ed. New York: Cambridge University Press, 1998. Collection of essays includes several accounts of mummy finds as well as a chapter on mummy research techniques.

Pringle, Heather. *The Mummy Congress: Science, Obsession, and the Everlasting Dead*. New York: Hyperion, 2001. Presents excellent discussion of the science of mummy studies, including a chapter on the Ice Maiden and a chapter on the destruction of Incan mummies by Spanish explorer Francisco Pizarro.

Reinhard, Johan. *Discovering the Inca Ice Maiden*. Washington, D.C.: National Geographic Society, 1998. Brief volume aimed at young readers details in simple terms the discovery of the Inca mummy and the treasures buried with her. Includes color photographs.

_____. *The Ice Maiden: Inca Mummies, Mountain Gods, and Sacred Sites in the Andes*. Washington, D.C.: National Geographic Society, 2006. Accounts of the discovery of the Ice Maiden and other archaeological expeditions in the Andes by the leader of the expedition that discovered the Peruvian Ice Maiden. Includes many interesting photographs.

See also: Ancient criminal cases and mysteries; Blunt force trauma; Forensic anthropology; Forensic archaeology; Kennewick man; Mummification.

Petechial hemorrhage

Definition: Bleeding from the capillaries into the skin or mucous membranes, which results in tiny (pinpoint) red marks.

Significance: The presence of petechial hemorrhages can help forensic pathologists to determine cause of death in many cases because such hemorrhages are often an indication of strangulation, hanging, or smothering.

Petechial hemorrhages, sometimes referred to as punctate hemorrhages, have been recognized for years as indicators of the increased pressure on the blood vessels in the head that occurs when the airway is obstructed. They have also been found to occur in many disorders and diseases that involve blood dyscrasias (abnormalities). The mechanism by which petechial hemorrhages occur was first delineated by J. G. Humble in 1949. Anything that leads to increased pressure within the capillaries can cause them to rupture, allowing blood to leak out into the skin or mucous membranes. Petechial hemorrhages are thus caused by tears in the blood vessels and fall into the category known as rhexis hemorrhages.

Forensic pathologists have long recognized the connection between petechial hemorrhages and asphyxiation. A pathologist will often make a diagnosis of "crush asphyxia" when findings include a history of traumatic compression of the chest or abdomen, swelling of the blood vessels due to overfilling (vascular engorgement), and the presence of petechial hemorrhages. It has been shown that if vascular congestion is not present (or possible), then petechial hemorrhages will not form at the site of the compression. Typically, no petechiae are found in areas underneath tight clothes, such as women's bras. The compression of the skin caused by a bra does not allow for vascular engorgement, so no petechial hemorrhages are found in this region, This "brassiere sign" (petechial hemorrhages over the upper chest with none in the area of the bra) is taken as an indicator of crush asphyxia.

Although petechial hemorrhages are often indicators of asphyxiation, particularly when they are present in the conjunctiva of the eye or on the face, they also occur in a wide variety of other conditions. Trauma that does not involve asphyxiation may also lead to petechial hemorrhage. In the case of shaken baby syndrome, the pinpoint red marks may be found on the retina or conjunctiva of the eye as well as on the earlobe. Low platelet counts (thrombocytopenia) or coagulopathies (defects in the body's blood-clotting mechanism) often lead to the existence of petechial hemorrhages, especially on the lower extremities. They are also seen as aftereffects of cardiopulmonary resuscitation (CPR). If CPR successfully restores blood flow to small blood vessels damaged by hypoxia, the vessels may easily rupture, resulting in petechial hemorrhages.

Robin Kamienny Montvilo

Further Reading

DiMaio, Vincent J., and Dominick DiMaio. *Forensic Pathology*. 2d ed. Boca Raton, Fla.: CRC Press, 2001.

Pyrek, Kelly M. *Forensic Nursing*. Boca Raton, Fla.: CRC Press, 2006.

Smith, David S. *Field Guide to Bedside Diagnosis*. 2d ed. Philadelphia: Lippincott Williams & Wilkins, 2007.

See also: Antemortem injuries; Asphyxiation; Blood residue and bloodstains; Choking; Drowning; Hanging; Hemorrhagic fevers; Homicide; Physical evidence; Shaken baby syndrome; Strangulation; Suffocation; Suicide.

Petrographic microscopy. *See* Polarized light microscopy

pH indicators. *See* Acid-base indicators

Phenolphthalein

Definition: Chemical that is the basis for the Kastle-Meyer test, a commonly used presumptive test for blood at crime scenes.

Significance: A positive reaction to phenolphthalein of a stain found at a crime scene suggests that the stain is probably blood; such information can facilitate an initial reconstruction of a crime and prompt follow-up.

In the presence of heme iron and hydrogen peroxide, phenolphthalein, which is clear in the reduced state, is converted to an oxidized state, which is pink. Because heme iron is present in hemoglobin, the protein that carries oxygen in red blood cells, a positive test can indicate the presence of blood. Such a test does not distinguish between human blood and animal blood, however; further testing is necessary to make that distinction and, if the blood is human, to determine whose blood it is. In addition, constituents of some plants, such as potatoes and horseradish, as well as oxidizing agents found in some cleansers, can catalyze the reaction. Accordingly, a phenolphthalein test is only presumptive for blood; a positive result must be confirmed by laboratory tests.

Typically, a forensic investigator performs the test by moistening a cotton swab with deionized water and rubbing the swab on the suspect stain, adding a drop of phenolphthalein solution to the swab, waiting thirty seconds, and then adding a drop of 3 percent hydrogen peroxide to the swab. A positive reaction will turn the swab a bright pink color within fifteen seconds. Often, a swab taken near the stain of interest is used as a control. If the swab turns pinkish before the hydrogen peroxide is added, the test is invalid. To ensure that the reagents have not deteriorated before use, the investigator validates the test using a known blood standard.

First introduced in 1901, the phenolphthalein test is fairly sensitive and quite specific. In addition, phenolphthalein does not destroy the sample, which can be kept and used in further tests at the lab. The use of phenolphthalein does not interfere with subsequent DNA tests. Furthermore, phenolphthalein is among the safest of the compounds used in presumptive tests for blood in the field; most others, including benzidine and orthotolidine, are known or probable carcinogens and thus pose a risk to investigators.

James L. Robinson

Further Reading

Geberth, Vernon J. *Practical Homicide Investigation: Tactics, Procedures, and Forensic Techniques.* 4th ed. Boca Raton, Fla.: CRC Press, 2006.

Lee, Henry C., Timothy Palmbach, and Marilyn T. Miller. *Henry Lee's Crime Scene Handbook.* San Diego, Calif.: Academic Press, 2001.

Owen, David. *Hidden Evidence: Forty True Crimes and How Forensic Science Helped Solve Them.* Richmond Hill, Ont.: Firefly Books, 2000.

See also: Acid-base indicators; Benzidine; DNA typing; Luminol; Orthotolidine; Presumptive tests for blood; Reagents; Serology.

Photocopier analysis. *See* Fax machine, copier, and printer analysis

Photograph alteration detection

Definition: Techniques used to determine whether photographs have been altered in any way to change the nature of the portrayal of their subjects.

Significance: People have altered photographs for many reasons since the invention of film photography, and forensic scientists have long been called upon to examine photographs for evidence of alteration. With the advent of digital photography, the ready availability of sophisticated tools and techniques for altering images has posed an increasingly difficult problem for investigators who must rely on photographs as evidence in criminal and other legal cases.

The alteration of a photograph taken with a film camera requires the use of brushing techniques that cover or chemically remove parts of the image. All basic methods of film photo alteration leave very obvious traces of the alteration process in the form of chemical marks and brushstrokes. Even skillful alteration of film photographic prints can generally be detected easily through the use of computer software that registers changes in lighting, positioning, or displacement of the subjects in the prints with respect to horizontal and vertical planes of reference. The alteration of digital images is usually more subtle. Digital images can be copied, edited, and shared without the loss of image quality. Software programs that allow users to alter digital images, such as Adobe Photoshop, are readily available and widely used.

In the past, criminal and civil courts were willing to admit video recordings and photographs as reliable evidence without much question. Given the ease with which digital im-

The picture at the top is an original photograph showing Spanish dictator Francisco Franco (center) walking with German chancellor Adolf Hitler during their meeting in a French town near the Spanish border in October, 1940. The government-controlled Spanish news agency altered the photography before releasing it to newspapers. In the altered version, at bottom, Franco's eyes are open, not closed, and his right arm is in a more relaxed position, making Franco look more comfortable in the German dictator's company. *(AP/Wide World Photos)*

ages can be altered, however, courts now require that photographs and digital video images undergo tests to determine if they have been altered before they can be admitted as evidence. Virtually all law-enforcement agencies in the United States routinely use specialized technology to determine the integrity of digital images.

Many images produced by digital cameras contain within them a kind of coding known as watermarking; this coding preserves records of the original images. Digital watermarks are not visible to the eye, but they can be detected through the use of certain software. Such software can tell users whether primary digital images have been altered by comparing the images with the information stored in their watermarks. Some law-enforcement agencies make use of sophisticated image-processing software to restore altered digital images to their original forms.

Because of the increasing ease of altering digital images and the possibility that forensic scientists' capability of detecting such alterations may be surpassed by new techniques of alteration, some observers have urged caution in the use of photographic evidence, and others have gone so far as to suggest that courts should not admit digital images as evidence. The use of the intentional alteration of images by forensic scientists, as in the digitizing of surveillance tapes to sharpen their images, has also come into question. For example, a dark spot on an image may sharpen under one resolution to reveal an object resembling a gun, whereas under another resolution the object may appear to be a knife, or it may be revealed to be simply a spot or blotch on the original image. Many have argued that evidence produced using such an unreliable technique should not be admitted in court.

Dwight G. Smith

Further Reading

Blitzer, Herbert L., and Jack Jacobia. *Forensic Digital Imaging and Photography*. San Diego, Calif.: Academic Press, 2002.

Russ, John C. *Forensic Uses of Digital Imaging*. Boca Raton, Fla.: CRC Press, 2001.

Tarantino, Chris. *Digital Photo Processing*. Indianapolis: Muska & Lipman, 2003.

Vacca, John R. *Computer Forensics: Computer Crime Scene Investigation*. 2d ed. Hingham, Mass.: Charles River Media, 2005.

See also: Art forgery; Counterfeiting; Direct versus circumstantial evidence; Eyewitness testimony; Forensic photography; Forgery; Handwriting analysis; Imaging; Sports memorabilia fraud; Steganography.

Physical evidence

Definition: Objects that are identifiable through several of the senses and are often used to prove facts in a court of law, such as establishing that a crime has been committed or a defective product has caused harm.

Significance: Forensic scientists analyze physical evidence collected from crime scenes and other locations to determine whether and how the evidence is relevant to criminal and civil investigations. Physical evidence may link suspects to crimes or civil wrongs or exonerate innocent persons.

Generally, physical evidence is defined as nonliving, although the sources of such evidence may be humans, animals, or plants. Body fluids—such as blood, semen, and saliva—and the DNA (deoxyribonucleic acid) extracted from them are examples of biological or serology evidence that may be considered physical evidence. Physical evidence is often divided into class evidence, which can be linked only to a type (or class) of items, and individual evidence, which can be linked to a specific individual, item, or civil wrong.

Physical evidence may include things that can be seen, whether with the naked eye or through the use of magnification or other analytical tools. Some of this evidence is categorized as impression evidence, including bite marks, fingerprints, footprints, knife cuts, tire tracks, and tool marks. Pattern evidence, a subcategory of physical evidence, might include blood spatter and burn patterns. Trace evidence is in most cases microscopic physical evidence that includes fibers, flakes, gunshot and bomb residue, hair, paint, plastic, pollen, soil, dust, and small fragments of physical objects such as glass, fingernails, fluids, and wood. Trace evidence might also include poisons that can be discovered only through body organ and tissue sampling.

Some physical evidence may be detected by smell or taste, often through the use of trained dogs. Such evidence might include accelerants, bombs, chemicals, and drugs. Among the most obvious kinds of physical evidence are weapons and other objects used to commit crimes, such as blunt instruments, guns and bullets, knives, ropes, and ligatures. Forged or altered documents are also physical evidence, as are actual objects or defective parts that caused harm in civil cases.

Forensic scientists are sometimes involved in gathering evidence of cybercrimes and civil wrongs committed with the use of computers. Although digital data evidence is not technically physical evidence, the physical objects used to create and transmit such data evidence are. Thus physical evidence includes computer hardware and peripherals as well as electronic devices such as cell phones and personal digital assistants.

Among the types of evidence generally not considered to be physical evidence are testimonial evidence from eyewitnesses, documentary evidence such as drawings or diagrams depicting crime scenes, digital evidence, audio evidence, and behavioral evidence from profiling.

Carol A. Rolf

The digital evidence stored within computers does not constitute physical evidence; however, computers themselves and other electronic hardware devices do. (© iStockphoto.com/Matjaz Boncina)

See also: Ballistic fingerprints; Crime scene search patterns; Cross-contamination of evidence; Direct versus circumstantial evidence; Disturbed evidence; DNA extraction from hair, bodily fluids, and tissues; Evidence processing; Fibers and filaments; Footprints and shoe prints; Gunshot residue; Hair analysis; Prints; Tire tracks; Tool marks.

Further Reading

Byrd, Mike. *Crime Scene Evidence: A Guide to the Recovery and Collection of Physical Evidence.* Wildomar, Calif.: Staggs, 2001.

Lee, Henry C., and Howard A. Harris. *Physical Evidence in Forensic Science.* 2d ed. Tucson, Ariz.: Lawyers & Judges Publishing, 2000.

Owen, David. *Hidden Evidence: Forty True Crimes and How Forensic Science Helped Solve Them.* Richmond Hill, Ont.: Firefly Books, 2000.

Physiology

Definition: Study of how living organisms and their parts function, including physical and chemical processes and factors.

Significance: One of the primary sciences at the root of the forensic sciences is physiology. Knowledge of how organisms function—particularly human bodies—contributes to many forensic procedures because it helps to establish cause in injuries and death. The physiology of dying is one important area of knowledge for forensic scientists; others include the physiology of drug and alcohol consumption, DNA analysis and polygraph testing, and the physiology of organisms such as plants and microbes.

The study of physiology begins with the cell, the fundamental unit that makes up living things. Groups of similar cells form tissues, and groups of tissues form organs. The organs combine into systems that make up higher-level living organisms. Some of the systems in the human body of particular interest to forensic scientists are the cardiovascular, nervous, digestive, and respiratory systems.

Human Physiology

The functions of the human body can contribute invaluable information that investigators can use in solving crimes. Human physiology plays a major role, for example, in determination of cause of death, DNA (deoxyribonucleic acid) analysis, blood spatter analysis, polygraph testing, and the effects of drug and alcohol consumption.

When a person dies, the physiological processes cease, and the cessation of these processes can provide valuable information about the time and cause of death. In an autopsy, a forensic pathologist completes a thorough investigation of the external and internal parts of the body. This investigation includes the evaluation of any wounds, the contents of the digestive system, and any residues on the body, such as gunpowder. Hair and nail samples are also analyzed, and toxicology tests are performed on the blood.

DNA stores a cell's information and directs its activities. A portion of the DNA molecule contains a code that directs its activities, and a portion of the molecule contains a unique code for each person. The primary use for DNA in forensics is thus the identification of persons. DNA can be used to identify crime victims or the perpetrators of crimes. By analyzing skin, blood, semen, or other body tissues collected from a victim's body, investigators may be able to make connections to suspects. DNA analysis has

proven to be a valuable technique in solving crimes.

Bloodstains and blood spatter patterns provide important clues in many crimes. Forensic scientists evaluate the blood evidence at crime scenes by applying knowledge about the forces that act on blood to affect its patterns on surfaces. The pumping of the heart generates pressure, causing blood to spray from a bad wound. Gravity causes blood to drip toward the ground. Movement of a wounded body can cause the blood to spray in different directions as a result of centrifugal force. Additionally, blood forms different kinds of patterns when it comes into contact with various kinds of surfaces.

Polygraph (lie detector) testing is a procedure in which a qualified tester evaluates a subject's physiological responses to questions to determine whether the person is telling the truth. The polygraph device measures several physiological responses: respiration, pulse rate, blood pressure, and skin perspiration. In general, when people are being deceptive they experience increases in blood pressure, heart rate, respiration rate, and perspiration; when they are being truthful, these measures all stay relatively constant. Although the polygraph does not provide a perfect test of truthfulness, qualified testers can get a good idea whether subjects are lying or telling the truth for each question asked.

With knowledge about how the body processes drugs and alcohol, forensic scientists can determine what substances individuals have used and in what amounts. In the body, these foreign substances are generally removed and broken down by the liver or excreted in the urine. Analyses of blood, saliva, urine, or hair samples can produce information about the presence of substances and, in some cases, the amounts ingested.

Physiology of Other Organisms

Forensic evidence is sometimes provided by nonhuman organisms such as plants, insects, and microbes. Because plants produce pollen and seeds and are fixed in their particular geographic locations, evidence of plant life can be used to connect possible suspects to crime scenes. For example, at a crime scene where specific plants are present, the perpetrator may unknowingly carry away seeds or pollen from those plants on body, shoes, or clothing; by analyzing such evidence, investigators can connect the person to the crime scene.

Insects can provide forensic evidence through experts' analysis of insect bite marks and waste products found on the bodies of crime victims or suspects. In addition, the types of insects found on human remains, as well as the activity patterns of those insects, can help determine the time and location of death. Some kinds of insect activity are also used in the determination of neglect and abuse in children and the elderly. The types of insects found splattered on vehicle windshields and radiator grills can provide information about where the vehicles have traveled.

Microbes—that is, microscopic organisms—can provide information about the origins of infections. Forensic scientists may also examine microbes and their DNA in cases of biological crimes, such as mailings of the spores that cause anthrax. By comparing the DNA of microbes used in a crime with the DNA of any such microbes found in a suspect's home, for example, scientists may be able to link the suspect to the crime.

Bradley R. A. Wilson

Further Reading

Breeze, Roger G., Bruce Budowle, and Steven E. Schutzer, eds. *Microbial Forensics*. Burlington, Mass.: Elsevier Academic Press, 2005. Reviews the relationships between microbe physiology and forensics.

Coyle, Heather Miller, ed. *Forensic Botany: Principles and Applications to Criminal Casework*. Boca Raton, Fla.: CRC Press, 2005. Contains information on plant physiology and its relationship to forensic science.

James, Stuart H., and Jon J. Nordby, eds. *Forensic Science: An Introduction to Scientific and Investigative Techniques*. 2d ed. Boca Raton, Fla.: CRC Press, 2005. Provides an overview of forensic science procedures, many of which are based on physiology.

Mozayani, Ashraf, and Carla Noziglia, eds. *The Forensic Laboratory Handbook: Procedures and Practice*. Totowa, N.J.: Humana Press, 2006. Covers most of the procedures based on physiology that are used in forensic laboratories.

Mozayani, Ashraf, and Lionel P. Raymon, eds. *Handbook of Drug Interactions: A Clinical and Forensic Guide*. Totowa, N.J.: Humana Press, 2004. Evaluates various drugs and describes their physiological effects on the body.

See also: Biometric identification systems; DNA analysis; Drug confirmation tests; Forensic pathology; Medicine; Nervous system; Polygraph analysis; Sobriety testing.

Poisons and antidotes

Definitions: A poison is any chemical or biological compound that can damage the body's organs or tissues. An antidote is any substance that can reverse or mitigate the damage done by a poison.

Significance: A forensic examination to determine cause of death may involve inspection of the body for poisonous residue or for the effects of poison on the body. Body tissues may also be subjected to toxicological analyses to identify any possibly poisonous substances present.

Many substances that are poisonous are, in fact, useful as medicines in the proper doses. The body can tolerate many poisonous substances; much depends on the amount of poison given and whether the body has been able to build up a tolerance to the substance. Some poisons, such as warfarin (a drug that keeps the blood from clotting), were developed as medicines but were later used as poisons. Poisoning can be acute (exposure on one occasion) or chronic (exposure over a period of time).

Types of Poisons

Poisons are generally divided into three large groups: biological poisons (such as plant substances), chemical poisons (such as insecticides and industrial substances), and drugs and pharmaceuticals. Biological poisons fall into three major categories: microbial toxins (produced by bacteria), phytotoxins (produced by plants), and zootoxins (produced by animals). These poisons are generally either ingested (as in the case of poisonous mushrooms) or taken in through the skin (such as through a bite or sting).

Chemical poisons, such as insecticides, herbicides, and industrial or household chemicals, generally cause body damage (skin damage or damage to the parasympathetic system, for example) but may also cause death by depressing the respiratory system. Organic compounds such as hydrocarbons, alcohols, or aldehydes are likely to cause damage involving the route through which they enter the body. For example, if inhaled, these compounds cause lung damage; if ingested, they cause damage to the gastrointestinal tract. Inorganic (generally metal) compounds such as mercury, lead, and cadmium can damage the brain, kidneys, nervous system, and gastrointestinal system. These types of poisons can accumulate in the body over a period of time and cause death.

Drugs and pharmaceuticals, which are generally ingested, tend to cause gastrointestinal irritation and may cause nausea and vomiting. Some compounds, such as morphine, can interfere with muscular activity, eventually causing death. Barbiturates can also depress the central nervous system, leading to respiratory failure and death.

How Antidotes Work

Antidotes work by counteracting the effects of poisons. Some poisons have specific antidotes, whereas other poisons have no known antidotes. One way to counteract a poison is to prevent the gastrointestinal tract from absorbing it. Activated charcoal can bind to a poison, making it difficult for the body to absorb it.

Another possible antidote is the introduction of a substance that keeps the body busy metabolizing it rather than the poison. For example, in ethylene glycol (antifreeze) poisoning, ethyl alcohol is administered. Ethyl alcohol is chemically similar to ethylene glycol, and the body be-

Graham Young, Poisoner

It has been said that one can be a successful poisoner or a famous poisoner, but not both. Somehow, Graham Young managed to achieve both success and fame with his uses of poison.

Young started experimenting with the effects of poisons on the human body when he was fourteen years old. He tested antimony and digitalis on members of his family, often making them violently ill. He escaped suspicion for quite some time, probably because he often ingested the food or drink he had poisoned and became sick, too. His stepmother eventually died from poisoning, and Young came under suspicion. He confessed to poisoning his stepmother as well as his father, sister, and a school friend, and he was subsequently sent to a secure psychiatric hospital for mentally unstable criminals. During his stay there, Young continued to study poisons and their effects and was suspected of continuing his experiments on his fellow inmates.

Released from the hospital in 1971, having been deemed "fully cured," Young began work at a large photography supply store. He began poisoning again; this time his victims were his supervisor and his coworkers. The illness his victims displayed was labeled as a strange flu, partly because of the enormity of Young's poisoning—he is thought to have poisoned up to seventy people during this time, mostly by lacing their tea with antimony or thallium. Only two became sick enough to die, however: a supervisor and a coworker whom Young particularly did not like.

Apparently, Young felt that his poisoning was not getting the attention it deserved, as he suggested to the company doctor that thallium poisoning could be the cause of the illness sweeping through his workplace. One of his coworkers knew of Young's interest in poisons, and he quickly became a suspect. After authorities found out about his previous poisoning conviction and discovered a diary listing in detail the persons he had poisoned and the amounts of poison he had given each, Young was convicted. He died in prison in 1990, at the age of forty-two. The official cause of death was a heart attack, but some speculation exists that his fellow inmates may have somehow caused his death because they suspected him of poisoning them.

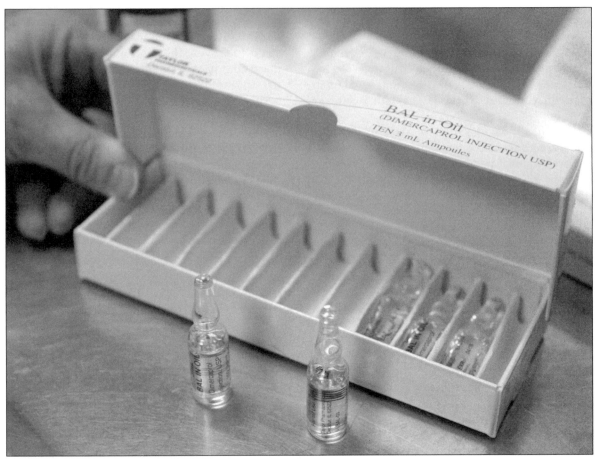

Kit containing vials of an antidote known as BAL (from "British Anti-Lewisite"), which was developed during World War I for use against heavy-metal poisons, such as mercury and arsenic. The antidote was still being used in the United States during the early twenty-first century. *(AP/Wide World Photos)*

gins to metabolize the ethyl alcohol quickly, leaving the ethylene glycol to pass through the system.

Other antidotes involve binding or trapping poison molecules or the body's receptors to those molecules. Atropine is used as an antidote to nerve gas, for example; it binds to the nervous system's acetylcholine receptors, preventing the nerve gas from doing so. Poisons that affect the skin can be counteracted with ointments that trap the poison molecules and keep them from being absorbed by the skin.

Emetics (substances that cause vomiting, such as syrup of ipecac) and cathartics (agents that cause diarrhea) are generally no longer recommended as antidotes for poison.

Marianne M. Madsen

Further Reading

Emsley, John. *The Elements of Murder: A History of Poison.* New York: Oxford University Press, 2005. Focuses on five deadly poisons (mercury, arsenic, antimony, lead, and thallium) and their use throughout history in murders.

Flanagan, Robert J., and Alison L. Jones. *Antidotes.* New York: Taylor & Francis, 2001. Covers the development and clinical uses of antidotes and their mechanisms of action.

Gupta, S. K., ed. *Emergency Toxicology: Management of Common Poisons.* New Delhi: Narosa, 2002. Discusses the treatment of poisoning cases, focusing on household products and industrial chemicals.

Klaassen, Curtis D., ed. *Casarett and Doull's*

Toxicology: The Basic Science of Poisons. 7th ed. New York: McGraw-Hill, 2007. Comprehensive work includes discussion of the principles, concepts, and mechanisms of modern toxicology.

Nelson, Lewis S., Richard D. Shih, and Michael J. Balick. *Handbook of Poisonous and Injurious Plants*. 2d ed. New York: Springer, 2007. Informative reference guide is intended for clinicians as well as laypersons interested in plant life and its possible dangers. Includes color photographs.

Stevens, Serita, and Anne Bannon. *Howdunit Book of Poisons: A Guide for Writers*. Cincinnati: Writer's Digest Books, 2007. Focuses on the use of poison as a plot point for mystery and crime writers. Includes information about how toxicologists uncover poisoning crimes.

See also: Ancient science and forensics; Arsenic; Biotoxins; Botulinum toxin; Carbon monoxide poisoning; Chemical terrorism; Forensic toxicology; Markov murder; Product tampering; Ricin; Toxicological analysis.

Polarized light microscopy

Definition: Technique that employs special filters to enhance microscopic images.

Significance: Polarized light microscopy is one of the microscopic techniques most commonly used by forensic scientists in the examination and identification of specimens. It is critical in the analysis of small evidence samples.

Although polarized light microscopy has been in use for almost two centuries, it remains one of the most powerful tools available for trace evidence analysis. Polarized light microscopy is a type of light microscopy that uses special filters to enhance the image of a sample. This technique is also known as petrographic or chemical microscopy.

Polarized light microscopy is generally one of the first methods chosen for characterizing and identifying various microscopic materials. By analyzing the optical properties of a sample with this technique, a forensic scientist can collect specific sample characteristics that cannot be obtained with other types of microscopy. Optical properties can provide much information about the structural features and composition of a specimen.

Polarized Light Microscopes

A polarized light microscope is equipped with two special filters, called polarizers, that help enhance the image of a specimen. One filter is referred to as the polarizer and the other is called the analyzer. The two polarizing elements are positioned in the optical path of the microscope. The polarizer is placed in the light

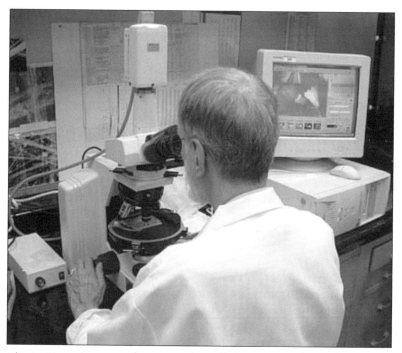

A scientist examines a sample using a polarized light microscope. *(State of California)*

path before the sample, such as underneath the microscope stage, with the preferred direction usually set left to right, or east to west. The analyzer is situated in the optical path in the body of the microscope above the objectives and is positioned between the sample and sample viewing. The analyzer is aligned opposite from the polarizer in a north-south direction. Both polarizer and analyzer can typically be rotated 360 degrees on most microscopes, and the analyzer can be moved into or out of the light path as required. Information can be collected using both plane-polarized light, in which only the polarizer is in place, or using crossed polarizers, in which both the polarizer and the analyzer are in place and positioned at right angles to each other.

Light is emitted from a source in all directions, but when this light is filtered through a polarizer, only light that vibrates in a specific direction can pass through the filter. In polarized light, the light waves all vibrate in the same direction. The direction in which light vibrates cannot be detected by the human eye, but it can be indicated by color effect or by intensity. Polarized light takes advantage of these features to enhance the image of the specimen. A common example of polarized light is polarized sunglasses, which reduce glare and improve visibility by filtering out all light except that traveling in one direction.

Optical Properties

Based on optical properties, materials can be divided into two general categories referred to as isotropic or anisotropic. Isotropic materials demonstrate the same optical properties in all directions; examples include gases, liquids, and certain glasses and crystals. Because they are optically the same in all directions, isotropic substances have only one refractive index. About 90 percent of all solid materials are anisotropic, however; that is, they have optical properties that vary with the orientation of incoming light and structure of the materials. Rather than having only one refractive index, as do isotropic materials, anisotropic materials have refractive indices that vary depending on the direction of incident light and the sample's structure.

When light interacts with an anisotropic sample, the light is split into component rays; this is called birefringence. Polarized light microscopy uses birefringence, or splitting of light, to cause light rays to interact in a specific way that generates information about the material being examined. When light hits anisotropic material, individual wave components are generated that vary in propagation direction and speed, and the light waves become out of phase. As out-of-phase light waves pass through the analyzer, they are recombined and are either added or subtracted through interference, and the light diffuses into various colors, known as interference colors. Interference colors are indicators of specific sample characteristics and can be used to identify samples. If the specimen is rotated, changes in brightness or color may be observed that can also help in sample identification.

Sample Analysis

The polarized light microscope is the instrument of choice for analyzing many types of small pieces of evidence (such as fibers, hairs, residues, inks, paints, illicit drugs, munitions, wood fragments, minerals, and soils) based on the specific appearance of different materials under polarized light. Information about important sample characteristics, such as shape, color, size, surface texture, and optical density, can be essential for determining the identity of an unknown specimen.

Polarized light microscopes are very sensitive and can be used for both quantitative and qualitative analyses. In addition to contributing important information about a sample's optical properties, polarized light microscopy can be used to make nondestructive analytical measurements. Enough information is generally collected from examination using polarized light microscopy to identify an unknown specimen or at least to reduce the number of possibilities. Additional chemical or structural analysis can follow to characterize the sample further or confirm the sample's identity. Polarized light microscopy is often combined with other techniques, such as spectroscopy, in a complete analytical scheme for examining forensic samples.

C. J. Walsh

Further Reading

Houck, Max M., and Jay A. Siegel. *Fundamentals of Forensic Science.* Burlington, Mass.: Elsevier Academic Press, 2006. General textbook geared toward both students and professionals covers many aspects of the forensic sciences. Includes an informative chapter on microscopy.

James, Stuart H., and Jon J. Nordby, eds. *Forensic Science: An Introduction to Scientific and Investigative Techniques.* 2d ed. Boca Raton, Fla.: CRC Press, 2005. Introductory text includes sections on polarized light microscopy as it relates to the analysis of trace evidence.

Mozayani, Ashraf, and Carla Noziglia, eds. *The Forensic Laboratory Handbook: Procedures and Practice.* Totowa, N.J.: Humana Press, 2006. Comprehensive textbook presents discussion of the use of polarized light microscopy in various types of sample analysis.

Petraco, Nicholas, and Thomas Kubic. *Color Atlas and Manual of Microscopy for Criminalists, Chemists, and Conservators.* Boca Raton, Fla.: CRC Press, 2004. Presents a collection of photomicrographs of specimens examined using polarized light microscopy. Includes introductory material on forensic microscopy.

Saferstein, Richard, ed. *Forensic Science Handbook.* 2d ed. Vol. 1. Upper Saddle River, N.J.: Prentice Hall, 2002. Provides discussion of the use of analytical instruments in forensic science, including a chapter that covers polarized light microscopy.

See also: Analytical instrumentation; Confocal microscopy; Fibers and filaments; Hair analysis; Micro-Fourier transform infrared spectrometry; Microscopes; Microspectrophotometry; Paint; Physical evidence; Scanning electron microscopy; Trace and transfer evidence.

Police artists. *See* Composite drawing

Police dogs. *See* Cadaver dogs; Canine substance detection; Scent identification

Police psychology

Definition: Variety of professional services offered by psychologists in law-enforcement settings.

Significance: The varied contributions of psychologists to the work of law enforcement have altered the ways in which certain police tasks are performed and have greatly improved the processes of law-enforcement personnel recruitment and evaluation.

The initial involvement of psychologists with law enforcement had its roots in the early twentieth century work of well-known cognitive psychologists Louis Thurstone and Lewis Terman, who applied the measures of IQ that they developed to the assessment of police officers. It was not until the latter part of the century, however, that psychologists began to work with police departments in a full-time capacity and to increase the variety of their services. Two of the early pioneers in this regard were Martin Reiser of the Los Angeles Police Department and Harvey Schlossberg of the New York City Police Department. Reiser was best known for his work in the development of forensic hypnosis techniques and the treatment of police stress. Schlossberg was the first police officer to obtain a doctoral degree in clinical psychology. He went on to become his police department's first full-time psychologist.

Psychological work in law enforcement is commonly related to four primary areas: applicant screening, officer counseling, performance of assessments of officers' fitness for duty, and participation in hostage negotiations.

Applicant Screening

The screening of applicants for law-enforcement jobs is typically accomplished in two stages: A battery of psychological instruments, including various personality tests, is administered, followed by an interview with a staff psychologist to review the results. Taking the tests can be stressful in itself, as the tests are typically given one after the other and several contain more than three hundred response items. By far the most heavily used (and most researched) instrument is the Minnesota Multiphasic Personality Inventory (MMPI). The items on this test are subdivided into scales that assess various aspects of psychopathology, and applicants who score high on one or more of these scales are questioned about their responses by the psychologist. Often, questioned applicants claim that they misunderstood the items; if the psychologist decides that an applicant's scores on the instrument's internal lie scales indicate a lack of candor, the applicant may be asked to take the test again. If pathological tendencies remain unexplained to the examining psychologist's satisfaction, this may be grounds for rejection.

The administration of psychological tests is typically part of a "screening out" recruitment model, which focuses on detecting applicants' inability to tolerate stress and prejudicial attitudes toward various groups officers may encounter in their work (including women, homeless people, gays, and members of racial or ethnic minority groups). The California Personality Inventory (CPI) is another popular test; it is oriented toward measuring adaptive or prosocial psychological tendencies. The CPI is often used when recruitment is done using a "selecting in" model, which aims to identify applicants with particular qualities or abilities that are desirable for police work. This may be especially relevant for those police forces that have adopted a "community policing" model, which emphasizes close work between law-enforcement personnel and community members on a variety of projects that address quality-of-life issues. Personality attributes such as warmth, empathy, insight, and creativity are important types of selection criteria in these circumstances.

In a crisis-intervention training session, a Waycross, Georgia, police officer (left) talks to a student pretending to be a suicidal person preparing to jump from a high ledge. *(AP/Wide World Photos)*

Counseling

The counseling aspects of police psychology focus on addressing the immediate needs of officers referred by supervisors. The most common problems are difficulties in dealing with the inherent stresses of the work and unresolved anger management issues. This part of the police psychologist's role is especially controversial among police officers themselves. Officers who receive counseling are typically not being evaluated on a voluntary basis, and, in many departments, it is routine at the initial consultation for the psychologist to authorize a temporary removal of the officer's gun. Many of the officers referred for counseling have family members who served long careers in law enforcement without ever having to face this issue, and it is traumatic for them. The weapon itself is an integral part of an officer's self-identity, and its removal, even for a temporary period, is a devastating blow to the officer's ego and affects the officer's reputation on the force.

Most police counselors function in a short-term capacity. That is, a counselor will assess an officer's initial problem and then may offer a limited number of therapy sessions in attempting to define the parameters of the problem further and develop an approach toward resolution. Longer-term therapeutic interventions are usually referred to outside psychologists or psychiatrists, even when a police department is large enough to employ its own psychologists on a full-time basis.

Fitness for Duty

A specialized form of short-term psychological services is the fitness-for-duty evaluation (FFDE). FFDEs are often oriented toward the assessment of stress tolerance or other possible difficulties that officers may be perceived to have in carrying out their jobs. Such evaluations may be required on a regular basis for personnel in high-stress units. FFDEs are often conducted routinely after any incidents involving the use of weapons, as part of efforts to screen for ongoing psychological difficulties in the aftermath of particularly stressful events.

A full evaluation of fitness for duty involves multiple data sources, including standardized psychological tests and clinical interviews, citizen complaints, background check reports, and records of any medical interventions. U.S. courts have generally upheld the right of police departments to require their personnel to undergo FFDEs when specific circumstances indicate that this practice will support the interests of public safety or maintain or increase the efficiency of the department's work.

It has been recommended that FFDEs be conducted by licensed psychologists who are knowledgeable about the relevant police psychology literature and related civil rights issues that affect law-enforcement agencies. The rationale justifying the evaluation of an officer's fitness for duty should be specific and based on alleged job behavior. The report that the evaluating psychologist later provides to law-enforcement executives should include only information that is directly relevant to the performance of the officer's job duties. FFDE sessions are sometimes recorded on audio- or videotape to protect departments from later allegations of arbitrariness or bias.

Participation in Hostage Negotiations

Psychologists' involvement in police hostage negotiations and on related crisis-intervention teams has been significant, especially since the early 1970's, when the Attica prison riot and the murder of the Israeli Olympic athletes at the Munich Olympic games received worldwide attention. Although psychologists' ultimate goal in hostage negotiations is to diffuse these situations through the use of an active system of creative problem resolution, the first thing psychologists must address is the emotionality of the hostage takers. This part of the intervention often proceeds in distinct stages: First, the negotiation team establishes communication with the hostage takers and convinces them that the team clearly hears and understands their demands (even though they do not agree with them); the negotiation team then lets as much time pass as possible to decrease the emotional level of the situation while investigators work to obtain more detailed information about what caused the situation, the present dangers and their likelihood of occurrence, and what can be done to and for the hostage takers when the immediate crisis is over. Only after these stages have successfully passed can psychologists begin the active work of problem resolution with optimal chances for success.

A large part of the police training provided by psychologists working in the areas of hostage negotiation and crisis intervention is conducted in a role-playing format. Much of this work is based on actual past incidents, frequently cases involving domestic violence, workplace violence, or suicide. Role-playing exercises in such training may last from several minutes to several hours; those of relatively long duration have obvious advantages in terms of their ability to simulate actual situations realistically. Online training modules have also been developed that take full advantage of both synchronous and asynchronous communication modes.

Eric Metchik

Further Reading

Reiser, Martin, and Nels Klyver. "Consulting with Police." In *The Handbook of Forensic Psychology*, edited by Irving B. Weiner and Allen K. Hess. New York: John Wiley & Sons, 1987. Reviews a variety of psychological interventions in law enforcement. Reiser is widely acknowledged as the leading pioneer in the development of this field.

Rostow, Cary D., and Robert D. Davis. *A Handbook for Psychological Fitness-for-Duty Evaluations in Law Enforcement*. New York: Haworth Clinical Practice Press, 2004. Presents a comprehensive structural analysis of all major aspects of law-enforcement FFDEs within the broader context of police psychology.

Rostow, Cary D., Robert D. Davis, and Judith P. Levy. "Police Psychology: The Influence of *Daubert* and Its Progeny." *Journal of Police and Criminal Psychology* 17, no. 2 (2002): 1-8. Includes analysis of important legal developments related to the qualification of expert witnesses and offers practical suggestions for how experts can meet the legal requirements.

Vecchi, Gregory M., Vincent B. Van Hasselt, and Stephen J. Romano. "Crisis (Hostage) Negotiation: Current Strategies and Issues in High-Risk Conflict Resolution." *Aggression and Violent Behavior* 10, no. 5 (2005): 533-551. Traces historical developments in the field of crisis negotiation and analyzes a specific model developed by the Federal Bureau of Investigation. Also discusses possible future trends in the field.

Walker, Lenore E. A., and David L. Shapiro. *Introduction to Forensic Psychology: Clinical and Social Psychological Perspectives*. New York: Kluwer Academic/Plenum, 2003. Provides a comprehensive, multidisciplinary review of key advances in the work of psychologists in criminal justice agencies.

See also: Criminal personality profiling; *Daubert v. Merrell Dow Pharmaceuticals*; Federal Law Enforcement Training Center; Forensic psychiatry; Forensic psychology; *Frye v. United States*; Hostage negotiations; Minnesota Multiphasic Personality Inventory; Polygraph analysis; Psychological autopsy; Training and licensing of forensic professionals; Trial consultants.

Pollen and pollen rain

Definitions: Pollen is the male reproductive structure of all flowering plants that is transported by wind, water, or animals to the female flower. Pollen rain is the release of vast amounts of pollen by male flowering plants of an ecological landscape.

Significance: Palynological analysis of pollen rain can be an important tool in crime investigations because it can help determine chronology and the type of ecological community within which an event may have occurred.

Pollen is the male gametophyte of a flowering plant. It originates in the anther of a flower, which consists of chambers called pollen sacs. Each pollen sac gives rise to microscopic grains of pollen. Pollen grains are not the equivalent of sperm in animals; rather, each pollen grain consists of at least two cells, a generative cell that produces the sperm to fertilize the female egg and a larger tube cell that provides the corridor to deliver the sperm to the egg.

Transfer of pollen to the female flower is accomplished via wind, water, or animals; windborne pollen is known as pollen rain. To facilitate dispersal by wind, pollen is small, lightweight, unscented, and generally inconspicuous. The spores released by mosses, ferns, and fungi are also considered part of pollen rain, and the study of such spores is part of forensic botany.

The volume of pollen rain released annually in any given area is enormous, with pollen covering the landscape in a very fine layer. Despite the abundance of pollen, this coating is invisible, or nearly so, except with the aid of a microscope. Pollen may become lodged in respiratory tracts and can accumulate on clothes, hair, and body. The pollen rain of a given area is called a pollen assemblage. Because each species of plant and fungus contributes its own unique pollen, such pollen assemblages are natural fingerprints of the vegetation in their areas; these fingerprints may differ significantly from one area to another.

Palynology is the examination and analysis of pollen assemblages. By comparing the pollen grains found on or in corpses, on suspects and their possessions, and on other objects, forensic palynologists can link particular persons with crime scenes based on the expected pollen rain for those areas.

Dwight G. Smith

Further Reading

Coyle, Heather Miller, ed. *Forensic Botany: Principles and Applications to Criminal Casework*. Boca Raton, Fla.: CRC Press, 2005.

Faegri, Knut, Peter Emil Kaland, and Knut Krzywinski. *Textbook of Pollen Analysis*. 4th ed. New York: John Wiley & Sons, 1989.

Horrocks, Mark, and Kevan A. J. Walsh. "Forensic Palynology: Assessing the Value of the Evidence." *Review of Palaeobotany and Palynology* 103 (1998): 69-74.

See also: Forensic botany; Forensic geoscience; Forensic palynology; Physical evidence; Trace and transfer evidence.

Polygraph analysis

Definition: Interrogation technique that measures physiological responses to detect deception.

Significance: Polygraph analysis, also known as lie detection, is widely used as part of law-enforcement investigations in the United States, although controversy exists regarding the reliability of the technique.

Polygraph analysis enjoys a rich history in the United States, where law-enforcement agencies have used it in interrogations with varying results since the early twentieth century. The reliability of the technique for detecting deception is the topic of ongoing controversy. Some proponents claim that polygraph analysis can detect deception with approximately 95 percent accuracy, whereas many scientists contend that the technique detects deception at rates only slightly better than chance.

History

William Moulton Marston is credited with inventing the discontinuous polygraph, which records physiological signals only at select times during an interrogation. As inventor and marketer, Marston brought great attention to the polygraph in the early twentieth century. He claimed that the polygraph was the end-all solution to difficulties with detecting deception during interrogation. Building on Marston's invention, John A. Larson developed a continuous polygraph, which he called a cardio-pneumo-psychograph, in 1921. Unlike Marston, however, Larson was critical of the polygraph and cautioned against its use in court proceedings. Mirroring Larson's viewpoint, the U.S. Supreme Court decided in *Frye v. United States* in 1923 that insufficient scientific support existed to allow polygraph results to be used as evidence in court proceedings.

In response to the *Frye* ruling, scientists worked toward developing scientifically validated polygraphy techniques. In 1930, Leonarde Keeler, an associate of Larson, and John E. Reid helped form the Scientific Crime Detection Laboratory of Northwestern University

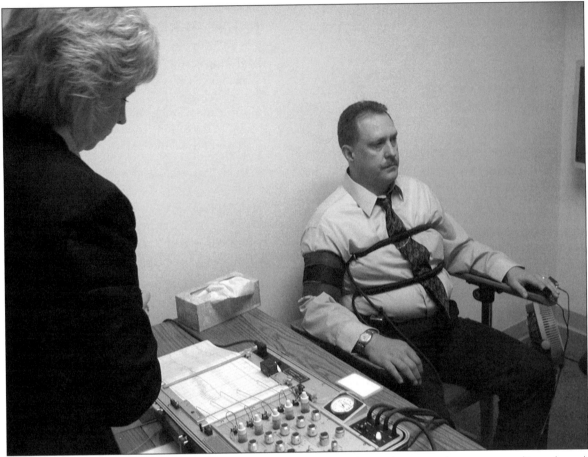

A police lieutenant (left) asks the questions and a police detective answers them as the two demonstrate the equipment used in a polygraph examination. *(AP/Wide World Photos)*

to enhance polygraph interrogation methods. Keeler later opened the first polygraphy training school in 1938. Reid followed suit, opening John E. Reid and Associates in 1947. These two schools became the most prominent polygraphy schools in the United States.

Equipment

The equipment used during a modern polygraph interrogation includes a physiological data acquisition device that measures respiration, blood pressure, pulse, and palmar sweating on a continuous basis. The traditional polygraph is a mechanical instrument that records physiological signals on a moving paper chart; following the interrogation, the chart is hand-scored by the polygrapher.

Increasingly, the traditional polygraph is being replaced by the computerized polygraph, which acquires, stores, and analyzes data in digital form. Computerized polygraphs often score charts by applying mathematical formulas based on the results of previous polygraph examinations.

Interrogation Techniques

Although most polygraphs measure the same physiological indicators, the interrogation techniques used by polygraphers vary greatly. The three most commonly used methods of interrogation are the irrelevant/relevant (I/R) test, the control question test (CQT), and the guilty knowledge test (GKT).

The I/R test was the original method of interrogation in early polygraphy, and it is still commonly used by some employers during personnel screening interviews. This technique uses a combination of task-irrelevant and task-relevant questions. An example of a task-relevant question is "Have you ever stolen an item valued at more than twenty dollars?" An example of a task-irrelevant question is "Is your name Bob?" The underlying rationale is that more marked physiological responses during task-relevant questions suggest deception. For instance, if an interview subject who was asked the two preceding questions had stolen an item valued at more than twenty dollars, that person would presumably show a greater physiological response to the relevant question than to the irrelevant question.

The CQT, which is a variant of the I/R test, is the most commonly used polygraphic technique in the United States. The CQT uses a combination of control, task-relevant, and task-irrelevant questions. An example of a control question is "Have you ever stolen an item valued at more than two dollars?" An example of a task-relevant question is "Did you steal one hundred dollars from Joe's wallet on December 17?" Control questions are designed to elicit known lies from just about everyone, thereby serving as a baseline with which to gauge the examinee's physiological "lie" response. The rationale is that guilty examinees should react more to task-relevant questions than to control questions because they are concerned about being caught for the specific crime in question, whereas examinees who are innocent of the crime in question will respond more to control questions because they are concerned about appearing to be criminal types.

The GKT technique investigates criminal guilt without attempting to identify a lie response. In this respect, it contrasts sharply with the I/R test and CQT. Although the GKT is used rarely by law-enforcement agencies in the United States, it is the preferred interrogation method in Japan. Instead of asking directly whether an examinee participated in a crime, the GKT attempts to assess concealed knowledge. It does so by asking specific questions about the crime followed by multiple-choice options. For example, if the walls of the room in which someone was beaten were painted blue, a GKT question might be "The paint in the room where the beating took place was: red, white, blue, or green?" The assumption is that guilty examinees will react more strongly to correct details of a crime, whereas innocent examinees will not.

Applications

Until the late 1980's, many American businesses used polygraphy as a tool for screening employees and job applicants, but with passage of the Employee Polygraph Protection Act of 1988, a federal law, private employers were prevented from using polygraphy in this way. Government agencies, contractors working with government agencies, and private-sector employees suspected of theft were exempted from this protection, however. Several government agencies, including the Federal Bureau of Investigation (FBI), the Central Intelligence Agency (CIA), the Department of Energy, and the National Security Agency, use the polygraph for employee screening on a regular basis.

Following the U.S. Supreme Court's decision in *Frye v. United States*, polygraph results were rarely introduced as evidence during court proceedings. In 1993, the Court's ruling in *Daubert*

Origins of the Polygraph

The Italian criminologist Cesare Lombroso is credited with developing the principles behind polygraph testing during the 1890's. A pioneer of modern scientific criminology methods, he sought to explain criminal behavior through human biology. He discovered that blood pressure increased in test subjects after they provided deceptive responses to questions. Later, William Moulton Marston and John A. Larson separately came to the conclusion that blood pressure and respiration are correlated. Larson constructed the actual recording device in 1921, but Leonarde Keeler and Walter Summers refined the direct predecessor of the modern polygraph testing device around 1924. Following their advances, investigators and employers began to use the polygraph as a matter of practice.

Douglas A. Orr

v. Merrell Dow Pharmaceuticals built on the *Frye* ruling by developing guidelines for introducing scientific evidence into court proceedings. The guidelines the Court established, collectively known as the *Daubert* standard, are as follows: Scientific evidence must be based on a testable theory or technique, the theory or technique must be peer-reviewed, the technique must have a known error rate, and the underlying science must be generally accepted by the scientific community. Following the *Daubert* decision, polygraph evidence became largely inadmissible in criminal proceedings. In half of U.S. state courts, polygraph evidence continues to be admissible in criminal proceedings when the defense and prosecution agree to the admissibility of the results before the test is taken. The results of polygraph analysis are commonly used in civil proceedings, however, and law-enforcement agencies often use the technique in screening criminal suspects.

Continuing Controversy

In 1997, David T. Lykken and William G. Iacono polled 363 scientists from the American Psychological Association and the Society for Psychophysiological Research concerning the use of GKT and CQT polygraph interrogation techniques. They found that although 75 percent of the scientists surveyed believed that the GKT is based on sound scientific evidence, only 33 percent held this view of the CQT. Moreover, only about 25 percent of the scientists polled believed that polygraph evidence should be allowed in a courtroom.

Critics of polygraph analysis assert that the technique rests on the faulty assumption of a "Pinocchio response"—that is, a specific physiological lie response or "signature" of deception. Scientific studies have found no evidence of such a response. Moreover, real-world studies of people who have been conclusively found either guilty or innocent of crimes suggest that the polygraph has a high false positive rate, meaning that it mistakenly classifies many innocent people as guilty. These findings have led many critics, such as Lykken and Paul Ekman, to refer to the polygraph as an "arousal detector" rather than a lie detector. They assert that many people may fail polygraph tests not because they are guilty of crimes but because they display nervousness, indignation, or surprise in response to the relevant questions.

Polygraph analysis may also be plagued by false negatives, or guilty individuals mistakenly classified as innocent. Some false negative results can be produced by "countermeasures"—tricks that help people "beat" the polygraph by allowing them to boost their physiological responses to irrelevant or control questions. Such countermeasures can be physical (such as biting down on one's tongue during these questions) or mental (such as performing complex mental arithmetic during these questions).

Attempts to study the validity of polygraph results are complicated by at least two major obstacles. First, laboratory studies cannot simulate the intense pressure of real-world polygraph interrogations, because the arousal associated with a lie generated for the purposes of a study probably differs from that associated with a lie generated to avoid imprisonment or even capital punishment. Second, studies of polygraph use in real-world settings may overestimate the accuracy of the results as applied to the general population, because many suspects are guilty of the crimes of which they have been accused. For example, if thirty-six of forty suspects in a study sample are guilty and all forty polygraph tests indicated guilt, one could claim that the polygraph was 90 percent accurate. These obstacles suggest that novel research methodologies are required to evaluate the validity of polygraphy in practice.

Patrick Sylvers and Scott O. Lilienfeld

Further Reading

Iacono, William G., and David T. Lykken. "The Validity of the Lie Detector: Two Surveys of Scientific Opinion." *Journal of Applied Psychology*, 82 (1997): 426-433. Reports on the results of a survey of several hundred expert psychologists regarding their opinions on the utility and admissibility of the polygraph in court.

Iacono, William G., and Christopher J. Patrick. "Polygraph ('Lie Detector') Testing: Current Status and Emerging Trends." In *The Handbook of Forensic Psychology*, edited by Irving

B. Weiner and Allen K. Hess. 3d ed. Hoboken, N.J.: John Wiley & Sons, 2006. Provides a comprehensive examination of the history and scientific evidence surrounding the polygraph.

Inbau, Fred E., John E. Reid, Joseph P. Buckley, and Brian C. Jayne. *Criminal Interrogation and Confessions*. 4th ed. Boston: Jones & Bartlett, 2004. Presents a good discussion of polygraph interrogation techniques.

Larson, John A. *Lying and Its Detection: A Study of Deception and Deception Tests*. Chicago: University of Chicago Press, 1932. Outlines Larson's critical evaluation of the polygraph as a device for lie detection.

Lykken, David T. *A Tremor in the Blood: Uses and Abuses of the Lie Detector*. 2d ed. New York: McGraw-Hill, 1996. Provides a comprehensive and critical review of the history, development, implementation, and scientific study of the polygraph.

Marston, William Moulton. *The Lie Detector Test*. New York: Richard R. Smith, 1938. Discusses Marston's beliefs regarding the infallibility of the polygraph.

National Research Council. *The Polygraph and Lie Detection*. Washington, D.C.: National Academies Press, 2003. Presents the findings of the council's review of scientific studies of the polygraph.

Raskin, David C., and Charles R. Honts. "The Comparison Question Test." In *Handbook of Polygraph Testing*, edited by Murray Kleiner. San Diego, Calif.: Academic Press, 2002. Reviews the CQT polygraph interrogation technique.

See also: Ancient science and forensics; Brainwave scanners; Courts and forensic evidence; *Daubert v. Merrell Dow Pharmaceuticals*; Expert witnesses; *Frye v. United States*; Interrogation; Physiology; Police psychology; Pseudoscience in forensic practice.

Polymerase chain reaction

Definition: Laboratory technique used to generate large numbers of copies of DNA for analysis.

Significance: The technique of polymerase chain reaction allows forensic scientists to use extremely small amounts of sample DNA to identify individual humans, animals, and other organisms. Such analyses are used for many purposes, including to link suspects to crime scenes, to identify the victims of mass disasters, to establish paternity, and to identify pathogens.

The molecule of life, DNA (deoxyribonucleic acid), is the unique genetic blueprint of an individual. DNA is present in virtually every cell in the body. The uniqueness of DNA, which is composed of two long strands, stems from the specific order (sequence) of its different nucleotide building blocks, which are linked together to form each strand. Because the nucleotide sequence of each person's DNA is unique (the only exception being identical twins, who have identical DNA), DNA analysis is an integral part of forensic investigations. DNA may be isolated from biological samples (such as blood, skin, semen, or hair) found at the scenes of mass disasters or crimes, from cheek cells swabbed from the insides of mouths (as may be taken from the parties in paternity determinations or from criminal suspects), or from the environment (as in the case of pathogens).

The specific sequence of nucleotides in several regions of the isolated DNA (short tandem repeats, known as STRs, or other specific sequences) is compared with the sequence in identical regions of a DNA standard. This standard comes from a known source; it may be from a predeath biological sample recovered from a disaster victim's personal effects, from a crime suspect, from a party involved in a paternity case, or, in the case of a pathogen, from a previously experimentally derived sequence. When a crime is being investigated, the standard may be on file in the Federal Bureau of Investigation's Combined DNA Index System (CODIS). Even if there is no match in a criminal case, such information may help exonerate a suspect.

Frequently, the amounts of DNA obtained at crime or disaster scenes and in other situations are insufficient to allow such comparisons. When this is the case, scientists can use the technique of polymerase chain reaction (PCR) to generate a large number of copies of the DNA for analysis. This technique is so sensitive that the DNA isolated from a single cell is sufficient to obtain the desired nucleotide sequence.

In PCR, the DNA to be copied is placed in a plastic test tube along with nucleotides, DNA polymerase, and two or more short sequences of single-stranded DNA (called primers) that define where DNA polymerase will begin working. DNA polymerase is an enzyme that adds nucleotides to the growing strand. The test tube is then placed in a machine that can vary the temperature of the test tube and its contents.

The test tube is first heated so that the two strands of the original DNA molecule will separate from each other. Each strand will act as a template for production of a new strand. The temperature is then slightly decreased to allow the DNA primers to bind to each template adjacent to the start of nucleotide addition. The temperature is then slightly increased, and DNA polymerase adds nucleotides until a new strand is synthesized on each template, producing two double-stranded DNA molecules after the first cycle that are identical to the original DNA molecule. Each time the steps are repeated, the DNA doubles: Four DNA molecules are produced after two cycles, eight DNA molecules are produced after three cycles, and so on. Repeating these steps thirty times results in about one billion copies of the amplified DNA region.

Jason J. Schwartz

Further Reading

McPherson, Michael, and Simon Møller. *PCR (The Basics).* 2d ed. New York: Taylor & Francis, 2006.

Rudin, Norah, and Keith Inman. *An Introduction to Forensic DNA Analysis.* 2d ed. Boca Raton, Fla.: CRC Press, 2002.

See also: CODIS; DNA fingerprinting; DNA profiling; DNA sequencing; DNA typing; Ebola virus; Electrophoresis; Louis XVII remains identification; Mitochondrial DNA analysis and typing; Paternity evidence; Pathogen genomic sequencing; Restriction fragment length polymorphisms; Short tandem repeat analysis; Y chromosome analysis.

Postconviction DNA analysis

Definition: Examination of DNA evidence in criminal cases that have already concluded with conviction of the accused.

Significance: The findings of postconviction DNA analysis can serve to affirm correct convictions, exonerate persons who have been wrongfully convicted, and identify the true perpetrators of crimes for which others were convicted. Such DNA analysis thus plays a vital role in maintaining the integrity of the criminal justice system.

The introduction of DNA (deoxyribonucleic acid) analysis revolutionized forensic science and provided law-enforcement agencies with a powerful tool for solving crimes. The proper use of DNA analysis can identify individuals with a higher degree of confidence than is possible with other forensic techniques, and such analysis has led to the conviction of many criminal offenders. Equally important, postconviction DNA analysis has resulted in the exoneration of many persons who had been wrongfully convicted of crimes. Postconviction analysis of DNA evidence may be conducted because access to such analysis was unavailable during the convicted offender's earlier trial or because advances in analysis techniques since the individual was convicted may provide better evidence than was available at the time of the trial.

Background

As a tool of forensic science, DNA analysis has a relatively short history. It began in 1985 in Great Britain, when Alec Jeffreys, a geneticist, stumbled onto the use of DNA markers (restriction fragment length polymorphisms, or RFLPs) for personal identification while searching for disease markers in human DNA. He saw the potential for the method's use in criminal and civil investigations and coined the term "DNA finger-printing," later explaining that he chose the term in a "deliberate move to emphasize the new forensic paradigm" that he foresaw. In April, 1985, Jeffreys was asked by Britain's Home Office to use DNA fingerprinting to solve an immigration dispute regarding the family identity of a boy. Although the blood group evidence supported the boy's claim of true kinship with the family, it was not convincing. The findings of the DNA analysis performed by Jeffreys and his colleagues supported the authenticity of the boy's claim.

The publicity that accompanied this case not only opened a floodgate of inquiries from immigrant communities over previously disputed cases but also led to the introduction of the use of DNA fingerprinting in paternity tests and many other applications. By 1986, the terms "DNA profiling" and "DNA typing" were also being used to refer to the technique. In the same year, DNA profiling saw its forensic debut in a murder case in Leicester, Jeffreys's hometown. This first admission of DNA typing evidence in a criminal court led to the exoneration of a young man who had falsely confessed to rape and murder. After that trial, the first-ever DNA-based manhunt subsequently brought the true perpetrator to justice; he was convicted in 1987. In the decades that followed, DNA typing became a standard tool of forensic science.

The Innocence Protection Act of 2004

This summary of section 411 of the Innocence Protection Act of 2004 (Title IV of the Justice for All Act of 2004) comes from the office of Senator Patrick Leahy of Vermont, who first introduced a version of this legislation in the U.S. Senate in 2000.

Federal postconviction DNA testing. Establishes rules and procedures governing applications for DNA testing by inmates in the Federal system. A court shall order DNA testing if the applicant asserts under penalty of perjury that he or she is actually innocent, and the proposed DNA testing may produce new material evidence that supports such assertion and raises a reasonable probability that the applicant did not commit the offense. Motions filed more than 5 years after enactment and 3 years after conviction are presumed untimely, but such presumption may be rebutted upon good cause shown. Penalties are established in the event that testing inculpates the applicant. Where test results are exculpatory, the court shall grant the applicant's motion for a new trial or resentencing if the test results and other evidence establish by compelling evidence that a new trial would result in an acquittal.

This section also prohibits the destruction of DNA evidence in a Federal criminal case while a defendant remains incarcerated, with certain exceptions. The government may destroy DNA evidence if the defendant waived the right to DNA testing; if the defendant was notified after his conviction became final that the evidence may be destroyed and did not file a motion for testing; if a court has denied a motion for testing; or if the evidence has already been tested and the results included the defendant as the source. . . . Intentional violations of these evidence-retention provisions to prevent evidence from being tested or used in court are punishable by a term of imprisonment.

Postconviction Exonerations

The power of DNA evidence to solve crimes and convict perpetrators is widely known, but the general public is perhaps less aware of the potential of such evidence to free wrongfully convicted individuals. The first person in the United States whose criminal conviction was overturned as the result of DNA evidence was a Chicago man named Gary Dotson. He was convicted in 1981 of a rape that never occurred and exonerated in 1989. The purported rape victim had recanted her testimony in 1985, but it was not until 1988 that DNA analysis positively excluded Dotson as the source of semen found on his accuser (the semen was that of the young woman's boyfriend, with whom she had consensual sex the day she claimed to have been raped). In 1993, Kirk Bloodsworth became the first person in the United States to escape a death sentence as the result of DNA analysis; he had been convicted of the 1984 rape and murder of a child, but postconviction DNA analysis proved that semen found on the victim was not his. The true perpetrator of the crime was eventually identified in 2003, also with the aid of DNA analysis.

Using postconviction DNA analysis to exonerate persons who have been wrongfully convicted is the central mission of the Innocence Project, an organization founded in 1992 by Barry Scheck and Peter Neufeld at the Benjamin N. Cardozo School of Law at Yeshiva University. The Innocence Project provides legal assistance to prisoners who could be proven innocent through DNA analysis, and it also works to publicize the fact that wrongful convic-

tions are not rare and isolated incidents but instead the predictable results of defects in the criminal justice system. Beyond simply freeing innocent people who are incarcerated, the Innocence Project attempts to reform the system that is responsible for their unjust imprisonment.

Regulations Governing Postconviction DNA Testing

Although thirty-eight U.S. states have laws in place that allow convicts access to DNA testing, many rules and regulations limit the ways in which postconviction DNA evidence can be used. In most cases, it is typical for states to require that any new evidence be brought to court within six months following a conviction in order to warrant a new trial. In the case of DNA evidence, the drawback of such a rule is obvious:

Gary Dotson (right), who spent eight years in prison for a rape he did not commit and became the first person in the United States whose criminal conviction was overturned as the result of DNA evidence, looks on during an Illinois Prisoner Review Board hearing in October, 2002, as his attorney, Lawrence Marshall, asks the board to grant his client a pardon. Dotson sought a pardon to erase the stigma of his conviction and to draw attention to problems in the justice system. *(AP/Wide World Photos)*

It excludes individuals who were convicted before DNA typing was available but for whom such typing may now provide important evidence relevant to their cases. Since the use of DNA evidence has become commonplace, many states have revised their statutes to allow for the presentation of evidence secured through postconviction DNA analysis even after convicted persons have exhausted all of their appeals.

The Innocence Project has made several suggestions for the improvement of state statutes related to postconviction DNA analysis. The organization asserts that state laws should provide for access to DNA testing wherever it can establish innocence, even in cases in which defendants have pleaded guilty; should set no absolute deadlines on when such access will expire; should provide access to currently available DNA technology, not dependent on whether such technology was available at the time of trial; should allow for flexibility in where and how DNA testing is conducted; should require the preservation of biological evidence for a reasonable period of time; and should require the disclosure of evidence that is in the custody of state officials.

In 2004, the U.S. Congress passed the Justice for All Act; this law includes a section, known as the Innocence Protection Act of 2004, that stipulates that all convicts with reasonable claims of innocence must be granted the opportunity to prove their cases in court using postconviction DNA testing. States seeking to qualify for funding under the Justice for All Act must allow convicted persons the level of access to postconviction DNA analysis specified in the act.

Ming Y. Zheng

Further Reading

Johnson, Paul, and Robin Williams. "Post-conviction DNA Testing: The United Kingdom's First 'Exoneration' Case?" *Science and Justice* 44, no. 2 (2004): 77-82. Examines in detail the first case in England in which postconviction DNA testing was used in a successful appeal by an imprisoned offender.

Kobilinsky, Lawrence F., Thomas F. Liotti, and Jamel Oeser-Sweat. *DNA: Forensic and Legal Applications*. Hoboken, N.J.: Wiley-Interscience, 2005. Presents a general overview of the uses of DNA analysis.

Lazer, David, ed. *DNA and the Criminal Justice System: The Technology of Justice*. Cambridge, Mass.: MIT Press, 2004. Thought-provoking collection of essays explores the ethical and procedural issues related to DNA evidence.

Rudin, Norah, and Keith Inman. *An Introduction to Forensic DNA Analysis*. 2d ed. Boca Raton, Fla.: CRC Press, 2002. Provides a good introduction to the history and application of DNA fingerprinting in forensic investigations.

Scheck, Barry, Peter Neufeld, and Jim Dwyer. *Actual Innocence: Five Days to Execution, and Other Dispatches from the Wrongly Convicted*. New York: Random House, 2000. Describes some of the most prominent and successful cases taken on by Scheck and Neufeld's Innocence Project.

See also: DNA analysis; DNA fingerprinting; DNA isolation methods; DNA profiling; DNA typing; Ethics of DNA analysis; Innocence Project; Mass graves; National DNA Index System; Pseudoscience in forensic practice; Rape.

Presumptive tests for blood

Definition: Laboratory tests used to examine items for stains that may be blood.

Significance: Presumptive tests are widely used in the initial screening of scenes and items for the presence of blood; thus the correct use of such tests and correct interpretation of both positive and negative results is vital in analysis and case management.

Because blood is frequently shed during violent crimes, the search for and identification of blood is an important part of the work of forensic scientists both in the laboratory and at the crime scene. The presence of blood and its locations can provide information about the event and circumstances being investigated. Analysts may, if the case circumstances warrant it, subject any bloodstains identified to DNA (deoxyribonucleic acid) profiling to determine from whom the blood could or could not have come; this information can also shed light on the event and circumstances.

The Appearance of Bloodstains

Although the detection of bloodstains may seem like a simple process, in reality it can be quite complex. Immediately after it is shed, blood is a red liquid. It starts to clot within a few minutes, and in relatively large quantities of liquid blood, a separation of blood into clotted red material and a light-colored liquid can be noted. In smaller amounts, blood dries before clotting is complete, and a shiny, slightly translucent red stain is observed. Bloodstains darken and change color to brown with time. Any treatment of the stain with water or smearing of the stain will dilute the blood, or decrease the amount present, which results in a color change. Any treatment of the blood with a cleaning agent or other chemical will alter the stain's color to a greenish shade.

The material on which a bloodstain is present also affects the stain's appearance. The texture and absorbency of some materials can obscure the physical appearance of blood, and the color of the background material affects the analyst's perception of the color of a stain.

The visual identification of a stain as possibly being blood is a useful start in a forensic examination, but additional work needs to be done before the stain can be identified as blood. To confirm the presence of blood, a forensic scientist will usually carry out a presumptive test.

The Chemical Basis of Presumptive Tests

Blood is a unique and complex biological fluid containing many different cell types and a wide range of circulating proteins, glycoprotein, and ions. One of these cell types is the red blood cell, or erythrocyte. The major protein component of the red blood cell is hemoglobin, which contains an iron ion and is responsible for binding oxygen and transporting it around the body. Hemoglobin is found only in blood, so being able to identify this protein in a stain allows the forensic scientist to identify the stain positively as blood.

When hemoglobin binds oxygen, it effectively acts as a type of oxidizing enyzme called a peroxidase, and this enzymatic activity is used in presumptive tests. Certain dyes are colorless but can be oxidized to yield a colored product. When such a dye is added to a possible bloodstain in the presence of an oxidant, the change in color shows that an oxidizing agent, such as hemoglobin, is present. Phenolphthalein is the dye component of the Kastle-Meyer presumptive test for blood; the dye changes from colorless to dark pink. Another example is tetramethylbenzidine, which is the dye component of a commercial test for blood in urine, the Combur-Test, which can also be used to detect bloodstains. The dye in this test changes from colorless to dark green. The luminol test is also a presumptive test, although one with a far more complex reaction pathway than that of more basic presumptive tests; the action of hemoglobin on luminol produces light.

Practical Limitations of Presumptive Tests

Sometimes, substances other than blood can cause the dye to change color in a presumptive test. These substances fall into two categories. First, any chemical that can react directly with the dye to oxidize it—that is, one that does not require the oxidizing action of hemoglobin on the oxidant—can give a positive result. Examples of these are metal salts, such as some copper salts or rust, hypochlorites, and bleaches.

Presumptive Test for Blood

A basic equation for a presumptive test for blood is as follows:

$$AH_2 + ROOH \xrightarrow{\text{Hemoglobin}} A + ROH + H_2O,$$

where AH_2 is the colorless dye, ROOH is the oxidizing agent (usually hydrogen peroxide), and A is the colored dye.

Forensic scientists refer to results like these, where positive results are given by substances other than blood, as false positives.

This sort of false positive can be excluded—that is, not thought of as coming from a possible bloodstain—by the application of the dye to the stain in the absence of the oxidizing agent. A positive result under those conditions means the stain is not blood, as the oxidizing agent is needed for hemoglobin to give a positive result in presumptive tests.

The other kinds of substances that give false positives are enzymes such as catalases or peroxidases, which can break down the oxidizing agent in the same way as hemoglobin. The most common of these are plant peroxidases, which are widespread in the plant kingdom and are found in cabbage, horseradish, and other fairly common plants.

Presumptive tests are very sensitive, giving positive results to blood dilutions of between 1 in 10^5 and 1 in 10^6 under ideal conditions. Given that forensic samples are usually not tested under ideal conditions, because most are on substrates that are dirty or contaminated to some extent, the actual sensitivity in the field is probably lower. The sensitivity means that the tests can be used to screen items for small amounts of blood or diluted blood as well as to test stains that look like blood to see if they might be blood.

As other substances can give positive results in such tests, it is not possible for a forensic scientist to say that a stain that gives a positive result in a presumptive test is definitely blood. Such a stain can be described as a probable bloodstain or similar. Confirmatory tests need to be conducted before an analyst can say definitively that any given stain is blood. These are typically immunological tests that are capable of detecting proteins specific to blood; most scientists agree that crystal and spectroscopic tests for hemoglobin can be regarded as confirmatory as well.

Douglas Elliot

Further Reading

Gaensslen, R. E. *Sourcebook in Forensic Serology, Immunology, and Biochemistry.* Washington, D.C.: National Institute of Justice, 1983. Presents a comprehensive and detailed history of presumptive testing.

Houck, Max M., and Jay A. Siegel. *Fundamentals of Forensic Science.* Burlington, Mass.: Elsevier Academic Press, 2006. Good general textbook includes a clear section on presumptive testing.

James, Stuart H., Paul E. Kish, and T. Paulette Sutton. *Principles of Bloodstain Pattern Analysis: Theory and Practice.* Boca Raton, Fla.: CRC Press, 2005. Provides some useful detail on presumptive testing and the biochemical makeup of blood.

Saferstein, Richard. *Criminalistics: An Introduction to Forensic Science.* 9th ed. Upper Saddle River, N.J.: Pearson Prentice Hall, 2007. General text includes information on confirmatory tests for blood.

Webb, Joanne L., Jonathan I. Creamer, and Terence I. Quickenden. "A Comparison of the Presumptive Luminol Test for Blood with Four Non-chemiluminescent Forensic Techniques." *Luminescence* 21, no. 4 (2006): 214-220. Presents comparisons of some standard presumptive tests used by forensic scientists.

See also: Benzidine; Blood residue and bloodstains; Crime scene investigation; DNA recognition instruments; Drug confirmation tests; Kidd blood grouping system; Luminol; Orthotolidine; Phenolphthalein; Reagents; Serology.

Printer analysis. *See* Fax machine, copier, and printer analysis

Prints

Definition: Impressions left on surfaces by hands (palm prints and fingerprints) and bare feet (sole prints and toe prints).

Significance: Fingerprints are routinely collected at crime scenes as means of identifying persons who were present during the crimes, but prints from the soles of feet and the palms of the hands are equally unique and revealing. Any prints that are recoverable at a crime scene may provide information important to the investigation.

Prints from bare feet found at crime scenes can be as telling as fingerprints, but in the United States such prints are less often employed than fingerprints because most people involved in crimes commonly wear some sort of covering—shoes or at least socks—on their feet. Where bare footprints or toe prints are available, they can be as valuable forensically as fingerprints because such prints contain the same ridges and valleys that characterize fingerprints and are as unique to each individual as fingerprints are.

Although bare footprints, toe prints, and palm prints are available less frequently at crime scenes than fingerprints, they can be invaluable to investigators of crimes. Even footprints left by people wearing shoes or socks can be telling in several ways. By measuring the length of a footprint, for example, a forensic anthropologist can arrive at an approximation of the height of the person who left it, because the length of a person's footprint represents roughly 15 percent of that person's height.

Palm prints are more frequently available than sole prints and, like fingerprints, the palm prints of each individual are unique. When palm prints are found at crime scenes, the corresponding fingerprints are often present as well.

Fingerprints

Fingerprint analysis is by far the most common way in which law-enforcement investigators connect particular persons with crime scenes. The technology used to accomplish such analysis has advanced considerably through the years, but the basic elements remain the same. Fingerprint analysts compare certain characteristics visible in the prints collected from crime scenes with the characteristics in prints from known sources to identify the persons who left the crime scene prints.

The basic patterns seen in all fingerprints on record fall into one of three major categories:

loop, whorl, or arch. The most common pattern is the loop, which is found in between 60 and 65 percent of all humans. The second most common is the whorl, found in 30 to 35 percent of all people. Approximately 5 percent of people have fingerprints with arches, and a very small percentage have a combination of the three patterns. Primates other than humans also have fingerprints and toe prints that are unique to each individual. Even identical twins have fingerprints different from those of their counterparts, although twins' prints are often quite similar.

The statistical probability that any two persons' fingerprints will be exactly alike is virtually zero. No two sets of fingerprints have ever been found to be identical, and fingerprint identification is considered valid in courts of law almost universally.

Even when a person's fingerprints are damaged by acid, fire, or surgery designed to eliminate them, prints identical to the original prints grow back on the affected fingers in a short time. Some criminals have attempted to destroy their fingerprints, but none has been known to succeed in doing so.

Classes of Prints

The fingerprints, palm prints, and bare footprints collected by forensic scientists fall into three classes: latent, visible, and plastic. Latent prints are those that are made when a hand or bare foot touches any surface, leaving behind a small amount of oily residue. Such prints are not necessarily immediately visible to the human eye, but forensic scientists can enhance their visibility by using a small brush to dust the surface with a powder specifically designed to highlight the ridges and valleys of these prints. After the prints are clearly visible, they are physically lifted from the surface with sterile transparent tape and transferred to special cards for transport to the laboratory for analysis. It is essential that crime scene investigators lift latent prints as quickly as they can, because the residue left behind on surfaces by hands and feet is mostly water and can evaporate very rapidly.

The visible prints found at crime scenes are usually made in some liquid or greasy medium, such as blood or oil. These prints can be seen without magnification. Plastic prints are those that are recovered from malleable materials, such as unfired clay or pastry dough. Both of these types of prints are photographed, and the photographs are transferred to print cards.

Forensic Uses of Footprints

In addition to suggesting the height of the person who made them, bare footprints or shoe prints made in sand or other soft surfaces can reveal the person's weight, through the depth of the impressions. Forensic scientists preserve such impressions by making plaster casts of them, and analysis of such casts often provides convincing evidence linking particular individuals to the scenes of crimes.

The foot impressions found at crime scenes are more often shoe prints than bare footprints, but shoe prints can also provide valuable information. Both footprints and shoe prints, for example, can reveal the direction in which the people who made them were traveling and approximately how fast they were moving (the prints left by the two feet of a person who is walking are closer together than the prints of a person who is running). The depth of foot impressions can suggest the weight of the person who left them and may also reveal whether the person was carrying something heavy.

Both shoe prints and bare footprints can reveal information about gait—that is, the way a person walks—that may help investigators to identify an individual. The angles of such prints, for example, can suggest the age and physical condition of the person who made them, such as whether the person is elderly or suffering from a condition such as arthritis.

Palm Prints and Sole Prints

When bare footprints are found at crime scenes, they are generally found in sand or in soft earth. Crime scene investigators must pre-

---

The FBI's Latent Print Operations Unit

Among the many specialized forensic services of the Federal Bureau of Investigation is the Latent Print Operations Unit (LPOU). Its advanced scientific examinations in the field of friction ridge analysis encompass the development and comparison of latent fingerprints, palm prints, and footprints. In addition to reporting its findings, the unit provides expert testimony in legal proceedings and offers training and forensic field support to law-enforcement agencies throughout the United States and other parts of the world.

Members of the LPOU have also participated in disaster relief work, helping to identify victims of such mass-casualty events as the space shuttle *Challenger* disaster of 1986, the Oklahoma City bombing of 1995, the terrorist attacks of September 11, 2001, Hurricane Katrina in 2005, and the Asian tsunami of 2004.

---

serve and collect such prints immediately, as they can quickly be degraded and washed away by rain, wind, or tides.

Footprints are generally much less commonly found at crime scenes than are fingerprints. Sometimes bare footprints are retrieved as visible prints from crime scenes where considerable blood has been shed, and in such cases they can provide strong evidence of the presence of particular persons at the scene. In similar situations where only shoe prints are found, the shoe prints can provide suggestive evidence that generally falls short of being incontrovertible.

Latent fingerprints are more likely to be recovered from crime scenes than are latent palm prints, although, in some instances, investigators are able to collect both fingerprints and palm prints. In cases in which a person committing a crime has grabbed a cylindrical piece of wood, such as a bedpost, both latent palm prints and fingerprints can often be retrieved.

R. Baird Shuman

Further Reading

Abbott, John Reginald. *Footwear Evidence: The Examination, Identification, and Comparison of Footwear Impressions*. Edited by Richard Germann. Springfield, Ill.: Charles C Thomas, 1964. Brief, classic work is remarkably thorough in detailing how forensic scientists deal with footwear impression evidence.

Bell, Suzanne. *Encyclopedia of Forensic Science*. New York: Facts On File, 2004. In addition to a strong section on fingerprints, provides valuable information on shoe prints, shoe impressions, footprints, and footwear impressions.

Bodziak, William J. *Footwear Impression Evidence: Detection, Recovery, and Examination*. 2d ed. Boca Raton, Fla.: CRC Press, 2000. Provides valuable fundamental information about how forensic scientists gather, preserve, and analyze the impressions left by shoes and other footwear found at crime scenes.

Conklin, Barbara Gardner, Robert Gardner, and Dennis Shortelle. *Encyclopedia of Forensic Science: A Compendium of Detective Fact and Fiction*. Westport, Conn.: Oryx Press, 2002. Offers an informative discussion of footprints, illustrated and replete with cogent examples, as well as extensive sections on tool marks, bite marks, and fingerprints.

Hilderbrand, Dwane S. *Footwear, the Missed Evidence: A Field Guide to the Collection and Preservation of Forensic Footwear Impression Evidence*. 2d ed. Wildomar, Calif.: Staggs, 2005. Provides information about all aspects of preserving, collecting, and interpreting footwear impressions.

Pentland, Peter, and Pennie Stoyles. *Forensic Science*. Philadelphia: Chelsea House, 2003. Includes excellent though brief sections on both fingerprinting and footprints. Intended for young adult readers.

Robbins, Louise M. *Footprints: Collection, Analysis, and Interpretation*. Springfield, Ill.: Charles C Thomas, 1985. Addresses footprint forensics from an anthropological point of view. Includes splendid illustrative drawings of Richard Gantt.

See also: Casting; Class versus individual evidence; Crime scene measurement; Ear prints; Fingerprints; Footprints and shoe prints; Integrated Automated Fingerprint Identification System; Physical evidence; Simpson murder trial; Sinus prints; Superglue fuming.

Product liability cases

Definition: Legal cases involving allegations that defective and dangerous products have harmed people and property.

Significance: Sophisticated evidence is necessary to prove that personal or property harm has resulted from defective products. Lawyers rely on forensic experts to conduct analyses of products suspected of being defective and prepare expert testimony to prove all elements of a legal theory or to defend an entity in the chain of distribution from liability. In addition, companies concerned with designing and manufacturing good-quality products rely on input from forensic scientists.

Manufacturers, wholesalers, distributors, retailers, assemblers, installers, and those who lease or rent products have the best ability to ensure that defective and dangerous products do not enter the marketplace. In the United States, when a defective product results in harm, the courts impose joint and several liability on the marketing participants as a matter of public policy. These deep-pocketed entities in the chain of distribution usually have insurance coverage and are able to spread the product liability risks and apportion damage costs among themselves better than those who suffer injury from defective products. Usually those who are not regularly in the business of selling or renting particular products, such as individuals who sell goods at yard or garage sales, are considered outside the chain of distribution and thus cannot be sued for product liability.

Historically, only those who had a buyer-seller relationship or were in privity of contract with a seller could sue, but U.S. states no longer limit those who have standing to sue under many of the product liability theories. This means that not only those who originally purchased a defective product have the right to sue but also any person who might foreseeably be harmed by the product may file a product liability action. This includes family members and friends of purchasers, remote purchasers, and any bystanders who suffer harm.

Causes of Action, Defects, and Remedies

Product liability cases are based on torts, or civil wrongs, and contract law. At least four significant causes of action are possible in a product liability case: strict product liability, negligence, misrepresentation or fraud, and breach of warranties. Some of the counts require plaintiffs to prove causation, whereas others do not. In every case, however, some proof must exist of a design, manufacturing, or warning defect or that the product is dangerous.

Companies conduct cost-benefit and risk analyses when determining the best designs for their products and whether reasonable alternative designs would avoid or reduce the risk of harm from the products. They balance the risks of potential harm against the costs of designs that will result in reasonably safe products while still ensuring that the companies can make a profit. Courts also consider cost-benefit analyses and reasonable alternative designs when a design defect is the issue in a product liability case. Plaintiffs may rely on forensic experts to prove that there is an alternative and safer design for the product, while defendants will try to show not only that no alternative design is reasonable but also that the alternative design suggested by the plaintiff is not cost-efficient.

Whenever a company manufactures a product with reasonable care but does not follow the intended design, a manufacturing defect may exist. When a product is seriously damaged or destroyed in an accident, forensic experts and those who attempt to reconstruct the accident may need to rely on the malfunction doctrine to prove product liability. The malfunction doctrine requires a plaintiff to eliminate all possible means of harm except for the product defect.

Warning defects consist of a lack of warnings or a failure to give adequate warnings concerning both the safe way to use a product and the potential dangers associated with the product, including those that are not obvious. It is impossible to warn against all potential risks of harm, but those in the chain of distribution have the responsibility to warn against foreseeable dangers in order to avoid liability based on a defective warning that renders a product unreasonably unsafe. Such warnings must be clear, understandable, and specific. Given the increasingly global nature of the marketplace, product instructions on use and warnings concerning dangers are usually provided in multiple languages, and many companies also use internationally understood symbols to warn of specific dangers.

Product liability cases are considered civil as opposed to criminal actions. Usually the plaintiffs who have personally been injured or whose property has suffered harm request monetary damages, but other remedies are available, including restitution and replacement of defective products. Moreover, when a court determines that monetary damages are not adequate, it may order relief such as an injunction that re-

A product liability case that drew a great deal of public attention involved motor vehicle accidents that were attributed to tread separation in Firestone Wilderness AT tires. This sport utility vehicle, which was equipped with the Firestone tires, was involved in a two-car accident that was apparently caused by malfunction of the tires. *(AP/Wide World Photos)*

quires the company to remove the defective product from the marketplace.

Strict Product Liability

As a matter of public policy, courts and legislatures have determined that consumers must be protected against harm from dangerous and unreasonably unsafe products. Plaintiffs thus may sue on the basis of strict product liability, originally a common-law tort that is now written into many U.S. state statutes. A strict product liability case involves liability without fault. A plaintiff need only show harm from an inherently dangerous, defective, or unreasonably unsafe consumer product that has not undergone substantial change since its purchase. A defendant cannot claim exercise of reasonable care to prevent injury or lack of intention to cause harm, as fault is not an issue in a strict product liability case.

In such a case, forensic experts are likely to testify about the inherent dangers of the consumer product that make it unreasonably unsafe and thus defective. An unreasonably dangerous product is one that exceeds the dangers expected by an ordinary consumer or a product for which a less dangerous alternative was economically feasible. In addition, the defense may call on forensic experts to testify regarding substantial changes made to the product between the time the product was purchased and the injury.

Not all injuries from dangerous and unsafe products may result in cognizable product liability claims. The potential dangers presented by some products are outweighed by the benefits they provide to society. For example, many modern prescription drugs have side effects, but the benefits of the drugs outweigh their potential harm, and as long as individuals have received adequate warnings, product liability cases involving such drugs are unlikely to be successful.

In addition, the dangers associated with other products, many of which have great utility, may be commonly known. These products are unavoidably dangerous, and there are no reasonable alternatives for making these products safe for their intended and ordinary purposes. Warnings of known dangers are unnecessary. A person harmed by such a product assumes the risk of harm, and a lawsuit based on product liability is usually dismissed. For example, everyone knows and expects that a knife is sharp; a person thus needs to be careful in using a knife to avoid harm.

Negligence

The tort of negligence requires proof of fault. Negligence requires evidence of four elements: that there was a reasonable duty of care owed by the defendant to the plaintiff to provide a safe product, that the defendant breached the duty of care, that because of the breach the plaintiff suffered harm, and that the breach was the foreseeable and proximate cause of the harm, as there was nothing else that intervened and could be blamed for the harm. Many things can go wrong with products in the chain of distribution. Manufacturers may fail to exercise due care in designing, assembling, inspecting, and testing component parts and consumer products before releasing them for sale in the marketplace. A retailer may carelessly sell a product that lacks adequate warnings for the ordinary consumer. Moreover, in some cases a claim could be based on negligence per se because a defendant failed to comply with statutory laws, such as providing required information on a food product label.

To succeed in a negligence action, the plaintiff must offer proof regarding the party responsible for causing the harm. Forensic experts are asked to develop this causal evidence and to determine whether the harm was foreseeable. Experts may also testify about the standard of care that is reasonable and expected of those who sell or lease similar products.

Misrepresentation

Misrepresentation is generally a tort action, although misrepresentation may also be alleged in a contract or warranty count. If misrepresentation is based on a careless act or an accident, the plaintiff must prove the elements necessary for negligence. However, if the misrepresentation is intentional or reckless, such as failure to recall a defective product from the marketplace with knowledge that the product is defective and potentially harmful, then the misrepresentation is based on fraud.

To prove fraudulent misrepresentation, a plaintiff must show that the defendant knew or was reckless in making affirmative statements about a product's quality that were not true or in concealing or failing to discover defects in a product that would be important and material to a consumer. The consumer must reasonably rely on the defendant's material misrepresentations in deciding to buy or lease the product or in continuing to use the product. The consumer's reliance on the misrepresentations must result in a detriment—a personal or property harm caused by the product. Generally, a person who did not purchase the product is unable to sue on a theory of misrepresentation because there is no proof of reasonable reliance on a misrepresentation.

Breach of Warranties

The final cause of action comes out of the commercial world of contracts, warranties, and a uniform statutory law known as the Uniform Commercial Code (UCC). At least three separate warranties are governed by the UCC: an express warranty, the implied warranty of merchantability, and the implied warranty of fitness for a particular purpose. A breach of any of these warranties relied on by a consumer in deciding to purchase or lease a product may provide the basis for a product liability claim. Sellers and lessors of products may exclude some or all of the warranties, although federal and state consumer protection laws may limit the ability to exclude all warranties and thus avoid liability for defective consumer products.

Sellers and lessors of products provide express warranties in many ways. A person expects a product to conform to models and samples. In addition, catalogs, advertisements, brochures, pictures, diagrams, and specifications of features are generally considered express warranties of what the consumer expects, even if no warranty was intended. Oral affirmations and written contract provisions made for the purpose of selling or leasing a product are also considered express warranties. Affirmations may include descriptive terms and often pertain to quality, how the product will perform, and conditions that may limit the express warranty. Purchasers may also infer express warranties because of a seller's or lessor's conduct that enticed them to buy or lease a product.

The implied warranty of merchantability means that the product must meet industry or government standards for similar products. The product must adequately perform and meet the expectations of a typical consumer. For example, a new car should enable a person to travel between locations. Some products must also be wholesome and safe for consumption before they are considered merchantable. If a person finds pieces of glass in a jar of baby food, the food clearly does not meet the consumer's expected quality standards. A consumer might expect to find a fish bone in a bowl of freshly made fish chowder, but not in fish sandwich made from a frozen fish fillet.

Some people purchase or lease products after seeking input from sellers or lessors. In such a case, the purchaser of the product wants to make sure that the product will satisfy specific needs and relies on the skill and expertise of the seller or lessor in deciding to purchase or lease the product. A consumer who is told that a product will meet specific needs has an implied warranty of fitness for a particular purpose that is breached when the product proves to be unfit for the intended purpose.

Defenses

In product liability litigation, several defenses are available to defendants to counter the multiple theories on which such cases are based. One defense is that the injured person abnormally misused the product and did not follow instructions for use or heed danger warnings. If, however, the misuse was foreseeable, this defense is not likely to be effective and the defendants are obligated to provide warnings.

Another defense might be assumption of the risk—that is, the defendant argues that the person claiming harm from a defective product was fairly warned of the dangers associated with the product and understood the dangers. The defendant must prove that despite the risks associated with the product, the injured plaintiff decided voluntarily to purchase or use the product and thus assumed any risk of harm from the product.

Contributory negligence is a common-law defense that bars all liability if a plaintiff contributes in any way to an injury from a product. Modern laws allow for comparative negligence as a defense, which is not as harsh as contributory negligence. Under the comparative negligence defense, plaintiffs who bear some responsibility for their own injuries from defective products have their damage awards reduced in proportion to their negligence when compared with the defendants' negligence in producing and selling dangerous and defective products.

Finally, most manufacturers that discover defects in their products attempt to limit their liability. If those in the distribution chain use reasonable efforts to notify purchasers of product defects, such as by publishing notices of product recalls in generally circulated newspapers or magazines or sending letters or notices of product recalls or defects to known purchasers, the purchasers are obligated to have the defects corrected. Purchasers cannot simply ignore such notices and file product liability claims if they are subsequently injured by the recalled products.

Forensic Expert Standards and Evidence Preservation

Product liability cases are quite complex, and forensic experts engage in many types of analyses to prove liability or to provide evidence for the defense. Expert witnesses, however, are subject to the so-called *Daubert* standard, a test laid out by the U.S. Supreme Court that requires a court to determine the reliability and credibility of scientific evidence based on objective standards, including the replicability of study results and the general acceptance by scientific peers of the expert's evidence or method of analysis.

Plaintiffs must also be sure to preserve defective products once they have caused harm. It may be necessary for a plaintiff to obtain a court order to gain control and possession over the product. If a plaintiff loses control over a product, it may be destroyed or altered, thus seriously compromising the ability of forensic experts to determine whether the injury was the result of a defective product.

Carol A. Rolf

Further Reading

Derthick, Martha A. *Up in Smoke: From Legislation to Litigation in Tobacco Politics*. 2d ed. Washington, D.C.: Congressional Quarterly Press, 2004. Discusses the product liability cases that were filed against tobacco companies for harm caused to individuals from smoking. Defenses such as comparative negligence and assumption of risk barred this litigation at first, but the states joined in the litigation and alleged failure by the tobacco companies to provide adequate warnings concerning the health risks of smoking. The litigation resulted in a master settlement agreement in which the tobacco companies agreed to pay billions in damages and to revise marketing and advertising.

Geistfeld, Mark A. *Principles of Products Liability*. New York: Foundation Press, 2006. Provides a complete discussion of the various product liability theories, doctrines, and defenses and applies these legal concepts to potential cases to develop insights into the specialized area of product liability and tort law.

Gooden, Randall L. *Product Liability Prevention: A Strategic Guide*. Milwaukee: ASQ Quality Press, 2000. Intended for organizations in the chain of product distribution to help them better understand how to prevent liability from defective products. Suggests many proactive approaches that companies can follow to ensure that they produce and sell high-quality products and thus avoid future liability.

Kiely, Terrence F. *Science and Litigation: Products Liability in Theory and Practice*. Boca Raton, Fla.: CRC Press, 2002. Clearly addresses the process of gaining court acceptance of expert scientific opinion in liability cases. Notes that many cases present questions of first impression, which means that no legal precedents or peer-reviewed studies exist on which courts can rely in determining that new technologies comply with legal standards of reliability and credibility.

Owen, David G. *Products Liability Law Hornbook*. St. Paul, Minn.: West, 2005. Provides a comprehensive review of liability and the legal theories and defenses pertaining to product liability litigation both in the United

States and in the global marketplace. Addresses several tangential topics, including the forensic analysis involved in determining product defects and in proving liability and causation through testimony at trials.

Owen, David G., and Jerry J. Phillips. *Products Liability in a Nutshell.* St. Paul, Minn.: West, 2005. Presents an excellent and easy-to-understand summary of the theories of liability, defenses, and various types of defects involved in product liability litigation.

Samuel, Andrew E. *Forensic Engineering: A Casebook on How to Find the Winning Line.* New York: Springer, 2006. Reviews actual product liability cases and the successful opinions and techniques used in those cases by experts. The material is at an introductory level and addresses multidisciplinary examples of litigation strategies.

Stallard, Eric, Kenneth G. Monton, and Joel E. Cohen. *Forecasting Product Liability Claims: Epidemiology and Modeling in the Manville Asbestos Case.* New York: Springer, 2004. Focuses on one of the largest and best-known class-action product liability cases ever brought in the United States. Discusses the case in terms of statistical forecasting of the number, timing, and nature of legal claims. Presents the mathematical models used in the case in understandable terms.

See also: Accident investigation and reconstruction; Courts and forensic evidence; Expert witnesses; Food and Drug Administration, U.S.; Food poisoning; Food supply protection; Product tampering; Silicone breast implant cases; Thalidomide; Toxic torts; Trial consultants.

Product tampering

Definition: Adulteration of consumer products with foreign substances that may cause serious harm, even risk of death, to those who use the products.

Significance: The absence of witnesses and the potential for broad public harm make product tampering one of the most challenging types of crimes for law-enforcement agencies to investigate. In such cases, it is important for authorities to determine quickly the extent of the tampering and the danger to the public at the same time they are working to identify suspects and remove any tainted products from stores.

Product tampering first became a public concern in the United States in September, 1982, when someone deliberately poisoned Extra-Strength Tylenol capsules with cyanide, leading to seven deaths in Chicago, Illinois. Subsequent laws such as the 1983 and 1994 Federal Anti-tampering Acts made product tampering a federal crime. Because these kinds of crimes typically have few witnesses, law-enforcement investigators must rely on physical evidence in tracking down suspects. They also face the task of determining where the tampering occurred. Most cases of product tampering involve foods and over-the-counter medicines that can be easily accessed at supermarkets or drugstores.

The motives for product tampering vary. Some perpetrators are motivated by the desire to create panic by killing members of the public, whereas others use tampering as a means of extortion, threatening to poison products unless particular demands are met. Still others use product tampering to commit murder for gain, such as to collect a victim's life insurance.

Initial Response

Under the Pure Food and Drug Act (1906) and the antitampering legislation passed in the early 1980's, the Food and Drug Administration (FDA) has the responsibility for investigating all cases of product tampering in the United States. When a case of tampering is reported, federal investigators descend on the retail outlet where the adulterated product was purchased or discovered to collect physical evidence.

All containers of suspect products are handled carefully to protect fingerprint evidence, because often those who commit this type of crime purchase certain products, take them to a private place to adulterate them, and then manage to get the products returned to the retail shelves. To protect the public, investigators usually remove all similar products from relevant locations and have them tested for contamination.

Narrowing the Investigation

Because product tampering can occur at the manufacturing, distribution, or retail level, investigators must examine each possibility. They must determine whether a case of tampering is limited to a single package, to packages at a particular retail outlet, or to an entire brand across an extensive geographic area.

Investigators may be aided by the footage from surveillance cameras at retail outlets. Given that it is known that some perpetrators purchase products, tamper with them, and then return them to the shelves, video evidence that a person has made repeated visits to a store and has been in the vicinity of the adulterated product can point to that person as a suspect. Computerized tracking of products sold in stores can also provide valuable information to investigators regarding when a tampered product was purchased and if it was returned to a store.

In 1993, false claims were made that syringes were being found in cans of Pepsi-Cola in Seattle, Washington, and then in other cities across the United States. Photos from a surveillance camera in a supermarket revealed the first incident to be a hoax; a woman could be seen opening a Pepsi can and slipping a syringe into it. She later claimed that she discovered the needle after she purchased the soft drink. This evidence tipped off investigators that other claims of tampering involving Pepsi cans might also be hoaxes.

Psychological profiling is another forensic tool used by investigators of product tampering. Such profiling can narrow the probable range of suspects according to age, gender, socioeconomic status, and educational background. The level of knowledge and chemical sophistication needed to succeed in the type of contamination committed can also add to a profile.

What and When

Investigators must quickly determine what foreign substance was added to an adulterated product so that they can locate possible sources for the poison and attempt to track down any persons who recently purchased it. During the 1991 investigation of the poisoning of Sudafed capsules in Washington State, an incident that resulted in the deaths of two people, investigators identified the type of cyanide used to contaminate the pills. They then were able to trace the cyanide back to a distributor and then to the husband of

---

Advice from the FDA

The U.S. Food and Drug Administration provides these tips for consumers.

How to Detect Product Tampering at the Grocery Store

- Carefully examine all food product packaging. Be aware of the normal appearance of food containers. That way you'll be more likely to notice if an outer seal or wrapper is missing. Compare a suspect container with others on the shelf.
- Check any antitampering devices on packaging. Make sure the plastic seal around the outside of a container is intact or that the safety button on the lid of a jar is down.
- Don't purchase products if the packaging is open, torn, or damaged. This includes products on the shelf or in the refrigerator or freezer sections of the grocery store.
- Don't buy products that are damaged or that look unusual. For example, never purchase canned goods that are leaking or that bulge at the ends. The same applies to products that appear to have been thawed and then refrozen.
- Check the "sell-by" dates printed on some products, and only buy items within that time frame.

How to Detect Product Tampering at Home

- When opening a container, carefully inspect the product. Don't use products that are discolored, moldy, have an off odor, or that spurt liquid or foam when the container is opened.
- Never eat food from packages that are damaged or that look unusual, such as cans that are leaking or that bulge at the ends.

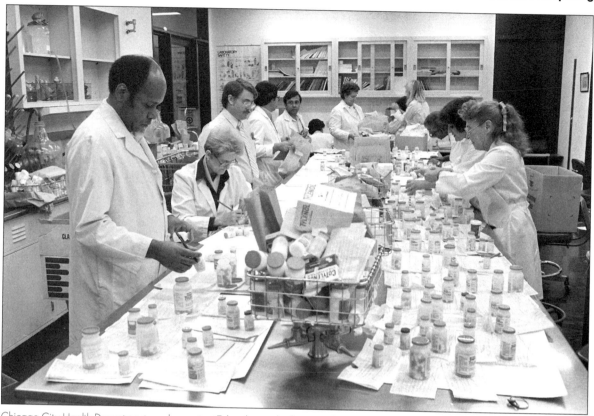

Chicago City Health Department employees test Tylenol capsules for cyanide content at a city laboratory in October, 1982. In September, 1982, seven people in the Chicago area died after ingesting cyanide-laced capsules of the over-the-counter medication. (AP/Wide World Photos)

one of the victims, who had purchased the cyanide in order to place it in his wife's medication.

Another crucial part of the investigation of product tampering is the determination of when the adulterating material was added to the product. Generally, chemical contaminants that are added to a product will change as they interact with the chemicals in the product. The rate of decomposition of the contaminant within the product thus provides clues regarding when the contaminant was added. Laboratory tests using spectroscopy can identify decomposition and narrow the period when the product was poisoned.

When contaminants are physical rather than chemical in nature, such as syringes in the Pepsi tampering hoaxes, investigators examine that evidence to find differences and similarities in the types of contaminants. In the Pepsi

hoaxes, investigators discovered that the syringes were of different types and sizes, suggesting that the tampering was not committed by a single individual.

Douglas Clouatre

Further Reading

Byrd, Mike. *Crime Scene Evidence: A Guide to the Recovery and Collection of Physical Evidence.* Wildomar, Calif.: Staggs, 2001. Discusses the types of evidence to be found and collected at crime scenes and the use of evidence samples in the investigation and prosecution of criminals.

Fisher, Barry A. J. *Techniques of Crime Scene Investigation.* 7th ed. Boca Raton, Fla.: CRC Press, 2004. Details the methods used in the collection and preservation of evidence found at crime scenes, including DNA and fingerprint evidence.

Murphy, Douglas B. *Fundamentals of Light Microscopy and Electronic Imaging*. 2d ed. New York: John Wiley & Sons, 2008. Explains the science and technology behind light microscopy in a straightforward manner accessible to nonscientists.

Trestrail, John Harris, III. *Criminal Poisoning: Investigational Guide for Law Enforcement, Toxicologists, Forensic Scientists, and Attorneys*. 2d ed. Totowa, N.J.: Humana Press, 2007. Describes the investigative techniques used to determine whether intentional poisonings have occurred and the types of poisons used in crimes.

See also: Chain of custody; Crime scene investigation; Criminal personality profiling; Federal Bureau of Investigation; Food and Drug Administration, U.S.; Product liability cases.

Profiling. *See* Criminal personality profiling; DNA profiling; Geographic profiling; Racial profiling

Pseudoscience in forensic practice

Definition: Use in forensic settings of disciplines that possess the superficial appearance of science but lack its substance.

Significance: On a daily basis, law-enforcement officials confront a host of challenges that often force them to make critical decisions under extreme time pressure and highly stressful circumstances. These decisions involve complex questions of innocence versus guilt, the profiling of criminal suspects, lie detection, the validity of eye-

witness testimony, and the interpretation of crime scene evidence, to name just a few. The accuracy of such techniques has the potential to determine crucial life-changing decisions, even capital punishment. As in many professions, individuals in law enforcement must evaluate techniques with a critical eye before using them. Like all disciplines that interpret data to make real-world decisions, forensic science can easily fall prey to the seductive charms of pseudoscience

Given the challenges of law-enforcement investigations, it is not surprising that forensic scientists have turned to psychology for assistance in evaluating the scientific support for the techniques they use. In the 1870's, Francis Galton, a cousin of Charles Darwin, experimented with a word-association test (in which a test examiner says a word, such as "money," and waits for a response from the subject) as a tool for lie detection. In the early twentieth century, Hugo Münsterberg performed experiments that demonstrated the fallibility of eyewitness testimony. Since that time, psychological researchers have spearheaded the development of scientifically grounded procedures to enhance the accuracy of forensic techniques. Nevertheless, the field of law enforcement continues to grapple with the pressing task of discriminating legitimate from illegitimate practices.

Central Characteristics of Pseudoscience

Pseudoscience differs from bona fide science in that pseudoscience does not "play by the rules" of science, even though it mimics some of the outward features of science. Philosopher of science Mario Bunge has suggested the categories of "research fields" and "belief fields" to distinguish science from pseudoscience, arguing that scientific practices are distinguished by scientific support as opposed to intuition or faith. For instance, experience alone is not sufficient for police officers to believe that their interrogation procedures produce accurate confessions; these procedures must be validated by scientific evidence.

In a scientific discipline, data must be reproducible—that is, replicable—across multiple studies, ideally studies conducted by independent investigators. In addition, most sciences display connectivity, meaning that they build on previous findings in a cumulative fashion. In contrast, most pseudosciences lack replicability and connectivity.

Science and pseudoscience are not always easy to distinguish, because they lie at opposite ends of a continuum, differing in degree rather than in kind. Nevertheless, a number of indicators can help locate practices, including those used in forensic settings, on the fuzzy spectrum between science and pseudoscience. Seven especially crucial indicators are described below.

Lack of Falsifiability and Overuse of Ad Hoc Maneuvers

Philosopher of science Karl Raimund Popper proposed that falsifiability is the key criterion distinguishing science from nonscience—that is, scientific claims can be shown to be wrong if evidence exists to contradict them. Statements such as "God created the universe" may be true or false, but they are not falsifiable using scientific methods because they cannot be refuted with observable evidence. As Popper observed, when research generates findings that seemingly falsify a given claim, pseudosciences often invoke ad hoc maneuvers—that is, escape hatches or loopholes—to explain away these negative findings.

In the case of fingerprint analysis, for example, some proponents claim an accuracy rate as high as 99.9 percent. They assert that a given fingerprint can be perfectly matched to an exemplar print, to the exclusion of all other possible sources of that print. When the technique fails, they often point to such special circumstances as distorted or insufficient prints or misuse of a fingerprint apparatus to explain why the findings did not support the claims. The repeated use of such ad hoc explanations after the fact to explain away negative findings renders a good deal of fingerprint analysis more pseudoscientific than scientific. In some cases, the limited use of ad hoc explanations can provide directions for future research, but pseudosciences invoke such explanations more often than not, rendering their claims virtually unfalsifiable.

An expert on the philosophy and nature of science, Austrian British philosopher Karl Raimund Popper (1902-1994) earned an international reputation with his publication of *The Logic of Scientific Discovery* in 1935. (AP/Wide World Photos)

Evasion of Peer Review

Mature sciences rely on a procedure called peer review as a safeguard against error. In peer review, submitted journal articles that evaluate scientific claims are read by outside experts (at least one, and typically three or more) who are entrusted with the task of subjecting the work to relatively impartial scrutiny. In many cases, the peer-review process results in outright rejection of articles; in others, articles are either rejected with an invitation to resubmit following substantial revisions or accepted provisionally.

Peer review is not a perfect filter against poor-quality research, but it is often an essential safeguard. Many pseudosciences bypass this safeguard, preferring to evaluate claims on their own. For example, graphology, the examination of handwriting to infer personality characteristics (not to be confused with forensic handwriting examination or analysis), has been used to profile child molesters and sadistic criminals although virtually no evidence exists to support the validity of this technique. Different and often contradictory schools of graphology have continued in isolation for centuries, ignoring the extensive scientific evidence that shows graphology to be an invalid means of assessing personality characteristics. Despite the overwhelming scientific literature debunking their claims, most graphology proponents continue to advance strong assertions without the restraint and objectivity afforded by the peer-review process.

Lack of Self-Correction

In the long run, science is self-correcting: Incorrect claims tend to be revised or weeded out, whereas correct claims tend to survive. In contrast, in pseudosciences, faulty claims tend to persist for lengthy periods of time, resulting in intellectual stagnation. For example, so-called truth serums are drugs, typically barbiturates, that supposedly elicit truthful information from reluctant individuals. Research has shown, however, that such drugs work in much the same way alcoholic beverages do: They reduce people's inhibitions, making them more likely to disclose both false and true information. The continued use of truth serums to elicit confessions and to unearth supposedly buried memories despite contrary evidence illustrates a lack of self-correction.

Confirmation Bias

Some psychologists, such as Carol Tavris, have argued that the scientific method is a safeguard against confirmation bias—the tendency of human beings to seek out evidence that supports their own hypotheses while ignoring, minimizing, or distorting evidence that does not. Most pseudosciences lack protections against confirmation bias. For example, the interrogation process used by many law-enforcement investigators lacks this safeguard. Investigators often form conclusions about a target suspect

prior to obtaining sound evidence, and the process of interrogation may become more about confirming those conclusions than about obtaining impartial information. Such presumptions can lead interrogators to close their minds toward alternative hypotheses and make them likely to seek out support selectively for their beliefs.

Research has shown that the presumption of guilt can influence investigators to adopt an interrogation style that elicits guilty behavior from suspects. Saul M. Kassin and Gisli Gudjonsson have described how suspicion of guilt on the part of interrogators can shape their behavior and lead suspects to act anxiously or defensively, thereby inadvertently confirming the interrogators' suspicions. If questioners increase their bodily movement during an interrogation, the suspect is likely to mimic them and in turn appear nervous and "guilty." As with any belief, interrogators' confidence in their beliefs or "hunches" that they are right about suspects can make it difficult for them to attend to data that do not support their beliefs.

Overreliance on Testimonial and Anecdotal Evidence

Informal testimonials and anecdotes suggesting that a technique is effective can sometimes provide justification for investigating that technique further in systematic studies, but they are never sufficient for concluding that a technique is effective. Many pseudosciences rely on informal personal evidence to validate their claims. For example, in more than 75 percent of cases in which postconviction analysis of DNA (deoxyribonucleic acid) evidence has demonstrated that the convictions were in error, eyewitness misidentification was a primary cause of the initial guilty verdicts. In such cases, law-enforcement officials relied too heavily on anecdotal testimony for proof of guilt. Individuals' subjective experiences are neither recorded nor preserved in memory exactly as the events occurred, and recollections can be contaminated at many steps between the witnessing of an event and the relayed testimony given at the police station or in the courtroom.

Extravagant Claims

Good scientists are aware that their claims are almost always provisional and might be overturned by later evidence; they are also careful not to overstate assertions in the absence of compelling evidence. In contrast, advocates of pseudoscience frequently advance extreme claims that greatly outstrip scientific evidence.

For example, some proponents of the polygraph or "lie detector" test make excessive claims regarding the accuracy of the device in detecting lies, asserting an accuracy rate of close to 100 percent. However, as psychologist David T. Lykken has observed, voluminous evidence suggests that polygraphs probably perform better than chance but are nowhere near as accurate as promoters claim. Because they measure physiological arousal rather than lying per se, they are especially prone to mislabeling innocent subjects as guilty. As with any tool or method, such extravagant claims should be seen as indicators that proponents of a given practice have overstated its ability and that the practice is operating outside the bounds of good science.

Ad Antequitem Fallacy

As the history of science shows, claims that have been around for a long time are not necessarily correct. For example, even though the practice of astrology is more than thirty-five hundred years old, there is no scientific support for astrologers' claims. Many pseudosciences fall prey to the *ad antequitem* fallacy: the error of concluding that because a claim is old, it must be valid. For example, hair comparison and blood type matching have been relied on in criminal cases since the nineteenth century, but the use of these techniques is based on relatively scant scientific validation. Scientific research has exposed these practices as lacking in specificity in identifying given individuals as having been present at crime scenes.

By keeping the indicators described above in mind, consumers of the forensic literature, including jurors, lawyers, judges, and police officers, can better distinguish science from pseudoscience. Moreover, knowledge of such indicators may help to bridge the wide gap between the law-enforcement and scientific communities and help ensure that forensic practices are based on solid research evidence.

Kristin E. Landfield and Scott O. Lilienfeld

Further Reading

Beyerstein, Barry. "Graphology." In *The Encyclopedia of the Paranormal*, edited by Gordon Stein. Amherst, N.Y.: Prometheus Books, 1996. Presents a penetrating discussion of how graphology falls outside the realm of bona fide science.

Cole, Simon A. "The Fingerprint Controversy." *Skeptical Inquirer* 31 (July/August, 2007): 41-46. Discusses the controversy surrounding identification through fingerprinting, focusing particularly on the absence of scientific validation and problems with the use of fingerprint analysis in the courtroom.

Huber, Peter W. *Galileo's Revenge: Junk Science in the Courtroom*. New York: Basic Books, 1991. Explains how scientific illiteracy is exploited in the courtroom, especially through the use of professional witnesses to advance unsupported pseudoscientific claims. Points to the scientific principles of publication, replication, verification, consensus, and peer review as defenses against courtroom junk science.

Kassin, Saul M., & Gisli Gudjonsson. "The Psychology of Confessions: A Review of the Literature and Issues." *Psychological Science in the Public Interest* 5 (November, 2004): 33-67. Provides a comprehensive look at the various decisions involved in identifying guilty parties and the psychological factors that contribute to false confessions.

Lilienfeld, Scott O., Steven J. Lynn, and Jeffrey M. Lohr, eds. *Science and Pseudoscience in Clinical Psychology*. New York: Guilford Press, 2003. Collection of essays highlights the indicators of pseudoscience and discusses the nature of both good and bad science, offering examples from within clinical and forensic psychology.

Lykken, David T. *A Tremor in the Blood: Uses and Abuses of the Lie Detector*. 2d ed. New York: McGraw-Hill, 1996. Offers a thorough and readable discussion of the history and pitfalls of lie detector tests, including a review of the scientific evidence on the polygraph.

Tavris, Carol, and Elliot Aronson. *Mistakes Were Made (But Not by Me): Why We Justify Foolish Beliefs, Bad Decisions, and Hurtful Acts*. Orlando, Fla.: Harcourt, 2007. Presents engaging discussion of how the human brain is predisposed toward self-justification, rendering humans prone to cognitive biases.

Wells, Gary L. "Helping Experimental Psychology Affect Legal Policy." In *Psychology and Law: An Empirical Perspective*, edited by Neil Brewer and Kipling D. Williams. New York: Guilford Press, 2005. Discusses how findings from psychological research can be applied to improving legal policies and suggests how scientific data can inform forensic practices in more productive ways.

See also: Ancient science and forensics; Celebrity cases; Courts and forensic evidence; Eyewitness testimony; Fingerprints; *Forensic Files*; Interrogation; Polygraph analysis; Truth serum; Wrongful convictions.

Psychological autopsy

Definition: Set of postmortem investigative procedures carried out to gain a better understanding of the psychological circumstances that may have contributed to a suicide.

Significance: Psychological autopsies allow researchers and investigators to gather information on suicidal behavior that cannot be obtained through the use of other methodologies. In addition to helping investigators determine the modes of death in cases of suicide, psychological autopsies can shed light on the reasons people commit suicide.

Edwin S. Shneidman, one of the founders of the field of suicidology, coined the term "psychological autopsy" to describe the procedure he developed with his colleagues at the Los Angeles County Medical Examiner's Office to assist medical examiners and coroners in clarifying equivocal deaths (deaths the causes of which are unknown). The psychological autopsy entails the analysis of medical autopsy and police reports, personal documents left behind by the deceased, and interviews with those who knew the deceased. Since the late twentieth century, the psychological autopsy has gained widespread usage in suicidology, and research studies of psychological autopsies have been conducted in several countries, including Sweden, Finland, Scotland, Taiwan, New Zealand, and Great Britain. The psychological autopsy has also become a widely used forensic investigatory tool.

Psychological Autopsies and Forensic Investigations

Psychologists conducting psychological autopsies compile information retrospectively about the behaviors, psychological states, and motives of deceased persons. For a death to be considered a potential suicide, evidence surrounding the death must show that the wound suffered could have been self-inflicted. Psychologists and law-enforcement officials must also determine that the deceased understood the consequences of the actions that led to the person's death (also called lethal intent).

During forensic investigations of possible suicides, the physical evidence should corroborate the findings of the psychological autopsies. For example, when it occurs, cadaveric spasm (instant rigor mortis) can help establish whether a death was homicide or a suicide. The presence of a weapon (such as a gun, knife, or razor blade) tightly clutched in the hand of the deceased as the result of cadaveric spasm strongly indicates suicide. The absence of cadaveric spasm, however, does not preclude suicide, as this phenomenon does not occur in every case. For reasons such as this, the careful consideration of both physical evidence and findings from psychological autopsies is critical to successful forensic investigations into possible suicides.

Elements of a Psychological Autopsy

A psychological autopsy includes semistructured interviews with relatives, friends, and other persons connected to the deceased. Another central component is a review of the medical and psychiatric histories of the deceased.

In analyzing the information gathered, the psychologist attempts to understand the final days and hours of the dead person's life. In doing so, the psychologist may rely on examination of the death scene as well as examination of such materials as the deceased's journals and suicide notes, books and music owned by the deceased, and the deceased's school, military, and employment records.

Many psychologists also gather information about the deceased person's family history of death and mental illness, familiarity with death methods, stress reaction patterns, involvement with alcohol or drugs, habits and routines, and relationship history when conducting a psychological autopsy. Of particular interest in this search for information is anything that indicates that the deceased person experienced any major life disruptions, such as the loss of a job or a loved one, in the days and hours leading up to the death.

Limitations of Psychological Autopsies

Despite the obvious utility of the psychological autopsy, much has been written about the limitations of this technique. Critics have noted, for example, that because the deceased are not available for questioning, psychologists must rely on interviews with those who knew them, and any of these people may contaminate the process by providing "biased" recollections.

The most commonly cited limitation or weakness of psychological autopsies is the lack of any standardized procedures for conducting them. Although psychologists have developed a guide with twenty-six categories to assist investigators in conducting psychological autopsies, not all of the categories are applicable to every case or are considered by every psychologist conducting a psychological autopsy. Despite these limitations, the psychological autopsy has proven to be an invaluable investigative tool, and findings from studies on psychological autopsies have

---

Admissibility of Psychological Autopsies in Court

Because no standard procedures and methods have been established for the conduct of psychological autopsies, testimony concerning the findings of these investigations is not always accepted in court. The *Daubert* standard of evidence, derived from the U.S. Supreme Court's decision in *Daubert v. Merrell Dow Pharmaceuticals* (1993), provides a two-pronged test for evaluating evidence presented by expert witnesses. In short, the relevance prong of the standard requires that the evidence "fit" the facts of the case, and the reliability prong requires that the evidence be derived from the scientific method. With *Daubert*, the Supreme Court made trial judges, specifically federal trial judges, the final gatekeepers of scientific evidence; thus decisions regarding the admissibility of the findings of psychological autopsies can vary from judge to judge.

---

led to innumerable advances in suicide prevention and the treatment of persons with suicidal tendencies.

James C. Roberts and Thomas E. Baker

Further Reading

Cohen, Ronald J., and Mark Swerdlik. *Psychological Testing and Assessment: An Introduction to Tests and Measurement.* 5th ed. New York: McGraw-Hill, 2002. Provides a fine introduction to widely used psychological tests and assessment procedures, including the psychological autopsy.

Eliopulos, Louis N. *Death Investigator's Handbook.* Expanded ed. Boulder, Colo.: Paladin Press, 2003. Widely used by homicide divisions in federal and local law-enforcement agencies for its useful information on crime scene processing and investigative techniques.

Joiner, Thomas. *Why People Die by Suicide.* Cambridge, Mass.: Harvard University Press, 2006. Provides a thorough overview of the major theories and evidence for why people commit suicide.

Maris, Ronald W., Berman, Alan L., and Morton M. Silverman. *Comprehensive Textbook of Suicidology.* New York: Guilford Press, 2000. Provides a clear and comprehensive overview of the field of suicidology.

Shneidman, Edwin S. *Autopsy of a Suicidal Mind.* New York: Oxford University Press,

2004. Shneidman and eight other renowned experts in the field of suicidology examine a suicide note provided to them by a distraught mother seeking to understand her son's death.

_____. *Lives and Deaths: Selections from the Works of Edwin S. Shneidman*. Edited by Antoon A. Leenaars. Philadelphia: Brunner/Mazel, 1999. Collection of thirty-seven articles by one of the founders of the field of suicidology.

See also: Antemortem injuries; Autoerotic and erotic asphyxiation; Autopsies; Coroners; Crime laboratories; Crime scene investigation; *Daubert v. Merrell Dow Pharmaceuticals*; Forensic psychology; Forensic toxicology; Hanging; Hesitation wounds and suicide; Suicide.

Psychopathic personality disorder

Definition: Psychological disorder characterized by egotistical, self-centered, impulsive, and exploitative behaviors, lack of remorse, and emotional callousness.

Significance: Psychopathic offenders are among the most physically violent, aggressive, and dangerous perpetrators of crimes. Although they make up only a small percentage of all offenders, they commit a disproportionate number of offenses and are often responsible for the most heinous of criminal acts. The ability to identify psychopaths accurately is thus critical to the protection of law-abiding citizens and the reduction of crime.

One of the most important and most influential treatises on psychopathic personality disorder was set forth in 1941 by Hervey Cleckley in his book *The Mask of Sanity: An Attempt to Reinterpret the So-Called Psychopathic Personality*. Cleckley outlined sixteen different core personality traits that define a psychopath, including pathological lying, superficial charm, lack of empathy, and egocentricity. Since the first edition of Cleckley's book was published, a wealth of research has examined a number of different issues germane to psychopathic personality disorder, including the potential causes and correlates of psychopathy, ways to assess and diagnose psychopathy, and how psychopathic personality disorder relates to violent offending. This line of research has shown that psychopathic criminals are qualitatively and quantitatively different from nonpsychopathic offenders.

Psychopathic criminals inflict more damage and commit more crimes than any other group of criminal offenders. Given their frequent involvement in antisocial behaviors, psychopaths are also at risk for being incarcerated for lengthy periods of time. Once imprisoned, however, they do not refrain from committing crimes; rather, they engage in a constellation of violent behaviors, ranging from assaulting other inmates to victimizing prison staff. Incarcerated psychopaths are frequently identified as the worst inmates in prison populations. When released from prison, psychopaths usually begin to offend again immediately. Some criminologists have estimated that, in the United States, 80 percent of psychopaths who have been released from incarceration are reconvicted of new crimes and returned to prison.

Not all psychopaths are criminals. Some find success in businesses that benefit from cutthroat practices; others make their way in the world as smooth-talking philanderers. All psychopaths, however, regardless of whether they are criminals per se, tend to inflict a great deal of harm on other persons and on society in general.

Assessment and Diagnosis

One of the more difficult issues facing clinicians is how to determine accurately whether an individual meets the criteria for being considered a psychopath. The most reliable and valid method of diagnosing psychopathy involves the use of some type of standardized actuarial assessment tool. Although a number of different instruments are available, the most widely used is the Psychopathy Checklist-Revised (PCL-R), developed by Robert D. Hare.

The PCL-R is administered by a doctoral-level clinician who conducts a face-to-face interview with the person being assessed for psychopathy. During the interview, which can last up to two hours, the clinician rates the person on twenty different traits.

Each trait is assigned a value ranging from zero to two, with higher scores indicating a greater likelihood that the person possesses that characteristic. A score of zero on a trait means that the person does not display the trait; a score of two means that the person definitely possesses the trait. When the interview is completed, the clinician tabulates the scores for all twenty traits; a person who receives a total score of thirty or higher is considered to be a psychopath. Overall, criminal offenders have an average PCL-R score of about twenty-two; nonoffenders, in contrast, have an average score of about five.

The twenty items that make up the PCL-R measure two different dimensions of psychopathy. Some items are designed to assess the personality traits of psychopaths, such as short-temperedness and impulsiveness; others indicate the extent to which the person leads an antisocial, unstable, and deviant lifestyle. Usually a person who scores high on one dimension also scores high on the other, but that is not always the case. In terms of the behaviors associated with these two dimensions, individuals who score high on the personality dimension are at much greater risk for becoming involved in acts of serious physical violence. The fact that psychopaths typically score high on both dimensions indicates their heightened propensity to engage in violent criminal acts and other types of antisocial behaviors.

Hare also developed a psychopathy checklist for adolescents ages twelve to eighteen, the Psychopathy Checklist: Youth Version (PCL:YV), which uses a semistructured interviewing platform to determine the extent to which an adolescent interviewee exhibits an array of psychopathic traits. Similar to the PCL-R, the PCL:YV is made up of twenty different items that tap behavioral, emotional, affective, and interpersonal traits often displayed by psychopathic adults. The PCL:YV has been shown to be a reliable and valid way of measuring psychopathy in

Traits of a Psychopath

In his classic work The Mask of Sanity, *published in 1941, Hervey Cleckley outlined sixteen different core personality traits that define a psychopath:*

- Superficial charm and good "intelligence"
- Absence of delusions and other signs of irrational thinking
- Absence of "nervousness" or psychoneurotic manifestations
- Unreliability
- Untruthfulness and insincerity
- Lack of remorse or shame
- Inadequately motivated antisocial behavior
- Poor judgment and failure to learn by experience
- Pathologic egocentricity and incapacity for love
- General poverty in major affective reactions
- Specific loss of insight
- Unresponsiveness in general interpersonal relations
- Fantastic and uninviting behavior with drink and sometimes without
- Suicide rarely carried out
- Sex life impersonal, trivial, and poorly integrated
- Failure to follow any life plan

samples of adolescents and is useful for examining the early development of psychopathic traits.

Prevalence and Offending Frequency

It is somewhat difficult to establish the prevalence of psychopathy in the general U.S. population because researchers studying psychopaths usually draw their samples from forensic populations. Some scholars, however, have calculated estimates of psychopathy in the adult population of the United States and have asserted that approximately 1 to 3 percent of male adults could be considered psychopaths, and about 1 percent of all female adults would meet the criteria for psychopathy.

The exploitative and aggressive behaviors displayed by psychopathic criminals are also relatively stable over long swaths of the life course. Psychopaths tend not to change their behaviors: Youthful psychopaths are likely to remain psychopaths as they mature into adulthood. This is especially true for those who score high on the personality dimension of the PCL-R.

Among the general public, psychopaths are a statistical aberration, but psychopaths are much more prevalent in prison populations. Although estimates vary, the general consensus is that psychopaths constitute about 20 percent of all incarcerated American prisoners, but they make up an even larger percentage of all inmates incarcerated for serious, violent crimes. Psychopathic criminal offenders not only commit a disproportionate percentage of the most serious acts of predation, but they also offend at much higher rates than do nonpsychopathic criminal offenders. In short, although psycho-

paths make up only a relatively small percentage of all offenders, they account for the vast majority of all criminal acts.

Causes and Treatment

The origins of psychopathy have long baffled scholars. Although it was once believed that social factors and environmental conditions were solely responsible for individuals' development of psychopathy and psychopathic traits, leading researchers now generally agree that biological and genetic factors play a large role in the process. Research has revealed, for example, that certain core psychopathic personality traits, such as impulsivity and callousness, are under significant genetic control. Evidence also suggests that brain abnormalities, such as problems with the amygdala, neuropsychological deficits, and a malfunctioning prefrontal cortex,

Serial killer Jeffrey Dahmer (center), flanked by his attorneys, at his 1991 murder trial in Milwaukee, Wisconsin. A textbook example of psychopathic personality disorder, Dahmer showed no remorse for the seventeen people he is believed to have killed. He often engaged in sex acts with his victims' bodies, many of which he dismembered, and he even ate parts of his victims. After being sentenced to fifteen consecutive life sentences plus ten years, he was beaten to death in prison by another inmate. *(AP/Wide World Photos)*

may be important factors in the etiology of psychopathy.

Given the vast amount of death and destruction caused by psychopathic criminals, great interest exists in whether treatment programs can have any impact on the violent behavioral patterns evinced by psychopaths. In general, violent and aggressive psychopaths are extremely nonresponsive to treatment efforts. Although some rehabilitation programs have reported success in reducing aggressive behaviors among psychopaths, this appears to be the exception rather than the rule. Psychopaths in treatment settings are known for resisting treatment, manipulating staff members, and victimizing fellow patients. Psychopathic criminals often leave treatment programs before completion, and even those who successfully complete such programs tend to have extremely high rates of recidivism. Some experts have argued that the only way to control psychopathic offenders is through incarceration.

Kevin M. Beaver

Further Reading

Babiak, Paul, and Robert D. Hare. *Snakes in Suits: When Psychopaths Go to Work.* New York: HarperCollins, 2006. Discusses the impacts of psychopathic personalities on corporate environments.

Blair, James, Derek Mitchell, and Karina Blair. *The Psychopath: Emotion and the Brain.* Malden, Mass.: Blackwell, 2005. Presents a cogent theoretical framework on which to base the argument that psychopaths have brain abnormalities.

Cleckley, Hervey. *The Mask of Sanity: An Attempt to Clarify Some Issues About the So-Called Psychopathic Personality.* 5th ed. Saint Louis: C. V. Mosby, 1976. Updated edition of the first book written about psychopaths, which was published in 1941. Provides one of the earliest and one of the most influential discussions about psychopathy and psychopaths.

DeLisi, Matt. *Career Criminals in Society.* Thousand Oaks, Calif.: Sage, 2005. Presents an excellent overview of habitual offenders, including psychopathic criminals.

Hare, Robert D. *Without Conscience: The Disturbing World of the Psychopaths Among Us.* New York: Guilford Press, 1999. Work by a leading expert on psychopathy provides a good introduction to the main concepts and issues relating to research in this field.

Meloy, J. Reid. *The Psychopathic Mind: Origins, Dynamics, and Treatment.* Lanham, Md.: Rowman & Littlefield, 1998. Comprehensive text discusses the causes of psychopathy and some different methods of treating psychopaths.

See also: Antipsychotics; Borderline personality disorder; Criminal personality profiling; Criminology; *Diagnostic and Statistical Manual of Mental Disorders*; Forensic psychiatry; Forensic psychology; Guilty but mentally ill plea; Minnesota Multiphasic Personality Inventory.

Psychotropic drugs

Definition: Broad group of substances that are capable of affecting human minds and behavior.

Significance: Forensic scientists are often called upon to determine whether psychotropic drugs are present in persons or at crime scenes as well as the exact nature of any such substances found.

Psychotropic drugs are also known as psychoactive substances. They include licit and illicit drugs as well as plants, foods, and household products not commonly thought of as drugs or druglike. Because of this breadth of forms, the potential range of effects of these substances is very broad. In general, however, psychoactive drugs have primary action on the central nervous system (brain and spine) and the behaviors and reactions it controls. These include processes such as attention, awareness, physical and other perceptions and feelings, emotions, concentration, learning, judgment, and thinking.

Drugs that are considered psychoactive are generally classified into groups based on the conditions they are legally used to treat and how they affect the body. Some common groupings include analgesics, antidepressants, antiepileptics, antiparkinsonian drugs, antipsychotics, anxiolytics, central stimulants, contraceptives, fertility drugs, general depressants, psychedelics, sedative-hyponotics, and tranquilizers. Substances of abuse can be classified into many of these categories as well; however, for diagnostic purposes, they are considered separately. Substances of abuse include alcohol, amphetamines, caffeine, cannabis (or marijuana), cocaine, hallucinogens (such as club drugs), inhalants, nicotine, opioids, phencyclidine (known as PCP), sedative-hypnotics, and anxiolytics.

Caffeine, hallucinogens, and inhalants illustrate the fact that psychotropic substances are not always found in pill or other common medicinal form. Caffeine is found in many everyday food items, including coffee, tea, and chocolate. Hallucinogens may be found in plants and fungi. Inhalants are found in household and workplace substances, such as gasoline, glue, lighter fluid, liquid correction fluid, paint, paint thinner, and varnish, as well as in the forms of amyl and butyl nitrate, general anesthetics, and nitrous oxide.

Common Uses

Psychotropic drugs have many positive uses. Various types of these substances are used in the treatment of mental illnesses such as attention-deficit/hyperactivity disorder (ADHD), depression, bipolar disorder, and schizophrenia. Antidepressants and mood-stabilizing drugs such as lithium are good examples of the psychoactive substances used for these purposes. Analgesics, including morphine, are used to treat pain. Other psychotropic drugs that are used to treat some complex conditions, such as epilepsy, have direct effects on the conditions they are used to treat as well as side effects that affect the mind.

Psychotropic drugs are also used recreationally and abused, but it is not only illicit recreational drugs that are of forensic interest. The most commonly used licit drugs—alcohol, caffeine, nicotine, and prescription drugs, including opioids—are also of interest to law enforcement. Alcohol, for instance, has long been related to crime; forensic scientists are often involved in determining the presence and amounts of alcohol in the blood in cases of persons accused of driving under the influence, public intoxication, and underage drinking. Caffeine intoxication may cause agitation, which, when combined with other circumstances, may lead to problems such as aggressive driving or verbal assault. Forensic scientists may conduct examinations of nicotine for cases related to accusations of smoking in restricted areas, such as on airplanes, or for lawsuits related to health damages caused by nicotine. Psychotropic drugs that are available by prescription, such as oxycodone, are often linked to crimes involving prescription forgery or improper prescribing of these substances by physicians.

Not all psychotropic drugs are prescription or illicit drugs. The caffeine found in coffee, tea, soft drinks, chocolate, and other commonly consumed beverages and foods is a powerful psychotropic drug that can alter behavior and become the object of dependencies. (© iStockphoto.com/José Luis Gutiérrez)

Continuing Controversies

In the United States, a number of controversies surround psychotropic drugs and their effects. These include long-running debates about the regulations attached to production of these substances as well as the laws concerning the distribution of such drugs and access to them. The characteristics of the users themselves also spark controversy. Although many psychotropic substances have been shown to be valuable in addressing suffering, debates continue about "good" and "bad" drugs, and the context of use is often ignored. Fierce disagreements are also ongoing regarding why, how, and when research on the value of any drug should be revisited.

Debates among lawmakers continue about which substances should be regulated, by what means, and to what extent. The process from drug production to end users is a long chain of events, and insufficiencies at any point can cause problems for those involved in the chain, costing them money. Decision making around the regulation of psychotropic drugs thus receives great scrutiny, because a delicate balance must be maintained in assigning who—producers, distributors, dispensers, users, the public at large—should pay the costs associated with any one drug and its impacts.

Many of the concerns about the users of psychotropic drugs tend to center on recreational users, focusing on how they should they be controlled, cured, or prosecuted. Some argue that users of these substances have certain moral or ethical weaknesses, but given that the use of psychoactive drugs—in one form or another—is the norm, this argument is ill founded. Another issue is the nonuse of these substances by individuals who might benefit from them under medical care and thus indirectly benefit society. Not all persons who might need psychotropic drugs are willing to take them, and some might take them only in certain circumstances, if they are able to make such judgments at all. If their refusal to use these substances will endanger their safety or the safety of others, should these persons be forced to take the drugs? Such matters are relevant to law enforcement in that they involve the balance of protecting individuals and society from harm while honoring hard-won civil liberties.

Nancy A. Piotrowski

Further Reading

Julien, Robert M. *A Primer of Drug Action: A Comprehensive Guide to the Actions, Uses, and Side Effects of Psychoactive Drugs*. 10th ed. New York: Worth, 2005. Describes how drugs are absorbed and processed by the body as well as their effects on the body and mind.

Kuhn, Cynthia, Scott Swartzwelder, and Wilkie Wilson. *Buzzed: The Straight Facts About the Most Used and Abused Drugs from Alcohol to Ecstasy*. 2d ed. New York: W. W. Norton, 2003. Easy-to-read guide provides basic information on commonly used drugs.

Rudgley, Richard. *The Encyclopedia of Psychoactive Substances*. New York: St. Martin's Press, 2000. Easy reference resource notes the histories, regions and patterns of use, and effects of various drugs.

Weil, Andrew, and Winifred Rosen. *From Chocolate to Morphine: Everything You Need to Know About Mind-Altering Drugs*. Rev. ed. Boston: Houghton Mifflin, 2004. Discusses the broad range of substances that affect the mind.

World Health Organization. *Neuroscience of Psychoactive Substance Use and Dependence*. Geneva: Author, 2004. Describes psychotropic drug effects at the level of neurotransmitters.

See also: Amphetamines; Antianxiety agents; Antipsychotics; Attention-deficit/hyperactivity disorder medications; Club drugs; Crack cocaine; Drug abuse and dependence; Drug classification; Halcion; Hallucinogens; Legal competency; Narcotics; Opioids.

Puncture wounds

Definition: Injuries made when pointed objects—such as knives, nails, needles, screwdrivers, or teeth—are forced into the body.

Significance: Deep or forceful puncture wounds can cause death, particularly if they affect internal organs such as the heart, liver, lungs, or kidneys.

Puncture wounds may appear insignificant, as little damage may be visible on the surface. Such wounds, however, may be deep even though they are not very wide (in contrast with cuts, which are wide but not necessarily deep). Deep puncture wounds may cause significant internal bleeding, and the weapons used to make the wounds may leave behind chemical residues that can cause infections that may lead to death.

The most significant types of puncture wounds examined by forensic scientists are generally knife wounds, as these are the most likely kinds of puncture wounds to cause death. Other types of materials may cause puncture wounds, however. These include glass, hypodermic and other needles, nails, screwdrivers, and even obscure objects such as hat pins. Puncture wounds may also be caused by other forces, such as when a falling body hits a fence stake or when a broken rib punctures a lung.

A puncture wound can be particularly dangerous if the tip of the instrument that made the wound has been treated with a poison or some other chemical. If the instrument is long, it can deposit these substances deep into the body, perhaps even into an organ. Even if no chemicals were present on the instrument, a puncture wound can heal over on the surface while bacteria are left to grow and fester inside the wound, causing infection and more internal damage. Puncture wounds that enter internal organs, known as penetrating puncture wounds, may cause irreparable organ damage that may not be obvious when the wound is first inflicted.

With careful examination during autopsy, a forensic pathologist can usually determine what type of weapon has caused puncture wounds. The pathologist may use X rays or other types of imaging, such as computed tomography (CT) scanning or magnetic resonance imaging (MRI), to determine the path or paths of the weapon through the body. The pathologist also examines the entry point of the instrument and inspects the decedent's clothing for holes and blood spatter patterns. (With puncture wounds, however, bleeding is often minimal.) Sometimes, especially if the weapon hit bone, the tip or some other small piece of the weapon may be left behind, giving the pathologist more evidence to use in determining the cause of the wound. Careful examination of a puncture wound can also help determine whether the wound was accidental, self-inflicted, or inflicted by an assailant.

Marianne M. Madsen

Further Reading

DiMaio, Vincent J., and Dominick DiMaio. *Forensic Pathology*. 2d ed. Boca Raton, Fla.: CRC Press, 2001.

James, Stuart H., and Jon J. Nordby, eds. *Forensic Science: An Introduction to Scientific and Investigative Techniques*. 2d ed. Boca Raton, Fla.: CRC Press, 2005.

Shkrum, Michael J., and David A. Ramsay. *Forensic Pathology of Trauma: Common Problems for the Pathologist*. Totowa, N.J.: Humana Press, 2007.

See also: Autopsies; Blood spatter analysis; Blood volume testing; Defensive wounds; Forensic pathology; Hesitation wounds and suicide; Knife wounds.

Quality control of evidence

Definition: Documented and demonstrable processes and procedures used to ensure the integrity of all items of evidence.

Significance: Demonstrable procedures for the collection, packaging, handling, transport, examination, and storage of items of evidence are crucial to ensuring that those items retain their evidential value. It is of the greatest importance that confidence can be placed in the integrity of an evidential item and any findings derived from it.

Quality-assurance programs have become commonplace in forensic organizations, and a number of accreditation bodies have been formed for the purpose of assessing the performance of forensic organizations against strict standards of practice. Accreditation allows organizations to demonstrate that they have been assessed and that their procedures were found to be satisfactory. They must also be able to demonstrate that those procedures are put into practice, however.

One of the most significant parts of any forensic organization's quality-assurance, or accreditation, program is that relating to the handling of evidence. The organization must be able to demonstrate that each item of evidence has been handled appropriately from the moment of its discovery up to its presentation in court for trial, and sometimes through subsequent appeals and retrials. If it can be demonstrated that an evidential item has been, or may potentially have been, compromised or contaminated in some way, the significance of its evidential value becomes questionable. Doubt about the handling of a single piece of evidence may also call into question the evidential value of any items held or handled in any way by the same specific laboratory or individual. This may also have ramifications for other cases involving that laboratory or individual.

Scene Security

When police personnel take control of a crime scene, they have a responsibility to take all reasonable steps to protect all potential evidence at the scene from deleterious change. Initially this involves ensuring that appropriate scene boundaries are put in place, a task that can be logistically difficult, particularly when a scene is outdoors.

After the scene parameters are in place, law-enforcement authorities must maintain control of the area to prevent entry to the scene by anyone other than those strictly required for processing and recording of the scene. Wherever possible, those individuals should all be well-trained, competent, and experienced crime scene personnel.

Chain of Custody

When an item of potential evidence is identified, its location within the crime scene and its conditions must be recorded. This is typically done through photography, scene sketches, and general notes. After possession is taken of the item, it becomes part of an official exhibits register.

The exhibits register, or evidence log, is a list of all items that come into the possession of the police, whether collected from a scene or by other means, in relation to an investigation. The register typically assigns a unique identifier to each item and records a description of the item along with information concerning where it was found and by whom and when it was physically seized. After an item is entered into the exhibits register, the register records the physical location of the item and every instance when custody of the item changes.

During the course of an investigation, items may be transferred between sections of an organization or between organizations in order for required examinations to occur. Each section or organization should have its own process in place for recording the chain of custody of any items within its possession.

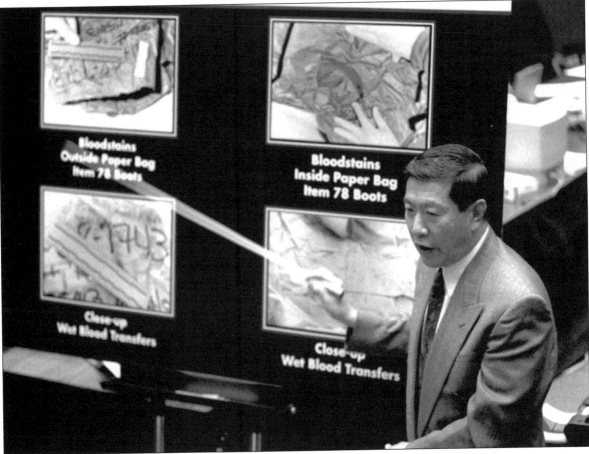

At O. J. Simpson's double-murder trial in 1995, Dr. Henry C. Lee, a renowned forensic scientist, was engaged by the defense to provide testimony that questioned the quality of the handling of evidence in the case by crime scene investigators. Here he explains how bloodstains were transferred from evidence items in the case to the paper sacks in which they were carried. *(AP/Wide World Photos)*

The Importance of Packaging

The method of packaging of an item of evidence is also crucial to maintaining its evidential value. Inappropriate packaging may destroy evidence. For example, the DNA (deoxyribonucleic acid) in biological fluids can rapidly degrade if stored in a moist environment, such as inside a sealed plastic bag; such evidence should therefore be stored in breathable packaging, such as paper bags. Flammable liquid residues in a fire debris sample, in contrast, should not be packaged in paper, as this allows them to evaporate; such residues should be packaged in airtight containers. It is important that all personnel who handle evidential items understand how packaging can affect the items and thus potentially affect the results of subsequent analyses.

Item Examination and Preservation of Item Integrity

During the laboratory examination of items of evidence—whether they are bullet fragments, bloodstains, or articles of clothing—some degree of physical handling of the items is inevitable. Following examination of an item, it is the responsibility of the examiner to be able to demonstrate that all reasonable steps were taken to ensure that the item was not detrimentally affected by the examination any more than was strictly necessary to perform the examination properly.

Crime laboratories often have strict requirements in place detailing what is considered to be acceptable practice in the examination of evidence. For example, the examination of items for DNA, particularly trace or contact DNA, can often involve elaborate precautions to prevent contamination. Examination spaces need to be thoroughly cleaned before and after items are examined. All equipment used must be either disposable or able to be cleaned thoroughly between item examinations. Examiners must wear disposable lab coats and gloves, face masks, and hair coverings to minimize their DNA contribution. This protective clothing must also be completely changed between the examinations of different items.

Records are kept of when an item was examined, who the examiner was, and where the examination took place. Any tests performed on an item are also recorded, as are the details of any subsamples collected.

Examination strategies for items involved in an investigation should also be considered. For example, if practical, a crime lab might schedule examinations of items from complainants, suspects, and scenes in a particular case to take place in different examination rooms on different days and by different analysts. This sort of strategy effectively eliminates any reasonable suggestion of cross-contamination occurring between case items.

R. K. Morgan-Smith

Further Reading

Adams, Thomas F., Alan G. Caddell, and Jeffrey L. Krutsinger. *Crime Scene Investigation*. 2d ed. Upper Saddle River, N.J.: Prentice Hall, 2004. Handbook for law-enforcement professionals focuses on excellence in the conduct of crime scene procedures, including the preservation of the integrity of evidence.

Inman, Keith, and Norah Rudin. *Principles and Practice of Criminalistics: The Profession of Forensic Science*. Boca Raton, Fla.: CRC Press, 2001. Provides an introduction to best practices in the forensic science profession. Includes discussion of evidence collection and preservation.

Pyrek, Kelly M. *Forensic Science Under Siege: The Challenges of Forensic Laboratories and the Medico-Legal Investigation System*. Burlington, Mass.: Elsevier Academic Press, 2007. Addresses the problems and challenges facing the field of forensic science, the history behind them, how they have been promulgated, and what could and should be done in the future to remedy them.

St. Clair, Jami J. *Crime Laboratory Management*. San Diego, Calif.: Academic Press, 2002. Presents excellent discussion of the unique needs and requirements involved in the management of forensic science laboratories.

See also: American Society of Crime Laboratory Directors; Chain of custody; Control samples; Courts and forensic evidence; Crime laboratories; Crime scene documentation; Crime scene investigation; Crime scene protective gear; Crime scene search patterns; Cross-contamination of evidence; Direct versus circumstantial evidence; Disturbed evidence; Evidence processing.

Quantitative and qualitative analysis of chemicals

Definition: Processes of identifying and measuring the individual components within chemical mixtures.

Significance: Analytical chemistry plays a major role in forensic laboratories. Techniques from the field of analytical chemistry are used to examine various types of physical evidence such as glass, soil, drugs, ink, paint, body fluids and tissues, explosives, and petroleum products. In forensic science, analysis of such evidence can be either qualitative or quantitative, depending on the information required, sample size, the technique used, and how the results are interpreted.

In chemical analysis, the components of a sample are identified and their concentrations determined. The main objective of qualitative analysis is to identify one or more substances or chemicals that may be present in a sample. The main goal of quantitative analysis is to determine how much of a particular chemical or substance is present in the sample. Most forensic analysis techniques currently in use are qualitative and are used to identify or confirm the presence or absence of certain materials. Subsequent analyses provide additional information, such as the amounts of component substances present in a sample. Forensics scientists conduct qualitative and quantitative analyses on chemical components of materials, objects, solutions, and biological specimens, including body fluids.

Qualitative Analysis

Qualitative analysis is an integral part of forensic science, with the primary goal to identify unknown substances and chemical elements present in a sample. Qualitative analyses are often used to confirm the presence or absence of certain materials in a sample. Although qualitative analysis can be used to separate components into categories, it is not useful for determining the amounts of certain compounds that are present. Comparison of samples is qualitative and can be conducted to determine whether the chemical compositions of two or more samples are similar.

Qualitative analyses are often based on physical properties, such as melting point, color, texture, density, and other properties that are distinctive for specific elements or compounds. Qualitative analyses are often conducted to determine whether illicit drugs or poisons are present in a sample. After it is known which substances are present, quantitative analysis follows to determine the concentration of each substance present in the sample.

Quantitative Analysis

When the presence of certain substances in a sample has been confirmed, the absolute or relative abundance of these compounds can be determined using quantitative techniques. Quantitative analysis is used to determine the quantity or concentration of a specific substance in a sample. For example, qualitative analysis is used to determine the presence of alcohol in the blood of a person suspected of driving under the influence; quantitative analysis is used to determine the amount of alcohol present in the blood (that is, the blood alcohol level).

Qualitative and Quantitative Analyses in Combination

A more complex analytical situation occurs when both qualitative and quantitative data are required. Although qualitative analyses are generally conducted for identification, in some situations quantitative information is also important. For example, reliable identification of a compound present in a sample is not possible unless a minimum amount of material is also present, which is quantitative information.

If comparing samples requires that the amount of a specific substance present in a sample be known in addition to the chemical elements that are present, then comparative qualitative methods also have quantitative features. Chemical analysts in forensic laboratories conducting qualitative analyses may also need to be involved with quantitative analysis.

Analytical Techniques

Many sophisticated laboratory techniques are used in forensic science for various types of chemical analyses. Some techniques are more suited for qualitative analysis, and others are more appropriate for conducting quantitative analysis. Some methods can be useful for both qualitative and quantitative analyses, depending on how the data are collected and analyzed. Techniques that are primarily used for qualitative analyses, such as substance identification, include "wet" chemical techniques to collect physical properties of sample components, some chromatographic techniques and spectroscopic methods, and DNA (deoxyribonucleic acid) analysis.

Although microscopy is generally qualitative in nature, it can be quantitative when used in combination with specific spectrophotometric measurements. Spectroscopy can be qualitative or quantitative or both, depending on the procedures used and the types of measurements collected. For example, ultraviolet and visible spectrophotometry is generally used as a screening tool to determine the presence or absence of suspected compounds, but it can also be quanti-

A chemist at the Centers for Disease Control and Prevention sets up a system using liquid chromatography coupled with mass spectrometry to analyze a sample. *(Centers for Disease Control and Prevention)*

tative in single-substance solutions or with appropriate standards. Other forms of spectroscopy, such as infrared (IR) or Fourier transform infrared (FTIR), are also recognized as useful for collecting quantitative measurements.

Chromatographic methods are used extensively in forensic science labs to analyze body fluids for the presence of illicit drugs, to analyze samples collected from crime scenes, and to analyze residues from explosives. Although thin-layer chromatography has generally been considered qualitative, many quantitative procedures involving this method are being developed. High-performance liquid chromatography (HPLC) has been used extensively for both qualitative and quantitative analyses of drugs, metabolites, explosives, marker dyes, and inks. Liquid chromatography coupled with mass spectrometry (LC-MS) is widely used in forensics for confirmatory and quantitative analyses and is a powerful tool for drug screening. Gas chromatography is also used for drug screening and can be used to quantify alcohol or illicit drugs in body fluids.

C. J. Walsh

Further Reading

Bogusz, M. J., ed. *Handbook of Analytical Separations*. Vol. 6 in *Forensic Science*, edited by Roger M. Smith. 2d ed. New York: Elsevier, 2007. Describes the applications of various separation methods used in forensic laboratories. Includes chapters devoted to methods of screening for various chemicals.

Harris, Daniel C. *Quantitative Chemical Analysis*. 7th ed. New York: W. H. Freeman, 2006. Widely used text covers all aspects of quantitative analytical chemistry.

Houck, Max M., and Jay A. Siegel. *Fundamentals of Forensic Science*. Burlington, Mass.: Elsevier Academic Press, 2006. Introductory textbook provides discussion of the basic methods of analysis used in forensic examinations.

Langford, Alan, et al. *Practical Skills in Forensic Science*. New York: Pearson Prentice Hall, 2005. Good introductory text addresses all of the various methods used in the forensic sciences. Includes several chapters on quantitative analyses, listed by technique.

Tebbett, Ian, ed. *Gas Chromatography in Forensic Science*. New York: Ellis Horwood, 1992. Provides an introduction to chromatography and then discusses specific issues regarding the uses of this technique in forensic chemistry, including in drug analysis, analysis of explosives, and toxicology.

See also: Acid-base indicators; Analytical instrumentation; Chromatography; Forensic toxicology; Gas chromatography; Mass spectrometry; Polarized light microscopy; Spectroscopy; Toxicological analysis; Ultraviolet spectrophotometry.

Questioned document analysis

Definition: Examination of documents to determine their origins or establish their authenticity.

Significance: Questioned document analysis has a broad scope, given that it can involve any item containing writing or symbols to convey meaning (such as a handwritten letter, a contract, or even graffiti on a lavatory wall). Forensic document examiners play important roles in the analysis of evidence in cases of fraud, forgery, counterfeiting, threats, and many other offenses.

The need for forensic document examiners emerged in the legal system as the courts needed help in handling, preparing, and interpreting document evidence. Document examiners employ many different methods depending on the questions they seek to answer. For example, is the signature on a given piece of art genuine? Were the diaries attributed to a particular person really written by that individual? Can a threatening letter be linked to a suspect? Was a page added to a business contract prior to or after the date of the original signature on the contract? A typical questioned document examination includes handwriting identification and analysis, analysis of printing devices, paper identification, ink identification, and examination of elements within the document such as indented markings, erasures, alterations, and obliterations. Document examiners also sometimes are called upon to analyze written materials that have been damaged by fire or water.

Both paper and print examinations involve the comparison of questioned items to known sources, which are called standards. Through this process, forensic document examiners may be able to link questioned materials to established sources. Forensic document examiners are often asked to determine the authenticity of documents based on the documents' purported dates, and comparisons with known standards can enable them to establish the histories and origins of such documents. Another common task performed by forensic document examiners is the assessment of whether multiple documents have a common origin—for example, to determine whether certain documents can be linked to materials that have been seized from a suspect.

The FBI's Questioned Documents Unit

In addition to its many other specialized forensic units, the Federal Bureau of Investigation operates the Questioned Documents Unit (QDU), which offers forensic support to fellow FBI units and other federal, state, and local law-enforcement agencies. This unit examines and analyzes handwritten, typed, and printed evidence collected during investigations. The QDU helps train federal, state, and local law-enforcement forensic examiners in its specialized field and disseminates information on document examination.

Knowledge of paper production processes and printing processes can help document examiners to identify class and individual characteristics in questioned documents. For instance, forensic document examiners are commonly asked to identify the types of printers used to produce particular documents. To do so, they might focus on watermarks, indentations, or accidental markings that result from the printing process.

By using scanners, microscopes, combinations of light sources and filters, and chemical testing techniques such as thin-layer chromatography (TLC), gas chromatography (GC), and mass spectrometry (MS), document examiners can identify the similarities in chemical properties in the elements used in documents. This often enables them to determine how and when the documents in question were created, and thus can lead to information on who created the documents.

Stephanie K. Ellis

Further Reading

James, Stuart H., and Jon J. Nordby, eds. *Forensic Science: An Introduction to Scientific and Investigative Techniques*. 2d ed. Boca Raton, Fla.: CRC Press, 2005.

Kelly, Jan Seaman, and Brian S. Lindblom, eds. *Scientific Examination of Questioned Documents*. 2d ed. Boca Raton, Fla.: CRC Press, 2006.

Storer, William H. "Questioned Documents." In *Introduction to Forensic Sciences*, edited by William G. Eckert. 2d ed. Boca Raton, Fla.: CRC Press, 1997.

See also: Document examination; Fax machine, copier, and printer analysis; Forensic accounting; Forensic linguistics and stylistics; Gas chromatography; Handwriting analysis; Hitler diaries hoax; Hughes will hoax; Mass spectrometry; Oblique lighting analysis; Paper; Thin-layer chromatography; Typewriter analysis; Writing instrument analysis.

R

Racial profiling

Definition: Law-enforcement practice of using race, ethnicity, or country of origin as a primary reason for detaining, questioning, or searching potential suspects.

Significance: As a single indicator of criminal intent, or in conjunction with a larger criminal profile, racial profiling is controversial and often leads to tensions between the police and targeted groups. Scientific investigation into the assumptions behind racial profiling has tended to debunk their validity.

Taking various forms, "profiling" is a modern investigative tool used by law enforcement to help investigate and prevent criminal activity. "Criminal profiles" are based on analyses of patterns of evidence left at crime scenes, as tangible physical evidence may offer clues to a culprit's motives, methods, and, in some instances, personality. "Racial profiling" differs in that it is not based on crime scene analyses. It is instead based on the notion that certain crimes are more likely to be committed by members of groups defined by race, ethnicity, or country of origin. A typical example would be the assumption that a person of Russian heritage is more likely than a person of Mexican heritage to belong to the Russian mob. Controversy would enter this kind of profiling, however, if law enforcement were to act on the assumption that *all* Russians might be members of the Russian mob. However, while all—or nearly all—members of the Russian mob are indeed likely to be Russians, not all Russians are likely to be mob members.

The rationale behind racial profiling is that members of certain racial and ethnic groups are more likely than other people to commit certain types of crime. For example, the fact that many African American youths commit drug crimes leads many people to think that African American youths in general are more likely than others

to commit such crimes. Acting on that assumption, law-enforcement officers might therefore be inclined to stop and question all young black men they encounter on the street solely because such youths seem to fit their profile of drug dealers. Such random stops occasionally do lead to the apprehension of drug dealers, but the practice also fosters police harassment of many innocent youths whose chief offense is being black.

Indeed, a common public perception in the United States is that law-enforcement officers frequently target innocent people who happen to be members of racial and ethnic minorities for traffic stops to check for possession of illegal drugs, violation of immigration laws, and other criminal activities. Such impressions are popularly supported by the publicizing of anecdotal accounts of famous African Americans, such as actors Wesley Snipes and Will Smith and football coach Tony Dungy, who have been stopped and harassed by police without apparent cause. Further contributing to public perceptions that law-enforcement officers are racially biased are numerous reports of nonwhite American citizens being detained at border crossings and airports under suspicion of carrying contraband drugs or engaging in possible terrorist activities.

Racial Profiling and the Law

Viewed by proponents as a useful tool in reducing crime and protecting law-abiding citizens, racial profiling has been at the center of many legal battles over the proper balance between protecting the rights and liberties of citizens and the need to fight crime. At issue is the right of citizens, guaranteed by the Fourth Amendment to the U.S. Constitution, "to be secure in their persons, houses, papers, and effects, against unreasonable searches and seizures." Several key U.S. Supreme Court rulings on the Fourth Amendment have directly or indirectly affected the use of racial profiling in police work. For example, in *Terry v. Ohio* in 1968, the Court ruled that police acting under reasonable suspicion could stop and quickly search persons without a warrant. This ruling gave police greater discretion in determining whom to stop, thereby increasing the potential for their using racial profiling to determine whom to stop.

Generally, however, using racial or ethnic identities as the only or primary reasons to approach, detain, or search suspects has been ruled illegal. Evidence obtained as the result of such a profile is generally regarded as in violation of the Fourth Amendment. For example, in *United States v. Brignoni-Ponce* (1975), the Supreme Court ruled that U.S. Border Patrol agents could not regard a person's ethnic appearance alone as justification to have a reasonable suspicion of criminal activity. Although immigration law was at issue in that particular case, the broader impact of the ruling was clear: Any law-enforcement officer's use of race or ethnicity as the sole basis for detaining a person violates that person's constitutional protections.

It is, however, permissible to use race, ethnicity, or country of origin as one element in a larger criminal profile in most situations. The behavior, rather than the race or ethnicity, of a suspect can always be a justifiable reason for police to detain or search the person. The Supreme Court ruling in *Whren et al. v. United States* (1996) made it legal for law-enforcement officers to use traffic violations as a pretext to check for other evidence of criminal activity. The impact of this ruling increased the discretionary power of the police and obscured potential racial motivations for stopping and searching nonwhite persons.

Political Responses

State and federal government responses to racial profiling have been mixed. In some instances, legislative bodies have increased the

discretionary powers of police, while others have attempted to reduce it to balance individual rights with crime control. Presidents Richard M. Nixon, Ronald Reagan, and George H. W. Bush all tended to support expanded discretionary powers of police in the national fight against illegal drugs. Opponents of racial profiling have claimed that their actions led to an increase in the illegal use of race to detain and search nonwhite persons. By contrast, President Bill Clinton strongly discouraged the use of racial profiling. He issued an executive memorandum to federal law-enforcement agencies requiring their officers to collect information on the race, ethnicity, and countries of origin of individuals whom they detained for the purpose of collecting data that would reveal investigative patterns at the federal level.

President George W. Bush also opposed racial profiling. With his support, the End of Racial Profiling Act was introduced in the U.S. Senate in February, 2004, but no further action was taken on the bill. Meanwhile, the terrorist attacks of September 11, 2001, renewed American fears about their safety and soon led to Congress's enactment of the Patriot Act of 2001, which increased discretionary powers for law enforcement for national security purposes. Many observers have criticized the

The Mathematics of Racial Profiling

The seductive appeal of racial profiling lies in the belief that if members of group X are disproportionately more likely than members of other groups to commit a particular crime, it makes sense to focus attention on group X in regard to that crime. However, if only a tiny percentage of group X members commit the crime, then such a focus may be ethically questionable, as it would burden the overwhelming majority of law-abiding members of group X. It is instructive to consider the mathematics of profiling.

If a particular crime that is committed by only 0.1 percent of the general population is committed by 1.0 percent of the members of group X, then any individual member of group X is ten times more likely to commit the crime than is a member of the general population. However, 99 percent of the members of group X are law-abiding with respect to this crime. Moreover, if all the members of group X constitute less than 10 percent of the total population, then less than half of the people who commit the crime in question are actually members of group X.

Patriot Act as an erosion of the constitutional rights of private citizens and a mechanism to justify using race or ethnicity as a primary reason for questioning and detaining suspects.

Applying Science to Racial Profiling

The science of racial profiling is in its infancy. It has mostly focused on whether nonwhite motorists are actually stopped and searched more frequently than white motorists and whether stereotypes of racial and ethnic minorities do in fact guide police in their discretionary decisions. Public awareness of the subject of racial profiling increased greatly during the early 1990's, after a black Washington, D.C., attorney named Robert Wilkins filed a suit against the Maryland State Police for subjecting him and his family to an illegal search based on a racial profile. The Wilkins case prompted experts to analyze Maryland traffic arrest patterns. They found that while white and black drivers exceeded the speed limit at the same rate, a much higher percentage of primarily black drivers were stopped and searched. Wilkins's case was settled out of court in 1996, but Maryland State Police implemented a no-tolerance policy on the use of race-based profiles and began to maintain records on the race and ethnicity of drivers stopped for traffic violations to track patterns of racial profiling.

Similar cases in other states have led to changes in police procedures and oversight by the federal government to eliminate highway stops based on the race of the driver. As other law-enforcement agencies began collecting racial and ethnic data during traffic stops, a consistent pattern emerged. Although black and Hispanic citizens are stopped and searched at higher rates than are white citizens, the rates at which they are found to be in possession of drugs and other evidence of illegal activity are equal to those of white citizens. Race and ethnicity thus are not the best predictors of illegal activity. Moreover, research into police decisions to use deadly force has found that proper training reduces the likelihood that race will be a factor in officers' decisions to shoot at suspects.

Kimberley A. McClure

Further Reading

Cole, David. *Terrorism and the Constitution: Sacrificing Civil Liberties in the Name of National Security.* 2d ed. New York: New Press, 2002. Presents a critical examination of the impulse to trade liberty for security in the United States since the terrorist attacks of September 11, 2001.

Costanzo, Mark. *Psychology Applied to Law.* Belmont, Calif.: Wadsworth, 2004. Contains a chapter on psychological perspectives of racial and criminal profiles that focuses on how law-enforcement officers use stereotypes to make discretionary decisions involving whom to stop and search, whom to investigate, and whom to arrest.

Davis, Kelvin R. *Driving While Black: Coverup.* Cincinnati, Ohio: Interstate International Publishing, 2001. Presents the author's personal account of how he was victimized by racial profiling.

Egendorf, Laura K., ed. *Terrorism: Opposing Viewpoints.* San Diego, Calif.: Thomson & Gale, 2004. Two sections focus on the use of racial profiling for national security purposes. Proponents argue that profiling could have prevented the terrorist attacks of September 11, 2001; the opposition argues that Americans are losing their civil liberties as the result of the Patriot Act of 2001 and increased discretionary powers of law enforcement.

Gaines, Larry, and Victor Kappeler. *Policing in America.* 4th ed. Cincinnati: Anderson, 2002. Excellent survey addresses the functions, culture, and discretionary authority of police officers. Includes an informative discussion of racial profiling.

Harris, David. *Profiles in Injustice: Why Police Profiling Cannot Work.* New York: New Press, 2002. Highly regarded work examines issues related to racial profiling.

Holbert, Steve, and Lisa Rose. *The Color of Guilt and Innocence: Racial Profiling and Police Practices in America.* San Ramon, Calif.: Page Marque Press, 2004. Provides an accessible account of anecdotal and scientifically based evidence of racial profiling and its effects and implications. Includes suggestions for addressing law-enforcement assumptions about race and crime.

Pampel, Fred C. *Racial Profiling*. New York: Facts On File, 2004. Provides a detailed historical account of the perceptions of racial profiling in the United States, legal summaries of important judicial decisions and their impact on racial profiling, and a useful glossary and bibliography on racial profiling.

Withrow, Brian L. *Racial Profiling: From Rhetoric to Reason*. Upper Saddle River, N.J.: Pearson Prentice Hall, 2006. Presents comprehensive discussion of racial profiling from a historical and contemporary perspective. Includes recommendations for research that can further understanding of the roles that race and ethnicity play in law enforcement and justice administration.

See also: Airport security; Anthropometry; Crime scene investigation; Criminal personality profiling; DNA database controversies; DNA profiling; Drug Enforcement Administration, U.S.; Ethics of DNA analysis; Federal Bureau of Investigation; Gang violence evidence; Geographic profiling.

A worker in protective clothing cleans out the 68,000-gallon pool used to store spent fuel rods from the high flux beam reactor of the Brookhaven National Laboratory on New York's Long Island. During the 1990's, the storage pool was suspected of leaking radioactive materials into the groundwater that provided Long Island's drinking water. *(AP/Wide World Photos)*

Radiation damage to tissues

Definition: Injury caused to the human body by energy waves as they pass through the body emitting ions.

Significance: Radiation damage may be a cause of death or injury that is not immediately obvious. By examining the pattern of damage in a body, a forensic pathologist can determine whether radiation caused the damage and, if so, what type of radiation was involved.

Radiation is everywhere, including in sunlight, and can pass through the body harmlessly. Certain types of radiation, however, can cause massive internal or external damage leading to death. Depending on the level or concentration of radiation, it may cause damage internally without noticeable external damage.

Types of Radiation

Radiation is either ionizing (ions are emitted into body tissues as the radiation passes through) or nonionizing. Nonionizing radiation is considered to be less dangerous because it passes through tissues without emitting any energy; sunlight is an example of this type of radiation. Types of ionizing radiation, which cause tissue damage as they emit ions into the tissues they penetrate, include alpha particle radiation, beta particle radiation, gamma rays, and X rays.

Different types of radiation damage body tissues in different patterns. For example, alpha particle radiation (often called alpha rays) causes an intense, local concentration of energy. Gamma radiation penetrates more deeply into the tissues, causing a more even and wide distribution of damage. By examining such damage patterns, a forensic pathologist can gain information about what type of radiation was involved in the radiation exposure.

Tissue Damage from Radiation

Radiation damages body tissues when ions are emitted into tissues. These ions are charged atomic particles, and they take electrons from atoms and molecules in the tissues, making those atoms and molecules unable to function. Radiation is most damaging to tissues when a concentrated amount of radiation destroys molecules in a small, defined area. This is why radiation can be used beneficially, for example, in destroying cancerous cells.

High levels or concentrations of radiation can cause massive burning of the skin and trigger death nearly immediately. However, low levels of radiation can be damaging as well. They may cause cell mutations or increase the likelihood that already mutated cells will reproduce at faster speeds. They may also cause internal damage that is not immediately obvious. The calculation of the amount of radiation absorbed by tissues is known as dosimetry.

Alpha rays generally do not penetrate below the first layer of dead skin cells and, as such, do not generally cause much tissue damage. Beta rays penetrate slightly deeper and cause damage such as surface burns to the skin (much like sunburn, but these burns take longer to heal). Although it is possible for beta rays to penetrate more deeply into the body, it is generally unlikely that these rays could cause much damage to internal organs. Gamma rays have the ability to penetrate deeply into the body and are much more likely to cause damage to internal organs than are the other types of ionizing radiation.

All cells in the body are not affected by radiation in the same way. Cells that divide rapidly or are more nonspecialized (relatively speaking) are affected at lower doses or concentrations of radiation than are cells that divide less rapidly or are more specialized. When radiation enters cells in the body, the cells can be affected in four different ways: They can remain undamaged and continue to function normally; they can become damaged, repair the damage, and continue to function normally; they can become damaged and repair the damage but be unable to continue functioning normally; or they can die and cease to function altogether.

Radiation damage is first noticeable in those cells that affect the body's rapidly changing tissues—cells in the intestines, skin, bone marrow, and reproductive organs, particularly the testicles. Damage to these tissues results in symptoms such as vomiting, burns, hair loss, changes in white blood cell count, and sterility. Long-term effects include eye cataracts, cancers, and genetic mutations.

Possible Sources of Radioactive Contamination

The Centers for Disease Control and Prevention provides this information on the possible sources and spread of radioactive contamination.

Radioactive materials could be released into the environment in the following ways:
- A nuclear power plant accident
- An atomic bomb explosion
- An accidental release from a medical or industrial device
- Nuclear weapons testing
- An intentional release of radioactive material as an act of terrorism

How Radioactive Contamination Is Spread

People who are externally contaminated with radioactive material can contaminate other people or surfaces that they touch. For example, people who have radioactive dust on their clothing may spread the radioactive dust when they sit in chairs or hug other people.

People who are internally contaminated can expose people near them to radiation from the radioactive material inside their bodies. The body fluids (blood, sweat, urine) of an internally contaminated person can contain radioactive materials. Coming in contact with these body fluids can result in contamination and/or exposure.

Acute Radiation Syndrome

An acute radiation dose (a large dose delivered to the whole body in a short period of time, such as in a radiation bomb blast or an accidental industrial exposure) can cause a pattern of damage referred to as acute radiation syndrome. This syndrome is characterized by damage to bone marrow, spleen, and lymph tissue, causing symptoms such as fatigue, fever, infections, and internal bleeding. The central nervous system is also affected, with damage to nerve cells causing symptoms such as confusion, coma, convulsions, loss of coordination, and shock. In addition, damage to the lining of the stomach and intestines causes symptoms such as bleeding ulcers, dehydration, diarrhea, digestive problems, electrolyte imbalance, nausea, and vomiting. An acute dose can also cause lasting damage to the thyroid gland, ovaries, and testicles.

Exposure to radiation can also have an effect on an embryo or fetus because as the fetus grows, its tissue cells are growing and dividing rapidly. If a pregnant woman is exposed to radiation, her child may have increased risks of mental problems or childhood cancers.

Marianne M. Madsen

Further Reading

Ahmed, Syed Naeem. *Physics and Engineering of Radiation Detection*. San Diego: Academic Press, 2007. Comprehensive textbook offers informative discussion of radiation detection. Appropriate for use by both students and professionals.

Byrnes, Mark E., David A. King, and Philip M. Tierno, Jr. *Nuclear, Chemical, and Biological Terrorism: Emergency Response and Public Protection*. Boca Raton, Fla.: CRC Press, 2003. Presents thorough discussion of the effects of radiation on the human body and addresses ways to reduce the risk of radiation poisoning in the event of terrorist use of nuclear weapons.

Holmes-Siedle, Andrew, and Len Adams. *Handbook of Radiation Effects*. 2d ed. New York: Oxford University Press, 2002. Provides information on all aspects of radiation, including its effects on the human body.

Knoll, Glenn F. *Radiation Detection and Measurement*. 3d ed. New York: John Wiley & Sons, 2000. Standard textbook discusses techniques for measuring radiation and various kinds of radiation detection equipment. Covers both basic principles and practical applications.

National Council on Radiation Protection and Measurements. *Management of Terrorist Events Involving Radioactive Material*. Bethesda, Md.: Author, 2001. Provides information on the ways in which radiation can damage human tissues.

Stabin, Michael G. *Radiation Protection and Dosimetry: An Introduction to Health Physics*. New York: Springer, 2007. Presents comprehensive discussion of radiation's effects and methods of protecting against them. Suitable both as an introduction to the field for students and as a practical handbook for health physics professionals.

See also: Decontamination methods; Dosimetry; Electromagnetic spectrum analysis; Environmental Measurements Laboratory; Nuclear detection devices; Nuclear spectroscopy; Silkwood/Kerr-McGee case.

Rape

Definition: Unlawful sexual intercourse with a person without that person's consent.

Significance: An inherently violent crime, rape is most often directed at women and children. The fact that rape is one of the most underreported crimes in the United States poses special problems for investigators as well as for attempts to prevent this crime and to collect data on its prevalence.

The crime of rape is one that generally involves offenders acting out issues of power and control over their victims. The sexual gratification experienced in normal sexual relations is generally a secondary motivation to those who commit rape. Most rape offenses fall into one of two mutually exclusive categories: cases in which

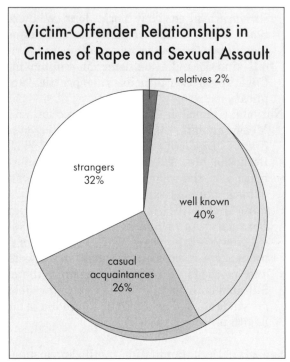

Victim-Offender Relationships in Crimes of Rape and Sexual Assault

- relatives 2%
- strangers 32%
- well known 40%
- casual acquaintances 26%

Source: U.S. Bureau of Justice Statistics, *Criminal Victimization.* Figures are based on all reported rapes and sexual assaults in the United States in 2002.

victims already know their assailants and those in which victims do not.

According to the National Crime Victimization Survey conducted by the U.S. Bureau of Justice Statistics, approximately two-thirds of all rape victims are assaulted by people whom they already know. This is particularly true in cases of "date rape," or acquaintance rape, which occur when offenders and their victims are together for social occasions. When rape victims are the spouses of their assailants, the assaults are termed marital rape or spousal rape. Assaults on persons under the legal age of consent are classified as statutory rape. The work of investigators in all these cases is made simpler by fact that victims can usually identify their attackers easily.

Serial and Stranger Rape

Serial rapists are predators who frequently stalk their victims and commit most of their offenses against strangers who are unlikely al-

ready to know them. Investigations of serial rape and other stranger rape cases thus have the added challenge of investigators' need to find evidence that identifies the offenders.

Serial rapists generally take great care to conceal their identities and disguise their appearance from their victims. This behavior increases the difficulty of identifying them. At the same time, however, each serial rapist tends to repeat predictable patterns of behavior—the offender's so-called modus operandi (MO), or method of operation. Offenders' distinctive MOs, trademark behaviors, and psychological signatures all provide evidence that helps investigators to connect similar rape cases and eventually track down the offenders.

Psychological Evidence

Building psychological profiles of offenders is central to most investigations of serial and stranger rapes. The Federal Bureau of Investigation (FBI) has developed a system called criminal investigative analysis that examines the known behavior of unidentified offenders and builds psychological profiles that can be used to link offenders' personality traits to physical evidence. The combination of criminal investigative analysis, physical evidence, and crime scene reconstruction provides the structure and direction for successful rape investigations. Most important, it provides a means for rape investigators, forensic profilers, and scientists to work collaboratively.

The FBI's National Center for the Analysis of Violent Crime (NCAVC) has developed a system for classifying the core behaviors of rapists. Psychological profiles alone do not enable investigators to identify specific suspects, but suspect profiles can help investigators find matches in databases of signature behaviors, travel distances, victim profiles, and similar information. The goal of comparative case analysis is to identify rape offenders by matching their psychological core behaviors, methods of operation, and psychological signatures with information in the databases. Among the behavioral variables of rapists that are entered into database records are the following: methods of approaching victims, techniques used to control victims, amounts of force used, sexual dynamics of the rapes themselves, methods of evading detection, and postoffense behaviors.

Rapist Typologies

The NCAVC places rapists in four primary categories based on their behavior: power-reassurance, power-assertive, anger-retaliatory, and anger-excitation. Rapists in the power-reassurance category generally execute surprise attacks and initially reassure their victims that no harm will come to them. These rapists also tend to pay compliments to their victims and act almost apologetically for the harm they are inflicting. Sometimes, they ask their victims to evaluate their sexual performance in order to meet their need to be reassured. They tend to use minimal physical force to achieve their objectives.

Rapists classified in the power-assertive category assume immediate and strong command over their victims, to whom they give specific sexual instructions. Tending to use profane language throughout their rapes, their goal is to demean and humiliate without regard for their victims' feelings, pain, or distress. Rapists in this category may carry weapons and generally use from moderate to excessive force in their attacks; they may apply brutal force to victims who resist.

Anger-retaliatory rapists initiate their sexual assaults with immediate applications of physical force and often use weapons of opportunity they find at the scenes. Their devastating blitz attacks combine with their angry and unsympathetic manner to overcome their victims rapidly. Male rapists in this category generally harbor deep-seated hatred of women. Their female victims serve as symbolic targets on whom they release their rage.

Anger-excitation rapists are sadists who often engage in violent, antisocial behavior to serve their obsessive and compulsive need to dominate others. In their initial approaches to their rape victims, they try to establish mutual trust. However, after they get their victims under control, the victims' distressed responses to the physical and emotional pain they are experiencing stimulates these rapists sexually. Investigators of crimes committed by anger-excitation rapists must be alert to signs indicating that the rapists are becoming more violent and possibly are escalating into serial killers.

Physical Evidence

Rape investigations are multidimensional, interdisciplinary, and team-oriented. Successful prosecutions of rape cases draw on the professional expertise and training of both investigation teams and forensic specialists. Sexual assault response teams of law-enforcement agencies typically include four members: first responders, investigator/detectives, victim advocates, and sexual assault nurse examiners. All of these specialists play roles in the collection of the forensic evidence that is critical to establishing that rape crimes have occurred.

Most of the physical evidence collected in rape investigations is found at the scenes of the crimes, on the bodies and clothing of the victims and the suspected offenders, and at so-called dump sites, where items connected with the crimes may have been discarded. Investigators look for trace evidence left on victims' clothing; signs of physical injuries to the victims, including bite marks and bruises; and trace evidence left by the offenders, including blood specimens, hair, semen, fibers, soil, and bits of vegetation.

The Geography of Serial Rape

The obsessive fantasies and compulsive personalities of rapists motivate some of them to commit multiple rapes. Those who become serial rapists tend to operate within limited geographic regions. Geographic information system (GIS) technology, or computerized crime mapping, can assist law-enforcement agencies in tracking the movements of such rapists. The distances that serial rapists travel between their crimes tend to be short—usually less than two miles—and rapists generally commit their first offenses close to their own homes or places of employment. Using GIS technology, investigators can build digital and statistical geographic profiles that can help to predict the locations where serial offenders may strike next and also help to locate where the offenders live or work.

To assist in organizing and protecting the evidence that is gathered, investigators use specially designed sexual assault evidence kits, which are commonly known as rape kits.

Medical examinations of rape victims are conducted by sexual assault nurse examiners and attending physicians. These teams make a special effort to gather biological evidence left on victims' bodies by their assailants; when such material contains DNA (deoxyribonucleic acid), analyses can result in DNA profiles that can be fed into the database of the Combined DNA Index System, better known simply as CODIS. Administered by the FBI, CODIS contains DNA profiles collected from throughout the United States, from samples taken from both convicted offenders and unsolved cases. An unfortunate limitation to this system, according to the National Institute of Justice, is that the evidence contained in hundreds of thousands of rape kits has never been processed, so the potential resulting DNA profiles have not been

sent to CODIS; hence a wealth of potentially valuable information on rapists is not available for comparison.

When rape victims are examined, large pieces of clean butcher paper are placed under them while they disrobe to reduce the chances of losing potentially valuable trace evidence that falls from their bodies and clothes. After the victims disrobe, their clothing is carefully examined for trace evidence. Each individual piece of clothing is packaged separately; moisture stains are dried out, and sheets of paper are inserted between folds of clothing for additional protection against cross-contamination.

When bite marks and other injuries are found on the bodies of rape victims during their examinations, photographs are carefully taken of the wounds as soon after the attacks as possible. Additional photographs taken about forty-eight hours later often prove valuable in documenting emerging bruise marks. Photographic evidence is often presented to juries in rape tri-

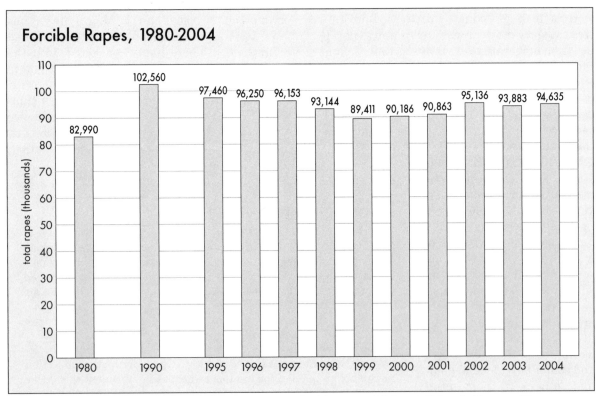

Forcible Rapes, 1980-2004

Source: Federal Bureau of Investigation, *Population-at-Risk Rates and Selected Crime Indicators*. Figures represent total completed and attempted rapes throughout the United States.

als to demonstrate the extent of physical injuries inflicted during assaults.

Thomas E. Baker and James C. Roberts

Further Reading

Dobbert, Duane L. *Halting the Sexual Predators Among Us: Preventing Attack, Rape, and Lust Homicide*. Westport, Conn.: Praeger, 2004. Presents a study of strategies that can be employed to prevent sexual assaults.

Hazelwood, Robert R., and Ann W. Burgess, eds. *Practical Aspects of Rape Investigation: A Multidisciplinary Approach*. 3d ed. Boca Raton, Fla.: CRC Press, 2001. Collection of essays describes the roles of police investigators, medical examiners, forensic scientists, crisis counselors, and public prosecutors in crimes involving rape.

Holmes, Stephen T., and Ronald M. Holmes. *Sex Crimes: Patterns and Behavior*. 2d ed. Thousand Oaks, Calif.: Sage Publications, 2002. Provides information from sociological studies of the characteristics of sex offenders.

National Institute of Justice. *The Future of Forensic DNA Testing: Predictions of the Research and Development Working Group*. Honolulu: University Press of the Pacific, 2005. Discusses advances in DNA collecting and testing as well as likely future uses of DNA analysis in law enforcement.

Rossmo, D. Kim. *Geographic Profiling*. Boca Raton, Fla.: CRC Press, 1999. A leading text in the field offers unique insights into criminal travel patterns, which often play important roles in criminal rape investigations.

Savino, John O., and Brent E. Turvey, eds. *Rape Investigation Handbook*. Boston: Elsevier Academic Press, 2005. Collection of essays by legal scholars, forensic scientists, and law-enforcement practitioners covers all aspects of the investigation of crimes of rape and demonstrates best practices in the field of rape case investigations.

Smith, Merril D., ed. *Sex Without Consent: Rape and Sexual Coercion in America*. New York: New York University Press, 2001. Collection focuses on the historical study of rape, exploring what rape meant to its victims and to American society at time times and places in the past.

Stuart, James H., and Jon J. Nordby, eds. *Forensic Science: An Introduction to Scientific and Investigative Techniques*. 2d ed. Boca Raton, Fla.: CRC Press, 2005. Presents comprehensive discussion of the techniques used by forensic scientists. Includes many useful illustrations and photographs.

Telsavaara, Terhi V. T., and Bruce A. Arrigi. "DNA Evidence in Rape Cases and the Debbie Smith Act: Forensic Practice and Criminal Justice Implications." *International Journal of Offender Therapy and Comparative Criminology* 50 (October, 2006): 487-505. Presents a detailed discussion of the growing backlog in analyses of the evidence contained in rape kits.

U.S. Department of Justice. *Using DNA to Solve Cold Cases*. Washington, D.C.: Government Printing Office, 2002. Brief practical guide is designed for criminal investigators who are responsible for working cold rape cases. Describes success stories and some of the limitations of using DNA evidence.

See also: CODIS; Criminal personality profiling; DNA profiling; Geographic information system technology; Living forensics; Paternity testing; Postconviction DNA analysis; Rape kit; Semen and sperm; Sexual predation characteristics; Strangulation; Violent sexual predator statutes.

Rape kit

Definition: Package of examination materials used by a doctor or nurse (examiner) for gathering evidence from a victim following a sexual assault.

Significance: The rape kit is part of the standardized protocol used in the collection and preservation of physical evidence following any alleged serious sexual assault. The evidence gathered and preserved through the use of a rape kit can aid in the criminal investigation and prosecution of the suspected assailant.

Christopher L. Morano, Connecticut chief state's attorney, announces the issuance of a new kit for the collection of evidence in sexual assault investigations at a news conference in October, 2004. The kit previously used in Connecticut is seen in Morano's right hand; the new kit, in his left hand, is aimed toward the collection of evidence of drug-facilitated sexual assault, which is often seen in cases of so-called date rape. *(AP/Wide World Photos)*

The standardization of approach provided by the rape kit—alternatively known as the sexual assault evidence kit or sexual assault forensic evidence (SAFE) kit—is thought to limit further physical and psychological trauma to the complainant (victim) by ensuring consistency of treatment. This evidence is gathered only after consent has been obtained from the complainant, who can give consent to just part of the examination and can withdraw consent at any time during the examination. Rape kit evidence can be gathered if the complainant (who may be male or female) consents to the examination but does not want to make a report to the police at that time, as the evidence can be stored for use in the future. A number of varieties of rape kits

have been developed, but the kind most commonly used in the United States is known as the Vitullo kit; it was developed by former Chicago police sergeant Louis R. Vitullo, who headed the Chicago Police Department's crime laboratory in the 1970's. The evidence gathered using a rape kit may help police to identify a suspect and may be used in court during any subsequent trial.

Conduct of the Examination and Contents of the Kit

The examination is conducted by a medical professional, typically a doctor or nurse, who may or may not have specialized knowledge or experience in working with sexual assault victims. In many U.S. states, rape kit exams are conducted by specially trained professionals who are part of sexual assault forensic examiner (SAFE) or sexual assault nurse examiner (SANE) programs. To secure the chain of custody after the examination is completed, the medical professional seals the rape kit in a box, which is then kept in a secure place until it is given to the police to be sent to the crime laboratory for analysis.

The rape kit typically contains instructions and forms, diagrams and checklists, slides, swabs, sterile urine collection containers, sterile sample containers, and self-sealing envelopes, bags, and labels. It is important that such materials are not "lick-sealed," as such cross-contamination would jeopardize the integrity of the evidence. For the same reason, all sample swabs and slides must be dry before they are placed in sterile containers.

How the Kit Is Used in the Examination

Prior to using the rape kit, the examiner collects a health history from the complainant; if relevant, a gynecological history is taken, including the date of last menstruation, type of usual contraception used, and last consensual sexual contact. It is important to the chain of evidence that the complainant is at no point left alone in the room once the examination has started, and neither the complainant nor anyone accompanying the complainant is allowed to handle the evidence. If the complainant wants to urinate or defecate prior to the examination, this material is gathered as part of the evidence, and the complainant is cautioned not to wipe the area until after the examination. The complainant is also advised not to remove any menstrual protection or contraceptive device from the body.

The complainant is asked to undress over a sheet of paper to minimize any loss of trace evidence (the paper is later examined for evidence that may have fallen from the complainant's clothing or body). The examiner then uses the rape kit to collect blood, semen, and other body fluid samples from the genitals, rectum, and mouth. The examiner combs the complainant's head and pubic area to collect samples of the complainant's hair and to look for any hairs or loose debris left by the perpetrator. Some hairs

may be plucked from these sites. The examiner scrapes under the complainant's fingernails to collect material that may contain skin cells, fibers, or other materials from the perpetrator. An ultraviolet light is used to identify any dried secretions on the complainant's skin, and swabs (moistened with a little water) are used to collect samples of any substances found. Each item of evidence is labeled and marked with a description of the sample, the complainant's name, the name of the examiner, the date, and the initials of everyone who handled the sample.

Photographs are taken of any injuries, bite marks, lacerations, or bruises on the complainant's body, and the clothes worn by the complainant are also preserved as evidence. The clothing and all photographs are packaged, sealed, and labeled to secure the chain of evidence.

Limitations of the Use of Rape Kits

Some physical evidence in sexual assault cases must be collected within seventy-two hours of the attack. In many U.S. jurisdictions, if an attack occurred more than ninety-six

---

Rape Kits Go Untested

The forensic analysis of rape kit evidence costs approximately five hundred to one thousand dollars per kit. In 2002, *The Oprah Winfrey Show* provided evidence suggesting that across the United States, the evidence collected in 300,000 to 500,000 rape kits was awaiting testing. Commenting on this backlog, the former police commissioner of New York City, Howard Safir, suggested that some 16,000 untested kits were in storage in New York and that this amounted to telling a woman, "You are not worth five hundred dollars." Also in 2002, the television newsmagazine *20/20* paid for half of the processing to test 50 rape kits in Baltimore, and the subsequent investigation solved five major crime cases and exonerated a wrongfully imprisoned man. The rape kit backlog was further investigated in 2003 by Court TV, and in 2007 the *Denver Post* reported on two cases in which rape kit evidence was lost before it could be tested.

hours prior to the examination, a rape kit is not deemed necessary. Despite the presumed scientific objectivity of the rape kit protocol, discretionary practices exist across the United States.

In some states, a complainant in a sexual assault case has the right to ask for the examination to be conducted by someone of the same gender as the complainant. The insufficient numbers of female medical personnel available in some areas may prevent some female complainants from being seen by female examiners in a timely manner. Another limitation of rape kit examinations is that the medical professional does not typically check for pregnancy or sexually transmitted infections; checks for these may need to be done at a later stage.

A rape kit can only help to determine if sexual contact has been made between certain people. It cannot provide evidence of consent or of *mens rea* (guilty mind). Severe injuries might suggest forced intercourse, but this cannot be proved by forensic evidence. Although rape kit evidence cannot prove guilt, it can exclude persons from suspicion; DNA (deoxyribonucleic acid) evidence gathered through the use of rapes kit has been used to clear innocent people.

Helen Jones

Further Reading

Campbell, Rebecca, Debra Patterson, and Lauren F. Lichty. "The Effectiveness of Sexual Assault Nurse Examiner (SANE) Programs: A Review of Psychological, Medical, Legal, and Community Outcomes." *Trauma, Violence, and Abuse* 6, no. 4 (2005): 313-329. Scholarly article describes the rape kit collection process in detail.

Carney, Thomas P. *Practical Investigation of Sex Crimes: A Strategic and Operational Approach*. Boca Raton, Fla.: CRC Press, 2003. A former commanding officer of the Manhattan Special Victims Squad presents case histories to illustrate the skills needed to investigate sex crimes effectively.

Hazelwood, Robert R., and Ann W. Burgess, eds. *Practical Aspects of Rape Investigation: A Multidisciplinary Approach*. 3d ed. Boca Raton, Fla.: CRC Press, 2001. Describes the roles of the police investigator, the medical examiner, the forensic scientist, the crisis counselor, and the prosecutor in crimes involving rape.

LeBeau, Marc A., and Ashraf Mozayani, eds. *Drug-Facilitated Sexual Assault: A Forensic Handbook*. New York: Academic Press, 2001. Collection of essays provides extensive information on this complex area of investigation and highlights the key issues surrounding evidence gathering.

Littel, Kristin. *Sexual Assault Nurse Examiner Programs: Improving the Community Response to Sexual Assault Victims*. Washington, D.C.: U.S. Department of Justice, 2001. Brief bulletin from the Justice Department's Office for Victims of Crime documents the impacts of specialist nurse training programs in providing services to victims of rape.

Savino, John O., and Brent E. Turvey, eds.. *Rape Investigation Handbook*. New York: Academic Press, 2005. Covers the investigative and forensic processes related to sex crimes and demonstrates best practices in the field of rape case investigations.

Telsavaara, Terhi V. T., and Bruce A. Arrigi. "DNA Evidence in Rape Cases and the Debbie Smith Act: Forensic Practice and Criminal Justice Implications." *International Journal of Offender Therapy and Comparative Criminology* 50 (October, 2006): 487-505. Discusses in some detail the backlog in the analysis of rape kit evidence.

See also: Bite-mark analysis; Cross-contamination of evidence; DNA extraction from hair, bodily fluids, and tissues; DNA fingerprinting; Evidence processing; Forensic nursing; *Mens rea*; Physical evidence; Rape; Semen and sperm; Trace and transfer evidence; Victimology; Violent sexual predator statutes.

Reagents

Definition: Substances that bring about chemical reactions when added to particular other substances.

Significance: Forensic scientists use reagents at crime scenes to discover "hidden" evidence, such as the presence of fingerprints that cannot be seen with the naked eye, and to conduct preemptive tests to determine whether substances present may be blood or other bodily fluids. Reagents are also useful for determining the presence of illegal substances, such as drugs.

Reagents are used to test questioned substances at crime scenes and in forensic laboratories. In the presence of the substances with which they are designed to react, reagents produce chemical reactions that usually involve color changes or other changes that can be seen, such as causing a substance to glow under a black light. If the substance with which a reagent is known to react is not present, the chemical reaction does not occur. For example, if a reagent known to react with blood does not react on a stain, that stain is not blood. If that reagent does react on a stain, the stain may be blood, but because other substances could cause the same reaction, the scientist cannot conclude that the stain is blood until further testing is done.

Chemical Reactions

Reagents react chemically with substances usually either through synthesis or through replacement. In synthesis, the reagent and the substance form a new substance. In replacement, the reagent acts on the substance by replacing some of the substance's elements with its own elements.

Forensic scientists must take care when preparing and using reagents. A reagent must be pure enough to react properly with the substance it is intended to detect, so it must be prepared according to strict procedures. In addition, because reagents may be carcinogenic, caustic, or explosive, scientists must handle them carefully; the use of protective clothing and equipment is recommended.

Uses in Biological and Chemical Labs

Many different reagents can be used to identify blood or other bodily fluids on different surfaces. The choice of reagent depends on the surface on which the bodily fluid is thought to be and whether the reagent is being used at the

crime site or in the laboratory. For example, some reagents work well on porous materials but are poor choices for nonporous materials. Other reagents may cause violent chemical reactions and therefore must be used only in laboratory settings.

Some of the reagents that identify blood are amido black, leuco crystal violet, luminol, and Takayama reagent. Amido black reacts with the protein in blood to produce a blue-black color, whereas leuco crystal violet, along with hydrogen peroxide, reacts with the hemoglobin or its derivatives in blood to produce a deep violet color.

Luminol reacts on the oxidizing activity of hemoglobin derivatives in blood to produce a blue-white chemiluminescent reaction (that is, it glows in the dark), so luminol tests must be conducted in darkness. The reaction produced by luminol does not last long (perhaps one to two minutes), and photographs of the tested area need to be taken quickly to preserve the results. Takayama reagent (a mixture of glucose, sodium hydroxide, pyridine, and deionized water) reacts with the hemoglobin in blood when heated to form pink needle- or rhomboid-shaped crystals that can be seen under a microscope.

Other reagents can identify other bodily fluids, such as semen. The reagent nuclear fast red stain, for example, stains spermatozoa so they are visible under a microscope.

Reagents can also identify illegal or poisonous substances. For example, copper sulfate reacts with ephedrine, pseudoephedrine, or norephedrine to produce a purple color, and cobalt thiocyanate reacts with cocaine or phencyclidine (PCP) to produce a blue color. A reagent made from solutions with sodium phosphate, chloramine-T, and a color reagent reacts with cyanide to produce a red color. The reagent used in the Dillie-Koppanyi test reacts with barbiturates to produce a violet color, and the Duquenois-Levine reagent, along with hydrochloric acid and chloroform, reacts with marijuana resins to produce a purple, then pink, color.

Uses with Impression Evidence

Powder or chemical reagents can be used to bring out fingerprints where none can be seen.

For example, ninhydrin is a reagent that reacts with some of the protein left behind by fingerprints. When ninhydrin is placed on a surface that has fingerprints, a deep blue/purple color highlights the prints. Gentian violet is another substance used to develop fingerprints. These types of reagents must be used with caution, however, because they destroy any DNA (deoxyribonucleic acid) evidence that may have been left behind with fingerprints.

Reagents can also be used with shoe prints to determine the type of soil in which the person wearing the shoe walked. For example, if the soil contains iron, ammonium/potassium thiocyanate will react with the iron to produce a reddish-brown color. Hydroxyquinoline reacts with calcium, magnesium, iron, aluminum, and other metals that may be present in small amounts in shoe or tire impressions to produce fluorescence that can be seen under an ultraviolet light. Iodine reacts with small amounts of waxy or oily substances on footprints or tire tracks and may be used in enhancing wet impressions.

Marianne M. Madsen

Further Reading

American Chemical Society Committee on Analytical Reagents. *Reagent Chemicals: Specifications and Procedures*. Washington, D.C.: American Chemical Society, 2005. Discusses the requirements and methods for determining the purity of analytical reagents.

Bell, Suzanne. *Forensic Chemistry*. Upper Saddle River, N.J.: Pearson Prentice Hall, 2006. Describes the methods that forensic scientists use involving chemistry and chemical reactions.

Cobb, Cathy, Monty L. Fetterolf, and Jack G. Goldsmith. *Crime Scene Chemistry for the Armchair Sleuth*. Amherst, N.Y.: Prometheus Books, 2007. Presents basic information on chemistry-related forensic techniques, including the use of reagents in identifying body fluids.

Johll, Matthew. *Investigating Chemistry: A Forensic Science Perspective*. New York: W. H. Freeman, 2007. Textbook designed for nonscience majors includes introductory material on basic chemical concepts, including the use of reagents, in crime solving.

Lundblad, Roger L. *Chemical Reagents for Protein Modification*. Boca Raton, Fla.: CRC, 2004. Discusses how protein modification relates to the analysis of individual amino acids.

Wang, Zerong. *Comprehensive Organic Name Reactions and Reagents*. New York: Wiley-Interscience, 2008. Describes the reactions, applications, and related reactions of reagents and provides experimental examples.

See also: Acid-base indicators; Benzidine; Blood residue and bloodstains; Crime scene screening tests; DNA isolation methods; Evidence processing; Footprints and shoe prints; Luminol; Microcrystalline tests; Orthotolidine; Phenolphthalein; Presumptive tests for blood; Semen and sperm; Tire tracks.

Restriction fragment length polymorphisms

Definition: Variations in the lengths of pieces of DNA cut with restriction enzymes.

Significance: Restriction fragment length polymorphisms are used as markers in gene mapping and to identify individuals in DNA fingerprinting. They are used to determine disease status, to test for paternity, and as forensic evidence to identify the sources of DNA samples.

Restriction fragment length polymorphisms (RFLPs) were the first DNA (deoxyribonucleic acid) typing to be used as forensic evidence. English geneticist Alec Jeffreys and his colleagues identified DNA fingerprints for forensic application in 1985. They examined regions of the human genome called minisatellites, which are made of a DNA sequence that is tandemly (end-to-end) repeated hundreds of times. These are also called variable number of tandem repeats (VNTRs). Individuals vary in the numbers of tandem repeats of that DNA sequence they have in their genomes.

In detecting these RFLPs, DNA is isolated from cells. A restriction enzyme (which makes sequence-specific cuts in DNA) is used to cut outside the repeating sequence. DNA is separated based on size through the use of gel electrophoresis. The DNA fragments are transferred from the gel to a membrane (called a Southern blot). A single-stranded, labeled DNA probe complementary to the repeating sequence is hybridized with the DNA on the membrane. The probe base-pairs with its complementary sequences on the membrane. This labeled probe allows the VNTR regions to be detected among all the DNA in the genome. The size of the fragment detected varies depending on the number of tandem repeats the individual has. This is length polymophism—length variation from individual to individual.

Samples of blood, semen, saliva, or other biological materials are often collected at crime scenes for later DNA analysis. As such a sample ages, dries, or is subjected to high temperatures, the DNA may degrade (break into smaller pieces). To use RFLPs, intact DNA of 20,000 to 25,000 base pairs is required. If DNA degraded to smaller sizes than this is used, a restriction fragment might not be generated, which could cause the false exclusion of a suspect. The minimum amount of DNA that is needed for detection using a radioactive or chemiluminescent probe is 10 to 50 nanograms.

RFLPs were used in the first forensic DNA profiling. As many as fifteen different loci could be examined. The Combined DNA Index System (CODIS), the system developed by the Federal Bureau of Investigation (FBI) for tracking DNA profiles, keeps DNA information from convicted felons for five RFLP loci.

The use of RFLPs for DNA fingerprinting is increasingly being replaced by polymerase chain reaction (PCR) methods, which amplify DNA. With PCR, many copies of short pieces of DNA can be made rapidly, and variations in sequences copied can be used to create a DNA profile. Because PCR can be done on degraded DNA, this newer method has widely replaced RFLPs in forensic applications.

Susan J. Karcher

Further Reading

Fisher, Barry A. J. *Techniques of Crime Scene Investigation*. 7th ed. Boca Raton, Fla.: CRC Press, 2004.

Gill, Peter, Alec J. Jeffreys, and David J. Werrett. "Forensic Application of DNA 'Fingerprints.'" *Nature* 318 (1985): 577-579.

Jones, Phillip. "DNA Forensics: From RFLP to PCR-STR and Beyond." *Forensic Magazine*, Fall, 2004.

Rudin, Norah, and Keith Inman. *An Introduction to Forensic DNA Analysis*. 2d ed. Boca Raton, Fla.: CRC Press, 2002.

See also: DNA analysis; DNA database controversies; DNA extraction from hair, bodily fluids, and tissues; DNA fingerprinting; DNA isolation methods; DNA typing; Electrophoresis; Ethics of DNA analysis; Paternity testing; Polymerase chain reaction; Short tandem repeat analysis; Soil.

RFLPs. *See* Restriction fragment length polymorphisms

Ricin

Definition: Poisonous protein extracted from beans of the plant with the botanical name *Ricinus communis* and the common name castor bean.

Significance: Given that the plant source for the highly toxic substance ricin is easy to obtain, concerns have arisen among law-enforcement and national security agencies that terrorists might attempt to use this toxin in attacks. Such fears are exacerbated by the fact that no antidote to ricin poisoning has been developed.

More than one million tons of castor beans are processed every year for their oil, and the poison ricin can be prepared from the waste created in this processing. Near the end of World War I, the U.S. Chemical Warfare Service extracted ricin from castor beans as part of a plan to produce a toxic weapon. The possession of ricin is illegal in the United States; ricin is listed as a restricted substance (select agent) in the U.S. Biological Weapons Anti-Terrorism Act of 1989.

Preparations of ricin generally appear as gray, off-white, or white powders. Ricin is a heat-resistant protein that consists of two protein subunits, an A chain and a B chain. The B chain is a lectin (carbohydrate-binding protein) and enables ricin binding and internalization by cells; the A chain is the lethal component. To be toxic, ricin has to enter cells, where the A chain enzymatically inactivates ribosomes, the protein-synthesizing machines of cells. The toxic dose of ricin for humans is approximately 500 micrograms; ricin is more toxic on a weight basis than most common nerve gases or chemical weapons. Ricin would be most dangerous as a weapon of terrorism in aerosolized form—that is, in the form of a fine powder that does not clump—as this form would enable the dispersion of the substance over a wide area.

Signs and Symptoms of Ricin Poisoning

The effects of ricin vary depending on how the poison enters the body. If ricin is inhaled, symptoms usually appear within a few hours to eight hours. These include difficulty breathing, fever, cough, nausea, profuse sweating, accumulation of fluid in the lungs, low blood pressure, and respiratory failure. If ricin is ingested with food or liquids, symptoms usually appear in less than six hours and include diarrhea, vomiting, severe dehydration, hallucinations, blood in urine, and seizures. Over the course of several days, liver, kidney, and spleen failure may result.

Time to death from ricin exposure depends on the dose and method of exposure; death may take place from thirty-six to seventy-two hours after initial exposure. Victims who survive past seventy-two hours often recover. Treatment consists of supportive care based on the route of entry of the ricin; for example, for ingested ricin, activated charcoal is administered orally. Other therapy includes provision of intravenous fluids, help in breathing, and medications for low blood pressure and seizures.

Criminal Cases Involving Ricin

Perhaps the most famous case of the use of ricin as a weapon is that of the assassination of Bulgarian dissident and exile Georgi Markov in London in 1978. Markov was a writer who worked for various Western European radio stations and was a persistent critic of the communist Bulgarian government. Agents of the Bulgarian government made three attempts on his life, and the third was successful. At a bus stop, Markov was reportedly stabbed in the thigh with an umbrella that had been specially fabricated to inject a small metal pellet that was designed to release ricin. He died a few days later. Because of Markov's verbalized suspicions about the incident, an autopsy was requested by Scotland Yard. The examination recovered a small metal sphere the size of a pinhead from Markov's body. The artifact, which was composed of expensive and finely machined metals, contained traces of ricin in an inner chamber.

Confirming Ricin Poisoning

In its fact sheet on ricin, the U.S. Centers for Disease Control and Prevention describes how authorities confirm cases of suspected ricin poisoning.

- If we suspect that people have inhaled ricin, a potential clue would be that a large number of people who had been close to each other suddenly developed fever, cough, and excess fluid in their lungs. These symptoms could be followed by severe breathing problems and possibly death.
- If in suspected situations where ricin may have been disseminated, preliminary environmental testing by public health or law enforcement authorities may detect ricin in powders or materials released into the immediate environment. Persons occupying such areas may initially be observed for signs of ricin poisoning.
- No widely available, reliable medical test exists to confirm that a person has been exposed to ricin.

Ricin is derived from the beans of the castor-oil plant, shown here at top right along with the leaf and flower head of the plant. *(© iStock-photo.com/Alex Bramwell)*

Less than two weeks before the attack on Markov, another Bulgarian dissident, Vladimir Kostov, was shot in Paris with a bullet carrying the same kind of pellet that killed Markov. The attempt on Kostov failed because the pellet did not lodge deeply in his body and was removed before it could deliver a lethal dose of ricin. The crimes against Markov and Kostov remain unsolved, but KGB defectors have claimed that the KGB provided technical assistance to the perpetrators.

In 1994 and 1995, members of a domestic American terrorist group, the Minnesota Patriots Council, were convicted of possession of ricin and of conspiring to kill law-enforcement officers. They had responded to an advertisement in a radical right-wing magazine offering the materials necessary to make ricin and instructions on how to make the toxin.

In February, 2004, ricin was detected in materials in the Washington, D.C., mail office of U.S. Senate Majority Leader Bill Frist. Three buildings were closed while investigations and tests for contamination were completed, and no human poisonings occurred. The case remains unsolved. Other cases involving small amounts of apparently homemade ricin made the news in the United States in 2006 and 2008, illustrating the relative ease with which this substance can be produced.

Forensic Detection of Ricin

Forensic techniques for the detection of ricin include the use of lateral-flow immunochromatographic devices for on-site detection as well as enzyme-linked immunosorbent assays in the laboratory. Other methods that have been employed for ricin detection and quantification, as it is a protein, include conventional amino acid sequencing and extremely sensitive and specific mass spectrometry techniques.

Oluseyi A. Vanderpuye

Further Reading

Audi, Jennifer, et al. "Ricin Poisoning; A Comprehensive Review." *Journal of the American Medical Association* 294, no. 18 (2005): 2342-2351. Focuses on the medical treatment of ricin poisoning.

Bullock, Jane, and George Haddow. *Introduction to Homeland Security*. 2d ed. Boston: Butterworth-Heinemann, 2006. Provides an informative overview of security measures, including coverage of issues relevant to protection against biological and chemical warfare agents.

Cook, David, Jonathan David, and Gareth Griffiths. "Retrospective Identification of Ricin in Animal Tissues Following Administration by Pulmonary and Oral Routes." *Toxicology* 223 (2006): 61-70. Discusses techniques used during death investigations for detecting ricin in different body fluids and organs.

Greenberg, Michael I. *Encyclopedia of Terrorist, Natural, and Man-Made Disasters*. Sudbury, Mass.: Jones & Bartlett, 2006. Presents examples of criminal uses of biological and chemical weapons.

Keyes, Daniel C., ed. *Medical Response to Terrorism: Preparedness and Clinical Practice*. Philadelphia: Lippincott Williams & Wilkins, 2005. Provides a review of clinical treatments for exposure to biological and chemical agents. Also discusses health care organizations' readiness for responding to terrorist attacks.

Lorberboum-Galski, Haya, and Philip Lazarovici. *Chimeric Toxins: Mechanisms of Action and Therapeutic Applications*. New York: Taylor & Francis. Reviews the research on ricin and many other poisonous substances in the context of their use as parts of medical therapies.

Rappuoli, Rino, and Cesare Montecucco, eds. *Guidebook to Protein Toxins and Their Use in Cell Biology*. New York: Oxford University Press, 1997. Technical handbook describes toxins similar to ricin as well as other classes of poisons derived from biological sources.

See also: Biodetectors; Biological terrorism; Biological weapon identification; Biological Weapons Convention of 1972; Biotoxins; Centers for Disease Control and Prevention; Forensic toxicology; Markov murder; Poisons and antidotes; Toxicological analysis.

Rigor mortis

Definition: Temporary stiffening of the cardiac and skeletal muscles that ensues shortly after death as the result of chemical changes within the muscular tissue. The limbs of the deceased may lock into position and become difficult to manipulate.

Significance: Together with algor mortis (cooling of body temperature) and livor mortis (discoloration from gravitational blood seepage), rigor mortis provides information that is useful in the assessment of time of death. In some cases, rigor mortis may be also useful for helping investigators determine whether bodies have been moved after death.

Rigor mortis (a Latin term meaning "the stiffness of death") was first studied systematically in the nineteenth century. Immediately after a human being dies, the body's muscles become limp, or flaccid. The circular sphincter muscles of the anus, for example, may relax to the point that defecation occurs. After a few hours, however (in some instances after a few minutes), the muscles grow rigid, locking the body into a fixed position. This stiffening occurs when, in the absence of oxygen and nutrients, the body's adenophine triphosphate (ATP) is depleted. This complex chemical energy source is critical for muscular contraction; without it, muscular fibers remain interlocked.

In a temperate climate with an ambient temperature of 70 degrees Fahrenheit, the rigidity of a body ideally proceeds, with some variations, according to chronological parameters. It generally progresses downward following Nysten's law (named for a nineteenth century researcher): It appears first in the small facial muscles (such as the muscles of the eyelids and jaws), then in the upper extremities, and then in the lower extremities. The facial muscles stiffen within thirty minutes to three hours after death; the entire body stiffens within six to twelve hours. After thirty-six hours (again in a temperate climate), rigor mortis tends to disappear in the same downward progression as the body begins to putrefy.

Although this multistaged biochemical process would seem to allow some precision in determining time of death, in fact no competent investigator would use information about rigor mortis in isolation to estimate time of death because the progression of rigor is subject to too many variables. Contrary to popular misconceptions fostered by films and television, observation of rigor mortis stages is one of the least reliable means of determining the postmortem interval; further, such observation is at all useful only before decomposition begins. When investigators base estimations of time of death on the progress of rigor mortis, they do not furnish specific times; rather, they make statements regarding probable intervals.

Cool ambient temperatures retard the progress of rigor mortis, and high temperatures accelerate it. How an individual died can also affect the progress of rigor. For example, if a person kicked at an attacker before dying, the ATP in the legs might be depleted first. Strychnine poisoning induces violent physical convulsions that would quickly deplete the supply of ATP and shorten the time for onset of rigor. Elevated body temperature caused by an infection would also accelerate the process.

David J. Ladouceur

Further Reading

DiMaio, Vincent J., and Dominick DiMaio. *Forensic Pathology*. 2d ed. Boca Raton, Fla.: CRC Press, 2001.

Innes, Brian. *Bodies of Evidence*. Pleasantville, N.Y.: Reader's Digest Association, 2000.

Nickell, Joe, and John F. Fischer. *Crime Science: Methods of Forensic Detection*. Lexington: University Press of Kentucky, 1999.

See also: Adipocere; Algor mortis; Autopsies; Decomposition of bodies; Forensic pathology; Livor mortis; Misconceptions fostered by media; Taphonomy.

Ritual killing

Definition: Murder of a human being as part of a religious, spiritual, or medicinal rite.

Significance: Although ritual killings are rare in the developed nations of the modern world, some traditional medicinal practices in the developing world still call for such practices, and occasional cases related to new religious movements are seen in developed nations. Behavioral profiling is a vital tool to aid investigators in the identification and classification of ritual killing cases. Through the analysis of patterned behaviors and common characteristics found among victims and offenders, law-enforcement investigators can better understand the features of the ritual killing phenomenon.

Ritual killing has been practiced by members of diverse civilizations for thousands of years. Various cultures throughout history have called for human sacrifices as ways to appease deities or ancestral spirits, to attain the support of supernatural forces for worldly gains, or to achieve spiritual transcendence. Such homicides are symbolic acts, and they are carried out in particular ways prescribed by cultural traditions.

Mexico's Aztec people are most infamous for engaging in ritual slaughter, but numerous other ancient cultures prescribed homicide rites to attain material or spiritual ends. In precolonial Borneo, headhunting was believed to ensure fertility and bountiful harvests. In Scandinavia, slave women were occasionally killed so that they could become the wives of recently deceased Viking warriors in the afterlife of Valhalla. Although the Old Testament itself contains numerous references to ancient forms of human sacrifice, the Abrahamic religions' condemnation of human sacrifice has been an important element in the widespread decline of the practice.

In modern times, nearly all religions and cultures have renounced human sacrifice. The few religious adherents who have remained faithful to or recently adopted human sacrifice are con-

Adolfo de Jesús Constanzo, a drug dealer and the leader of a black magic cult in Matamoros, Mexico. He and his followers committed at least twelve ritual murders intended to enable them to become invincible and to evade law-enforcement authorities. (AP/Wide World Photos)

sidered marginal and not representative of their larger communities.

African Medical Murder

Throughout much of southern and western Africa, a type of ritual killing occurs that adherents believe to be medicinal, although the practice is maintained and perpetuated by traditional religious beliefs. *Muti* killing, a term derived from the Zulu word for medicine, is ritual murder in which the vital organs of live victims are removed to be used in sacred medicines created by traditional healers.

Various traditional African medicines are made from animal organs or plants, but the most powerful medicine is considered to be that made from human remains, as the luck of others can be taken and transferred. Adherents be-

lieve that such medicine will bring wealth, success, power, or fertility and ward off drought, illness, and myriad other evils. It is desirable for the organs to be removed from conscious victims, as screams of pain are thought to strengthen the potency of the medicine. As they are necessary for the removal of organs from live individuals, knives are the exclusive weapon of choice. The most common body parts removed are the eyes, head, tongue, genitalia, hands, heart, and breasts. As the explicit purpose is merely to obtain the organs, murder is not a necessary part of the ritual, although the victims nearly always die as a result. Rarely is any effort made to conceal these homicides; the bodies of victims are typically left out in the open near sources of running water.

The most desirable victims are healthy and young, as this is thought to create the most potency. They are most frequently poor, young, indigenous males. Typically, at least three parties are involved in the ritual: the traditional healer, the client seeking assistance from the healer, and the assassin. The killing is set in motion when the client, usually a member of a traditional community, visits a healer for help in achieving some type of personal gain. The client is usually not involved in the murder and purchases the medicine afterward for a substantial fee. The healer prescribes a specific medicine and approaches a third party or parties to commit the crime; the murder is almost never carried out by the healer. Assassins are most likely to be males over thirty years old from lower socioeconomic backgrounds; they typically work together in small teams. The killers, motivated by profit, dedication to tradition, or both, often know their victims and may even be related to them.

Ritual Killing in Developed Nations

Law-enforcement personnel in developed nations are often unfamiliar with the practices of ritual killing and thus do not know how to go about investigating crimes that appear to include elements of ritual. In some cases, the nature of bodily dismemberment may allow investigators to determine whether or not a ritual killing has taken place, and offender profiling and victimology (study of victims' behavior) may be instrumental in their assessment of possible suspects.

Although ritual homicide and suicide are rare in developed nations, some marginal religious movements have engaged in these practices in order to accomplish material or spiritual ends. In 1997, for example, thirty-nine members of the Heaven's Gate religious cult committed mass suicide because they believed that they would be transported to a "level beyond human" as a result. It may be argued that the 1978 deaths of more than nine hundred members of Jim Jones's People's Temple in Jonestown, Guyana, constituted a form of ritual killing, as some of those who died committed suicide willingly by ingesting a poisoned fruit-flavored drink and others were forced to drink the liquid or were shot.

Ritual killings in the name of demoniac spirits have also occurred in the West. One such case involved murders committed by a drug-dealing so-called black magic cult in Matamoros, Mexico, in 1989. Charismatic leader Adolfo de Jesús Constanzo and his followers committed numerous ritual murders intended to enable them to become invincible and evade law-enforcement authorities. Body parts of the group's victims were found floating in a ceremonial pot along with dead spiders and scorpions.

In the United States, the concept of ritual killing is perhaps most commonly associated with satanic cults, which have been alleged to have established organized networks that engage in ceremonies in which victims (often children) are brainwashed, abused, and killed. Claims of such widespread ritual abuse remain unsubstantiated, however, and most authorities believe that descriptions of so-called satanic cults have been greatly exaggerated. Although an organization known as the Church of Satan exists, its theology rejects both animal and human sacrifice.

Eric Madfis

Further Reading

Adinkrah, Mensah. "Ritual Homicides in Contemporary Ghana." *International Journal of Comparative Criminology* 5 (2005): 29-59. Examines twenty-four cases of ritual murder committed in Ghana between 1990 and 2000 and discusses socioeconomic influences, demographics, motivations, and general patterns of the crimes.

Green, Miranda. *Dying for the Gods: Human Sacrifice in Iron Age and Roman Europe.* Charleston, S.C.: Tempus, 2002. Analyzes the reasons for and functions of human sacrifice throughout much of ancient history. Includes descriptive case studies.

Labuschagne, Gerard. "Features and Investigative Implications of *Muti* Murder in South Africa." *Journal of Investigative Psychology and Offender Profiling* 1 (2004): 191-206. A South African police commander details the offender and victim characteristics associated with *muti* murder and provides guidelines for investigating this crime.

Richardson, James T., Joel Best, and David G. Bromley, eds. *The Satanism Scare.* New York: Aldine de Gruyter, 1991. Excellent reader presents discussion of the social construction of the fear of Satanism and satanic ritual abuse in the United States.

See also: Child abduction and kidnapping; Crime scene investigation; Homicide; Suicide; Victimology.

Sacco and Vanzetti case

Dates: Murder committed April 15, 1920; Sacco and Vanzetti executed August 23, 1927

The Event: After two Italian immigrants were charged with murder, ballistics evidence played an important role in their prosecution.

Significance: The guilt or innocence of Nicola Sacco and Bartolomeo Vanzetti continues to be a subject of ongoing discussion, as is the forensic evidence presented at their trial and retested several times thereafter.

On April 15, 1920, in a small town near Boston, the paymaster and a security guard at a shoe factory were shot and robbed of more than $15,000. On May 5, 1920, two Italian immigrants, Nicola Sacco and Bartolomeo Vanzetti, were arrested for the crime; the two were carrying guns. When they were eventually indicted for the murder of the guard, Alessandro Berardelli, twentieth century America's most notorious political trial was set in motion. The trial of Sacco and Vanzetti took place in the midst of the Red Scare, when federal and state authorities in the United States moved aggressively against any signs of radical political activity.

The Trial

Sacco and Vanzetti's trial opened in Dedham, Massachusetts, on May 31, 1921. By far the most controversial evidence presented in the case was that dealing with guns and bullets; the trial became a battle of the experts as testimony was presented on both sides about the new field of forensics encompassing ballistics and firearms identification.

The prosecution presented expert testimony concerning one of the four bullets (designated bullet III) found in the body of Berardelli. No one disputed that the bullet had been fired from a Colt automatic or that Sacco was arrested carrying a Colt automatic. The prosecution's key witness, Captain William Proctor, testified that bullet III was "consistent with being fired from that [Sacco's] pistol." (Two years later, however, after he allegedly had a dispute with the prosecutor, Proctor provided an affidavit to the defense stating that he found no evidence that bullet III had actually been fired from Sacco's gun.) The defense presented testimony from two ballistics experts who challenged the prosecution's expert's testimony. (Years later, however, one of the defense experts changed his testimony and said that a shell casing found at the scene was fired from Sacco's gun.)

The Verdict

On July 14, 1921, after five and one-half hours of deliberations, the jury returned guilty verdicts against both defendants, and Sacco and Vanzetti were subsequently sentenced to death. The convictions immediately prompted protests in the United States as well as in France and Italy, and posttrial legal motions and appeals continued for years.

A key defense motion for a new trial alleged that Captain Proctor, by arrangement with the prosecution, had given intentionally misleading testimony. The defense claimed that despite Proctor's testimony that bullet III was "consistent" with having been fired from Sacco's Colt, Proctor had confided earlier to the district attorney that he did not believe the bullet came from the defendant's gun. The trial judge denied this motion, and his ruling was upheld by the Massachusetts Supreme Court in 1926.

After being overwhelmed by pleas for clemency for Sacco and Vanzetti, Massachusetts governor Alvan T. Fuller appointed a three-person advisory commission to investigate the case. The commission hired Colonel Calvin Goddard, a pioneer in the field of ballistics who had written a seminal article titled "Forensic Ballistics" in which he described a new method of firearms investigation. This technique employed the comparison microscope developed by Goddard's colleague Philip O. Gravelle, which allowed for simultaneous microscopic side-by-side comparisons of two objects.

In the presence of one of the ballistics experts who had testified for the defense, Goddard fired a bullet from Sacco's gun and then used a comparison microscope to examine the ejected casing next to each of the casings found at the scene of the crime. The first two casings from the crime scene did not match Sacco's gun, but the third one did. Both of the defense experts agreed that the two cartridges had been fired from the same gun.

When the commission concluded that Sacco and Vanzetti were guilty beyond a reasonable doubt, Governor Fuller denied them clemency. Last-ditch appeals to the Massachusetts and U.S. Supreme Courts failed, and on August 23, 1927, the two men were executed. Both continued to proclaim their innocence to the very end.

The Aftermath

In October, 1961, forty years after Sacco and Vanzetti's trial, the Massachusetts State Police Laboratory examined the ballistics evidence using techniques much improved over those available earlier and concluded that bullet III was in fact fired from Sacco's Colt automatic. Critics, however, noted that these results meant nothing if bullet III was substituted years before to frame the defendants.

In 1982, Professor Regis Pelloux of the Massachusetts Institute of Technology conducted new tests in which he compared bullet III with the other three bullets found in Berardelli's body. He found both differences and similarities but concluded that the differences could be explained by deformation that occurred as the bullets entered the victim's body. In 1983, renowned forensic scientist Henry C. Lee demon-

Bartolomeo Vanzetti (left) and Nicola Sacco, manacled together and surrounded by guards and onlookers, approaching the Massachusetts courthouse where they were sentenced to death in 1921. Appeals challenging the validity of the expert testimony used against them delayed their executions until 1927. (Library of Congress)

strated that the six Peters cartridges taken from Sacco when he was arrested were made on the same machine that made the two Peters fired cartridge cases found at the crime scene. In 1988, a reporter for the *Boston Globe* newspaper disclosed that a police sergeant had admitted that the prosecution's ballistics experts had switched the murder weapon.

Some scholars have continued to dispute the conclusiveness of the ballistics evidence in this case, asserting that bullet III might have been planted by prosecutors. Others have pointed out that bullet III matched perfectly with the autopsy report on the victim. Those who believe the defendants were correctly convicted have argued that if the prosecution witnesses had been part of a conspiracy to frame Sacco, they would not have been so restrained in their testimony; some have also asserted that the prosecutor would have been highly unlikely to jeopardize his entire career by falsifying evidence in the case.

Stephen F. Rohde

Further Reading

Frankfurter, Felix. *The Case of Sacco and Vanzetti: A Critical Analysis for Lawyers and Laymen*. 1927. Reprint. Buffalo, N.Y.: William S. Hein, 2003. Classic work by the future U.S. Supreme Court justice makes the case for a new trial by carefully marshaling evidence of unfairness at the trial and pointing to others as possible perpetrators of the crime.

Russell, Francis. *Sacco and Vanzetti: The Case Resolved*. New York: Harper & Row, 1986. Updated examination of the case defends the author's first book (cited below) against the onslaught of criticism it received from supporters of the defendants. Argues that Vanzetti was an accessory after the fact.

_____. *Tragedy in Dedham: The Story of the Sacco-Vanzetti Case*. New York: McGraw-Hill, 1962. Initial work of one of the preeminent proponents of the view that Sacco was guilty but Vanzetti was either innocent or marginally involved.

Topp, Michael M. *The Sacco and Vanzetti Case: A Brief History with Documents*. New York: Palgrave Macmillan, 2005. Places the case in its historical context by providing documents from the time. Includes an informative introduction and a chronology of the case.

Young, William and David E. Kaiser. *Postmortem: New Evidence in the Case of Sacco and Vanzetti*. Amherst: University of Massachusetts Press, 1985. Comprehensive critique of the evidence against Sacco and Vanzetti takes full advantage of the forensic techniques developed in the years after the case. Advances the theory that bullet III was fraudulently substituted to frame the defendants.

See also: Ballistic fingerprints; Ballistics; Chain of custody; Firearms analysis; Microscopes.

Saliva

Definition: Complex fluid mixture secreted from the salivary glands into the mouth or oral cavity.

Significance: Saliva is an extremely useful tool in many forensic applications, in part because collection of saliva samples is relatively simple and noninvasive. Even small samples of saliva will yield the blood types of the donors as well as DNA for comparative purposes.

Saliva contains water, electrolytes, mucus (consisting of mucopolysaccharides and glycoproteins), various enzymes, and opiorphin, a painkilling substance. Saliva has many functions in the human body. It aids digestion by moistening food, binding it together so that it may be more effectively chewed. It also lubricates food, permitting swallowing and easy passage of food down the esophagus, thereby minimizing irritation of the lining of the oral cavity. The salivary enzyme amylase initiates digestion of carbohydrates such as starch, and the mix of saliva with molecules in food and liquid aids tasting, as the molecules more readily interact with taste buds located on the tongue.

Saliva aids oral hygiene by flushing food

debris from the mouth. It contains the enzyme lysozyme, which destroys many bacteria, thereby acting as a disinfectant; however, many pathogenic bacteria can thrive in the mouths of humans and other animals. Saliva also functions as a protective barrier, as when nausea reflexively triggers saliva flow, which coats the oral lining and teeth before vomiting occurs so that acidity is minimized.

The amount and type of saliva secretion is controlled by the autonomic nervous system. Increased stimulation leads to increased blood flow to the salivary glands, which stimulates production and release of saliva. Sympathetic stimulation results in an increased amount of mucus in the saliva, and parasympathetic stimulation results in increased volume of watery saliva production (serous saliva).

Saliva samples are often important in criminal investigations. Collection of saliva is relatively simple and noninvasive, and only a small amount is needed for determination of an individual's blood type and for extraction of DNA (deoxyribonucleic acid) for comparisons. Saliva can also reveal the drugs an individual has taken; in some cases, even simple contact with certain drugs can be detected through analysis of saliva.

Saliva samples also permit evaluation of general health, and saliva tests have been developed for the detection of certain medical ailments, such as human immunodeficiency virus (HIV), and other health problems. Saliva samples that reveal the presence of viral, bacterial, or systematic diseases may link their donors to crime scenes or to objects.

Dwight G. Smith

Further Reading

Idowu, O. R., and B. Caddy. "A Review of the Use of Saliva in the Forensic Detection of Drugs and Other Chemicals. *Journal of the Forensic Science Society* 22 (1982): 123-135.

Mandel, I. D. "The Diagnostic Uses of Saliva." *Journal of Oral Pathology and Medicine* 19 (1990): 119-125.

Sweet, D., and D. Hildebrand. "Saliva from Cheese Bite Yields DNA Profile of Burglar: A Case Report." *International Journal of Legal Medicine* 112 (April, 1999): 201-203.

Walsh, D. J., et al. "Isolation of Deoxyribonucleic Acid (DNA) from Saliva and Forensic Science Samples Containing Saliva." *Journal of Forensic Sciences* 37 (1992): 387-395.

See also: Bite-mark analysis; DNA analysis; DNA extraction from hair, bodily fluids, and tissues; DNA isolation methods; DNA recognition instruments; Evidence processing; Hantavirus; Oral autopsy; Serology.

Sarin

Definition: Highly toxic liquid substance used as a chemical weapon.

Significance: Concerns that terrorists could employ sarin in chemical attacks have increased law-enforcement agencies' attention to this substance. The United Nations classifies sarin as a weapon of mass destruction.

Sarin was discovered in the 1930's during a search for new insecticides. Its extreme toxicity to humans led to its development as a chemical weapon by Nazi Germany and other nations, and huge quantities were manufactured and stored. In the 1980's and later, sarin was used several times in warfare and in terrorist attacks. The United Nations Chemical Weapons Convention of 1993 bans the manufacture and storage of chemical weapons including sarin, which is also known as isopropyl methylphosphonofluoridate or GB. Various nations— including the United States and Russia—have been gradually destroying stockpiles of munitions with sarin in accordance with the Chemical Weapons Convention. The United States has taken significant steps to provide members of its armed forces with means of protection from sarin attacks.

Toxic Effects

A so-called nerve gas, sarin is one of several chemical agents that exert toxic effects through the ability to bind to and inactivate the vital enzyme acetylcholinesterase (AChE). AChE exists in nerves and acts as a catalyst for hydrolysis of acetylcholine, the chemical that is released at nerve endings and that causes muscle contraction. Only a small amount of AChE is present in nerves, but it is very effective in catalyzing the destruction of acetylcholine.

When AChE is inactivated by sarin or a similar nerve agent, the acetylcholine builds up and causes uncontrolled muscle contractions. Symptoms of poisoning by sarin include pain in the eyes, blurred vision, runny nose, incontinence, respiratory failure, convulsions, coma, and death. The eyes are particularly sensitive; the pupils react to sarin by shrinking to pinpoints (meiosis). Sarin absorbed through the skin or inhaled as vapor or aerosol is toxic to different degrees, depending on exposure.

Dispersal

Sarin may be dispersed as a vapor or as an aerosol. The volatility of sarin permits a significant concentration of vapor at ambient temperatures, but this volatility also means that it may not persist in the environment. Toxic concentrations are more effectively achieved in confined spaces.

Aerosol dispersal of sarin, which requires some type of sprayer, can achieve higher concentrations than vapor dispersal. All types of dispersal tend to leave traces of sarin or its degradation products on surfaces, including clothing, from which forensic samples may be obtained for identification.

Detection and Treatment

Methods for the detection of sarin in military situations include test papers, test kits, and electronic devices. The M8 test paper for soldiers is impregnated with three dyes and responds with three color changes characteristic of different classes of chemical warfare agent. The M256A1 test kit contains a simple apparatus for sampling and applying chemical tests. Among more sophisticated methods are those that use small mass spectrometers, about the size of a brick; these devices can sample the ambient air directly and detect individual compounds. Also under development are even smaller detectors that use AchE on a silicon chip or compounds with fluorescence that reacts to nerve agents.

Treatment of sarin poisoning follows removal of the victim from contaminated clothing and all other contact with the toxic substance. Atropine may be given by injection to provide some relief from symptoms, as it inhibits binding of excess acetylcholine at some receptors. Diazepam may be administered to control the muscular spasms caused by the nerve agent, and pralidoxime methanesulfonate (P2S) is helpful in removing it from AChE.

Prophylaxis consists of drugs administered before sarin exposure occurs to increase resistance and reduce

Terror Attacks in Japan

In November, 1994, members of the religious movement Aum Shinrikyo sprayed sarin aerosol near a pond in a park in the city of Matsumoto in Japan. Sarin's precursor chemicals, such as isopropanol, trimethylphosphite, methyl iodide, and sodium fluoride, have legitimate industrial uses, and in 1994 it was possible for individuals to purchase these materials openly (access to many has since been restricted). The cult members had obtained chemicals sufficient to prepare sarin in quantity. In the Matsumoto attack, 5 people were killed and 274 were injured. The police were initially unsure what had happened, but eventually forensic investigators detected sarin in the water of the pond.

A few months later, on March 20, 1995, Aum Shinrikyo carried out a sarin attack on three major lines of the Tokyo subway system; the terrorists boarded subway trains and punctured plastic bags of impure sarin. This time it took police investigators only two hours to collect a sample and identify sarin using the method of gas chromatography-mass spectrometry (GC-MS). The attack killed 12 people and injured thousands. The dead exhibited extreme lividity, bronchial congestion, meiosis, and pulmonary edema. Some victims showed reduced cholinesterase activity in the blood. This attack stimulated research on forensic methods for detecting nerve agents and on possible courses of treatment for poisoning by such agents.

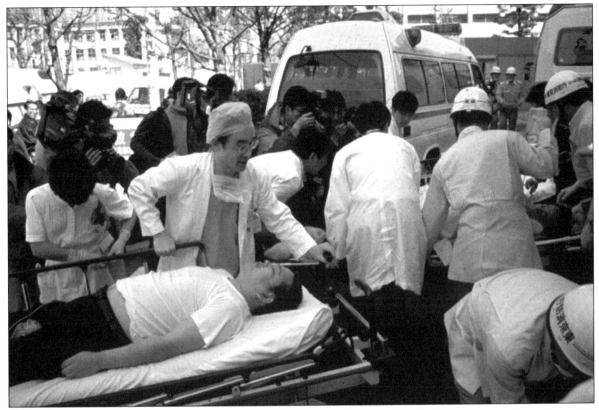

Tokyo subway passengers arrive at a hospital after being injured by sarin gas that was released in the subway system by members of the Aum Shinrikyo cult on March 20, 1995. The attack killed twelve and injured thousands. *(AP/Wide World Photos)*

the severity of possible symptoms. Among the drugs used are atropine and pyridostigmine bromide.

John R. Phillips

Further Reading

Croddy, Eric A., with Clarisa Perez-Armendariz and John Hart. *Chemical and Biological Warfare: A Comprehensive Survey for the Concerned Citizen.* New York: Copernicus Books, 2002. Addresses the uses of sarin and other nerve agents as weapons.

Marrs, Timothy C., Robert L. Maynard, and Frederick R. Sidell, eds. *Chemical Warfare Agents: Toxicology and Treatment.* 2d ed. Hoboken, N.J.: John Wiley & Sons, 2007. Presents a technical discussion of the factors affecting the toxicity of agents. Includes description of tests done with sarin on volunteers.

Mauroni, Al. *Chemical and Biological Warfare: A Reference Handbook.* 2d ed. Santa Barbara, Calif.: ABC-CLIO, 2007. Comprehensive survey of chemical and biological weapons includes a valuable annotated bibliography that includes citations to Internet sites.

Suzuki, Osamu, and Kanako Watanabe, eds. *Drugs and Poisons in Humans: A Handbook of Practical Analysis.* New York: Springer, 2005. Collection of highly technical articles discusses analytic techniques. Includes information on procedures for the analysis of sarin and its degradation products through gas chromatography and mass spectrometry.

Tucker, Jonathan B., ed. *Toxic Terror: Assessing Terrorist Use of Chemical and Biological Weapons.* Cambridge, Mass.: MIT Press, 2000. Presents twelve case studies of the use of chemical and biological agents by terrorist groups, identifying terrorists' patterns of behavior and strategies to combat them.

White, Peter, ed. *Crime Scene to Court: The Es-*

sentials of Forensic Science. 2d ed. Cambridge, England: Royal Society of Chemistry, 2004. General work provides good discussion of forensic science principles.

See also: Analytical instrumentation; Chemical agents; Chemical terrorism; Chemical warfare; Chemical Weapons Convention of 1993; Nerve agents; Nervous system; Soman.

Satellite surveillance technology

Definition: Commercially owned and operated Earth-orbiting satellites capable of producing high-resolution photographs of the ground from space.

Significance: Most surveillance requires either the person doing the surveillance or the equipment used to be in proximity to the target being watched, so there is risk that the target will become aware of the surveillance. The use of satellite technology, however, enables law-enforcement and other agencies to conduct surveillance that is undetectable by the targets.

Shortly after the first artificial satellites were placed into Earth orbit, plans were made for surveillance satellites. Such spy satellites were used by the military and intelligence agencies of national governments to monitor the activities of other nations from space. Commercial uses for imaging satellites eventually led to the development of remote-sensing satellites capable of monitoring land usage. With advances in technology, commercial satellites have been created with capabilities far in excess of those held by military satellites of only several years ago. Modern commercial satellites are capable of capturing images with resolutions of one meter (a little more than three feet) or less, meaning that they are capable of distinguishing between objects at least one meter apart.

The proliferation of high-resolution commercial satellites has led to a market for the data

they collect. Several police agencies in the United States have contracted to use Digital-Globe's QuickBird satellites to acquire high-resolution images. This type of surveillance can provide police with information such as the approximate numbers of people involved in suspected gang or drug-trafficking activities and their patterns of movement. Satellite-captured images can also provide law-enforcement agencies with information on the locations of fences, walls, trees, vehicles, and other obstacles in particular areas, which can be very useful, for example, when special weapons and tactics (SWAT) teams are preparing for raids. Alternative methods of surveillance, such as by aircraft, could alert suspects to police activity and potentially put officers at risk. Satellite surveillance also enables federal authorities to monitor national borders in remote regions that are difficult to monitor in other ways.

Commercial satellite technology began as remote sensing to monitor land usage, and law-enforcement agencies still use satellites for this purpose: to look for cultivated fields of marijuana or other controlled substances. Such surveillance can also be done by aircraft, but a single satellite can cover more area in more locations than a small fleet of aircraft. Also, satellites offer complete stealth surveillance, whereas aircraft can often be heard or spotted by persons on the ground. In addition, unlike aircraft, which must be fueled and flown on specific missions, satellites are always on duty. All that authorities need is to access the images.

Some privacy advocates have challenged law-enforcement agencies' uses of satellite surveillance as violations of the right to protection from unlawful searches guaranteed in the Fourth Amendment to the U.S. Constitution. Most law-enforcement agencies, however, argue that surveillance through satellite images does not require warrants. So far, the courts have permitted warrantless satellite surveillance.

Raymond D. Benge, Jr.

Further Reading

Bamford, James. "Big Brother Is Tracking You. Without a Warrant." *The New York Times*, May 18, 2003, p. 140.

Jasani, Bhupendra, and Gotthard Stein, eds. *Commercial Satellite Imagery: A Tactic in Nuclear Weapon Deterrence.* New York: Springer, 2002.

Peterson, Julie K. *Understanding Surveillance Technologies: Spy Devices, Their Origins, and Applications.* Boca Raton, Fla.: CRC Press, 2001.

See also: Closed-circuit television surveillance; Federal Rules of Evidence; Flight data recorders; Forensic photography; Geographic information system technology; Imaging; Night vision devices.

Scanning electron microscopy

Definition: Technique in which a high-powered scanning electron beam is used to achieve high-resolution imaging of microscopic samples.

Significance: Forensic scientists are often asked to compare various kinds of materials to determine whether the materials have a common origin. Scanning electron microscopy allows analysts to view samples at high magnification so that they can compare the surface characteristics of the samples to see if they are consistent with each other.

The scanning electron microscope was invented in 1938 by Manfred von Ardenne. The instrument is capable of distinguishing objects that are 3 nanometers apart, compared with 200 nanometers for simple light microscopes. Because of this, scanning electron microscopy (SEM) can be used for imaging and comparing very small surface characteristics.

In forensic science, SEM is typically used for comparing known samples to unknown samples recovered from crime scenes. SEM can be used to compare virtually any kind of materials, but in forensic laboratories it is most commonly used for imaging tool marks, fibers, minerals, soil samples, and gunshot residue.

The scanning electron microscope consists of an electron gun mounted atop a series of electromagnetic lenses and scanning coils, a sample holder, and a detector. The electron gun produces a high-powered electron beam that is focused by condenser lenses and scanned back and forth across the sample being imaged. The beam penetrates into the sample and causes the

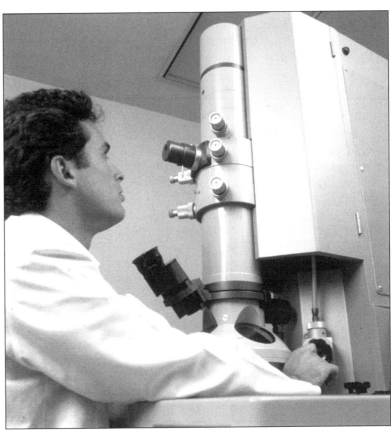

A technician uses a scanning electron microscope to examine a sample. *(Custom Medical Stock Photo)*

production of four things: low-energy secondary electrons (SEs), backscatter electrons (BSEs), X rays, and heat. The SEs are ejected from just under the surface of the sample, enter the detector, and are converted electronically to an image of the sample surface. Flat areas of the sample appear dark, and elevated areas appear lighter.

Some instruments also contain backscatter detectors that produce images using BSEs. These images have lower resolution than SE images but they are unique in that in these images heavier compounds appear brighter than lighter compounds. For example, a mixture of calcium carbonate and magnesium carbonate would appear simply as small grains when viewed in SE mode, but when viewed in BSE mode, the grains of calcium carbonate would appear brighter because calcium is a heavier element than magnesium.

SEM is often coupled with energy-dispersive spectroscopy (EDS), which provides an elemental profile of the section of the sample being viewed. This is especially useful for comparisons of items that look the same under SE mode, such as two pieces of paper. An analyst who is trying to determine whether two pieces of paper are consistent with each other may first view the two samples under SEM. If they appear different, the samples can be said to be inconsistent. If the samples appear similar, the analyst could perform EDS to see if the samples contain all the same trace elements. It may be found, for example, that one piece of paper has trace amounts of copper in it and the other does not. In that case, the two samples may be determined inconsistent even if they appear similar under SEM.

Lisa LaGoo

Further Reading

Flegler, Stanley S., John S. Heckman, and Karen L. Klomparens. *Scanning and Transmission Microscopy: An Introduction*. New York: Oxford University Press, 1993.

Goldstein, Joseph, et al. *Scanning Electron Microscopy and X-Ray Microanalysis*. 3d ed. New York: Kluwer Academic/Plenum, 2003.

Li, Zhigang R. *Industrial Applications of Electron Microscopy*. New York: Marcel Dekker, 2003.

See also: Analytical instrumentation; Document examination; Energy-dispersive spectroscopy; Fax machine, copier, and printer analysis; Fibers and filaments; Geological materials; Gunshot residue; Imaging; Microscopes; Paint; Paper; Tool marks; Trace and transfer evidence.

Scent identification

Definition: Use of specially trained dogs to identify particular persons by their unique odors.

Significance: In some cases, criminal investigators use trained scent identification dogs to connect crime scene evidence with suspects.

The canine sense of smell can be as much as ten thousand times more sensitive than the human sense of smell, and dogs' ability to discriminate among odors is sometimes useful during criminal investigations. Traditionally, police have used canines' olfactory skills to track or trail criminal suspects as well as missing persons. Dogs can track a person by following indicators of a fresh track, such as the odors of crushed vegetation and disturbed ground. To trail an individual, a dog needs a scent sample of the quarry.

A trailing dog uses the scent of a known person to identify that person's location. If presented with the scent of an unknown person, a trained dog can identify that person in a crowd. This is the basis of scent identification.

Human Scent

Research has shown that humans have stable and unique odor profiles and that dogs can be trained to recognize unique scents in mixtures of other odors. Studies with bloodhounds indicate that genetics plays a key role in determining the uniqueness of a person's scent. Although dogs can discriminate among members of human families, identical twins, who essentially have the same genes, pose a problem for dogs. It has been suggested that a human's scent profile, or "odortype," may be determined by the expression of genes in the major histocompatibility complex, the genes that also control immune responses through recognition of "self" and "nonself."

Other elements that may contribute to the uniqueness of an individual's scent include nutrition, hygiene, and state of health. Such secondary factors may become significant if a dog must distinguish between identical twins.

Studies with Dutch and German scent identification dogs have found that the age of a scent sample affects a dog's performance. Dogs faultlessly matched odors collected on the same day of the testing, but they made mistakes when presented with scent samples that had been stored for two weeks. After this initial drop in performance level, the dogs' accuracy remained steady even with scent evidence up to six months old. These results show that scent has a volatile component.

Using gas chromatography-mass spectrometry, scientists have analyzed the volatile components of human odor signatures. They have found that the distinctiveness of humans' scents arises from a combination of common compounds that differ in amounts from person to person. In addition, they have discovered that some compounds are unique to certain people.

The Federal Bureau of Investigation (FBI) has supported bloodhound research workshops in which the durability of human scent has been examined. One study showed that a dog could use the scent of a mailed letter to locate the letter writer's house six months after the person had moved out of the house. Another study found that bloodhounds could detect human scent on bomb fragments and identify the individual who had handled the bomb before it exploded.

The Scent Identification Lineup

The durability of human scent can combine with the sensitivity of the canine nose to allow criminal investigators to link a suspect and crime scene evidence in a scent identification lineup. This technique is relatively new to law-enforcement agencies in the United States, but it has become established in Europe. The Netherlands National Police Agency, for example, has formulated a protocol for the scent lineup that is accepted by the Dutch courts.

The basic Dutch police scent lineup proceeds as follows. A scent identification dog and its han-dler enter a test room that contains six stainless-steel scent-carrier tubes, each 10 centimeters (about 4 inches) long, clamped to platforms; one of these tubes has been handled by a suspect, and the other five have been handled by adults who are not associated with the suspect. After several quality-assurance tests are conducted, the suspect identification stage begins with the dog sniffing a scent evidence object collected from the scene of the crime. The dog then smells the scent-carrier tubes. If the dog picks the scent-carrier tube handled by the suspect in two tests, the police conclude that the scent evidence object and the suspect share an "odor similarity."

The scent lineup protocol requires that the dog's handler be unaware of who touched the scent-carrier tubes. This protects the findings from being invalidated by the possibility that the handler gave any nonverbal, or even unconscious, suggestion to the dog.

Scent Identification Evidence in U.S. Courts

The identification of a person by scent has an important limitation: Scent can be transferred from one person or object to another. Although scent identification can establish a direct or indirect link between an individual and crime scene evidence, it cannot prove that the individual participated in a crime.

In the United States, scent identification is usually not considered to be enough evidence to justify an arrest. Rather, a scent identification is viewed as one indicator of reasonable suspicion. Investigators must seek corroboration of a scent identification to meet the standard of probable cause before they can arrest the identified person.

Judges in the United States have expressed different opinions about the admissibility of scent lineup evidence. In some jurisdictions, judges view scent identification as sufficiently reliable to be presented during trial, whereas judges in other jurisdictions require the presentation of scientific evidence that every person has a scent so unique that it provides an accurate basis for identification. Although judges disagree about the scientific proof of reliability, scent identification offers a valuable tool for criminal investigation.

Phill Jones

Further Reading

Harvey, Lisa M., et al. "The Use of Bloodhounds in Determining the Impact of Genetics and the Environment on the Expression of Human Odortype." *Journal of Forensic Sciences* 51, no. 5 (2006): 1109-1114. Reports on research findings that indicate bloodhounds rely primarily on genetically determined cues when differentiating among humans.

Harvey, Lisa M., and Jeffrey W. Harvey. "Reliability of Bloodhounds in Criminal Investigations." *Journal of Forensic Sciences* 48, no. 4 (2003): 811-816. Examines the bloodhound's ability to trail and to discriminate among the scents of different humans.

Schoon, Adee, and Ruud Haak. *K9 Suspect Discrimination.* Calgary, Alta.: Detselig Enterprises, 2002. Discusses methods for training scent identification dogs and presents a history of canine scent detection in police investigations.

Syrotuck, William G. *Scent and the Scenting Dog.* 4th ed. Mechanicsburg, Pa.: Barkleigh Productions, 2000. Explores the canine sense of smell and discusses the challenges faced by scent identification dogs.

Tomaszewski, Tadeusz, and Piotr Girdwoyn. "Scent Identification Evidence in Jurisdiction." *Forensic Science International* 162, nos. 1-3 (2006): 191-195. Presents a survey of scent identification practices in the United States, the Netherlands, Germany, and Poland.

See also: Buried body locating; Cadaver dogs; Canine substance detection; Cross-contamination of evidence; Physical evidence.

Secret Service, U.S.

Date: Established on July 5, 1865

Identification: Federal agency created to combat counterfeit currency throughout the United States after the Civil War. After 1902, the agency's expanded mission included protective details for U.S. presidents and vice presidents and their families; it later began to offer protection to U.S. presidential candidates as well as to foreign dignitaries.

Significance: One of the oldest federal law-enforcement agencies in the United States, the Secret Service has shut down many illegal money operations and has investigated numerous other forms of fraud in addition to carrying out its widely known function of protecting past and current presidents, vice presidents, and their families.

The U.S. Secret Service was founded on July 5, 1865, as a law-enforcement bureau of the U.S. Department of the Treasury with the mission of combating counterfeiting and the distribution of fake treasury notes and currencies. During the nineteenth century, the federal government's systems for creating, distributing, and tracking currency were in disarray, inviting fraud and other illegal activities. Throughout the early nineteenth century, each U.S. state had at least one version of its own exclusive coin and paper currencies. In fact, during this time, it was rumored that more than one-third of all paper currency in circulation in the United States was counterfeit.

During its first thirty years, the Secret Service investigated and closed down countless illegal money operations throughout the continental United States. Aside from targeting numerous counterfeiting scandals, the agency began to investigate various cases that fell outside the duties outlined in its initial charter. Throughout the history of the Secret Service, numerous U.S. presidents have ordered the agency to investigate both individuals and groups suspected of involvement with many kinds of fraud and other activities deemed threatening to the government or the general public; the subjects of such investigations have ranged from members of the U.S. government to individual American citizens. Among those most frequently investigated by the Secret Service have been groups known for their antigovernment rhetoric; the Ku Klux Klan is a notable example.

Investigation

The primary investigative mission of the Secret Service continues to be focused on crimes that deal specifically with counterfeiting; these include crimes involving nonfinancial federal documents as well as money and finance-related documents. Since the early 1980's, however, Congress has expanded the investigative responsibilities of the Secret Service, which now include the investigation of credit card fraud, crimes involving forgery, various forms of cybercrime, crimes related to American financial institutions, money laundering (both domestic and international), and major cases of identity theft. The Secret Service is the only federal agency that Congress has explicitly designated as having investigative jurisdiction over major identity theft cases.

In 2000, following the Columbine High School massacre in 1999, the Secret Service added the investigation of major incidents of school violence in the United States to its traditional duties of fighting counterfeiting and other financially related crimes. The assess-

---

Forensic Services of the Secret Service

The U.S. Secret Service provides the following information about the agency's forensic services.

The U.S. Secret Service is home to an advanced forensic laboratory, which includes the world's largest ink library. Secret Service forensic analysts examine evidence, develop investigative leads and provide expert courtroom testimony. . . .

Forensic examiners analyze questioned documents, fingerprints, false identification documents, credit cards, and other related forensic science areas. Examiners also are responsible for coordinating photographic and graphic production, as well as video, audio, and image enhancement services. Much of the technology and techniques utilized by examiners is exclusive to the U.S. Secret Service. . . .

The forensic services utilized by the Secret Service include a number of specialties:

- **Identification:** The Secret Service has access to a full range of fingerprint-related services using the most up-to-date chemical and physical methods, including the utilization of state-of-the-art equipment for the development of latent prints. Specialists provide technical expertise and training in all fingerprint-related matters to the Secret Service field offices and other law enforcement agencies. They also provide expert testimony in federal, state, and local courts.
- **Forensic Automation:** Forensic automation analysts provide advanced automated/computer support to all U.S. Secret Service protective and investigative elements, as well as for outside requests that have

originated within Secret Service field offices. This responsibility is computer intensive and utilizes internal and external networks to identify fingerprints, handwriting, counterfeit identity documents, and financial documents. . . .
- **Polygraph:** The Secret Service has distinguished itself as having one of the premier polygraph programs in existence. Highly trained personnel use their skills and the latest technology available to enhance U.S. Secret Service protective missions, criminal investigations, and hiring needs. The examiners assigned to the program are considered experts in the psychology of deception and provide investigative expertise for all cases under the agency's jurisdiction. . . .
- **Questioned Documents:** The Secret Service has long been recognized as one of the foremost questioned document laboratories in the world. The primary goal of analysts is to support field investigations by providing expert forensic analyses of evidence developed during investigations, writing reports of the scientific findings, and providing subsequent expert testimony in court proceedings. . . .
- **Visual Information:** The Secret Service utilizes a unique blend of technologies providing expertise in forensic photography, graphic arts, multimedia operations, audio/image enhancement, voice identification, and 3-D modeling and simulation.

---

ment of threats of school violence also became a high priority for the Secret Service.

Protection

In 1901, after William McKinley became the victim of the third presidential assassination in U.S. history, Congress made an informal request for Secret Service agents to provide protection for U.S. presidents, and in 1902 the agency took on the full-time responsibility of protecting the president. It was not until 1906, however, that Congress passed a federal law that made protection of the president of the United States a major duty of the Secret Service and provided funds for that purpose. In 1917, another law added Secret Service protection for the president's immediate family and made it a federal offense for anyone to make verbal or written threats against a president or any member of the president's family.

The protective role of the Secret Service has grown a great deal since its inauguration. Two divisions of Secret Service personnel are responsible for various protective assignments. One of these is made up of special nonuniformed agents who act as bodyguards for various government officials. These agents all train for years before they are handpicked to receive this duty assignment. The second group consists of uniformed officers who carry out their duties much as do regular police officers. Established in 1922, this uniformed force is a noticeable presence as its members provide security at federal facilities, foreign embassies, the vice president's home, and the White House.

Among those persons for whom the Secret Service provides protection details are the current president and vice president and their immediate families, former presidents (and their spouses) who have been out of office for no more than ten years, all presidential and vice presidential candidates and their families up to 120 days before the general election, U.S. dignitaries acting on behalf of the United States in foreign countries, and foreign ambassadors who are visiting the United States. In addition, the Secret Service provides protection to any other individuals the president considers to be in need of such protection.

Paul M. Klenowski

Further Reading

Johnson, David R. *Illegal Tender: Counterfeiting and the Secret Service in Nineteenth Century America*. Washington, D.C.: Smithsonian Institution Press, 1995. Provides a history of the Secret Service with a focus on the agency's war on counterfeiting.

Melanson, Philip H. *The Secret Service: The Hidden History of an Enigmatic Agency*. Rev. ed. New York: Carroll & Graf, 2005. Revealing and candid history presents an interesting perspective on the Secret Service.

Neal, Harry Edward. *The Secret Service in Action*. New York: Elsevier/Nelson Books, 1980. Provides a detailed look at the role of the Secret Service and how that role changed over the course of the agency's first one hundred years.

Petro, Joseph, with Jeffrey Robinson. *Standing Next to History: An Agent's Life Inside the Secret Service*. New York: Thomas Dunne Books, 2005. Memoir by a former agent allows an interesting glimpse into the workings of the agency.

U.S. Secret Service. *Moments in History, 1865-1990*. Washington, D.C.: Department of the Treasury, 1990. Offers a unique look at the important role of the secret service agent over the years.

See also: Computer crimes; Counterfeit-detection pens; Counterfeiting; Document examination; Forgery; Identity theft; National Crime Information Center.

Semen and sperm

Definitions: Semen is a viscous fluid that results from a combination of secretions from the seminiferous tubules and glands such as the prostate, seminal vesicles, and Cowper's glands. Spermatozoa (sperm) are reproductive cells carrying male genetic material; they are uniquely found in the fluid of semen.

Significance: Semen is one of the most commonly analyzed types of biological evidence collected during criminal investigations, particularly cases involving sexual assault. DNA analysis of semen samples can link suspects to crimes or eliminate innocent persons from suspicion.

In 1677, Dutch scientist Antoni van Leeuwenhoek became the first person to report the observation of spermatozoa under a microscope. Sperm, the reproductive cells that carry male genetic material, are morphologically distinctive in that they are characteristically elongated cells divided into regions called head, midpiece, and tail. The sizes of spermatozoa and shapes of the heads vary among species; in human spermatozoa, the heads are oval in shape.

Composition of Semen

General ranges are known for how many spermatozoa are found in a given volume of semen and the amount of semen typically produced. This information can be applicable in the strategies used for testing biological evidence and for reconstructing events at a crime scene. It can also influence the approach taken to extract and analyze DNA (deoxyribonucleic acid) from a semen stain.

Other cells in semen are epithelial cells from the linings of the male reproductive tract. Although these make up less than 1 percent of the volume of semen, they can be sufficient to make DNA typing possible for semen lacking spermatozoa due to congenital conditions or vasectomy. The spermatozoa are usually the main source of DNA in semen that is tested forensically to provide evidence for the source of the semen. It is of forensic importance that spermatozoa DNA can be extracted under conditions different from those used for other types of cells, because this means that a semen component of DNA can be separated from female DNA, thus making it easier to identify the origin of the semen.

The liquid portion of semen is called seminal plasma; it contains certain organic substances in relatively high concentrations, including ascorbic acid, citric acid, fructose, prostaglandins, phosphoryl choline, spermine, and spermidine. Zinc is an element present in particularly high concentrations in semen relative to other body fluids. Certain proteins are found in higher concentrations in semen than in other sources; the most useful of these in terms of forensic testing are prostatic acid phosphatase, prostate-specific antigen (PSA), and semenogelin.

Detection of Semen and Sperm

As a biological stain, semen survives as evidence detectable by biochemical and DNA typing techniques for several years. The survival of DNA in semen stains has allowed for the analysis of evidence in items more than ten years old. Under a forensic lamp that emits blue light, semen stains and some other body fluids fluoresce, which is helpful in their detection at crime scenes or on evidence such as clothing. Additional tests may then be performed to determine whether given stains are semen.

A commonly used presumptive, or screening, test for semen looks for activity of the enzyme acid phosphatase in stains. Acid phosphatase is found at levels four hundred times higher in semen than in other body fluids. In the presence of acid phosphatase, an acid solution of fast blue and alpha-naphthyl phosphate will turn blue-purple. An investigator may sample a stain by rubbing it with a swab or moist piece of filter paper and then adding a drop of the acid solution to the swab or paper; a positive result produces a blue or purplish color within thirty seconds. Where no stains are visually apparent, an area containing a suspected semen stain can be divided into sectors for systematic searching using the acid phosphatase detection technique. This method is not a conclusive indication of the presence of semen, however; other approaches must be used to identify semen definitively for a court of law.

One confirmatory test for semen relies on the special staining and microscopic observation of spermatozoa. The sample can be taken from a crime victim or from a stain on material such as cloth that has been extracted in water after gentle stirring. A drop of the extract is placed on a microscope slide, processed to cause adherence of any cells to the slide, and stained with picroindigocarmine and fast red. This procedure characteristically stains spermatozoa heads red and midpieces a green to yellow color, leading to the name "Christmas tree stain."

A forensic scientist in the DNA section of the Seattle crime laboratory of the Washington State Patrol tests a shirt for semen. As a biological stain, semen survives as evidence detectable by biochemical and DNA typing techniques for several years. *(AP/Wide World Photos)*

Spermatozoa can remain alive and moving for four to six hours in the living female body. Intact nonmotile spermatozoa may still be found in the female body up to six days after deposition.

After certain periods of time, nonmicroscopic techniques are not useful in the identification of stains as semen. Another limitation of microscopic techniques is that they do not detect semen that does not contain sperm, such as the semen produced by vasectomized males. In cases where semen stains are aged or suspected to be from vasectomized males, immunological techniques may be used that detect substances that are highly abundant or relatively unique to semen and present in semen from both vasectomized and nonvasectomized males. The most widely used confirmatory immunological test

for semen uses antibodies that are specific for PSA. The test format is a type of cassette called a lateral flow immunochromatographic assay. PSA is found in highest abundance in semen, so that at levels detectable in semen, other body fluids are apparently negative for PSA content.

Another immunological test that works by the same principles detects the presence of a protein called semenogelin, which has not been found in any other biological fluids and tissues tested. Semenogelin also appears to be unique to humans and perhaps other higher primates and therefore is potentially the most specific immunological test for semen available.

Oluseyi A. Vanderpuye

Further Reading

Baechtel, F. S. "The Identification and Individualization of Semen Stains." In *Forensic Science Handbook*, edited by Richard Saferstein. Vol. 2. Englewood Cliffs, N.J.: Prentice Hall, 1988. Discusses semen identification and the use of classical serological techniques for analyzing whether a semen stain originated from a given person.

Gaensslen, R. E. *Sourcebook in Forensic Serology, Immunology, and Biochemistry*. Washington, D.C.: National Institute of Justice, 1983. Presents a comprehensive review of the fundamentals and practice of forensic serology relevant to semen evidence.

Jones, Edward L. "The Identification of Semen and Other Body Fluids." In *Forensic Science Handbook*, edited by Richard Saferstein. 2d ed. Vol. 2. Upper Saddle River, N.J.: Prentice Hall, 2005. Discusses the forensic science techniques used in relation to semen evidence.

Nash, Jay Robert. *Forensic Serology*. New York: Chelsea House, 2006. Provides background information on the use of serology in the forensic sciences and discusses various techniques used in the handling of semen evidence.

Saferstein, Richard. *Criminalistics: An Introduction to Forensic Science*. 9th ed. Upper Saddle River, N.J.: Pearson Prentice Hall, 2007. Introductory textbook includes a chapter that provides a general introduction to serology and discusses semen analysis.

See also: Biohazard bags; Crime scene screening tests; DNA extraction from hair, bodily fluids, and tissues; DNA isolation methods; DNA recognition instruments; Evidence processing; Immune system; Lasers; Locard's exchange principle; Paternity testing; Postconviction DNA analysis; Rape; Rape kit; Serology; Y chromosome analysis.

Separation tests

Definition: Techniques used to separate the chemical components in sample mixtures so that they can be identified.

Significance: Forensic scientists often need to separate evidence sample mixtures into their individual chemical components to determine precisely what the substances are and to distinguish among samples that may initially look very similar.

Forensic laboratories use a number of different techniques to separate samples into their individual chemical components. These include filtering methods, extraction methods, and thin-layer chromatography. Filtering is a simple and rapid method of separating the components that make up sample mixtures. A solid sample is placed in a filter funnel lined with filter paper that is positioned over a beaker. A solvent is poured over the sample and collected in the beaker after it passes over the sample. Sample components that are soluble in the solvent pass through the filter paper in the solvent and are collected with the solvent in the beaker. Components that are insoluble remain in the filter paper. Although this method is simple to perform, the success of filtering depends on the solubility of sample components in the solvent.

Another procedure used to separate sample components is extraction. One of the most routinely used of the many different extraction methods is liquid-liquid extraction. In this case, the sample is in solution form and an extraction solvent is added. The extraction solvent is chosen based on the chemistry of the target component; the component should be soluble in the ex-

traction solvent and should prefer to exist in that solvent. In addition, the extraction solvent should not mix with the original solvent; that is, the solvents should form two separate layers. With the correct choice of extraction solvent, the target component moves from the sample solution into the extraction solvent, which is then removed. The component has thus been extracted into this solvent and can be analyzed further.

Thin-layer chromatography (TLC) provides another means to separate complex samples that contain numerous components of interest. As with all chromatography techniques, separation is achieved based on differences in the interaction of sample components with a mobile and a stationary phase. In TLC, the stationary phase is typically a solid adsorbent coated onto a thin plate of silica, and the mobile phase is a liquid. The sample is applied to the TLC plate, which is then introduced into a small volume of the mobile phase. The mobile phase travels up the plate by capillary action, dissolving the sample and hence carrying the sample up the plate.

Separation of components occurs because of differences in attraction for the stationary and mobile phases. Components that have stronger attraction for the stationary phase spend more time in that phase and therefore do not travel as quickly as components with less attraction for the same phase. In TLC, this is seen as component spots on the plate—spots close to the bottom of the plate indicate components that did not travel far and hence had greater attraction for the stationary phase. The plate is removed from the mobile phase and dried, and then the distance that the components have traveled is determined. The numbers of components present in a known standard and in the questioned sample are compared, as are the distances corresponding components in both samples traveled.

TLC can be used in the analysis of a variety of different types of evidence. For example, two inks or two fibers may both appear blue to the naked eye when in fact they are composed of different dyes. Using TLC, dyes in the inks or fibers may be separated into the individual dye components and compared. Illicit drug samples may contain cutting agents that may or may not be illegal. TLC can be used to separate the illegal drug from these other substances before further analysis is performed to confirm the identity of the drug.

Ruth Waddell Smith

Further Reading

Bell, Suzanne. *Forensic Chemistry*. Upper Saddle River, N.J.: Pearson Prentice Hall, 2006.

Bogusz, M. J., ed. *Handbook of Analytical Separations*. Vol. 6 in *Forensic Science*, edited by Roger M. Smith. 2d ed. New York: Elsevier, 2007.

Saferstein, Richard. *Criminalistics: An Introduction to Forensic Science*. 9th ed. Upper Saddle River, N.J.: Pearson Prentice Hall, 2007.

Sherma, Joseph, and Bernard Fried, eds. *Handbook of Thin-Layer Chromatography*. New York: Marcel Dekker, 2003.

See also: Analytical instrumentation; Chromatography; Document examination; Fibers and filaments; Microcrystalline tests; Presumptive tests for blood; Serology; Thin-layer chromatography.

September 11, 2001, victim identification

Date: Terrorist attacks occurred on September 11, 2001

The Event: Following the devastation caused by terrorist attacks on the World Trade Center in New York City and the Pentagon in Arlington, Virginia, experts used several forensic techniques to identify the dead.

Significance: This investigation was unique in that it involved a very high number of deaths at three very different scenes separated by great distances. The contributions of forensic science to the recovery and identification of the victims were important both because they aided in the in-

vestigation of these crimes and because they made it possible for the family members of victims to lay their loved ones' remains to rest.

In the aftermath of the four plane crashes that took place on the morning of September 11, 2001, authorities had to create a plan quickly to manage victim identification. Because the deaths were caused by acts of terrorism, jurisdiction over the bodies went to the Office of the Armed Forces Medical Examiner (OAFME), a division of the Armed Forces Institute of Pathology. The OAFME, however, did not have sufficient human resources to deal with so many separate incidents of such great magnitude all at once. A decision was thus made to honor the request made by authorities in New York City and allow the New York medical examiner's office to handle the victims who died at the World Trade Center. The OAFME would handle the remains at the Pentagon as well as those at the site of the crash in a field near Shanksville, Pennsylvania.

Search and Recovery

At any death scene, no matter what the details or the scope, the most important, and therefore first, step taken by first responders is always to check for and treat survivors. Any loss of evidence that occurs because medical personnel enter a scene to treat victims is considered acceptable. Immediately after the attacks, massive searches began for any possible survivors at the Pentagon and at the World Trade Center site (later referred to as Ground Zero); it was clear that United Airlines Flight 93, which crashed in Pennsylvania, had no survivors.

A rescue operation is very different from a scene search, as time is of the essence. At both the Pentagon and Ground Zero, search efforts had to be stopped often because of fires in the buildings and fears of continued structural collapses. All rescue workers had to leave these scenes every time the areas were deemed too dangerous; after the risks had subsided, they resumed their previous positions. The initial searches in both areas were thus extremely slow and time-consuming.

The OAFME conducts autopsies at a mortuary located on Dover Air Force Base in Delaware, approximately one hundred miles east of the Pentagon, but the first bodies from the crash sites did not arrive at the OAFME facility until two days after the attacks, on September 13, 2001. The remains varied in condition from full-bodied corpses to fragments of muscle and bone. Some remains were burned; some were crushed. Many were commingled; that is, parts from two or more bodies were mixed together. The victim remains recovered from Ground Zero were much more fragmented than those recovered at the Pentagon, as they had been subjected to the tremendous forces of the collapse of the World Trade Center buildings.

Methods of Identification

Even when bodies in need of identification are relatively fresh and complete, visual identification is not considered accurate enough for official purposes. Following the September 11 attacks, most of the remains recovered were in pieces, and visual identification was of no use at all. The purpose of the autopsies performed on the remains was victim identification.

Three main forensic methods produce results that are accepted as positively identifying deceased persons: fingerprint analysis, forensic odontology (analysis of teeth and dentistry), and DNA (deoxyribonucleic acid) analysis. Each on its own is sufficient for identification, and each involves a process of comparing elements of remains with antemortem (prior to death) documents or records of persons who could possibly be the deceased. For every piece of remains that was brought into the Dover mortuary, all three methods were conducted whenever possible.

The Events of September 11, 2001

Within approximately ninety minutes on the morning of September 11, 2001, four hijacked U.S. airline jets were crashed, resulting in approximately 3,000 deaths. At 8:46 A.M., American Airlines Flight 11 was flown into the north side of the north tower of the World Trade Center, striking between the ninety-fourth and ninety-eighth floors of the 110-story building. At 9:02 A.M., United Airlines Flight 175 crashed into the south side of the south tower of the World Trade Center, hitting between the seventy-eighth and eighty-fourth floors. Three buildings in the World Trade Center complex eventually collapsed as the result of the structural failure caused by these collisions. At 9:59 A.M. the south tower, designated as 2 World Trade Center, fell, followed by the north tower, named 1 World Trade Center, at 10:28 A.M. These collapses eventually caused the third building, 7 World Trade Center, to fall at approximately 5:20 P.M. Including the passengers on the two planes, approximately 2,750 victims died at the World Trade Center on that day.

Shortly after the first two planes struck the twin towers of the World Trade Center, at 9:37 A.M. American Airlines Flight 77 was flown into the western side of the Pentagon in Arlington, Virginia. If many sections of that side of the building had not been empty because of a scheduled renovation, the loss of life could have been much worse; as it was, 184 people in the building and on the plane that struck it died at the Pentagon.

A passenger uprising aboard United Airlines Flight 93 prevented the hijackers of that flight from reaching their designated target. Instead, at 10:03 A.M. the plane crashed in a field outside of Shanksville, Pennsylvania. All 40 passengers and crew members were killed.

Managing the Remains

All remains that arrived at Dover Air Force Base followed the same flow and were seen by workers at the same stations. When each body bag arrived, its paperwork was reviewed; the paperwork noted where the remains were from, how they were found, and any identifying numbers given to them. The remains were then renumbered using an OAFME system, so they could be tracked through the stations. A checklist that accompanied the remains throughout the process was annotated with the OAFME number to ensure that no station was missed and to document the reason any given station may not have been able to work on the remains (such as the fingerprint station explaining that the remains included no hands).

The first station was a security scanning machine much like the kind used at airports. The body bag was placed on the conveyor belt, and the X-ray machine allowed for an initial look inside the bag. This preliminary step allowed the workers to check for any hazards in a bag, such as sharp metal objects, before they opened it. After the remains were taken off the belt, pictures were taken of the closed bag to document how it arrived. The bag was then opened and pictures were taken of the body or parts inside.

Steps in the Identification Process

The next station was the first of the identification process, the anthropology station. Foren-

A forensic scientist opens a freezer containing the remains of victims of the September 11 terrorist attacks at a facility in Springfield, Virginia, in August, 2002. Above his head and on the rear wall are the names of the World Trade Center victims that he and other scientists were working to identify through DNA samples. *(AP/Wide World Photos)*

sic anthropologists examine skeletal remains to determine the sex, age, and race of the deceased. In this particular case, the anthropology station's function was to characterize and document the remains in each bag. If, for example, a bag was found to contain two right arms, this was noted so that the workers at the rest of the stations would know that the bag contained commingled remains. If a bag contained only a hip and upper leg bone, then it could skip the fingerprint and forensic odontology stations.

The fingerprinting station was next. Fingerprints were taken of every recoverable finger, and analysts from the Federal Bureau of Investigation (FBI) later compared the prints with the antemortem fingerprint records available for those on the list of possible victims. Many of those who died at the Pentagon on September 11 were in the military, and thus their fingerprints were on file and accessible. The FBI also conducted searches for fingerprint records that may have existed for all of the nonmilitary victims.

The remains next moved to the forensic odontology station. Forensic odontologists compare oral X rays and castings of the teeth of decedents with antemortem dental records. Tooth enamel is one of the hardest substances produced by the human body; it can survive when the rest of the body is crushed, decomposed, or severely burned. Elements such as the positions of teeth in the jaw, the shapes of fillings, and the lengths of the roots of teeth can all contribute to the identification process.

The next step was to X-ray the remains. Although the primary purpose of the X rays taken was to assist the pathologists with their work in performing the autopsies that followed, comparisons of X rays were also sometimes used in the identification process. For victims with X rays in their medical records, radiologists could compare antemortem and postmortem X-ray images. Unique injuries, healing mechanisms, or medical procedures revealed in X rays could help to identify individuals.

The third method of positively identifying remains, DNA analysis, was begun when the remains were brought into autopsy. Nuclear DNA is found in cells that contain nuclei, such as the cells in blood, skin, and saliva. Nuclear DNA is

Victims of the 9/11 Terrorist Attacks

Place	Male	Female	Unknown	Total
World Trade Center	2,128	621	—	2,749
Pentagon	108	71	5	184
Somerset County, Pennsylvania	20	20	—	40
Totals	2,256	712	5	2,973

Source: Federal Bureau of Investigation, *Crime in the United States,* 2002.

the most common type used for DNA testing, but it is somewhat fragile and can easily be damaged, especially by decomposition. Another type of DNA, mitochondrial DNA, can be used in a different test comparison that can also identify remains. Unlike nuclear DNA, the offspring receives mitochondrial DNA only from the mother, and since there is no mixing with the father's mitochondrial DNA, usually little change is seen from generation to generation. Mitochondrial DNA is much sturdier than nuclear DNA and can withstand decomposition changes. It can be recovered from both bone and teeth even after hundreds of years. Because mitochondrial DNA is maternal in its delivery, mitochondrial DNA from a decedent must be compared with mitochondrial DNA from a family member on the decedent's mother's side to make a match.

Success Rate

Following the unprecedented national tragedy of the September 11 attacks, identifying the victims was an extremely high priority. The OAFME was able to identify positively all 184 victims from the Pentagon scene as well as each of the 40 victims from the Pennsylvania field. The New York medical examiner's office had similar success with the remains recovered from the World Trade Center site.

The volume of the remains examined, the number of agencies involved, and the number of volunteer workers who helped with the identification process went beyond anything either of the medical examiners' offices had ever before experienced. By using established forensic methods for positively identifying remains, they were able to give the victims' families a

sense of resolution by returning the remains of their loved ones to them for burial.

Russell S. Strasser

Further Reading

DiMaio, Vincent J., and Dominick DiMaio. *Forensic Pathology.* 2d ed. Boca Raton, Fla.: CRC Press, 2001. One of the best reference sources available in the field of forensic pathology. Covers autopsies, types of death, and body decomposition, and also provides good explanations of the methods used to identify remains.

Grant, Nancy, David Hoover, Anne-Marie Scarisbrick-Hause, and Stacy Muffet. "The Crash of United Flight 93 in Shanksville, Pennsylvania." In *Beyond September 11th: An Account of Post-disaster Research.* Boulder: Natural Hazards Center, University of Colorado, 2003. Focuses specifically on the crash in Pennsylvania. Discusses jurisdictional issues and the problems that arose regarding the search for and recovery of the remains to be identified.

Keiser-Nielsen, Søren. "Dental Identification: Certainty v. Probability." *Forensic Science* 9, no. 2 (1977): 87-97. Somewhat dated article nevertheless provides a very good overview of the field of forensic odontology and the procedures used.

Lowe, Seana, and Alice Fothergill. "A Need to Help: Emergent Volunteer Behavior After September 11th." In *Beyond September 11th: An Account of Post-disaster Research.* Boulder: Natural Hazards Center, University of Colorado, 2003. Conveys well the chaos created by this tragedy, as the sheer numbers of people who wanted to help made some processes (including the identification of victims) difficult.

Ritter, Nancy. "Identifying Remains: Lessons Learned from 9/11." *NIJ Journal* 256 (January, 2007) 20-25. Reviews the techniques used to identify human remains in the aftermath of the September 11 attacks. Expresses clearly the difficulties associated with handling large numbers of both victims and volunteers.

Rubinoff, Daniel, Stephen Cameron, and Kipling Will. "A Genomic Perspective on the Shortcomings of Mitochondrial DNA for 'Barcoding' Identification." *Journal of Heredity* 97, no. 6 (2006): 581-594. Argues against some of the identification powers of mitochondrial DNA when attempting to trace heritage back through generations. While technical, it does give a good explanation of the mitochondrial DNA process.

Simpson, David M., and Steven D. Stehr. "Victim Management and Identification After the World Trade Center Collapse." In *Beyond September 11th: An Account of Post-disaster Research*. Boulder: Natural Hazards Center, University of Colorado, 2003. Good overview addresses the processes used to identify the victims at the World Trade Center. Compares the work with other identification cases.

See also: Airport security; Anthrax letter attacks; Asian tsunami victim identification; DNA analysis; Fingerprints; Forensic anthropology; Forensic odontology; Mitochondrial DNA analysis and typing; Oral autopsy; World Trade Center bombing.

Serology

Definition: Study of the properties and components of biological fluids such as blood, saliva, cerebrospinal fluid, and semen.

Significance: Much of the physical evidence analyzed by forensic scientists in criminal investigations is biological in nature, and serological methods are used on this biological evidence. Forensic serologists use antibodies or separation techniques to identify and measure biological molecules and materials for legal purposes.

In forensic science, serology is typically used to identify biological evidence related to crimes such as sexual or physical assault, homicide, kidnapping, and robbery. Contact between victims and offenders as well as between people and objects during crimes can lead to the transfer of biological materials, as noted by Locard's exchange principle. Serological evidence may prove or disprove statements by suspects, victims, or witnesses and may associate evidence with suspects or victims. The types of biological evidence most often subjected to serological analysis include the biological fluids blood, saliva, and semen.

Composition and Markers of Biological Fluids

Different types of biological evidence analyzed by serology have distinctive cellular and molecular compositions. Blood contains cells as well as both biological and inorganic molecules and ions. Blood cells are divided into two major groups: red blood cells (erythrocytes), which are major sources of blood group antigens but contain no DNA (deoxyribonucleic acid), and white blood cells, which contain DNA and B-lymphocyte subpopulations that produce antibodies that are widely used tools in serology.

Hemoglobin is a substance specific to red blood cells and absent from other body cells. Reactivity with hemoglobin forms the basis of most forensic tests for blood. Blood contains a great variety of proteins, some of which display inherited variations in structure and therefore were historically used in forensic serology to exclude or associate bloodstains with individuals before the rise of DNA typing. Certain of these proteins are also found in other biological fluids.

Spermatozoa are a unique cellular component used to identify semen in biological evidence. Spermatozoa exhibit unique morphology in that each has a compact region or "head" containing most of the organelles, a short cylindrical region or midpiece, and an elongated whiplike appendage or "tail." Proteins specific for semen include prostate-specific antigen (PSA) and semenogelin. Certain other biological molecules, however, including various proteins, oligosaccharides, prostaglandins, and basic compounds, are relatively specific or abundant in this biological fluid.

Saliva is a viscous fluid that contains buccal cells from the lining of the mouth, which are the main source of DNA in saliva. Substances in saliva include many proteins, such as alpha amylase, mucins, and proline-rich proteins, as well as other biological molecules and inorganic compounds. The enzyme alpha amylase is uniquely abundant in saliva.

Tests for Biological Fluids

Most tests for the detection and identification of blood are based on reactions with hemoglobin from erythrocytes. Several screening tests are color tests that rely on the ability of hemoglobin to transfer oxygen from hydrogen peroxide to another substance that either changes color (for example, pink for phenolphthalein, green for tetramethylbenzidine) or causes the production of light (chemiluminescence), as in the case of luminol. To identify stain material as blood conclusively after one of these presumptive tests, a forensic scientist may perform a microcrystalline test. In such a test, a trace scraping of the stain is gently heated with particular chemicals; if blood is present, microscopic examination will reveal the formation of crystals of characteristic shapes and sizes.

Immunology-based methods are used to identify the species of origin of bloodstains. Some methods, such as lateral-flow immunoassay, use monoclonal antibodies against human hemoglobin to identify human blood. Another method uses immunoprecipitation of human blood proteins by antibodies against human blood (serum) proteins on extracts of the stain evidence in an agarose medium.

A presumptive test for semen relies on detection of the enzyme acid phosphatase, which is more abundant in semen than in other biological fluids. One confirmatory test for semen involves microscopic examination of material after treatment with the "Christmas tree" (picroindigocarmine) stain, which marks intact spermatozoa with characteristic green, yellow, and red colors in specific regions. Other specific semen tests are immunochromatographic ones that use monoclonal antibodies to PSA or to semenogelin, an apparently human/primate- and sperm-specific protein.

Until 2006, only presumptive tests were available for detection of saliva, and these relied on the detection of alpha amylase enzyme activity on colored starch or other colorimetric substrates. An immunochromatographic test became available in 2006 that appears to be confirmatory and uses a monoclonal antibody specific for the salivary form of alpha amylase.

Blood Group Typing

Human blood groups were the first genetically based systems used by forensic scientists to gain information on who might or might not be the sources of biological evidence. Identification of blood groups from evidence samples involves the use of defined antibodies to agglutinate (clump together) erythrocytes based on the type of inherited blood group carbohydrates on the erythrocyte. ABO and Rh blood group antigens are the major systems used. Several other types of blood groups (such as Lewis and MN antigens), involving other genetically inherited structures, have been used in forensic serology. Blood group typing of dried bloodstains and other body fluids is achieved through various methods of extracting stains and testing the extracts for their ability to inhibit agglutination.

Inherited differences (polymorphisms) exist in proteins found in blood and other biological fluids. By using serological techniques to identify which variants of proteins are present in biological evidence, scientists can help to associate victims or suspects with particular items of evidence or exclude victims or suspects from consideration. Electrophoretic analyses identify protein variants based on the differing degrees to which they move in an electric field while in a medium such as agarose or polyacrylamide. Some polymorphic blood proteins include transferrin, Gc (group-specific component), phosphoglucomutase, and haptoglobin. Better testing is achieved when the serologist analyzes several polymorphic proteins in a sample to arrive at a statistical calculation of a probability that the stain did or did not originate from a particular individual.

Oluseyi A. Vanderpuye

Further Reading

Baechtel, F. S. "The Identification and Individualization of Semen Stains." In *Forensic Science Handbook*, edited by Richard Saferstein. Vol. 2. Englewood Cliffs, N.J.: Prentice Hall, 1988. Discusses semen identification and the use of classical serological techniques for analyzing whether a semen stain originated from a given person.

Gaensslen, R. E. *Sourcebook in Forensic Serology, Immunology, and Biochemistry*. Washington, D.C.: National Institute of Justice, 1983. Presents a comprehensive review of the fundamentals and practice of forensic serology.

Houck, Max M., and Jay A. Siegel. *Fundamentals of Forensic Science*. Burlington, Mass.: Elsevier Academic Press, 2006. Good general textbook includes a chapter that succinctly describes the field of forensic serology and its relevance.

Nash, Jay Robert. *Forensic Serology*. New York: Chelsea House, 2006. Provides background information on the use of serology in the forensic sciences and discusses various techniques of forensic serology.

Saferstein, Richard. *Criminalistics: An Introduction to Forensic Science*. 9th ed. Upper Saddle River, N.J.: Pearson Prentice Hall, 2007. Introductory textbook includes a chapter that covers immunology basics and the history and methods of forensic serology.

Whitehead, P. H. "A Historical Review of the Characterization of Blood and Secretion Stains in the Forensic Laboratory, Part One: Bloodstains." *Forensic Science Review* 5 (June, 1993): 35-40. Discusses the development and application of serological techniques over time.

See also: Blood residue and bloodstains; Blood spatter analysis; DNA typing; Electrophoresis; Epidemiology; Immune system; Kidd blood grouping system; Multisystem method; Paternity evidence; Paternity testing; Physical evidence; Saliva; Semen and sperm.

Sex determination of remains

Definition: Process of discerning the sex of a decomposed human body based on knowledge of the physiological and behavioral differences between the sexes.

Significance: The sexual dimorphism of human beings allows forensic scientists to accomplish one of the most important initial steps in ascertaining the identity of unknown human remains—the determination of sex.

Male and female human beings exhibit significant anatomical and behavioral differences. For example, male humans are on average larger and stronger than female humans, and female humans gestate, bear, and nurse the young. For forensic investigators, challenges in determining the sex of human remains occur primarily when bodies are badly decomposed. Remaining tissues may contain DNA (deoxyribonucleic acid) that is not too degraded to allow for analysis; in such cases, routine forensic DNA analysis to determine the identity of the remains based on short tandem repeat (STR) markers includes a marker for sex determination such as the one within the gene for dental enamel (amelogenin).

When sufficient skeletal remains are available, forensic scientists may determine sex by using methods that exploit the structural differences associated with muscularity and size in men and with childbearing in women. Teeth are not sufficiently different between the sexes for forensic purposes. Sex differences in skeletal remains are relatively trivial at birth, and using such remains to determine the sex of juveniles is difficult at best. Some early differences between boys and girls do occur in the pelvis, but reliable sex differentiation is not possible until after the anatomical changes associated with puberty. The methods that forensic scientists use to assess sex differences in skeletal remains fall into two categories: anthroposcopic or qualitative characteristics (eyeball) and metric traits (quantification). Metric measures have more influence in court because they allow more accurate specification of degrees of reliability.

Sexually Dimorphic Regions of the Skeleton

Accuracy at determining sex is from 90 to 100 percent with the entire skeleton but declines to 90-95 percent, 80-90 percent, and about 80 percent, respectively, with only the pelvis, only the skull, and only the long bones. The impact of giving birth on the shape of the pelvis makes it the most reliable bone for differentiating the sexes. Most of the sex-specific features reflect how a woman's pelvis is designed to permit the fetus to exit the woman's body within the constraints of bipedal walking. The infe-

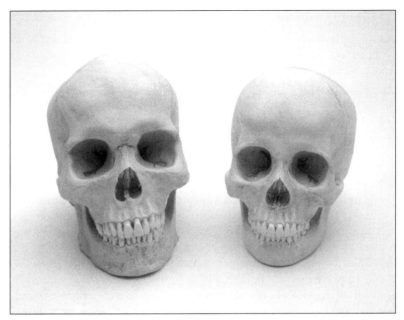

Male (left) and female human skulls. After the pelvis, skulls are the second-most-useful parts of human skeletal systems for determining sex. However, ethnic ancestry complicates such determinations because male and female skull characteristics vary among the world's major ethnic divisions. *(Digital Stock)*

rior bony pelvis must be angled out of the way, and these pressures result in different morphologies (structures) and angles that for some features, in combination or alone, can be as accurate as 96 percent. The pelvis is also the best bone for use in any attempt to determine the sex of the remains of a juvenile.

The skull is the second most useful structure for determining sex, but some traits vary depending on the ancestral origins of the individual. Some features typical of European-derived female skulls, such as relatively high forehead and smaller size, are shared with some Asian male skulls. Some overlap also exists between male and female skull traits within populations, although typically male skulls are not only larger but also more rugged in appearance. These average differences are partly a function of age. Young male skulls look more feminine because of less developed muscle attachments, and older female skulls can look more masculine after menopause. More reliable is the use of computer software that determines sex based on discriminant function analysis of a series of measures between points on a skull.

Postcranial bones can also be used to determine sex, although with less success. Overlap exists in skeletal characteristics of men and women, less so in the shoulders and feet than in the lower limbs, but, again, measures can vary depending on the population. Differences are dependent in part on genetic differences among ancestral populations and in part on environmental influences, particularly nutrition. Malnourished individuals can be smaller and less muscular than those who are better nourished, so poor nutrition can sometimes increase the overlap between male and female skeletal characteristics, because men are often more sensitive to this kind of stress.

Limitations of Metric Methods

Metric methods for determining sex from skeletal remains involve measuring between points on a structure, such as the skull, and then entering the measures into a software program that performs discriminant function analysis and predicts the sex of the unknown individual based on the resulting value. Formulas vary in terms of which measurements are necessary; this provides flexibility in the case of incomplete bones.

The data used in these discriminant function analyses have been generated from skeletal collections for which the sexes of individuals are known; most have been derived from studies on the Hamann-Todd Human Osteological Collection at the Cleveland Museum of Natural History and the Robert J. Terry Anatomical Skeletal Collection at the National Museum of Natural History in Washington, D.C. The specimens in both of these collections were gathered in the Midwest during the first half of the twentieth century; thus the individuals represented experienced diets and disease ecologies significantly different from those of modern Americans. In addition, the collections do not represent the diversity of ancestral origins found in the population of the United States in the twenty-first century.

Because the functions derived from these collections are losing their utility, the University of Tennessee at Knoxville set up the Forensic Anthropology Data Bank in 1986 to centralize the growing amounts of information available on skeletal remains in modern populations. Most forensic anthropologists compare unknown individuals to populations in this database with the help of FORDISC, a forensic anthropology software program.

Joan C. Stevenson

Further Reading

Burns, Karen R. *Forensic Anthropology Training Manual*. Upper Saddle River, N.J.: Prentice Hall, 2006. Comprehensive textbook includes discussion of sex differences for each region of the human skeleton.

Butler, John M. *Forensic DNA Typing: Biology, Technology, and Genetics of STR Markers*. 2d ed. Burlington, Mass.: Elsevier Academic Press, 2005. Very readable textbook introduces this complex subject to novices.

Byers, Steven N. *Introduction to Forensic Anthropology*. 3d ed. Boston: Pearson/Allyn & Bacon, 2008. Comprehensive, accessible textbook includes a chapter on sexing skeletons.

Klepinger, Linda L. *Fundamentals of Forensic Anthropology*. Hoboken, N.J.: John Wiley & Sons, 2006. Excellent textbook includes a chapter on sex identification of skeletal remains.

Scheuer, Louise, and Sue Black. *The Juvenile Skeleton*. Burlington, Mass.: Elsevier Academic Press, 2004. Describes the subtle sex differences that can be observed in juvenile skeletons.

White, Tim D., and Pieter A. Folkens. *The Human Bone Manual*. Burlington, Mass.: Elsevier Academic Press, 2005. Well-illustrated volume is the next best thing to studying an actual skeleton. Includes discussion of sex differences.

See also: Anthropometry; DNA analysis; DNA extraction from hair, bodily fluids, and tissues; Forensic anthropology; Forensic sculpture; Osteology and skeletal radiology; Short tandem repeat analysis; Skeletal analysis; University of Tennessee Anthropological Research Facility; Y chromosome analysis.

Sexual predation characteristics

Definition: Characteristics of criminal offenders who exhibit a pattern of pursuing nonconsenting persons for the purpose of acting out aggressive sexual fantasies that commonly include themes of domination, control, and revenge.

Significance: The behaviors of sexual predators range along a continuum from coercive sexual acts, such as rape, to sadistic torture and homicide. These individuals prey on victims they perceive as weak and vulnerable, such as women and children. Law-enforcement investigations of cases involving sexual predators must take into account the compulsive and deep-seated nature of such offenders' sexual urges and fantasies.

Sexual predators derive intense sexual pleasure from pursuing, overpowering, and forcing their victims to comply with their deviant fantasies. Sexually violent predators make up a subgroup of sexual offenders. These individuals engage in violent and sometimes deadly sexual activities with their victims. Over time, the severity of their deviant fantasies may escalate as these perpetrators require increasing degrees of control or victim suffering to achieve sexual gratification. Over the courses of their criminal careers, some sexual predators perfect their patterns so that they gain access to many victims while eluding capture by the authorities.

Sexually violent predators tend to share a number of characteristics. For example, research has found that many of these offenders have experienced severely troubled childhoods, often including verbal, physical, and sexual abuse. Most are Caucasian males who typically began their offending in early to mid-adolescence, if not before, and have experienced problems with substance abuse.

The crimes of sexual predators are often motivated by the sexual gratification they receive from inflicting pain, mutilating, and displaying the bodies of their victims in sexually suggestive positions. These acts often lead to or involve the death of the victims; however, sexual stimulation, not murder, is the perpetrators' primary goal. Victims may be sexually penetrated, but it is not uncommon for these offenders to use penetration with foreign objects in place of or in addition to penetration with penis or fingers. Sexual penetration does not always occur during such crimes, however; at times, this can make it difficult for investigators to determine that the crimes were sexually motivated.

Types of Sexual Predators

Research into sexual predation has identified two broad types of offenders, distinguished according to the offender's level of social adjustment, the amount of planning that goes into each crime, and the offender's behavior with the victims. Those classified as "organized" sexual predators consciously plan their crimes and choose their victims in order to have significant control. These offenders spend a considerable amount of time trying to conceal their crimes so that they avoid being caught and often travel significant distances to find their victims and commit their crimes. They are socially adept and able to function in intimate sexual relationships.

The sexual predators classified as "disorganized" are typically socially inadequate and engage in their crimes impulsively, typically in response to particular stressors. They are opportunistic, so they are not selective when choosing their victims and rarely expend much effort in concealing their crimes. Their behavior is often erratic or haphazard because of their lack of planning; if they need weapons, they are likely to use whatever weapon is available at the scenes of their crimes.

Research regarding sexual predation has typically focused on male sex offenders because perpetrators of violent crimes, particularly sexual crimes, are typically male adults. Female sex offenders do exist, however; for the most part, their offenses occur with children under the age of six. It has been suggested that the rate of sexual offending by women is higher than crime reports indicate because such crimes by women often go unreported or unnoticed owing to societal views on sexual offenses.

Managing Sexual Predators

"Sexually violent predator" is a legal term assigned to certain sex offenders. In most U.S. states, in order to be labeled a sexually violent predator, a person must be convicted of committing sexually violent acts on at least two victims. Additionally, the individual must be diagnosed with a mental disorder that places that person at risk of committing additional sexually violent acts. In some states, those convicted offenders who are labeled as sexually violent predators may be incarcerated in state mental facilities for some period of time after they have completed their court-mandated sentences in correctional facilities. Forensic psychologists or psychiatrists then assess the mental status of such offenders and testify in court on the results of their assessments and on their opinions concerning the level of treatment the offenders should receive.

Jocelyn M. Brineman and
Richard D. McAnulty

Further Reading

Hudson, Kirsty. *Offending Identities: Sex Offenders' Perspectives on Their Treatment and Management*. Portland, Oreg.: Willan, 2005. Reports on a study in which the author interviewed convicted sex offenders about their experiences in one of three treatment groups and their perceptions of their treatment. Includes discussion of the offenders' perspectives on their crimes.

Purcell, Catherine E., and Bruce A. Arrigo. *The Psychology of Lust Murder: Paraphilia, Sexual Killing, and Serial Homicide*. Boston: Elsevier/Academic Press, 2006. Discusses sexually motivated murder by examining theories ranging from developmental issues to behavioral motivations. Specific accounts involving Jeffrey Dahmer are offered to enable comparisons of the validity of a number of models.

Ressler, Robert K., Ann W. Burgess, and John E. Douglas. *Sexual Homicide: Patterns and Motives*. Lexington, Mass.: Lexington Books, 1988. Gathers information on sexually motivated crimes in relation to the backgrounds of the criminals in support of the motivational model of sexual homicide.

Salter, Anna C. *Predators: Pedophiles, Rapists, and Other Sex Offenders—Who They Are, How They Operate, and How We Can Protect Ourselves and Our Children*. New York: Basic Books, 2003. Based on interviews with both sex offenders and their victims, examines how the offenders operated and how the victims were deceived. Also discusses prevalence and incarceration rates.

Schlank, Anita, ed. *The Sexual Predator: Legal Issues, Clinical Issues, Special Populations*. Kingston, N.J.: Civic Research Institute, 2001. Collection of essays by both prosecutors and defense attorneys focuses on the issues surrounding civil commitment cases involving sexually violent predators.

Schlesinger, Louis B. *Sexual Murder: Catathymic and Compulsive Homicides*. Boca Raton, Fla.: CRC Press, 2004. Discusses the historical background of sexual homicide and the difficulties in the identification and classification of sexual murders and their perpetrators.

See also: Actuarial risk assessment; Competency evaluation and assessment instruments; Cyberstalking; Expert witnesses; Forensic psychiatry; Forensic psychology; Internet tracking and tracing; Megan's Law; Psychopathic personality disorder; Rape; Victimology; Violent sexual predator statutes.

Shaken baby syndrome

Definition: Signs and symptoms in an infant or young child resulting from violent shaking, including subdural hematomas, cerebral edema, and retinal hemorrhages.

Significance: The incidence of shaken baby syndrome in the United States has been estimated to range between six hundred and fourteen hundred cases a year. The actual number may be much higher, however, as many cases may not be brought to the attention of medical professionals. In addition, it is easy to miss the diagnosis of shaken baby syndrome, as generally no external injuries are visible. Forensic scientists must be aware of the signs and symptoms associated with the syndrome so that cases of child injury and death caused by abuse do not go unnoticed.

In the early 1970's, John Caffey used the term "whiplash shaken infant syndrome" to describe the injuries caused in young children by violent shaking that are now commonly known as shaken baby syndrome (SBS). Others have used terms such as "shaken impact syndrome" and "shaken/slammed baby syndrome" to emphasize that impact of the child's head against a hard or soft surface—such as a floor, wall, or mattress—often occurs in addition to the shaking.

Infliction of Injuries

In a typical scenario leading to SBS, an infant or toddler's caretaker, irritated by the child's incessant crying, grabs the small victim by the shoulders or chest and shakes the child forcefully back and forth. The child's relatively large head, which is poorly supported by weak neck muscles, rolls around repeatedly. At the same time, the brain is exposed to acceleration, deceleration, and rotational forces that cause the bridging veins to shear, leading to the formation of subdural hematomas and swelling of the brain.

In milder cases, the baby becomes drowsy and ceases to cry. The abuser, having obtained the desired result, is likely to repeat the shaking on other occasions when again the irritable infant cannot be consoled. More severe manifestations of SBS, which tend to lead to contact with physicians, include vomiting, apnea, seizures, loss of consciousness, and death. Survivors of SBS require long-term follow-up, as they frequently face behavioral, learning, and developmental challenges later in life.

Forensic Evaluation

The collection and preservation of evidence and the notification of appropriate authorities are necessary steps toward the successful prosecution of child abusers. In cases in which SBS is suspected, examining physicians need to search purposefully for clinical signs of maltreatment. When a small child has been shaken violently, retinal hemorrhages are generally present in both eyes. Accuracy in diagnosing retinal hemorrhages demands that an ophthalmologist evaluate the patient. A detailed description of the findings accompanied by drawings and photographs constitutes valuable evidence.

Another hallmark of SBS, subdural hematoma, is revealed only through imaging of the head, either by computed tomography (CT) or by magnetic resonance imaging (MRI). CT or MRI scanning will also help detect the presence of cerebral edema.

When SBS is suspected, examining physicians should obtain X rays to look for old and new fractures, specifically of the skull, ribs, collarbone, and long bones. On rare occasions when bruising, swelling, and lacerations are present, documentation with the help of body diagrams and appropriately dated and labeled forensic photographs can be helpful in court. Additionally, health care workers need to obtain and document detailed testimony from the caretakers of suspected victims of SBS. In cases of SBS,

the severity of victims' injuries usually does not correlate with caretakers' descriptions of what happened to the children, and contradictory statements or changing stories are often given.

Health professionals should be aware of the caretaker-related risk factors associated with child maltreatment. Although female babysitters have been shown to be responsible for a high incidence of abuse, severe child abuse often occurs at the hands of male caretakers—the abused children's stepfathers or biological fathers or the boyfriends of the children's mothers. Perpetrators are often alone with the children at the time injuries occur. Other factors that have been found to be associated with child

Pediatrician Daryl Steiner, a noted champion of protecting children against parental abuse, testifying in a child abuse trial in Mansfield, Ohio, in 2005. Steiner used a doll to demonstrate to the jury how a baby can be shaken in a way that produces the brain damage associated with shaken baby syndrome. *(AP/ Wide World Photos)*

maltreatment include poverty, drug abuse, significant life stressors, spousal abuse, low-birth weight infants, and young, unmarried mothers.

Autopsies should be performed in cases of unexplained infant death. Ideally, the pathologists assigned to such cases should be trained in pediatric forensic science.

The Courts and SBS

All U.S. states mandate that suspected child abuse be reported to the appropriate authorities, but health care workers are often reluctant to report suspected cases. Most child abuse cases are heard in civil court, the main focus of which is child safety. Civil court requires only a "preponderance" of proof to decide that abuse has taken place. Criminal courts become involved when death or severe injury has occurred; for convictions, the criminal system requires proof beyond a reasonable doubt.

The American judicial system struggles with rulings in cases of SBS. Judges and prosecutors often lack extensive knowledge about child abuse, and juries are reluctant to believe the presented evidence. In addition, the laws are poorly tailored to deal with violent infant death. Frequently abusers are not convicted, and those that are often receive mild sentences. One highly publicized case involving SBS was that of the young British au pair Louise Woodward, whom a jury found guilty of second-degree murder in the death of the child who had been in her care, eight-month-old Matthew Eappen. The presiding judge later reduced the conviction to involuntary manslaughter.

Elisabeth Faase

Further Reading

Kellogg, Nancy, and the Committee on Child Abuse and Neglect. "Evaluation of Suspected Child Physical Abuse." *Pediatrics* 119 (2007): 1232-1241. Presents guidelines for medical professionals to use in the evaluation of suspected child abuse.

Monteleone, James A., and Armand E. Brodeur, eds. *Child Maltreatment.* 2d ed. St. Louis: G. W. Medical Publishing, 1998. Medical text presents analysis of the mechanism of brain injury in SBS. Includes images of subdural hematomas.

Morey, Ann-Janine. *What Happened to Christopher: An American Family's Story of Shaken Baby Syndrome.* Carbondale: Southern Illinois University Press, 1998. Narrative account of the case of an actual SBS victim and his family includes medical, social, and legal details pertaining to SBS.

Peinkofer, James. *Silenced Angels: The Medical, Legal, and Social Aspects of Shaken Baby Syndrome.* Westport, Conn.: Auburn House, 2001. Provides comprehensive discussion of SBS from the perspective of a clinical social worker.

Reece, Robert M., and Cindy Christian, eds. *Child Abuse: Medical Diagnosis and Management.* 3d ed. Elk Grove Village, Ill.: American Academy of Pediatrics, 2007. Medical text presents detailed description of retinal hemorrhages and the kinds of bone fractures seen in child abuse.

See also: Brain-wave scanners; Child abduction and kidnapping; Child abuse; Forensic pathology; Forensic photography; Living forensics; Medicine; Petechial hemorrhage.

Sherlock Holmes stories

Identification: A fictional consulting detective based in London, Sherlock Holmes first appeared in Sir Arthur Conan Doyle's *A Study in Scarlet*, published in 1887. By the time he made his last appearance in a work by Doyle in 1927, he was the most widely known fictional detective in the world.

Significance: With Sherlock Holmes, Doyle popularized the figure of the forensic investigator, introducing empirical investigative methods to a worldwide audience. In turn, Holmes offered a model for forensic scientists.

Sir Arthur Conan Doyle (1859-1930) began medical studies at the University of Edinburgh in 1876. Forensic medical investigation had been introduced there during the late eighteenth century, and a new kind of scientist was overturning the tradition-burdened medicine and law-enforcement practices of the past. Among these scientists was Dr. Joseph Bell, an eminent surgeon and occasional forensic investigator who became Doyle's mentor. Bell argued for the full use of the senses in the observation of evidence; he insisted that investigators should draw conclusions from evidence alone and reject unsupported theories. Earlier investigators had too frequently formed theories and then sought evidence to support them.

Doyle several times acknowledged Holmes's debt to Bell, but whether Bell and Holmes were pioneers is doubtful. In the nineteenth century, forensic science was far more advanced in some parts of Europe than it was in England or the United States. Holmes, for example, often called on Bell's ability to identify a man's occupation from his appearance, but French forensic scientist Auguste Ambroise Tardieu had published on this subject as early as 1849, referring to similar work by earlier investigators. Holmes's interest in toxicology was similarly anticipated; Matthieu-Joseph-Bonaventure Orfila, a Spaniard, published a work in 1813 that is considered to be a founding document in the field of forensic toxicology. In 1891, Holmes stories began to appear regularly in *The Strand Magazine*. By 1893, Hans Gross's *System der Kriminalistik (Criminal Investigation*, 1906) had appeared. The Holmes stories nevertheless impressed scientists. Edmond Locard (1877-1966), the pioneer of forensic science who originated the dictum that came to be known as Locard's exchange principle, advised his students to read Doyle's detective fiction.

Through the Holmes stories, Doyle popularized scientific ideas. Sherlock Holmes first ap-

Illustration of Sherlock Holmes (right) and Dr. Watson drawn by Sidney Paget for *The Strand Magazine* in 1892.

peared at a time when the United States, England, and Europe were experiencing terrorist attacks, assassinations, and other social turmoil, and the stories offered hope that science and reason could find a path to social order and justice. When Doyle attempted to kill Holmes off in "The Adventure of the Final Problem" (1893), thousands dropped their subscriptions to *The Strand*; thousands more renewed when Holmes returned in *The Hound of the Baskervilles* (serialized in the magazine, 1901-1902). The Sherlock Holmes character, which went on from Doyle's original publications to be featured in countless plays and films, helped to create worldwide acceptance of the principles of forensic science.

Betty Richardson

Further Reading

Costello, Peter. *Conan Doyle Detective: True Crimes Investigated by the Creator of Sherlock Holmes*. New York: Carroll & Graf, 2006.

Stashower, Daniel. *Teller of Tales: The Life of Arthur Conan Doyle*. New York: Henry Holt, 1999.

Wagner, E. J. *The Science of Sherlock Holmes: From Baskerville Hall to the Valley of Fear, the Real Forensics Behind the Great Detective's Greatest Cases.* Hoboken, N.J.: John Wiley & Sons, 2006.

See also: Crime laboratories; Crime scene investigation; Forensic geoscience; Forensic toxicology; Literature and forensic science; Locard's exchange principle; Misconceptions fostered by media; *Silence of the Lambs, The*; Training and licensing of forensic professionals.

Short tandem repeat analysis

Definition: Determination of the number of repetitive DNA sequences two to seven base pairs in length that are found at particular locations on chromosomes in long arrays, the exact number of which typically varies among individuals in a population.

Significance: Short tandem repeat analysis represents a rapid and straightforward way to identify the persons to whom samples of DNA belong and is widely used for the identification of DNA samples collected at crime scenes, in paternity testing, and in the identification of human remains.

Since the 1990's, the analysis of short tandem repeats (STRs; also called microsatellites) as a method of DNA (deoxyribonucleic acid) identification has gained prominence over the original restriction fragment length polymorphism (RFLP) protocol developed in 1985. The original method required that a relatively large amount of nondegraded DNA (about 100 nanograms) be isolated from a forensic sample and took several days to process. It measured the variation in the number of repeating units of DNA that were typically fifteen to fifty base pairs in length, also called minisatellites. This process is also referred to as the analysis of variable number of tandem repeats (VNTRs).

STR analysis has several advantages over the RFLP protocol: It requires about one hundred times less DNA, it can be completed within a few hours, and it exhibits less sensitivity to DNA degradation. The first two advantages come about mainly because of the coupling of this procedure with the polymerase chain reaction (PCR), also developed during the 1980's. PCR allows for the rapid amplification of trace amounts of DNA using a set of DNA "primers" that bind to the sequence of interest and use it as a template to make millions of copies. The final advantage is the result of the decreased size of the DNA fragments that are analyzed, typically only a few hundred base pairs in length. It follows that, as the length of DNA being analyzed decreases, so does the probability that it has been degraded.

The short length of the fragments used in STR analysis does introduce one limitation. Because the variability in these shorter fragments within a population is less compared with RFLP analysis, more of them must be analyzed to provide the same assurances of an exact identification. This drawback has been circumvented by the development of "multiplex" systems for PCR. Here eight to sixteen pairs of PCR primers are combined in one reaction, each set labeled with a different fluorescent dye so that the products can be discriminated.

Another modification that has been made to improve STR analysis is the use of capillary gel electrophoresis, instead of the traditional "slab" gels, to separate out the resulting DNA fragments. This technique, developed in conjunction with the Human Genome Project, is much faster than slab gels and particularly amenable to the use of fluorescently labeled primers.

James S. Godde

Further Reading

Griffiths, Anthony J. F., et al. *Introduction to Genetic Analysis.* 9th ed. New York: W. H. Freeman, 2008.

Strachan, Tom, and Andrew P. Read. *Human Molecular Genetics 3.* New York: Garland Press, 2004.

See also: Anastasia remains identification; Bacterial biology; CODIS; DNA analysis; DNA extraction from hair, bodily fluids, and tissues; DNA fingerprinting; DNA profiling; DNA typing; Electrophoresis; Paternity testing; Polymerase chain reaction; Restriction fragment length polymorphisms; Y chromosome analysis.

The Silence of the Lambs

Date: Premiered on January 30, 1991
Identification: Motion-picture thriller about investigators' pursuit of a serial killer that presents an iconic portrayal of criminal personality profiling.
Significance: The success of *The Silence of the Lambs*, a film based on Thomas Harris's best-selling novel of the same title, led many people, particularly women, to pursue careers in federal law enforcement and forensic psychology. The film's portrayal of criminal personality profiling influenced public ideas about the criminally insane and heightened interest in the law-enforcement tactics used to apprehend such offenders.

The Silence of the Lambs, directed by Jonathan Demme, pits Clarice Starling (played by Jodie Foster), a Federal Bureau of Investigation (FBI) special agent in training, against "Buffalo Bill," a serial killer (the character, portrayed by Ted Levine, is an amalgamation of three real-life serial killers). The FBI's apprehension of Buffalo Bill hinges on the assistance of incarcerated killer—and brilliant psychiatrist—Hannibal Lecter (played by Anthony Hopkins).

With little physical evidence available except for the discovery of a death's-head moth in the throat of one of Buffalo Bill's dead victims, the federal agents investigating the case rely on criminal personality profiling in attempting to determine the identity of the killer. Although Lecter is a master of con games and psychological sadism and Starling is still in training, the FBI sends Starling, alone, to gather information from Lecter, who is being held in an insane asylum.

During the 1990's, numerous books were published about criminal personality profiling. Many were written by FBI agents who were central to developing the FBI's Behavioral Science Unit (later renamed the Behavioral Analysis Unit) and established methods for using criminal profiling as an investigative tool. Thomas Harris routinely consulted with FBI agents when creating the characters for his novels, including *The Silence of the Lambs*. Similarly, for added credibility, the makers of the book's film adaptation sought consultation from retired FBI special agent John Douglas.

The Silence of the Lambs has nevertheless been criticized as a rather unrealistic portrayal of the conditions under which FBI agents, and specifically criminal profilers, work. In fact, Robert K. Ressler, former director of the FBI's acclaimed Violent Criminal Apprehension Program (Vi-CAP), objected to the movie's script because he perceived it as an unrealistic portrayal of the bureau's agents. Ressler pointed out that profilers for the FBI are highly experienced, trained investigators, not new recruits. They are not "supersleuths," he said, adding that profiling is not a magical or mystical process. Rather, it requires the systematic, objective analysis of crime scenes. This analysis involves psychological principles and is conducted by experienced investigators who ultimately derive lists of personality and behavioral characteristics of the offenders. Local law-enforcement personnel then use this information in the detection and apprehension of the offenders.

Despite the implausibility of the "go it alone" investigative style into which Clarice Starling is thrust in *The Silence of the Lambs*, as well as the questionable efficacy of criminal profiling generally, the film has inspired many potential law-enforcement agents and remains a virtual recruitment tool for the FBI's Behavioral Analysis Unit.

Nickie D. Phillips

Further Reading
Douglas, John. *Mindhunter: Inside the FBI's Elite Serial Crime Unit*. New York: Pocket Books, 1995.

Nathan, Gregory. "Offender Profiling: A Review of the Literature." *British Journal of Forensic Practice* 7 (August, 2005).

Ressler, Robert K., and Tom Shachtman. *Whoever Fights Monsters: My Twenty Years Tracking Serial Killers for the FBI*. New York: St. Martin's Press, 1992.

See also: Criminal personality profiling; Forensic psychiatry; Forensic psychology; Literature and forensic science; Misconceptions fostered by media; Sherlock Holmes stories.

Silencers for firearms

Definition: Devices that reduce the peak sound pressure levels of gunshots.

Significance: By using silencers on firearms, criminals can substantially reduce the sounds of gunfire and thus reduce the likelihood that those sounds will reveal their locations or the types of guns being fired.

The term "silencer" is something of a misnomer, as many silencers reduce but hardly eliminate the sound of gunshots. "Sound suppressor" is a more accurate term. First developed during the twentieth century, sound suppressors are widely used by firearms owners in a number of nations, including Finland, France, Sweden, and the United Kingdom. They are often used to protect neighbors from unnecessary noise in locations where guns are fired on a regular basis (such as target ranges).

Sound suppressors are less commonly used in the United States, in part because the federal National Firearms Act of 1934 required owners to register the devices with the federal government and to pay a hefty tax. The motive for stringent regulation of sound suppressors at that time may have been fear that sound suppressors could facilitate the poaching of animals during a period when hunger and malnutrition were widespread in the nation. According to U.S. law, any device that reduces the sound of a firearm by at least three decibels is considered a "silencer." Most U.S. states allow their residents to possess silencers in accordance with federal law, and the criminal use of lawfully owned silencers by ordinary citizens in the United States is essentially nil.

A silencer may be attached to a gun's barrel (muzzle silencer) or may be built into the barrel itself (integral silencer). Silencers achieve sound suppression in a variety of ways. "Wet" suppressors contain grease or other liquid coolants; "dry" suppressors may use baffles to contain sound energy.

Sound suppressors typically reduce gunshot sounds by about fifteen to twenty decibels. Contrary to many media portrayals, the suppressed sound can still be more than four times louder than a chainsaw. When used in conjunction with simultaneous sounds in the surrounding area (such as traffic noise), however, silencers can be effective in masking the sound of gunshots.

In a heavily silenced firearm, the sound of the bullet flight may be louder than the sound of the gunshot, thereby making it more difficult for a

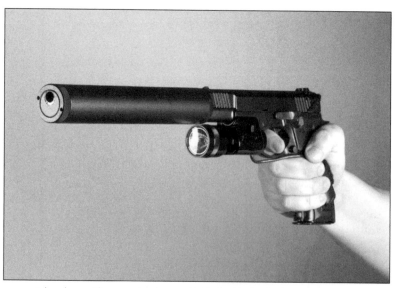

A handgun with a muzzle silencer. (© Vadim Kozlovsky/Dreamstime.com)

witness to identify the origin of the gunshot. Snipers find silencers useful in that they help to maintain the snipers' concealed positions by reducing the visible muzzle flash of gunshots and by reducing recoil.

David B. Kopel

Further Reading

Paulson, Alan C. *Sporting and Tactical Silencers*. Vol. 1 in *Silencer: History and Performance*. Boulder, Colo: Paladin Press, 1996.

Paulson, Alan C., N. R. Parker, and Peter G. Kokalis. *CQB, Assault Rifle, and Sniper Technology*. Vol. 2 in *Silencer: History and Performance*. Boulder, Colo: Paladin Press, 2002.

See also: Assassination; Ballistics; Bureau of Alcohol, Tobacco, Firearms and Explosives; Firearms analysis; Misconceptions fostered by media.

Silicone breast implant cases

Date: 1977-1999

The Event: Women throughout the United States filed individual and class-action lawsuits against the manufacturers of silicone gel-filled breast implants, alleging that injuries and illnesses resulted when the products ruptured or leaked. Suits filed during the 1990's led to huge monetary awards for damages to women who claimed injury from silicone breast implants, often because the manufacturers had concealed safety information from implant recipients.

Significance: Numerous scientific studies of silicone breast implants have shown that there is no significant link between such implants and the diseases experienced by the plaintiffs who brought lawsuits against the manufacturers, but these cases nonetheless resulted in the largest proposed product liability settlement in American legal history. In addition, the beginning of federal regulation of medical devices in the United States may be attributed to the silicone breast implant cases.

The first silicone gel-filled breast implant was introduced in 1962. By 1964, Dow Corning Corporation, the largest manufacturer of such implants, had established its Medical Products Division in order to market silicone breast implant products. Between 1962 and 1991, nearly two million women had received silicone breast implants in North America alone. Of these women, 80 percent received the implants for cosmetic reasons; the remaining 20 percent received the implants as part of breast reconstruction surgery following mastectomies.

As increasing numbers of breast augmentation surgeries were performed, problems with silicone implants began to become evident, including hardening and occasional rupture; cases of enlargement of the lymph nodes in implant sites were also observed. At the same time, some recipients of silicone implants began to develop an array of more serious disorders that they suspected were related to the implants. Some recipients developed systemic connective-tissue diseases, including scleroderma, systemic lupus erythematosus, rheumatoid arthritis, and other nonspecific autoimmune ailments. The silicone breast implant lawsuits focused on the alleged link between the silicone implants and connective-tissue diseases.

Background

The first suit, which was filed in 1977, resulted in a $170,000 settlement against Dow Corning. In *Hopkins v. Dow Corning Corporation* (1991), a jury found that the plaintiff's mixed connective-tissue disease was linked to her ruptured silicone breast implants and awarded the plaintiff $7.3 million. The bulk of that award ($6.5 million) can be attributed to the jury's desire to punish the conduct of Dow Corning, which had concealed its knowledge that its silicone implants could leak and failed to disclose the adverse results of animal testing the company had conducted.

In response to *Hopkins* and other cases, certain manufacturers of breast implants and their suppliers set aside funds of $4.25 billon to deal with potential legal suits. The fund was used as the basis for a global settlement whereby women who had received implants were given a deadline to decide whether they would join a class-action suit that guaranteed a settlement of $200,000 to $2 million if they agreed not to litigate or would litigate separately. Despite the settlement offer, 12,359 individual lawsuits were filed against Dow Corning by the end of 1993. In 1995, Dow Corning filed for Chapter 11 bankruptcy protection, which halted all pending litigation.

In 1997, a jury in the first class-action suit against Dow Chemical, which owned half of Dow Corning, found that the company had fraudulently concealed the dangers of silicone and failed to investigate properly the health risks associated with silicone implants. Facing the bankruptcy of Dow Corning, the plaintiffs agreed in 1998 to an offer of $3.2 billion to settle numerous injury claims; this step allowed Dow Corning to emerge from bankruptcy proceedings. Given the scientific evidence, most silicone breast implant cases after 1998 did not result in awards of punitive damages, but juries still concluded that the manufacturers were liable for concealing evidence and failing to warn recipients.

The Scientific Evidence Presented

To establish that silicone breast implants constitute a risk factor for the development of immune system-related disorders, epidemiological studies must show that recipients of these implants as a distinct group develop these disorders at a higher rate than do women without implants or any normal population of women. The first such study, the results of which were published in 1994, failed to demonstrate any such heightened risk or increased development of disorders, and statistical analyses continue to demonstrate that no evidence exists of any causal link or association between breast implants and any of the individual connective-tissue diseases, all connective-tissue diseases combined, or any other autoimmune conditions.

As most commentators have observed, insufficient scientific evidence exists to support the conclusion that the silicone breast implants caused the alleged injuries. Evidence is too sparse even to support the argument that the implants increased the likelihood of the recipients' developing these conditions. For example, one study noted that patients with insulin-dependent diabetes and those who depend on dialysis have increased exposure to silicone because silicone accumulates in their bodies. In these individuals, no systemic illnesses or any illnesses similar to those experienced by women with the silicone implants developed; thus, these illnesses are probably not attributable to silicone.

It is extremely difficult to establish a causal link involving illnesses and a product. In *Livshits v. Natural Y Surgical Specialties, Incorporated* (1991), the plaintiff was initially able to demonstrate a "cause-and-effect" link, but later the court substantially reduced the award of damages when the testimony of the plaintiff's expert witness was disqualified. The expert had testified that the plaintiff's silicone implant had caused an acceleration of the cancer that occurred in the plaintiff's breast. A study published in June, 1992, however, revealed that silicone was linked only to connective-tissue sarcomas that appeared in limited numbers in rodent species susceptible to cancer. The court found this study to be clear evidence that the silicone implant did not cause the acceleration of the plaintiff's cancer and therefore reduced the plaintiff's award.

Some commentators still adhere to their belief that the implants caused the disorders sustained by these women. They argue that scientific evidence may show no link between silicone breast implants and specific classic autoimmune diseases, but the research has not addressed possible connections of the implants to atypical autoimmune diseases or the severe complications that arise locally at the sites of implants.

No definitive scientific evidence has shown whether removing silicone breast implants changes the course of connective-tissue diseases. One study found some improvement in seven of twelve patients after the removal of implants, but no firm conclusions can be drawn from this small sample.

The Food and Drug Administration's Response

In 1976, in response to public pressures regarding the lack of safety testing of silicone breast implants, the Medical Devices Amendment was added to the Federal Food, Drug, and Cosmetic Act. This amendment required the U.S. Food and Drug Administration (FDA) to review and approve new medical devices for safety. It had no effect on silicone breast implants, however, as they had already been on the market for almost fifteen years.

For years, the FDA failed to act on growing concerns related to breast implants, allowing manufacturers, in essence, to regulate themselves. In 1988, the FDA classified the implants as Class III devices, which meant that manufacturers were required to provide detailed data as to product safety and design. The data, however, were not due until 1991, at which point the FDA concluded that many manufacturers had submitted insufficient safety data and requested more. In 1992, after hearings before two independent advisory committees, the FDA placed a moratorium on the use of silicone gel-filled breast implants other than in research because of inadequate data on their safety. In 2006, silicone implants received FDA approval for use in breast reconstruction in women of any age and in breast augmentation (often cosmetic) in women twenty-two years or older.

Vivian Bodey

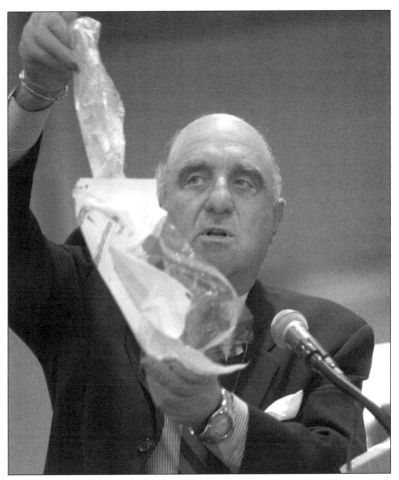

Dr. Edward Mehmed, testifying before a federal advisory panel in October, 2003, shows the remains of a silicone gel breast implant that he removed from one of his patients. *(AP/Wide World Photos)*

Further Reading

Angell, Marcia. *Science on Trial: The Clash of Medical Evidence and the Law in the Breast Implant Case*. New York: W. W. Norton, 1997. Argues that there was no medical consensus or evidence to support the contention that implants could cause widespread illness and that the courts should have relied on scientific evidence instead of awarding such large sums of money. Intended for a general audience.

Bar-Meir, Eran, Michael Eherenfeld, and Yehuda Shoenfeld. "Silicone Gel Breast Implants and Connective Tissue Disease: A Comprehensive Review." *Autoimmunity* 36 (June, 2003): 193-197. Presents an in-depth discussion of epidemiological studies that have been unable to establish an association between silicone gel breast implants and autoimmune disease.

Janowsky, Esther C., Lawrence L. Kupper, and Barbara S. Hulka. "Meta-analyses of the Relation Between Silicone Breast Implants and the Risk of Connective-Tissue Diseases." *New England Journal of Medicine* 342, no. 11 (2000): 781-790. Presents a detailed statistical analysis of several studies of the relationship between silicone breast implants and the risk of connective-tissue and autoimmune diseases to determine whether there was some statistical basis in alleging the relationship.

Stewart, Mary White. *Silicone Spills: Breast Implants on Trial*. Westport, Conn.: Praeger, 1998. Focuses on the stories of specific women while also providing good accounts of some of the cases as they wound their way through the courts. Nontechnical work intended for a general audience.

U.S. Food and Drug Administration. "Silicone Gel-Filled Breast Implants Approved." *FDA Consumer Magazine*, January/February, 2007. Presents a concise summary of the history of silicone breast implants and concludes that no convincing evidence exists to show that breast implants are associated with connective-tissue disease or cancer.

See also: *Daubert v. Merrell Dow Pharmaceuticals*; Epidemiology; Expert witnesses; Food and Drug Administration, U.S.; Immune system; Product liability cases.

Silkwood/Kerr-McGee case

Date: Silkwood died on November 13, 1974

Identification: An employee of the Kerr-McGee plutonium fuel-rod processing plant, Karen Silkwood was a union activist who gained notoriety after she died under mysterious circumstances while actively engaged in a campaign to publicize serious worker safety violations in her employer's plant near Crescent, Oklahoma.

Significance: Silkwood's dramatic and unexplained death, which was apparently connected to the safety hazards she was investigating, drew national attention to dangers in the nuclear power industry. Investigations established that Kerr-McGee had committed serious safety infractions that contributed to Silkwood's poor health and possibly even her death.

A divorced mother of three, Karen Silkwood (1946-1974) began working at the Kerr-McGee Corporation's new nuclear reactor fuel-rod processing plant near Crescent, Oklahoma, in August, 1972. There, she helped to produce plutonium pellets. Among the tasks she performed in the plant's metallography laboratory were quality-control checks on plutonium pellets that she held up to unexposed X-ray film. Pellets in which plutonium was distributed evenly throughout produced no "hot spots" on the film and passed the quality-control checks. Silkwood also polished fuel-rod welds to check for cracks and inclusions.

As an employee of the Kerr-McGee plant, Silkwood belonged to the Oil, Chemical, and Atomic Workers Union (OCAW). In November, 1972, only a few months after she had been hired, her union's contract with Kerr-McGee expired. The local union branch then went on strike, demanding higher wages and improved training and health and safety programs. After ten weeks, the strike ended when Kerr-McGee issued a sign-or-be-fired ultimatum. Meanwhile, the strike had strengthened Silkwood's bonds to her union, and she was developing concerns regarding worker safety in her plant.

The Trouble Begins

During the spring of 1974, Kerr-McGee fell so far behind in production that it initiated twelve-hour shifts and seven-day workweeks to catch up. The accelerated work pace caused a dramatic increase in accidental contaminations and spills, and Silkwood's worries about worker safety heightened. On July 31, 1974, Silkwood herself was accidentally contaminated while working in the emission spectroscopy lab. Tests using Atomic Energy Commission (AEC) standards showed a slight air-filter contamination in the lab. However, results of the test seemed confusing because the contamination occurred only on Silkwood's shift, not on the shifts before or after hers.

In August, 1974, Silkwood was elected to the local union's bargaining committee and assigned to address the topics of health and safety for the impending contract negotiations. Taking her new responsibilities seriously, she began studying work conditions at Kerr-McGee carefully. In September, she and two other local union officials met with officials of the national union and the AEC to discuss evidence of the dangerous conditions in the plant that she had observed. She also revealed her suspicions that company officials were altering the plant's quality-control records to make sure production levels remained high. She specifically faulted Kerr-McGee for falsifying inspection records to hide the improper handling of fuel rods and the improper assignment of poorly trained workers to perform tasks during a production speedup. If her charges could be proven to be true, Kerr-McGee would have been found to be guilty of fraud. Silkwood was then advised to gather more documentation at the plant secretly. At that same meeting, she learned for the first time that plutonium is carcinogenic.

Silkwood's Contamination

Several months later, Silkwood discovered that she herself had become contaminated with nearly forty times the legal limit for plutonium contamination. Curiously, the plutonium contamination did not seem to come from any holes in the protective gloves she had used and was greater on a day when she had only been doing office work and had no contact with nuclear materials. When she arrived for work on November 7, plant inspectors found Silkwood so dangerously contaminated that she was even exhaling contaminated air. A health team accompanied her to her home, where traces of plutonium were found in her bathroom, her refrigerator, and other places. Silkwood and her housemate were then sent to Los Alamos National Laboratory for more extensive examinations, and their house was thoroughly decontaminated.

The Forensic Mystery

The important question for forensic investigators to answer was how Silkwood could have become so seriously contaminated within such a short period. Silkwood herself charged that Kerr-McGee operatives were conducting a smear campaign to discredit her criticisms of safety conditions at their plant by putting plutonium in the urine and feces sample jars they gave her. That, she claimed, accounted for the plutonium contamination found in her bathroom that occurred when she spilled a urine sample there on the morning of November 7. She pointed out that samples taken at her home showed dramatically higher levels of contamination than those taken in "fresh" jars either at the Kerr-McGee plant or at Los Alamos.

Kerr-McGee responded by accusing Silkwood of deliberately contaminating herself in order to discredit the company. Making such an accusation was a dangerous strategy for the company to pursue, as it suggested that the company's security procedures were so lax that employees could smuggle nuclear material out of the plant. To complicate the issue, forensic investigators later determined that the soluble plutonium to which Silkwood had been exposed was not the same kind to which she could have had any kind of access in the plant for several months. The plant stored the type of plutonium with which she had been contaminated in a vault to which only Kerr-McGee managers had access.

Silkwood's Death

At the time Silkwood was contaminated by plutonium, Silkwood claimed to have assembled a large file of documents that supported her charges of irregularities in the Kerr-McGee plant. She was scheduled to meet with a *New York Times* reporter and a national union official to publicize her findings. On November 13, 1974, she showed a binder and packet of documents to attendees at a union meeting in Crescent, Oklahoma. Afterward, she left the meeting alone, intending to drive to Oklahoma City, thirty miles away, to present the documents to the *Times* reporter and union official.

Silkwood never reached Oklahoma City. Later that evening, her dead body was found in her car, which had apparently run off the road and hit a culvert. Police on the scene concluded that her death resulted from a single-car crash caused by her falling asleep at the wheel. They claimed to find no glass or debris to indicate that any other vehicles were involved. They also claimed to find some methaqualone (quaaludes) and marijuana in Silkwood's car, but none of the documents she was believed to be carrying. A coroner found enough traces of methaqualone in her blood to cause her to become drowsy.

Despite a lack of hard evidence, many people believed that Silkwood was murdered to keep her from publicizing her charges against Kerr-McGee. Independent investigators argued that another vehicle could have forced her car off the road without leaving any evidence of its involvement in the accident. They also dispute the suggestion that Silkwood was asleep at the time of the accident by pointing out that the position in which her steering wheel was bent indicated that she must have been awake and alert, trying to control her car.

Investigation and Trial

Both the AEC and the Oklahoma state medical examiner requested that the Los Alamos Tissue Analysis Program examine Silkwood's internal organs. Medical examiners found extensive plutonium contamination, with the greatest damage in her lungs and smaller amounts in her gastrointestinal organs. Such contamination was not consistent with the type of exposure to plutonium that Silkwood would have had during her normal tasks in the Kerr-McGee plant.

In November, 1976, Silkwood's father and children filed a wrongful-death civil suit against Kerr-McGee, seeking $160,000 in damages. The suit charged the corporation with negligence in handling plutonium and both Kerr-McGee and the FBI with a conspiracy to deprive Silkwood of her civil rights. Throughout the legal proceedings' discovery period, the Silkwood family's attorneys were impeded by insufficient funds and a lack of cooperation from the defendants. They dropped the conspiracy charges before the suit went to trial and shifted their focus to proving negligence. The plaintiffs also amended their complaint to $1.5 million in compensatory damages and $10 million in punitive damages.

The Silkwood case, through which the family sought to improve safety in the nuclear industry and to educate the public on the dangers of nuclear energy, was not only a civil trial but also a social movement. Under the direction of attorney Gerald Spence, the Silkwood legal team sought to prove several issues: that plutonium was ultrahazardous and that Kerr-McGee was responsible for its proper care, that Karen Silkwood had been contaminated with plutonium that originated at Kerr-McGee, that she had not contaminated herself, that her contamination injured her between November 5 and 13, 1974, and that Kerr-McGee was negligent in failing to protect its workers. The trial did not cover the details of Silkwood's death.

The trial began in March, 1979, and lasted ten weeks. The plaintiffs called nineteen witnesses to testify on the dangers of plutonium, working conditions at Kerr-McGee, and Karen Silkwood's character. The defense team called twenty-four witnesses to testify that Silkwood had deliberately contaminated herself with non-Kerr-McGee plutonium and that the contamination had not injured her. Moreover, the defense argued that her contamination fell under workers' compensation laws.

Aftermath of the Silkwood/Kerr-McGee Case

Despite a standing offer of a large cash reward for new information in the case, the full circumstances of Karen Silkwood's death remain unresolved. In December, 1983, Hollywood drew more attention to the case and to the dangers of nuclear energy with their version of the story in the film *Silkwood*, directed by Mike Nichols and starring Meryl Streep in the title role. The film earned five Academy Award nominations. One year later, a coalition of nuclear safety groups established the Karen Silkwood Awards to keep her memory alive by honoring safety crusaders in the nuclear industry. Silkwood may have lived an ordinary life, but her death initiated a social movement that not only changed the public perception of nuclear energy but also ultimately resulted in federal changes to the industry's regulation.

Jennifer Davis

In May, 1979, both sides rested. While meeting with the judge, Kerr-McGee conceded that Silkwood had, in fact, been contaminated by its own plutonium. The judge then set a precedent by defining plutonium as ultrahazardous. On May 18, 1979, after twenty-one hours of deliberation, the jury found Kerr-McGee negligent in an off-site contamination incident and awarded Silkwood's estate $500,000 in compensatory damages, $5,000 in property damages, and $10 million in punitive damages.

Kerr-McGee appealed the verdict to the Tenth Circuit Court of Appeals, contending that the first trial had violated federal and state regulations and that the first judge had erred in declaring plutonium ultrahazardous. On December 11, 1981, the appellate court concurred and lowered the award to only the $5,000 in property damages. Silkwood's team then appealed to the U.S. Supreme Court. On January 11, 1984, that Court ruled that victims of radiation injuries could sue nuclear power companies.

The Supreme Court's decision severely limited the federal monopoly on nuclear power by placing companies under state tort laws that could hold companies liable for punitive damages for gross negligence. The decision not only vindicated Karen Silkwood but also stood as a victory for states, which were given some regulatory control of the nuclear industry. In an out-of-court settlement in August, 1986, the Silkwood case finally ended with a $1.38 million agreement. Kerr-McGee contended that it settled to avoid more costly litigation.

Richard L. Wilson and Jennifer Davis

Further Reading

James, Stuart H., and Jon J. Nordby, eds. *Forensic Science: An Introduction to Scientific and Investigative Techniques*. 2d ed. Boca Raton, Fla.: CRC Press, 2005. Provides an excellent overview of the forensic sciences for general readers.

Kohn, Howard. "Malignant Giant." *Rolling Stone*, June 11, 1992, 92-97. Includes excerpts from the March 27, 1975, article that sparked an anti-nuclear power movement in the United States. Also discusses the impact of the case on the magazine.

_____. *Who Killed Karen Silkwood?* New York: Summit Books, 1981. Early compilation of *Rolling Stone* articles covers the struggles of Silkwood's family and supporters and theories about her death. Includes a discussion of the evidence against Kerr-McGee.

Raloff, Janet. "Silkwood: The Legal Fallout." *Science*, February 4, 1984, 74-79. Discusses the importance of the U.S. Supreme Court ruling in the Silkwood case for state regulation of the nuclear industry.

Rashke, Richard. *The Killing of Karen Silkwood: The Story Behind the Kerr-McGee Plutonium Case*. 2d ed. Ithaca, N.Y.: Cornell University Press, 2000. Provides a detailed look at the events surrounding Silkwood's death and the first trial. Based on information drawn from extensive interviews and available sources. A preface and three short chapters explore what has been learned about Silkwood since the book's initial publication.

See also: Courts and forensic evidence; Dosimetry; Environmental Measurements Laboratory; Forensic pathology; Forensic toxicology; Journalism; Nuclear detection devices; Quantitative and qualitative analysis of chemicals; Radiation damage to tissues.

Simpson murder trial

Date: January 24-October 3, 1995

The Event: Indicted for the 1994 murders of his former wife Nicole Brown Simpson and her friend Ronald Goldman, O. J. Simpson used his wealth and celebrity to assemble a so-called dream team of defense lawyers. He was acquitted at trial after his attorneys successfully attacked much of the forensic evidence presented by the prosecution.

Significance: Simpson's televised murder trial brought issues of legal procedure and forensic investigation to the attention of millions of viewers on a daily basis for months, even as it exerted a distorting influence on the proceedings. His acquittal brought home to legal professionals the need for higher standards in the collection, interpretation, and presentation of forensic evidence, but it also revealed how legal processes can be influenced by celebrity and race. In addition, it highlighted the education gap between forensic professionals and the public from which juries are drawn.

During O. J. Simpson's murder trial, the prosecution produced what it called a "mountain" of evidence to demonstrate Simpson's guilt, and the defense explained the evidence away in terms of a police conspiracy to frame Simpson. Reporter Jeffrey Toobin may have been right when he observed that "the sheer number of associations between Simpson and the evidence made the evidence seem too complex when in fact it merely showed just how guilty Simpson was."

The Evidence

Evidence of Simpson's guilt included the victims' blood in his vehicle and on his socks, and his own blood at the murder scene and at his home. It included hair like Simpson's on Goldman's shirt and on a knit cap. It included fiber like the carpet in Simpson's Ford Bronco on the knit cap and on a glove. It included bloody shoe prints in Simpson's size, which were traced to a rare brand of shoes he denied owning. (Later, at Simpson's civil trial, photographs of him wearing such shoes materialized.) It included a bloody glove at the crime scene and the glove's mate at Simpson's estate. It included motive, opportunity, guilty behavior (the Bronco "escape," an apparent suicide note), and suspicious circumstances (unexplained wounds on Simpson's left hand). Some additional evidence—for example, Simpson's statements in an early interview

A key moment in O. J. Simpson's trial came when prosecutors asked him to put on a glove found at the murder scene and its mate. The obvious difficulty Simpson had in squeezing his hands into the gloves is believed to have damaged the prosecution's case severely. *(Sam Mircovich/Reuters/Landov)*

with police—was not presented.

The prosecution emphasized how much evidence remained unrefuted by the defense's claims of police conspiracy, incompetence, and racism. The defense, intoning "garbage in, garbage out," insisted that things "didn't fit" and that there was "something wrong" with the prose-

> ## California's Definition of "Reasonable Doubt"
>
> It is not a mere possible doubt because everything relating to human affairs, and depending on moral evidence, is open to some possible or imaginary doubt. It is that state of the case which, after the entire comparison and consideration of all the evidence, leaves the minds of the jurors in that condition that they cannot say they feel an abiding conviction to a moral certainty of the truth of the charge.
>
> *Instructions to jurors in California courts*

cution's case. For those appalled by the verdict, the idea of a vast police conspiracy was absurd and the appeal to racism without foundation, and much evidence withstood even those suspicions. Those who celebrated the acquittal felt the "something wrong" with the prosecution's case tainted everything, even if exactly what was wrong had not been identified; enough had gone wrong with the investigation by the Los Angeles Police Department (LAPD), and with the prosecution's witnesses, to justify reasonable doubt about whether the prosecution had met its burden of proof, even if one supposed Simpson probably guilty.

Reasonable Doubt

Opinions on the Simpson case divided largely along racial lines because the life experience of many African Americans made it seem reasonable, and that of many whites made it seem unreasonable, that racial motivations could lead authorities to trump up charges against a famous black man. It made sense to the prosecution to argue that LAPD detective Mark Fuhrman's lies about his use of racial epithets did not mean that he had planted evidence, although the law does suppose that a witness who lies about one matter may be willing to lie about others.

Some believed that the prosecution had not met its burden of demonstrating guilt beyond a reasonable doubt. As others viewed it, the evidence of guilt was overwhelming, so doubt could not be reasonable. If there could be no reasonable doubt, then the jury was willful or incompetent or both. This was the jury both sides had accepted, however.

After Simpson's acquittal, some commentators suggested that the jury system itself re-

quired amendment. A later jury, in the civil trial (October 23, 1996-February 4, 1997), found the evidence compelling and found Simpson "liable" for the attacks. Was this outcome the result of better (or worse) lawyering, stricter judging, absence of cameras, racial makeup of the jury, difference in standard of proof?

Not only did the two juries disagree, the experts continued to disagree. Critics such as attorneys Vincent Bugliosi and Daniel Petrocelli have expressed their beliefs that the specious doubts raised by the defense in the criminal trial have been dispelled. In contrast, forensic pathologist Michael Baden, who testified as an expert witness for the defense at the criminal trial, years later lamented that blood drops on Nicole Brown Simpson's back were not collected and suggested that "if the coroner's staff at the murders had not turned over Nicole's body, we might know beyond a reasonable doubt who killed those innocent people." Baden went on to plead for better protection of crime scenes and more careful collection, preservation, and testing of trace evidence. Renowned criminalist Henry C. Lee, whose expert testimony for the defense exerted immense influence on the jury, has continued, despite years of severe criticism, to view Simpson's acquittal as a victory for the objectivity of forensic science.

Edward Johnson

Further Reading

Baden, Michael, and Marion Roach. *Dead Reckoning: The New Science of Catching Killers*. New York: Simon & Schuster, 2001. Popular account of modern forensic advances makes several comments about the Simpson case.

Bugliosi, Vincent. *Outrage: The Five Reasons*

Why O. J. Simpson Got Away with Murder.
New York: W. W. Norton, 1996. Presents a
detailed argument for Simpson's guilt along
with a scathing analysis of why the case was
lost.

Erzinçlioglu, Zakaria. *Every Contact Leaves a
Trace: Scientific Detection in the Twentieth
Century.* London: Carlton Books, 2000. General discussion of forensics by a distinguished entomologist includes an oddly confused account of some of the evidence in the
Simpson case.

Lange, Tom, and Philip Vannatter, as told to
Dan E. Moldea. *Evidence Dismissed: The Inside Story of the Police Investigation of O. J.
Simpson.* New York: Pocket Books, 1997.
Two leading detectives in the case describe
their investigation.

Lee, Henry C., with Thomas W. O'Neil. *Cracking
Cases: The Science of Solving Crimes.* Amherst, N.Y.: Prometheus Books, 2002. Discusses the famous criminalist's thoughts on
the Simpson case in chapter 3.

Petrocelli, Daniel, with Peter
Knobler. *Triumph of Justice:
The Final Judgment on the
Simpson Saga.* New York:
Crown, 1998. Definitive work
on Simpson's civil trial highlights flaws in the criminal trial
and explains how lead attorney
Petrocelli was able to secure
judgment against Simpson.

Toobin, Jeffrey. *The Run of His
Life: The People v. O. J. Simpson.* New York: Random House,
1996. Account by the reporter
whose story in *The New Yorker*
first revealed the defense's strategy to "play the race card."

See also: Blood residue and bloodstains; Blood spatter analysis;
Chain of custody; Cross-contamination of evidence; DNA analysis;
DNA extraction from hair, bodily
fluids, and tissues; Footprints and
shoe prints; Hair analysis; Homicide; Journalism; Trace and transfer evidence.

Sinus prints

Definition: X rays of the bony ridges inside
human skulls and the spaces they create.

Significance: Called "prints" because they resemble fingerprints in being unique to
each human being, sinus prints are valuable both to medicine and to forensic anthropology, which uses them to identify
bodies.

The uniqueness of the human sinus region was
initially discovered by surgeons, who noticed in
viewing preoperative X rays that the configuration of the sinus region varies from person to
person, with no two exactly alike. Unlike other
bones in the body, which are fairly standard
across individuals, the sinus areas of different
persons' skulls differ, and this can make surgery
in this area difficult. For this reason, preoperative X rays are taken when patients undergo si-

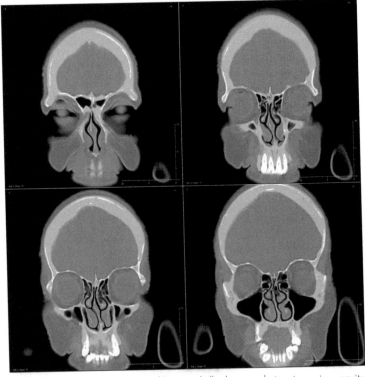

Computed tomography images of human skulls showing their unique sinus cavity
shapes. (© Trout55/Dreamstime.com)

nus surgery so the surgeons can familiarize themselves with the patients' unique sinus cavities before surgery begins.

Forensic anthropologists sometimes use sinus prints to identify bodies. Other X rays may also assist with identification, particularly X rays of skeletal anomalies, such as broken bones. Even when bodies are not identified immediately, X rays can be used to help identify them years later.

Although each person's sinus print is unique, it can be difficult to identify a dead body from one postmortem sinus print alone. A sinus print made prior to death must also exist, and it must be accessible to law enforcement. For these reasons, sinus prints are used more often to confirm suspected identities than to identify individuals without other forms of identification.

Although sinus prints have been used for forensic identification since the early twentieth century, this technique is rarely mentioned, even in the forensic science literature. In one of the most famous instances of this method of identification, sinus prints were used to verify the identity of President John F. Kennedy after he was assassinated in 1963. A comparison of sinus prints made before and after Kennedy's death confirmed that the body subjected to autopsy was, indeed, that of the late president of the United States.

Ayn Embar-Seddon and
Allan D. Pass

Further Reading

Asherson, Nehemiah. *Identification by Frontal Sinus Prints: A Forensic Medical Pilot Survey*. London: Lewis, 1965.

Larheim, T. A., and P.-L. Westesson. *Maxillofacial Imaging*. New York: Springer, 2006.

See also: Autopsies; Class versus individual evidence; DNA fingerprinting; Ear prints; Fingerprints; Forensic anthropology; Osteology and skeletal radiology; September 11, 2001, victim identification; University of Tennessee Anthropological Research Facility.

Skeletal analysis

Definition: Examinations by forensic anthropologists of bones that are subjects of criminal investigations.

Significance: Because skeletons and teeth are the hardest and most durable parts of human bodies, they are often the only parts that investigators recover after victims of crimes have been dead for long periods of time. Forensic anthropologists are trained to identify skeletal remains and interpret the unique evidence they contain; they can often help identify homicide victims and reconstruct the circumstances of both their lives and their deaths.

Forensic anthropology is the application of physical anthropological knowledge to evidence used in the legal process. The field is one of the recognized subdisciplines of the American Academy of Forensic Science. Practitioners in the field are frequently called upon to identify skeletal, badly decomposed, or otherwise unidentified human remains. Often, their first task is to apply techniques developed within physical anthropology to determine whether unidentified remains are human. After confirming that remains are, in fact, those of human beings, they try to answer other questions about the identities of the decedents, the manner of their deaths, and whether they were victims of foul play.

Forensic anthropologists frequently work alongside forensic pathologists, odontologists, and other investigators. They not only help identify decedents but also help determine their manner of death and how long they have been dead—the so-called postmortem interval. Although these professionals may initially be called upon to assist in locating and recovering suspicious human remains, they do most of their work on skeletons after they are recovered. Using the evidence they find in bones, they build decedents' biological profiles, which include their sex, age, ancestry, stature, and unique identifying features, such as former injuries.

Human Skeletons

The bone matter in skeletons is made up of two primary materials: a hard mineral salt known as hydroxyapatite and a more flexible organic material, collagen. Hydroxyapatite gives bones their structural support and torsion strength, and collagen gives them their elasticity and tensile strength. Bones in living bodies are also living matter. They are innervated and receive nutrients from the bodies' blood supplies. Like other living tissues, they produce waste from metabolic processes associated with their growth and development.

In addition to their structural support function, the muscles, ligaments, and tendons that are connected to the skeleton permit the body's animation. Skeletons also house the bone marrow that produces the vital red blood cells. Because living bones are replaced at a rate of about 10 percent per year and are constantly being re-formed by the mechanical forces exerted on them, they effectively record information about the body after an individual's death. The analytical techniques that forensic anthropologists use help bones speak for the dead.

Methods of Identifying Bones

Determining whether recovered bones belong to human beings requires a detailed knowledge not only of the morphology of all the bones in human skeletons but also of all types of animal bones with which human bones might be confused. Because there are only two sexes, one might expect that determination of a given decedent's sex should be correct approximately 50 percent of the time. However, given the critical functional differences between male pelvises and female pelvises, which are modified by childbirth, as well as general sexual differences in the muscle masses attached to

The Major Bones of the Human Skeleton

bones, forensic experts should be able to identify the sex of unknown decedents from skeletal evidence in more than 95 percent of cases they investigate.

Methods of determining age from bones are more complex than those used for determining sex. Many criteria are employed to estimate the age of a decedent from a skeleton. Moreover, matching the estimated age at time of death of a body with the age of a long-missing person can be further complicated by uncertainty about the missing person's age at time of death. This latter complication is especially relevant to identifying the skeletal remains of children, whose bones change more quickly than those of adults. If the bones of what appears to have been a three-year-old child were recovered several years after a two-year-old child disappeared, those remains might belong to the missing child, but making such a match would pose special difficulties.

Age is best determined through the employment of multiple criteria. Among infants and children, for example, the numbers of bones, the presence or absence of specific bones, and the degree of bone development can all be important in estimating age at time of death. Infant humans have approximately four hundred bones; however, as the children grow older, the shapes and numbers of their bones change. Some of the bones fuse to others at growth plates, and the predictable timing of such events can be used to estimate age at time of death. The emergence of deciduous, or "baby," teeth and their gradual replacement by permanent teeth are also developmental events that occur at predictable ages.

The ages of middle-aged adults and older persons can be estimated based on changes in the appearance of the pubic bones of the pelvis, suture closures among their skull bones, the presence and degree of development of arthritis, and combinations of a host of degenerative changes that normally occur in human bones as individuals age. It is more difficult to estimate the ages of adult decedents than young decedents, however, because as human beings age, many other variables can affect their skeletal development. These variables include individual genetics, dietary differences, and exposure to disease and physical traumas.

Determining the ancestry of decedents from

Queen Hatshepsut

Skeletal remains can tell many stories about their owners' lives by providing information on age, health history, birth defects, and injuries. Skeletal analyses can even provide information on remains that are almost unimaginably old. A dramatic example is what has been learned from the bones of the legendary Queen Hatshepsut (c. 1525-c. 1482 B.C.E.), who ruled Egypt in her own right almost thirty-five hundred years ago. Inscriptions and written records chronicle her achievements as queen. Her bones chronicle the fact that she died at about the age of fifty from the ravages of metastatic bone cancer.

Dwight G. Smith

---

their skeletal remains is the most difficult aspect of creating biological profiles. Skulls must be present and in reasonably good condition to enable a host of measurements and observations to be collected. The data that are collected are then compared with measurements and other information gathered from large numbers of people of known ancestry and stored in databases. The results of multiple discriminant statistical procedures, along with researchers' experience and expertise in assessing the wide range of human skeletal variation, assist in identifying the ancestry of unknown decedents.

Estimating the stature of decedents from their skeletal remains is comparatively easy and involves the application of only basic mathematics. Forensic anthropologists simply measure the longest bones recovered in a set of skeletal remains and multiply the lengths by figures listed in the most relevant regression tables. The main challenge is in choosing which formulas to use from among the many available. Allowing for differences in sex, age, and ancestry, different formulas are used for the various long bones of the body.

Other unique skeletal features of decedents used to help identify remains include dental work, orthopedic prostheses, and records of fractures. In some cases, the cause of death itself or other injuries sustained around the time of death leave evidence on skeletons. Examples include perimortem injuries, evidence of sharp force or blunt force traumas, bullet wounds, and manual strangulation. For example, the recovered skull of a person known to have been shot through the head is likely to contain persuasive evidence of the decedent's cause of death.

Turhon A. Murad

Further Reading

Burns, Karen R. *Forensic Anthropology Training Manual*. Upper Saddle River, N.J.: Prentice Hall, 2006. General textbook on forensic anthropology includes discussion of sex differences for each region of the human skeleton.

Gill, George W., and Stanley Rhine. *Skeletal Attribution of Race: Methods for Forensic Anthropology*. Albuquerque: Maxwell Museum of Anthropology, University of New Mexico, 2004. Contains images of skull and face-form variations useful for determining ancestry.

Katzenberg, M. Anne, and Shelley R. Saunders, eds. *The Biological Anthropology of the Human Skeleton*. New York: John Wiley & Sons, 2000. Assortment of essays provides a comprehensive overview of issues relating to skeletal analysis. Includes a focused discussion of forensic science as applied to skeletal remains.

Krogman, Wilton Marion. "A Guide to the Identification of Human Skeletal Material." *FBI Law Enforcement Bulletin* 8, no. 8 (1939): 3-31. Classic essay on skeletal analysis that helped prompt the development of modern forensic anthropology. Krogman later wrote the standard textbook on skeletal analysis.

Krogman, Wilton Marion, and Mehmet Yasar Iscan. *The Human Skeleton in Forensic Medicine*. 2d ed. Springfield, Ill.: Charles C Thomas, 1986. Updated and expanded version of Krogman's standard textbook, which he first published in 1962.

Martini, Frederic H., Michael J. Timmons, and Robert B. Tallitsch. *Human Anatomy*. 6th ed. San Francisco: Pearson/Benjamin Cummings, 2008. Comprehensive anatomy text provides a detailed introduction to the skeletal system.

Scheuer, Louise, and Sue Black. *The Juvenile Skeleton*. Burlington, Mass.: Elsevier Academic Press, 2004. Focuses on the special characteristics of the skeletons of infants and children and includes explanations of subtle sex differences that can be observed.

Schwartz, Jeffrey H. *Skeleton Keys: An Introduction to Human Skeletal Morphology, Development, and Analysis*. New York: Oxford University Press, 2007. Presents an in-depth look at the skeletal system.

White, Tim D., and Pieter A. Folkens. *The Human Bone Manual*. Burlington, Mass.: Elsevier Academic Press, 2005. Compact volume offers essential information about skeletal identification for use by professional anthropologists, forensic scientists, and researchers. Contains hundreds of drawings and photographs.

See also: Anthropometry; Body farms; Decomposition of bodies; Forensic anthropology; Forensic sculpture; Gestational age determination; Mitochondrial DNA analysis and typing; Osteology and skeletal radiology; Sex determination of remains; Sinus prints.

Skeletal radiology. *See* Osteology and skeletal radiology

Sketch artists. *See* Composite drawing

Smallpox

Definition: Contagious viral disease characterized by high fever and a pustular rash that may cover the body.

Significance: Given the severity of certain forms of smallpox and the present-day lack of immunity to it among the world's population, the disease has the potential to be used as a weapon for mass devastation.

Smallpox is caused by a viral agent, a member of a family known as the poxviruses. Other viruses in the family include a variety of agents with the surname "pox" (monkeypox, cowpox) and vaccinia, but smallpox is the only one that naturally infects humans and has the potential of causing the deaths of a significant number of its victims. The virus is highly transmissible through contact with infected persons, both through oral secretions and through objects contaminated with the virus.

History of Smallpox

Smallpox is among the most ancient of human diseases, dating back at least to the times of the pharoahs in twelfth century B.C.E. Egypt. Likewise, the disease was prevalent in Southeast Asia and China during this era. The first written description of a disease that was likely smallpox is found in the fourth century C.E., in the writings of Eusebius of Caesarea; the first recorded epidemic of the disease in the Middle East came a century later. Common in Europe by the sixteenth century, smallpox was transported to the Americas by Spanish explorer Hernán Cortéz (c. 1520); it wreaked havoc there on the native populations and opened the way for Spanish conquest.

Although the cause of smallpox was unknown in the eighteenth century, it was clear even to the casual observer that the illness was devastating to populations that had never been previously exposed; mortality could approach levels as high as 90 percent among such peoples. In Europe, where the disease had by then been known for centuries, mortality still remained at a level of 20-30 percent in the most severe outbreaks. Survivors generally exhibited severe scarring at the sites of "pocks" that had covered the body.

Two forms of the disease were apparent. The more severe type, referred to above, was known as *Variola major*. A less severe type, *Variola minor*, exhibited a much lower mortality rate, as low as 1-2 percent. The basis for the difference

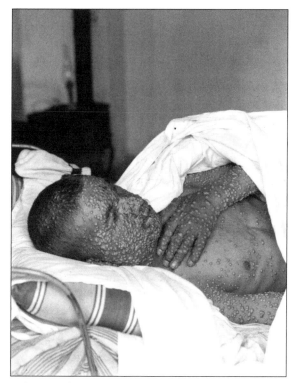

Early twentieth century smallpox patient with an advanced case of the disease showing the pustules that characterize it. *(Library of Congress)*

between the two forms remains unknown, as scientists have been unable to find much to distinguish the viruses associated with the two forms.

Evidence that the disease could be prevented originated with the Chinese, who, sometime around the eleventh century C.E., carried out a practice called variolation, in which smallpox crusts prepared as powders were inhaled or swallowed. The procedure was not always successful, but in many cases it did provide a measure of protection against the disease.

The practice of variolation spread through Persia (present-day Iran) and across the Middle East and Eastern Europe with the growing Muslim empire. Mary Wortley Montagu, wife of the British ambassador to Turkey and herself disfigured by the disease, had her son variolated in 1718. The practice, brought back to London with her return, was eventually described in writings that became part of the proceedings of the Royal Society of London for the

Improvement of Natural Knowledge. These proceedings were read in Boston by the American physician Zabdiel Boylston as well as by the Reverend Cotton Mather, and variolation made its way into North America.

Variolation became a widespread practice in Western Europe during the eighteenth century, as published reports provided evidence for the efficacy of the procedure and physicians from the Continent traveled to London and learned of the practice. Although it never became completely safe, variolation was increasingly accepted as a means of protecting people from the devastation of smallpox.

Smallpox and Biological Warfare

Evidence for the intentional use of smallpox as a biological weapon is mainly anecdotal. The earliest example may have been the introduction of the disease among Native American populations during the French and Indian War (1754-1763). Devastation of the Aztecs by smallpox during Spain's sixteenth century conquest was likely the result of accidental infection (although it clearly benefited the conquerors), but it clearly demonstrated the lack of resistance within isolated populations. The disease had appeared periodically in other native populations, creating a fear among these peoples similar to their fear of European weapons.

The French in North America were cognizant of the effects of smallpox among their Native American enemies, and at least one leader, Charles le Moyne de Longueuil, suggested its use as a weapon in the 1750's. During the French and Indian War in North America, the Americans and their British allies had mixed success in fighting Native American warriors who were often allied with the French. In 1763, British commander Sir Jeffrey Amherst reportedly approved providing native tribes with blankets that had been contaminated with the smallpox agent. Whether the blankets were ever actually distributed is unknown, but the following year some of the tribes experienced a smallpox epidemic.

Debate Concerning Smallpox Vaccination

The World Health Organization (WHO) in 1980 declared that smallpox had been eradicated, and the world was now free of the disease. Unlike most other viruses, smallpox is maintained only within the human population, so with the absence of disease, vaccination of susceptible individuals was no longer required. The United States ended its own requirement to vaccinate children against smallpox in 1972, as the disease was no longer found in the Western Hemisphere by that time. Around the world, most persons born since the 1980's have no immunity against the disease.

In 1980, the World Health Assembly (the major decision-making body of the WHO) recommended the destruction of all stocks of the smallpox virus, with the exception of reference laboratories in the United States, Great Britain, the Soviet Union, and South Africa. South Africa subsequently destroyed its stocks voluntarily, and Great Britain transferred its stocks to the Centers for Disease Control and Prevention in Atlanta, leaving only two sites in the world with remaining samples of the virus.

With an increase of terrorism in the twenty-first century, fears that terrorist groups could gain access to smallpox virus stocks and use the disease as a weapon resulted in controversy over whether vaccination among the general population should resume. Vaccination of both military personnel and health care workers was resumed to a limited extent. The likelihood that a terrorist group could obtain access to smallpox viral stocks is unknown, but the rapid dissemination of the illness—even prior to the onset of symptoms—lends a level of justification for real concern over the use of smallpox as a weapon of terrorism.

In 2001, the American Medical Association (AMA) declared smallpox one of the diseases that might be exploited by terrorists. With the absence of actual disease, however, the danger of severe side effects associated with vaccination outweighs the likelihood of exposure to smallpox; the AMA has estimated that large-scale vaccination could result in three hundred deaths per year in the United States alone.

Despite the use of variolation, smallpox remained common in North America in the decades that followed. The beginning of the American Revolutionary War in 1775 provided another opportunity for smallpox to have an effect on the ability of armies to fight. The British army, with its common soldiers representing the lower echelons of English society, was largely immune to the disease, either through required variolation or natural exposure, whereas the Americans were largely susceptible. An outbreak of the disease among American troops who invaded Canada was significant in eliminating the Americans as an effective fighting force. Certainly the Americans' sheer fatigue and lack of training, as well as weather conditions, played their roles, but illness was an important element in reducing the numbers of American troops.

General George Washington several times had to decide whether to require variolation of his men. Smallpox was clearly deadly, but the side effects of variolation could include not only temporary incapacitation but also development of actual smallpox, and from there the disease could spread to others. No evidence exists that the British intentionally practiced biological warfare on the Americans, but military decisions throughout the war were often affected by either the presence or the fear of smallpox. Variolation had been banned in several of the American colonies prior to the revolution, largely because of fears that the practice could cause outbreaks of the disease; Washington reversed the ban and required the inoculation of his troops during the war to protect them against a disease to which his opponents were already immune. In particular, inoculation of the Americans during the Siege of Boston in 1775 may have played an important role in maintaining Washington's army as a fighting force.

Smallpox remained a problem in North America, and not only in the northeastern region. In the years after the American victory over the British at Yorktown in 1781, smallpox repeatedly spread from Central America into what is now Texas and the American Southwest, frequently devastating Native American tribes. The precise numbers of deaths are un-known, but the elimination of thousands of natives and their villages certainly played a role later in the ability of colonists to subdue those populations.

Eradication of Smallpox

Variolation was a useful tool for fighting smallpox, but it was far from safe. During the 1790's, the British country physician Edward Jenner began to test a new procedure, the use of material from a bovine form of the pox, cowpox, as a means to immunize persons against smallpox. Although Jenner has been given proper acknowledgment for the thorough testing and publicizing of the practice that became known as vaccination (from the Latin word for cow, *vacca*), his work was not unprecedented. As early as the 1770's, Jenner was informed of the protection associated with cowpox by English dairymaids who had developed lesions as a result of milking cows that had the infection on their udders. Jenner first tested the efficacy of vaccination on himself and his family, and then on local children—with the approval of their parents. He found that vaccination with material prepared from the pustules of cowpox provided effective immunization against smallpox. Although the subsequent widespread use of the practice revealed some small degree of danger from side effects, vaccination was far superior to variolation.

Jenner had his opponents, and vaccination was far from universally accepted. It became clear, however, that the incidence of smallpox was significantly reduced in populations that had been extensively vaccinated. Eventually, compulsory vaccination became the rule, not only in England but also in the Americas. By the 1940's, smallpox had largely disappeared from most of Europe and North America. The disruption of World War II slowed many nations' abilities to control the disease, but in the years following the war, eradication of smallpox became a goal of the newly created World Health Organization (WHO).

Unlike many viral diseases, smallpox in its "natural state" is found only in humans. The lack of any animal reservoir meant that with interruption of the spread of infection in the human population there was hope for actual elimination of the disease. In 1948, the WHO began a program aimed at eradication of the disease, the goal being to immunize anyone who had come into contact with a smallpox victim rather than relying on "simple" mass inoculation. The principle behind the decision was to prevent the spread of the illness beyond the focus of infection, thus breaking the chain and eliminating the local outbreak.

The final push to eradicate smallpox began in 1967; that year, 131,000 cases of the disease were reported worldwide. Over the next ten years, the numbers of reported cases continued to fall, and the last natural case of the disease was diagnosed in Somalia in October, 1977. Other than a single accidental infection owing to a laboratory accident in 1978, no cases of smallpox have occurred in the world since then, indicating the first eradication of a human disease.

With the elimination of smallpox, vaccination against the disease is no longer routinely practiced, and many among the world's population may very well lack any natural immunity to the disease. Although the smallpox virus is no longer available in the general population, viral stocks remain in laboratories in both the United States and Russia. No stores of smallpox virus are believed to be located anywhere else, but with increased attention to the possibility of terrorist threats, fears have grown that persons with malicious intent could somehow obtain samples from the existing stocks to create their own form of biological weapon.

The question of whether the smallpox viral stocks should be destroyed has been much debated and remains unresolved. Proponents of destruction argue that with the absence of widespread immunity, even an accidental infection started by a careless researcher could unleash the virus into a "virgin" population, with results that might be comparable to those experienced by Native Americans in earlier centuries. Opponents of stock elimination argue that further research on the DNA (deoxyribonucleic acid) of the virus may shed light on the mechanism by which the virus causes disease, perhaps even leading to the production of a safer means of vaccination.

Richard Adler

Further Reading

Allen, Arthur. *Vaccine: The Controversial Story of Medicine's Greatest Lifesaver*. New York: W. W. Norton, 2007. History of vaccination includes discussion of smallpox, as it was the first major human disease controlled through immunization of the population.

Behbehani, Abbas. "The Smallpox Story: Life and Death of an Old Disease." *Microbiological Reviews* 47 (December, 1983): 455-509. Provides a history of the disease and tells the story of its eradication.

Carrell, Jennifer Lee. *The Speckled Monster: A Historical Tale of Battling Smallpox*. New York: Dutton, 2003. Presents a partially fictionalized account of the roles played by the Reverend Cotton Mather and physician Zabdiel Boylston in the introduction of variolation as a means to control smallpox in early eighteenth century Boston.

Fenn, Elizabeth. *Pox Americana: The Great Smallpox Epidemic of 1775-1782*. New York: Hill & Wang, 2001. Discusses the role played by smallpox during the American War of Independence, including speculation regarding its possible use in biological warfare on the part of the British.

Glynn, Ian, and Jenifer Glynn. *The Life and Death of Smallpox*. New York: Cambridge University Press, 2004. Covers the history of the disease as well as the story of its eradication.

Hopkins, Donald. *The Greatest Killer: Smallpox in History*. Chicago: University of Chicago Press, 2002. Focuses on the effects of smallpox epidemics on the history of human civilization.

See also: Anthrax; Biodetectors; Biological terrorism; Biological weapon identification; Biotoxins; Bubonic plague; Centers for Disease Control and Prevention; Ebola virus; Epidemiology; Hantavirus; Medicine; Nipah virus; Pathogen transmission; Viral biology.

Smoke inhalation

Definition: Breathing in of gases, vapors, and particles created by combustion (burning) or pyrolysis (breakdown of material by heat in the absence of enough oxygen to support combustion).

Significance: By examining the airways of a person who has died in a fire, a forensic pathologist can determine the cause of death and whether the individual was dead before the fire started or died during the fire.

Smoke inhalation has been known to be potentially deadly for centuries. For example, the Roman writer and naturalist Pliny reported in the first century C.E. that prisoners were executed by being placed over a smoking fire. Of the people who die in fires, two to three times as many die from smoke inhalation as die from burns. When large numbers of people are killed in a fire, deaths most often occur because people are trapped in the building and succumb to smoke inhalation. For example, all eighty-seven deaths in the 1990 fire at the Happy Land social club in New York City were caused by smoke inhalation, and up to half of the one hundred people who died in the Station nightclub fire in West Warwick, Rhode Island, in 2003 were killed by smoke.

How Smoke Inhalation Causes Death

Smoke inhalation damages the body in multiple ways, all of which may cause or contribute to death. Inhaling hot smoke burns the tissues that line the airways. Thermal burns from smoke tend to occur only in the mouth and upper part of the trachea (windpipe). Nevertheless, if the smoke is hot enough, when it reaches the larynx (voice box), it can trigger a spasm that closes the windpipe and causes asphyxiation.

If the smoke contains toxic gases, it can also cause chemical burns. When a fire burns certain synthetic polymers, such as PVC (polyvinyl chloride) pipe, poisonous hydrogen chloride gas is created; burning wool, silk, nylon, and polyurethane create deadly hydrogen cyanide gas. Exposure to either of these gases can cause death. In addition, soot and particles in smoke can trigger a reaction in the airways similar to an asthma attack. The airways narrow, and the individual begins to wheeze in an attempt to get enough air.

One of the most common causes of smoke inhalation death is carbon monoxide (CO) poisoning. In a normally functioning lung, oxygen from the air is transferred to a molecule called hemoglobin that is found in red blood cells. Hemoglobin holds the oxygen as the red blood cell travels through the circulatory system. When the red blood cell reaches an oxygen-deficient cell, hemoglobin releases the oxygen molecule and picks up a molecule of carbon dioxide (CO_2). CO_2 is a normal cellular waste product. The red blood cell carries it to the lungs, where it is released and breathed out of the body. The hemoglobin molecule then picks up another oxygen molecule and the cycle repeats.

In a fire, a large amount of carbon monoxide, a colorless, odorless gas, is produced through incomplete combustion, or pyrolysis. Hemoglobin binds to CO two hundred times more easily than it binds to oxygen. When CO enters the lung, it rapidly binds to hemoglobin, making it impossible for the hemoglobin to pick up any oxygen molecules. Once the CO is bound to hemoglobin, it remains tightly attached, so that over time less and less oxygen can be picked up in the lungs and carried to cells, and little CO_2 is removed.

When the level of CO in a person's blood reaches about 30 percent, the person becomes confused; this state may contribute to the inability to escape from a fire. As the amount of CO increases (many victims of smoke inhalation have as much as 80 percent of their hemoglobin bound to CO), the body is simply too depleted of oxygen for cells to continue to function. Breathing air with 100 parts per million of CO can be fatal in half an hour; air with 5,000 parts per million of CO causes death within a few minutes. Carbon monoxide poisoning causes asphyxiation at the cellular level.

Signs of Foul Play

Typically in the United States, when a person dies in a fire, an autopsy is performed to determine the cause of death whether the fire was accidental or arson is suspected. In addition to looking for external burns, the pathologist looks for signs of damage to the tissues lining the airways. The presence of soot in the lungs indicates that the victim was breathing after the fire started. The amount of CO bound to hemoglobin in the blood may also be measured after death.

Sometimes fires are set to cover up or destroy evidence of other crimes, such as murder. As long as remains recovered from a fire scene include airways that can be examined, however, a forensic pathologist can determine whether the victim was alive at the time the fire started. If death occurred before the fire began, the body will show no signs of airway burns, even if the external body is charred. No soot or particulate matter will be found in the airways and lungs, and the level of CO in the blood will be less than 15 percent.

Martiscia Davidson

Further Reading

Faith, Nicholas. *Blaze: The Forensics of Fire*. New York: St. Martin's Press, 2000. Discusses how fire and arson investigators work and how forensic scientists contribute to solving the crime of arson.

MacDonald, Jake. "After the Inferno: Winnipeg's Arson Squad Can Tell How a Fire Started and Often Who Started It, by Sifting Through the Ashes and Reading Scorch Marks on the Wall." *Saturday Night*, May 20, 2000, 24-32. Examines how fires are investigated. Includes discussion of how doctors recognize death by smoke inhalation.

Redsicker, David R., and John J. O'Connor. *Practical Fire and Arson Investigation*. 2d ed. Boca Raton, Fla.: CRC Press, 1997. Provides comprehensive coverage of all aspects of fire investigations, with emphasis on fires that cause deaths.

Shusterman, Dennis. "Predictors of Carbon Monoxide and Hydrogen Cyanide Exposure in Smoke Inhalation Patients." *Journal of Toxicology: Clinical Toxicology* 34 (January, 1996): 61-72. Reports the findings of a research study that looked at the levels of carbon monoxide and cyanide in the blood of smoke inhalation victims.

Tanner, Robert. "New Science Challenges Ar-

son Convictions." *The Washington Post*, December 31, 2006; p. A08. Details the case of a false conviction based partially on smoke inhalation evidence.

See also: American Academy of Forensic Sciences; Arson; Asphyxiation; Autopsies; Carbon monoxide poisoning; Chicago nightclub stampede; Choking; Forensic pathology; Suffocation.

Sobriety testing

Definition: Measures taken by law-enforcement officials to determine whether persons are intoxicated in situations in which being intoxicated is dangerous or unlawful.

Significance: The results of sobriety testing by police officers are often used as evidence in court and may be the primary evidence in cases involving charges such as driving while intoxicated or driving under the influence of alcohol or other drugs.

Many different kinds of testing can reveal the presence or absence of intoxicating substances in the human body. Urine and blood tests can effectively screen for the presence of drugs or alcohol in a person's system, but these tests are not generally convenient for providing information in the field when a law-enforcement officer suspects that someone may be under the influence. Instead, especially during traffic stops, field sobriety tests are used.

A law-enforcement officer may administer a field sobriety test any time the officer has reason to believe that a driver may be intoxicated. Among the many signs that indicate an individual may be under the influence of alcohol are the smell of alcohol on the breath, intoxicated demeanor, and slurred speech. These signs, however, are subjective. To increase the standardization of field sobriety testing across the United States, the National Highway Traffic Safety Administration (NHTSA) created the Standardized Field Sobriety Test (SFST), a set of recommended field test procedures.

The SFST consists of three separate tests,

the results of which the administering officer evaluates on a variety of factors. The first test is designed to measure the subject's horizontal gaze nystagmus (HGN), which is the jerking of the eye that occurs when the eye moves from one side to the other. This occurs naturally and cannot be controlled voluntarily. During the HGN test, the officer asks the subject to follow the movement of a small object, such as a finger or pen, with his or her eyes. The officer moves the object horizontally in front of the subject's face and assesses the individual's ability to follow the object as well as the amount and location of the jerking movements of the eyes. Compared with a person who is not intoxicated, a person who is intoxicated will show more jerking movement when the gaze is more centered.

An officer administers the horizontal gaze nystagmus test, part of the Standardized Field Sobriety Test, to a person suspected of driving under the influence of alcohol. During this test, the officer asks the subject to follow the movement of a small object with his or her eyes, and the officer assesses the individual's ability to follow the object as well as the amount and location of the jerking movements of the eyes. *(© iStockphoto.com/Frances Twitty)*

The other tests in the SFST are the one-leg stand test and the walk-and-turn test. Both are designed to test the subject's ability to do two or more things at the same time. During the walk-and-turn test, the officer asks the subject to take nine steps, heel to toe, in a straight line and then turn and take nine steps back. During the one-leg stand test, the subject attempts to stand on one leg while counting. During both of these tests the officer uses a predetermined set of guidelines to assess the subject's ability to perform the specified tasks. The subject's failure on a set number of attributes results in a determination that the subject is intoxicated. Research has shown that officers who use the three tests of the SFST together make correct determinations of intoxication in more than 90 percent of cases.

Helen Davidson

Further Reading

Haggin, Daniel J. *Advanced DUI Investigation: A Training and Reference Manual*. Springfield, Ill.: Charles C Thomas, 2005.

Wilson, Mike, ed. *Drunk Driving*. Detroit: Greenhaven Press, 2007.

See also: Breathalyzer; Drug abuse and dependence; Drug and alcohol evidence rules; Drug confirmation tests; Mandatory drug testing; National Transportation Safety Board.

Soil

Definition: Earth's outer crust, which consists of rocks and humus, serves as ground for vegetation, and houses a wide array of materials, including glass and metals.

Significance: Soil is the structural matrix or home for bacteria, plants, fungi, and nematodes, all of which are living organisms and all of which exist in the soils of different areas in varying identifiable combinations. Because soil is ubiquitous material and is easily transferred from one place to another, soil evidence often plays a role in criminal investigations. By comparing soil samples, forensic scientists can link persons and objects to crime scenes.

Soil has been used as material evidence in crime scene investigations since the 1890's. For many years, basic microscopy and morphological analyses were the primary means of soil comparison, but increasingly sophisticated techniques have greatly enhanced forensic scientists' ability to compare the contents of soil samples. Depending on the type of case and the other types of evidence available, physical examination of soil alone might provide the complementary information needed. Soils can be classified into different types based on their physical characteristics. Geologists, for example, classify soils according to particle size distribution, pH, color, and moisture content as well as other physical features. The analysis of soils for forensic purposes, however, often requires more detail than simple physical examination can provide. Forensic scientists look at soil not as an isolated material but as a group of materials, including any particles and any organisms that are part of a given sample.

Chemical Analyses

The quantities of soils found at crime scenes are not necessarily abundant, and small samples often limit the techniques forensic scientists can use to perform some physical analyses. Small sample size is not an impediment to analysis of soil's content, however. Scientists can chemically analyze soils for trace elements and metals using techniques such as mass spectrometry (MS), which establishes a relationship between the mass and the ratio of the elements in a sample. MS technology is often coupled with other, more sensitive technologies to elucidate the elemental composition of a wide array of samples, ranging from the simplest to the most complicated matrices, including, but not limited to, drugs,

An investigator collects soil samples. Because soil is easily transferred from one place to another, soil evidence often plays a role in criminal investigations. (© iStockphoto.com/Bart Coenders)

chemical warfare agents, and environmental samples. Some of the technologies used in combination with MS are inductively coupled plasma (ICP-MS), gas chromatography (GC-MS), liquid chromatography (LC-MS), glow discharge (GD-MS), and capillary electrophoresis (CE-MS).

Other analysis methods that do not involve mass spectrometry can provide similar results, such as inductively coupled plasma-optical emission spectrometry (ICP-OES) and atomic absorption spectroscopy (AAS). These various techniques provide different separation matrices and principles, and analysts must decide which should be used based on the type of sample being analyzed, the limit of detection, and the output resolution requirement.

Environmental samples have to be digested before being introduced into the instrument of choice. Once they are introduced either as a liquid (slurry) or a microspray, the ions are separated on the provided separation matrix based on their mass-to-charge ratio. The number of ions produced for a specific mass is assumed to be proportional to the amount present in the sample; these data are constantly transferred to a computer and analyzed by software that produces a mass spectrum. The masses are then compared to those in reference libraries or in the literature to determine the different elements present in the sample. These methods provide relatively fast, highly specific, and sensitive multielemental analytical information.

Molecular Analyses

When the amount of soil recovered at a crime scene is sufficient for both physical and chemical analyses, a more specific soil profile can be obtained, and this can help establish soil uniqueness. In some instances, however, the recovered amount of soil is too minute to allow either physical or chemical analysis. In such cases, information on soil content may be obtained through DNA (deoxyribonucleic acid) analysis of microbial, fungal, and plant genomes present in the soil. Recent studies have shown that such analysis can provide unique information about the organism or material in question. Novel molecular techniques coupled with separation technologies used for human DNA analysis have been able to provide unique

soil "fingerprints" that can be compared with known samples.

Specific markers exist in the DNA of every organism. Plants have sequences repeated in tandem, as is the case with humans. Microbes and fungi contain conserved and variable regions throughout their genomes; the differences encountered in the variable regions are what give each organism its unique identity. Ribosomal ribonucleic acid (rRNA) has been the marker of choice in the analysis of microbial communities because, unlike protein markers, rRNA is ubiquitous.

Terminal restriction fragment length polymorphism (TRFLP) and amplicon length heterogeneity (ALH) have both proven successful in determining the microbial community composition of soils. The first uses labeled primers that will bind to the ends of specific primer sequences to be amplified using polymerase chain reaction (PCR). The PCR product is then cut with restriction enzymes; these molecular scissors recognize specific sequences and cut the DNA wherever a specific site is recognized. Because the sequences of the organisms are different, different patterns are obtained. ALH uses fluorescently labeled universal primers to amplify the variable regions within the genome. Both techniques use high-resolution genetic analyzers to separate the obtained fragments. The results are recorded by a camera and transferred to a computer, which makes the pattern available to the analyst for subsequent comparisons.

Lilliana I. Moreno

Further Reading

Conklin, Alfred R. *Introduction to Soil Chemistry: Analysis and Instrumentation*. Hoboken, N.J.: John Wiley & Sons, 2005. Textbook describes the chemical properties of soil and the different methods that can be used to analyze soil samples.

Heath, Lorraine E., and Venetia A. Saunders. "Assessing the Potential of Bacterial DNA Profiling for Forensic Soil Comparisons." *Journal of Forensic Sciences* 51, no. 5 (2006): 1062-1068. Discusses the use of microbial DNA in establishing differences and similarities in soil material.

Moreno, Lilliana I., et al. "Microbial Meta-genome Profiling Using Amplicon Length Heterogeneity-Polymerase Chain Reaction Proves More Effective than Elemental Analysis in Discriminating Soil Specimens." *Journal of Forensic Sciences* 51, no. 6 (2006): 1315-1322. Compares and contrasts the different methods of soil analysis to determine which is better suited for forensic comparisons.

Petraco, Nicholas, and Thomas Kubic. "A Density Gradient Technique for Use in Forensic Soil Analysis." *Journal of Forensic Sciences* 45, no. 4 (2000): 872-873. Describes the preparation of soils for physical characterization based on density.

Pye, Kenneth. *Geological and Soil Evidence: Forensic Applications.* Boca Raton, Fla.: CRC Press, 2007. Provides guidance regarding the potential value and limitations of geological and soil evidence in forensic investigations. Very informative.

Ruffell, Alastair, and Jennifer McKinley. "Forensic Geoscience: Applications of Geology, Geomorphology, and Geophysics to Criminal Investigations." *Earth-Science Reviews* 69 (March, 2005): 235-247. Focuses on the history and improvements of methods for the analysis of soil and the application of soil analysis to crime scene settings.

See also: Atomic absorption spectrophotometry; Bacterial biology; Forensic archaeology; Forensic botany; Forensic geoscience; Forensic palynology; Gas chromatography; Geological materials; High-performance liquid chromatography; Laser ablation-inductively coupled plasma-mass spectrometry; Mass spectrometry; Restriction fragment length polymorphisms.

Soman

Definition: Highly toxic colorless liquid that has potential for use as a chemical weapon.

Significance: Concerns that terrorists could employ chemical agents in attacks have increased law-enforcement agencies' at-tention to substances such as soman. The manufacture and storage of soman are banned by the United Nations Chemical Weapons Convention of 1993.

The nerve agent soman was first prepared in 1944 in Germany as part of that nation's chemical warfare program. Soman, which has a camphorlike odor, is chemically similar to sarin, but more toxic. Nerve agents such as soman act as inhibitors of the enzyme acetylcholinesterase (AChE). The neurotransmitter acetylcholine is released at nerve endings and causes muscle contraction. In the normal course of affairs, the acetylcholine is soon destroyed by a reaction catalyzed by AChE. If this enzyme is disabled in its function by binding to a nerve agent, the continued presence of acetylcholine produces the symptoms of poisoning: pain and watering in the eyes, contracted pupils (meiosis), respiratory failure, runny nose, incontinence, convulsions, coma, and death.

Although soman is twice as toxic as sarin and more persistent in the environment, the U.S. Army decided in 1948 to develop sarin as a weapon instead of soman. The manufacture of soman would have been more costly, and the lack of a sufficiently effective antidote was felt to be a disadvantage in case of accidental exposures. The Soviet Union, however, did manufacture soman, using captured German technology.

Soman has apparently not been used in warfare or terrorism. Soman poisoning leaves detectable traces on, around, or in the bodies of victims, and blood samples can be tested for AChE levels, which are abnormally low in individuals exposed to the agent. The U.S. military employs test kits and instruments that can detect nerve agents and provide warnings. In the laboratory, soman can be detected through the use of gas chromatography-mass spectrometry (GC-MS) or capillary column gas chromatography using a chiral medium.

Treatment of nerve agent poisoning involves injection of atropine and administration of pralidoxime chloride (2-PAM chloride). This treatment needs improvement, and research in the area is active. A complicating factor that is particularly prominent with soman is an irreversible reaction known as aging, which renders the soman-AChE complex inactive to pralidoxime within about ten minutes of exposure.

During the Persian Gulf War of 1991, U.S. soldiers were given pyridostigmine bromide (PB) as a prophylactic measure in the mistaken belief that Iraq might attack with soman. Carbamates such as PB bind reversibly with AChE and block the soman so that when exposure to the nerve agent ends, AChE can re-form. Nerve agent scavengers such as exogenous AChE can also provide protection.

John R. Phillips

General H. Norman Schwarzkopf with U.S. troops during the Gulf War of 1991. During that conflict, pyridostigmine bromide was distributed to many U.S. troops because of fears that Iraqi forces might use soman as a weapon. *(AP/Wide World Photos)*

Further Reading

Croddy, Eric A., and James J. Wirtz, eds. *Weapons of Mass Destruction: An Encyclopedia of Worldwide Policy, Technology, and History*. Santa Barbara, Calif.: ABC-CLIO, 2005.

Hoenig, Steven L. *Handbook of Chemical Warfare and Terrorism*. Westport, Conn.: Greenwood Press, 2002.

Somani, Satu M., and James A. Romano, Jr., eds. *Chemical Warfare Agents: Toxicity at Low Levels*. Boca Raton, Fla.: CRC Press, 2001.

Suzuki, Osamu, and Kanako Watanabe, eds. *Drugs and Poisons in Humans: A Handbook of Practical Analysis*. New York: Springer, 2005.

Tucker, Jonathan B. *War of Nerves: Chemical Warfare from World War I to al-Qaeda*. New York: Pantheon Books, 2006.

See also: Centers for Disease Control and Prevention; Chemical agents; Chemical terrorism; Chemical warfare; Nerve agents; Nervous system; Sarin; Tabun.

Spectroscopy

Definition: Techniques for producing and analyzing spectra formed by the emission or absorption of electromagnetic radiation accompanying changes between the energy levels of atoms and molecules.

Significance: Using spectroscopy, forensic scientists examine the spectra of evidence samples obtained from crime scenes or related locations to analyze their chemical content and determine the energy levels and molecular structures of the materials. Such analysis may enable investigators to link crime scene materials to suspects.

Forensic scientists use a variety of spectroscopic methods over a large range of frequencies, and their spectroscopic analyses yield a wide variety of information about trace evidence—including soils, glass, drugs, pigments, dyes, inks, fuels, and explosives—found at crime scenes or related locations. The underlying principle of all spectroscopic techniques is that substances selectively absorb certain frequencies of electromagnetic radiation and reflect or transmit others.

One way of classifying spectra is according to whether the radiation is in the infrared (IR), ultraviolet (UV), visible, X-ray, or microwave region of the electromagnetic spectrum. In forensic applications, IR spectroscopy is the most common spectroscopic method used, because most substances absorb IR very selectively. The IR spectra of thousands of substances have been cataloged and stored in computer databases to be used for comparison tests with IR spectra from suspected evidence obtained at crime scenes or related locations. UV and visible spectral analysis are used for some types of evidence, particularly drug samples and arson accelerants found in fire scene debris.

Mass spectrometry (MS) is used to identify unknown substances under investigation. Components of substances are typically separated using chromatography and are then sent into a high-vacuum chamber to be ionized by high-speed electrons. Ion fragments pass through a magnetic field, and the shapes of their parabolic trajectories determine their mass-to-charge ratios. No two substances have the same fragmentation patterns and trajectories. MS acts as a "fingerprint" for analyzed trace evidence.

X-ray fluorescence (XRF) spectroscopy has been used to help identify weapons used in crimes and in analyzing debris that has resulted from explosions. XRF has been successful in identifying paint, leather, plastic, glass, and ceramic samples in forensic studies. The method can reveal the elements contained in pigments of various colors of paint as well as chromium and other elemental content in leather. It has been used to identify the presence of arsenic in glasses and lead in enamels. XRF has also been used successfully to identify hidden fingerprints at crime scenes.

Raman spectroscopy (RS) has proven very useful in identifying fiber, ink, dye, and resin evidence. RS is based on the fact that when light from a high-intensity laser is reflected off a material, a small fraction of the reflected light is shifted to a frequency slightly different from

that of the original laser light. From this frequency shift, the sample material can be identified. The RS spectra act as "optical fingerprints" for molecular composition. The method can even differentiate between the compositions of inks of the same color.

Alvin K. Benson

Further Reading

James, Stuart H., and Jon J. Nordby, eds. *Forensic Science: An Introduction to Scientific and Investigative Techniques*. 2d ed. Boca Raton, Fla.: CRC Press, 2005.

Saferstein, Richard. *Criminalistics: An Introduction to Forensic Science*. 9th ed. Upper Saddle River, N.J.: Pearson Prentice Hall, 2007.

Tilstone, William J., Kathleen A. Savage, and Leigh A. Clark. *Forensic Science: An Encyclopedia of History, Methods, and Techniques*. Santa Barbara, Calif.: ABC-CLIO, 2006.

See also: Analytical instrumentation; Electromagnetic spectrum analysis; Energy-dispersive spectroscopy; Fourier transform infrared spectrophotometer; Infrared detection devices; Mass spectrometry; Micro-Fourier transform infrared spectrometry; Microspectrophotometry; Nuclear spectroscopy; Scanning electron microscopy; Ultraviolet spectrophotometry.

Sperm. *See* Semen and sperm

Sports memorabilia fraud

Definition: Sale of sports memorabilia falsely claimed to have been autographed or used by a sports celebrity.

Significance: Forgers and other scam artists have taken advantage of the high interest in sports memorabilia among the American public to make a great deal of money selling fraudulent autographs and supposedly game-used sports equipment. Law-enforcement agencies have increased their efforts to address this form of fraud.

Heightened interest in professional sports, a good economic climate in which many people had disposable income, and the explosion of on-line marketing came together in the 1990's to create an expanded interest in sports collectibles in the United States. With rising interest and prices, forgeries of sports figures' autographs became increasingly common. According to the Federal Bureau of Investigation (FBI), the sports memorabilia market in the early twenty-first century generated more than one billion dollars in sales annually in the United States. Reputable auction houses such as Christy's and Sotheby's, along with many online companies, began holding sales of sports collectibles. Prices soared for memorabilia such as trading cards, autographed pictures, programs, helmets, jerseys, balls, pucks, and other paraphernalia that had been used in competition (referred to by collectors as "game-used" items). As interest and prices increased, forgeries and fraudulent memorabilia flooded the sports collectibles marketplace. The problem expanded from the United States to involve forgers and suppliers in Europe and Asia as well.

Sports Souvenir Forgery and the Law

Forgery has always been illegal, and many law-enforcement agencies maintain divisions to investigate art and document forgery. For several reasons, however, the forging of autographs on sports memorabilia presented new problems for law enforcement. First, most current sports figures do sign autographs, so hundreds of legitimate autographs of a single celebrity may be in existence. This makes it difficult or impossible to prove a direct link between any particular autograph and the sports figure. Second, compared with art, autographs are relatively easy to forge, and, unlike signatures on legal documents, the autographs of sports figures initially did not require authentication, such as witnesses or notarizing. Third, many sports souvenirs are sold through the Internet, which eliminates the opportunity for buyers to examine the goods in person or seek second opinions before they buy and geographically separates buyer and seller, making prosecution for forgery difficult. Finally, many sports forgeries sell for little enough money that duped buyers, should they

---

Operation Bullpen

The following is excerpted from an overview of Operation Bullpen, a sports memorabilia investigation carried out by the Federal Bureau of Investigation, provided on the FBI's Web site.

In 1997, the FBI in San Diego utilized information from Operation Foul Ball and other sources to institute an undercover operation designed to infiltrate the nationwide memorabilia fraud network. Together with the U.S. Attorney's Office and the Internal Revenue Service, an undercover scenario was devised in which an Undercover Agent would pose as a distributor of American memorabilia in Asia. This scenario enabled the FBI to purchase evidence without causing the sale of forged items to the public. It also made the criminals more likely to openly discuss the counterfeit nature of the memorabilia, because it was "going overseas" beyond the reach of U.S. law enforcement agencies. To support this "cover story," the FBI established the Nihon Trading Company in Oceanside, California. . . .

The key evidence in this investigation were recorded statements which provided evidence of the individuals' involvement in forging, fraudulently authenticating, and/or distributing the materials. In Operation Bullpen, referred to as Phase I, the San Diego Division of the FBI conducted well over 1,000 consensually recorded audio and video tapes. During the consensually recorded conversations, numerous co-conspirators made incriminating statements which illuminated the nature and common practices involved with sports memorabilia fraud. For example, one of the conspirators liked to joke to the Undercover Agent how Mickey Mantle still has one arm out of the grave signing autographs. Other conspirators were noting how Wilt Chamberlain was still available for signing weeks after his death.

A special agent of the Federal Bureau of Investigation displays a "certificate of authenticity" for a baseball purportedly signed by Mother Teresa at a news conference held in San Diego, California, on February 14, 2001, to announce the bureau's arrest of a ring of counterfeiters involved in producing millions of dollars' worth of fake sports trading cards. In the foreground is a printer's proof of a counterfeit card featuring Sammy Sosa. (AP/Wide World Photos)

discover they have been swindled, are unlikely to report it to the police.

California was the first U.S. state to pass a law specifically aimed at curbing sports souvenir fraud. The Autographed Sports Memorabilia Statute of 1992 required dealers selling sports figures' autographs to provide certificates of authenticity (COAs) to buyers. Using this law, a group of buyers who had bought forged autographs online sued the Internet auction company eBay, which is based in California, for not providing COAs. They lost their suit when the court decided that eBay is a market-

place, not a dealer, and is therefore exempt from the law. Before long, in any case, COAs lost much of their value, as forgers soon learned that with a little practice and good computers they could easily manufacture false COAs.

In 1997, the FBI began an investigation of sports autograph forgery in San Diego, California, called Operation Foul Ball. This effort broke up five southern California forgery rings and resulted in the conviction of twenty-six individuals. The FBI next initiated a national investigation called Operation Bullpen, which set up a false import-export company in order to infiltrate wholesale providers of fraudulent sports memorabilia. By 2001, raids in twelve U.S. states broke up thirteen memorabilia forgery rings and two sports card forgery rings. Thirty-six individuals were eventually convicted. Despite the involvement of the FBI, however, sports souvenir forgery continues to be a major international problem.

Protecting Against Fraud

In response to Operation Bullpen, Major League Baseball (MLB) became the first sports league to take concerted action to prevent memorabilia fraud. MLB created its own authentication program, which requires the presence of an independent witness to an autograph by any MLB player; at the time an autograph is witnessed, a numbered hologram is placed on the item so that its ownership can be tracked in a database. A number of reputable sports memorabilia companies began using similar procedures; some also videotape sports stars throughout their autograph-signing sessions.

Despite these measures, forgery is rampant. Following Operation Bullpen, the FBI reported finding warehouses full of fraudulent sports memorabilia. The agency estimated that in 2003 at least half the autographed sports and celebrity items sold were fakes, and that the proportion increased to 75 to 80 percent for items sold on eBay. Among the sports figures most popular with forgers are Muhammad Ali and Mark McGwire; it has been estimated that more than 99 percent of the purported Ali and McGwire signatures for sale are forgeries.

To decrease their chances of buying fraudulent items, consumers should buy from reputable dealers or auction houses and should ask for proof of authenticity or evidence that provides a solid link between the sports figure and the autographed item. Consumers should also educate themselves about the history of pens and balls, as these items change over time. For example, if an autograph of an old-time ballplayer is signed with a Sharpie pen, it is a forgery, because Sharpies are relatively new writing instruments. Consumers should also consider the prices being asked for the items they are seeking—if the price of an item is too good to be true, the item is probably a fake. In addition, consumers should avoid collecting the autographs of stars who are having exceptional seasons or who have died unexpectedly, as the incidence of forgeries is highest with the best-known and most newsworthy individuals. Finally, consumers who suspect that any sports memorabilia being offered for sale is fraudulent should report the matter to the police.

Martiscia Davidson

Further Reading

Brayer, Ruth. *Detecting Forgery in Fraud Investigations: The Insider's Guide.* New York: ASIS International, 2000. Provides an introduction to the detection of forged documents. Intended for readers with some background in forensics and the legal aspects of forgery cases.

Nausbaum, David. "Forgeries, Theft Take Some of the Thrill out of Collectibles." *Los Angeles Business Journal*, July 10, 2006, 11. Presents an analysis of the problem of sports forgeries and makes suggestions for combating the problem.

Nickell, Joe. *Detecting Forgery: Forensic Investigation of Documents.* 1996. Reprint. Lexington: University Press of Kentucky, 2005. Excellent introduction to the topic approaches forgery from an investigative perspective. Presents the technical aspects of analyzing documents while discussing several famous forgery cases.

Walton, Kenneth. *Fake: Forgery, Lies, and eBay.* New York: Simon Spotlight Entertainment, 2006. Autobiographical account of memorabilia fraud by a reformed eBay forger.

Williams, Pete. *Sports Memorabilia for Dummies.* Foster City, Calif.: IDG Books Worldwide, 1998. Provides a basic introduction to the pastime of collecting sports souvenirs.

See also: Art forgery; Check alteration and washing; Counterfeiting; Forgery; Handwriting analysis; Hitler diaries hoax; Questioned document analysis; Secret Service, U.S.; Writing instrument analysis.

Spot tests. *See* Crime scene screening tests

Steganography

Definition: Method of hiding information within written documents or electronic files in ways that are not obvious to anyone except the intended recipients.

Significance: In examining electronic evidence in cases of computer-related crimes, forensic scientists may determine that steganography has been used to pass sensitive information in innocent-looking documents or other electronic files.

The term "steganography" comes from two Greek words, *steganos*, meaning "covered," and *graphos*, meaning "writing"; that is, steganography is the science of covered, or hidden, writing. Steganography differs from cryptography. In cryptography, the presence of hidden information is clear even though the information cannot be read easily because it is encoded. In steganography, the presence of hidden information is disguised in an ordinary-looking document that gives no clue to its presence. The hidden information may or may not be encoded, but the strength of steganography is that the presence of the secret information is not apparent.

The information does not call attention to itself, and uninitiated viewers simply see the cover document and are not stimulated to look for additional information in it.

Steganography has a long history. The ancient Greeks are reported to have tattooed secret messages on the shaved heads of slaves, then, after the hair grew back, sent the slaves to deliver the hidden messages. During World War II, spies conveyed secret information in ordinary letters by writing between the visible lines in invisible ink that became visible only when the paper was heated. Photographic microdots were also used during World War II and after, over the course of the Cold War. One of these tiny dots could be substituted for a period at the end of a sentence in a document; the recipient would then remove the dot and enlarge it to retrieve the information it contained.

Modern steganographic techniques involve the insertion of hidden information into computer files. Information can be inserted into text documents, into picture files such as JPEG files, or into audio files such as MP3 files. The secret information is hidden from the ordinary viewer or listener, but the intended recipient can extract the information using a special program and password. Many techniques have been developed for hiding electronic data in computer files using easily available software. The hidden data generally replace irrelevant or relatively unimportant bits in the original file. Data are most successfully hidden when the size of the secret message is small compared with the size of the cover file.

The science of detecting information that has been hidden in this way is called steganalysis. Computer forensics experts can detect data hidden with steganography by using programs designed for this purpose. In their simplest form, these programs compare original (clean-copy) files with altered (data-inserted) files, but many more sophisticated methods of steganalysis have also been developed.

Persons involved in computer-related crime may use steganography to conceal information about their activities from both casual observers and police investigators. Also, steganography may be used in industrial espionage to export sensitive information from company computers

to competitors. This method of passing hidden messages has many other potential uses as well.

Martiscia Davidson

Further Reading

Katzenbeisser, Stefan, and Fabien A. P. Petitcolas, eds. *Information Hiding Techniques for Steganography and Digital Watermarking*. Norwood, Mass.: Artech House, 2000.

Radcliff, Deborah. "Quick Study: Steganography—Hidden Data." *Computerworld*, June 10, 2002.

Wayner, Peter. *Disappearing Cryptography: Information Hiding—Steganography and Watermarking*. 2d ed. San Francisco: Morgan Kaufmann, 2002.

See also: Computer crimes; Computer forensics; Cryptology and number theory; Document examination; Internet tracking and tracing; Photograph alteration detection; Tattoo identification.

Stimulants

Definition: Broad group of substances that share the capacity to activate and excite the human central and peripheral nervous systems as well as the cardiovascular system.

Significance: Many people make regular use of nonmedical, legal stimulants such as caffeine, but stimulants are also often misused. Crimes related to the use and distribution of illicit stimulants—including fraud, forgery, robbery, and even murder—occupy many of the resources of law-enforcement agencies and are costly to society.

Drugs that have stimulant properties are many in number and varied in form. All forms of cocaine and amphetamines are classified as stimulants, including concoctions that can be created in small clandestine labs, such as methcathinone, made from amphetamine and cathinone, and the street drug known as crystal or ice, a kin of methamphetamine made from seemingly innocuous and easily available ingredients. Other drugs that stimulate the nervous and cardiovascular systems include widely used substances such as nicotine and caffeine as well as less commonly known substances such as khat leaves (the leaves of the plant *Catha edulis*), which are chewed to deliver mild stimulating effects.

Use and Abuse

Stimulant drugs have a limited number of legitimate uses, such as in the treatment of attention-deficit/hyperactivity disorder (ADHD). Appetite-suppressing drugs (also known as anorectics) used in the treatment of obesity are also stimulants, as are drugs used in the treatment of narcolepsy, a disorder characterized by random immediate onset of sleep. Stimulants are not widely employed in the treatment of other medical problems, as the use of these drugs has not received much support in terms of the balance of benefits over risks. The primary risks of stimulant use include raised blood pressure and the possibility of the development of a substance-use disorder, such as abuse or dependence.

Stimulants have addiction potential because they are reinforcing drugs. Users typically experience feelings of euphoria and power, decreased need for sleep, relief from fatigue, decreased appetite, increased talkativeness, and increased energy. These effects alone qualify stimulants for classification as performance-enhancing drugs, not only for athletes but also for others who may need these benefits, such as workers who need to stay awake during long shifts or long-distance truck drivers. For individuals who are easily distracted, such as those with ADHD, stimulants also tend to decrease distractibility, allowing them to focus their attention. In addition, stimulants may increase sexual interest and excitement and, because of decreased fatigue, improve sexual performance.

The typical routes of administration for recreational stimulants (nasal inhalation, inhalation through smoking, and intravenous injection) tend to promote rapid effects on the body and strengthen the association of taking the drugs with its effects. In general, the quicker a drug takes effect, the easier it is for the body and mind to associate the drug with the experienced pleasure and the greater the addiction potential.

Dangers and Side Effects

The problems associated with stimulant use are numerous. Aside from the desirable effects described above, stimulant intoxication can cause much less attractive effects, including paranoia, anxiety, panic, psychosis, rapid pulse rate, hyperalertness, restlessness, insomnia, confusion, hallucinations, agitation, aggression, violence, and suicidal or homicidal tendencies. It is not uncommon for stimulant use to be associated with crimes related to personal and interpersonal injury, assaults, and accidents.

Stimulant abusers often suffer physical problems such as worn-down teeth (from bruxism, or teeth grinding), injuries from the compulsive repetitive handling or manipulation of objects or the body (for example, facial picking), arrhythmias, heart damage, and even seizures. When withdrawing from stimulants, individuals may experience feelings of confusion and depression, increased fatigue, and other symptoms.

Many of the symptoms of stimulant use, abuse, and dependence mimic the problems of other mental health disorders. Because of this, persons who seek help for such symptoms resulting from stimulant use are often treated as if they have some of these other problems. For example, they may be treated initially for sleep problems, anxiety, depression, or psychosis with drugs such as sleep aids, antianxiety agents, antidepressants, and antipsychotics. As they cease stimulant use and detoxify, their symptoms often resolve or decrease, and they consequently can stop these treatments. In some cases, however, after chronic stimulant use, the damage done can be more lasting, and treatments may need to be maintained.

Legal Issues and Crime

The manufacturers, distributors, and users of illegal stimulants are all participants in various forms of crime. Manufacturers take part in the illegal procurement of component parts of these drugs and threaten the public health with the dangerous conditions they create in clandestine labs (where poor ventilation can lead to explosions or fires) and with the toxic chemicals they dump into the environment. They also commit crimes such as battery, assault, and murder at times to protect their illegal labs from being discovered or disturbed.

Once the drugs are made, illegal trafficking and sales become part of the picture, as does the potential for money laundering and other financial crimes. For end users, crimes related to intoxication are common, including driving under the influence, as are acts of violence and aggression related to paranoia and other psychological effects. Stimulant users sometimes commit crimes as a result of drug-induced feelings of power and euphoria, which may lead them to believe they are smarter than everyone else and can break laws without fear of being caught. Such users may commit fraud, forgery, crimes of opportunity, and even murder.

Nancy A. Piotrowski

Further Reading

Inaba, Darryl S., and William E. Cohen. *Uppers, Downers, All-Arounders: Physical and Mental Effects of Psychoactive Drugs*. 5th ed. Ashland, Oreg.: CNS, 2003. Provides an easy-to-read overview of a broad spectrum of stimulants, including look-alikes and over-the-counter drugs.

Julien, Robert M. *A Primer of Drug Action: A Comprehensive Guide to the Actions, Uses, and Side Effects of Psychoactive Drugs*. 10th ed. New York: Worth, 2005. Reliable, long-standing text provides information on how particular drugs affect individuals at different life stages, from youth to old age.

Solanto, Mary V., Amy F. T. Arsnten, and F. Xavier Castallanos, eds. *Stimulant Drugs and ADHD: Basic and Clinical Neuroscience*. New York: Oxford University Press, 2001. Presents a technical discussion of how stimulant drugs have been used to treat attention-deficit/hyperactivity disorder. Notes the drugs' effects on behavior and their side effects, as well as relevant brain effects.

Weil, Andrew, and Winifred Rosen. *From Chocolate to Morphine: Everything You Need to Know About Mind-Altering Drugs*. Rev. ed. Boston: Houghton Mifflin, 2004. Presents a down-to-earth discussion of drugs that affect the mind. Easy to read.

Weinberg, Bennette Alan, and Bonnie K. Bealer. *The World of Caffeine: The Science and Culture of the World's Most Popular Drug*. New York: Routledge, 2002. Social history of caffeine addresses the stimulant's presence in a variety of commonly consumed products and its impacts.

See also: Amphetamines; Antianxiety agents; Antipsychotics; Attention-deficit/hyperactivity disorder medications; Club drugs; Crack cocaine; *Diagnostic and Statistical Manual of Mental Disorders*; Drug abuse and dependence; Drug classification; Forensic toxicology; Hallucinogens; Illicit substances; Performance-enhancing drugs.

STR. *See* Short tandem repeat analysis

Strangulation

Definition: Intentional act of applying pressure to a body part to cut off or restrict the flow of blood or air, resulting in loss of consciousness, injury, brain damage, or death.

Significance: Strangulation is a deliberate criminal act that takes place during such crimes as murder, sexual assault, domestic violence, and child abuse. Recognition of the signs of strangulation can aid forensic pathologists in determining cause of death and can help first responders get proper treatment for surviving victims.

Strangulation is used by a perpetrator to silence or kill the victim. Strangulation occurs during sexual assault, rape, domestic violence, child abuse, and other criminal acts. It is estimated that at least 50 percent of rape victims have been strangled.

A deputy coroner testifying in a trial in Ohio in early 2007 uses a drawing and his hands to demonstrate how a murder victim was strangled. (AP/Wide World Photos)

The act of strangulation entails applying pressure to a certain part of the body to reduce or stop blood flow to the brain or restrict oxygen in an airway. The brain needs oxygen to survive. Without oxygen, a person may lose consciousness, sustain brain injury or brain damage, or die. The perpetrator's hands or an object, such as a rope or cord, may be used to force restriction of oxygen at the victim's neck.

Only eleven pounds of pressure applied for ten seconds to the neck is necessary to force the restriction of oxygen to cause unconsciousness. Death can occur in four to five minutes with thirty pounds of pressure to the neck. Death can also result within thirty-six hours after strangulation if internal neck swelling is not diagnosed or treated.

After strangulation, injuries to the body may or may not be visible, but internal injuries could have taken place. Internal neck swelling is serious because it can jeopardize the airway passage needed for breathing. Persons who have been strangled and sustained no visible injuries have been known to die several weeks after strangulation as the result of undiagnosed brain damage. For these reasons, it is extremely important for first responders to ask crime victims if they were strangled, with or without loss of consciousness.

Signs of strangulation that should prompt medical attention include red spots on the skin (from capillaries bursting), bloodred eyes, neck swelling (subtle to severe), difficulty swallowing or breathing, vomiting blood, voice loss or raspy voice, coughing, and neck pain. Other signs that a person has been strangled include rope or cord burns, red vertical or horizontal line marks on the skin, scratches and bruises on the neck, and symptoms of brain injury, such as confusion, memory problems, mood changes, or personality changes. It is imperative that investigators carefully document and photograph any signs of strangulation injury.

Mary Car-Blanchard

Further Reading

Spitz, Werner U., ed. *Spitz and Fisher's Medico-legal Investigation of Death: Guidelines for the Application of Pathology to Crime Investigation.* 4th ed. Springfield, Ill.: Charles C Thomas, 2006.

Strack, Gael B., and George McClane. *How to Improve Your Investigation and Prosecution of Strangulation Cases.* San Diego, Calif.: San Diego City Attorney and San Diego City Police, 1999.

See also: Autoerotic and erotic asphyxiation; Autopsies; Choking; Defensive wounds; Forensic photography; Hanging; Homicide; Petechial hemorrhage; Rape; Suffocation.

Structural analysis

Definition: Evaluation of the engineering and construction of buildings and other structures.

Significance: When structures fail or are deliberately damaged, forensic scientists are often involved in conducting analyses to determine exactly what occurred. Structural analyses can reveal whether structural failures were caused by design flaws, by properties of the physical components used, or by other factors. In cases of deliberate destruction by explosive or mechanical means, structural analyses can determine the nature of the criminal acts and provide investigators with information about possible suspects.

The analysis of architectural structures such as buildings, bridges, and highways involves the evaluation of the physical and chemical properties of their material components and the engineering theory behind the ways in which these components are put together, which includes concern with the mechanics of the components' elasticity and their response to natural laws such as the law of gravity. Construction design involves applied theoretical frameworks of physics, chemistry, and mathematics. Generally, when structural deformations and design failures occur, engineers and physicists perform structural analyses; when catastrophic structural failures take place that may have been caused deliberately, forensic engineers become involved in such analyses. Forensic engineers are also sometimes involved in examining structural failures that have led to property damage or personal injury lawsuits; they may be called upon to determine whether such failures resulted from poor design, problems with construction, or lack of maintenance.

Architectural Design and Construction

The designs of structures begin with architects and engineers: Architects provide the artistic designs, and engineers detail the construction elements required to achieve those designs. Construction engineers determine the types and amounts of materials needed for structural projects. Typically, they use computer models to conduct extensive tests and determine how much of each material will be required; they examine the spatial relationships among the components to be used, the amount of weight or pressure each beam or other part can hold, and how the completed structure will function. Usually, engineers construct computer models of each design component and test each virtually under all potential conditions and stresses, such as varying load structures, earthquakes, and strong winds. These tests serve to identify any potential weaknesses that need to be eliminated in structural designs.

Forensic Engineering

Forensic engineering is a highly specialized branch of forensic science that is involved in the analysis of buildings and other constructed artifacts in legal cases of property damage, injury, and death. Most often, forensic engineers are called upon in cases concerned with liability issues resulting from property damage. In such cases, they help to determine the causes of structural failures.

The first task of a forensic engineer in a case of structural failure is to determine whether the structure of interest met all local, state, and federal building regulations, where applicable. For example, if the case concerns a house or business, the engineer must find out whether the structure met all building codes specified by the planning and zoning regulations of the town in which it was located. The engineer then goes on to examine systematically the individual components of the structure and how they related to one another.

One of the most common applications of forensic science in cases of structural failure is the analysis of damaged structures in which fires of suspicious origin are implicated. In such cases, forensic experts—both engineers and fire investigators—examine what remains of the structures to determine the fires' origins. They look at burn patterns and gather evidence for chemical analyses to identify the possible presence of accelerants, which can point to arson.

Forensic engineers are also involved in maintaining safe structures by conducting materials tests and analyses of building codes and reconstruction costs. By analyzing completed existing structures, forensic engineers can provide those responsible for maintaining the structures with recommendations for repairs and improvements that can help the structures remain safe while performing in an efficient manner.

Legal Issues

Legal cases that involve structural or architectural failures are decided under the laws of product liability, which are based in the legal concept that consumers must be protected from harm caused by dangerous or unreasonably unsafe products. Under product liability laws, manufacturers and distributors are responsible for injuries or property damage resulting from poor design of their products (including buildings and components of buildings such as doors and windows). For example, if a bridge was designed to withstand certain load specifications but forensic engineers determine that it failed under lesser pressure, the construction company that built the bridge would be deemed responsible under product liability laws and would be liable to pay compensation for damages and injuries resulting from the structural failure.

Dwight G. Smith

A material research engineer cuts a sample of metal to be analyzed from steel beams recovered from the World Trade Center after the terrorist attacks of September 11, 2001. The National Institute of Standards and Technology began an extensive study of the structural failure of the World Trade Center buildings in 2002. (AP/Wide World Photos)

Further Reading

Bosela, Paul A., and Norbert J. Delatte, eds. *Forensic Engineering: Proceedings of the Fourth Congress.* Reston, Va.: American Society of Civil Engineers, 2007. Collection of technical articles presented at a conference of forensic engineers covers a wide range of topics, including natural hazards, residential investigations, performance of transportation facilities, and historical cases.

Brown, Sam, ed. *Forensic Engineering: An Introduction to the Investigation, Analysis, Reconstruction, Causality, Prevention, Risk, Consequence, and Legal Aspects of the Fail-

ure of Engineered Products. Humble, Tex.: ISI, 1995. Provides a thorough treatment of all aspects of building failure.

Day, Robert W. *Forensic Geotechnical and Foundation Engineering*. New York: McGraw-Hill, 1999. Covers the investigation and evaluation of building damage caused by geological changes, including settlement and expansion of soil and earthquakes. Aimed at professional engineers.

Noon, Randall K. *Forensic Engineering Investigation*. Boca Raton, Fla.: CRC Press, 2001. Comprehensive handbook discusses the procedures investigators follow in criminal cases of structural failure.

See also: Accident investigation and reconstruction; Arson; Blast seat; Bomb damage assessment; Burn pattern analysis; Electrical injuries and deaths; Improvised explosive devices; Oklahoma City bombing; Product liability cases; World Trade Center bombing.

Suffocation

Definition: Severe deprivation of the oxygen supply needed by the body to sustain life.

Significance: Death by suffocation often causes no exterior signs of trauma. During an autopsy, a forensic pathologist may be able to discover signs of chemicals in the lungs or other damage that would lead to a determination of suffocation as the cause of death.

The body can be deprived of oxygen to the point of death in a variety of ways, including through compression of the chest, interference with oxygen absorption, displacement of oxygen in the lungs, and smothering. Suffocation may occur intentionally, as in cases of murder or suicide, or it may occur accidentally.

Compression of the chest to the point of limiting the lungs' ability to expand can cause suffocation. This type of suffocation is a cause of death in situations involving panicked crowds (the most common cause of death in such disasters is suffocation, not trampling, as is often believed), accidents in which the victims are buried in substances such as sand or grain, and accidents in which objects fall on victims' chests. In the combat exercise known as "body scissors," the legs are used to compress an opponent's chest, depriving that person of oxygen. Snakes such as boa constrictors and pythons use this type of suffocation to kill their prey.

The body's absorption of oxygen can be interfered with chemically or physically. Chemical interference can be caused by agents such as carbon monoxide (often from car exhaust) or phosgene (a toxic compound used as a weapon during World War I, but now used as an industrial reagent). These agents interfere with the body's ability to absorb oxygen by bonding with blood cells in place of oxygen.

Another form of interference with oxygen absorption is physical displacement. This occurs when a type of gas takes the place of oxygen in the lungs. Some of the types of gases that can displace oxygen are hydrogen cyanide and potassium cyanide, which were previously used in gas chambers for execution and as chemical weapons and are now used in industrial applications. Displacement may also occur with smoke and other types of fumes or with another substance, such as water. In addition, oxygen may be displaced from the lungs in a vacuum or an extremely low-pressure environment; in such an environment, oxygen is literally sucked out of the lungs.

Smothering is a means of suffocation that involves the obstruction of the flow of air into the lungs. For example, an attacker may cover the mouth and nose of a victim with a physical object, such as a hand, a pillow, or a plastic bag. In some cases, such action may be combined with chest compression.

Marianne M. Madsen

Further Reading

Baden, Michael, and Marion Roach. *Dead Reckoning: The New Science of Catching Killers*. New York: Simon & Schuster, 2001.

Lyle, D. P. *Forensics and Fiction: Clever, Intriguing, and Downright Odd Questions from Crime Writers*. New York: St. Martin's Press, 2007.

Shkrum, Michael J., and David A. Ramsay. *Forensic Pathology of Trauma: Common Problems for the Pathologist.* Totowa, N.J.: Humana Press, 2007.

See also: Asphyxiation; Autoerotic and erotic asphyxiation; Carbon monoxide poisoning; Chicago nightclub stampede; Choking; Drowning; Hanging; Inhalant abuse; Petechial hemorrhage; Smoke inhalation; Strangulation.

Suicide

Definition: Act of intentionally killing oneself through one's own effort or with the assistance of another.

Significance: Suicide is one of the leading causes of unnatural death in the world, particularly among teenagers. It is a phenomenon that affects every nation as well as every culture. The strategic use of suicide in warfare and terrorism has become commonplace in the past century, and the topic of assisted suicide has become a source of great controversy.

Suicide has been a part of human society since history has been recorded, and the ethical implications of the act have been debated since ancient times. The scholars of ancient Greece addressed the legitimacy of suicide; Plato rejected the act based on a religious rationale, but Socrates disagreed and ultimately committed suicide. Under the Roman Empire, many soldiers committed suicide after defeat in war or to avoid capture by enemies. Later, Christianity altered views on suicide to mirror the sacrifices made by Jesus Christ. Specifically, Christians typically honored those who committed suicide as a sacrifice for a larger cause, such as in war, but they held in contempt those who used suicide as a way to escape the law or for other reasons deemed cowardly.

Suicide has been used as a strategy in warfare throughout history. During World War II, the Japanese sent what were termed kamikaze pilots to fly bombs into U.S. ships. The North Vietnamese also used suicide tactics against American soldiers during the Vietnam War. Moreover, although suicide is at odds with Islamic law, some Muslims use suicide attacks on their enemies under the notion of martyrdom warfare. The difference between suicide and martyrdom is that martyrdom is undertaken for a higher purpose, whereas suicide is undertaken to escape the hardships of life.

Across cultures, suicide remains a problem in the twenty-first century, with concerns increasing about suicide among teenagers. Moreover,

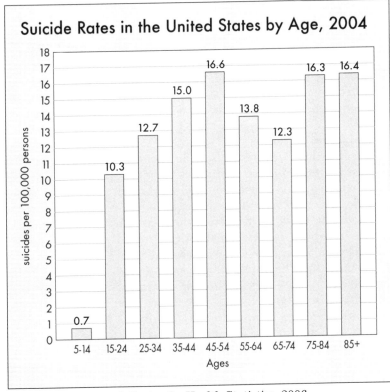

Suicide Rates in the United States by Age, 2004

Source: U.S. National Center for Health Statistics, 2006.

Euthanasia

Passive euthanasia involves aiding the termination of other persons' lives by withdrawing life-support assistance, such as medical treatments, medications, respirator equipment, respirators, nutrition, and water. Active euthanasia involves the administration of treatments or medications designed to end life. Euthanasia is considered to be voluntary when victims request it and involuntary when persons other than the victims request it. Physician-assisted suicide differs from active voluntary euthanasia in that physicians do not perform the actual killings but merely provide the means for suicide, such as prescriptions for lethal doses of drugs. In some jurisdictions, all forms of euthanasia are illegal.

Little systematic research has been done to examine why some people choose assisted suicide over unassisted suicide. However, in contrast to the pattern for suicide in general, about two-thirds of the persons who apply for assistance with suicide in those jurisdictions where the practice is legal are women.

Steven Stack

international debates are ongoing regarding the morality of assisted suicide, or euthanasia, with strong views being expressed on both sides of the topic of the "right to die."

Investigating Suicide

Investigations regarding suicide typically take two forms: research that seeks to explain the phenomenon of suicide and investigations into deaths that appear to have been self-inflicted. Attempts to understand and explain suicide have been undertaken at both micro and macro levels. Macro-level research on the topic has centered on the impact of the social structure on suicide rates across cities and even nationally. Theorists such as Émile Durkheim have attempted to show correlations between factors such as war periods and the Great Depression on suicide rates in the United States. In contrast, micro-level research has attempted to understand individual-level factors that may lead to suicide. For instance, researchers have examined the relationship between suicide and the social pressures placed on teenagers as well as that between suicide and the family problems encountered by adults. Suicide researchers are careful to separate attempted suicides in which the persons survive from completed suicide; many contend that the two are completely separate phenomena with completely separate causes.

Forensic pathologists are typically the members of the criminal justice system who oversee investigations into deaths that are suspicious or unnatural. In the United States, coroners or medical examiners (depending on the state) conduct investigations of unnatural deaths and order lab tests and autopsies on the bodies. However, law-enforcement officers and criminalists often collect data at death scenes that can be just as valuable or even more valuable than autopsy and toxicology test results in determining whether deaths are attributable to suicide, accident, or murder. When an automobile fatality occurs, for instance, police officers may need to conduct exhaustive interviews with other drivers and then with the family and friends of the deceased in order to rule out suicide. At the very least, police investigators have a critical role in collecting the evidence that forensic pathologists use in making their determination.

Because of the myriad circumstances in which unnatural or suspicious deaths may occur, forensic pathologists typically have wide-ranging expertise. They routinely have to make decisions regarding the likely ways in which many kinds of wounds were inflicted on bodies, including bullet wounds, stab wounds, wounds caused by blunt force trauma, and burns. Moreover, when suicide is suspected, pathologists sometimes focus on the life histories, psychiatric data, and other information on the backgrounds of the deceased. Such psychological autopsies can aid in the determination of cause of death, but it should be noted that the use of this technique has been greatly exaggerated in popular media depictions of the work of pathologists.

Brion Sever

Further Reading

Durkheim, Émile. *Suicide: A Study in Sociology*. Translated by John A. Spaulding and

George Simpson. 1951. Reprint. New York: Free Press, 1997. Classic work examines suicide from a sociological viewpoint, focusing on macro-level trends. Warns against using statistics to attempt to understand the causes of suicide.

Gorsuch, Neil. *The Future of Assisted Suicide and Euthanasia.* Princeton, N.J.: Princeton University Press, 2006. Lists the arguments for and against the legalizing of assisted suicide and places the phenomenon within an international context.

Holmes, Ronald, and Stephen Holmes. *Suicide: Theory, Practice, and Investigation.* Thousand Oaks, Calif.: Sage, 2005. Analyzes the theories surrounding the causes of suicide and examines how suicides are investigated. Includes actual suicide notes in discussion of the motives underlying suicide.

Joiner, Thomas. *Why People Die by Suicide.* Cambridge, Mass.: Harvard University Press, 2005. In-depth discussion of the determinants of suicide includes analysis of the differences between those who attempt suicide but survive and those who complete suicide.

Picton, Bernard. *Murder, Suicide, or Accident: The Forensic Pathologist at Work.* London: Hale, 1971. Focuses on the difficulty faced by forensic pathologists in distinguishing deaths by suicide from deaths resulting from murder and accidents.

See also: Autoerotic and erotic asphyxiation; Autopsies; Borderline personality disorder; Celebrity cases; Drowning; Forensic entomology; Forensic pathology; Forensic toxicology; Hesitation wounds and suicide; Psychological autopsy; Ritual killing.

Superglue fuming

Definition: Use of cyanoacrylate vapors to visualize latent fingerprints.

Significance: Fingerprints and palm prints are often critical pieces of evidence encountered at crime scenes. Because most fingerprints are not visible to the naked eye and are easily destroyed, the fuming of prints with the vapors of superglue (cyanoacrylate) has become common. This technique makes permanent what would otherwise be transient pieces of evidence.

Forensic scientists have used superglue fuming since 1982 to visualize latent fingerprints and palm prints on nonporous surfaces such as metals and plastics. The developed prints are white and provide especially good contrast with dark-colored surfaces. Dyes such as rhodamine can be used to enhance the contrast of prints with light backgrounds and can cause prints to fluoresce when viewed under the appropriate conditions.

How Fuming Works

Superglue, like many adhesives, is a polymer. A polymer is a type of molecule that exists in the form of long chains of repeating units, called monomers. Superglue consists almost entirely of cyanoacrylate ester, which consists of carbon, hydrogen, oxygen, and nitrogen and polymerizes (forms long chains) rapidly in the presence of minute amounts of water.

When superglue vapor comes in contact with a fingerprint on a nonporous surface, it quickly begins polymerizing. Layers of polymer build up until the minute details of the fingerprint are visible. Because the vapor interacts only with the fingerprint, the area around the details remains free of superglue. In addition to enabling visualization of the fingerprint, the superglue makes the print permanent, thus preserving it.

Procedure

Superglue fuming is often performed in a fuming tank. The item to be fumed is suspended or propped inside a glass tank, such as an aquarium, so that the area of the item suspected to contain a fingerprint or palm print is not touching any surface of the tank. A source of superglue vapor is also required. The superglue may be vaporized in one of two ways: Either a small amount of sodium hydroxide, a very strong base, is added to the unpolymerized glue or the glue is heated. Crime labs typically employ the heating method, as it tends to be more efficient, but methods of heating the glue vary from lab to lab. The heat source can be anything from a lightbulb to a small warming plate (of the kind designed to hold a coffee mug) to a cup of boiling water.

To begin the fuming, a small amount of superglue (roughly the size of a quarter) is typically placed on an aluminum foil tray, which is then placed above the heat source inside the fuming tank, along with the item to be fumed. The tank is then sealed, and the vapor is allowed to fill the chamber. The vapor interacts with the object in the tank and develops any prints that might be present on the surface. The fuming is allowed to progress for anywhere from less than an hour to six hours, depending on the efficiency of the heat source, the lab's protocols, the size of the tank, and the object being fumed.

A handgun hanging inside a superglue fuming tank, above the small warming plate used to heat the glue. Fingerprints are developed and preserved by the fuming process. *(AP/Wide World Photos)*

When the fuming is complete, the heat source is turned off and the tank is opened. The fumed object can then be removed and examined for developed prints.

Another fuming technique involves the use of a handheld fuming wand, which contains solid superglue along with a butane torch. The torch heats the superglue and causes it to vaporize quickly. These fumes can be directed onto the surface of interest, and high-quality prints can be developed in minutes. An advantage to this method is that most handheld fuming wands are portable, so they can be taken to crime scenes and used to fume large objects that cannot be transported to the lab. Such wands can also be used as vapor sources in traditional fuming tank setups.

Safety Considerations

Although superglue is nontoxic—it is even sometimes used to seal surgical wounds—the vapors given off during the fuming process will bind to skin, eyes, and mucous membranes if these are left unprotected. Persons wearing contact lenses should not come into close proximity to superglue fuming because of the possibility that the lenses will bond to the eyes. The fumes themselves can also be very irritating. To prevent exposure, laboratories generally conduct superglue fuming in chemical fume hoods, and those performing the procedure wear safety goggles and gloves and make sure that none of their skin is exposed.

If a fume hood is not available, such as when a fuming wand is used at a crime scene, extra care must be taken to ensure that no one is exposed to the fumes. In addition to wearing the kinds of personal protective gear noted above, the person using a fuming wand often employs a face mask to avoid inhaling the vapors.

Lisa LaGoo

Further Reading

Champod, Christophe. *Fingerprints and Other Ridge Skin Impressions*. Boca Raton, Fla.: CRC Press, 2004. Comprehensive discussion of fingerprint evidence includes detailed information on superglue fuming.

Gardner, Ross M. *Practical Crime Scene Processing and Investigation*. Boca Raton, Fla.:

CRC Press, 2005. Guide to investigating crime scenes focuses on practical applications of forensic techniques. Discusses the different kinds of tank setups used in superglue fuming.

Genge, N. E. *The Forensic Casebook: The Science of Crime Scene Investigation*. New York: Ballantine, 2002. Easy-to-read overview of crime scene investigation features a section on fingerprints that discusses methods of print visualization, including superglue fuming.

Jackson, Andrew R. W., and Julie M. Jackson. *Forensic Science*. 2d ed. Upper Saddle River, N.J.: Pearson Prentice Hall, 2008. Provides a broad overview of forensic science and includes basic information on superglue fuming of fingerprints.

Saferstein, Richard. *Criminalistics: An Introduction to Forensic Science*. 9th ed. Upper Saddle River, N.J.: Pearson Prentice Hall, 2007. Excellent introductory textbook covers most forensic disciplines. Includes in-depth information on fingerprints.

See also: Ear prints; Fingerprints; Imaging; Integrated Automated Fingerprint Identification System; Prints.

T

Tabun

Definition: Highly toxic liquid used as a chemical warfare agent.

Significance: Concerns that terrorists could employ chemical agents in attacks have increased law-enforcement agencies' attention to substances such as tabun. The manufacture and storage of tabun are banned by the United Nations Chemical Weapons Convention of 1993.

Tabun, which was discovered in Germany in the 1930's during a search for new insecticides, is the earliest and most easily manufactured of the so-called nerve gases. Although it has been superseded as a chemical weapon by agents such as VX, its relative ease of manufacture makes it attractive to some nations that might consider using it as a weapon.

Tabun was manufactured and stored in multiton quantities in Nazi Germany during World War II, but it was never used in combat. During the Iran-Iraq War (1980-1988), however, Iraq used the agent against Iranian troops. In 1984, a team sent to Iran by the United Nations found tabun in a dud bomb that Iraq had dropped inside Iran's borders. The team also visited a field hospital where several patients were recovering; they exhibited symptoms consistent with poisoning by tabun, although no detailed tests were done.

Like other organophosphorus nerve agents, tabun is an inhibitor of the vital enzyme acetylcholinesterase (AChE). When tabun is absorbed through the skin or the vapor or aerosol of the agent is inhaled, the chemical binds to AChE. The normal function of AChE is to catalyze a reaction that removes acetylcholine from the nerve endings, where it activates muscle contraction. Inhibition of the enzyme allows accumulation of acetylcholine, which causes sweating, runny nose, incontinence, visual impairment (including pain and contraction of the pupils, or meiosis), respiratory failure, convulsions, coma, and death. The degree of danger depends somewhat on the mode of exposure and the weight of the individual, but very small amounts of nerve agents such as tabun are toxic.

Signs of exposure to tabun in victims include abnormally low AChE levels in the blood. Traces of the agent may also be found in the victims' bodies. Methods have been developed for detecting nerve agents in biological samples at the picogram level using gas chromatography-mass spectrometry (GC-MS) or capillary gas chromatography. Members of the American armed forces use a handheld device, the chemical agent monitor (CAM), that detects nerve agents under field conditions through ion mobility spectrometry.

Treatment of nerve agent poisoning involves injections of atropine and administration of pralidoxime chloride (2-PAM chloride). The oxime tends to displace the nerve agent from the AChE, but it must be given quickly, because a reaction known as aging soon makes the AChE-nerve agent combination irreversible. Drugs given before exposure (prophylaxis) include carbamates (physostigmine, pyridostigmine) and enzymatic organophosphate scavengers.

John R. Phillips

Further Reading

Croddy, Eric A., and James J. Wirtz, eds. *Weapons of Mass Destruction: An Encyclopedia of Worldwide Policy, Technology, and History*. Santa Barbara, Calif.: ABC-CLIO, 2005.

Hoenig, Steven L. *Handbook of Chemical Warfare and Terrorism*. Westport, Conn.: Greenwood Press, 2002.

Somani, Satu M., and James A. Romano, Jr., eds. *Chemical Warfare Agents: Toxicity at Low Levels*. Boca Raton, Fla.: CRC Press, 2001.

Suzuki, Osamu, and Kanako Watanabe, eds. *Drugs and Poisons in Humans: A Handbook of Practical Analysis*. New York: Springer, 2005.

Tucker, Jonathan B. *War of Nerves: Chemical Warfare from World War I to al-Qaeda*. New York: Pantheon Books, 2006.

See also: Centers for Disease Control and Prevention; Chemical agents; Chemical terrorism; Chemical warfare; Chemical Weapons Convention of 1993; Nerve agents; Nervous system; Sarin; Soman.

Tape

Definition: Manufactured product that consists of a long strip of a backing film with an adhesive applied to one side that allows the film to be stuck to a surface.

Significance: Law-enforcement investigators may encounter various kinds of adhesive tapes as evidence in a range of cases, including homicides, kidnappings, drug trafficking cases, and cases involving explosive devices. By analyzing tape evidence recovered from crime scenes, comparing the physical and chemical properties of the samples with pieces or rolls of tape recovered from suspects or from other items, forensic scientists can provide investigators with valuable information.

Pressure-sensitive adhesive tapes are generally composed of several layers: a release coating, a backing film, and an adhesive coating. The release coating is a very thin layer that prevents the tape from sticking to itself when wound on a roll. The backing film is commonly a type of polymer, such as polyethylene, polypropylene, or polyvinyl chloride, but paper and cloth tapes are also available. The type of adhesive coating used depends on the specific application of the tape, with the most common types of adhesives being natural rubber, styrenated rubber, and acrylic polymers. Packaging tape and electrical tape are the most common types of tapes that forensic scientists encounter in their work.

The first stage of the examination of a tape evidence sample consists of a comparison of the physical characteristics of the recovered and control samples. This includes comparison of the color, surface texture, width, and thickness of the backing film and the adhesive layer. Optical properties such as birefringence and fluorescence are also compared for some tapes. The forensic scientist may use microspectrophotometry to compare the colors of the tapes objectively. Surface striations may also be visible on the film; these are imparted to the tape during its manufacture. Examination of these striations can be carried out in a way that is analogous to a tool-mark comparison.

A range of analytical techniques are then applied to the backing film and to the adhesive

By comparing the physical and chemical properties of tape evidence recovered from crime scenes with pieces or rolls of tape from known sources, forensic scientists can provide investigators with valuable information. (© iStockphoto.com/Daniel Norman)

layer to determine their chemical compositions. The choice of techniques used depends on the instrumentation available. Techniques commonly applied include Fourier transform infrared (FTIR) spectroscopy, pyrolysis gas chromatography (PyGC), X-ray fluorescence (XRF), and scanning electron microscopy with energy-dispersive spectroscopy (SEM-EDS). If cloth tapes are being examined, the fibers present in the tape are also analyzed.

A conclusive match of the recovered and control tape samples is possible if a physical fit is found between the fractured ends of the two samples. A correspondence of striations on the surface of the film may also prove a conclusive match if it can be shown that the marks alter during the manufacture of the particular tape being examined. Otherwise, a correspondence of physical and chemical features results in a match of class characteristics; the evidential value of such a class match is determined through reference to surveys of similar types of tapes.

Sally A. Coulson

Further Reading

Maynard, Philip, Katrina Gates, Claude Roux, and Chris Lennard. "Adhesive Tape Analysis: Establishing the Evidential Value of Specific Techniques." *Journal of Forensic Sciences* 46, no. 2 (2001): 280-287.

Saferstein, Richard. *Criminalistics: An Introduction to Forensic Science.* 9th ed. Upper Saddle River, N.J.: Pearson Prentice Hall, 2007.

See also: Fibers and filaments; Fourier transform infrared spectrophotometer; Fracture matching; Gas chromatography; Mass spectrometry; Microspectrophotometry; Physical evidence; Tool marks.

Taphonomy

Definition: Study of postmortem changes in organisms from the time of death to the point of discovery.

Significance: Postmortem events alter the condition of human remains and may leave evidence that can potentially be confused with trauma. The study of human decomposition also provides important clues that aid in the estimation of the time since death.

The term "taphonomy" was coined in 1940 by the Russian paleontologist Ivan Yefremov to describe the "laws of burial." Taphonomists attempt to understand events that occur to organisms after death, a period defined as the postmortem interval. Early research in the field of taphonomy focused on the study of fossils, especially the conditions that determine how and why certain organisms are preserved in the fossil record. Since the 1980's, taphonomy has become an important research area in forensic science, focusing on the study of postmortem changes in human remains and estimation of the time since death (TSD), also known as the postmortem interval. This emerging field, known as forensic taphonomy, applies the principles of taphonomy to the study of human decomposition. TSD studies are usually undertaken by anthropologists, entomologists, or pathologists who have forensic expertise, but the examination of postmortem changes in human remains is an interdisciplinary study and may involve a number of different specialists.

Goals of Forensic Taphonomy

Forensic taphonomy addresses several important medicolegal issues, including estimation of the TSD and the study of postmortem changes in human remains caused by decomposition, transport, weathering, or fire. TSD estimation can aid in narrowing down the search for a missing person or can be used to exclude potential suspects from consideration who have alibis for the time when an alleged homicide occurred.

When a corpse is exposed to the environment for a long period of time, estimation of the TSD becomes increasingly difficult. Over time, insects, bacteria, plants, animal scavengers, and other aspects of the physical environment alter remains. Postmortem changes to remains can potentially be misinterpreted as perimortem wounds—that is, trauma inflicted at or around the time of death.

Different taphonomic processes also leave distinct signatures, so the ability to differentiate postmortem changes from perimortem trauma is critical. For example, tooth marks on bone from animal scavenging should not be misinterpreted as perimortem trauma. Taphonomic studies require close examination of the condition of the remains and any alterations caused by the environment. Humans are also considered taphonomic agents, as a perpetrator may be involved in transporting or altering (for example, mutilating or dismembering) remains after death.

Stages of Decomposition

When human remains are discovered, one of the first questions asked is, How long has the victim been dead? Decomposition typically occurs in the following predictable sequence of stages: the fresh stage, the bloat stage, the active decay stage, the advanced decay stage, and the dry or skeletal stage. The rate of decay, however, is influenced by a number of factors in the immediate environment, such as temperature, humidity, moisture, availability of insects and animal scavengers, and soil conditions. Bodies that are found indoors or that are buried decompose at slower rates than remains that are deposited on the surface of the ground. In the case of a recent death, medicolegal investigators examine the body for early signs of decomposition.

Changes during the fresh stage of decomposition generally occur within the first few days postmortem. Immediately after death, the body cools until it reaches ambient temperature, a process known as algor mortis. Pooling of blood into the capillaries of the skin, or livor mortis, follows and is fixed by approximately twelve

An entomology doctoral student at the University of Florida's Institute of Food and Agricultural Sciences examines a colony of blowfly maggots as she conducts research into the growth rates of maggots at various temperatures. Information from such studies can help crime scene investigators determine time of death based on the maggots found on bodies. (AP/Wide World Photos)

hours after death. Rigor mortis, the hardening of the muscles, begins about two hours after death but may last for up to twenty-four hours.

The bloat stage is marked by the buildup of gases within the body, which causes the abdomen to be distended. The skin also becomes discolored and marbled in appearance. This process may last for several days up to a month after death. Carrion-feeding insects such as blowflies and flesh flies also typically arrive at a corpse within minutes after death. The maggots from these flies use the body as a food source for several weeks to months.

During the active decay stage, maggots, beetles, and other insects reduce the mass of the corpse, and the chest cavity begins to collapse. In the advanced decay stage, remains are nearly skeletonized owing to insect and animal scavenger activity. Finally, in the dry or skeletal decay stage, the skeletonized remains are devoid of soft tissue and odor. Postmortem changes are somewhat predictable within a given region; however, the rate of decomposition is highly variable from region to region.

Taphonomic Studies

Although some taphonomic studies occur within laboratory settings, most research is conducted outdoors with the remains of nonhuman animals, such as pigs. In some locations, however, donated human cadavers are used to study decomposition rates; the Anthropological Research Facility at the University of Tennessee, Knoxville, popularly known as the Body Farm, is perhaps the most widely known example of this kind of research center.

With the establishment of increasing numbers of outdoor taphonomic research facilities in different locations, scientists have been able to gain reliable data on variations in decay rates. These studies, which contribute to an in-depth understanding of the process of human decomposition, provide law-enforcement investigators with information they need to make more accurate estimates of time since death.

Eric J. Bartelink

Further Reading

Galloway, Alison, et al. "Decay Rates of Human Remains in an Arid Environment: Retrospective Study of Decay Rates in the Southwestern United States." *Journal of Forensic Sciences* 34 (May, 1989): 607-616. Reports on the findings of a scientific study of decay rates.

Haglund, William D., and Marcella H. Sorg, eds. *Advances in Forensic Taphonomy: Method, Theory, and Archaeological Perspectives*. Boca Raton, Fla.: CRC Press, 2002. Detailed edited volume focuses on theoretical and practical applications of taphonomy in medicolegal settings.

_____. *Forensic Taphonomy: The Postmortem Fate of Human Remains*. Boca Raton, Fla.: CRC Press, 1997. Collection of essays highlights case studies and research dealing with taphonomy in medicolegal settings.

Komar, Debra A. "Decay Rates in a Cold Climate Region: A Review of Cases Involving Advanced Decomposition from the Medical Examiner's Office in Edmonton, Alberta." *Journal of Forensic Sciences* 43 (January, 1998): 57-61. Reports on the findings of a study of variability in decay rates of remains found in cold climates.

Lyman, R. Lee. *Vertebrate Taphonomy*. New York: Cambridge University Press, 1994. Provides a comprehensive overview of the science of taphonomy for archaeologists, physical anthropologists, and paleontologists.

See also: Adipocere; Algor mortis; Body farms; Decomposition of bodies; Forensic anthropology; Forensic archaeology; Forensic entomology; Livor mortis; Rigor mortis; Skeletal analysis; University of Tennessee Anthropological Research Facility.

Tarasoff rule

Definition: Duty of mental health professionals to warn third parties known to be the subjects of threats of injury or death by patients.

Significance: When California's highest court imposed liability on mental health professionals for serious injuries to third parties known to be the subject of threats by patients, the court held that the public interest in protecting individual safety overrides the maintenance of confidentiality between therapist and patient.

Prior to the 1976 decision of the California Supreme Court in *Tarasoff v. Regents of the University of California*, no law in the United States recognized a therapist's duty toward individuals with whom the therapist had no formal relationship. A therapist had discretion concerning any warning to a third party about a dangerous individual. Maintaining confidentiality within the confines of the therapist-patient relationship was paramount. Following the court's ruling in *Tarasoff*, mental health professionals were charged with the responsibility to take reasonable steps to prevent violence threatened by their patients by warning third parties as well as the appropriate authorities.

Because the court failed to provide guidelines concerning when warnings would be required and left it up to therapists to determine whether patients would in fact act on their threats, the duty imposed on therapists was subject to much conjecture and speculation. When the decision was first handed down, opponents predicted that it would lead to unwarranted hospitalizations and ineffective calls to police and potential victims. They also suggested that therapists might become wary and avoid potentially violent patients, who in turn would be reluctant to talk with therapists about their violent thoughts. Several decades have demonstrated that those fears were unrealistic, however.

Subsequent case law has also clarified a workable solution concerning when a therapist is required to issue a warning to a third party. When a patient expresses a threat of serious harm to an identifiable victim, the legal obligation to protect the intended victim against such danger is imposed on the therapist. That duty may require the therapist to take one or more steps, such as warning the intended victim or others of the danger, notifying law-enforcement authorities, and taking whatever additional actions are necessary, depending on the nature of the case.

Facts of the Case

Prosenjit Poddar was a graduate student from India, studying at the University of California at Berkeley. In the fall of 1968, he met Tatiana (Tanya) Tarasoff at a folk-dancing class. They saw each other weekly throughout that fall, and on New Year's Eve, Tarasoff kissed Poddar. He interpreted this kiss to indicate the existence of a serious relationship between them. When Tarasoff learned of Poddar's feelings, she told him of her involvement with other men and indicated that she was not interested in entering into an intimate relationship with him. In part because of their different cultures, Poddar did not understand Tarasoff's explanation and underwent a severe emotional crisis. He spoke to a friend about his love for Tarasoff and his uncontrollable desire to kill her.

During the summer of 1969, Tarasoff went to Brazil. After she left, Poddar began to improve and, at a friend's suggestion, sought help from the university's health service. He began psychotherapy under the care of a staff psychologist, Dr. Lawrence Moore. During his ninth session with Moore, Poddar confided that he was going to kill Tarasoff when she returned from Brazil. Two days later, Moore personally notified campus police officers that Poddar was capable of harming himself or others; he also wrote a letter to the chief of the campus police in which he stated that Poddar was an acute and severe paranoid schizophrenic and a danger to himself and others. The campus police took Poddar into custody, but they released him when he promised to change his attitude and stay away from Tarasoff. Poddar stopped his therapy.

When Tarasoff returned from Brazil in October, 1969, Poddar continued to stalk her. On October 27, armed with a pellet gun and a kitchen knife, Poddar shot Tarasoff and repeatedly and fatally stabbed her. Afterward, he called the police, confessed, and asked to be handcuffed. Moore's diagnosis of Poddar was confirmed the following day.

The Decision

Poddar was charged with Tarasoff's murder, and he pleaded not guilty by reason of insanity. A jury convicted Poddar of second-degree murder, and he appealed on multiple grounds. The appellate court focused on jury instruction errors made in the trial court and reduced Poddar's conviction to manslaughter. Two years later, the California Supreme Court vacated the judgment, held that the jury instruction error was prejudicial, and remanded the case for retrial. Poddar was not retried. Rather than conduct another lengthy trial, the state released Poddar on the condition that he leave for India and not return to the United States. He did so; he later married in India.

Tarasoff's parents filed a wrongful-death civil action simultaneously against the university's police department, the Regents of the University of California, and the university's health service for failing to warn their daughter about Poddar's desire to kill her. At trial, the case was dismissed because of the absence of a cause of action (legal reason for suing) owing to the physician-patient privilege of confidentiality. Specifically, the court ruled that a physician has a duty only to the patient, not to third parties; therefore, no duty was owed to Tarasoff.

The intermediate appellate court upheld the trial court's decision, but the California Supreme Court reversed, holding that the case stated a cause of action and must be heard. The Supreme Court reasoned that the therapist has a duty to use reasonable care to give threatened persons whatever warnings are necessary to avert foreseeable danger. The duty extends from the patient to the intended victim. Addressing the defendants' assertion that a warning constitutes a breach of the trust inherent in confidential communications, the court recognized the public interest in supporting effective treatment of mental illness and protecting patients' right to privacy and confidentiality but concluded that the public interest in safety from violent assault outweighs these considerations, stating, "The protective privilege ends where the public peril begins."

The initial California Supreme Court decision in 1974 held that the campus police could be found liable for their failure to warn Tarasoff, but at the rehearing in 1976, the police were released from all liability. The holdings with respect to the psychotherapists were essentially the same in both cases and were predicated on the same arguments. The second decision provided therapists greater latitude to "protect" intended victims rather than to "warn" them. It should be noted that the case was never decided on the merits because it was settled for an undisclosed sum of money.

In evaluating the imposition of liability, the California Supreme Court noted the discretion given to psychiatrists to use their best judgment in determining whether patients are dangerous. Courts will generally defer to this discretion. In cases in which patients verbally demonstrate intent to harm others, however, psychiatrists are liable for injuries that arise from patients' carrying out their threats.

Tarasoff's Impact

The court's ruling in *Tarasoff* expanded the legal concepts of duty and foreseeability. Despite initial concerns regarding therapists' inability to predict violent behavior accurately and the effect of breach of confidentiality, these matters have not had the adverse impacts initially feared and predicted. Ultimately, the *Tarasoff* case stimulated greater awareness of violent patients' potential for carrying out such behavior. That, in turn, stimulated closer scrutiny and better documentation concerning this issue.

Since the *Tarasoff* decision, other interesting related questions have arisen, such as whether clergy who engage in pastoral counseling activities have a duty to protect third parties. Because in pastoral counseling there is little or no "control" over the penitent as there is over the patient in psychotherapy, the legal arguments used in *Tarasoff* do not apply to this situation. Scholars feel, however, that most members of the clergy in their discretion will take necessary steps to notify either potential victims or the appropriate authorities.

The *Tarasoff* rule imposes civil liability. The question of criminal liability has not been

---

Excerpt from the Court's Decision in *Tarasoff*

We conclude that the public policy favoring protection of the confidential character of patient-psychotherapist communications must yield to the extent to which disclosure is essential to avert danger to others. The protective privilege ends where the public peril begins.

Our current crowded and computerized society compels the interdependence of its members. In this risk-infested society we can hardly tolerate the further exposure to danger that would result from a concealed knowledge of the therapist that his patient was lethal. If the exercise of reasonable care to protect the threatened victim requires the therapist to warn the endangered party or those who can reasonably be expected to notify him, we see no sufficient societal interest that would protect and justify concealment. The containment of such risks lies in the public interest.

studied extensively, but one scholar has argued that the breach of the duty to warn should lead to criminal liability for the felony committed by the patient. Furthermore, the duty was reformulated as a duty to treat dangerousness, not as a duty to prevent harm to third parties. It should be noted, however, that no jurisdiction has prosecuted a therapist criminally for a violation of the *Tarasoff* duty to warn.

Although the *Tarasoff* rule applies only in California, it has been considered in every U.S. state, although it is not followed everywhere. Some states have refused to follow *Tarasoff* out of a need to protect the confidential disclosure of information, barring disclosure of any information to third parties. Others follow *Tarasoff* but limit third-party liability to situations in which specific intended victims are named. Still others require that the intended victim be directly threatened by a patient, and some impose a duty on the psychiatrist to take action to prevent the patient from carrying out the threat, including seeking commitment of the patient or obtaining police detention. Most states have extended the therapist's duty to identifiable victims only, and not to the general public. A minority of courts have recognized a broader duty to protect the public from the danger imposed by a patient.

Marcia J. Weiss

Further Reading

Appelbaum, Paul S. *Almost a Revolution: Mental Health Law and the Limits of Change.* New York: Oxford University Press, 1994. Discusses important reforms in mental health law: changes in civil commitment laws, the *Tarasoff* duty to warn, the rights of mental patients to refuse treatment, and changes in the insanity defense

Beis, Edward B. *Mental Health and the Law.* New York: Aspen, 1984. Explains in lay terms the legal aspects of the mental health system and the legal responsibilities of mental health professionals. Useful as a guide to the standards of care and treatment required by the law.

Blum, Deborah. *Bad Karma: A True Story of Obsession and Murder.* New York: Atheneum, 1986. Details the relationship between Poddar and Tarasoff, illustrating their clash of cultures.

Buckner, Fillmore, and Marvin Firestone. "'Where the Public Peril Begins': Twenty-five Years After *Tarasoff.*" *Journal of Legal Medicine* 21, no. 2 (2000): 187-222. Offers interesting and complete commentary on the case from the perspective of a quarter century after the ruling.

Frost, Lynda E., and Richard J. Bonnie, eds. *The Evolution of Mental Health Law.* Washington, D.C.: American Psychological Association, 2001. Collection of articles includes discussion of the duty to warn.

Hermann, Donald H. J. *Mental Health and Disability Law in a Nutshell.* St. Paul, Minn.: West, 1997. Succinct summary of the law is intended for use as a reference and study guide by students, lawyers, and mental health professionals.

Slobogin, Christopher. "*Tarasoff* as a Duty to Treat: Insights from Criminal Law." *University of Cincinnati Law Review* 75 (2007): 101-117. Excellent scholarly treatment of the hypothesis that breach of the *Tarasoff* duty could also lead to criminal liability.

See also: Actuarial risk assessment; Courts and forensic evidence; *Diagnostic and Statistical Manual of Mental Disorders*; Forensic psychiatry; Forensic psychology; Guilty but mentally ill plea; Living forensics; Medicine.

Tattoo identification

Definition: Process in which permanent body art and markings are used as information to help determine identity.

Significance: Law-enforcement professionals can use tattoos to identify unknown persons in a number of ways. Tattoos on the bodies of unknown deceased persons can help forensic scientists identify those persons, and information from witnesses about the tattoos seen on criminal perpetrators can help identify suspects. The tattoos worn by particular persons can also help to provide information about group membership, which can be used to trace identity.

Tattooing is a process in which ink or a substance containing dye is introduced into the dermis, a deep layer of the skin that does not regularly renew itself in the way the outer layer of skin, the epidermis, does. The ink or dye is usually deposited in the dermis through the use of an electric machine that produces very rapid movement of a needle (up to three thousand times per minute), although tattooing can also be accomplished by an individual using less professional methods. The dye is not soluble, and as the epidermis is shed, the tattoo remains visible. Tattoos do, however, often fade perceptibly over time.

Distinctive tattoos can be helpful to law-enforcement personnel when they need to identify unknown persons, including suspects and victims of crimes. (© iStockphoto.com/Barry Crossley)

Human beings have used tattoos for thousands of years for a variety of religious, cultural, and individual reasons. Governments have also used tattoos at various times throughout history to identify convicts, prisoners of war, and other groups, such as Nazi Germany's tattooing of prisoner numbers on those held in concentration camps during World War II. In the United States, the numbers of persons getting tattoos to make personal statements of identity or group membership are believed to be on the increase. As of 2003, 16 percent of American adults reported having one or more tattoos, with women and men about equally likely to be tattooed. In general, personal tattoos in the United States are becoming larger and more prominently displayed, with increasing use of vibrant colors.

Identification of Suspects

The knowledge that a criminal suspect has a tattoo may be extremely valuable to an investigator in identifying that individual. Many tattoos are placed on areas of the body that are easily visible to others, such as the arms, hands, face, throat, or neck. Additionally, tattoos are often brightly colored, and many feature easily recognizable and memorable items, objects, or words.

After a crime has been committed, it can often be difficult for witnesses to provide investigators with a clear description of the perpetrator, given that people who commit crimes often attempt to disguise some or all of their features, using gloves, hats, masks, and other devices. A tattoo that is not completely covered, or is momentarily exposed, can provide an important clue to a criminal perpetrator's identity. Witnesses often have blurry or differing memories of events, but they may be able to recall seeing a tattoo of an easily recognizable object, such as a well-known cartoon character, even when they cannot provide police with information on the perpetrator's eye color, height, or distinguishing facial features.

In addition to being useful for positive identification if a suspect is found, tattoos can give investigators possible leads. Many groups—such as street gangs, biker groups, and military divisions—have their own individualized tattoos that members get to identify themselves as part of their groups. If the perpetrator of a crime has a recognized group tattoo, this can give investigators a good lead on where to seek additional information.

Because tattoos are generally permanent, they can also be used to identify persons who may have changed or aged significantly since the most recent description or photograph available to investigators. Tattoos are also much more difficult to conceal than hair color, eye color, or other features commonly used to describe individuals. Some tattoos are even used to cover up marks—such as scars, birthmarks, or even other tattoos—that might be used as identification.

Although it is not common, tattoos can be removed by a complex and expensive laser procedure that often requires repeated visits to a doctor or specialist. Because this procedure is available, law-enforcement authorities cannot always rule out an identification because the individual does not have a specific tattoo.

Identification of Human Remains

Tattoos are often extremely valuable evidence in the identification of human remains. When an individual is reported missing, any information about tattoos or other body modifications (such as piercings) that person has can be useful in helping investigators determine the identity of any human remains that are discovered. Even when a specific identification of unknown remains is not possible, tattoos on the body can help by providing starting points for investigation. For example, tattoos may indicate group membership or may indicate that the deceased was a regular customer at a local tattoo shop. Tattoos are usually visible until the body is significantly decomposed.

During investigations of major catastrophes involving large numbers of victims, such as the tsunami that hit Thailand in 2004 or the terrorist attacks on the World Trade Center in 2001, identification of victims is often strongly aided by the examination of tattoos. Also, forensic anthropologists often find tattoos helpful in the identification of bodies recovered from mass graves. When the mass graves are of recent origin, examination of tattoos may enable the identification of individual victims. When the mass graves are ancient, examination of tattooing may help to identify the groups or tribes to which the individuals in the graves belonged.

Helen Davidson

Further Reading

Cox, Margaret, et al. *The Scientific Investigation of Mass Graves*. New York: Cambridge University Press, 2008. Presents a penetrating discussion of the techniques of identifying remains recovered from mass graves and also addresses the ethical issues involved.

Fenske, Mindy. *Tattoos in American Visual Culture*. New York: Palgrave Macmillan, 2007. Provides a history of tattooing in the United States, with a special focus on the cultural aspects of the tattoo through history.

McCartney, Carole. *Forensic Identification and Criminal Justice: Forensic Science, Justice, and Risk*. Portland, Oreg.: Willan, 2006. Discusses the forensic and legal issues involved in identification.

Rush, John A. *Spiritual Tattoo: A Cultural History of Tattooing, Piercing, Scarification, Branding, and Implants*. Berkeley, Calif.: Frog, 2005. Presents the history of tattooing and other body modifications, along with discussion of the functions tattooing has fulfilled in ancient and modern societies.

Thompson, Tim, and Sue Black, eds. *Forensic Human Identification: An Introduction*. Boca Raton, Fla.: CRC Press, 2007. Provides information about various techniques used by forensic experts to identify individuals both alive and deceased. Includes a section on identification using tattoos and other body modifications.

See also: Asian tsunami victim identification; Composite drawing; Croatian and Bosnian war victim identification; Decomposition of bodies; Gang violence evidence; Mass graves; September 11, 2001, victim identification; Skeletal analysis; Steganography.

Taylor exhumation

Date: June 17, 1991

The Event: The body of Zachary Taylor was exhumed after more than 140 years so that an autopsy could be performed to determine whether the twelfth president of the United States died of poisoning, as many had long speculated.

Significance: The sudden death of Zachary Taylor in the sixteenth month of his presidency caused considerable speculation. If Taylor was poisoned, as many presumed he was, those who were responsible were never brought to account. Although the autopsy performed in 1991 was intended to settle the question of Taylor's cause of death, the results failed to convince some historians that Taylor was not murdered.

The deaths of presidents, especially when sudden and unexpected, often give rise to conspiracy theories. On July 4, 1850, President Zachary Taylor attended a ceremony for the laying of the cornerstone for the unfinished Washington Monument. The day was hot and humid, but Taylor, presumably wishing to look presidential, dressed in a heavy coat and wore both a necktie and a hat. Ravaged by thirst, he consumed large quantities of warm water from a pitcher left in the sun. He also drank a large glass of cold milk and overindulged in some cherries and pickles.

Back at the White House, he shed his warm clothing and showed signs of an illness diagnosed as cholera morbus, a general classification of the digestive ills that plagued many Washingtonians during the sweltering summers. He spent a miserable night fighting nausea and diarrhea but was well enough the following day to work in his office. The following day, however, he fell ill again. The doctor who was summoned treated Taylor with opium and with a medication that contained mercury; both treatments were aimed at calming his digestive system and settling his upset stomach.

On July 9, Taylor's condition worsened to the point that it was publicly announced that the president was probably near death. At ten o'clock on that Tuesday night, Taylor, aware he was dying, called his family to his bedside; within an hour, he died. Vice President Millard Fillmore succeeded him, taking the oath of office the following day.

Taylor was buried on July 13 in Washington's Congressional Cemetery, where his remains rested until they were transferred to Louisville, Kentucky, on October 25, 1850. He remained buried there, with his wife's remains interred beside him after her death in 1852, until the two were disinterred on May 6, 1926, and moved to a newly constructed mausoleum in the Zachary Taylor National Military Cemetery in Louisville.

During the late 1980's, historians began to speculate that Zachary Taylor had been poisoned—with either arsenic or strychnine—by supporters of slavery who had been outraged by Taylor's support of the Compromise of 1850, which enabled California and New Mexico to enter the union as nonslave states. Two notable people who opposed the president's stance on this issue were Senator Henry Clay and Taylor's vice president, Millard Fillmore. Finally, in 1991, Taylor's great-great-great-grandson, Dabney Taylor, encouraged the exhumation of Taylor's remains for postmortem examination.

The Application of Forensic Science

On June 17, 1991, the body of Zachary Taylor was exhumed and transported to the Oak Ridge National Laboratory in Tennessee. Even though it had been interred for 141 years, it was reasonably well preserved. Two pathologists, Larry Robinson and Frank Dyer, conducted an autopsy on the remains, examining the bones and hair of the dead president for any toxic materials that might have contributed to his death. After Robinson and Dyer completed their work, the medical examiner of Kentucky reviewed their autopsy report and, being in agreement with the findings, issued a statement declaring that Taylor had died from natural causes and that trace elements of arsenic found in his body were one-thousandth the quantity needed to kill anyone.

This was not the end of the matter, however. Michael Parenti and other historians questioned the validity of Robinson and Dyer's autopsy findings. Parenti asserted that the pathol-

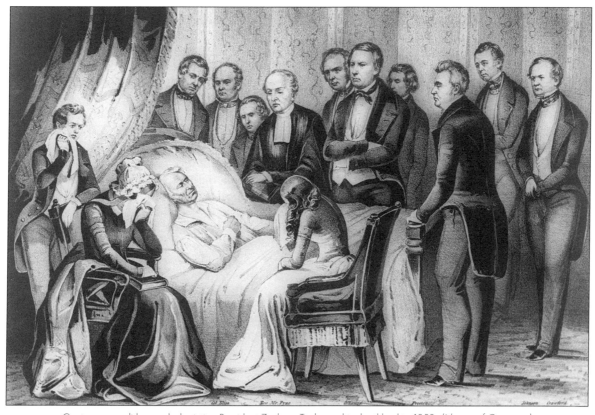

Contemporary lithograph depicting President Zachary Taylor on his deathbed in 1850. *(Library of Congress)*

ogists did not test hair very close to Taylor's scalp, hair that would have grown in the period during which the president was dying and that, had Taylor been poisoned, would have contained concentrations of toxic elements far in excess of what was found in the autopsy. Based on this argument, a request was made to the National Park Service in 1997 to exhume Taylor's body a second time for a more thorough autopsy. The request was rejected.

R. Baird Shuman

Further Reading

Bauer, K. Jack. *Zachary Taylor: Soldier, Planter, Statesman of the Old Southwest*. Newtown, Conn.: American Political Biography Press, 1994. Offers an extensive assessment of Taylor's career and his election as president on the Whig ticket.

Bumgarner, John R. *The Health of the Presidents: The Forty-one United States Presidents through 1993 from a Physician's Point of View*. Jefferson, N.C.: McFarland, 1994. Considers each U.S. president from George Washington to Bill Clinton from a medical standpoint.

Deem, James M. *Zachary Taylor*. Berkeley Heights, N.J.: Enslow, 2002. Presents a brief overview of Taylor's life, aimed primarily at adolescent readers. Factually solid, eminently readable.

Joseph, Paul. *Zachary Taylor*. Edina, Minn.: Abdo, 2002. Provides an accessible introduction to Taylor's life and politics.

Kops, Deborah. *Zachary Taylor: America's Twelfth President*. New York: Children's Press, 2004. An overview of the life, presidency, and death of Zachary Taylor directed toward young readers.

Parenti, Michael. *History as Mystery*. San Francisco: City Lights Books, 1999. Chapter 6 of this discussion of historical mysteries focuses on the death of Zachary Taylor and raises serious questions about the 1991 autopsy.

See also: Arsenic; Beethoven's death; Drug confirmation tests; Exhumation; Food poisoning; Lincoln exhumation; Louis XVII remains identification; Nicholas II remains identification; Poisons and antidotes.

Telephone tap detector

Definition: Device that indicates the presence of an eavesdropping device on a telephone line.

Significance: In criminal and terrorist investigations, high-stakes legal proceedings, industrial espionage, and other activities, knowing the content of telephone conversations can provide evidence against criminals or business and personal advantages to competitors or adversaries. For those who believe they may be targeted for telephone surveillance, the ability to detect the presence of a tap on a telephone line provides an important defense.

Wiretapping is the accessing of telephone conversations by direct interception of the telephone signal. Historically, wiretap laws in the United States were designed to protect the content of telephone conversations. Initiating a telephone wiretap required a court order and a high level of proof that the wiretap was essential to a law-enforcement investigation. The Patriot Act, which was passed following the 2001 terrorist attacks on the Pentagon and on the World Trade Center in New York City, made it easier for law-enforcement agencies in the United States to tap telephones. All the Patriot Act requires is that the requesting agency certify that information likely to be obtained from the tap is relevant to an investigation.

Traditional telephone tap detectors are devices that, when spliced into telephone lines, indicate when the voltage on the lines changes. When a tap detector is installed, it is set to monitor the voltage on the line when it is assumed to be untapped. If a physical tap is placed on the line, the voltage will decrease. Other events, such as listening in on a phone extension, will also cause the voltage to decrease. Changes in telephone transmission and telephone tapping technologies have, however, rendered traditional telephone tap detectors almost useless against all but the crudest types of taps. Despite this, some electronics retailers continue to sell voltage-change telephone tap detectors.

Changes in telephone technology have made it easier to intercept telephone calls as well as more difficult to detect taps or interceptions. For example, older analog cellular telephone conversations can sometimes be picked up on police scanners. Others can be picked up by nearby baby monitors. There is no way for the telephone users to detect whether someone is listening in on these conversations. Most telephone transmissions are now digital, however, which has reduced this problem. Digital transmissions, although often encoded, must by law be made available to law-enforcement agencies with legal authority to wiretap.

Voice over Internet Protocol (VoIP) technology allows telephone conversations to be carried

The Patriot Act and Electronic Surveillance

Title III of the Patriot Act of 2001 permits law-enforcement officers to enter buildings covertly for the purpose of installing the listening devices needed for electronic surveillance. Covert entry is authorized, however, only when Title III warrants are issued. To obtain warrants, law-enforcement officers must show the following:
- Probable cause that specific offenses are about to occur, have occurred, or are occurring
- That evidence is like to be obtained by the intercept or wiretap
- That all other investigative techniques either have failed or will fail to provide the necessary evidence or that they are too dangerous to employ
- That the locations of the proposed wiretaps are sites of criminal activity
- That telephones are being used to conduct criminal activity at those sites

on over the Internet. VoIP communications are not generally covered under traditional wiretap laws. These transmissions can be intercepted in sophisticated and difficult-to-detect ways similar to those used to intercept other kinds of electronic data transmitted between computers.

As of 2008, telephone taps of either landlines or cellular telephones initiated by telephone companies at the request of law-enforcement agencies were virtually undetectable. Many illegal telephone taps are also difficult to impossible to detect, despite the claims made by companies selling traditional wiretap detectors.

Martiscia Davidson

Further Reading

Diffie, Whitfield, and Susan Landau. *Privacy on the Line: The Politics of Wiretapping and Encryption.* Cambridge, Mass.: MIT Press, 2007.

Olejniczak, Stephen P. *Telecom for Dummies.* Indianapolis, Ind.: Wiley, 2006.

See also: Dial tone decoder; Electronic bugs; Electronic voice alteration; Internet tracking and tracing; Voiceprints.

Thalidomide

Definition: Sedative drug prescribed for pregnant women in the late 1950's and early 1960's to combat morning sickness until it was found to cause serious physical deformities during fetal development.

Significance: When taken by pregnant women between the twentieth and fortieth days of gestation, thalidomide causes severe birth defects. The thalidomide tragedy showed that governments need to be scrupulous in determining the possible risks posed by new drugs before granting permission to manufacturers to market those drugs. Forensic scientists must investigate unusual medical conditions that appear in the population as rapidly as possible so that regulations can be put in place to avert disaster.

Prior testing of thalidomide had been seriously flawed when the drug was introduced into West Germany during the late 1950's, marketed vigorously as an antidote against a variety of human ailments, including morning sickness. By 1959, an estimated one million Germans were using the drug on a daily basis, and some German pharmacies allowed the purchase of thalidomide without a prescription. An advertisement by the German company selling the drug misleadingly declared that thalidomide was an antidote for morning sickness, that it relieved tensions associated with pregnancy, that it could be taken as often as necessary, and that it would harm neither pregnant women nor their unborn children.

Discovering Deformities

In December, 1961, William McBride, an Australian physician, reported in a major medical journal that he had attended the births of a number of babies who showed severe physical abnormalities and whose mothers had used thalidomide. Shortly thereafter, German physicians reported similar outcomes and presented pictures of newborns with various deformities, including some with finlike appendages attached to their shoulders instead of arms and hands.

At that time, thalidomide was being sold in forty-six countries under fifty-one different brand names. It has been estimated that between five thousand and ten thousand newborns suffered serious defects throughout the world as the result of their mothers' use of thalidomide. The injuries occurred primarily in Western Europe, Canada, Australia, and Japan. In West Germany, after prolonged court hearings, more than twenty-eight hundred persons received compensation for the harm they suffered as a result of the use of thalidomide

In the United States, the drug company Richardson-Merrell applied to the Food and Drug Administration (FDA) in 1960 for approval to market thalidomide. The application went to Dr. Frances Kelsey, who possessed a doctorate in pharmacology and a medical degree but had been working at the FDA for only a month. Kelsey was pressured by her superiors and by the drug company to approve thalidomide, but

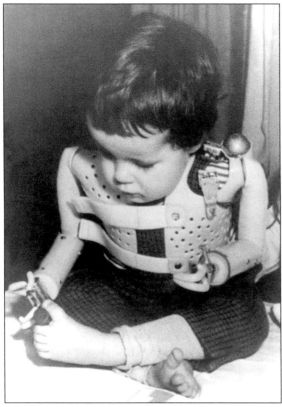

A three-year-old girl, born in the early 1960's without arms to a German mother who took the drug thalidomide. The girl uses power-driven artificial arms. *(AP/Wide World Photos)*

she insisted that better test results had to be obtained before she would recommend approval. As a result of Kelsey's stance, only seventeen cases of thalidomide-related deformity among newborns occurred in the United States. In 1962, Kelsey was awarded the President's Award for Distinguished Federal Civilian Service for her firm stand against federal approval of thalidomide.

Remedial Actions

The powerful lesson that emerged from the dire consequences of the failure to block the marketing of thalidomide outside the United States was that governments must be vigilant in monitoring new products produced by drug companies and should strongly resist companies' efforts to enhance their profits by bringing drugs into the marketplace prematurely. In addition, forensic specialists need to analyze the

reported results of tests on new drugs carefully to ensure that the testing has been conducted on adequate samples of animals and humans and that the results are accurately presented.

Following the thalidomide disaster, an important step was taken toward protecting the public in the United States with the passage in 1962 of the Kefauver-Harris Amendment, a measure that had been languishing in congressional committees through many sessions. The bill eliminated a previous provision of U.S. law that allowed drug companies to sell new drugs to the general public if the FDA did not say otherwise for six months after the drugs were submitted to the FDA for approval. Since passage of the amendment, drug companies can sell new drugs only after the FDA has affirmed that the products are safe and effective on the basis of "substantial evidence." Such evidence must include the results of carefully conducted scientific trials using matched groups where possible; that is, during the testing of a new drug, persons in one group undergo treatment with the drug while those in another are given a placebo, a harmless pill that resembles the drug being tested.

In 1998, the FDA approved thalidomide for limited uses. It has been shown to provide dramatically effective treatment for complications of Hansen's disease (leprosy); trials found relief of symptoms in more than 70 percent of those given the drug, compared with only 2.5 percent of those who were administered a placebo. Thalidomide has also been approved for use in the treatment of the symptoms of acquired immunodeficiency syndrome (AIDS), some forms of cancer, and various skin conditions.

Gilbert Geis

Further Reading

Mason, David. *Thalidomide: My Fight*. London: Allen & Unwin, 1976. Tells the story of Mason's daughter, Louise, who suffered the absence of limbs as a result of her mother's use of thalidomide. Mason led the campaign in Britain for compensation to thalidomide victims.

Roskies, Ethel. *Abnormality and Normality: The Mothering of Thalidomide Children*. Ithaca, N.Y.: Cornell University Press, 1972.

Presents an analysis of the experience of Canadian victims of thalidomide injuries. Considers the reactions of family members, neighbors, and hospitals and addresses the psychological consequences of the injuries.

Sjöström, Henning, and Robert Nilsson. *Thalidomide and the Power of Drug Companies.* New York: Penguin Books, 1972. Offers details of the self-interested behavior of the drug companies in the marketing of thalidomide and their opposition to compensation claims.

Stephens, Trent D., and Rock Brynner. *Dark Remedy: The Impact of Thalidomide and Its Revival as a Vital Medicine.* Cambridge, Mass.: Perseus, 2001. Traces the history of thalidomide from its creation to its therapeutic uses in the twenty-first century.

Teff, Harvey, and Colin R. Munro. *Thalidomide: The Legal Aftermath.* Farnborough, England: Saxon House, 1976. Provides details of the litigation that resulted from the claims for compensation by thalidomide victims.

See also: Actuarial risk assessment; Antianxiety agents; Autopsies; Barbiturates; Chemical agents; Control samples; Product liability cases.

Thanatology

Definition: Study of death among human beings, including investigation of the circumstances surrounding deaths of individuals, the grief experienced by loved ones, and larger social attitudes toward death.

Significance: The field of thanatology is interdisciplinary, including such areas of study as religion, medicine, psychology, sociology, psychiatry, social work, anthropology, and pharmacology. Much of the work of thanatologists focuses on palliative care for dying individuals and their families, which involves treating pain and addressing the physical, psychosocial, and spiritual issues related to death.

The term "thanatology" derives from the Greek word for death, *thanatos.* Thanatology explores how questions about the meaning of life and death affect the dying and their loved ones, recognizing that these questions are relevant to the psychological health of individuals, families, communities, and cultures. Because death is such a broad and complex subject, thanatology relies on holistic knowledge and practice.

Evolution of Thanatology

During the mid-twentieth century, many Americans considered death a taboo topic, to the extent that death was an unacceptable topic for scholarly research, public education, or public discussion. Eventually, however, this attitude was challenged by the initiatives of a number of pioneers, including Cicely Saunders, William Lamers, and Elisabeth Kübler-Ross. In 1967, Saunders founded St. Christopher's Hospice in London, England; St. Christopher's is often credited as being the first hospice. Saunders emphasized that dying is not simply a biomedical or physical event; it also has psychosocial, familial, and spiritual implications. At St. Christopher's, she tried to create a homelike, family-centered atmosphere that would allow dying persons to live life fully, free from debilitating pain and incapacitating symptoms. In 1974, Lamers founded a hospice in Marin County, California, that viewed home care as the model of hospice treatment and stressed psychosocial care and the use of volunteers.

The hospice movement is based on the recognition that the dying process is part of the normal process of living, and hospice care focuses on enhancing the quality of remaining life. From their beginnings in the mid-1960's, hospice programs expanded quickly; within forty years, more than eight thousand hospices were in operation all around the world. Both the hospice philosophy and the growth of hospices improved the treatment of dying persons and encouraged the study of the dying process.

The growth of the hospice movement was in part a reaction to medicine-driven care that abandoned those who were no longer responsive to treatment. In addition, the movement resonated with persons who were beginning to question consumerism and those who were seeking a return to nature. Hospice care affirms life and neither hastens nor postpones death. It seeks to preserve and promote the inherent potential for growth within dying individuals and their families during the last phase of life.

In *On Death and Dying*, first published in 1969, Kübler-Ross wrote of natural death at a time when many people were becoming increasingly averse to the medical profession's technological and impersonal approach to care of the dying. She posited that dying persons go through five stages: denial, anger, bargaining, depression, and acceptance. Through case vignettes, she made a powerful plea for humanistic care for dying persons. Although research has found that the five stages she delineated are not characteristic of all dying individuals, Kübler-Ross's call for humanistic care in the last stage of life is an enduring legacy.

Dr. Elisabeth Kübler-Ross was a pioneer in the field of thanatology. Her book *On Death and Dying* (1969) made a strong plea for humanistic care for dying persons. *(AP/Wide World Photos)*

Issues and Resources

Technological advances have raised many issues surrounding death, such as how long people live, when they know that they are dying, and where they typically die. Among the end-of-life decisions that dying persons and their family members often face are decisions regarding advance care plans, life-support options, giving and receiving communications about the dying person's medical condition, and who will make health care decisions when the dying person is no longer able to do so. In addition, dying persons and their families may discuss the topics of autopsy, organ donation, and euthanasia. Within a diverse society, culturally meaningful thanatology practice requires a commitment to personal and professional assessment in response to the challenges presented by cultural differences in death, dying, and bereavement.

One resource in the field of thanatology is the Association for Death Education and Counseling (ADEC), one of the oldest interdisciplinary professional organizations for persons who work with the dying. Dedicated to promoting excellence in death education, care of the dying, grief counseling, and research in thanatology, ADEC provides information, support, and resources to its multicultural, multidisciplinary membership and, through its members, to the public. ADEC has a two-level program in which individuals can become certified in thanatology or fellows in thanatology. Certification status indicates that a person has special educational training in the field. Fellow status recognizes that a person has met specific knowledge requirements (as measured through a standardized test) and has demonstrated competence in teaching, research, or clinical practice through a professional portfolio.

Lillian M. Range

Further Reading

Balk, David, ed. *Handbook of Thanatology: The Essential Body of Knowledge for the Study of Death, Dying, and Bereavement*. New York: Routledge, 2007. Comprehensive text presents wide-ranging discussion of death-related issues. Includes sections on dying, end-of-life decision making, loss, traumatic death, and death education.

Becvar, Dorothy S. *In the Presence of Grief: Helping Family Members Resolve Death, Dying, and Bereavement Issues*. New York: Guilford Press, 2001. Provides a detailed portrait of death through case studies and personal stories of grief and struggle.

Corr, Charles A., Clyde M. Nabe, and Donna M. Corr. *Death and Dying, Life and Living*. 5th ed. Belmont, Calif.: Wadsworth, 2006. Thorough text covers all aspects of death and dying, including chapters on developmental issues, legal concerns, and challenges of the twenty-first century.

DeSpelder, Lynne Ann, and Albert Lee Strickland. *The Last Dance: Encountering Death and Dying*. 7th ed. New York: McGraw-Hill, 2004. Highlights the main issues in thanatology in a comprehensive and readable way.

Kübler-Ross, Elisabeth. *On Death and Dying*. 1969. Reprint. New York: Charles Scribner's Sons, 2003. Classic work focuses on the lessons that the dying can teach their doctors, nurses, and clergy, as well as their own family members.

See also: Antemortem injuries; Autopsies; Coroners; Forensic nursing; Forensic pathology; Homicide; Opioids; Physiology; Psychological autopsy; Suicide.

Thin-layer chromatography

Definition: Technique used to separate chemical compounds into their individual components.

Significance: By using thin-layer chromatography to determine the chemical components that make up particular substances, forensic scientists can help to identify the origins of those substances or link samples found at crime scenes to potential suspects.

Using thin-layer chromatography (TLC), forensic scientists can analyze the dye composition of fibers, poisons in food, pigments contained in plant specimens, or the ingredients in chemical weapons, explosives, or drugs. This method can also be used to detect the presence of a controlled substance in urine or blood.

TLC involves a stationary phase (a solid) and a mobile phase (a liquid or gas). As the name suggests, the technique uses a thin layer of silica gel, alumina, or cellulose coated on a piece of flat and inert glass, acetate, metal, or plastic. The silica gel or alumina is the stationary phase. The mobile phase is the solvent used.

First, a solution containing the sample of interest is "spotted" or applied to the TLC plate alongside reference or control spots (of solutions containing known substances) near the bottom of the plate. The plate is dipped into a solvent, often ethanol or water, such that the plate is minimally submerged. The chamber containing the solvent and plate is covered. By capillary action, the solvent travels up the TLC plate. The spots are dissolved and moved up by the solvent. This is called chromatographic development. The rate and distance of movement depend on the molecular forces and solubility of the chemical compounds in the solvent. Solutes (the compounds contained within a spot) with a greater affinity for the solvent will tend to spend more time with the solvent than solutes with less affinity for the solvent.

Colorless substances can also be separated by TLC. One common method involves the addition of a fluorescent compound such as manganese-activated zinc silicate to the adsorbent and visualization under a black light. Another method is the use of iodine vapors as a general unspecific color reagent.

The movement of the solvents can be determined through the calculation of a retention factor value. Retention factor values of known and unknown compounds can be compared to provide an index of similarity. Compounds with similar retention factor values tend to share solubility characteristics.

Rena Christina Tabata

Further Reading

Hahn-Deinstrop, Elke. *Applied Thin-Layer Chromatography: Best Practice and Avoidance of Mistakes*. Translated by R. G. Leach. 2d ed. Weinheim, Germany: Wiley-VCH, 2007.

Sherma, Joseph, and Bernard Fried, eds. *Handbook of Thin-Layer Chromatography*. New York: Marcel Dekker, 2003.

See also: Chromatography; Column chromatography; Fax machine, copier, and printer analysis; Forensic toxicology; Quantitative and qualitative analysis of chemicals; Questioned document analysis; Separation tests.

Tire tracks

Definition: Impressions left by vehicle tires on semisoft surfaces.

Significance: Tire tracks are often found at crime scenes, and analysis of such tracks can provide important information for investigators. Tracks can reveal the size and weight of a vehicle as well as the brand, model, and size of the tire; these details may link a suspect's vehicle to a crime scene.

By examining tire tracks, forensic investigators can determine the distance between two or more wheels of a vehicle, which can allow them to estimate the size, weight, and wheelbase of the vehicle. In addition to this information, the tread impressions that tires leave in soft soil, mud, dust, or snow reveal identifiable patterns: solid design elements interspersed with grooves. Databases containing pictures of the thousands of different tread designs in existence are widely available, and forensic investigators can use these to find matches for the tire tread impressions found at crime scenes. By finding a tire tread match, investigators can deduce the brand, style, and size of the tire, which also gives them a general idea of the type of vehicle on which the tire is likely mounted.

Because tires on motor vehicles do not wear evenly, they develop unique use patterns. If a suspect's vehicle is located, wear patterns seen in tire impressions from the crime scene can be compared to wear patterns on the vehicle's tires, often with enough accuracy to identify the vehicle positively as having been at the crime scene.

Forensic scientists record tire tread impressions either by photographing them or by casting them. Photography is usually the method of choice when the impressions are less than one-fourth inch deep and tracks at the scene are not confusingly overlapped. Photographs are first taken of the general scene, to place the location of the tracks in context. A ruler is then placed next to each tread impression to indicate scale, and close-up photographs are taken. When impressions are photographed in snow, they are first gently sprayed with a product called Snow Print Wax or colored spray paint to increase contrast.

Casting is a method of making a three-dimensional copy of an impression. This is the method of choice for deep or confusing impressions. Powdered casting material is mixed with water and gently poured into the impression.

Investigators gather tire-track evidence outside a church destroyed by an arson fire in Panola, Alabama, in early 2006. *(AP/Wide World Photos)*

After the material dries, it is removed from the scene and cleaned by technicians. The resulting cast can then be compared to tires in the tire design database or to tires on a suspect's vehicle. Courts generally accept tire impression photographs and casts that match a suspect's vehicle as physical evidence that the vehicle was present at the crime scene.

Martiscia Davidson

Further Reading

Bodziak, William J. *Tire and Tire Track Evidence: Recovery and Forensic Examination.* Boca Raton, Fla.: CRC Press, 2008.

Rainis, Kenneth G. *Hair, Clothing, and Tire Track Evidence: Crime-Solving Science Experiments.* Berkeley Heights, N.J.: Enslow, 2006.

Staggs, Steven. *Crime Scene and Evidence Photographer's Guide.* 2d ed. Wildomar, Calif.: Staggs, 2005.

See also: Casting; Footprints and shoe prints; Forensic photography; Physical evidence; Reagents; Trace and transfer evidence.

Tool marks

Definition: Impressions or abrasions made by tools when they contact surfaces.

Significance: Tools are often used in the commission of crimes, and the marks made by these tools can be valuable pieces of evidence. Trained examiners can gain information about the physical specifications of individual tools from the marks they create, and these specifications can be compared with tools known to be in the possession of suspects.

Broadly defined, a tool is any object used to gain a physical advantage. Because criminal offenders often use tools to gain access to areas to which they would not otherwise have access, tool marks are commonly found at crime scenes, particularly on items such as window and door frames and safes.

Class and Individual Characteristics

When conducting tool-mark analysis, forensic scientists compare tools and their marks by examining class characteristics, which narrow down the type and perhaps even brand of a tool, and individual characteristics, which can directly match a tool to a mark. For example, if a crowbar was used to pry a window open, the tool mark found on the window frame might show that the profile of the tool consisted of two 1.5-centimeter edges with a 4-millimeter gap between the edges. These class characteristics can be used to eliminate all crowbars that have profiles that do not fit those specifications. Continuing the example, if a suspect is identified and a crowbar is found in that person's possession that has a profile consisting of two 1.5-centimeter edges separated by a 6-millimeter gap, that crowbar could be eliminated as the one used to pry the window open. If the suspect is found to have a crowbar consistent with the tool mark, however, further analysis would have to be performed, with the examiner comparing individual characteristics.

Individual characteristics on tools are typically the results of tiny imperfections or damage. When a tool has imperfections that were introduced in the manufacturing process, this can result in microscopic striations, or lines, in any marks the tool makes. The marks made by a damaged tool will also exhibit striations, and these are often more pronounced than striations due to manufacturing. No two tools will have exactly the same pattern of striations in their tool marks. Because of this, a microscopic comparison of striations made by a known tool to striations found in a tool mark from a crime scene can be used to determine whether the two tool marks are consistent—that is, whether they had to have come from the same tool.

Methods of Analysis

If a tool mark found at a crime scene is on an object that can be transported back to the crime lab, the object is collected. If a tool mark appears on a surface that cannot be taken back to the lab, such as a floor or wall, a cast of the mark is made so that the details of the mark can be analyzed at the lab.

Each tool mark collected is first examined for

different types of class characteristics as the scientist attempts to gain information about the type of tool that was used to create the mark. If a suspect has been identified, a search warrant may then be obtained for tools in that person's possession so that the tools can be compared with the specifications of the tool that made the evidence tool mark. Any tools identified are brought back to the crime lab and used to make tool marks in the same material as the object containing the questioned tool mark. The forensic scientist then compares the marks on a microscopic level to see if the striations are consistent with each other.

Evidentiary Value

The utility of tool-mark analysis has long been accepted among forensic scientists, but the evidentiary value of such analysis has come into question because it is difficult for scientists to assign measures of statistical significance to their findings. The difficulty in assessing statistical significance stems from a lack of defined criteria for pronouncing that a match has been made between a known tool mark and a questioned tool mark. That is, no standard has been set regarding a minimum number of striations that must be consistent for an identification to be considered definitive. Rather, all striations have to match, regardless of how many are present.

Problems have also arisen in the field as a result of a perceived subjectivity in the interpretation of tool-mark evidence. Accusations have been made for some time that the comparison of tool marks constitutes more of an art than a science. Despite these allegations, however, toolmark analysis continues to play an important role in crime scene investigations.

Lisa LaGoo

Further Reading

Gardner, Ross M. *Practical Crime Scene Processing and Investigation.* Boca Raton, Fla.:

The FBI's Firearms-Toolmarks Unit

The Federal Bureau of Investigation operates many highly specialized forensic investigation units, including the Firearms-Toolmarks Unit (FTU). This division applies advanced scientific techniques to examinations of firearms, components of ammunition, bullet trajectories, gunshot residue, tool marks, and other related forms of physical evidence. In addition to collecting, analyzing, and processing evidence used in FBI investigations, the FTU serves as a liaison in the fields of tool-mark and firearm analysis with other national and international forensic laboratories and law-enforcement agencies, for which it also provides training.

CRC Press, 2005. Guide to investigating crime scenes focuses on practical applications of forensic techniques. Includes discussion of the surfaces on which tool marks are typically found.

Genge, N. E. *The Forensic Casebook: The Science of Crime Scene Investigation.* New York: Ballantine, 2002. Easy-to-read overview of crime scene investigation includes a short section on tool marks as well as an interview with an examiner.

Mozayani, Ashraf, and Carla Noziglia, eds. *The Forensic Laboratory Handbook: Procedures and Practice.* Totowa, N.J.: Humana Press, 2006. Practical guide to the procedures carried out in forensics labs provides basic information on tool-mark analysis and the evidentiary value of the findings.

Saferstein, Richard. *Criminalistics: An Introduction to Forensic Science.* 9th ed. Upper Saddle River, N.J.: Pearson Prentice Hall, 2007. Excellent introductory textbook addresses most forensic disciplines. Contains several sections on tool marks and other kinds of impression evidence.

Thurman, James T. *Practical Bomb Scene Investigation.* Boca Raton, Fla.: CRC Press, 2006. Presents information regarding the examination of tool marks found in close proximity to explosion scenes.

See also: Bite-mark analysis; Casting; Class versus individual evidence; Control samples; Document examination; Federal Bureau of Investigation Laboratory; Fracture matching;

Lindbergh baby kidnapping; Lock picking; Microscopes; Physical evidence; Scanning electron microscopy.

Toxic torts

Definition: Civil wrongs that involve personal injuries caused by toxic substances.
Significance: Forensic scientists play a major role in conducting scientific studies to show causal relationships between toxic substances and personal injuries and to assist the government in regulating toxic substances to prevent toxic tort litigation.

Toxic torts, environmental lawsuits, and product liability cases are often linked together as modern causes of action that have experienced tremendous growth in the United States since World War II owing to rapid rates of industrial and technological change. Toxic tort cases involve complex issues of proof—that particular toxic substances cause specific harms. The scientific evidence necessary to demonstrate causation is not easily admissible in a court of law, and admissibility requires satisfaction of the standards set forth in *Daubert v. Merrell Dow Pharmaceuticals* (1993). Plaintiffs who suffer personal injury from toxic substances thus may not always receive justice because of the difficulties in showing causation. In addition, some injuries caused by toxic substances may not manifest themselves until long after exposure to the substances, and future litigation may be barred by statutes of limitation and issue preclusion because courts have already rendered final decisions in the cases.

History

Toxic tort litigation grew out of common-law tort actions, especially nuisance, negligence, and strict liability claims. Historical examples of common-law claims for injuries caused by environmental pollution include claims filed in England in the early years of the Industrial Revolution. These causes of action were based on allegations that smoke, odors, noise, and toxic substances were affecting the health and welfare of individuals. Modern-day toxic tort cases are usually based on a theory of negligence. If the toxic substance is ultrahazardous, however, strict liability may apply.

Although toxic tort litigation concerns private personal injuries, toxic substances are regulated by society through public law. The U.S. Congress has charged the Environmental Protection Agency with carrying out and enforcing the provisions of many of the federal laws that regulate the manufacture, sale, and use of toxic substances and the disposal of such substances in the air, water, and soil. Those involved in public regulation and enforcement, however, have not been able to keep up with the ever-growing list of toxic substances capable of causing personal injuries. Complex toxic tort litigation is thus on the rise despite the government's attempt to prevent toxic torts.

Toxic Substances

Toxic substances include any substances that could cause injury to a person's bodily integrity. Generally, harmful biological and chemical substances such as hazardous wastes and asbestos have been considered to be toxic substances, but radiological and other injurious substances as well as natural products such as tobacco may also be considered toxic.

New products and substances are constantly entering the global marketplace, many times with little regulation, and some substances may not be deemed toxic and personally injurious for years after they are introduced. Such findings are usually made after lengthy scientific investigation, study, and analysis. When a finding of toxicity is made about a particular product, the U.S. government usually steps in and removes the product from the marketplace or requires that manufacturers provide specific warnings concerning its toxicity and its proper use. By that time, however, it may already be too late for many people who have been exposed to the product, as many incurable diseases linked to toxic substances can take long periods to appear.

Proof

The most difficult element of proof in toxic tort litigation is causation. Forensic experts conduct research and provide expert testimony to show that exposure to certain toxic substances causes specific personal injuries. Initially, much of the reasoning in toxic tort lawsuits is based on deductive guesswork about what appears to be the most obvious cause of a particular harm—the existence of a toxic substance. However, the legal system does not allow scientific guesses as evidence, so forensic scientists must satisfy the *Daubert* standard by showing that their opinions concerning causation are reliable.

When a substance is implicated in a toxic tort lawsuit for the first time, a pioneering scientist must attempt to show that the substance caused the personal injury or will cause additional harm in the future. Forensic scientists are usually able to identify suspect toxic substances such as asbestos and tobacco that might be linked to human harm such as cancer. Making a scientifically reliable connection between a toxic substance and a personal injury, however, is very difficult, particularly when other factors may be at play. Moreover, because of ethical considerations, human subjects are rarely involved in scientific studies concerning the effects of toxic substances. Instead, animal studies are often used, and the results of such studies are not as reliable.

Carol A. Rolf

Further Reading

Chiodo, Ernest P. *Toxic Tort: Medical and Legal Elements*. Philadelphia: Xlibris, 2007. Compares and contrasts the medical and legal issues in toxic tort litigation and suggests techniques to ensure the admissibility of scientific evidence.

Cranor, Carl F. *Toxic Torts: Science, Law, and the Possibility of Justice*. New York: Cambridge University Press, 2006. Explores the use of scientific evidence in toxic tort litigation and the complexities associated with the admissibility of such evidence.

Eggen, Jean MacChiaroli. *Toxic Torts in a Nutshell*. 3d ed. St. Paul, Minn.: West, 2005. Introductory text highlights theories of liability, defenses, and damages in toxic tort and environmental litigation.

Madden, M. Stuart, ed. *Exploring Tort Law*. New York: Cambridge University Press, 2005. Collection of essays presents an exploration of tort law that is both historical and global, including discussion of modern litigation that encompasses toxic tort lawsuits and class actions.

Madden, M. Stuart, and Gerald W. Boston. *Law of Environmental and Toxic Torts: Cases, Materials, and Problems*. 3d ed. St. Paul, Minn.: Thomson/West, 2005. Textbook explains theories, elements of proof, and difficulties in proving causation in toxic tort litigation, especially for injuries not yet in evidence.

Rudlin, D. Alan, ed. *Toxic Tort Litigation*. Chicago: American Bar Association, 2007. Outlines theories, evidence admissibility, settlement, and procedural issues in toxic tort litigation. Also includes detailed information related to several toxic substances.

See also: Biotoxins; Chemical agents; Courts and forensic evidence; *Daubert v. Merrell Dow Pharmaceuticals*; Forensic toxicology; International Association of Forensic Toxicologists; Mycotoxins; Product liability cases; Toxicological analysis.

Toxicological analysis

Definition: Methodologies used to identify and quantify the presence of drugs (including alcohol) and toxins in samples and to interpret the significance of the results.

Significance: In forensic science, toxicological analysis encompasses aspects of sample preparation, chemical analysis, and interpretation of results. Toxicology plays a vital role in a wide range of different case types encountered in forensic work, including death investigations (criminal or otherwise), impaired driving, sexual assault, and drug use in sports or in other matters involving questions about human performance.

Toxicology departments are among the busiest in most forensic laboratories, owing to the pervasiveness of drug and alcohol use and the potential for the involvement of these substances in a wide range of case types. Toxicological analysis may be performed on a variety of sample types, including materials of biological and nonbiological origin. Typical biological samples include blood, urine, visceral tissues (such as tissues from the liver), stomach contents, hair, and saliva. Nonbiological samples may include portions of food and/or beverages, syringes, and other items. The analysis may be qualitative (for example, simple identification of the presence of a substance within a sample) or quantitative, where the amount or concentration of a toxin contained within the sample is important for toxicological interpretation.

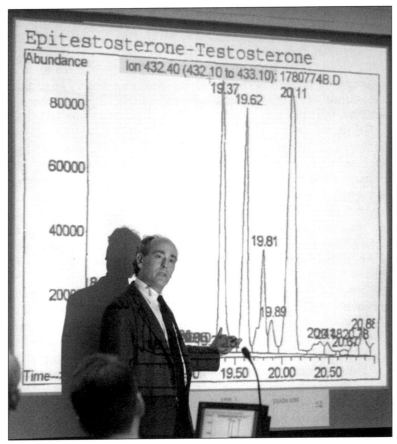

At an arbitration hearing in May, 2007, concerning doping allegations against 2006 Tour de France champion Floyd Landis, a toxicologist testifies about abnormalities on a chart of urine test results from the French government's National Laboratory for Doping Detection. (AP/Wide World Photos)

Procedures

After properly collected, handled, and documented samples are obtained and submitted to the laboratory, toxicological analysis often occurs in four distinct phases. The first stage involves consideration of the circumstances of the case and any requests for particular analyses from the submitting agencies (coroner or medical examiner, police agencies). In this step, details about particular symptomatology or events that occurred in the case provide some guidance for the toxicologist in deciding which drugs or toxins to analyze for, which sample types are suitable (pending availability) for analysis, and which methods to use.

Next, samples generally undergo some form of preparation to remove residual impurities prior to chemical analysis, given the chemical complexity of samples typically encountered in forensic work (such as decomposed tissues).

This sample preparation process typically involves some combination of homogenization, dilution, and selective extraction of the compounds of interest from the background material into a pure solvent. Extraction generally involves manipulation of the chemical conditions (such as pH, solvent, or temperature) to favor diffusion of drugs or toxins from the sample matrix into another phase. For example, acidic drugs may be ionized as a result of proton loss at elevated pH values.

Extraction may then first require a reduction of pH in a blood sample, ensuring that the acidic drug remains uncharged and therefore more soluble in an organic solvent that is immiscible (incapable of mixing) with the blood. Adding such a solvent to a blood sample creates two phases: an aqueous blood phase and an organic phase. Shaking this mixture results in diffusion of the drug into the organic phase, leaving many of the blood constituents in the aqueous phase. Similar approaches may be used to isolate basic compounds or neutral (that is, neither acidic nor basic) compounds.

Multiple extraction cycles may be performed on the same sample, or multiple, different extraction steps may be performed in series in an effort to create the "cleanest" extract possible. In many cases, extracts are then concentrated through evaporation of the extraction solvent to improve the sensitivity of detection in the subsequent analysis step.

Analysis of prepared samples then generally occurs by instrumental methods, including spectrophotometry, gas chromatography, liquid chromatography and mass spectrometry. It should be noted that, despite even the best sample preparation efforts, prepared extracts still usually contain multiple chemical compounds. Consequently, most instrumental analyses used in toxicological analysis include some sort of separation of the constituents of the extract mixture (for example, through gas or liquid chromatography). Forensic scientists may use these methodologies qualitatively, quantitatively, or in combination to provide as much information about the chemical makeup of extracts as possible.

Interpretation of Results

After all of the analyses of a given extract have been conducted and have been thoroughly reviewed for scientific completeness, the analytical results are collected and interpreted collectively for their toxicological significance. Here, important considerations include drug concentrations, the sample type in which they were measured (that is, a given drug concentration in a blood sample may have toxicological implications that are different from the implications for the same concentration in a urine sample), any potential drug interactions (such as the combination of alcohol and other depressant drugs), and the circumstances of the case, including any special considerations (such as the stability of a given drug under a particular set of storage conditions). Generally, the toxicologist must conduct a thorough review of the scientific literature to assess the effects of different drugs at different concentrations and under different circumstances.

After the four phases of analysis are complete, the toxicologist prepares a report detailing which samples were analyzed, the analytical findings, and the methods by which the results were obtained. This report also contains the toxicologist's conclusions and statements regarding sample handling, continuity of evidence, and chain of custody. The scientist may then be called upon to provide testimony as an expert witness and further questioned about the contents of the report.

James Watterson

Further Reading

Baselt, Randall C. *Disposition of Drugs and Chemicals in Man*. 7th ed. Foster City, Calif.: Biomedical Publications, 2004. Describes the properties and associated tissue concentrations of a wide range of toxic compounds and discusses the techniques used to analyze these chemicals.

_____. *Drug Effects on Psychomotor Performance*. Foster City, Calif.: Biomedical Publications, 2001. Comprehensive reference work presents information on the impairing effects of a wide range of therapeutic and illicit drugs.

Brunton, Laurence L., John S. Lazo, and Keith L. Parker, eds. *Goodman and Gilman's the Pharmacological Basis of Therapeutics*. 11th ed. New York: McGraw-Hill, 2006. Authoritative advanced textbook explains basic pharmacological principles and the specific pharmacological features of therapeutic agents. Includes some discussion of illicit agents.

Karch, Steven B., ed. *Drug Abuse Handbook*. 2d ed. Boca Raton, Fla.: CRC Press, 2007. Describes the pharmacological, physiological, and pathological aspects of drug abuse in general, and individual chapters address specific compounds, such as alcohol, as well as specific issues related to drug abuse, such as workplace drug testing.

Levine, Barry, ed. *Principles of Forensic Toxicology*. 2d ed., rev. Washington, D.C.: American Association for Clinical Chemistry, 2006.

Introductory textbook describes the analytical, chemical, and pharmacological aspects of a variety of drugs of forensic relevance.

See also: Alcohol-related offenses; Analytical instrumentation; Drug abuse and dependence; Forensic toxicology; Gas chromatography; High-performance liquid chromatography; Homogeneous enzyme immunoassay; Illicit substances; International Association of Forensic Toxicologists; Mass spectrometry; Poisons and antidotes; Sherlock Holmes stories; Toxic torts; Ultraviolet spectrophotometry.

Toxicology. *See* Forensic toxicology

Trace and transfer evidence

Definitions: Trace evidence is evidence present in very small amounts, requiring careful attention, and often special techniques, to detect. Transfer evidence is evidence that has moved from one person or object to another (for example, from a crime victim to the perpetrator or vice versa).

Significance: Trace evidence and transfer evidence often take the form of fibers, hairs, soils, paint chips, and other tiny pieces of material that must be carefully collected from crime scenes and transported to the laboratory for analysis. The information gained from forensic analysis of such evidence can help law-enforcement investigators to link suspects to crime scenes.

Although trace evidence and transfer evidence are conceptually distinct, the terms "trace" and "transfer" are frequently applied to the same materials, the debris (hairs, fibers, dust, glass and paint fragments, and other materials, natural and manufactured) that French forensic pioneer Edmond Locard characterized as containing the "mute witnesses" of criminal truth. Locard's exchange principle, widely regarded as the fundamental idea behind forensic science, insists that "every contact leaves a trace." This transfer—blood on a door handle, for example—need not be unperceived, but it is the difficult-to-perceive transfer (the "trace") that is likely to survive attempts to scrub away evidence of mischief.

"Trace" Versus "Transfer"

When surfaces touch, transfer evidence is produced, although transfer can occur without direct contact. Surfaces pick up matter and leave matter behind, or disturb the material already there, or both. Stepping in the mud may leave behind a shoe print (possibly one with great individuality); it also may take away material from the mud and leave behind material from the shoe.

Transfer evidence thus can be viewed as including both "pattern transfer" evidence, such as imprints and impressions (of fingerprints, shoe prints, tire tracks, and so on), and "trace transfer" evidence, such as hairs, fibers, glass fragments, soil, and blood. The former is often referred to simply as "pattern evidence," the latter as "trace evidence." The phrase "trace, or transfer, evidence" (occasionally further abbreviated to just "trace evidence") is sometimes used as a loose label for both.

As a practical matter, what falls into the category of trace evidence is influenced by bureaucratic factors such as crime lab organization, including spatial layout, equipment distribution, staffing contingencies, and funding requirements. "Trace" functions to some extent as a catchall category, and so the kinds of evidence that fall into that category can vary enormously. As one trace analyst has put it, "Trace analysis is the section of the crime lab where, if they don't know where to send it, they send it to us."

Problems with Trace Evidence

Some problems related to the use of hair, fiber, and other trace and transfer evidence in criminal cases have involved familiar concerns about proper quality control in the collection, preservation, testing, and documentation of evidence. Other problems have arisen owing to the professional or moral failings of individual "experts" who have overstated the significance of "matches." Despite much loose talk about two or more items "matching" or "being similar," and about results "corroborating" or being "consistent with" a certain hypothesis, much trace evidence at best rules out certain possibilities.

More decisive, positive implications depend heavily on judgments about probabilities. How likely is it that a fiber found on a murder victim came from the carpet in a vehicle belonging to the defendant? Given a glass fragment found on a suspect that is similar to the glass in a crime victim's home, when is it reasonable to conclude that it comes from that source? Forensic scientists devote much effort to trying to establish relevant numbers, and many statistical mistakes can be made in reasoning about these matters. Calculating the likelihood of variation among items of a given kind (such as hairs or glass fragments) is part of the problem and part of why it is important that forensic scientists conduct comparisons using control samples.

The emergence of DNA (deoxyribonucleic acid) analysis has played a role in decreasing the emphasis on trace and transfer evidence. It has also prompted recognition of serious flaws in both the scientific and the judicial utilization of results. In establishing the innocence of numerous individuals who have been convicted of crimes, DNA evidence has provided an indictment of the evidence (often hairs, fibers, or other trace evidence) on the basis of which those individuals were originally convicted. This development has contributed to a decline in the prestige attached to the analysis of trace evidence.

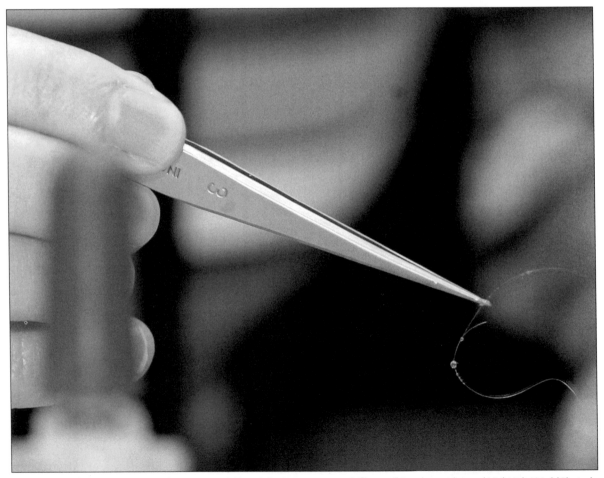

A technician in the Georgia Bureau of Investigation's Trace Lab examines a strand of hair collected as evidence. *(AP/Wide World Photos)*

The Future of Trace Evidence

In announcing a symposium on trace evidence sponsored by the Federal Bureau of Investigation (FBI) and the National Institute of Justice (NIJ) in 2007, Sandra Koch of the FBI Laboratory's Trace Evidence Unit noted that "collection, preservation, analysis, and eventual use in court [of trace/transfer evidence] have declined in recent years." Half a decade earlier, retired forensic scientist Larry Ragle had lamented that "it has become more difficult for the lab personnel to justify spending the time it takes to characterize trace evidence, hairs, and fibers, or even to train new scientists in the techniques," and that in some jurisdictions "crime scene investigators no longer spend the time to search for and collect the standards necessary for comparison should trace evidence be important as the investigation progresses."

Trace evidence stands in the shadow of the rapid advance of DNA analysis, but it might nonetheless have a brighter future. The progress of nanotechnology (the science of ultrasmall— molecular-scale—particles and processes) may be expected to lead to the identification of yet subtler class characteristics of materials as well as to increased ability to detect individualizing features of wear and idiosyncrasies of manufacture in what were formerly indistinguishable mass-produced objects. (Whether such developments will have practical application within the context of underfunded and overtasked crime labs is another question.)

Moreover, trace evidence and transfer evidence are important for their role in the maintenance of an open-minded, holistic approach to forensics. As one crime lab director has observed:

> It used to be that when our firearms unit received a bullet, the first thing they'd do would be they'd wash it off so they could see all their little grooves and markings so they could do their comparison. . . . [They now realize that] there might be blood on there that's important. . . . Directors of crime labs have to . . . not lose the ability of people to recognize evidence beyond their one little specialty.

Edward Johnson

Further Reading

Aitken, Colin G. G., and Franco Taroni. *Statistics and the Evaluation of Evidence for Forensic Scientists.* 2d ed. Hoboken, N.J.: John Wiley & Sons, 2004. Provides extensive discussion of the statistical issues involved in the interpretation of trace and transfer evidence.

Fisher, Jim. *Forensics Under Fire: Are Bad Science and Dueling Experts Corrupting Criminal Justice?* New Brunswick, N.J.: Rutgers University Press, 2008. Surveys the weaknesses that exist in some areas of forensic science, including the analysis of hair and fiber evidence.

Fletcher, Connie. *Every Contact Leaves a Trace: Crime Scene Experts Talk About Their Work from Discovery Through Verdict.* New York: St. Martin's Press, 2006. Presents commentary from more than eighty professionals in the field of forensic science, with a focus on the difference between their real-life work and depictions of forensic work in the popular media. Includes an extensive discussion of trace evidence.

Houck, Max M., ed. *Mute Witnesses: Trace Evidence Analysis.* San Diego, Calif.: Academic Press, 2001. Collection of essays presents a variety of viewpoints on central concerns in the handling and interpretation of trace evidence.

_____. *Trace Evidence Analysis: More Cases in Mute Witnesses.* Burlington, Mass.: Elsevier Academic Press, 2004. Second anthology edited by Houck discusses a variety of cases involving trace evidence.

Kelly, John F., and Phillip K. Wearne. *Tainting Evidence: Inside the Scandals at the FBI Crime Lab.* New York: Free Press, 1998. Recounts the effects of incompetence, dishonesty, and cover-up in a number of trace evidence cases handled by the nation's most prestigious forensic lab.

Lee, Henry C., Timothy Palmbach, and Marilyn T. Miller. *Henry Lee's Crime Scene Handbook.* San Diego, Calif.: Academic Press, 2001. Discusses proper evidence collection, preservation, and assessment. Lee is one of the best-known practitioners of forensic science in the United States.

Ragle, Larry. *Crime Scene*. Rev. ed. New York: Avon Books, 2002. Provides detailed information on the procedures used in the collection, testing, and interpretation of trace and other evidence.

See also: Animal evidence; Blood residue and bloodstains; Class versus individual evidence; Crime scene protective gear; Cross-contamination of evidence; Defensive wounds; Fibers and filaments; Forensic geoscience; Glass; Gunshot residue; Hair analysis; Hit-and-run vehicle offenses; Locard's exchange principle; Paint; Semen and sperm; Soil.

Training and licensing of forensic professionals

Definition: Education in forensic techniques and certification of competence in the practice of such techniques.

Significance: Professionalization implies that self-regulation, in some cases supplemented by laws, should determine appropriate standards for the education and certification of those who practice the profession. The standards of competence for forensic professionals, however, are in many cases unspecified or vary by jurisdiction, or from field to field, or are only loosely connected with evidential standards. This situation has prompted both demands for greater professionalization of the field of forensic science and worries about the restrictive effects of excessive regulation.

In the late nineteenth century, when Sir Arthur Conan Doyle created his master detective character Sherlock Holmes, who used his multifarious knowledge and his powers of ratiocination to clarify mysteries that had flummoxed Scotland Yard's energetic but imperceptive Inspector Lestrade, the idea of applying science to the solution of crime was largely speculative. Since that time, forensic science has developed sophisticated techniques and given birth to a variety of professional organizations, but still only limited agreement exists on exactly what forensic professionals should know, or even what constitutes competence in the field. Debate continues concerning how should modern criminalists—the heirs of both Holmes and Lestrade—should be trained and certified.

Varying Standards

In the early twenty-first century, the profession of private investigator is licensed throughout the United States, but forensics as a field is wide open. Some specialists, such as medical examiners, are subject to certification, and many specialists are regulated by their own professional organizations, but some observers have argued that greater unification and professionalization of those who have business with forensic issues is in order.

The problem is that "forensic science" is not a natural science; rather, forensic science includes any science that is useful, more or less often, in settling facts of interest in the courtroom. Over time, new sciences emerge and old "sciences" sometimes fade. In the era of Alphonse Bertillon (1853-1914), knowing how to measure various human physical features, such as ears, was important, but fingerprinting largely displaced that older system of identification. More recently, fingerprinting has seen its own preeminence challenged by DNA (deoxyribonucleic acid) "fingerprinting" as well as by worries about accuracy and puzzles created by computerization.

In addition to disagreements about the criteria for training and the necessity and scope of licensing, disagreements exist even about standards for evidence. With regard to fingerprints, for example, no standard has been established regarding the minimum number of points of commonality that must be present for examiners to consider a match reliable. Various nations have differing requirements, and requirements in the United States vary across states and even across police jurisdictions within states.

In the courtroom, these issues are reflected in debates about who can or should be accorded expert witness status. Leading British forensic entomologist Zakaria Erzinçlioglu (1951-2002) at the time of his death was conducting a vigorous campaign for the British courts to rethink who ought to be able to function as expert witnesses in those courts.

In 1995, the American Academy of Forensic Sciences (AAFS), concerned by the wide variation in certification standards used by different boards, undertook to make the credentialing process for forensic scientists more rational. As a result, the AAFS in 2000 established the Forensic Specialties Accreditation Board (FSAB) as a way of "accrediting the certifiers." The FSAB considered and rejected the idea of allowing accreditation through independent organizations, such as the National Commission of Certifying Agencies or the American Board of Medical Specialties, because "the forensic community would be unwisely delegating its professional oversight responsibility to non-forensic organizations."

Georgia Private Investigator Bill

The complex issues in the area of licensing are illustrated by the controversy in 2006 over a bill passed by the Georgia state legislature (2006 H.B. 1259) making it (with limited exceptions) a felony to engage in the private detective business without a license. This included "obtaining or furnishing . . . information" about crimes or the "securing of evidence . . . to be used before any court." The bill was supported by the Georgia Association of Professional Private Investigators as a way to improve the image of private investigators and "protect the public" from untrained, fly-by-night amateurs. "We have all seen them," the president of that organization wrote. "They spring up. . . . They screw up the investigation and their actions result in their clients losing their cases. . . . Meanwhile the 'investigator' has decided that this is not as much fun as they had thought and . . . moved on."

Computer consultants argued that the bill would unreasonably require them to be licensed

---

Recommendations for Education and Training

In June, 2004, the National Institute of Justice published a special report titled Education and Training in Forensic Science: A Guide for Forensic Science Laboratories, Educational Institutions, and Students. *The report, created by the Technical Working Group for Education and Training in Forensic Science, makes the following recommendations concerning training in the forensic sciences.*

Undergraduate degree. Undergraduate forensic science degree programs are expected to deliver a strong and credible science foundation that emphasizes the scientific method and problem-solving skills. Exemplary programs would be interdisciplinary and include substantial laboratory work, as most employment opportunities occur in laboratory settings. Natural sciences should dominate undergraduate curriculums and be supported by coursework in specialized, forensic, and laboratory sciences and other classes that complement the student's area of concentration.

Graduate degree. Graduate programs can move students from theoretical concepts to discipline-specific knowledge. Exemplary curriculums can include such topics as crime scenes, physical evidence, law/science interface, ethics, and quality assurance to complement the student's advanced coursework. Graduate programs should be designed with strong laboratory and research components. Access to instructional laboratories with research-specific facilities, equipment, and instrumentation and interaction with forensic laboratories are required to enhance the graduate-level experience. By emphasizing written and oral communication and report writing, graduate programs can prepare students for future courtroom testimony.

Forensic scientists have an ongoing obligation to advance their field through training and continuing professional development. Training programs should include written components (e.g., instructor qualifications, student requirements, performance goals, and competency testing), and their content should contain several core and discipline-specific elements guided by peer-defined standards. Continuing professional development . . . should be structured, measurable, and documented.

as private investigators and that in general the bill's provisions were inconsistent with the (sometimes) legally recognized right of scientific experts to examine evidence and testify to their findings. Moreover, as computer commentator Mark Rasch sensibly and cynically observed, "Internet based crimes occur across jurisdictions, but licensing boards' authority does not. So a company performing computer forensics in Georgia, run by a licensed PI in Georgia who had to examine a hard drive in California, theoretically would either have to obtain a license in California or retain the services of a California PI to do the work. Is this a full employment program for former cops?"

In May, 2006, Governor Sonny Perdue vetoed the bill, noting that it "fails to exclude from the private investigator licensing requirement many professions that collect information or may be called as expert witnesses in court proceedings." Although computer forensics consultants celebrated the veto as a victory, the political issue about increasing the penalty was not dead, and in any event unlicensed investigation remained illegal (albeit a misdemeanor) under existing law. Other states, of course, have other laws, some similar and some not. The larger issues—about what constitutes competence in matters of forensic science, who should have the authorization to train and to certify that competence, and how to ensure national (and, increasingly, international) commensurability—remain unresolved.

Edward Johnson

Further Reading

Barnett, Peter D. *Ethics in Forensic Science: Professional Standards for the Practice of Criminalistics*. Boca Raton, Fla.: CRC Press, 2001. Presents a concise treatment of the ethical issues affecting the training and licensing of forensic professionals.

Hallcox, Jarrett, and Amy Welch. *Bodies We've Buried: Inside the National Forensic Academy, the World's Top CSI Training School*. New York: Berkley Books, 2006. Describes the National Forensic Academy's ten-week training course for law-enforcement agents. Topics of the training include the identification, collection, and preservation of evidence.

Inman, Keith, and Norah Rudin. *Principles and Practice of Criminalistics: The Profession of Forensic Science*. Boca Raton, Fla.: CRC Press, 2001. Provides an introduction to "good practices" (including ethics) in the forensic science profession.

Rasch, Mark. "Forensic Felonies." *Security Focus*, April 24, 2006. Commentary helped to sound the alarm (from computer consultants' point of view) about the proposed Georgia felony penalty for unlicensed investigation.

Robberson, John. "President's Pen." *The Connection: Official Newsletter of the Georgia Association of Professional Private Investigators*, April, 2006, 3. Presents professional private investigators' explanation of their support for the Georgia bill changing unlicensed investigation from a misdemeanor to a felony.

See also: American Academy of Forensic Sciences; American Society of Crime Laboratory Directors; Computer forensics; *Daubert v. Merrell Dow Pharmaceuticals*; DNA fingerprinting; Ethics; Expert witnesses; Federal Bureau of Investigation Forensic Science Research and Training Center; Federal Law Enforcement Training Center; Fingerprints; International Association for Identification; International Association of Forensic Toxicologists; Pseudoscience in forensic practice; Sherlock Holmes stories.

Trial consultants

Definition: Persons with expertise that can be applied to courtroom settings who aid attorneys in preparing and executing trial strategies.

Significance: Among the various services provided by trial consultants, the one perhaps most relevant to forensic science is that of preparing expert witnesses to give courtroom testimony. Forensic scientists are often called to testify in court regarding the findings from their examination of evidence, and they may work with trial consultants beforehand so that they can present their testimony in the most effective manner.

Most law schools focus on teaching legal theory, legal writing, argumentation, bar exam preparation, and other practical matters of being a lawyer. Law schools do not generally include much instruction in disciplines such as psychology, sociology, statistics, anthropology, judgment and decision-making sciences, presentation technology, marketing, or market research. Many of these disciplines however, have proven helpful to attorneys as they seek to develop and carry out strategic arguments at trial. Since the 1980s, the gap between expertise in the law and expertise in these other areas has been filled by a growing number of specialists known as trial consultants.

Jury Selection

One area in which trial consultants have specialized is jury selection. Using psychological principles, consultants aid attorneys by identifying the characteristics of potential jurors that they believe will cause the jurors to be more or less likely to be sympathetic to the attorneys' clients or arguments. By examining the attitudes and experiences of the people in the pools from which jurors are selected, jury consultants draw conclusions about how each would be likely to decide given cases. With this information, attorneys can attempt to have excused from juries any persons they believe will be inclined to be unsympathetic toward their clients.

Preparation of Expert Witnesses

Attorneys frequently call on forensic scientists and other experts in scientific and technical fields such as physics, chemistry, biology, and psychology to testify in court. These experts are not always skilled at public speaking, and they can seem uneasy on the witness stand. Trial consultants often help to prepare experts so that they appear relaxed and confident as they present their testimony, which can aid their credibility with jurors. Sometimes this involves rehearsing with experts in simulated courtroom settings. Trial consultants also explain to expert witnesses the best ways for them to get particular messages across and how to avoid becoming flustered or confused under cross-examination.

Presentation Materials

Some trial consultants specialize in producing visual aids that attorneys use in presenting the facts of cases to juries. Photographs, time lines, charts, graphs, documents, and animations are among the types of visual materials that trial attorneys may need to convey facts clearly to juries. If such materials are confusing or even just difficult to see, jurors may fail to grasp the points the attorneys are trying to make. Many trial consulting firms can produce much higher-quality visual aids than trial attorneys could make on their own because these firms employ graphic artists and creative designers.

Pretrial Research

One way in which trial consultants gather information to help plan the strategies to be used in jury trials is by conducting research. Such research can take a wide variety of forms, from simple surveys to complete mock trials. The aim in each case is to discover how members of the public, ideally persons similar to the potential jurors, will view the case, the attorney, and the arguments that will be presented.

One of the methods that trial consultants often use in conducting research is the focus group. The consultant for a case recruits members of the public and pays them to listen to the case, both the arguments presented by the side that hired the consultant and the arguments that may be made by the opposing side. After the focus group members have heard all the arguments, they may be asked to discuss the case with a moderator, to respond to questionnaires about the case, or even to conduct a mock deliberation. The consultant records and then analyzes all of the feedback from the group.

Often, consultants find out through focus groups and other kinds of pretrial research that members of the public do not see cases in the same ways the attorneys do. Such research may reveal particular weaknesses in attorneys' arguments or even problems with the ways in which people react to the attorneys themselves.

Dr. Jo-Ellan Dimitrius (right), seated next to an attorney while serving as a consultant during the jury selection phase of former professional basketball player Jayson Williams's manslaughter trial in 2004. A specialist in predicting the behavior of jury members, Dimitrius has consulted in more than one thousand trials and has coauthored books on jury selection and "reading" people. She also appeared in a brief documentary about the making of the motion picture *Runaway Jury* (2004). *(AP/Wide World Photos)*

Pretrial research can also uncover weaknesses in the ways in which attorneys and witnesses present information, especially if the information is complicated.

Controversy

Trial consulting is a relatively new field, and it has been the source of controversy. For example, some members of the legal community have raised questions about whether attorneys who employ consultants have an unfair advantage, given that many clients cannot afford to pay for their attorneys to hire consultants. Also, some observers have expressed concern about the fact that, unlike the legal profession, the field of trial consulting is largely unregulated, and consultants need no special licensing or certification. Of the many services offered by trial consultants, those involving jury selection are perhaps

the most controversial; it has been argued that consultants' input into the jury selection process may be seen as a violation of the right to an impartial jury trial, as provided for in the Sixth Amendment to the U.S. Constitution.

Robert Bockstiegel

Further Reading

Ball, David. *Theater Tips and Strategies for Jury Trials*. 3rd ed. Notre Dame, Ind.: National Institute for Trial Advocacy, 2003. Volume for attorneys, written by a trial consultant, discusses approaches to jury persuasion based in theater concepts.

Cotterill, Janet. *Language and Power in Court: A Linguistic Analysis of the O. J. Simpson Trial*. New York: Palgrave Macmillan, 2003. Draws on transcripts from Simpson's murder trial as well as interviews conducted after the trial with Simpson and jurors in the case to examine the importance of the role of the language used in the courtroom. Includes discussion of the jury selection process.

Kassin, Saul M., and Lawrence S. Wrightsman. *The American Jury on Trial: Psychological Perspectives*. New York: Hemisphere, 1988. Discusses all aspects of the American jury system, from jury selection to jurors' decision-making processes.

Mauet, Thomas A. *Trials: Strategy, Skills, and the New Powers of Persuasion*. New York: Aspen, 2005. Volume aimed at attorneys focuses on courtroom strategy and the art of juror persuasion.

Posey, Amy J., and Lawrence S. Wrightsman. *Trial Consulting*. New York: Oxford University Press, 2005. Describes the growth of the profession of trial consulting and explains the primary activities performed by trial consultants, including witness preparation, the conduct of focus groups and mock trials, and jury selection.

See also: Competency evaluation and assessment instruments; Courts and forensic evidence; Criminology; Expert witnesses; Eyewitness testimony; Legal competency; *People v. Lee*; Police psychology; Simpson murder trial.

Truth serum

Definition: Any of a number of drugs that depress the cerebral nervous system and reduce inhibitions.

Significance: The search for methods to secure intelligence, confessions, and details of criminal acts led law-enforcement agencies to employ pharmaceutical products such as scopolamine and barbiturates (notably sodium amytal and sodium thiopental) to try to induce persons to reveal information that they would not disclose voluntarily. The designation "truth serum" is misleading, however, as subjects under the influence of such drugs may lie.

Success sometimes results when the persons interrogated come to believe that they can only tell the truth.

The term "truth serum" was introduced into forensic language during the 1920's by Dr. Robert House of Ferris, Texas. When House administered scopolamine to induce what was called "twilight sleep" to ease the difficulties of childbirth, he noticed that the drug made patients talkative and that they often revealed information that they otherwise would not have disclosed.

In 1963, the U.S. Supreme Court ruled in *Townsend v. Sain* that information acquired in interrogation after the use of a "truth serum" is not admissible in court in criminal cases. Charles Townsend, a heroin addict suspected of murder, suffered severe withdrawal pains while being interrogated by law-enforcement investigators. After a police doctor injected Townsend with scopolamine and phenobarbital, allegedly to treat the effects of the opiate withdrawal, Townsend confessed to the murder. The Court declared that, because of the use of "truth serum," Townsend's confession failed to meet the constitutional requirement that it be voluntary.

Two developments that followed the terrorist attacks on New York City and the Pentagon on September 11, 2001, focused renewed attention on the use of truth serum in the United States. The first was a U.S. Supreme Court opinion that stated that the fight against terrorism might require "heightened deference to the judgment of the political branches with respect to matters of national security" (*Zadvydas v. Davis*, 2001). Second, William Webster, a former chief of the Central Intelligence Agency (CIA) and the Federal Bureau of Investigation (FBI), urged the Pentagon to administer truth serum drugs to defiant Taliban and al-Qaeda prisoners to obtain information that could prevent fresh terrorist attacks. Webster's critics maintained that the use of truth serum constitutes a violation of international treaties in that such use invades the privacy of, inflicts indignity on, and compromises the bodily integrity of the subject.

Gilbert Geis

Further Reading

Geis, Gilbert. "In Scopolamine Veritas: The Early History of Drug-Inducted Statements." *Journal of Criminal Law, Criminology, and Police Science* 50 (November/December, 1959): 347-357.

Horsley, J. Stephen. *Narco-analysis: A New Technique in Short-Cut Psychotherapy.* London: Oxford University Press, 1948.

Moenssens, Andre A. "Narcoanalysis in Law Enforcement." *Journal of Criminal Law, Criminology, and Police Science* 52 (November/December, 1961): 453-458.

Winter, Alison. "The Chemistry of Truth and the Literature of Dystopia." In *Literature, Science, Psychoanalysis, 1830-1970: Essays in Honour of Gillian Beer*, edited by Helen Small and Trudi Tate. New York: Oxford University Press, 2003.

_____. "The Making of 'Truth Serum.'" *Bulletin of the History of Medicine* 79, no. 4 (2005): 500-533.

See also: Barbiturates; Brain-wave scanners; Drug abuse and dependence; Ethics; Interrogation; Polygraph analysis; Pseudoscience in forensic practice.

A scientist at the Rocky Mountain Laboratory of the U.S. Public Health Service performs necropsies on tularemia-infected guinea pigs during the early 1940's. The animals were injected with water from mountain streams suspected as sources of the disease. *(Library of Congress)*

Tularemia

Definition: Infection caused by the bacterium *Francisella tularensis*.

Significance: Commonly known as rabbit fever, tularemia is a disease endemic in North America as well as parts of Europe and Asia. Its relevance to forensic science lies chiefly in its potential for use as a bioweapon.

Tularemia is a naturally occurring disease. Its primary hosts are rabbits, prairie dogs, muskrats, and other small mammals, but it can also be transmitted by ticks and deerflies. After infection, onset is rapid. Symptoms include headache, fatigue, dizziness, and nausea. If untreated, tularemia may result in death.

The U.S. Centers for Disease Control and Prevention (CDC) regards *Francisella tularensis* as a viable bioweapon agent because tularemia is highly infective and incapacitating yet has relatively low lethality, a consideration in its possible deployment near a civilian population. The bacterium is easy to distribute both as an aerosol and in municipal drinking water supplies. Aerosol release would have the most widespread effect on public health, especially if done in urban settings. *F. tularensis* is classified as a Category A agent, which means it has serious potential for inducing terror in a population (other Category A agents include *Yersinia pestis*, the bacterium that causes plague; *Variola major*, the virus that causes smallpox; *Bacillus anthracis*, the bacterium that causes anthrax; and *Clostridium botulinum*, the bacterium that causes botulism). Japan, the Soviet Union, and the United States have all stockpiled *F. tularen-*

sis in the form of offensive weapons at different times in their histories. It is now known that the Soviet army used the pathogen against the Germans during World War II in the Battle of Stalingrad.

Because the early symptoms of tularemia are similar to those of many ordinary or seasonal infections, an attack using *F. tularensis* on the general population in any given area in the United States could easily take health authorities by surprise. With an incubation range of one to fourteen days and average onset of symptoms taking from three to five days, an attack might not be immediately detected. Security measures that have been taken against this possibility include the installation in thirty U.S. cities of sensors that constantly monitor the air for deadly pathogens. If epidemiologists suspect the deliberate or unexplained release of the tularemia organism, standard practice is for them to contact the appropriate law-enforcement agencies immediately.

One of the things that makes the possibility of the use of the tularemia pathogen as a weapon particularly worrisome is that no vaccine against the disease is available to the general public, in contrast to other possible bioterror agents such as anthrax and smallpox. Some comfort is provided by the availability of potent and effective antibiotics against tularemia.

Robert Klose

Further Reading

Dembek, Zygmunt F., Ronald L. Buckman, Stephanie K. Fowler, and James L. Hadler. "Missed Sentinel Case of Naturally Occurring Pneumonic Tularemia Outbreak: Lessons for Detection of Bioterrorism." *Journal of the American Board of Family Practice* 16 (July/August, 2003): 339-342.

Dennis, David T., et al. "Tularemia as a Biological Weapon: Medical and Public Health Management." *Journal of the American Medical Association* 285 (June 6, 2001): 2763-2773.

Siderovski, Susan Hutton. *Tularemia*. New York: Chelsea House, 2006.

See also: Bacteria; Bacterial biology; Bacterial resistance and response to antibacterial agents; Biological terrorism; Biological warfare diagnosis; Biological weapon identification; Biological

---

Symptoms and Spread of Tularemia

The Centers for Disease Control and Prevention provides the following information about tularemia.

What Are the Symptoms of Tularemia?

Symptoms of tularemia could include:

- sudden fever
- chills
- headaches
- diarrhea
- muscle aches
- joint pain
- dry cough
- progressive weakness

People can also catch pneumonia and develop chest pain, bloody sputum and can have trouble breathing and even sometimes stop breathing.

Other symptoms of tularemia depend on how a person was exposed to the tularemia bacteria. These symptoms can include ulcers on the skin or mouth, swollen and painful lymph glands, swollen and painful eyes, and a sore throat.

How Does Tularemia Spread?

People can get tularemia many different ways:

- being bitten by an infected tick, deerfly or other insect
- handling infected animal carcasses
- eating or drinking contaminated food or water
- breathing in the bacteria, *F. tularensis*

Tularemia is not known to be spread from person to person. People who have tularemia do not need to be isolated. People who have been exposed to the tularemia bacteria should be treated as soon as possible. The disease can be fatal if it is not treated with the right antibiotics.

Weapons Convention of 1972; Biosensors; Biotoxins; Chemical Biological Incident Response Force, U.S.; Pathogen genomic sequencing.

Typewriter analysis

Definition: Process by which experts examine typewritten documents to determine information about the typewriters on which the items were produced.

Significance: Typewriter analysis can play a vital role in any investigation involving a document believed to have been produced on a typewriter, such as a ransom note, threat letter, or forged document. Although typewriter analysis has faded in importance since the use of computers and printers has become widespread, forensic scientists are still called upon at times to analyze documents produced on typewriters.

Handwriting is widely understood to differ from person to person, making the source of a handwritten note or document easily identifiable. In contrast, many people believe that typewritten documents all look the same and that finding the sources of documents created on typewriters should be difficult, if not impossible. Although typed documents are less easy to distinguish from one another than handwritten documents, an expert in typewriter analysis can determine a lot of useful information from a single typewritten document.

The processes used in typewriter analysis differ slightly depending on the document in question and the goal of the investigation. If the goal

is to determine the originator of a document, a single specific typewriter may need to be identified. If the goal is to determine whether an important historical document is a forgery, determining pertinent information about the type of machine used, and when it first became available, may be enough.

To determine whether a typewritten document was created on a certain machine, an expert compares a sample document typed on the machine in question to the relevant document. The comparison can be made to a document known to have been created on that machine, such as a letter or bill, or it can be made to a document typed solely for the purpose of comparison.

The expert compares the two documents side by side, sometimes using a hand magnifier or a high-powered microscope. The first determination to be made is usually whether the two documents came from machines of the same make and model. To determine this, the expert compares the two documents in terms of the spacing between letters, the shapes of the letters,

The unique traits that distinguish individual typewriters are much more pronounced in documents made using early models, which could not sustain the uniformity over time of later models. Individual keys tended to become increasingly dirty, chipped, and misaligned, and some keys made lighter impressions than others. Although modern computers have displaced typewriters—which are no longer manufactured in the United States—typewriter analysis remains important in investigations involving historical documents. (© iStockphoto.com/José Luis Gutiérrez)

the spacing between lines of type, and other attributes.

Although typewriters of the same make and model will produce very similar documents, individual typewriters can have attributes that make them specifically identifiable. Some of these traits may have come from the factory, such as a slightly misshapen letter. More commonly, they occur over time and with wear of the typewriter. Different letters, and even different parts of letters, wear differently. This means that any document typed on a particular machine will show the same slight imperfections in particular letters. An expert can use such imperfections to determine whether the typewriter used to create the comparison document also created the document in question.

Helen Davidson

An Early Case Solved by Typewriter Analysis

On its Web site, the Federal Bureau of Investigation describes a case solved through typewriter analysis in an article titled "The Birth of the FBI's Technical Laboratory: 1924 to 1935":

Harrington Fitzgerald, Jr., a mental patient in a Pennsylvania veterans' hospital more than one hundred miles away from his nearest relatives, opened and quickly sampled the box of chocolates from "Bertha." Perhaps he thought the November 1933 delivery was an early Christmas present; if so, it was the last one he received. Fitzgerald died soon after eating the first poisoned treat. As the crime occurred on federal property, Agents of the U.S. Bureau of Investigation [the FBI's predecessor] investigated. Mr. Fitzgerald's sister, Sarah Hobart, quickly became the primary suspect and so Agents solicited samples of her handwriting. These samples along with the package's wrapper and card were sent to Headquarters for analysis in the Bureau's new Technical Laboratory.

There, Special Agent Charles Appel, a balding, meticulous investigator, received the evidence and began to compare the handwriting samples to the note card. He reported that the note from "Bertha" and the Hobart samples revealed no match. More analysis could be done, he suggested, if the investigating Agents would obtain samples from Hobart's husband and track down the family's typewriter. Diligent detective work led Philadelphia Agents to a typewriter Mrs. Hobart had conveniently sent in for repair at a local shop. Using samples of type from the Hobart machine, Appel quickly determined that it was the machine on which the mailing label on the package of poisoned candy was typed. Confronted with the evidence, Sarah Hobart confessed.

Further Reading

Koppenhaver, Katherine M.. *Forensic Document Examination: Principles and Practice.* Totowa, N.J.: Humana Press, 2007.

Vastrick, Thomas W. *Forensic Document Examination Techniques.* Altamonte Springs, Fla.: Institute of Internal Auditors Research Foundation, 2004.

See also: Document examination; Fax machine, copier, and printer analysis; Federal Bureau of Investigation Laboratory; Forensic linguistics and stylistics; Forgery; Paper; Questioned document analysis; Unabomber case; Writing instrument analysis.

U

Ultraviolet spectrophotometry

Definition: Analytical chemistry technique used as a screening tool in classifying chemical compounds.

Significance: Forensic scientists often use ultraviolet spectrophotometry when conducting preliminary screening to identify classes of compounds, such as in drug screening, detection of explosives, toxicology, paint analysis, and soil discrimination.

Ultraviolet (UV) spectrophotometry is a nondestructive, sensitive technique that measures light absorbed by a sample in the ultraviolet spectral region. UV spectrophotometry has two general uses in forensics: screening and quantitation. Although not useful as a confirmatory test, UV spectrophotometry is a good preliminary screening method to identify classes of organic compounds with aromatic rings or conjugated systems. These structural features are common in many types of drugs and other controlled substances and in many materials used in explosives.

UV spectrophotometry can be used as a screening tool to identify a class or group of compounds in a sample. Although scientists can determine the presence or absence of suspected compounds using this technique, UV spectrophotometry has limited specificity because structurally related compounds can generate similar spectra. Many compounds, including various drug groups, produce characteristic spectra, but these spectra typically do not provide enough detail for specific compound identification; they are most useful for determining a class of compounds present in a sample. UV spectrophotometry is thus most useful for single-component analysis of samples with known or suspected composition, such as pharmaceuticals.

Different compounds have varying capacities to absorb UV light, so mixtures of compounds can complicate analysis. For example, a compound that absorbs UV light strongly combined with a controlled substance that is a weak UV absorber may generate a spectrum that masks the presence of the controlled substance. Specific compound identification requires more precise chemical analytical tools that can provide structural detail, such as infrared (IR) spectroscopy or mass spectrometry (MS).

UV spectrophotometry can also be used to quantify a substance in a sample. The amount of UV light absorbed by a sample corresponds to the concentration of a particular substance in the sample. A forensic scientist can use such a quantitative procedure, for instance, to compare the concentration of a substance in a sample that is suspected of being tampered with to the concentration of the same substance in a known, unaltered sample. These measurements can be followed with more thorough analyses using other techniques to determine the actual concentration and identity of the substance in question.

UV spectrophotometry can be used to identify controlled substances and drugs of abuse, such as amphetamines and methamphetamine. This technique can also be used to detect compounds that might be found in explosives, such as compounds that contain nitro groups attached to aromatic rings. Forensic scientists also use UV spectrophotometry in analyzing soils and paints as well as in quantifying DNA (deoxyribonucleic acid). For analysis of small samples, UV spectrophotometry can be combined with a microscope in the technique known as microspectrophotometry.

C. J. Walsh

Further Reading

Bell, Suzanne. *Forensic Chemistry*. Upper Saddle River, N.J.: Pearson Prentice Hall, 2006.

Houck, Max M., and Jay A. Siegel. *Fundamentals of Forensic Science*. Burlington, Mass.: Elsevier Academic Press, 2006.

James, Stuart H., and Jon J. Nordby, eds. *Forensic Science: An Introduction to Scientific and Investigative Techniques*. 2d ed. Boca Raton, Fla.: CRC Press, 2005.

See also: Analytical instrumentation; Electromagnetic spectrum analysis; Energy-dispersive spectroscopy; High-performance liquid chromatography; Microspectrophotometry; Quantitative and qualitative analysis of chemicals; Spectroscopy.

Unabomber case

Date: Bombings took place between May, 1978 and April, 1995

The Event: Unabomber was the name given to the unknown perpetrator of a series of bombings in the United States that targeted primarily victims associated with universities and airlines. Many of the explosive devices were sent through the U.S. mail.

Significance: The Unabomber case brought ecoterrorism to the attention of American law-enforcement agencies and led to one of the largest manhunts in the history of the Federal Bureau of Investigation.

Ted Kaczynski, the Unabomber, carried out one of the longest single-handed strings of bombings in the history of terrorism. From 1978 to 1995, he delivered at least sixteen bombs to targets, some through the U.S. mail and others through hand delivery. In a little less than seventeen years, Kaczynski killed three people and wounded twenty-three, succeeding in inserting terror into the psyches of many Americans. At the end of his reign of terror, *The New York Times* and *The Washington Post* published a long essay written by Kaczynski in exchange for a halt to the bombings. Kaczynski was captured the next year and eventually pleaded guilty in 1998 to federal charges related to the bombings. He received a sentence of four life terms, escaping the death penalty that federal prosecutors originally sought.

Kaczynski's Early Life

Ted Kaczynski was born on May 22, 1942, in Chicago, and in his childhood, educators at Evergreen Park Central School deemed him a gifted student. It has been reported that he scored 157 on an IQ test when he was ten years old. He was allowed to skip the sixth grade and to take classes with older students. In his journal, Kaczynski stated that being placed into classes with older children caused considerable difficulty in his life; he was verbally taunted and found that he was unable to fit in socially.

Kaczynski attended high school at Evergreen Park Community High School. Although he excelled academically, he continued to struggle socially, feeling isolated from other students. He briefly experienced some social fame in high school when he constructed a pipe bomb in one of his science classes, but he generally remained a loner throughout his high school career. His isolation was exacerbated when he was allowed to skip the eleventh grade and graduated from high school at the age of fifteen. Kaczynski was then accepted into Harvard University and began classes there in 1958 at the age of sixteen.

Kaczynski struggled in social relationships throughout college and felt particularly uncomfortable interacting with women. He again excelled in academics, however, and graduated in 1962. He then moved to the University of Michigan in Ann Arbor, where he received both a master's degree and a Ph.D. in mathematics. Some of his professors there later described him as ambitious, talented, and gifted. While in graduate school, he also taught undergraduate classes and published a number of articles. It has been reported that Kaczynski had confusion about his gender during graduate school, experiencing fantasies of being a female, and that he contemplated a sex change at this time. Instead of addressing that issue, however, he sought psychiatric help for anxiety.

Kaczynski took a job as assistant professor of mathematics at the University of California at Berkeley in 1967, but he did not relate well to his students. Despite attempts by administrators to persuade him otherwise, he resigned from his position in 1969, and his professional life began to spiral downward in conjunction

This widely circulated sketch of the suspected Unabomber was created by forensic artist Jeanne Boylan for the Federal Bureau of Investigation before Ted Kaczynski was apprehended in 1996. *(AP/Wide World Photos)*

with his social life. After his resignation, Kaczynski returned to Illinois and lived in a small house owned by his parents. He was largely unemployed during this period, working random jobs and borrowing money from his parents to get by.

In the 1970's, Kaczynski lived as a hermit, interacting with only a few people and slipping deeper into social isolation and anger, which he directed against the technological advancement of society. His relationships with family members became increasingly odd, as he accused them of emotional abuse and persistently sought apologies. Some psychologists who have reviewed Kaczynski's life believe that he was showing signs of schizophrenia.

Kaczynski began writing about the evils of technology, including its control over individuals. He also began planning to kill people in an apparent attempt to make a statement about the evils of technology. In 1978, at the same time he was starting to put his desire to commit terrorism into motion, Kaczynski was working with his brother and father at a foam-rubber factory.

Bombings and Investigation

The first bomb that Kaczynski aimed at another person was placed in a package left at the University of Illinois at Chicago in 1978; the package carried the return address of Professor Buckley Crist at Northwestern University. The package was found and sent back to the professor, who was suspicious of receiving a returned package that he had never mailed. A campus police officer at the university, Terry Marker, then opened the package and it detonated, causing Marker minor injuries.

Kaczynski followed this initial attack with attempted bombings of airlines in 1979. He sent several bombs in the mail to airline officials and placed a bomb in the cargo hold of an American Airlines flight from Chicago to Washington, D.C. That bomb did not explode because of a defective timer, but it did begin to smoke while the flight was in the air, causing the pilot to undertake an emergency landing. Officials of the Federal Bureau of Investigation (FBI) stated afterward that the bomb was easily strong enough to bring down the airplane. Although the FBI initially thought that the attempted airline bombings might be the work of a disgruntled airline employee, the psychological profile of the Unabomber (the term comes from the FBI's designation of the case as UNABOM, for "university and airline bomber") pointed to an intelligent man who was possibly an academic.

Kaczynski continued his bombings in the early to mid-1980's, and his desire to cause serious harm to others became a reality. In 1985, one of his bombs caused John Hauser, a graduate student at the University of California, Berkeley, and member of the U.S. Air Force, to lose several fingers and the vision in one eye. Kaczynski then targeted two computer stores, one in 1985 and one in 1987. Computer store owner Hugh Scrutton became the first person to die in one of the Unabomber's attacks on December 11, 1985.

For unknown reasons, Kaczynski took a six-year hiatus from his bombings before launching new attacks in 1993. That year, one of his devices seriously injured David Gelernter, a computer science professor at Yale University, and another caused Charles Epstein, a geneticist, to lose fingers. He continued his attacks in 1994 and 1995; his bombs killed advertising executive Thomas J. Mosser, whose company had helped Exxon repair its image after the *Exxon Valdez* oil spill, and Gilbert P. Murray, the president of the California Forestry Association, an organization that lobbies for the timber industry.

Manifesto and Capture

In 1995, Kaczynski began to mail letters to former victims in which he threatened dire consequences if his paper titled "Industrial Society and Its Future" was not published in a significant newspaper or newspapers. This work,

which later became known as the Unabomber manifesto, was published by *The New York Times* and *The Washington Post* on September 19, 1995. The overriding themes of the work were antigovernment, anti-big business, and antitechnology.

Law-enforcement authorities' investigation of the Unabomber was at a standstill at the time the manifesto was published, with nothing to go on but a sketch artist's rendering of a man in sunglasses and a hooded jacket or sweatshirt, some fingerprints, and few other clues. The fingerprints that investigators lifted from some of the bombs were later found not to match Kaczynski's, leading some to speculate that the prints may have been part of Kaczynski's purposeful attempts to mislead investigators. The FBI had also changed its profile of the Unabomber, describing the likely suspect as a

Federal agents escort Ted Kaczynski (center) from the federal courthouse in Helena, Montana, on April 4, 1996. Kaczynski was charged with one count of possession of bomb components during the court appearance. *(AP/Wide World Photos)*

The Unabomber's Forensic Psychiatric Evaluation

The following excerpt from a forensic psychiatrist's report, dated January 16, 1998, details the procedures undertaken to determine Ted Kaczynski's competency to stand trial.

During this evaluation, Mr. Kaczynski was interviewed by Sally C. Johnson, Chief Psychiatrist and Associate Warden of Health Services for the Federal Correctional Institution in Butner, North Carolina. During this evaluation, Mr. Kaczynski was interviewed by the examiner on eight occasions at the Sacramento County Jail, with a total interview time of approximately 22 hours. The interviews took place either in the lineup room conference area or in confidential attorney visiting booths on the second or eighth floor. At the start of the initial interview and briefly during subsequent interviews on 01/12/98 and 01/13/98, the defense attorneys were present to answer Mr. Kaczynski's questions regarding the evaluation process. In addition to the clinical interviews, formal review was conducted of previous medical evaluations, as well as previous neuropsychological and psychological testing results. Additional

psychological testing administered during this evaluation included the Minnesota Multiphasic Personality Inventory-2 (01/12/98), the Millon Clinical Multiaxial Inventory-II (01/12/98), the Beck Depression Inventory (01/15/98), and the Draw a Person Picking an Apple from a Tree projective drawing (01/15/98). Psychological testing administered during this evaluation was administered by Dr. Johnson. Scoring and interpretation of tests were accomplished with the assistance of psychology staff at FCI Butner.

At the outset of this evaluation and repeatedly throughout the week, the purpose of the evaluation and limits of confidentiality of information provided were discussed with Mr. Kaczynski. He was informed that the information and the observations made would provide the basis for completion of a report which would be available to the Judge, as well as the Defense and Prosecuting Attorneys. He was advised that a provision was in place to protect the privacy of any en camera materials. He demonstrated an adequate understanding of this information.

---

blue-collar mechanic who might work in the airlines industry.

After the manifesto was published, Ted Kaczynski's brother, David Kaczynski, contacted authorizes to tell them about his suspicion that his brother was the Unabomber. He had previously seen letters written by his brother that he believed were similar to the manifesto, and forensic linguists in the FBI were able to match these writings with the manifesto. Ted Kaczynski was arrested on April 3, 1996, in the mountains of Montana, where he had been living in a small cabin.

Although Kaczynski was diagnosed with paranoid schizophrenia, it was determined that he was competent to stand trial. He pleaded guilty before the case went to trial, however, and was sentenced to life in prison without the possibility of parole. He later made an attempt to withdraw his plea, but his request was denied and the court's decision was upheld on appeal.

Brion Sever

Further Reading

Arnold, Ron. *Ecoterror: The Violent Agenda to Save Nature—The World of the Unabomber.* Bellevue, Wash.: Free Enterprise Press, 1997. Argues that conservation and ecology movements have become increasingly dangerous and attempts to link the Unabomber's crimes to a radical environmental agenda.

Chase, Alston. *Harvard and the Unabomber: The Education of an American Terrorist.* New York: W. W. Norton, 2003. Discusses the societal and personal environment in which Kaczynski came of age to explore his motivations. Includes photographs.

Graysmith, Robert. *Unabomber: A Desire to Kill.* Washington, D.C.: Regnery, 1997. Presents a full account of Kaczynski's life and crimes.

Waits, Chris, and Dave Shors. *Unabomber: The Secret Life of Ted Kaczynski.* Helena, Mont.: Farcountry Press, 1999. Interesting work is coauthored by a man who was Kaczynski's neighbor in Montana for twenty-five years. Includes photographs.

See also: Bomb damage assessment; Bombings; Crime scene sketching and diagramming; Criminal personality profiling; Federal Bureau of Investigation; Forensic linguistics and stylistics; Handwriting analysis; Improvised explosive devices; Oklahoma City bombing; Typewriter analysis.

University of Tennessee Anthropological Research Facility

Date: Established in 1972

Identification: Facility at which forensic anthropologists conduct research on the decomposition of human remains and the identification of skeletal or badly decomposed bodies.

Significance: The Anthropological Research Facility at the University of Tennessee provides human identification services and death investigation training to arson investigators, county medical examiners, and various federal, state, and local law-enforcement agencies.

Dr. William M. Bass is credited with establishing the University of Tennessee's Anthropological Research Facility in 1972. Soon after Bass began working at the University of Tennessee in 1971, the state medical examiner asked him to do some consulting work on several death investigations. Although Bass had been trained as a forensic anthropologist, he had limited experience with cases involving human decomposition. In addition, little research had been conducted to document the stages of human decomposition. As a result, Bass and the faculty of the Anthropology Department at the University of Tennessee created the Anthropological Research Facility, now commonly known as the Body Farm, so that forensic anthropologists

could study postmortem decomposition of human remains.

The Body Farm is located on a three-acre tract of land close to the university's Knoxville campus; it hosts about 120 bodies at any given time. The Body Farm serves as a primary research facility for doctoral students in forensic sciences and as a training site for crime scene investigators, law-enforcement officers, morticians, dental experts, emergency medical personnel, decontamination experts, and anthropologists. Research at the Body Farm has helped forensic anthropologists to document the decomposition of the human body in relation to weather, water, indoor versus outdoor settings, clothing, insects, small mammals, and other variables.

The University of Tennessee also houses the nation's largest modern bone collection, the William M. Bass Donated Skeletal Collection. Data on the skeletal remains in the collection are entered into the University of Tennessee's Forensic Anthropology Data Bank. This database is the primary tool that forensic anthropologists across the United States use to determine age, sex, stature, ancestry, and other unique characteristics from skeletal remains.

The University of Tennessee's Forensic Anthropology Center inspired the formation of the National Forensic Academy (NFA), one of the leading law-enforcement investigation training centers in the United States. The NFA offers an intensive ten-week training program designed to educate law-enforcement agents in evidence identification, collection, and preservation. The primary goal of the NFA is to prepare law-enforcement officers to recognize crucial components of crime scenes and improve the process of evidence recovery and submission.

Kimberly D. Dodson

Further Reading

Bass, Bill, and Jon Jefferson. *Beyond the Body Farm: A Legendary Bone Detective Explores Murders, Mysteries, and the Revolution in Forensic Science.* New York: William Morrow, 2007.

_____. *Death's Acre: Inside the Legendary Forensic Lab the Body Farm Where the Dead Do Tell Tales.* New York: G. P. Putnam's Sons, 2003.

Hallcox, Jarrett, and Amy Welch. *Bodies We've Buried: Inside the National Forensic Academy, the World's Top CSI Training School.* New York: Berkley Books, 2006.

See also: Autopsies; Body farms; Crime laboratories; Crime scene documentation; Crime scene investigation; Decomposition of bodies; Evidence processing; Forensic anthropology; Forensic sculpture; Sex determination of remains; Skeletal analysis; Taphonomy.

U.S. Army Medical Research Institute of Infectious Diseases

Date: Founded on January 27, 1969
Identification: Federal medical research laboratory equipped to handle high-level hazardous biological materials.
Significance: With the increasing threat of both domestic and international bioterrorism, the U.S. Army Medical Research Institute of Infectious Diseases has been instrumental in training and providing diagnostic support to federal, state, and local law-enforcement agencies while maintaining its primary mission of finding medical ways to protect military personnel from biological weapons.

The U.S. Army Medical Research Institute of Infectious Diseases (USAMRIID), located at Fort Detrick in Frederick, Maryland, was established to perform basic and applied research on ways to prevent and treat biological threats to American military personnel. USAMRIID replaced the U.S. Army Medical Unit at Fort Detrick, which conducted research on offensive biological weapons. Offensive research was discontinued in 1969, and American stockpiles of biological weapons were destroyed in the early 1970's.

To contain dangerous and highly transmissible organisms safely, USAMRIID has a biosafety level 4 (BSL-4) laboratory and BSL-4 patient ward for treating infected individuals. BSL-4 is the most secure level of biohazard laboratory. Access to BSL-4 facilities is strictly limited, and complex engineering features of these facilities prevent the escape of hazardous material. USAMRIID also contains lower-security BSL-2 and BSL-3 laboratories. The facility employed about 750 scientists and support personnel in 2006, with the number expected to grow to 1,300 by the end of the decade.

USAMRIID is the lead laboratory for the U.S. Biological Defense Research Program, the primary mission of which is to protect and treat members of the armed forces who are exposed to infectious agents such as *Bacillus anthracis* (the bacterium that causes anthrax), *Clostridium botulinum* (the bacterium that causes botulism), and Ebola and other dangerous viruses. Some biological threats are exotic organisms that service members might encounter only when they are deployed to foreign lands, whereas others, such as anthrax, are potential agents of bioterrorism that could be released on either military or civilian populations.

Research at USAMRIID involves the development of vaccines against biohazards, establishment of treatment regimens for infected individuals, and development of decontamination procedures. The organization works with other institutions, including the U.S. Centers for Disease Control and Prevention and the World Health Organization, in conducting research and surveillance and in responding to biological threats. In developing vaccines, USAMRIID collaborates with private industry. Vaccine research often results in health benefits to civilians as well as to military personnel.

In the twenty-first century, USAMRIID has become increasingly involved in working with law-enforcement organizations on domestic bioterrorism. For example, in September, 2001, when letters containing anthrax spores were sent through the mail to several American media outlets and politicians, USAMRIID analyzed more than 31,000 samples of suspect material submitted by law-enforcement agencies as part of Operation Noble Eagle. Since 2001,

Nicknamed the "Eight Ball," this one-million-liter steel sphere was built at Fort Detrick in 1952 to measure the virulence of anthrax spores and other airborne bacteria. The device was not used after 1969, when the U.S. military began to dismantle its offensive biological weapons program. *(AP/Wide World Photos)*

USAMRIID has provided training for many thousands of law-enforcement agents in the handling of potential biohazards and decontamination of biocontaminated sites. The institute also provides diagnostic support for law-enforcement agencies across the United States.

Martiscia Davidson

Further Reading

Linden, Caree V. "Bio-warfare Detectives." *Soldiers Magazine*, May, 2005, 42-45.

Preston, Richard. *The Demon in the Freezer: A True Story.* New York: Random House, 2002.

Wheelis, Mark, Lajos Rózsa, and Malcolm Dando, eds. *Deadly Cultures: Biological Weapons Since 1945.* Cambridge, Mass.: Harvard University Press, 2006.

See also: Anthrax; Anthrax letter attacks; Biological weapon identification; Biological Weapons Convention of 1972; Centers for Disease Control and Prevention; Chemical Biological Incident Response Force, U.S.; Epidemiology.

ValuJet Flight 592 crash investigation

Date: Airliner crashed on May 11, 1996

The Event: On May 11, 1996, ValuJet Flight 592, en route from Miami International Airport to Hartsfield International Airport in Atlanta, Georgia, crashed minutes after takeoff. The plane dived into the Florida Everglades, complicating the investigation into the causes of the crash as well as recovery of the remains of the passengers and crew.

Significance: The forensic investigation into the crash of ValuJet Flight 592 focused on causes and effects. The ultimate impact of the disaster was a shift in the Federal Aviation Administration's mandate from "promotion" to "safety" in the civil aviation industry.

ValuJet was one of several discount airlines created during the reconfiguration of the passenger airline industry following the bankruptcy of such major carriers as Pan American World Airways, Eastern Airlines, and several others. On May 11, 1996, one of ValuJet's DC-9-32 aircraft was carrying 105 passengers and 5 crew members. Within minutes of takeoff, the copilot requested clearance from the control tower for the plane to return to Miami because of fire and smoke in the passenger cabin and cockpit. Soon after, however, the plane plunged into the Everglades, reportedly at an angle of some 75 degrees. The Miami-Dade County Police Department began search-and-rescue operations in the dangerous alligator- and snake-infested terrain, which was also covered with flammable aviation fuel, only to determine that there were no survivors.

Candalyn Kubeck, the first American female chief pilot to die in an accident, was in command of Flight 592. The plane, which was built in 1969, had been found to have several violations during ValuJet's two and one-half years of operations, but it had never been grounded.

The Investigation

The plane's flight data recorder, which measured eleven types of aircraft movement and control settings, was recovered on May 13. The voice recorder, or "black box," was retrieved on May 15. The cockpit tape had recorded a brief, unidentified sound some six minutes after takeoff and indicated that the crew had been informed of fire and smoke conditions in the passenger cabin about twenty-two seconds later. Eleven seconds after that, the copilot requested clearance to return to Miami, but the plane crashed four minutes later, barely 20 miles west of the airport.

The search for human remains and wreckage ended on June 10. Some 75 percent of the aircraft was recovered, and the Metro-Dade County medical officer reported that by then the remains of 36 of the 110 crash victims had been identified.

The radio message of fire and smoke on board was confirmed by the state of the wreckage. Suspicions focused on the nature of the cargo stored in the plane's forward hold, which included more than one hundred oxygen generators, the safety devices used in aircraft to provide oxygen to passengers when cabin pressure is lost. The investigators concluded that a chemical reaction inside one or more of the generators had ignited and in turn set fire to three aircraft tires also stored in the hold; from that point, the fire spread quickly. It was not clear, however, whether these conditions compromised the plane's controls first or whether the conflagration had disabled the crew.

The investigators also discovered that ValuJet, in the interest of keeping expenses down, had farmed out maintenance and loading operations to a subcontractor: SabreTech, based in Phoenix, Arizona. It was also found that ValuJet had exercised very little supervision over this subcontractor. The oxygen generators had not been properly packed, lacked safety caps, and were incorrectly labeled as empty rather than as hazardous cargo as they should have been, given that the chemical reaction that creates oxygen in such generators can also create heat of up to 500 degrees Fahrenheit. The fire that occurred on the plane was further evidenced by the fact that the recovered debris included a scorched seat frame, two heat-damaged oxygen generators, and a partially burned aircraft tire.

The Federal Aviation Administration (FAA) shut down ValuJet on June 17, 1996, for an indefinite period after an intensive thirty-day investigation had uncovered "serious deficiencies" in the airline's operations. These deficiencies included failure to perform repairs properly, failure to document repairs, flying aircraft known to have serious maintenance problems, and ignoring FAA safety directives. ValuJet was required to pay two million dollars as part of the cost of having its fleet reinspected. When ValuJet resumed operations several months later, it had merged with another company and was known as AirTran Airways. In December, 2001, SabreTech faced 220 charges of murder and manslaughter involving the 110 victims of ValuJet Flight 592. The case was settled out of court, however, with SabreTech pleading no contest and agreeing to donate one-half million dollars to charity.

Final NTSB Report

All of these and other matters contributing to the tragedy were brought out in the report of the National Transportation Safety Board (NTSB) of August 19, 1997. In the report, the NTSB criticized the FAA for failing to enforce its ten-year-old recommendation that smoke detectors and fire suppression systems be installed in all aircraft cargo holds. The NTSB also expressed doubt whether ValuJet's maintenance chief at the time of the crash, David Gentry, was properly qualified for his position and criticized ValuJet's lack of supervision over SabreTech.

Underlying the problems noted by the NTSB was the cozy relationship between the airline industry and the FAA as well as the U.S Department of Transportation (DOT) as a whole, which is responsible for the public's transportation safety. This is a general problem because often those responsible for overseeing airline industry matters themselves come from the ranks of the industry; this built-in conflict of interest makes the authorities sympathetic to the problems of the airlines in a highly competitive environment and thus unwilling to treat the airlines too harshly.

Politics also played a role. The airline industry is a significant financial contributor to the campaigns of many U.S. senators and members of Congress who sit on important committees dealing with civil aviation, a situation that leads to considerable reciprocal back-scratching. Thus, even crusaders among the regulators (such as Mary Schiavo, former inspector general of the U.S. Department of Transportation) were largely ignored when they charged that crucial negative reports on ValuJet's earlier violations preceding the crash of Flight 592 had

ValuJet's Older Fleet

The ValuJet budget airline was started in late 1993, and by the time of the crash of Flight 592 in May, 1996, it had increased its fleet to fifty-one airplanes, mostly used DC-9s, following spectacular growth and profitability. The average age of planes in ValuJet's fleet was more than twenty-six years, about fifteen years older than the aircraft of major U.S. carriers. The plane on Flight 592 had been built in 1969 and had returned to airports seven times in the previous two years because of safety problems.

According to experts, older aircraft are not necessarily less safe than newer aircraft, but older planes do require more rigorous maintenance. To a large extent, however, ValuJet's profitability rested on its ability to cut costs—and at times corners as well. To save money, instead of using its own maintenance workers, ValuJet had contracted with an outside firm, SabreTech, and did not provide appropriate supervision of SabreTech's work. One of the consequences of the crash of Flight 592 was that the Federal Aviation Administration began to investigate the performance of such relatively inexpensive subcontractors.

Robert Francis, vice chairman of the National Transportation Safety Board, stands amid some of the wreckage of ValuJet Flight 592 gathered in a hangar by investigators. *(AP/Wide World Photos)*

been suppressed so that the flying public would not be alarmed.

Consequences

On May 23, 1996, all passenger planes were forbidden to carry the kind of generator suspected of causing the ValuJet crash (although empty generators were exempted from the ban). Schiavo resigned from the Department of Transportation in July, 1996, and went public with her complaints. In part as a result of the crash of Flight 592, the U.S. Congress reworded the dual mandate with which the Federal Aviation Administration had originally been entrusted, namely, to promote civil aviation and ensure its safety. The FAA mandate became to promote safety as a priority but also to encourage the development of civil aviation.

Peter B. Heller

Further Reading

Calder, Simon. *No Frills: The Truth Behind the Low-Cost Revolution in the Skies*. London: Virgin Books, 2002. Describes the lack of adequate government controls that led to the crash of ValuJet 592.

Cobb, Roger W., and David M. Primo. *The Plane Truth: Airline Crashes, the Media, and Transportation Policy*. Washington, D.C.: Brookings Institution, 2003. Presents one of the most thorough accounts of the ValuJet disaster available.

Fallows, James. *Free Flight: From Airline Hell to a New Age of Travel*. New York: PublicAffairs, 2001. Explains the crash of ValuJet 592 as a sequence of misfortunes, each of which was individually so trivial that no one was able to foresee the deadly synergistic effect.

Krause, Shari Stamford. *Aircraft Safety: Accident Investigations, Analyses, and Applications*. 2d ed. New York: McGraw-Hill, 2003. Uses various case studies to discuss the numerous causes that underlie airplane accidents.

Schiavo, Mary, with Sabra Chartrand. *Flying Blind, Flying Safe*. New York: Avon Books, 1997. The former inspector general of the U.S. Department of Transportation lambastes the Federal Aviation Administration and former DOT employees for playing politics at the expense of the flying public's safety.

See also: Accident investigation and reconstruction; Airport security; Autopsies; Flight data recorders; National Transportation Safety Board.

Victimology

Definition: Study of victims of crimes and the nature of victimization.

Significance: Information about the victims of crimes forms an important element of criminal investigations. Any attempt to understand individual crimes is incomplete without an understanding of the victims.

The term "victimology" was coined by the German American psychiatrist Fredric Wertham (1895-1981) in 1949. In its broadest sense, the term applies to the study of all persons who suffer losses of any kind through their own acts or the acts of others or of nature. However, in the narrower sense in which victimology pertains to the forensic sciences, the term applies mainly to the study of victims of crimes perpetrated by others. Any given crime involves both a perpetrator and a victim. The study of perpetrators has long been a primary focus of criminology, and a large body of knowledge has been built in this area. By contrast, the scientific study of crime victims has received less attention. However, since the last decades of the twentieth century, interest in the roles played by victims of crime has greatly increased.

Possible reasons for the lag in the scientific study of victims compared with the study of crime and its perpetrators might include the perception that victims play a relatively insignificant role in crimes as well as the tendency among many people to fault the victims themselves for their misfortunes. Studies begun during the 1940's sought to establish typologies of victims. Two of the earliest researchers in this field, Hans von Hentig and Benjamin Mendelsohn, are considered the founders of victimology as a subdiscipline.

Mendelsohn, an attorney who began his research during the 1950's, discovered in the interrogations of crime victims and other witnesses he conducted while preparing his cases that interpersonal relationships often existed between victims and offenders. From that discovery, he developed a six-stage classification of victims. His categories ranged from completely innocent victims to those who were more guilty than the alleged offenders; he also described what he called "pretend victims."

Studies of victimology during the 1970's began considering the levels of responsibility of victims in the process of their victimization. Stephan Schafer and L. A. Curtis considered what they called functional responsibilities of the victim. These ranged from no responsibility

to total responsibility. During the 1980's, Benjamin Mendelsohn expanded on his earlier work with his general victimology theory, which developed the concepts of self-victimization, social victimization, and technological victimization.

Andrew Karmen authored the definition used in modern victimology, which encompasses the crimes, potential victim-offender relationships, victim experiences with the justice system, and other social groups within victims' communities. The major omission of Karmen's definition is the study of the victim. Advocation of a focus on the victim is one of the areas of controversy within victimology.

Evolution of Victim Responsibilities

In primitive human societies, members who were victimized by others were generally expected to take responsibility for exacting revenge and recovering whatever they may have lost. As the victims themselves were responsible for achieving justice, their societies generally provided neither rules for protection of their members nor officials to enforce rules. When victims needed help in exacting revenge and recovering their losses they turned to their relatives, fellow clan members, or fellow tribesmen, depending on the contexts of the situations.

In cases of severe crimes, blood feuds or family feuds often developed. Such feuds could last for long periods and were difficult to terminate. As societies developed more complex institutions of government, they generally worked to prevent feuds by formalizing rules for restitution. An example can be seen in the Code of Hammurabi; this set of laws, issued by Hammurabi during his reign as king of Babylon, from approximately 1792 to 1750 B.C.E., changed the role of victims by making the state responsible for administering punishments to perpetrators and restoring losses to victims. During medieval Europe's age of feudal barons and monarchs, crimes came to be defined as acts against the state. Consequently, the state itself received whatever compensation or restitution was taken from perpetrators of crimes. The victims of the crimes then became witnesses for the state.

During the early colonial era in North America, victims of crimes were made responsible for investigations and had to pay for the warrants that sheriffs needed to make arrests. Moreover, the victims were also responsible for procuring attorneys to prosecute the accused. After the United States achieved its independence and adopted the U.S. Constitution (1789) and the Bill of Rights (1791), justice systems changed considerably. Crimes were redefined as acts against the state (in the broad sense), which represented its citizens, and the state itself became the victim. State and local governments established offices of public prosecutors, who acted on the behalf of government and society. This transformation gave government the incentive to create investigative bodies within law-enforcement agencies and helped to launch the modern forensic sciences needed by those bodies.

Meanwhile, public prosecutors assumed responsibility for determining what charges should be levied against persons accused of committing crimes. Prosecutors also determined the sanctions and punishments that should be sought in criminal cases. These changes left the actual victims of the crimes with the responsibility only to file formal complaints with police. The police, in turn, were responsible for investigating complaints, finding and analyzing evidence, and forwarding their findings to the prosecutors. Victims were then left to become witnesses in whatever criminal prosecutions developed.

Victim Movements

During the 1960's, concepts of victim rights again changed, along with the rise of new social movements. These changes began with the Civil Rights movement, an amorphous nonviolent mass movement calling attention to the historical victimization of members of ethnic and racial minorities in the United States. This movement was soon followed by the anti-Vietnam War movement, which revealed that political and governmental systems and controls could be changed by common citizens. The third major movement was the women's liberation movement, which addressed the victimization of people based on their gender. It was followed by the law-and-order movement, the first to draw attention to victims of crime.

Other developments during the 1960's also affected victims of crime. For example, the state of California established one of the earliest victims' compensation programs. During the 1970's, volunteer programs began arising to aid victims of domestic violence, rape, and

The Victims of Crime Act

Passed into law on October 12, 1984, this federal legislation established the Crime Victims Fund to help finance state compensation programs as well as assist victims of federal crimes. Demonstrating the federal commitment to assist crime victims, the Victims of Crime Act (VOCA) quickly became a key component in the funding of programs throughout the United States.

During the early 1980's, President Ronald Reagan supported the growing movement for the right of crime victims to receive fair treatment. In 1981, he proclaimed an annual National Victims of Crime Week. In April, 1982, he established the President's Task Force on Victims of Crime, which made sixty-eight recommendations to help victims. During the following October, he signed the Victim and Witness Protection Act, which increased penalties on those who tried to intimidate victims or witnesses, mandated restitution to victims from offenders, and required the consideration of victim impact statements at sentencing in federal criminal trials.

The Victims of Crime Act of 1984 established the Crime Victims Fund, which at first had a cap of $100 million per year. Each state was to receive at least $100,000, and 5 percent of the fund would go to victims of federal crimes. Rather than coming from taxpayers, revenues for the fund are obtained from fines, penalty fees, forfeitures of bail bonds, and literary profits from convicted offenders. By 1988, the fund was supporting fifteen hundred programs a year, and its maximum was increased to $150 million. VOCA was well received by the American public, and the law's success encouraged states to do more to assist victims.

Thomas T. Lewis

other crimes through the creation of safe houses. As these efforts became better organized, national associations arose in what might be called a movement for victims' rights. During the early 1980's, President Ronald Reagan responded to this movement by ordering the creation of the President's Task Force on Victims of Crime. This significant development was followed by passage of the federal Victims of Crime Act of 1984, which created a system for funding compensation paid to victims of crime.

Assessing Victimization

Scientific studies of victims must be conducted without bias or prejudgments. It is important that researchers examine tangible evidence when attempting to determine the extent to which victims are responsible for their own victimization. The roles of victims may range from no responsibility to shared responsibility to provocation. Without sufficient information about the victims' roles, analyses of crimes are incomplete and may possibly be in error.

The primary sources for measuring crime and victimization are the Federal Bureau of Investigation's (FBI) Uniform Crime Report (UCR), the National Incident-Based Reporting System (NIBRS), and the U.S. Bureau of Justice Statistics' National Crime Victimization Survey (NCVS). The UCR is an annual crime report that has been prepared by the FBI since 1930. Its value to studies of victimization is limited by its emphasis on street crimes reported by law enforcement. By contrast, the NIBRS records victim information for many offenses. Although the NCVS is administered nationally and seeks to cover both reported and unreported crimes and victimizations, its data include only persons at least twelve years of age and exclude many persons who are in military service or residents of some institutions.

The scientific study of victims has shown that crime is not a random event. If it were, then it would affect all persons, regardless of their gender, race, ethnicity, socioeconomic class, or location. Studies of victims have shown that the most frequently victimized category of persons comprises male adolescents who are members of racial and ethnic minorities and live in eco-

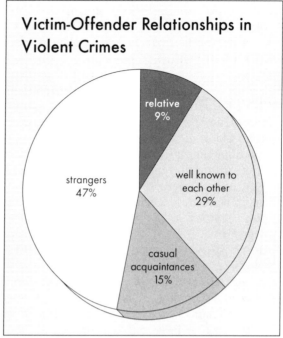

Source: U.S. Bureau of Justice Statistics, *Criminal Victimization.* Percentages reflect data for all violent crimes reported in the United States in 2002.

nomically depressed urban areas. Studies have shown that many victims and perpetrators of crimes share the same characteristics and are known to one another. These findings challenge the often-presented image of crime as an interracial phenomenon; rather, it is more often intraracial.

Richard L. McWhorter

Further Reading

Carney, Thomas P. *Practical Investigation of Sex Crimes: A Strategic and Operational Approach.* Boca Raton, Fla.: CRC Press, 2003. A former commanding officer of the Manhattan Special Victims Squad presents case histories to illustrate the skills needed to investigate sex crimes effectively.

Cohen, Lawrence E., and Marcus Felson. "Social Change and Crime Rate Trends: A Routine Activity Approach." *American Sociological Review* 44 (1979): 588-608. Explains how people's everyday behaviors can increase their likelihood of becoming crime victims.

Curtis, L. A. *Criminal Violence: National Patterns and Behavior.* Lexington, Mass.: D. C. Heath, 1974. Provides an early discussion into the function of victim responsibilities.

Doerner, W. G., and S. P. Lab. *Victimology.* 4th ed. Dayton, Ohio: Anderson, 2005. Popular survey text provides an introduction to the field of victimology, with a focus on the possible mental health disorders resulting from different types of criminal victimization.

Hentig, Hans von. *The Criminal and His Victim: Studies in the Sociobiology of Crime.* New Haven, Conn.: Yale University Press, 1948. Early discussion by a father of victimology presents a typology of victims.

Karmen, Andrew. *Crime Victims: An Introduction to Victimology.* Belmont, Calif.: Wadsworth/Thomson Learning, 2001. Introductory text focuses on victims' rights and functions in the American criminal justice system.

Mendelsohn, Benjamin. "Victimology and Contemporary Society's Trends." *Victimology* 1 (1976): 8-28. Essay by an early pioneer in victimology discusses a wide range of issues in the field.

Miethe, T. D., R. C. McCorkle, and S. J. Listwan. *Crime Profiles: The Anatomy of Dangerous Persons, Places, and Situations.* 3d ed. Los Angeles: Roxbury, 2006. Discusses the most frequent offender, victim, and situational characteristics of seven major types of crimes and presents some possible theoretical explanations.

Schafer, Stephan. *The Victim and His Criminal: A Study in Functional Responsibility.* New York: Random House, 1968. Considers the interaction between victim and criminal in a typology of victim precipitation.

See also: Criminology; Cyberstalking; Defensive wounds; *Diagnostic and Statistical Manual of Mental Disorders*; Forensic psychology; Living forensics; Rape; Rape kit; Ritual killing; Sexual predation characteristics.

Violent sexual predator statutes

Definition: Laws that prevent the release of dangerous sex offenders into the community after they complete their prison sentences, instead requiring them to be committed to secure psychiatric facilities.

Significance: Violent sexual predator statutes have been a source of legal controversy because they extend the confinement of offenders who have already served their maximum sentences. These laws have also been a source of controversy among mental health professionals who question the indefinite hospitalization of offenders for whom no effective treatments are available.

In 1990, in response to the rape and sexual mutilation of a six-year-old boy by a formerly incarcerated sex offender, Washington State enacted the Community Protection Act (CPA). Regarded as the first modern violent sexual predator statute, the CPA permits prosecutors to initiate civil commitment proceedings against certain types of sex offenders. Incarcerated sex offenders who are found to have mental disorders that place them at risk to commit additional sex offenses in the future can be involuntarily committed to secure psychiatric facilities after they complete their prison sentences. Those who are committed to psychiatric facilities can be released from those facilities only when psychiatric professionals find that they no longer pose any danger to the community.

Several U.S. states already had passed laws that were similar to Washington State's CPA, but the earlier laws had been repealed or fallen into disuse. After enactment of the CPA, however, more than one dozen states and the District of Columbia passed violent sexual predator statutes modeled on the CPA. These laws differ in specific provisions from state to state, but they have two basic characteristics in common: the application of the civil commitment process to sex offenders and the designation of certain sex offenders as violent sexual predators.

Common Characteristics

Violent sexual predator statutes use the civil commitment process to continue to confine sex offenders after they have completed their prison sentences. Civil commitment has traditionally been used in the involuntary hospitalization of individuals who are at imminent risk to hurt themselves or others owing to severe mental disorders such as major depression, schizophrenia, or bipolar disorder. For example, individuals who are actively considering suicide can be civilly committed to mental health facilities until they are sufficiently recovered that they no longer pose an immediate risk to themselves. Civil commitment has traditionally been used to confine persons only briefly, providing safety to them and to society until their crises have passed and their conditions have stabilized.

Violent sexual predator statutes are an unusual application of the civil commitment process. Most sex offenders do not have severe mental disorders, nor do they have to be diagnosed with such disorders in order to be civilly committed under existing violent sexual predator statutes. Violent sexual predator statutes do not require offenders to be at imminent risk of harming others, nor are the periods of commitment intended to be brief. Instead, violent sexual predator statutes are meant to confine offenders who are likely to pose long-term risks to the community, and the periods of confinement are indefinite.

State laws vary in their definitions of which sex offenders are eligible for civil commitment and in the processes by which they assign the status of violent sexual predator to imprisoned offenders. In most states, to be designated as violent sexual predators, offenders must have committed violent sexual offenses against strangers (rather than friends or family members) and must be judged to have some kind of mental abormality or personality disorder that makes it likely they will commit similar offenses in the future.

Typically, a prosecutor must initiate civil commitment proceedings against an offender while the offender is still incarcer-ated. This process begins with a probable cause hearing. If probable cause is established, the offender undergoes a psychiatric evaluation; that is, mental health professionals are called upon to render opinions as to whether or not the offender meets the definition of a violent sexual predator as specified in the statute. If the evaluation indicates that the offender meets the definition, the case moves to a jury trial, where the offender has an opportunity to mount a defense and demonstrate that he or she is not a violent sexual predator. If the jury finds that the offender should be designated a violent sexual predator, the offender is transferred to a secure psychiatric facility upon completion of his or her original prison sentence. The period of confinement is not specified. The offender can petition for release when mental health professionals judge that the offender is no longer a danger to the community.

U.S. States Holding Persons Under Violent Sexual Predator Laws, 2006

State	Number Held
Arizona	414
California	558
Florida	942
Illinois	307
Iowa	69
Kansas	161
Massachusetts	121
Minnesota	342
Missouri	143
Nebraska	18
New Jersey	342
North Dakota	75
Pennsylvania	12
South Carolina	119
Texas	69
Virginia	37
Washington	305
Wisconsin	500
Total	4,534

Source: Data from Kathy Gookin, *Comparison of State Laws Authorizing Involuntary Commitment of Sexually Violent Predators: 2006 Update.* Olympia: Washington State Institute for Public Policy, August, 2007.

Legal Challenges

Since the inception of violent sexual predator statutes, critics have questioned the constitutionality of these measures. The issue was first heard before the U.S. Supreme Court in *Kansas v. Hendricks*. Hendricks, a convicted child molester, was the first offender confined in Kansas under that state's violent sexual predator statute. He challenged his psychiatric confinement, arguing that it amounted to a second incarceration for his sex offense, which would be a violation of the prohibition against double jeopardy found in the Fifth Amendment to the U.S. Constitution. The Supreme Court ruled against Hendricks in 1997, holding that violent sexual predator statutes do not qualify as punishment because their purpose is not to punish the offender but rather to protect the public. The case established the constitutionality of existing violent sexual predator statutes and paved the way for the enactment of such statutes in states where they were being considered.

A second ruling by the Supreme Court regarding violent sexual predator statutes, *Kansas v. Crane*, concerned the degree to which offenders must be unable to control their sexual behavior in order to be deemed violent sexual predators. Crane, a convicted sex offender confined under the Kansas statute, argued that the state had not successfully demonstrated that he was incapable of controlling his illegal sexual behavior. The Court ruled against Crane in 2002, holding that the state does not have to demonstrate that offenders are incapable of control; rather, the state need only demonstrate that offenders have serious difficulty controlling their illegal sexual behavior. This lower threshold for demonstrating offenders' dangerousness may make successful prosecution of violent sexual predator cases easier.

Challenges for Mental Health Professionals

The implementation of violent sexual predator statutes poses challenges to the mental health professionals who must evaluate sex offenders for their civil commitment trials and who must treat those offenders later designated as violent sexual predators. First, "violent sexual predator" is a legal term, not a diagnosable mental disorder, so no standard set of psychiatric signs and symptoms exists for mental health professional to assess while conducting an evaluation for civil commitment. Second, evaluating whether or not a sex offender should be designated a violent sexual predator requires the mental health professional to address the future dangerousness of the offender. Predicting the future actions of individuals with accuracy is difficult, and the prediction of dangerous actions that occur infrequently, such as sexual offenses, is especially difficult. Third, treating sex offenders committed under violent predator statutes is complicated by the fact that no psychotherapy has been scientifically demonstrated to treat this group of offenders effectively. Furthermore, offenders confined under violent sexual predator statutes are entitled to refuse treatment, but they still cannot be released until they are judged to pose no risk to the community.

Damon Mitchell

Further Reading

La Fond, John Q. *Preventing Sexual Violence: How Society Should Cope with Sex Offenders.* Washington, D.C.: American Psychological Association, 2005. Provides an overview and analysis of strategies used to manage sex offenders, including violent sexual predator statutes.

Mercado, Cynthia C., Robert F. Schopp, and Brian H. Bornstein. "Evaluating Sex Offenders Under Sexually Violent Predator Laws: How Might Mental Health Professionals Conceptualize the Notion of Volitional Impairment?" *Aggression and Violent Behavior* 10 (2005): 289-309. Presents an analysis of the impact of *Kansas v. Hendricks* and *Kansas v. Crane* on psychological evaluations conducted for violent sexual predator hearings.

Prentky, Robert A., Eric S. Janus, and Michael S. Seto, eds. *Sexually Coercive Behavior: Understanding and Management.* New York: New York Academy of Sciences, 2003. Collection of research articles discusses the reasons for sex offending and the treatment and assessment of sex offenders. Also analyzes various policies and strategies used to manage sex offenders.

Terry, Karen J. *Sexual Offenses and Offenders: Theory, Practice, and Policy.* Belmont, Calif.: Wadsworth, 2006. Textbook provides overviews of sex offender typology and treatment as well as discussion of public policies related to sex offending.

Winick, Bruce J., and John Q. La Fond, eds. *Protecting Society from Sexually Dangerous Offenders: Law, Justice, and Therapy.* Washington, D.C.: American Psychological Association, 2003. Collection presents legal and psychiatric analyses of the strategies and laws used to manage sex offenders, including violent sexual predator statutes.

See also: Antianxiety agents; Forensic psychiatry; Forensic psychology; Internet tracking and tracing; Megan's Law; Rape; Sexual predation characteristics.

Viral biology

Definition: Subspecialty of biology that focuses on viruses, tiny nonliving microbes that serve as receptacles for nucleic acids (RNA or DNA) and are dependent on prokaryotic or eukaryotic hosts for replication.

Significance: Viral biologists have knowledge of the structure, genetics, and replication of viruses as well as the skills needed to identify associated viral pathology. These skills are becoming increasingly significant to forensic science, given growing threats of biocrime, acts of bioterrorism, and emerging and reemerging viral diseases. The domains of viral biology and forensic science appear to overlap in the areas of biosecurity and epidemiology of infectious disease.

In contrast to the epidemiological and diagnostic requirements of public health and private practice, respectively, microbial forensics (the

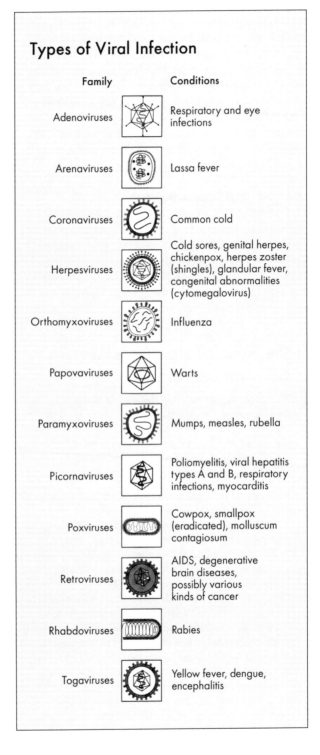

Types of Viral Infection

Family		Conditions
Adenoviruses		Respiratory and eye infections
Arenaviruses		Lassa fever
Coronaviruses		Common cold
Herpesviruses		Cold sores, genital herpes, chickenpox, herpes zoster (shingles), glandular fever, congenital abnormalities (cytomegalovirus)
Orthomyxoviruses		Influenza
Papovaviruses		Warts
Paramyxoviruses		Mumps, measles, rubella
Picornaviruses		Poliomyelitis, viral hepatitis types A and B, respiratory infections, myocarditis
Poxviruses		Cowpox, smallpox (eradicated), molluscum contagiosum
Retroviruses		AIDS, degenerative brain diseases, possibly various kinds of cancer
Rhabdoviruses		Rabies
Togaviruses		Yellow fever, dengue, encephalitis

branch of forensic science that deals with microorganisms) demands more detailed characterization of microbes in order to determine the origins of pathogens or toxins (identification) and who or what organizations were responsible for their dissemination (attribution). Microbial forensic scientists use genetic and nongenetic assays to attribute a source or to discount one and to determine whether an event occurred naturally (for example, through the spread of an infectious disease) or as the result of an inadvertent release of a toxin or pathogen, a biocrime, or an act of bioterrorism.

Methods and Technologies

Forensic microbiological investigations are essentially similar to standard forensic investigations in that they involve crime scene investigation, attention to chain of custody, and strict adherence to protocols for evidence collection, preservation, and shipping. The evidence sam-

ples analyzed in relation to a suspected biocrime or act of bioterrorism may include liquids, powders, and organic matter as well as fingerprints, hair, and fibers. Given that the goal is to provide physical evidence for use in legal proceedings, an effective microbial forensics program mandates validation of each step in the investigation, from sample collection to interpretation of results, in order to guarantee that quality-assurance practices are being implemented.

In 1999, when West Nile virus disease was found in the state of New York, apparently the first time it had occurred in the United States, authorities worried that a biocrime had been committed. Microbial forensic techniques helped scientists determine that the emerging West Nile virus disease had been spread by mosquitoes and was a natural occurrence. The technologies scientists use in such cases include polymerase chain reaction (PCR) assays, which amplify samples, and sequencing to identify pathogens. Information obtained from PCR and sequencing of nucleic acids may then be evaluated through phylogenetic studies, which are used to infer relationships between organisms and may help characterize novel viral strains, as was demonstrated in 1999 when a new strain of the human immunodeficiency virus (HIV) was identified in Africa.

Phylogenetic studies may also help determine whether a viral strain was introduced through negligent or criminal action. For example, forensic scientists were able to identify the source of an HIV infection in a case of sexual abuse of a child even after several years had passed; they compared the nucleotide sequences of the child with those of her abuser and found that the strain of HIV

The National Biodefense Analysis and Countermeasures Center

The U.S. Department of Homeland Security's National Biodefense Analysis and Countermeasures Center (NBACC), created after the anthrax letter attacks perpetrated in the eastern United States in the fall of 2001, provides biosafety level 4 (BSL-4) laboratory space for biological threat characterization and bioforensic research. The NBACC describes its primary research areas as follows:

Biological Threat Characterization Center (BTCC) conducts studies and laboratory experiments to
- better understand current and future biological threats,
- assess vulnerabilities to the nation, and
- determine potential impacts to guide the development of countermeasures against these threats.

As mandated by Presidential Directive "Biodefense for the 21st Century," the BTCC will prepare a biennial risk assessment report comparing the risk from various biothreat agents.

National Bioforensic Analysis Center (NBFAC) conducts bioforensic analysis of evidence from biocrimes and terrorism to
- attain a "biological fingerprint" to identify perpetrators and
- determine the origin and method of attack.

NBFAC is designated in "Biodefense for the 21st Century" to be the lead federal facility to conduct and facilitate the technical forensic analysis and interpretation of materials recovered following a biological attack in support of the appropriate lead federal agency.

Biodefense Knowledge Center (BKC) supports collaboration and data sharing among policy makers, scientists, first responders, and other stakeholders requiring timely and authoritative biodefense information.

was the same. (Deoxyribonucleic acid, or DNA, and ribonucleic acid, or RNA, are composed of nucleotides.) Previously, a group of hemophiliac patients who had received pooled blood plasma and were later infected with HIV were shown to have been infected from the same source—that is, contaminated plasma. In another case, genetic analysis showed that a New Jersey dentist and five of his patients harbored the same strain of HIV, indicating that the dentist was the source of the infection.

Bioterrorism and Emerging Viral Diseases

Advances in sanitation, the discovery of vaccines for diseases such as smallpox, and, in the early 1940's, the development of penicillin as an antibiotic resulted in growing optimism in the public health community that infectious disease—the number one killer worldwide—would soon be controlled. In the late twentieth century, however, the world began to experience the greatest pandemic of all time, that of HIV and acquired immunodeficiency syndrome (AIDS). Within less than three decades, approximately fifty million persons had been infected worldwide and twenty million were dead, and HIV/AIDS, along with its cohort, tuberculosis, threatens to kill hundreds of millions more. Molecular epidemiologists are focusing on understanding drug-resistant strains of HIV and tuberculosis so that they can discover ways to combat them. Virologists are studying the blood from survivors of the catastrophic influenza epidemic of 1918 to understand why the flu was so deadly and to prepare for the possibility of another pandemic caused by the avian influenza virus H5N1.

At no time in history has the dilemma of the application of science for either the good or the detriment of humankind been more apparent as the specters of bioterrorism and emerging viral diseases underscore the need for biosecurity and biosurveillance around the world. (Emerging viral diseases may be caused by previously unknown viruses or by known viruses that have newly appeared or reappeared in particular locales or populations or have mutated, become drug-resistant strains, or developed new modes of transmission.) The National Institute of Allergy and Infectious Diseases (NIAID) has cate-

gorized agents responsible for the emergence and reemergence of highly virulent and contagious infectious viral diseases across the globe and has classified a host of pathogens as "agents with bioterrorism potential," including Ebola and Marburg hemorrhagic viruses, the smallpox virus and related pox viruses, hantaviruses, Lassa virus, and bacteria such as *Bacillus anthracis* (which causes anthrax) and *Yersinia pestis* (which causes plague), all of which may be weaponized.

The Laboratory Response Network—involving the Centers for Disease Control and Prevention (CDC), the Association of Public Health Laboratories, and the Federal Bureau of Investigation (FBI), with links to laboratories across the United States—was created specifically to respond to acts of bioterrorism and outbreaks of emerging infectious disease. In 2003, the U.S. Department of Homeland Security launched the National Bioforensic Analysis Center to serve as a resource for the analysis of microbial evidence derived from acts of bioterrorism.

Cynthia Racer

Further Reading

Budowle, Bruce, et al. "Quality Sample Collection, Handling, and Preservation for an Effective Microbial Forensics Program." *Applied and Environmental Microbiology* 72 (October, 2006): 6431-6438. Discusses the collection and preservation techniques required for a successful microbial forensic investigation and emphasizes the interactions among various governmental agencies in such an investigation.

Budowle, Bruce, Randall Murch, and Ranajit Chakraborty. "Microbial Forensics: The Next Forensic Challenge." *International Journal of Legal Medicine* 119 (November, 2005): 317-330. Provides a comprehensive review of the subfield of microbial forensics, including discussion of bioterrorism and biocrime, the pathogenic organisms used in these crimes, and the techniques employed to characterize them.

Carter, John B., and Venetia A. Saunders. *Virology: Principles and Applications.* Hoboken, N.J.: John Wiley & Sons, 2007. Presents a clear and accessible introduction to virology, explaining virus structure, replication, and genetics.

Ellison, D. Hank. *Handbook of Chemical and Biological Warfare Agents.* 2d ed. Boca Raton, Fla.: CRC Press, 2007. Excellent reference source for information on agents used in chemical and biological warfare, including blood agents.

Lederberg, Joshua, ed. *Biological Weapons: Limiting the Threat.* Cambridge, Mass.: MIT Press, 1999. Examines the dangers posed by biological weapons as well as the ways in which the United States has tried to decrease those dangers.

Nathanson, Neal. *Viral Pathogenesis and Immunity.* 2d ed. Burlington, Mass.: Elsevier Academic Press, 2007. Covers the essentials of viral biology: pathogenesis and host responses to viral infections as well as virus-host interactions.

See also: Anthrax; Anthrax letter attacks; Biological warfare diagnosis; Biological weapon identification; Biological Weapons Convention of 1972; Biotoxins; Ebola virus; Epidemiology; Hantavirus; Hemorrhagic fevers; Nipah virus; Pathogen genomic sequencing; Smallpox.

Voice alteration. *See* Electronic voice alteration

Voiceprints

Definition: Visual representations of individuals' voices based on biometric measurements.

Significance: Law-enforcement investigators use voiceprint analysis to determine the likelihood that particular individuals are the persons speaking in recorded conversations. In the United States, the admissibility of voiceprints as evidence varies from state to state.

The principle underlying the use of voiceprints, also called sound spectrograms, for identification is that each individual has a unique voice; that is, each person's voice has particular characteristics that allow the voice to be distinguished from every other voice. Each person's voice is affected by the size and shape of the person's vocal cords, mouth, throat, teeth, and nasal cavity. In addition, voice uniqueness derives from the movement of the tongue, lips, and jaw muscles during speech. When a speaker's voice is analyzed by an instrument known as a sound spectrograph, which maps the voice onto a graph to produce a visual representation, the resulting voiceprint is, according to proponents of the technology, as unique as a fingerprint. This technology is one of several that has been used to authenticate the claim that Osama Bin Laden is the speaker on audiotapes released by al-Qaeda.

History

In 1941, Bell Telephone Laboratories in New Jersey developed the sound spectrograph, a device that analyzes sound frequencies and wavelengths and creates visual records of sounds in the form of graphs. Although intelligence agencies were interested in the technology as a way to identify enemy agents from recorded telephone conversations, progress toward the identification of individual speakers was slow until the early 1960's. At that time, police in New York City became interested in using voice analysis to assist in identifying a caller who was repeatedly phoning in bomb threats to airlines. They asked Lawrence Kersta, a Bell Labs engineer, to determine whether a comparison of sound spectrograms, which Kersta later called voiceprints, could be used to identify a suspect positively as the caller. Kersta experimented with visual pattern matching of voiceprints and concluded that when an unknown voiceprint was compared with that of a known speaker, the likelihood of a match could be determined with more than 99 percent accuracy.

Kersta's results were not universally accepted, and other researchers found a lower degree of accuracy, but in the early 1970's, law-enforcement agencies began trying to enter voiceprints into evidence in criminal cases.

Some courts accepted voiceprint evidence; others threw it out on the grounds that the technology had not been adequately proven. Although the American Board of Recorded Evidence, an advisory board of the American College of Forensic Examiners, published standards in 1997 for the comparison of voice samples and certifies speaker identification examiners, voiceprint evidence is not uniformly admissible in American courts.

Controversies Surrounding Voiceprint Evidence

From the beginning, voiceprint evidence has been a topic of controversy. Although Kersta claimed almost perfect accuracy in identifying speakers, his experiments were performed under ideal conditions with high school girls as subjects. Other experimenters, working under different, less ideal conditions, reported lower accuracy rates. Currently, the results of voiceprint comparisons are classified, based on the numbers of similarities in the samples, as positive identification, probable identification, positive elimination, probable elimination, or unable to determine. In a study of two thousand forensic voiceprints, the Federal Bureau of Investigation (FBI) found 0.31 percent false identifications and 0.53 percent false eliminations.

Among the questions that have plagued voiceprint evidence are whether voiceprints of the same person change over time and whether a voice can be disguised to fool the spectrograph. Studies have shown quite conclusively that although a person's voice may sound different to listeners as the person ages, the frequency and wavelength of the sound remains essentially unchanged. Disguising or distorting the voice, however, can make voiceprint comparison invalid. A trained examiner will recognize that one voice sample has been artificially altered, and this may force an "unable to determine" finding. Courts have ruled that it is not a violation of suspects' rights to compel them to provide acceptable voice samples.

Standards and Training

Certain conditions must be met for the results of voiceprint comparisons to be considered valid. Several minutes of speech from both the known speaker and the unknown speaker must be available for analysis. Ideally, the samples should contain many of the same words and phrases. The style of speech in the samples must be similar—for example, one cannot be shouted and the other whispered. Relaxed, normal conversation produces the most accurate results. The quality of both recordings must be good (for instance, clear and free of excessive background noise). In addition, the analyst must be a trained voiceprint technician. The analyst should make both a visual comparison of the voiceprints and an auditory comparison of the samples to listen for vocal tics, phrasing, and accent similarities and differences.

Minimum training for a voiceprint technician involves completing a two- to four-week course, performing a minimum of one hundred voice comparisons under the direct supervision of an expert, and passing an examination given by experts in the field. Voiceprint technicians who serve as expert witnesses often have additional training, including academic research in forensic linguistics or forensic phonetics. The International Association of Forensic Linguists and the International Association of Forensic Phonetics and Acoustics publish the *International Journal of Speech Language and the Law*, which presents research findings and reports on legal cases involving speaker identification through voice samples.

Martiscia Davidson

Further Reading

Dornman, Andy. "Biometrics Becomes a Commodity." *IT Architect*, February 1, 2006, 46. Discusses the current state of biometric technology, including fingerprints and voiceprints.

"Forensic Science, No Consensus." *Issues in Science and Technology* 20 (Winter, 2004): 5-9. Forum with contributions by various scholars analyzes the problems associated with forensic laboratory work, including voiceprint analysis.

Hollien, Harry. *Forensic Voice Identification*. San Diego, Calif.: Academic Press, 2002. Covers the science behind voice identification and gives practical information on speech recordings, voice stress analysis, and speaker identification.

James, Stuart H., and Jon J. Nordby, eds. *Forensic Science: An Introduction to Scientific and Investigative Techniques.* 2d ed. Boca Raton, Fla.: CRC Press, 2005. Basic introductory text presents information on all aspects of forensic science, including voice identification techniques.

Tanner, Dennis C. *Medical-Legal and Forensic Aspects of Communication Disorders, Voice Prints, and Speaker Profiling.* Tucson, Ariz.: Lawyers & Judges Publishing, 2007. An expert in the field of speech forensics details the science of speech production and how voice identification can be used in both routine situations and those involving individuals with accents, speech disorders, or intoxication.

See also: Biometric identification systems; Electronic voice alteration; Forensic linguistics and stylistics; *Frye v. United States.*

W

Water purity. *See* Air and water purity

Wildlife forensics

Definition: Analysis of animal tissues in addition to such traditional forensic evidence as fingerprints associated with wildlife poaching and smuggling.

Significance: Crimes committed against wildlife might remain unsolved without forensic evidence to prove connections among animal victims, human hunters, and scenes where animals were slain or captured. Scientific proof from bloodstains, antlers, and animal by-products enables law-enforcement personnel to identify and seek legal prosecution of suspects in crimes involving animals.

Forensic examination of wildlife-related evidence became crucial during the late twentieth century because of increased governmental awareness worldwide of the poaching and smuggling of endangered and protected species. As demand for exotic pets and animal goods led wildlife traders to expand their trafficking activities and populations of some species dwindled, the 1973 Convention on International Trade in Endangered Species of Wild Fauna and Flora (CITES) established uniform criteria for global enforcement of laws protecting vulnerable species. The United States enforced the Endangered Species Act of 1973 and forbade importation of Asian elephant ivory beginning in 1976 and African elephant ivory starting in 1989. Scholarly articles featuring wildlife forensics appeared in journals such as *Forensic Science International* and in conference proceedings.

Establishing Resources

Before the National Fish and Wildlife Forensics Laboratory was established in 1989, approximately 90 percent of wildlife poachers in the United States were not punished because evidence of their crimes was unavailable unless game wardens had witnessed their actions. Law-enforcement personnel needed scientific evidence that they could present in court if they were going to be able to prosecute crimes committed against wildlife. Most forensics laboratories did not pursue investigations related to wildlife crimes.

In 1979, the U.S. Fish and Wildlife Service hired Ken Goddard to serve as the agency's chief forensic investigator. Goddard, a biochemist who had worked in law-enforcement crime laboratories, applied his experience and expertise to the apprehension of poachers. He requested that the U.S. government establish a wildlife forensics laboratory so that he could perform his work more effectively. The result, the National Fish and Wildlife Forensics Laboratory in Ashland, Oregon, became the sole laboratory investigating wildlife crimes in the United States and globally.

Serving as director of the laboratory, Goddard recruited a staff of scientists who specialized in morphology, pathology, criminalistics, and toxicology. Differentiating between police forensic work, which focuses on one species, and wildlife forensic investigations, which may involve thousands of species, the National Fish and Wildlife Forensics Laboratory assembled sophisticated technology and a diverse collection of specimens, including skeletons, feathers, and blood, to aid in its work of identifying wildlife victims, particularly when evidence consists of only fragments or bloodstains. The laboratory also established a DNA (deoxyribonucleic acid) and protein database to aid in species identification.

The National Fish and Wildlife Forensics Laboratory's collaborative approach helped to establish an innovative scientific field, incor-

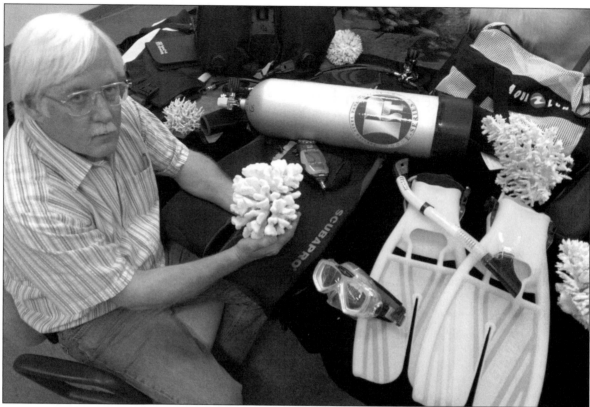

Ken Goddard, director of the National Fish and Wildlife Forensics Laboratory, displays gear and materials he used to develop protocols for criminal investigations on coral reefs. Goddard joined with the International Coral Reef Initiative to offer training in such investigations in October, 2006. *(AP/Wide World Photos)*

porating existing technologies and biological and chemical procedures and inventing methods to conduct original investigations. Forensic ornithologists, veterinarians, and wildlife specialists enhanced the laboratory's capabilities.

Scientific Investigations

For the forensic scientists at the wildlife laboratory, a case begins when a sample arrives and is cataloged. Wildlife forensic evidence takes varied forms, from entire carcasses to pieces of bone; it may include dried fluids, pelts, raw meat, and products made from animal materials. Morphologists evaluate specimens to identify their species; this work sometimes requires comparisons with samples from known species in the laboratory's collection. The scientists frequently use scanning electron microscopes to scrutinize samples for structures to determine

species. Species identification clarifies whether or not the animal is legally protected; crocodiles, for example, are a protected species, whereas alligators are not.

Serologists analyze blood samples, using mass spectrometry to weigh hemoglobin protein molecules to identify species. Genetic fingerprinting is useful when bloodstains at scenes or on poachers' clothing are the sole available evidence. Investigators may use DNA analysis to connect the body parts of an animal recovered in separate locations. Wildlife forensic investigators also compare saw marks, such as on antlers and heads, to match severed wildlife pieces. DNA analysis may also be used to associate meat with a crime scene. Forensic scientists can determine whether poached animals were born in the wild or captively bred, as some hunters claim, if the DNA of the animals' alleged parents is available for testing. DNA evidence can also enable investigators to identify the weapons used to kill animals.

Pathologists at the wildlife forensics laboratory examine evidence to determine the causes of animals' deaths. Experts in criminalistics evaluate bullets found inside animals, tire tracks, and other evidence found at crime scenes to supplement the information acquired from biological and chemical examinations. Such evidence can link together an animal victim, a human suspect, and the place where the crime occurred.

Wildlife forensic scientists have devised techniques for evaluating animal goods. For example, Edgard O. Espinoza and Mary-Jacque Mann developed a simple way for customs agents to appraise the Schreger lines in ivory (lines that are visible in cross sections of ivory) by measuring the lines' angles to determine if the ivory came from an elephant's tusk or some other source. Ivory with Shreger line angles of 115 degrees or greater comes from banned sources, whereas ivory with line angles of 90 degrees or less is legal. This method has exposed poachers who had falsely identified their ivory as originating from legal sources and has resulted in a reduction in elephant poaching.

Wildlife forensics investigators have also analyzed bile acids to identify different kinds of animal bladders that have been harvested for folk medicines. It is illegal to kill bears for this purpose, but the harvesting of pig bladders is legal. Researcher Stephen Busack has been able to identify some reptiles by scale shapes and patterns even when tanning and dying processes have obliterated the skins' original pigments.

The National Fish and Wildlife Forensics Laboratory's successes have encouraged forensic investigators to establish similar facilities in other locations, including internationally, but the laboratory in Ashland remains the only one of its kind devoted entirely to wildlife.

Elizabeth D. Schafer

Further Reading

Espinoza, Edgard O'Niel, and Mary-Jacque Mann. *Identification Guide for Ivory and*

Determining New Species-Defining Characteristics

A writer for the National Fish and Wildlife Forensics Laboratory offers this explanation of one of the lab's most difficult tasks, determining new species-defining characteristics.

If the federal wildlife special agents and game wardens and conservation officers who comprise our user groups seized (for example) whole elephants as evidence, attached an evidence tag to their tails, and dragged them into a courtroom, we wouldn't need a $4.5 million wildlife crime laboratory.

You would recognize that animal as an elephant.

And we would recognize it as an elephant.

And I would wager that we could get the average jury of 12 to agree that it is an elephant, based upon certain commonly-accepted species-defining morphological characteristics, such as the trunk, the tusks, the large ears, the even larger rear end, the small tail, etc.

But the thing is, these wildlife officers don't seize whole elephants and send them to our laboratory for identification (a fact for which, I might add, we are all extremely grateful!); rather, they seize wildlife pieces, parts and products in which the commonly-accepted species-defining characteristics are no longer present.

So what we have to do, as a wildlife crime laboratory, is conduct an extensive amount of research to come up with new species-defining characteristics that will allow us to testify in court that this piece, part or product originated from a specific species of animal, and not from any other possible species in the entire world . . . which, if you stop to think about it, is quite a trick.

Oh yes, one other thing: there are no established cookbooks for our work. Wildlife forensics is very much in its infancy as a branch of forensic science, so we will be working with a lot of other wildlife experts and police-type forensic scientists to conduct our research and bring our profession forward to assist wildlife officers at the federal, state and international levels in enforcing wildlife laws.

Ivory Substitutes. 3d ed. Baltimore: World Wildlife Fund, 2000. Describes forensic techniques for differentiating ivory specimens originating from elephants and other animals.

Jackson, Donna M. *The Wildlife Detectives: How Forensic Scientists Fight Crimes Against Nature*. Photographs by Wendy Shattil and Bob Rozinski. Boston: Houghton Mifflin, 2000. Features the techniques used in the National Fish and Wildlife Forensics Laboratory's investigation of the 1993 poaching of an elk in Yellowstone National Park.

Knight, Jonathan. "Cops and Poachers." *New Scientist*, January 22, 2000, 40-43. Article about Goddard emphasizes the importance of species identification for wildlife forensic evidence.

Luoma, Jon R. "The Wild World's Scotland Yard." *Audubon* 102 (November/December, 2000): 72-80. Presents a detailed account of the achievements of the scientists at the National Fish and Wildlife Forensics Laboratory.

Repanshek, Kurt. "Tracking Poachers with Forensic Science." *Technology Review* 98 (August/September, 1995): 22-23. Focuses on technological applications developed to prove wildlife crimes.

See also: Animal evidence; Blood residue and bloodstains; Courts and forensic evidence; Crime laboratories; Direct versus circumstantial evidence; DNA analysis; DNA banks for endangered animals; Forensic botany; Hair analysis; Mass spectrometry.

World Trade Center bombing

Date: February 26, 1993

The Event: A car bomb exploded inside the parking garage below New York City's World Trade Center's north tower, killing six people and injuring more than one thousand. The explosion also disrupted public services and necessitated a massive cleanup effort.

Significance: An intense forensic investigation by agents of the Federal Bureau of Investigation led to the arrest and conviction of four suspects. In the absence of eyewitnesses to the bombing, the convictions rested mostly on forensic evidence extricated from the blast's rubble, telephone and bank records, and other documentary evidence. The bombing itself was regarded as an act of international terrorism that prompted changes in security measures in the United States.

At 12:17 P.M. on February 26, 1993, a huge bomb exploded in the underground parking garage below the north tower of New York City's World Trade Center. Like its twin, the 110-story tower was part of a complex in which fifty thousand people worked on a typical day. The Trade Center complex also hosted as many as eighty thousand visitors a day.

The explosion blasted a hole almost one hundred feet wide that extended through four sublevels of concrete and ruptured sewer and water mains. The blast, which was felt several miles away, forced the evacuation of thousands of people from the building. It cut off telephone service to a large part of Lower Manhattan and ruptured nearby power lines. Without electrical power, most local radio and television stations could not broadcast throughout much of the following week.

In response to the chemical and biological hazards left in the wake of the blast, crews from the federal government's Environmental Protection Agency and Occupational Safety and Health Administration cleaned up the sewage, acid, fumes, and asbestos. The bomb itself had contained at least twelve hundred pounds of urea nitrate, a fertilizer that had been used only once in 73,000 explosions previously investigated by the Federal Bureau of Investigation (FBI).

The Investigation

Four days after the blast, *The New York Times* received a letter from a group calling itself the Liberation Army Fifth Battalion. The group was unknown to law-enforcement agen-

New York City police and firefighters inspect the bomb crater inside the World Trade Center parking garage on February 27, 1993, one day after the terrorist attack that killed six people and injured more than one thousand. *(AP/Wide World Photos)*

cies, but the FBI authenticated the letter as having come from a West Bank Palestinian named Nidal A. Ayyad. Its message called the bombing attack a response to the American support of Israel and American interference in Middle Eastern affairs. It also threatened further attacks if the U.S. government failed to change its Middle Eastern policies.

Many government agencies responded to the bombing by sending investigation teams to the site. The first team to arrive at the scene was composed of FBI agents and specialists from the FBI's explosives unit. During the seven days following the bombing, more than three hundred law-enforcement officers sifted through the 2,500 cubic yards of debris created by the blast. A bomb technician working for the federal Bureau of Alcohol, Tobacco, Firearms and Explosives (ATF) found the part of a nearly destroyed van with a vehicle identification number (VIN).

That information made it possible to trace the van to the agency that had rented it and from there to the renter, another West Bank Palestinian named Mohammed A. Salameh.

Reconstructing the Crime

As law-enforcement investigators worked to reconstruct what had happened, other evidence pointed to the rental van as the source of the blast within the building. In addition to finding chemical residues in the air, ATF agents discovered physical evidence of "feathering," or stretching, of the van and dimpled metal near the van that had been liquefied by the heat of the blast and had shot out, leaving small indentations in nearby objects. This physical evidence indicated that the van itself was at the center of the blast.

Other forensic investigators collected detailed documents that would lead to the apprehension of the primary suspects in the case. In

The Fates of the Conspirators

Four West Bank Palestinian Muslim militants were eventually arrested and tried for their parts in the World Trade Center bombing. All four had been influenced by the blind Egyptian cleric Sheikh Omar Abdel Rahman, who had once been implicated in the 1981 assassination of Egyptian president Anwar el-Sadat. Most of the conspirators also had connections with El Sayyid A. Nosair, an Egyptian convicted of assault and weapons charges for a shooting at the time of militant Rabbi Meir Kahane's assassination in 1990.

On March 4, 1993, authorities made the first arrest, of Mohammed A. Salameh. Arrests of three other suspected conspirators—Nidal A. Ayyad, Mahmoud Abouhalima, and Ahmad M. Ajaj—followed. Abdul Rahman Yasin, an American of Iraqi heritage, was questioned by the FBI but afterward fled to Iraq. He was later indicted and in 2001 was placed on the FBI's most-wanted list. Since then, he has remained a fugitive. The five-month trial of the accused conspirators began in the U.S. federal district court in Manhattan in October, 1993. On March 4, 1994, all four were found guilty on thirty-eight counts of conspiracy to blow up the building, and each man was sentenced to 240 years in prison without the possibility of parole.

Long after the bombing, fugitives and additional suspects were apprehended, extradited, and eventually tried. Ramzi Yousef, a Kuwaiti national who was believed to be the mastermind of the bombing, was located in Pakistan and returned to New York in February, 1995. He was considered to be a trained professional terrorist, unlike those he recruited, entering countries under different aliases with false papers, cash, and connections. Eyad Ismail was traced to Jordan and returned to New York in July, 1995. Yousef and Ismail were subsequently tried and found guilty of conspiracy for their roles in the World Trade Center bombing. In 1996, Yousef was sentenced to life in prison, and in 1998, Ismail received a sentence of 240 years in prison; both sentences included no possibility of parole.

1991, a Kuwaiti national named Ramzi Yousef, who appeared to be the mastermind behind the bombing, apparently began planning the attack with his uncle, Khalid Shaikh Mohammed, a member of the radical Muslim group al-Qaeda who helped fund the conspiracy. Their goal was to cause one of the Trade Center's towers to fall on the other, maximizing the damage. Police later found bomb-making instructions in the luggage of Yousef's partner, Abdul Rahman Yasin, an American of Iraqi heritage.

The bomb contained urea pellets, sulfuric acid, aluminum azide, nitroglycerin, magnesium azide, and bottled hydrogen. The conspirators also added sodium cyanide to the mixture in the hope that cyanide gas would be disseminated throughout the building's ventilation system.

After the attack, inquiries into how it occurred found that security in the Trade Center garage had been seriously lacking, despite the fact that the Port Authority had identified the tower's garage as one of three places of security concern in 1985. Security in the Trade Center was afterward greatly improved. However, the enhanced measures would prove useless when hijacked jetliners were flown into the towers on September 11, 2001. On that occasion, the goals of the earlier bombing were achieved when the intense fire damage inflicted by the airplanes carrying large amounts of jet fuel caused both towers to collapse completely.

Sheryl L. Van Horne

Further Reading

Behar, Richard. "The Secret Life of Mahmud the Red." *Time*, October 4, 1993, 54-61. Describes the role of defendant Mahmoud Abouhalima in the World Trade Center bombing.

Caram, Peter. *The 1993 World Trade Center Bombing: Foresight and Warning*. London: Janus, 2001. Documents the long-term security risk of the building. Written by a police officer who was an antiterrorist officer.

Dwyer, Jim, Deidre Murphy, Peg Tyre, and David Kocieniewski. *Two Seconds Under the World: Terror Comes to America—The Conspiracy Behind the World Trade Center*

Bombings. New York: Crown, 1994. Discusses some conspiracy theories surrounding the bombing while accounting for the facts of the crime through the use of information and police data about the act as well as interviews with confidential sources.

Pellowski, Michael J. *The Terrorist Trial of the 1993 Bombing of the World Trade Center: A Headline Court Case*. Berkeley Heights, N.J.: Enslow, 2003. Details the events leading up to the bombing as well as the capture of the suspects and their trials.

Reeve, Simon. *The New Jackals: Ramzi Yousef, Osama Bin Laden, and the Future of Terrorism*. Boston: Northeastern University Press, 1999. Explains how Yousef and Bin Laden, who were trained militarily, have used terrorism for religious and political purposes.

Simon, Jeffrey D. *The Terrorist Trap: America's Experience with Terrorism*. 2d ed. Bloomington: Indiana University Press, 2001. Examines the history of terrorist acts against the United States. Chapter 1 treats the 1993 World Trade Center bombing under the title "Welcome to Reality."

Weaver, Mary Anne. "The Trail of the Sheikh." *The New Yorker*, April 12, 1993, 71-89. Discusses the shadowy, blind Muslim cleric Sheikh Omar Abdel Rahman, mentioned as a key figure in various terrorist plots, and examines his Egyptian connections.

See also: Blast seat; Bomb damage assessment; Bombings; Bureau of Alcohol, Tobacco, Firearms and Explosives; Driving injuries; Federal Bureau of Investigation; Federal Bureau of Investigation Laboratory; First responders; Improvised explosive devices; Oklahoma City bombing; Paper; September 11, 2001, victim identification; Structural analysis.

Writing instrument analysis

Definition: Examination of documents and writing instruments with the aim of determining which specific instruments were used to create the documents of interest.

Significance: Handwritten documents often play important roles in criminal investigations and court cases. Through writing instrument analysis, forensic scientists can gather information about documents (such as wills, ransom notes, or threatening letters) that can help investigators link the documents to suspects.

Law-enforcement investigators sometimes encounter pieces of written evidence that can potentially provide important information about individuals or crimes. In some instances, a document may be integral to the case, such as a ransom note or forged document. At other times, a scribbled note might be a clue to the identity of a criminal for whom investigators are searching. In these cases, any information that can be gathered about the documents and how they were produced can be helpful to investigators. Information linking a suspect to a written document may also be used as evidence during a trial. Although the numbers of handwritten documents figuring prominently in law-enforcement investigations have diminished over time, as first the widespread adoption of typewriters and later the common use of computers and printers greatly reduced the frequency with which many people handwrite any documents, writing instrument analysis remains an important function of forensic science.

Types of Writing Instruments

Many different types of writing instruments may be used in the creation of a document. These include objects that are generally thought of as writing instruments, such as pens and pencils, as well as less commonly used instruments, such as crayons, spray paint, or lipstick. Anything that can be used to create a mark on a surface may be considered a writing instrument.

The most common writing instruments are mass-produced pens and pencils. For many years, the fountain pen was the most common writing instrument, but it was largely replaced in 1954, when the ballpoint pen was introduced. Fiber-tip or porous-point pens, roller-ball pens, and gel pens are also commonly used types of pens. Available pencil types include traditional graphite pencils, colored pencils, and mechanical pencils. Each pencil type is available in a wide range of lead sizes and softnesses. Each type of pen or pencil leaves specific, telltale signs of its identity on any document it is used to create.

Identification Techniques

The techniques used in identifying a writing instrument depend on the goal of the investigation and the availability of writing samples. In some cases, the goal of the investigator is to determine whether a particular document could have been created using a certain writing instrument. In such a case the writing instrument is generally available to create sample documents for comparison. The examiner then compares the original and sample documents, using the naked eye as well as the microscope, and conducts any relevant chemical tests.

If no suspected writing instrument has been identified, the examiner must try to determine as much information as possible using the available document. The first step in the attempt to determine what specific writing instrument was used is a visual inspection of the document. This inspection can usually provide information about the type of writing instrument used, such as whether the writing was created with a pen, pencil, highlighter, crayon, or other instrument.

The next step is to use a microscope to examine the document in more detail. Under the microscope, clues to the identity of the writing instrument that are not apparent to the naked eye become visible. For example, different types of writing instruments can be identified by the lines, marks, and indentations they leave in the writing surface. A pen that uses a ball to disperse ink leaves indentations from the ball in the paper that are visible under the microscope. A pen that does not use a ball, such as a fountain pen or a felt-tip pen, does not leave such indentations.

In some cases, an examiner is able to determine only the type of pen or other writing instrument that was used. In other cases, however, the examiner may be able to identify a specific writing instrument based on imperfections specific to that instrument. A pen tip that is bent or cracked, for example, will produce writing that is likely to show individual characteristics that can be identified by an expert.

The type of ink used can also help the examiner to determine the writing instrument that was used to create a given document. Inks may be tested in many different ways. Some tests involve wetting the sample with a solution and examining the way the ink spreads. An examiner may need to avoid such methods in some cases—for instance, if the goal of the examination is to validate a historic document or only a very small amount of sample is available to study—as they effectively destroy a section of the sample.

Helen Davidson

Further Reading

Bauchner, Elizabeth. *Document Analysis*. Philadelphia: Mason Crest, 2006. Provides an overview of the various components associated with forensic document analysis and includes chapters on important cases, such as the investigation of documents purported to be Adolf Hitler's diaries.

Brunelle, Richard L., and Kenneth R. Crawford. *Advances in the Forensic Analysis and Dating of Writing Ink*. Springfield, Ill.: Charles C Thomas, 2003. Discusses the forensic uses of ink identification and dating, with sections on the admissibility of evidence and chemical techniques.

Ellen, David. *Scientific Examination of Documents: Methods and Techniques*. 3d ed. Boca Raton, Fla.: CRC Press, 2006. Presents information about all aspects of the forensic analysis of handwritten and typewritten documents, including analysis of typewriters, computer printers, and photocopiers. Also describes how this type of evidence functions in the courtroom.

Koppenhaver, Katherine Mainolfi. *Forensic Document Examination: Principles and Practice*. Totowa, N.J.: Humana Press, 2006. Comprehensive text discusses the various steps involved in document, handwriting, and writing instrument analysis, including information on preparing reports and equipping a laboratory.

Nickell, Joe. *Pen, Ink, and Evidence: A Study of Writing and Writing Materials for the Penman, Collector, and Document Detective*. New Castle, Del.: Oak Knoll Press, 2003. Provides an in-depth look at different types of writing instruments and inks, including discussion of the history and development of writing instruments.

See also: Check alteration and washing; Chromatography; Document examination; Fax machine, copier, and printer analysis; Forensic linguistics and stylistics; Forgery; Handwriting analysis; Hitler diaries hoax; Paper; Questioned document analysis; Typewriter analysis.

Wrongful convictions

Definition: Cases in which persons who are in fact not guilty of the crimes of which they are accused are nonetheless convicted of those crimes.

Significance: Judges and juries must weigh all the evidence placed before them when they make decisions about defendants' guilt or innocence. It is important to recognize that the intentional misuse or unintentional misinterpretation of forensic evidence can lead to the criminal conviction of innocent persons.

Forensic science has made significant contributions to attempts to rectify the problem of wrongful convictions in the United States. Modern understanding of DNA (deoxyribonucleic acid) and advances in DNA analysis technology, in particular, can be credited with aiding the courts in exonerating hundreds of innocent individuals who had been wrongly convicted. Ironically, these exonerations have often involved the use of one form of forensic evidence (particularly DNA evidence) to discredit earlier findings based on other forms of forensic evidence (such as blood typing, fingerprints, ballistics, bite marks, foot prints, or hair comparisons). In cases of exoneration, what typically occurs is that evidence preserved from the incarcerated person's original trial is reanalyzed using modern DNA technology, and this new analysis proves conclusively that the individual is not linked to the crime.

Researchers have studied the case files of many persons proved to have been wrongfully convicted to understand the ways in which the criminal justice system can malfunction. This work has provided a wealth of information on the factors associated with wrongful conviction.

The Double-Edged Sword

For the criminal justice system, forensic science is a double-edged sword. On one hand, when properly used, it can be a powerful tool that serves justice; forensic scientists help police, prosecutors, defense attorneys, judges, and juries do what they are supposed to do—that is, exonerate the innocent and convict the guilty. On the other hand, when the forensic evidence presented in a courtroom is faulty, it can mislead the judge or jury and result in the conviction of an innocent person. The stakes are high when forensic science enters the courtroom, as it is often the testimony of forensic scientists that ultimately sways the judge or jury in the determination of guilt or innocence.

Although some criminal cases are tried without the benefit of forensic evidence, possibly with only eyewitness testimony, the vast majority of criminal cases rely on the expert testimony of forensic scientists, who present to the court their opinions regarding what the physical evidence means in terms of the defendant and the crime. Because evidence involving genetic materials (such as blood, skin, and semen) is available in less than 20 percent of all cases, the most powerful tool available to forensic science—DNA analysis—is not used in more than 80 percent of criminal cases. In cases where genetic material is not available for analysis, scientists are usually called upon to analyze fingerprints, handwriting, ballistics, tool marks, and samples of materials such as paints, plastics, glass, and fibers.

It has been found that in many cases of wrongful conviction, a forensic scientist who appeared as an expert witness for the prosecution played a pivotal role, presenting erroneous and damning conclusions about the evidence. Such faulty forensic science is particularly harmful to an innocent suspect because judges and jurors assign great importance to the testimony of laboratory scientists who swear to the accuracy of the evidence they present. Jurors routinely give such evidence much more weight than other evidence. An expert who testifies that the forensic evidence essentially identifies the accused as the perpetrator of a crime often exhibits the same type of influence on the judge or jury as does an eyewitness who points at the accused in the courtroom and says, "That's the person I saw do the crime." The testimony of a forensic scientist can often mean the difference between conviction and acquittal to a wrongly accused defendant.

Misrepresentation of Scientific Findings

Faulty forensic science can contribute to a wrongful conviction in two ways: through unintentional or intentional misrepresentation of the scientific findings. Forensic scientists can unintentionally present faulty findings in the courtroom for a variety of reasons. Research into cases of wrongful conviction has found that the work of forensic technicians in some police crime laboratories is plagued by uneven training and questionable objectivity. Poorly trained or lazy technicians can conduct forensic tests that yield inaccurate results.

Forensic scientists can also commit unintentional errors in the form of inadvertent mislabeling or switching of samples, mistaken recording of data, inaccurate transcription of results, and loss of evidence. Sometimes the results of scientific tests are themselves accurate but unintentional misinterpretation of the data harms the wrongfully accused. In sum, faulty scientific testimony resulting from either erroneous lab tests or erroneous conclusions based on valid lab tests can lead to wrongful convictions.

Willie "O" Pete Williams answers a question during a news conference at the office of the Georgia Innocence Project in Atlanta on January 25, 2007. The project presented DNA evidence to free Williams from prison after he had served twenty-one years following a wrongful conviction for rape. (AP/Wide World Photos)

Repercussions of Wrongful Convictions

Wrongful convictions carry high personal and social prices. First, they compromise public safety. When a falsely accused person is convicted of a crime, that individual is punished in place of the one who actually committed the offense. Therefore, for virtually every person wrongfully convicted of a crime, a corresponding guilty person has not been brought to justice and may continue to commit crimes.

Wrongful convictions also undermine the public's confidence in the criminal justice system. Media stories about individuals who have been exonerated after languishing in prison for years can shake citizens' faith in the ability of the system to separate the innocent from the guilty and to do justice. The resulting damage to the symbolic status of the criminal justice process and loss of confidence in the criminal justice system can have serious and widespread negative consequences. For example, if jurors become skeptical of police testimony or prosecutorial judgment, they may be more likely to acquit guilty individuals. A loss of confidence in the criminal justice system may also lead to an increase in vigilantism.

In addition, when innocent persons are convicted of crimes and incarcerated, several separate injustices occur. Primarily, the wrongfully convicted suffer unjustly, subjected to the horrors of prison life, perhaps facing execution. The families of persons who are wrongfully convicted also suffer, enduring separations—husbands from wives, parents from children, and brothers from sisters—as well as public shame and often substantial losses in income. Moreover, family members typically exhaust all their available resources in attempting to correct their relatives' wrongful convictions. Other participants in the criminal justice process may also suffer. Jurors, witnesses, police officers, prosecutors, defense attorneys, and judges often experience significant distress when they discover that their actions contributed to sending innocent persons to prison.

Sometimes forensic experts intentionally misrepresent the scientific findings in court. In a study of sixty-two wrongful convictions, the Innocence Project (a nonprofit organization founded at the Benjamin N. Cardozo School of Law to assist prisoners who could be proven innocent through DNA testing) found that so-called rigged lab tests often contributed to erroneous convictions. The study determined that "fraudulent science" (intentional fabrication of evidence by a forensic specialist) contributed to 33 percent of the wrongful conviction cases analyzed. Several wrongfully convicted individuals have been exonerated because it was eventually discovered that the forensic scientists who testified at their trials had "made up" or "dry labbed" their results to satisfy the prosecutors and advance their own careers. ("Dry labbing" refers to the practice among corrupt scientists of writing reports regarding scientific findings without conducting any tests.)

Intentional misrepresentation of scientific findings can also occur when forensic experts cross the line from science to advocacy in their testimony, perhaps by exaggerating the results of their tests in ways that are devastating to defendants. Defense attorneys often make no effort to investigate the validity of experts' testimony or to challenge their findings, sometimes because they lack the resources to perform needed tests and sometimes because they are lazy or incompetent.

Indirect Effects of Forensic Error

It has been recognized for years that faulty forensic science can contribute directly to wrongful conviction, but for a long time little attention was paid to the degree to which faulty forensic science can indirectly lead to wrongful conviction by contaminating seemingly independent nonscientific evidence. For example, eyewitnesses who have misidentified a criminal suspect may become increasingly confident in their identification once they discover that forensic scientific tests (whether erroneous or not) have verified their statements. Given that "witness confidence" has been demonstrated to have a strong influence on jurors' perceptions that identification testimony is correct, erroneous conclusions by forensic scientists in such cases are particularly dangerous. In sum, faulty forensic findings may influence and encourage other participants in a trial (witnesses, police officers, prosecutors) to rely more strongly on their own erroneous conclusions.

The damage done by faulty forensic science not only affects the original trials of wrongfully suspected individuals but also continues to plague them when their cases are being appealed. Even when it is discovered that erroneous scientific testimony was offered at trial, the prosecutor will typically say that the testimony amounts to "harmless error" and that the conviction would have occurred even if the faulty evidence had not been presented. The prosecutor will usually suggest that other evidence presented at the trial—such as eyewitness testimony or the defendant's lack of a provable alibi—is enough to legitimate the conviction. What is often unrecognized (and sometime unrecognizable) at the appellate level is the effect that the erroneous expert testimony had on the other witnesses in the trial.

Reducing Forensic Error

Given that human beings will always make mistakes, the phenomenon of wrongful conviction is unlikely ever to be eliminated totally. It is, however, possible to reduce the amount of faulty forensic science presented in courtrooms and thereby reduce the likelihood of wrongful convictions. Forensic science is subject to the influence of human error at every step, beginning with the collection of evidence and on through the storing, testing, and interpretation of that evidence. Forensic scientists must diligently apply their training and ensure that the testimony they offer in court is as scrupulously accurate as humanly possible. Forensic experts who intentionally misrepresent their data should be prosecuted to the fullest extent of the law.

Government standards regarding the training of forensics laboratory personnel and the preservation and handling of evidence have been strengthened in the United States over the years, and aggressive enforcement of these standards should reduce error. Also, lawyers have the responsibility and obligation to their clients to challenge flawed scientific testimony; law schools and continuing education seminars should promote training for attorneys that will help them better recognize and challenge specious forensic testimony.

Robert J. Ramsey

Further Reading

Connors, Edward, Thomas Lundregan, Neal Miller, and Tom McEwan. *Convicted by Juries, Exonerated by Science: Case Studies in the Use of DNA Evidence to Establish Innocence After Trial.* Washington, D.C.: National Institute of Justice, 1996. Government research report discusses a study initiated to identify and review cases in which convicted persons were released from prison as a result of posttrial DNA testing of evidence.

Gross, Samuel R., et al. "Exonerations in the United States, 1989 through 2003." *Journal of Criminal Law and Criminology* 95, no. 2 (2005): 523-560. Analyzes 340 individual exonerations during the period covered. Notes that the data suggest that the total number of miscarriages of justice in the United States in the preceding fifteen years must run to the thousands, perhaps tens of thousands, in felony cases alone.

Huff, C. Ronald, Arye Rattner, and Edward Sagarin. *Convicted but Innocent: Wrongful Conviction and Public Policy.* Thousand Oaks, Calif.: Sage, 1996. Examines the full range of cases in the United States in which innocent people have been falsely accused, convicted, and incarcerated and describes the variety of missteps in the criminal justice system that can lead to unjust imprisonment.

Radelet, Michael L., Hugo Adam Bedau, and Constance E. Putnam. *In Spite of Innocence: Erroneous Convictions in Capital Cases.* Boston: Northeastern University Press, 1992. Useful collection of case studies reveals the factors commonly associated with wrongful conviction. Includes a glossary of legal terms.

Ramsey, Robert J., and James Frank. "Wrongful Conviction: Perceptions of Criminal Justice Professionals Regarding the Frequency of Wrongful Conviction and the Extent of System Errors." *Crime and Delinquency* 53 (July, 2007): 436-470. Presents an analysis of data from a survey of criminal justice professionals—including prosecutors, defense attorneys, and judges—that solicited their perceptions of the causes and extent of wrongful convictions.

Scheck, Barry, Peter Neufeld, and Jim Dwyer. *Actual Innocence: Five Days to Execution, and Other Dispatches from the Wrongly Convicted.* New York: Random House, 2000. Describes some of the most prominent and successful cases taken on by Scheck and Neufeld's Innocence Project. Also offers commentary on the shortcomings of the American system of criminal justice.

Zalman, Marvin. "Cautionary Notes on Commission Recommendations: A Public Policy Approach to Wrongful Convictions." *Criminal Law Bulletin* 41, no. 2 (2005): 169-194. Discusses the need to create state-level blue-ribbon committees to examine wrongful convictions and make recommendations. Also addresses other strategies for understanding and reducing wrongful convictions, such as expansion and strengthening of interest groups and policy networks concerned with wrongful conviction and reforms of appellate procedures.

See also: CODIS; Crime scene investigation; Criminalistics; *Daubert v. Merrell Dow Pharmaceuticals*; DNA analysis; Ethics; Evidence processing; Eyewitness testimony; False memories; *Frye v. United States*; Innocence Project; Postconviction DNA analysis; Questioned document analysis; Trace and transfer evidence.

X

X-ray diffraction

Definition: Technique for studying crystal structure by deflecting X rays off the atomic planes of a substance.

Significance: Because each crystalline substance has a unique X-ray diffraction pattern, this technique allows forensic scientists to analyze the "fingerprints" of evidence found at crime scenes and related locations.

X-ray diffraction (XRD) is a significant tool for the analysis of solid materials encountered in forensic science. Analysis of trace amounts of materials, including fibers, hair, minerals, metals, dust, pollens, blood, drugs, dyes, polymers, explosives, firearms discharge residues, soil, and paint, can help establish links between suspects and victims and between suspects and crime scenes; conversely, such analysis can eliminate some persons from suspicion.

Crystal structures serve as three-dimensional diffraction gratings for X rays. Most X rays impinging on a crystal pass straight through, but some are scattered from the crystalline planes and form an interference pattern on exposed film that is uniquely related to the atomic arrangement and subsequent identity of the substance. In addition to enabling the analysis of large amounts of a material, XRD can be employed to analyze small samples, smears, and minute contact traces of a substance. The way a sample is prepared for XRD analysis and the XRD method employed are determined by the type, amount, and consistency of the trace specimen; the involved surface where the specimen was found; and the forensic questions raised by the criminal offense.

The majority of physical evidence materials recovered at crime scenes and related locations are typically crystalline or semicrystalline in nature; thus forensic scientists can analyze and identify them using XRD methods. Other evidence can be converted to crystalline form. With blood evidence, for example, iodine is used for this purpose; other compounds are used to convert other kinds of specimens to crystalline form. Samples of recovered evidential materials are typically converted to powder form for study using an X-ray powder diffractometer. Nonpowder samples can also be analyzed using XRD.

Forensic scientists use XRD patterns as a screening tool to examine fiber trace evidence and to sort the evidence into groups based on type of fiber. This discriminates the type of fiber and preserves the fabric, which may contain stains of evidential value. The nondestructive nature of XRD analysis is a very important advantage of this technique when the forensic evidence must be preserved.

Among other advantages of XRD methods in forensic science are their ability to identify the unique character of patterns produced by crystalline material, their ability to distinguish between elements and their oxides, and their ability to identify chemical compounds, polymorphic forms, and mixed crystals in a nondestructive manner. In many cases, XRD methods are the only methods that allow detailed differentiation of crime scene materials under laboratory conditions.

With advances in computer automation, the analysis of X-ray diffraction patterns has become increasingly easy and fast. The International Center for Diffraction Data has more than forty thousand digitized diffraction patterns in its database that forensic scientists can use to help identify critical specimens found at crime scenes and related locations.

Alvin K. Benson

Further Reading

James, Stuart H., and Jon J. Nordby, eds. *Forensic Science: An Introduction to Scientific and Investigative Techniques.* 2d ed. Boca Raton, Fla.: CRC Press, 2005.

Mozayani, Ashraf, and Carla Noziglia, eds. *The Forensic Laboratory Handbook: Procedures and Practice.* Totowa, N.J.: Humana Press, 2006.

Robertson, James, and Michael Grieve, eds. *Forensic Examination of Fibres.* 2d ed. Philadelphia: Taylor & Francis, 1999.

See also: Analytical instrumentation; Art forgery; Blood residue and bloodstains; Fax machine, copier, and printer analysis; Forensic toxicology; Gunshot residue; Nuclear spectroscopy; Spectroscopy.

Y

Y chromosome analysis

Definition: DNA analysis technique that focuses on the Y chromosome, which determines male sex in human beings.

Significance: Analyses of Y chromosome markers and mitochondrial (maternally inherited) DNA are important for forensic, genealogical, archaeological, and anthropological studies because they can be conducted even with very small or degraded samples of genetic material.

The Y and the X chromosomes are sex chromosomes. Within the twenty-three pairs of human chromosomes, one pair in a female human has two X chromosomes and one pair in a male human has an X and a Y chromosome. The Y chromosome is the smallest human chromosome—about fifty million base pairs, or 2 percent of the total DNA (deoxyribonucleic acid) in cells.

Two small regions (called the pseudoautosomal regions) at the tips of the X and Y chromosomes are homologous. The pseudoautosomal regions of the X and Y chromosomes pair during meiosis. The rest of the Y chromosome (95 percent) is present in just one copy (is haploid) and does not have a homologous copy with which to pair, so there is no genetic recombination for the majority of the Y chromosome. Because no genetic recombination occurs, the Y markers can be tracked through generations.

The nonrecombining portion of the Y chromosome has been shown to have different kinds of polymorphisms that mutate at different rates. Short tandem repeats (STRs) on the Y chromosome are such polymorphic markers. These short sequences are three to five nucleotides long and are repeated a variable number of times (five to thirty times) in different individuals. Polymerase chain reaction (PCR), a DNA amplification method, is used to amplify the particular Y-STR through the use of primers specific for that STR. A large number of different STRs are amplified in a single reaction through the use of primers specific to each STR (multiplex PCR). The amplified DNA is sized using gel electrophoresis to enable the identification of which allele (copy of a gene) of the Y-STR an individual has. Single nucleotide polymorphisms (SNPs) are also used. Kits to PCR-amplify Y-STRs are commercially available, and numerous Y sequences have been collected for comparisons in the Y Chromosome Haplotype Reference Database.

Y-STRs are important to extract male-specific information from a sample when sperm are not present. Such a sample from a crime scene may take the form of a mixture of blood from a male perpetrator and a female victim or male saliva on a female victim. Y chromosome markers are also used in paternity testing and in missing persons investigations. Further, the lack of recombination makes Y markers useful in human migration and evolutionary studies comparing male humans over lengthy periods.

Because PCR can amplify a small amount of DNA, small and degraded samples can be analyzed for Y-STRs. One disadvantage of Y chromosome analysis is that loci are not independent of one another, so haplotypes (the alleles at all the tested loci) must be examined. Also, unless a mutation has occurred, paternal lineages have the same Y-STR haplotype, so fathers, sons, brothers, uncles, and paternal cousins cannot be distinguished from each other by Y-STR analysis.

Susan J. Karcher

Further Reading

Gusmão, Leonor, et al. "DNA Commission of the International Society of Forensic Genetics (ISFG): An Update of Recommendations on Use of Y-STRs in Forensic Analysis." *Forensic Science International* 157 (2006): 187-197.

Hanson, Erin K., and Jack Ballantyne. "Comprehensive Annotated STR Physical Map of Human Y Chromosome: Forensic Implications." *Legal Medicine* (Tokyo) 8 (March, 2006): 110-120.

Kobilinsky, Lawrence F., Louis Levine, and Henrietta Margolis-Nunno. *Forensic DNA Analysis*. New York: Chelsea House, 2007.

Willuweit, Sascha, and Lutz Roewer. "Y Chromosome Haplotype Reference Database (YHRD): Update." *Forensic Science International: Genetics* 1, no. 2 (2006): 83-87.

See also: DNA database controversies; DNA extraction from hair, bodily fluids, and tissues; DNA typing; Ethics of DNA analysis; Mitochondrial DNA analysis and typing; Polymerase chain reaction; Short tandem repeat analysis.

Appendixes

Guide to Internet Resources

The sites listed below were visited by the editors of Salem Press in April, 2008. Because URLs frequently change and sites move, the accuracy of these addresses cannot be guaranteed; however, long-standing sites—such as those of university departments, national organizations, and government agencies—generally maintain links when sites move or otherwise upgrade their offerings.

General

Crime and Clues
http://www.crimeandclues.com

Crime scene technician Daryl W. Clemens maintains this site, which provides introductory-level material for people interested in forensic science. The site, which is updated frequently, features full-text articles on various forensic science topics written by experts. The topics covered range from general discussions to descriptions of specific techniques and types of evidence.

Forensic-Evidence.com
http://www.forensic-evidence.com

This information center is maintained by Andre A. Moenssens, Douglas Stripp Missouri Professor of Law Emeritus at the University of Missouri, Kansas City, School of Law. The site focuses on the legal and evidentiary aspects of forensic science as applied in courts and educational systems and includes discussion of personal privacy issues. The information provided may be especially useful to lawyers, forensic scientists, and educators.

Kruglick's Forensic Resource and Criminal Law Search Site
http://www.bioforensics.com/kruglaw

Created by Kim Kruglick and sponsored by Forensic Bioinformatics, this site is devoted primarily to the legal aspects of applied forensic science. The site includes the text of court opinions and statutes as well as links to sites that focus on criminal law and the death penalty, links to legal search engines, and information on general research links. The site also offers helpful "primers" to help students and nonscientists understand the technical aspects of forensic science.

National Forensic Science Technology Center
http://www.nfstc.org

This site describes the programs of the National Forensic Science Technology Center, which is an independent, nonprofit corporation established in 1995 by the American Society of Crime Laboratory Directors to provide high-quality systems support, training, and education to American forensic science professionals.

Reddy's Forensic Page
http://www.forensicpage.com

Maintained by Reddy P. Chamakura, a retired forensic scientist who spent thirty-six years with the New York City Police Department Police Laboratory, this site highlights news stories involving forensic science. It also provides an extensive compilation of links to resources including associations, journals, mailing lists, and job opportunities as well as Web sites devoted to subspecialties in forensic medicine, applications, investigative techniques, research programs, and laboratories.

Zeno's Forensic Site
http://forensic.to/forensic.html

This site, maintained by Zeno Geradts, a forensic scientist with the Digital Evidence Section of the Netherlands Forensic Institute, is particularly helpful for locating articles on forensic science topics by professionals in the field. It also includes information on multiple subareas of forensic science, medicine, psychology, and psychiatry, as well as more general information resources.

Forensic Subspecialties

Accredited Psychiatry and Medicine: Medical and Psychiatric Experts

http://www.forensic-psych.com

This site is devoted to discussion of the work of forensic psychiatrists, particularly in their role as expert witnesses in legal matters. Topics addressed include employment litigation, product liability, and professional ethics. The site includes the full text of the American Academy of Psychiatry and the Law's Ethical Guidelines for the Practice of Forensic Psychiatry.

Bloodspatter.com

http://www.bloodspatter.com

This site, maintained by J. Slemko Forensic Consulting, provides information on actual cases involving blood evidence as well as links to sites with related subject matter. The site also features a tutorial on bloodstain pattern analysis.

C.A.S.T. Website: Shoe Print and Tire Track Examination Resources

http://members.aol.com/varfee/mastssite/home.html

Chesapeake Area Shoeprint and Tire Track (C.A.S.T.), a consortium of forensic footwear and tire-track examiners, maintains this site, which is devoted to promoting the analysis of footwear and tire-track evidence at crime scenes. The site provides links to databases and to manufacturers, experts, vendors, trade associations, and professional societies connected to this forensic discipline.

Emily J. Will, Forensic Document Examiner

http://www.qdewill.com

Will, a certified document examiner, includes on her site introductory information about the work of forensic document examiners and handwriting identification experts. Articles on the site discuss the instruments that document examiners use (such as infrared equipment and digital microscopes) as well as the techniques they employ. An article on famous cases involving document analysis is included, as are links to sites with related material.

Ethics in Science

http://www.chem.vt.edu/chem-ed/ethics

This site lists links to articles describing selected cases of misconduct by scientists as well as links to science ethics resources and essays on ethics in science. A section of the site is devoted to ethics-related articles in forensics written by D. H. Garrison, Jr., who works in the Forensic Services Unit of the Grand Rapids, Michigan, Police Department.

FirearmsID.com

http://firearmsid.com

Maintained by Scott Doyle, who works for the Kentucky State Police as a firearms and toolmark examiner, this site presents informative articles about specific firearms and their uses, firearms safety procedures, and other topics related to firearms. It also features discussion forums and information about careers in forensic science.

Forensic Art

http://www.forensicartist.com

This site provides information on and case examples of many aspects of forensic art, including two- and three-dimensional facial reconstruction, computer-enhanced reconstruction, and composite drawing. It also features links to many sites with related content as well as a link to the Doe Network, a volunteer organization dedicated to the identification of missing persons and cold-case crime victims in North America, Australia, and Europe.

Forensic Botany

http://myweb.dal.ca/jvandomm/forensicbotany

Created in 2002 by Jennifer Van Dommelen for a class at Dalhousie University in Halifax, Nova Scotia, this site provides wide-ranging information on the field of forensic botany, which entails the application of the science of botany to the resolution of legal questions. The site reviews the techniques used by scientists in the subdisciplines of palynology, anatomy and dendrochronology, limnology, systematics, ecology, and molecular biology. It also provides links to sites featuring related material.

Forensic Dentistry Online

http://www.forensicdentistryonline.org

This site serves as a comprehensive information center for professionals in forensic odontology. It features numerous articles on the various applications of forensic dentistry as well as links to professional organizations and journals.

Forensic DNA Glossary

http://www.forensicdna.com/emailforms/
DNAGlossary.html

The work of Norah Rudin and Keith Inman, two widely respected experts in the field, this glossary provides helpful basic information about the uses and applications of DNA analysis in forensic science.

Forensic Entomology: Insects in Legal Investigations

http://www.forensicentomology.com

Dr. J. H. Byrd created this site to "assist in the education of crime scene technicians, homicide investigators, coroners, medical examiners, and others involved in the death investigation process." The site features articles that describe the use of entomology as a tool of forensic science, detailing the activities of forensic entomologists. It also provides a list of relevant literature, a list of board certified forensic entomologists, and links to sites containing related material.

Forensic Mathematics

http://dna-view.com

This site, maintained by Charles H. Brenner, a consultant in forensic mathematics, provides extensive technical information concerning the mathematics involved in the interpretation of DNA analysis results.

How Do Bullets Fly?

http://www.nennstiel-ruprecht.de/bullfly

This well-illustrated article by Ruprecht Nennstiel details the basics of bullet motion and explains bullet trajectories and impacts. It also includes discussion of experimental techniques for the observation of small arms fire.

Latent Print Examination: Fingerprints, Palmprints, and Footprints

http://onin.com/fp

Maintained by Ed German, a forensic scientist with more than thirty years of experience working in government crime laboratories, this site offers an abundance of information on latent print analysis as well as helpful links to sites covering related material.

Molecular Expressions

http://micro.magnet.fsu.edu

This site is maintained by the Optical Microscopy Division of the National High Magnetic Field Laboratory, a joint venture of the Florida State University, the University of Florida, and the Los Alamos National Laboratory. It provides in-depth information on optical microscopy and includes collections of color photographs taken through optical microscopes.

Ridges and Furrows

http://ridgesandfurrows.homestead.com

This site contains excellent introductory material about fingerprint analysis as well as more technically oriented material on topics such as skin anatomy and the histology of thick skin, enhancement of latent prints using digital technology, and latent print identification. Numerous links to sites with related material are also provided.

Scientific Working Group on Friction Ridge Analysis, Study and Technology

http://www.swgfast.org

The Scientific Working Group on Friction Ridge Analysis, Study and Technology (SWGFAST) is one of several scientific working groups sponsored by the Federal Bureau of Investigation Laboratory Division that are devoted to improving forensic science practices and building consensus among federal, state, and local forensic laboratories and practitioners. This site provides numerous documents produced by SWGFAST concerning guidelines and standards for friction ridge examination, also known as latent print examination.

Short Tandem Repeat DNA Internet Data Base (STRBase)

http://www.cstl.nist.gov/biotech/strbase

This site, created by John M. Butler and Dennis J. Reeder of the Biochemical Science Division of the National Institute of Standards and Technology, features highly technical information on topics related to the use of short tandem repeat (STR) analysis for genetic mapping for identity testing, including sequence information on each STR system, population data, and commonly used multiplex STR systems. The site provides a comprehensive listing of addresses of scientists and organizations as well as materials and techniques used.

World Wide Web Virtual Library: Forensic Toxicology

http://home.lightspeed.net/~abarbour/
  vlibft.html

This segment of the World Wide Web Virtual Library is maintained as a public service by Alan D. Barbour, a Fellow of the American College of Forensic Examiners and a consulting forensic toxicologist. The site is primarily a list of links to numerous sites devoted to forensic science, including forensic toxicology sites, general forensic science sites, and sites providing education and career guidance in forensic science fields.

Indexes to Periodical Publications

AFTE Journal Keyword Index

http://www.afte.org/ExamResources/
  journalindex.htm

Rocky Stone of the Albuquerque, New Mexico, Police Department compiled this keyword index of articles that have been published in the journals of the Association of Firearm and Tool Mark Examiners (AFTE). The site makes the index available for download in two formats.

American Journal of Forensic Medicine and Pathology

http://www.amjforensicmedicine.com

The "Archive" section of this site provides listings of the articles published in the *American Journal of Forensic Medicine and Pathology* since 1996. Abstracts of the articles may be viewed for free; fees are charged for access to the articles themselves. This journal features original articles on new examination and documentation procedures, focusing on forensic scientists' expanding role in medicolegal practices.

Canadian Society of Forensic Science Journal

http://ww2.csfs.ca/csfs_journal.aspx

This site provides an index to original papers, commentary, and reviews in the various branches of forensic science published by the *Canadian Society of Forensic Science Journal* since 1995. Abstracts of the articles may be viewed for free; fees are charged for access to the articles themselves.

FBI Law Enforcement Bulletin

http://www.fbi.gov/publications/leb/leb.htm

This site makes available past issues of the Federal Bureau of Investigation's monthly publication dating from 1996. Full issues are available for either HTML or PDF download.

Forensic Science Communications

http://www.fbi.gov/hq/lab/fsc/current/
  index.htm

The "Back Issues" section of this site provides access to all articles that have appeared in *Forensic Science Communications* since the journal began publishing in 1999. This peer-reviewed journal is published quarterly by the Federal Bureau of Investigation Laboratory Division.

Information Bulletin for Shoeprint/ Toolmark Examiners

http://www.intermin.fi/intermin/hankkeet/
  wgm/home.nsf

An index to past issues of the *Information Bulletin for Shoeprint/Toolmark Examiners* is available in the "IBSTE" section of this site, which is maintained by the bulletin's publisher, the Expert Working Group Marks (EWGM), one of the forensic science working groups of the European Network of Forensic Science Institutes. The EWGM focuses on such impression evidence as tool marks, shoe prints, tire marks, marks made by bare feet, and manufacturing marks. Full issues of the bulletin are available for PDF download on the site.

Journal of Forensic Sciences
http://www.aafs.org

The "Journal of FS" section of this official site of the American Academy of Forensic Sciences (AAFS) provides access to a searchable index of issues of the *Journal of Forensic Sciences* from 1972 through 2005 (information on more recent issues is available online only to AAFS fellows, members, and affiliates). Abstracts of the articles may be viewed for free; fees are charged for access to the articles themselves.

National Criminal Justice Reference Service Abstracts Database
http://www.ncjrs.gov/abstractdb/search.asp

This site provides access to summaries of many thousands of resources housed in the National Criminal Justice Reference Service (NCJRS) Library, including reports from all levels of government, research reports, books, and journal articles. It is also the only comprehensive collection that includes the *Journal of Forensic Identification* in its index. This database has direct access only to abstracts, but when full texts of items are available online, links are provided.

Professional Organizations and Government Agencies

American Academy of Forensic Sciences
http://www.aafs.org

American Board of Forensic Document Examiners
http://www.abfde.org

American Board of Forensic Odontology
http://www.abfo.org

American Board of Forensic Toxicology
http://www.abft.org

American Society of Crime Laboratory Directors
http://www.ascld.org

American Society of Questioned Document Examiners
http://www.asqde.org

Armed Forces Institute of Pathology
http://www.afip.org

Association of Firearm and Tool Mark Examiners
http://www.afte.org

Bureau of Alcohol, Tobacco, Firearms and Explosives, U.S.
http://www.treas.gov

Bureau of Legal Dentistry
http://www.boldlab.org

Canadian Society of Forensic Science
http://ww2.csfs.ca

Centers for Disease Control and Prevention
http://www.cdc.gov

Drug Enforcement Administration, U.S.
http://www.usdoj.gov/dea/index.htm

Environmental Measurements Laboratory
http://www.eml.st.dhs.gov

European Network of Forensic Science Institutes
http://www.enfsi.eu

Federal Bureau of Investigation
http://www.fbi.gov

Federal Law Enforcement Training Center
http://www.fletc.gov

Food and Drug Administration, U.S.
http://www.fda.gov

Forensic Science Service
http://www.forensic.gov.uk

Forensic Science Society
http://www.forensic-science-society.org.uk

International Association for Craniofacial Identification
http://www.forensicartist.com/IACI

International Association for Identification
http://www.theiai.org

International Association of Bomb Technicians and Investigators
http://www.iabti.org

International Association of Forensic Nurses
http://www.iafn.org

International Association of Forensic Sciences
http://www.iafs2005.com

International Association of Forensic Toxicologists
http://www.tiaft.org

Interpol
http://www.interpol.int

National Institute of Justice
http://www.ojp.usdoj.gov/nij

National Transportation Safety Board
http://www.ntsb.gov

Secret Service, U.S.
http://www.secretservice.gov

Society of Forensic Toxicologists
http://www.soft-tox.org

Dwight G. Smith

Television Programs

American Justice (Documentary, A&E, 1997-   ). This long-running nonfiction crime series, hosted by journalist Bill Kurtis, presents evidence from various criminal cases and challenges the viewer to think critically about law-enforcement investigative techniques, the facts of each case, and the constitutional rights of the accused. The cases featured are often controversial, and the program aims to stimulate critical analysis of the evidence and the judicial process, calling into question the snap judgments that casual observers often make about the innocence or guilt of suspects.

Anatomy of a Crime (Documentary, Court TV, 2000-2002). This show went behind the scenes to look at the fast-paced lives of criminal investigators, often featuring dramatic footage such as the point of view from a police car during a high-speed chase. The program depicted the procedures carried out by police in the course of investigating various kinds of crimes, including human trafficking and drug smuggling. It also raised issues regarding the news and entertainment media's coverage of crime and related events.

Arrest & Trial (Documentary, USA, 2000-2001). Each episode of this series used both reenactments and actual footage to follow the stories of real-life crimes from their commission through their investigation and prosecution. The investigative portion of each episode described the uses of forensic science in the case. This program was created by Dick Wolf, who also created the *Law & Order* dramatic crime series.

Autopsy (Documentary, HBO, 1994-   ). This program features Dr. Michael Baden, former chief medical examiner of New York City, who has been involved as an expert witness in a number of famous criminal cases, including the O. J. Simpson murder trial. In each episode, Baden explains the autopsy results and other forensic evidence related to a particular death.

Bones (Drama, Fox, 2005-   ). This series features the criminal cases that come before Dr. Temperance Brennan, a forensic anthropologist, and her team of forensic experts—each a specialist in a particular area—at the fictional Jeffersonian Institute in Washington, D.C. In solving crimes, the team works with Special Agent Seeley Booth of the Federal Bureau of Investigation. The crimes that Dr. Brennan and her team investigate are often unusual, and the technologies they use to examine the evidence are highly sophisticated.

Cold Case (Drama, CBS, 2003-   ). This program focuses on the work of a special team within the Philadelphia Police Department that investigates cold cases—that is, cases in which the leads or evidence trails have gone cold. Many of the crimes investigated in the show are years or even decades old. In each episode, an unsolved crime is somehow brought to the team's attention, and the investigators take a new look at the old evidence, which can sometimes be reexamined with forensic techniques that have been developed since the crime was committed. The types of forensic evidence that have figured into the program's plots have included fingerprint analysis, DNA analysis, ballistics, and blood evidence.

Cold Case Files (Documentary, A&E, 1999-   ). This program, hosted by journalist Bill Kurtis, shows the hard work that police investigators put into solving real-life cases that have eluded solution for years, sometimes for decades. Many of the cases featured, which are described through interviews with participants, have been solved through the application of forensic techniques that were not available to investigators at the times the crimes were committed, particularly DNA analysis.

Crime and Punishment (Documentary, NBC, 2002-2004). This program, created by Dick Wolf, who also created the dramatic crime series *Law & Order* and its spin-offs, followed the work of district attorneys in San Diego, California, as they prepared and prosecuted actual criminal cases. Unlike many true-crime programs, it used no narration, interviews, or reenactments. Instead, the attorneys were seen carrying out their actual work of interviewing witnesses, gathering evidence, and presenting their cases in court.

Crime 360 (Documentary, A&E, 2008-   ). This program features the re-creation of crime scenes and the depiction of the likely sequences of events that took place at the scenes through computer-generated imagery (CGI). The details portrayed in the CGI animated segments are based on the information gathered from scientific examination of the evidence in each case.

Criminal Minds (Drama, CBS, 2005-   ). In this program, a team of specialists within the Federal Bureau of Investigation's Behavioral Analysis Unit employs criminal personality profiling to aid local police departments in apprehending serial rapists and murderers. The team members examine crime scenes, analyze victimology, and interview witnesses to understand the motivations and emotional triggers of the criminal perpetrators.

Crossing Jordan (Drama, NBC, 2001-2007). This series focused on the crime-solving efforts of medical examiners and other specialists working at the Boston medical examiner's office. In addition to analyzing evidence from autopsies as well as materials found on the bodies that entered their morgue, the characters often visited crime scenes and interviewed witnesses to further their investigations. Many different forensic science techniques and technologies were featured in the program.

CSI: Crime Scene Investigation (Drama, CBS, 2000-   ). This is the program credited with bringing cutting-edge forensic science into American homes while at the same time glamorizing and distorting the work of forensic scientists in the minds of the public. Each episode follows forensic scientists of the Las Vegas Crime Lab as they collect and examine the evidence from one or more crimes and then interpret the evidence to aid the police investigations. The focus is on the use of forensic techniques to determine how the crimes were committed, in contrast to many crime dramas' emphasis on other investigative techniques. The success of *CSI* led to two

spin-off series: *CSI: Miami* (2002-   ) and *CSI: NY* (2004-   ).

Dr. G: Medical Examiner (Documentary, Discovery Health Channel, 2004-   ). Featuring Dr. Jan Garavaglia, a forensic pathologist who works out of a county medical examiner's office in Orlando, Florida, this show demonstrates the various forensic procedures used to investigate mysterious or suspicious deaths, including toxicology screening and autopsy. Most of the cases described relate to criminal events.

The First 48 (Documentary, A&E, 2004-   ). The title of this program refers to the importance of speed in police efforts to solve crimes or find missing persons. Each episode offers unprecedented access to homicide detectives during the first forty-eight hours after a murder is committed, following the investigators and observing their evidence-gathering techniques during this crucial period.

Forensic Files (Documentary, Court TV, 2000-   ). Each episode of this program discusses the forensic techniques used in the analysis of evidence from a given crime or mysterious death. Using dramatic reenactments and interviews, the program shows how forensic science provides investigators with the information they need to solve cases.

In Justice (Drama, ABC, 2006). Inspired by the work of the Innocence Project, this short-lived series was a departure from other crime-based dramas in that it focused on the cases of persons convicted of crimes they did not commit. The investigators and attorneys of the fictional National Justice Project attempted in each episode to overturn the conviction of a wrongfully incarcerated person. Team members reinvestigated the crime, sometimes finding new evidence. They also reexamined old evidence, in some cases applying forensic techniques that had been unavailable at the time of the person's original trial, particularly DNA analysis.

Law & Order (Drama, NBC, 1990-   ). This program, the longest-running crime show in television history, explores the two major sides of the American criminal justice system's response to crime: The first half of each episode is devoted to the police investigation of a crime, usually a homicide, and the second half focuses on the legal issues involved in the prosecution of the suspect arrested by the police. In the first half, the New York City police detectives are usually guided in their investigation, at least in part, by an autopsy report on the victim from a forensic pathologist as well as reports from various crime lab technicians regarding their analyses of the evidence gathered from the crime scene (such as ballistic evidence and fingerprints). The courtroom scenes in the second half of the show often touch on issues of evidence admissibility and the presentation of forensic evidence by expert witnesses.

Law & Order: Criminal Intent (Drama, NBC, 2001-   ). This spin-off series focuses on psychological techniques of criminal investigation, which include behavioral profiling and forensic psychology. Although the detectives of the New York City Police Department's Major Case Squad also rely on autopsy reports and other information provided by forensic specialists who examine physical evidence in their cases, this program is concerned primarily with the motivations of persons who commit crimes and the need for investigators to understand those motivations.

Law & Order: Special Victims Unit (Drama, NBC, 1999-   ). This spin-off series depicts the work of a special New York Police Department unit that is devoted to the investigation of sexually based crimes, such as rape, incest, and child pornography. The program highlights how medical personnel use rape kits to gather evidence from victims following sexual assault and how DNA analysis and other forensic techniques can be applied to the conviction of sexual offenders.

Medical Detectives (Documentary, TLC, 1995-1999). This program featured real cases in which medical investigators attempted to solve criminal cases with very little information to go on. In 2000, Court TV (now truTV) picked up this series and widened its scope to create *Forensic Files*.

NCIS (Drama, CBS, 2003-   ). This program features the work of a team from the Naval Criminal Investigative Service, which investigates crimes involving members of the U.S. Navy or Marines. The team includes a forensic specialist, a computer scientist, and a medical examiner, and their analyses of the evidence play a large role in guiding each investigation.

The New Detectives (Documentary, Discovery Channel, 1996-1999). This program featured the work of world-renowned forensic scientists and depicted how they used everything from anthropological data to high-tech forensic screening devises to solve crimes around the United States.

Quincy, M.E. (Drama, NBC, 1976-1983). One of the first programs to deal with forensic science, this show focused on the crime-solving activities of a medical examiner who worked to collect evidence on suspicious deaths that occurred in the Los Angeles area. The lead character's skills enabled him to uncover clues from the smallest pieces of evidence. Although it originally presented stories involving typical criminal events, many later episodes emphasized political and social injustices in the American criminal justice system.

Snapped (Documentary, Oxygen, 2004-   ). This series focuses on the cases of real-life women who committed horrendous crimes, including the murders of their husbands, their husbands' mistresses, and their children. Although much of each episode is devoted to discussion of the drama surrounding the lives of the women who committed these crimes, some attention is given to the investigative techniques used by law-enforcement agencies to solve the crimes.

Unsolved Mysteries (Documentary, NBC, 1987-2002). This program, hosted by actor Robert Stack, presented the known facts related to a variety of unsolved criminal cases as well as cases of missing persons and paranormal phenomena. It featured interviews with persons involved in the cases as well as dramatic reenactments. Viewers were encouraged to contribute any information that could help solve the cases presented, and many did. It has been estimated that nearly 40 percent of the cases featured on the program were solved through help from viewers.

Women's Murder Club (Drama, ABC, 2007-2008). This program, set in San Francisco, featured a group of four women—a police inspector, an assistant district attorney, a reporter, and a medical examiner—who worked together to solve cases of homicide. The information provided by the medical examiner often played an important role in guiding the investigations.

Jennifer L. Christian

Key Figures in Forensic Science

Victor Balthazard (1872-1950). A Paris, France, native whose innovative work with ballistics and hair follicles aided forensic investigations, Balthazard studied at the École Polytechnique prior to becoming an artillery officer in 1893. Interested in medical research, by 1904 he quit his military career to focus on forensic medicine endeavors, and he subsequently was named Paris's chief medical examiner. A 1909 murder initiated Balthazard's scientific study of hair when he found hair evidence on the victim. Using a microscope, Balthazard compared that evidence with hair collected from a suspect; the comparison resulted in the first forensic use of human hair evidence offered as proof of a suspect's guilt. Balthazard contributed to the knowledge of ballistics in forensic science: He asserted that not only bullets but also casings and cartridges are marked by the guns that fire them, and he proved his hypothesis by making microscopic comparisons of those objects. Forensic investigators accepted Balthazard's ideas, which offered them options to study the variety of ballistics evidence found at crime scenes. Balthazard also examined blood spatter patterns to investigate crimes.

William M. Bass (1928-   ). Creator of the University of Tennessee's Anthropological Research Facility, informally called the Body Farm, Bass was born in Staunton, Virginia. He studied psychology at the University of Virginia, where he also enrolled in anthropology classes. After completing a bachelor of arts degree in 1951, Bass served in the U.S. Army until 1953, then began graduate work at the University of Kentucky, where he earned a master of science degree in anthropology by 1956. Continuing his academic training at the University of Pennsylvania, Bass received his doctoral degree in 1961 and began teaching as an anthropology professor at the University of Kansas. In 1971 he became the head of the Anthropology Department at the University of Tennessee in Knoxville, and in 1972 he established the Body Farm. The facility, located near the university's hospital, offers forensic scientists and students in forensic anthropology the opportunity to study in depth the process of the decomposition of the human body.

Alphonse Bertillon (1853-1914). Best known for his pioneering work applying science to criminal identification, Bertillon was born in Paris, France, where his father, Louis Adolphe Bertillon, was a prominent physician and anthropologist. Bertillon began working for the Parisian police department in 1878. Assigned tasks related to arrest records describing criminals, Bertillon dismissed written and photographic techniques as ineffective. He devised a system of anthropometry—that is, measurement of skulls, arms, feet, fingers, and other body parts—to supplement photography of criminals' faces. Despite initial rejection of his idea, Bertillon convinced the police to try his method, and in 1883 it helped to establish a standardized identification for a man who had used various aliases when previously arrested. In 1892, Bertillon gained international recognition when his measurement method identified a wanted fugitive suspected of bombing a judge's home. The Bertillon system, also known as *bertillonage*, later lost favor for identification because it was often impractical for use in identifying suspects at crime scenes, measurements were inconsistently recorded, and it was useless to describe the measurements of twins and other skeletally similar criminals—such persons could be distinguished from one another only through fingerprinting.

Edgard O. Espinoza (1953-   ). An innovator in wildlife forensic science, Espinoza was born in Concepción, Chile. In 1975, he emigrated to California, where he studied medical technology at Loma Linda University, earning a bachelor of science degree in 1978. Enrolling in graduate school at the University of California, Berkeley, Espinoza focused on forensic science studies, completing master's and doctoral degrees in 1984 and 1988, respectively. He taught forensic sciences at

Sacramento State University and provided forensic expertise to aid law-enforcement investigations. Employed at the National Fish and Wildlife Forensics Laboratory since 1989, he held various positions, including chief of the Criminalistics Section. With colleague Mary-Jacque Mann, Espinoza determined how to evaluate Schreger lines in ivory to aid customs agents in distinguishing banned elephant ivory imports from legal ivory sources, and Espinoza and Mann published *Identification Guide for Ivory and Ivory Substitutes* in 1991. Espinoza also developed a technique using mass spectrometry to analyze minute amounts of blood evidence to identify the animal species from which the blood came according to the hemoglobin proteins present.

Henry Faulds (1843-1930). A pioneer in fingerprint analysis, Faulds was born at Beith in Ayrshire, Scotland. He studied at the University of Glasgow and Anderson's College, aspiring to become a physician and a medical missionary. Faulds pursued missions in India and then in Japan, starting a mission hospital in the Tsukiji district of Tokyo. He became intrigued by fingerprints pressed into pottery and began collecting fingerprints; subsequently, his examination of fingerprints led to solutions in two criminal cases. After a theft near his home, Faulds identified a servant as the culprit by comparing fingerprint evidence on a cup with prints in his collection. In another case, Faulds compared the fingerprints of an arrested suspect with fingerprints from the crime scene and found they did not match; another person was identified whose fingerprints were those at the crime scene. In an article published in the October, 1880, issue of the journal *Nature*, Faulds stressed the value of fingerprint analysis for apprehending criminals. Experimenting with removing fingerprints, he noted that the ridges on fingers are resilient and do not change despite trauma. In 1905, Faulds published *Guide to Finger-Print Identification*. His efforts to convince European police to adopt fingerprinting as a method of identification were largely unsuccessful, however.

Francis Galton (1822-1911). An English scientist who contributed basic fingerprint information to forensic science, Galton was born in Birmingham, England. After reading the commentary on fingerprint identification published in the scientific journal *Nature* by Henry Faulds and William James Herschel, Galton wanted to create a classification method for fingerprints. He wrote to Herschel, who gave Galton his collection of fingerprints. Galton also collected fingerprints from people in London. Examining those samples, he realized that all ten fingerprints on a person vary, that aging does not affect fingerprints' patterns, and that every fingerprint is distinctive, with duplication impossible even in twins. Galton suggested classifying fingerprints simply according to their loops, arches, and whorls. In 1892, he published a book on the topic titled *Finger Prints*. As a result of Galton's work, British law-enforcement authorities began considering securing suspects' fingerprints in addition to using anthropometry, the measurement method of identification created by Alphonse Bertillon. Realizing that his fingerprint classification was not fully functional for effective forensic use, Galton stopped his work in this area, and most law-enforcement personnel continued to use anthropometry.

Alexander O. Gettler (1883-1968). Known for establishing innovative forensic toxicology methods, Gettler was born in Austria and emigrated to the United States when he was a child. He earned a diploma from City College of New York in 1904 and then attended Columbia University, completing a master's degree in chemistry in 1910 and a doctorate in chemistry in 1912. He became chief chemist at Bellevue Hospital in 1915, and in 1918, medical examiner Charles Norris named Gettler chief toxicologist at the New York City Medical Examiner's Office. Analyzing evidence chemically, Gettler conducted research assessing levels of alcohol in blood and how alcohol consumption influences driving ability. He also developed a method for measuring chloride in blood to determine whether drowning was the cause of death when bodies were found in water. Forensic investigators worldwide adopted that technique. Gettler created the first graduate forensic toxicology program in the United States at New York University, where he taught chemistry until 1950, when he became professor emeritus. Gettler retired as chief toxicologist in April, 1959. During his career, he wrote numerous scholarly articles on toxicology and testified in court many times regarding his analyses of forensic evidence. The American Academy of Forensic Sciences named an award in Gettler's honor.

Calvin Goddard (1891-1955). An innovator in the forensic examination of ballistics evidence, Goddard was born in Baltimore, Maryland. After earning a bachelor's degree at The Johns Hopkins University in 1911, Goddard completed his medical degree there in 1915 and then joined the U.S. Army Medical Corps. Five years later, he was honorably discharged and took the position of assistant director of The Johns Hopkins Hospital. In 1924, Goddard left Maryland for a Cornell Medical School professorship. A year later, Goddard, a gun enthusiast, moved to New York City to work at the Bureau of Forensic Ballistics, where he initiated methods to connect guns with fired bullets by comparing the unique marks etched on bullets as they are discharged from firearms. Goddard next directed Northwestern University's Scientific Crime Detection Laboratory, aspiring to provide educational and laboratory resources for law-enforcement personnel nationwide. At Northwestern's law school, Goddard taught courses featuring police science, an emerging academic subject. He established the innovative *American Journal of Police Science* in 1930. His later career involved military laboratory work in the United States and Asia, extending his influence on forensic ballistics.

Ken Goddard (1946-   ). A wildlife forensics pioneer, Goddard was born in San Diego, California. He enrolled at the University of California, San Diego, in 1964, and later transferred to the University of California, Riverside, where he completed a bachelor of science degree in 1968. While he studied biochemistry in graduate school at California State University, Los Angeles, where he earned a master's degree in 1971, Goddard

realized that research did not appeal to him. He decided to pursue forensic work, so that his scientific knowledge would aid law enforcement. He worked as a crime laboratory forensic scientist for several California sheriff's and police departments until 1978, when he applied for a position to oversee a national forensics program for the U.S. Fish and Wildlife Service. Goddard became director of the National Fish and Wildlife Forensics Laboratory in 1989. In addition to his work in wildlife forensics, he has written crime novels that incorporate elements of forensic science.

Bernard Greenberg (1922-   ). Considered a founder of forensic entomology, Greenberg was born in New York City. He earned a bachelor of arts degree from Brooklyn College in 1944 and then served in the U.S. Air Force until 1946. He then undertook graduate studies at the University of Kansas, where he completed a master of arts degree in 1951 and his doctorate three years later. He accepted a position teaching biology as an assistant professor at the University of Illinois Medical Center in Chicago. Eventually, Greenberg's research concerning flies resulted in law-enforcement personnel seeking his expertise, starting with a 1976 murder case. Greenberg consulted and testified regarding forensic evidence involving insects and cadavers, particularly the use of insect evidence to determine time since death, establishing the scientific basis for forensic entomology. Greenberg published the two-volume work *Flies and Disease* (1971-1973) and cowrote, with John Charles Kunich, *Entomology and the Law: Flies as Forensic Indicators* (2002). In 1981, Greenberg served as scientific governor of the Chicago Academy of Sciences. He retired as professor emeritus in 1990.

Hans Gross (1847-1915). An innovative jurist who recognized the value of the scientific examination of evidence to the legal process, Gross, born in Graz, Austria, pursued education that qualified him to accept a position as an examining judge. Realizing that law-enforcement officers of his time, the mid-nineteenth century, focused on policing civil unrest more than they did on investigating crimes, Gross took it upon himself to secure and examine the evidence in the cases before him so he could deliver effective legal judgments. He relied on scientific approaches to evaluate suspects and the evidence associated with their alleged crimes. Gross also applied science when considering legal proceedings for civil issues. In 1893, Gross published *System der Kriminalistik* (*Criminal Investigation*, 1906), which was based on his forensic insights and work. The book gained him global recognition for his views regarding science as an effective investigation technique. Gross, who lectured at the University of Graz and the University of Prague, urged scientists and law-enforcement personnel to seek improved forensic methods using proven technology and scientific developments instead of relying on obsolete techniques and tools. Sir Arthur Conan Doyle studied Gross's ideas for details he elaborated in his Sherlock Holmes stories.

Edward R. Henry (1850-1931). A forensic fingerprint pioneer, Henry, born in London, worked for the Indian Civil Service in Calcutta as police inspector. Frustrated by the limitations of the measurement system of identification created by Alphonse Bertillon (anthropometry, also known as *bertillonage*), Henry knew that palm prints and fingerprints were used in India to notarize legal documents. He had read about the ideas of Henry Faulds and Francis Galton concerning fingerprints, and he had met Galton in England. Henry gathered fingerprint data and contemplated how best to organize them. He had an epiphany in December, 1896, and created a classification system that differentiated fingerprints by whorls, radial and ulnar loops, and plain and tented arches, recognizing their variations, as well as by the numbers of ridges composing those shapes. Henry compared fingerprinting with *bertillonage* measurements and proved that fingerprinting, with his classification method, identified criminals more accurately. In 1897, Henry's fingerprint technique became the standard identification process used in India, and the Indian government published his work *Classification and Uses of Fingerprints*. Henry

subsequently took the position of police commissioner in London. Police in the United States and Europe soon appropriated and improved on aspects of Henry's classification techniques.

Alec Jeffreys (1950-   ). The originator of DNA (deoxyribonucleic acid) fingerprinting, Jeffreys was born in Oxford, England. Jeffreys's father, an inventor, encouraged Jeffreys's scientific interests by buying him a chemistry set and microscope. Jeffreys enrolled in Oxford's Merton College, completing his biochemistry degree in 1972. He pursued graduate work in genetics and earned his doctoral degree in 1975. Jeffreys conducted postdoctoral genetic research at the University of Amsterdam until 1977, when he returned to England to conduct research on DNA in the University of Leicester's genetics department. While experimenting with DNA components in September, 1984, Jeffreys realized that DNA bands differ significantly and could be useful for purposes of identification, much like fingerprints. His work in genetic fingerprinting led to significant changes in the field of forensic science. DNA comparisons were first used publicly to resolve issues of identification in immigration and paternity cases. Law-enforcement authorities then requested that Jeffreys use so-called DNA fingerprinting in two unsolved 1980's murders; the resulting analysis identified the killer and exonerated another suspect. Jeffreys and other scientists subsequently improved on Jeffreys's original methods with techniques such as polymerase chain reaction (PCR).

Paul L. Kirk (1902-1970). A pioneer in criminalistics in the United States, Kirk was born in Colorado Springs, Colorado. He graduated from Ohio State University with a bachelor's degree in 1924 and then earned a master's degree at the University of Pittsburgh the following year. In 1927, he completed a doctorate in biochemistry at the University of California, Berkeley. Kirk stayed at Berkeley to teach and conduct research in criminalistics, and he also agreed to serve as an adviser to California's state crime laboratory, the first such lab established by a state government in the United States. Kirk helped the university to develop a criminology program that came to be influential in forensic practices. He urged law-enforcement investigators to acquire scientific knowledge and to learn about the varied kinds of forensic evidence they might encounter and consider how such evidence might be connected to crime victims. Kirk wrote several books, including *Crime Investigation: Physical Evidence and the Police Laboratory Interscience* (1953). He also developed a transportable forensic laboratory that inspired the creation of similar kinds of equipment for use by law-enforcement personnel.

Alexandre Lacassagne (1843-1924). Sometimes referred to as the father of forensic science, Lacassagne was born in Cahors, France. Trained as a physician, he traveled to North Africa to treat military troops; during his time there, he examined soldiers' injuries caused by bullets and realized that tattoos could be used to identify soldiers who had been killed. When he returned to France, Lacassagne taught forensic medicine as a pathology professor at the University of Lyon. As a result of his research and experiences, Lacassagne devised useful methods of identifying unidentified bodies by examining their skeletal and dental conditions. By 1889, Lacassagne concluded that bullets could be connected to the firearms that discharged them based on the grooves etched into bullets by the weapons' barrels, providing the theoretical basis for the science of ballistics. Lacassagne also investigated the physical evidence used to prove that people were dead, noting that the skin appears purple when blood stops circulating. His investigations of rigor mortis and body temperature contributed to the forensic techniques used to calculate time since death when bodies are discovered.

Karl Landsteiner (1868-1943). A scientist who recognized the forensic value of basic blood characteristics, Landsteiner was born in Vienna, Austria. He began his unexpected forensic medical achievements when he enrolled at the University of Vienna, aspiring to become a physician. Completing a degree in 1891, he focused his research on serology. His aim was to improve the techniques of blood transfusion, which was a very risky practice for patients receiving blood. Landsteiner discovered the existence of four human blood groups—a discovery with practical applications, as patients requiring transfusions could receive blood that matched their types and would not cause dangerous reactions. Forensic investigators recognized the value of Landsteiner's discovery for the identification of crime victims and suspects through the testing of blood evidence for type. After completing his blood type research, Landsteiner studied viruses and poliomyelitis. When World War I ended, he moved to the Netherlands and then to New York City, where he conducted research with Alexander S. Wiener to detect blood's rhesus (Rh) factor; this work also enhanced forensic identification methods. Landsteiner won the 1930 Nobel Prize in Physiology or Medicine for his research concerning blood types.

John A. Larson (1892-1965). Known for innovating the basic elements of a forensic polygraph tool, Larson was born in Shelbourne, Nova Scotia. He acquired his education in the United States, studying at Boston University, where he completed a bachelor's degree by 1914 and a master's degree the next year. Moving to California, Larson enrolled in graduate school at the University of California, Berkeley, to pursue doctoral work to become a criminologist. He earned a doctoral degree in 1920, followed by a medical degree in 1928 from Rush Medical College. In addition to pursuing his education, Larson secured employment with the police department in Berkeley, qualifying for the rank of sergeant. Berkeley police chief August Vollmer assigned Larson the task of creating a machine that could evaluate the truthfulness of a person being interviewed. Larson created a prototype polygraph that included a band that wrapped around the interviewee's arm to note fluctuating blood pressure. Vollmer served as Larson's first subject, showing how his lies affected the polygraph. Inspired by Larson's device, a number of inventors subsequently designed more complex polygraphs.

Leone Lattes (1887-1954). A contributor to the science of the forensic analysis of blood evidence, Lattes was born in Turin, Italy. He advanced his medical studies by visiting European universities, particularly in Germany, where he became intrigued with investigating blood after he met with serological researcher Max Richter. Returning to Turin, where he conducted research at the Institute of Forensic Medicine, Lattes focused on learning about blood types. In 1915, a man whose wife thought his bloody shirt proved he had been unfaithful asked Lattes to determine the source of the blood on the shirt. Lattes acquired the shirt three months after it had been stained. Because no technique for analyzing bloodstains yet existed, Lattes assessed the stain by wetting it to identify the blood type. The type matched that of the man, and Lattes concluded that the man had bled on his shirt. Later, while experimenting with blood flakes mixed with fresh blood, Lattes noted that the blood became lumpy if the samples were not of the same blood type. Forensic scientists recognized the value of Lattes's method for quick assessment of bloodstains, and that technique has retained its investigative value.

Edmond Locard (1877-1966). Originator of the principle of forensic science that holds that "every contact leaves a trace," Locard was born in France. As a young adult, intrigued by the incorporation of science into Sir Arthur Conan Doyle's Sherlock Holmes stories, Locard decided to pursue criminology professionally. He enrolled in the University of Lyon, where he took courses from Alexandre Lacassagne and Alphonse Bertillon. After completing degrees in legal and medical studies, Locard began employment with Lacassagne, where he remained through 1910, when he became director of the Lyon police laboratory. He used forensic evidence and techniques to prove the guilt of thieves, counterfeiters, and murderers. Despite an accused murderer's alibi in 1912, Locard evaluated skin cells he collected from the suspect's fingernails and detected the presence of a unique cosmetic the victim had worn. That forensic evidence caused the suspect to admit he had lied. Locard focused on dust as essential forensic trace evidence, studying variations and specifying how investigators should collect it. He also developed poroscopy, or the assessment of the distribution of pores in fingerprints.

James Marsh (1794-1846). An English chemist, Marsh devised a technique and testing device that forensic investigators could use to determine whether arsenic was present in organisms. The technique, known as the Marsh test, employed zinc and either sulfuric or hydrochloric acid to form hydrogen gas, which reacts with arsenic. During the early nineteenth century, arsenic was a favored poison used by murderers, and law-enforcement authorities needed an accurate way to prove whether that toxin had caused deaths. Starting in 1822, Marsh lived in Woolwich and worked as the Royal Arsenal's chemist. He also secured employment assisting Michael Faraday, evaluating weaponry for the Royal Military Academy. In 1836, Marsh testified at a legal proceeding, using his toxicology testing expertise to present evidence convincingly. An article he wrote describing his test for arsenic appeared in the October, 1836, issue of the *Edinburgh New Philosophical Journal*. Marsh's peers recognized the value of the test and adapted it when needed; such significant forensic toxicologists as Matthieu-Joseph-Bonaventure Orfila are known to have employed the technique. Marsh's testing procedure remained useful into the twentieth century, but it was rendered obsolete when more advanced toxicological tests were developed.

Alan R. Moritz (1899-1986). A prominent forensic pathologist, Moritz was born in Hastings, Nebraska. He earned three degrees at the University of Nebraska: a bachelor of science degree in 1920, a master's degree the next year, and a medical degree in 1923. He subsequently moved to Cleveland, Ohio, where he held several pathology positions during his career at Lakeside Hospital and Western Reserve University School of Medicine. Moritz accepted a professorship at Harvard University in 1937. That year, he discovered that by applying a mixture of amyl acetate and nail polish to hair follicles on microscope slides, he could create a clearer microscopic view of the follicles in the dried chemicals than was possible with the raw follicles alone. He provided his pathology expertise to investigations conducted by the Massachusetts State Police Force until 1949, when he returned to Cleveland. Moritz's widely read article "Classical Mistakes in Forensic Pathology" appeared in the December, 1956, issue of the *American Journal of Clinical Pathology*. Moritz testified regarding forensic evidence in such notable trials as the Sam Sheppard murder case and served on the Warren Commission, which was established to investigate the assassination of President John F. Kennedy in 1963.

Matthieu-Joseph-Bonaventure Orfila (1787-1853). An important figure in the development of forensic toxicology, Orfila was born in Mahón on Spain's island of Minorca. After completing courses in chemistry and other sciences in his native country, Orfila moved to Paris, France, to complete his medical studies. Teaching at the University of Paris medical school, Orfila also investigated the chemistry of such poisons as arsenic. He wrote *Traité des poisons tirés des règnes minéral, végétal et animal: Ou, Toxicologie générale* (1813-1815; treatise on poisons drawn from the mineral, plant, and animal kingdoms, or general toxicology), which was the first text to examine scientifically the physiological and psychological effects of poisons and to explain how medical and legal personnel could determine whether persons had been poisoned and what toxins had damaged their systems. Because of his expertise in poisons, Orfila was called upon to testify at the 1840 murder trial of Marie Lafarge, who was accused of poisoning her husband, Charles. After criticizing a chemist's testimony regarding circumstantial arsenic evidence in the victim's home, Orfila used the Marsh test to examine the victim's internal organs for arsenic. The results·of the test were positive, and Marie Lafarge was convicted.

Albert S. Osborn (1858-1946). A pioneer in the field of forensic document examination,

Osborn was born in Sharon, Michigan, and grew up on his parents' farm. Uninterested in becoming a farmer, Osborn studied penmanship at a Lansing, Michigan, college and then accepted a teaching position at the Rochester Business Institute in New York in 1882. Osborn soon became a legal consultant, evaluating documents for evidence of forgery; he established an office in New York City. He became frustrated when judges dismissed his insights regarding the documents he evaluated, so he began writing essays describing his techniques to educate legal professionals. His reputation as a document expert was enhanced when he testified regarding typed documents concerning the federal government's deployment of naval vessels in 1908. In 1910, he published *Questioned Documents*, now considered a classic source in the field. In 1935, Osborn testified in court regarding his evaluation of the messages sent to the famous aviator Charles A. Lindbergh demanding ransom for Lindbergh's kidnapped son; he stated that suspect Bruno Hauptmann's handwriting matched the notes, contributing to the prosecution's successful conviction of Hauptmann.

Sydney Alfred Smith (1883-1969). Born in New Zealand, Smith influenced the practices of forensic science on several continents during his career. He enrolled at the University of Edinburgh after moving to Scotland in 1908. Completing his degree with honors in 1912, Smith began to pursue graduate work with Scottish forensic medicine expert Harvey Littlejohn. He earned a public health diploma and master's degree by 1914, then served during World War I. Following the war, he worked for the Egyptian Ministry of Justice and initiated a forensic medicine program at the University of Cairo. Smith helped to create an internationally renowned forensic medicine laboratory there and became an expert in bullet wounds and ballistics. He created a comparison microscope for use in his ballistics investigations. In 1925, Smith published *Forensic Medicine: A Text-Book for Students and Practitioners*, and in 1928 he became a forensic medicine professor at his alma mater when Littlejohn died. He remained at the University of Edinburgh for the next quarter century. Smith emphasized that forensic scientists should master specialties within the field and collaborate, sharing their diverse skills and knowledge to evaluate criminal evidence effectively.

Clyde Snow (1928-   ). An innovator in the field of forensic anthropology, Snow was born in Fort Worth, Texas. As a child, he observed his physician father and a deputy as they determined the identity of a human skeleton they found while hunting. Snow graduated from New Mexico Military Institute in 1947, then completed a bachelor of science degree four years later at Eastern New Mexico University. He took medical courses at Baylor University and pursued zoology graduate work at Texas Tech University, where he earned a master's degree in science in 1955. In 1967, he received a doctoral degree in anthropology from the University of Arizona. Named director of the Federal Aviation Administration's Physical Anthropology Laboratory in 1968, Snow worked on identifying the victims of airplane crashes by assessing skeletal remains. He expedited searches for information by creating computer databases of victim descriptions and descriptions of skeletal evidence. After he retired in 1979, he worked with human rights groups to identify the remains exhumed from mass graves worldwide, gathering evidence to prosecute war criminals. Snow's achievements contributed to the acknowledgment of the field of forensic anthropology by the American Academy of Forensic Sciences and encouraged many anthropologists to pursue forensic investigations.

Bernard Spilsbury (1877-1947). Born in Leamington Spa, Warwickshire, England, Spilsbury helped to influence public opinion concerning the value of forensic science. He studied natural science at Oxford University's Magdalen College, earning a bachelor's degree in 1899. He then took medical courses at St. Mary's Hospital Medical College, intending to become a general practitioner. Instead, he became interested in forensic science, largely owing to the influence of St. Mary's Hospital toxicologists and pathologist Augustus Joseph Pepper, who hired Spilsbury to conduct pathology and anatomy work. By 1905, Spilsbury completed his medical studies and began to pursue a career as a resident assistant pathologist working with Pepper, who frequently assisted law-enforcement personnel with forensic investigations. In 1908, Spilsbury became the Home Office chief pathologist after Pepper's retirement from that position. Spilsbury gained acclaim for his forensic skills and expertise as he testified in notable court cases; he specialized in poisoning cases, particularly cases involving arsenic. His testimony helped to convict murderers who might otherwise have been acquitted, and this increased the public's acceptance of the value of forensic science.

Alfred Swaine Taylor (1806-1880). An important contributor to the shaping of forensic legal perceptions, Taylor was born in Northfleet, Kent, England. He served as an apprentice in London and then took medical courses at Guy's Hospital and St. Thomas' Hospital; he also studied briefly in Paris, France, in 1925, earning a degree three years later. He traveled to advance his medical experiences, returning to England in 1831 after studying injuries caused by firearms during Paris revolts. In London he taught forensic medicine at Guy's Hospital. Applying his medical expertise to legal issues, Taylor published *Elements of Medical Jurisprudence* (1843), *Medical Jurisprudence* (1845), and *The Principles and Practice of Medical Jurisprudence* (1865). Valued for his expertise, Taylor appeared frequently in courtrooms to offer testimony about his evaluation of evidence. At an 1859 trial, Taylor stated that a murdered woman had been poisoned with arsenic. The defendant's attorneys disputed Taylor's testimony, noting that his forensic investigation included copper tools that might have been the source of the arsenic in the tested sample. Taylor's flawed testing method resulted in the defendant's being exonerated, and this led to some distrust of forensic investigations among the public and questioning of the competence of forensic professionals.

Mildred Trotter (1899-1991). A forensic anthropology innovator, Trotter was born in Monaca, Pennsylvania. Enrolling at Mount Holyoke College in 1916, she studied zoology, earning a bachelor's degree in 1920. Trotter accepted a research fellowship at Washington University School of Medicine in St. Louis, Missouri, while attending graduate school to become an anatomist. She received a master of science degree in 1921 and a doctorate three years later. Trotter studied physical anthropology at the University of Oxford for a year before returning to teach and conduct research at Washington University, where she became the first woman to hold the rank of full professor. Starting in 1948, she assisted the American Graves Registration Service's Central Identification Laboratory in Hawaii and provided her anthropological expertise to the U.S. Army in the Philippines during 1951. She focused on researching the human skeleton, investigating maturation and skeletal variations affected by gender and ethnicity. Her findings initiated the method used by forensic anthropologists to determine the approximate height of a deceased person through measurement of the femur (thighbone) when only partial remains are available.

Paul Uhlenhuth (1870-1957). A native of Hannover, Germany, Uhlenhuth studied medicine and became a surgeon for German troops during the late nineteenth century. In 1900, he moved to Berlin to work at the Institute for Infectious Diseases, where he conducted research with renowned bacteriologist Robert Koch, who investigated tuberculosis. Koch encouraged Uhlenhuth to focus on serological research, and Uhlenhuth detected how proteins varied in blood samples from diverse animal subjects. He developed a serum, containing antibodies, to test blood, noting that animal serum clotted with human blood. His findings provided forensic investigators with a technique to determine whether blood evidence, fresh or dried, originated from humans or animals, thus enabling law-enforcement authorities to disprove some suspects' claims that blood found on their garments and weapons came from animals rather than humans. Uhlenhuth conducted his test for the trial of Ludwig Tessnow, who was accused of killing some children. Tessnow claimed that the stains police found on his clothing were wood dye, not blood, but Uhlenhuth determined that they were human blood, and this testimony resulted in Tessnow's conviction. After that legal success, many forensic investigators employed Uhlenhuth's serum analysis.

August Vollmer (1876-1955). An influential figure in the development of forensic science in the United States, Vollmer was born in New Orleans, Louisiana. He served in the U.S. Army during the Spanish-American War, deployed as a scout in the Philippines, prior to moving to Berkeley, California. As chief of the Berkeley Police Department during the early twentieth century, Vollmer valued forensic science and was interested in developments in the field. He hired college-educated personnel who had scientific experience and encouraged police officers to use science in their investigations. He established a police school specifically to train officers in how to collect and assess evidence that could be useful for the legal prosecution of cases. In 1916, Vollmer assisted professors at the University of California at Berkeley in creating a pioneering criminology program. In 1921, he helped initiate research into polygraphy when he asked Berkeley police sergeant John A. Larson to build a machine that could detect when interviewees were lying. Vollmer established a crime laboratory at Berkeley in 1923 that became a resource for forensic investigation for both Berkeley police and other law-enforcement groups. Throughout his career, Vollmer mentored police officers who later became police chiefs across the United States and incorporated the use of forensic science in their departments.

Alexander S. Wiener (1907-1976). A serology expert, Wiener was born in Brooklyn, New York. After completing a bachelor's degree in biology at Cornell University in 1926, Wiener earned a medical degree four years later at Long Island College of Medicine. He then served as director of the blood transfusion division at the Jewish Hospital in Brooklyn. In 1938, New York's chief medical examiner, Thomas Gonzales, named Wiener to direct the state's first laboratory devoted to serology investigations, a position he held until 1976. Wiener collaborated with Karl Landsteiner in comparing blood antigens in humans with those produced by monkeys, resulting in the 1940 finding of the rhesus (Rh) factor. Emphasizing serology as a forensic tool, Wiener evaluated evidence for law enforcement, identifying suspects based on blood types. He wrote several books, including *Blood Groups and Blood Transfusion* (1935). Wiener and his father, attorney George Wiener, contributed to the drafting of state legislation regarding blood group evidence in paternity and criminal cases.

Jeffries Wyman (1814-1874). Frequently credited as the founder of forensic anthropology, Wyman was born in Chelmsford, Massachusetts. Growing up in Charlestown, where his physician father oversaw the McLean Asylum for the Insane, Wyman was fascinated by scientific topics. He studied at Harvard College, earning a degree in 1833, then enrolled at Harvard Medical School, graduating four years later. Wyman subsequently taught anatomy at Harvard and became curator of the Peabody Museum of Archaeology and Ethnology. Wyman's involvement in forensic activities began when a janitor found body parts, bones, and dentures scattered in an anatomy vault and in the office of Harvard medical professor John White Webster. Wyman guided investigators to evaluate the evidence to determine whether they were the remains of Dr. George Parkman, who had vanished on November 23, 1849, around the time he had attempted to collect a debt Webster owed him. Wyman and his colleagues concluded that the bones and dentures were similar to Parkman's physique and jaw shape, and Webster was convicted of the killing.

Paolo Zacchia (1584-1659). Considered a forensic medicine pioneer, Zacchia was employed as the Vatican's physician, providing medical care for popes. Historians credit him with writing the first known scientific text discussing issues that formed the foundation of forensic medicine. From 1651 onward, Zacchia recorded his experiences with a variety of medical processes associated with forensic science, including wound analysis, autopsies, and testing fluids from victims and criminals, and he related his legal concerns in eleven volumes he collectively titled *Quaestiones medico-legales* (questions of legal medicine). Zacchia comprehensively discussed medical and legal aspects of historical and contemporary cases that occurred during the Renaissance in his innovative work, which retained usefulness among forensic researchers through the eighteenth century.

Elizabeth D. Schafer

Time Line

Year   Event

1194   The Office of the Coroner is established by King Richard I in England as a means of collecting fines owed to the Crown. The work of the office includes determining causes of deaths, as murder and suicide are illegal.

1198   Pope Innocent III issues a proclamation condemning the forging of papal bulls and threatening forgers with excommunication. The proclamation outlines six elements that judges should look for in detecting forgeries.

1248   Perhaps the first book applying medical knowledge to legal situations, *Xi Yuan Ji Lu* (various English translations of the title include *The Washing Away of Wrongs* and *Collected Cases of Injustice Rectified*), by scholar Song Ci (Sung Tz'u), is published in China.

1662   Londoner John Graunt collects mortality statistics and becomes the first to quantify patterns of disease in a population.

1686   Italian anatomist Marcello Malpighi notes the presence of consistent patterns on human fingertips.

1747   Scottish physician James Lind applies epidemiological observations in identifying the causation of scurvy and suggesting treatment for the disease.

1761   Italian anatomist Giovanni Battista Morgagni publishes the first medical text on autopsies, *De Sedibus et Causis Morborum per Anatomen Indagatis* (*The Seats and Causes of Diseases Investigated by Anatomy*, 1769).

1775   Paul Revere identifies the remains of General Joseph Warren by examining Warren's dentures, which Revere had made.

1813   Spanish chemist Matthieu-Joseph-Bonaventure Orfila publishes the first volume of a work on toxicology that addresses testing for poisons, *Traité des poisons tirés des règnes minéral, végétal et animal: Ou, Toxicologie générale* (1813-1815; treatise on poisons drawn from the mineral, plant, and animal kingdoms, or general toxicology).

1818   British book illustrator Thomas Bewick uses engravings of his own finger- and thumbprints as a means of identifying his work.

1823   Bohemian physiologist Jan Evangelista Purkyně writes a paper describing a number of friction ridge patterns found in a variety of fingerprints.

1835   British policeman Henry Goddard matches a bullet used in a murder back to its weapon by identifying a defect in the mold in which the bullet was made.

1840   The Marsh test, developed by James Marsh in 1836 as a means of detecting arsenic, becomes the first analytical method of toxicology introduced during a criminal trial.

1843   The M'Naghten rule is formulated. It states that defendants are not criminally responsible if at the times of their crimes they suffered from diseases of the mind that rendered them unable to discern the difference between right and wrong or were delusional and justified their criminal behavior as legitimate self-defense.

1848   British anesthetist John Snow begins his research into cholera; by 1854, his findings lead to the understanding of the causation of the disease.

1850's Englishman Sir William James Herschel begins using fingerprints as a means of identification on contracts during his work in India.

1865   The U.S. Secret Service is created to protect American currency and to investigate and combat counterfeiting.

1866   Dynamite is first developed, made from nitroglycerin, diatomaceous earth, and sodium carbonate wrapped in distinctive red paper.

1871   Italian criminologist Cesare Lombroso theorizes that criminals can be identified by their physical traits. Although most of his theory centers on the sizes of skulls and the lengths of bones, Lombroso later comes to be known as the father of criminal profiling.

1874   English chemist C. R. Alder Wright first produces heroin while conducting laboratory experiments with morphine.

1878   U.S. anatomist Thomas Dwight publishes the first work on forensic anthropology, an essay titled "Identification of the Human Skeleton: A Medico-legal Study."

1882   French criminologist Alphonse Bertillon begins to develop a system of identification based on the measurement of many dimensions of individuals' bodies.

1882   Scottish scientist Henry Faulds begins studying fingerprints after noticing those left on clay sculptures by artists. He concludes that every fingerprint is unique.

1889   French criminologist Alexandre Lacassagne matches a bullet to the gun that fired it by comparing the rifling marks on the bullet to those in the barrel of the firearm.

1890's The findings of experiments conducted by James McKeen Cattell, Alfred Binet, William Stern, and others suggest that eyewitness testimony is often unreliable and incomplete.

1891   Englishman Sir Edward R. Henry is appointed inspector-general of police in Bengal, India, where he develops a system to classify and analyze fingerprints and to apply such analyses to criminal prosecutions. In 1897, the Indian government publishes Henry's work *Classification and Uses of Fingerprints*.

1892   English anthropologist Sir Frances Galton regroups Jan Evangelista Purkyně's fingerprint categories into four basic patterns in his book *Finger Prints*.

1893   Austrian criminologist Hans Gross, in his book *System der Kriminalistik* (*Criminal Investigation*, 1906), expresses the importance of trace evidence in criminal investigations.

1897   George A. Dorsey becomes the first anthropologist to apply osteology in a criminal trial when he testifies regarding fragments of human bone found in a vat at the Luetgert sausage factory in Chicago.

1898   British mathematician Karl Pearson uses bone measurements to estimate an unidentified individual's antemortem height.

1900   Albert Llewellyn Hall publishes an article titled "The Missile and the Weapon" in the *Buffalo Medical Journal*, in which he presents the first analysis of the marks imparted to bullets by the rifling in gun barrels.

1900   Austrian biologist Karl Landsteiner identifies three human blood groups, which he names A, B, and C. The groups are later labeled A, B, and O.

1901   The use of the chemical phenolphthalein in presumptive tests for blood is introduced.

1901   The Fingerprint Branch at New Scotland Yard is created.

1903   Russian botanist Mikhail Semyonovich Tsvet invents chromatography as a tool for helping him to separate plant pigments. The technique is later applied to the separation of many different kinds of chemical mixtures into their individual components.

1904   The use of the chemical benzidine in presumptive tests for blood is introduced.

1906   The Food, Drug and Insecticide Administration (later named the Food and Drug Administration) is established in the United States.

1908   The Bureau of Investigations (renamed the Federal Bureau of Investigation in 1935) is created.

1908   With the publication of his book *On the Witness Stand: Essays on Psychology and Crime*, Hugo Münsterberg helps to popularize the notion that the application of psychology could be an asset for the legal system.

1908   German chemist Georg Popp becomes the first to use forensic geoscience in a criminal investigation when he compares soil samples from a crime scene to the soil on a suspect's shoes to disprove the suspect's alibi.

1910   French criminologist Edmond Locard establishes the first modern scientific laboratory for the investigation of crime in Lyon, France.

1912   The use of the chemical orthotolidine, also known as o-tolidine, is introduced in presumptive tests for blood.

1913   Psychological services are provided to inmates at a U.S. correctional facility for the first time.

1914   The U.S. Congress passes the Harrison Narcotic Drug Act, which regulates the manufacturing and distribution of heroin and other drugs.

1915   The International Association for Identification is formed.

1916   Joseph Goldberger of the U.S. Public Health Service begins two years of studies to identify the causation of pellagra.

1917   Lewis Terman becomes the first American psychologist to use psychological testing in the selection process for police officers.

1917   Mustard gas, a blister agent, is first employed as a weapon by Germany during World War I.

1920's William Moulton Marston becomes the first professor of legal psychology at American University.

1920   Two Italian immigrant laborers, Nicola Sacco and Bartolomeo Vanzetti, are arrested for the armed robbery and murder of two people in South Braintree, Massachusetts. Ballistics evidence plays an important role in their conviction and eventual execution for the crime.

1921   American medical student and police officer John A. Larson develops a continuous polygraph machine, which he calls a cardio-pneumo-psychograph.

1921   Philip O. Gravelle invents the comparison microscope, which allows forensic scientists to conduct simultaneous microscopic side-by-side comparisons of two objects.

1923   The ruling of the Court of Appeals for the District of Columbia in *Frye v. United States* introduces a new standard for the admissibility of new or novel scientific evidence in court. According to this "general acceptance" standard, expert testimony is admissible only if the scientific principle, theory, or discovery on which it is based is "sufficiently established to have gained general acceptance in the particular field in which it belongs."

1923   The first American police department criminal laboratory is established in Los Angeles, California, by August Vollmer.

1923   The International Criminal Police Commission (later renamed the International Criminal Police Organization) is established in Vienna, Austria. Commonly known as Interpol, it becomes the largest international police organization in the world.

1924   The Federal Bureau of Investigation (FBI) establishes a central database of fingerprints against which law-enforcement agencies can seek to match prints found in their local investigations.

1925   Sir Austin Bradford Hill studies the difference in mortality rates between people living in urban settings and those living in rural environments.

1925   The Geneva Protocol outlaws the use of biological weapons.

1931   Harold E. Burtt publishes *Legal Psychology*, the first textbook on the subject.

1931   French criminologist Edmond Locard publishes the first volume of his magnum opus *Traité de criminalistique* (1931-1936; treatise on criminalistics), a six-volume work in which he proposes the idea that becomes known as Locard's exchange principle, concerning the transfer of trace evidence.

1932   The Federal Bureau of Investigation Laboratory is established in the United States.

1932   The infant son of pioneer aviator Charles A. Lindbergh is abducted from the nursery of the family's home. Handwriting exemplars and forensic evidence concerning wood are pivotal in the eventual arrest and conviction of Bruno Hauptmann for the crime.

1934   The National Firearms Act of 1934 requires owners of firearms to register the devices with the federal government.

1936   Tabun, the earliest and most easily manufactured nerve gas, is discovered in Germany during experiments to develop new insecticides.

1938   The nerve agent sarin, which is about twice as deadly as tabun, is invented in Germany.

1938   German physicist Manfred von Ardenne invents the scanning electron microscope, which is capable of distinguishing objects three nanometers apart.

1939   American anthropologist Wilton Marion Krogman illustrates the importance of osteology to law enforcement with the publication of his article "A Guide to the Identification of Human Skeletal Material."

1940   Russian paleontologist Ivan Yefremov coins the term "taphonomy" and describes this field as the study of events that occur to organisms after death.

1944   The nerve agent soman is first prepared in Germany as part of that nation's chemical warfare program.

1947   The Environmental Measurements Laboratory is established by the U.S. Health and Safety Division of the Atomic Energy Commission to monitor local and global radiation levels and operate an emergency response group.

1948   The American Academy of Forensic Sciences is formed.

1949   J. G. Humble describes the mechanism by which petechial hemorrhages occur.

1950's The Identi-Kit is introduced for use in the composite drawing of suspects' faces based on information provided by eyewitnesses; this tool features numerous transparencies with choices for face shape, eyes, nose, and so on, to be used in creating composite images.

1951   F. H. Allen describes the Kidd blood grouping system, which is used for typing blood based on specific proteins, known as the Kidd blood antigens.

1952   The first edition of the American Psychiatric Association's *Diagnostic and Statistical Manual of Mental Disorders* is published; the work provides an authoritative scheme that mental health professionals use to classify psychological disorders.

1954   In *Holland v. United States*, the U.S. Supreme Court upholds the use of circumstantial evidence as a basis for conviction in a criminal case.

1957   Australian aeronautical researcher David Warren creates the first flight data recorder that can record data from all of an aircraft's basic operating systems.

1957   The International Association of Forensic Sciences is established.

1960's Martin Reiser of the Los Angeles Police Department becomes one of the first full-time police psychologists in the United States.

1960's Correctional psychology becomes recognized as a profession as a result of the efforts of Stanley Brodsky, Robert Lewinson, and Asher Pacht.

1960's Leland C. Clark develops the first enzyme electrodes, an achievment that eventually leads to the creation of more advanced versions for applications in biotechnology and forensic science.

1960   In *Dusky v. United States*, the U.S. Supreme Court rules that to be deemed competent to stand trial, individuals must have a minimum level of understanding of the legal proceedings and the ability to assist their attorneys in their own defense.

1962   Forensic anthropologist Wilton Marion Krogman publishes *The Human Skeleton in Forensic Medicine*, a work that expands on his seminal 1939 article on the topic of the identification of human skeletal material.

1962   The American Law Institute drafts the Model Penal Code, which includes an important formulation of an insanity defense standard.

1963   The U.S. Supreme Court rules in *Townsend v. Sain* that information acquired during interrogation after the use of a "truth serum" is not admissible in court in criminal cases.

1963   The first patent issued for a flight data recorder in the United States is granted to James Ryan.

1963   U.S. president John F. Kennedy is assassinated in Dallas, Texas. Lee Harvey Oswald is charged with the crime but is never tried, as he is murdered by Jack Ruby two days later. Forensic science plays an important role in the investigation of this high-profile crime, particularly in the autopsy and in the determination of the trajectories of the bullets fired.

1963   The International Association of Forensic Toxicologists is founded.

1964   American police official Alfred V. Iannarelli publishes *The Iannarelli System of Ear Indentification*, in which he asserts that external ears have unique shapes and that ear features can be classified with a system similar to that used to classify fingerprints.

1965   All U.S. commercial airlines are required to install in their aircraft cockpit voice recorders that can capture the last thirty minutes of crew voice communications and noise on any flight.

1966   In *Miranda v. Arizona*, the U.S. Supreme Court rules that individuals in law-enforcement custody must be informed of their Fifth Amendment right against self-incrimination and their Sixth Amendment right to counsel before any questioning can take place.

1966   The International Reference Organization in Forensic Medicine is established by William G. Eckert.

1967   The National Crime Information Center, a central U.S. database for crime-related information maintained by the FBI, begins operations.

1967   The National Transportation Safety Board is established in the United States.

1969   In *Frazier v. Cupp*, the U.S. Supreme Court rules that police or other law-enforcement agents can lie to suspects in order to further their investigations.

1969   The National Institute of Justice is established in the United States.

1969   The U.S. Army Medical Research Institute of Infectious Diseases is founded.

1969   The U.S. National Central Bureau of Interpol is established to facilitate cooperation between American law-enforcement agencies and Interpol.

1969   President Richard M. Nixon issues an executive order outlawing research into offensive biological weapons in the United States.

1970   The Controlled Substances Act establishes rules and regulations for the federal control of drugs in the United States in terms of drug classifications and punishments for violations of the legislation's provisions.

1970   The Federal Law Enforcement Training Center is founded in the United States.

1972   British army troops attack civilian protesters during a march of the Northern Ireland Civil Rights Association in Londonderry, and fourteen protesters die as a result. Later forensic investigations into the events seek to determine whether the soldiers involved were attacked with firearms and nail bombs before they began shooting.

1972   Forensic anthropology becomes an established area of study with the creation of the Physical Anthropology Section of the American Academy of Forensic Sciences.

1972   The Anthropological Research Facility, which soon comes to be known as the Body Farm, is created at the University of Tennessee under the leadership of forensic anthropologist William M. Bass.

1972   The Biological Weapons Convention is opened for signature; the international agreement is intended to end the production of biological weapons worldwide.

1972   Pediatric radiologist John Caffey coins the term "whiplash shaken infant syndrome" to describe the injuries caused in young children by violent shaking; the syndrome later comes to be widely known as shaken baby syndrome.

1972   The Bureau of Alcohol, Tobacco and Firearms (ATF) is established as a division of the U.S. Department of the Treasury; it is later renamed the Bureau of Alcohol, Tobacco, Firearms and Explosives.

1973   The Drug Enforcement Administration is established in the United States.

1974   The use and manufacture of the carcinogenic chemical benzidine, long employed in presumptive tests for blood at crime scenes, are banned in the United States by the Environmental Protection Agency.

1974   The American Society of Crime Laboratory Directors is founded.

1975   The California court case *People v. Marx* helps to establish evidentiary standards for the use of forensic odontology in trials.

1976   A will purportedly handwritten by billionaire Howard Hughes and left anonymously at the headquarters of the Church of Jesus Christ of Latter-day Saints in Salt Lake City, Utah, is filed with a county court in Las Vegas, Nevada, a few weeks after Hughes's death. The will, which includes a provision giving $156 million to Melvin Dummar, owner of a small Utah gas station, is challenged in court and, after evidence is presented regarding fingerprint analysis and analyses of handwriting and ink, is ruled a forgery.

1976   Whitfield Diffie and Martin Hellman develop an algorithm that allows two people to create a shared symmetric computer encryption key.

1976   *Quincy, M.E.*, a fictional television drama about a coroner who uses forensics to solve crimes, premieres on NBC.

1977   The FBI begins using the first computerized automated fingerprint identification system.

1978   American forensic scientists Brian Wraxall and Mark Stolorow develop the multisystem method, which enables the simultaneous analysis of three different blood isozymes from a single bloodstain.

1978   Ted Kaczynski, who will become known as the Unabomber, sends his first bomb through the U.S. mails. He continues sending bombs, primarily to people associated with universities and airlines, until 1995. Forensic scientists study the bombs for clues to the bomber's identity.

1978   Georgi Markov, a defector from Communist Bulgaria, is poisoned with ricin in London, England. Forensic science is instrumental in determining the cause of death and the method used in the murder.

1979   The U.S. Fish and Wildlife Service hires American biochemist Ken Goddard to serve as the agency's first forensic investigator.

1979   Bite-mark evidence plays a crucial role in the first trial of serial killer Ted Bundy for murders committed at Florida State University's Chi Omega sorority house. Bundy is found guilty and sentenced to death.

1980   English forensic investigator Stuart Kind performs calculations relating the locations and times of thirteen murders purportedly committed by the Yorkshire Ripper.

1980   During the Iran-Iraq War (1980-1988), Iraq uses the nerve agent tabun against Iranian troops. The use of the chemical weapon is confirmed in 1984 when a United Nations team finds tabun in an unexploded Iraqi bomb within Iranian borders.

1981   The FBI establishes its Forensic Science Research and Training Center.

1982   Forensic scientists begin using cyanoacrylate vapors to visualize and preserve latent fingerprints and palm prints.

1983   American chemist Kary Mullis develops the polymerase chain reaction (PCR) method for copying strands of DNA.

1983   German journalist Gerd Heidemann claims to have come across diaries kept by Nazi chancellor Adolf Hitler during the period 1932-1945. The diaries are initially authenticated by World War II historians but are ultimately proven to be forgeries when tests show that the paper and ink used were not available during Hitler's lifetime.

1984   The Computer Fraud and Abuse Act is passed in the United States, making it a federal offense to cause damage to a computer connected to the Internet.

1985   British geneticist Alec Jeffreys discovers the use of DNA markers (restriction fragment length polymorphisms, or RFLPs) for personal identification while searching for disease markers in DNA. He recognizes the potential for the method's use in criminal and civil investigations and coins the term "DNA fingerprinting."

1986   The space shuttle *Challenger* explodes in flight, killing all seven crew members. The forensic investigation that follows determines that the accident was caused by the failure of an O-ring seal.

1986   American physician Harry McNamara describes "living forensics," the application of clinical medicine to cases of trauma that require forensic investigation.

1986   The University of Tennessee at Knoxville establishes the Forensic Anthropology Data Bank to centralize the information available on skeletal remains in modern publications.

1987   Englishman Colin Pitchfork is the first criminal offender to be caught as the result of mass DNA screening.

1989   The National Fish and Wildlife Forensics Laboratory is established in the United States.

1990   Washington State enacts the Community Protection Act, which is regarded as the first modern violent sexual predator statute.

1990   The U.S. Congress passes the Anabolic Steroid Control Act of 1990, which criminalizes the nonmedical use of anabolic steroids.

1990   The FBI establishes the Combined DNA Index System (CODIS).

1991   The first U.S. patent is issued for a counterfeit-detection pen, which uses ink that changes color through a chemical reaction when it comes into contact with counterfeit bills.

1991   Remains suspected to be those of Russian czar Nicholas II and his family, executed in 1918, are sent from Russia to the Forensic Science Service laboratory in England and to Carnegie Mellon University in the United States. DNA testing results in a 95 percent certainty that the remains are those of the Russian imperial family.

1991   American geneticist C. Thomas Caskey develops the short tandem repeat (STR) method, a type of polymerase chain reaction process for DNA strand replication.

1991   The FBI selects short tandem repeat analysis over restriction fragment length polymorphism analysis as the preferred method of DNA evidence analysis.

1991   The body of Zachary Taylor, twelfth president of the United States, is exhumed by coroner Richard Greathouse so that tests can be performed to find out whether Taylor was in fact poisoned more than 140 years previously. Although arsenic is detected in the remains, the levels found are well below the levels considered to be toxic to human beings.

1991   The Integrated Ballistics Identification System (IBIS), a searchable database that enables identification of firearms through comparisons of ballistic fingerprints, is developed in Canada.

1991   The Forensic Science Service is established in England.

1992   The professional title "forensic nurse" is established at a meeting of a group of sexual assault nurse examiners (SANEs) in Minneapolis, Minnesota. From this meeting, the International Association of Forensic Nurses (IAFN) is formed to promote and support forensic nursing.

1992   An FBI proposal to expand federal wiretapping laws to include intercepting suspects' computer and online activities is defeated because of objections from groups concerned with protecting civil liberties.

1992   The Innocence Project is founded at the Benjamin N. Cardozo School of Law at Yeshiva University; the organization is devoted to helping wrongfully convicted prisoners use DNA evidence to prove their innocence.

1993   In *Daubert v. Merrell Dow Pharmaceuticals*, the U.S. Supreme Court rules that trial judges have the responsibility for determining the admissibility of expert testimony on scientific evidence, based on the credibility and relevance of the evidence.

1993   The civil case *Anderson v. PG&E* (the so-called Erin Brockovich case) begins. The suit deals with claims that the Pacific Gas and Electric Company illegally dumped chemicals and contaminated the drinking water in Hinkley, California, with hexavalent chromium.

1993   The U.S. government establishes ten regional Disaster Mortuary Operational Response Teams (DMORTs) to provide local agencies with added expertise in the location, recovery, and identification of deceased individuals after disasters.

1993   The Chemical Weapons Convention is opened for signature; the international agreement bans the manufacture and storage of chemical weapons such as soman and tabun.

1993   Kirk Bloodsworth becomes the first wrongfully convicted person in the United States to escape a death sentence as the result of postconviction DNA analysis. His 1984 conviction for the rape and murder of a child is overturned when DNA testing proves his innocence.

1994   Bite-mark evidence provides important corroboration in the trial of Jesse Timmendequas when a bite mark on Timmendequas's hand is shown to match the dentition pattern of seven-year-old Megan Kanka. Timmendequas is found guilty of murdering the child.

1994   The Substance Abuse and Mental Health Services Administration establishes guidelines for the drug testing of federal employees in the United States.

1994   The first evidentiary use of nonhuman DNA occurs in Canada when investigators find the hairs of a cat on the jacket of a man accused of murdering his wife, disproving the suspect's alibi.

1994   The first of the statutes known as Megan's Law is enacted, requiring convicted sex offenders to register with authorities for the purpose of community notification.

1995   The American Nurses Association officially recognizes forensic nursing as a nursing subspecialty.

1995   Timothy McVeigh uses a variation of an ammonium nitrate/fuel oil explosive to attack the Alfred P. Murrah Federal Building in Oklahoma City; the explosion kills 168 people and injures more than 600 others. Investigators are able to collect enough evidence to tie McVeigh and his coconspirators to the bombing.

1995   The Aum Shinrikyo religious cult uses homemade sarin to attack subway commuters in Tokyo, Japan. Nearly five thousand people are hospitalized as a result, and twelve deaths are attributed to the attack. Within two hours of the attack, investigators are able to collect a sample of the substance used, and forensic scientists use gas chromatography-mass spectrometry to identify it as sarin.

1995   The European Network of Forensic Science Institutes is created.

1995   The remains of a fully clothed mummy are discovered on Mount Ampato, Peru. Forensic anthropologists later determine that the girl was most likely about fourteen years old when she died, probably as a result of a human sacrifice, in the fifteenth century.

1995   Former football star O. J. Simpson faces charges of murdering two people in a highly publicized criminal trial that brings forensic science, and DNA testing in particular, into popular consciousness.

1995   *Medical Detectives*, a television series portraying actual forensic cases, premieres on TLC (The Learning Channel).

1996   The Church Arson Task Force is formed to coordinate federal, state, and local law-enforcement efforts to address an increase in arson cases involving churches attended by African Americans.

1996   Prehistoric human remains are found on the bank of the Columbia River near Kennewick, Washington. Forensic examination of the remains reveals that they are approximately 9,800 years old and raises some mysteries as to their origins.

1997   The Joint Commission on Accreditation of Healthcare Organizations begins requiring that hospital staff be trained in the identification of victims of abuse, violence, and neglect and in the collection and preservation of physical evidence from victims for potential legal proceedings.

1997   The Federal Aviation Administration requires that all flight data recorders on U.S. planes be capable of recording at least eighty-eight points of flight data.

1997   In *Kansas v. Hendricks*, the U.S. Supreme Court rules that violent sexual predator statutes that use the civil commitment process to continue to confine sex offenders after they have completed their prison sentences do not qualify as punishment because their purpose is not to punish offenders but to protect the public.

1997   In *General Electric v. Joiner*, the U.S. Supreme Court emphasizes the discretion of trial judges in making decisions to exclude or admit expert testimony.

1998   Mitochondrial DNA analysis is used to identify the remains of the Vietnam War service person interred in the Tomb of the Unknowns at Arlington National Cemetery as First Lieutenant Michael Blassie of the U.S. Air Force.

1998   The FBI's DNA Analysis Units are formed.

1998   The FBI establishes the National DNA Index System.

1998   Retired professor Eugene A. Foster leads a team in testing DNA samples in an attempt to determine whether Thomas Jefferson, third president of the United States, fathered any children by Sally Hemings, one of his slaves. The tests results indicate that a male in Jefferson's line, possibly Thomas Jefferson himself, was the father of at least one of Hemings's children.

1999   The Identity Theft and Assumption Deterrence Act makes identity theft a felony.

1999   In *Kumho Tire Company v. Carmichael*, the U.S. Supreme Court extended trial judges' authority in determining the admissibility of expert testimony by expanding the areas of consideration from scientific methods to all cases in which technical expertise is involved.

1999   The term "forensic epidemiology" is first used in an official context during the presentation of an epidemiologist as an expert witness during a legal proceeding.

1999   Microbial forensic techniques help scientists determine that the first U.S. outbreak of the West Nile virus is a natural occurrence and not an act of bioterrorism.

1999   The FBI launches the Regional Computer Forensics Laboratory in San Diego, California, to assist state, local, and federal law-enforcement agencies in evaluating electronic evidence.

1999   The FBI launches the largest computer forensic case to date when the Melissa virus attacks commercial, government, and military computer systems. David L. Smith of Aberdeen, New Jersey, is arrested for the crime.

1999   The FBI's Integrated Automated Fingerprint Identification System becomes operational.

2000   The American Academy of Forensic Sciences establishes the Forensic Specialties Accreditation Board to accredit the certifiers of forensic fields.

2000   William Walsh, chief scientist at the Pfeiffer Treatment Center in Warrenville, Illinois, tests hair samples from composer Ludwig van Beethoven (who died in 1827) and finds extremely heavy lead deposits. Walsh surmises that lead poisoning may have caused Beethoven's many illnesses and death.

2000   *Forensic Files*, a television series focusing on actual forensic cases, premieres on Court TV.

2000   Scientists announce that mitochondrial DNA analysis has positively identified a heart that had been kept in a jar near Paris, France, since the late eighteenth century as that of King Louis XVII, who died at the age of eight.

2000   *CSI: Crime Scene Investigation*, a fictional television drama about a team of investigators who use forensics to solve crimes, premieres on CBS. The show becomes so popular that it spawns two spin-off series, *CSI: Miami* in 2002 and *CSI: NY* in 2004.

2001   In the case of *People v. Lee*, the New York Court of Appeals holds that the decision regarding whether or not to admit expert testimony at trial regarding the reliability of eyewitness identification is at the discretion of the trial court judge.

2001   Terrorists crash hijacked airliners into the twin towers of the World Trade Center in New York City, into the Pentagon in Arlington, Virginia, and into a field near Shanksville, Pennsylvania, killing approximately three thousand people in all. Forensic odontology and DNA testing play major roles in the process of identifying the victims.

2001   Several letters containing spores of *Bacillus anthracis*, the bacterium that causes anthrax, are mailed by an unknown assailant to news media offices and to two U.S. senators, and ultimately five of the twenty-two people who become infected with anthrax die. Biosensors enable early detection of the anthrax bacterium in letters sent to the Hart Senate Office Building in Washington, D.C., and those potentially exposed there receive prophylactic treatment with antibiotics. Eventually, DNA testing finds that the strain of anthrax used matches a strain produced at Fort Detrick in Frederick, Maryland.

2001   The American Psychological Association stipulates that education for a forensic psychology specialty should be in applied psychology and recommends areas of specialization in clinical psychology, counseling psychology, neuropsychology, and school psychology, with advanced instruction in law and justice.

2002   In the wake of the previous year's anthrax letter attacks, the American Academy of Microbiology formulates standards for evidence collection and analysis of molecular tests for microbial forensics.

2002   The FBI establishes the Scientific Working Group for Microbial Genetics and Forensics to facilitate the identification of organisms used in biocrimes or bioterrorist attacks.

2002   In *Kansas v. Crane*, the U.S. Supreme Court rules that states are not required to show that criminals have no control over their sexual impulses in order to label them violent sexual predators; rather, states need only demonstrate that offenders have serious difficulty controlling their illegal sexual behavior.

2002   *Time* magazine names three forensic auditors—Cynthia Cooper, Coleen Rowley, and Sherron Watkins—as joint "Persons of the Year."

2003   The space shuttle *Columbia* disintegrates during reentry, killing all seven crew members. DNA testing and forensic odontology play important roles in the identification of the remains.

2003   The FBI, in partnership with the U.S. Department of Homeland Security, launches the National Bioforensic Analysis Center to serve as a resource for the study of microbial evidence linked to acts of bioterrorism.

2004   More than thirteen hundred children and adults are held hostage in a middle school in Beslan, a town in the Russian Federation republic of North Ossetia-Alania, by a group of armed terrorists demanding the withdrawal of Russian troops from Chechnya. On the third day of the siege, Russian security forces storm the school, and the resulting fight destroys the building and leaves nearly four hundred people dead. DNA analysis plays an important role in identifying the victims, many of whom are badly burned.

2004   A massive earthquake triggers tsunamis that devastate the coastlines of several Asian countries and kill as many as 250,000 people. Forensic odontology becomes pivotal in the process of identifying the victims.

2004   The U.S. Congress passes the Justice for All Act, which stipulates that all convicts with reasonable claims of innocence must be granted the opportunity to prove their cases in court using DNA testing.

2004   The U.S. Congress passes the Anabolic Steroid Control Act of 2004, which strengthens legal penalties for the distribution and possession of anabolic steroids and encourages education for children regarding the dangers of steroid abuse.

2005   In London, England, bombings in the public transit system kill fifty-two passengers and injure more than seven hundred others. The explosive used is determined to be triacetone triperoxide, which is made from common ingredients that may be obtained relatively easily and is almost undetectable by substance-detection dogs or by conventional bomb-detection systems.

2005   A survey conducted by the National Association of Counties finds that 58 percent of U.S. county law-enforcement agencies list methamphetamine as their number one drug problem.

2005   Turkish and Moroccan hackers release the Zotob Internet worm to steal credit card numbers from infected computers worldwide. Investigators gather data (including IP addresses, e-mail addresses, names linked to those addresses, and hacker nicknames), and less than eight days after the worm hits the Internet, two suspects are arrested.

2006   A forensic team led by Spanish geneticist José Antonio Lorente uses mitochondrial DNA analysis to identify remains held at the Cathedral of Seville, Spain, as those of fifteenth century explorer Christopher Columbus.

2008   Russian forensic scientists who had performed analyses on DNA extracted from teeth, bones, and other fragments of remains recovered in 2007 near the site where remains of members of the last Russian imperial family were found in 1991 announced that they had positively identified the remains as those of Czar Nicholas II's children Alexei and Maria.

2008   The FBI's Integrated Automated Fingerprint Identification System begins development of the Next Generation Identification (NGI) system to increase the efficiency of identifying criminals, suspected terrorists, and undocumented aliens attempting to enter the United States. The NGI will incorporate such biometric identification features as facial recognition, iris scans, palm authentication, and possibly applications using DNA data.

Russell S. Strasser

Bibliography

Contents

General Studies

Block, Eugene B. *Science vs. Crime: The Evolution of the Police Lab*. San Francisco: Cragmont, 1979. Tribute to the evolution of criminal investigation includes chapters that focus on such aspects of forensic science as fingerprints, hair analysis, ballistics, bloodstain characteristics, and document analysis.

DiMaio, Vincent J., and Dominick DiMaio. *Forensic Pathology*. 2d ed. Boca Raton, Fla.: CRC Press, 2001. Explains the theory and science behind all types of techniques applied in the practice of forensic pathology. Topics covered include time of death, premortem violence, blunt trauma to the head and body, airplane casualties, deaths in nursing homes, and suicide.

Evans, Colin. *The Casebook of Forensic Detection: How Science Solved One Hundred of the World's Most Baffling Crimes*. Updated ed. New York: Berkley Books, 2007. Describes the world of forensic scientists and the investigative methods that were used in specific criminal cases. The one hundred case studies presented are categorized according to the forensic techniques that were most useful in solving the cases. Within categories, the cases are arranged in chronological order. Very entertaining and informative.

Gardner, Ross M. *Practical Crime Scene Processing and Investigation*. Boca Raton, Fla.: CRC Press, 2005. Demonstrates the author's expertise in forensic science investigation, honed over the course of his career with the U.S. Army Criminal Investigation Division. Outlines an eighteen-step crime scene investigation process.

Geberth, Vernon J. *Practical Homicide Investigation Checklist and Field Guide*. Boca Raton, Fla.: CRC Press, 1997. Instructional guide, useful for both experts and beginners, has been called the bible of homicide investigation and is used by many U.S. law-enforcement agencies. Explains in detail the process by which forensic analysts solve crimes. Includes graphic pictures of crime scenes and bodies of homicide victims.

Genge, N. E. *The Forensic Casebook: The Science of Crime Scene Investigation*. New York: Ballantine, 2002. Focuses primarily on crime scene investigation but also discusses the analysis of bodies, explosives, computer crimes, animal examiners, and forensic photography. Informative appendixes include a listing of forensic science degree programs in the United States.

Gerber, Samuel M., ed. *Chemistry and Crime: From Sherlock Holmes to Today's Courtroom*. Washington, D.C.: American Chemical Society, 1983. Collection of essays begins with discussion of crimes featured in fictional works that involve a knowledge of chemistry. Subsequent chapters focus on the history of forensic science and on specific chemistry-related techniques scientists use to analyze evidence samples. The final chapter presents the results of a two-year study of physical evidence used in police investigations.

Gerstenfeld, Phyllis B., ed. *Criminal Justice*. 3 vols. Pasadena, Calif.: Salem Press, 2006. Comprehensive reference work provides clear and authoritative treatment of all aspects of the American criminal justice system, including the role of forensic science in the work of law enforcement and the courts.

Gilbert, James N. *Criminal Investigation*. 7th ed. Upper Saddle River, N.J.: Pearson Prentice Hall, 2007. Well-organized volume begins with chapters on the history of criminal investigation and basic concepts before discussing the investigative method, the writing of reports, and law-enforcement interviewing techniques. Individual chapters are then devoted to the forensic investigation of specific kinds of crimes: burglary, robbery, homicide and aggravated assault, sexual assault, larceny, drug investigation, and gang investigation. Suspect identification and courtroom proceedings are also addressed, and the final chapter offers insights into likely future developments in criminal investigation.

Girard, James E. *Criminalistics: Forensic Science and Crime*. Sudbury, Mass.: Jones & Bartlett, 2008. Provides clear explanations of the basic chemistry and biology involved in the processes of forensic science for readers with no scientific background. Individual sections are devoted to criminalistics, trace evidence, pattern evidence, chemical evidence, biological evidence, and terrorism.

Houck, Max M., and Jay A. Siegel. *Fundamentals of Forensic Science*. Burlington, Mass.: Elsevier Academic Press, 2006. Good general textbook offers basic introductions to all areas of the forensic sciences, including crime scene investigation, forensic analytical tools, and the methods and techniques used in forensics laboratories.

James, Stuart H., and Jon J. Nordby, eds. *Forensic Science: An Introduction to Scientific and Investigative Techniques*. 2d ed. Boca Raton, Fla.: CRC Press, 2005. Respected introductory text presents clear information on all aspects of forensic science as well as discussion of the positions and expectations of forensic scientists within society.

Karagiozis, Michael Fitting, and Richard Sgaglio. *Forensic Investigation Handbook: An Introduction to the Collection, Preservation, Analysis, and Presentation of Evidence*. Springfield, Ill.: Charles C Thomas, 2005. Reviews the history and basic principles of forensic science and its relationship to the American criminal justice system before addressing specific areas of the field, such as biological evidence, criminal profiling, and death investigation. Features informative appendixes and an extensive glossary.

Lee, Henry C., and Jerry Labriola. *Dr. Henry Lee's Forensic Files*. Amherst, N.Y.: Prometheus Books, 2006. As a criminalist who has worked on many high-profile cases, Lee offers an insider's view of the examination of forensic evidence and the presentation of such evidence in court. Interesting book reviews five of Lee's most famous cases, including the Scott Peterson and Elizabeth Smart murder cases.

Miller, Hugh. *What the Corpse Revealed: Murder and the Science of Forensic Detection*. New York: St. Martin's Press, 1999. Reviews the forensic investigations behind sixteen murders that led to identification of the perpetrators. This engaging and interesting work has received some criticism because a number of the real-life facts of the cases have been altered, but the investigative techniques depicted are accurate and well explained.

Nickell, Joe, and John F. Fischer. *Crime Science: Methods of Forensic Detection*. Lexington: University Press of Kentucky, 1999. Covers an impressive number of topics, from the history of forensic science to the modern science laboratory. Each topic is addressed in a fairly basic manner, and a practical and informative case study appears at the end of each chapter.

Peterson, Joseph L., ed. *Forensic Science: Scientific Investigation in Criminal Justice*. New York: AMS Press, 1975. Collection of articles by experts in various subspecialties of forensic science and criminal justice addresses such topic areas as the role of science in a legal system, the development of forensic science laboratories, and the availability of science in the administration of criminal justice.

Platt, Richard. *Crime Scene: The Ultimate Guide to Forensic Science*. New York: Dorling Kindersley, 2003. Introductory work serves to explain to nonscientists a wide range of topics in forensic science, including assessment of crime scenes, body identification, evidence analysis, and identification of suspects. Case studies help to illustrate important points.

Saferstein, Richard. *Criminalistics: An Introduction to Forensic Science*. 9th ed. Upper

Saddle River, N.J.: Pearson Prentice Hall, 2007. Excellent introductory textbook provides clear and concise explanations of the technical terms, complex tests, and theories involved in forensic science. Presents comprehensive coverage of both the basics and the advanced methods used during forensic investigations.

_____, ed. *Forensic Science Handbook*. 2d ed. 2 vols. Upper Saddle River, N.J.: Prentice Hall, 2002-2005. Amazingly complete work discusses nearly every method and technique used by forensic scientists, including those related to toxicology tests, DNA analysis, document examination, drug identification, fiber examination, and firearms identification. An excellent resource for beginners in the field and seasoned scientists alike.

Wilkes, Roger, ed. *The Giant Book of Murder: Real Life Cases Cracked by Forensic Science*. London: Constable & Robin, 2000. Collection describes the forensic science applied in thirty-two true murder cases, highlighting the advances that have been made in the field over time.

Zonderman, Jon. *Beyond the Crime Lab: The New Science of Investigation*. Rev. ed. New York: John Wiley & Sons, 1999. Illuminates the history behind modern techniques of forensic science and discusses the various kinds of investigative cases that have particularly benefited from advances in the science. Ends with a discussion of the ethical and constitutional implications of the use of some modern tools of surveillance and identification.

Ballistics

Dodd, Malcolm J. *Terminal Ballistics: A Text and Atlas of Gunshot Wounds*. Boca Raton, Fla.: CRC Press, 2006. Sections focus on "hardware," or the inner workings of many types of firearms; on the injury patterns to skin, bones, and internal organs associated with specific types of firearms; and on the techniques that forensic scientists use in ballistics analysis. Includes a glossary.

Heard, Brian J. *Handbook of Firearms and Ballistics: Examining and Interpreting Forensic Evidence*. New York: John Wiley & Sons, 1997. Describes different types of firearms and ammunition and explains clearly the forensic examination of ballistics and firearms evidence. Includes discussion of the testimony of expert witnesses in cases involving such evidence.

Hueske, Edward E. *Practical Analysis and Reconstruction of Shooting Incidents*. Boca Raton, Fla.: CRC Press, 2006. Comprehensive work addresses nearly all aspects of crime scene analysis involving firearms. Begins by explaining the theory of reconstruction and the mathematics behind ballistics and then introduces the equipment, tests, and techniques used to collect and examine firearms evidence. Also includes discussion of firearms wound characteristics, blood spatter analysis, and ricochet phenomena and presents examples from actual cases.

Meyers, Charles. *Silent Evidence: Firearms (Forensic Ballistics) and Toolmarks—Cases from Forensic Science*. Boone, N.C.: Parkway, 2004. Presents thorough coverage of firearms forensics by describing and explaining the ballistics evidence from thirteen real-world cases. Addendum titled "A Primer on Firearms and Toolmark Identification" presents background on the forensic discipline of ballistics.

Warlow, Tom. *Firearms, the Law, and Forensic Ballistics*. 2d ed. Boca Raton, Fla.: CRC Press, 2005. Begins with an introduction to different types of explosives and firearms and then presents up-to-date information on legislation in the United States concerning firearms. The chapters that follow address specific aspects of forensic ballistics analysis, both in the laboratory and at the crime scene, and the presentation of ballistics evidence in court.

Bloodstain Evidence

Bevel, Tom, and Ross M. Gardner. *Bloodstain Pattern Analysis with an Introduction to Crime Scene Reconstruction*. 3d ed. Boca Raton, Fla.: CRC Press, 2008. Well-illustrated, interesting work focuses on the reproduction of the scenes of violent crimes. Explains different types of bloodstains and how they are caused and also describes the computer technology used to re-create crime scenes based on bloodstains and blood spatter.

Haag, Lucien C. *Shooting Incident Reconstruction*. Burlington, Mass.: Academic Press, 2006. Comprehensive volume covers the philosophy and theory behind studies of bloodstain and blood spatter analysis as well as the science of ballistics and the trajectory of moving objects, illustrating why bloodstain analysis is such a respected area of forensic science. Includes an extensive glossary.

James, Stuart H., and William G. Eckert. *Interpretation of Bloodstain Evidence at Crime Scenes*. 2d ed. Boca Raton, Fla.: CRC Press, 1999. Excellent reference work presents a history of the discipline of bloodstain analysis and then walks readers through the entire process of dealing with blood evidence at crime scenes, using specific case studies to illustrate important points. A valuable resource for law-enforcement personnel.

James, Stuart H., Paul E. Kish, and T. Paulette Sutton. *Principles of Bloodstain Pattern Analysis: Theory and Practice*. Boca Raton, Fla.: CRC Press, 2005. Provides complete discussion of bloodstain and blood spatter analysis, including information on testing techniques, chemical treatment, report writing, and applications of the findings of analyses in the court system. Useful appendixes include trigonometric tables, scene and laboratory checklists, and information on court decisions related to blood analysis and testing.

Wonder, A. Y. *Blood Dynamics*. New York: Academic Press, 2001. Focuses on the accurate identification of eight bloodstain pattern types. Introductory chapter discusses blood characteristics and probable and possible bloodstain patterns.

DNA Analysis

Brown, T. A. *Gene Cloning and DNA Analysis: An Introduction*. 5th ed. Malden, Mass.: Blackwell, 2006. Explains in clear language the science of DNA analysis and the techniques used in such analysis. Excellent resource for students or professionals.

Butler, John M. *Forensic DNA Typing: Biology, Technology, and Genetics of STR Markers*. 2d ed. Burlington, Mass.: Elsevier Academic Press, 2005. Provides an overview of some introductory-level basics, but is primarily intended for readers with some scientific background. Discusses DNA typing systems, the Y chromosome, mitochondrial DNA markers, statistical genetic analysis of DNA data, and technological development in DNA analysis. Uses examples from high-profile cases in discussing specific techniques.

Robertson, J., A. M. Ross, and L. A. Burgoyne, eds. *DNA in Forensic Science: Theory, Techniques, and Applications*. New York: Ellis Horwood, 1990. Begins with a primer on DNA and then delves into topics such as isolation techniques, DNA probing techniques, human identification through DNA typing, and paternity testing. Closes with a discussion of the legal implications of DNA profiling.

Rudin, Norah, and Keith Inman. *An Introduction to Forensic DNA Analysis*. 2d ed. Boca Raton, Fla.: CRC Press, 2002. Basic introductory work explains the techniques and procedures of DNA analysis in terms that nonscientists can understand. Includes case studies and discussion of U.S. Supreme Court decisions related to DNA analysis.

Document Analysis

Ellen, David. *Scientific Examination of Documents: Methods and Techniques*. 3d ed. Boca Raton, Fla.: CRC Press, 2006. Provides in-depth discussion of handwriting elucidation and analysis as well as the analysis of instruments used to create documents, including typewriters, printers, and photocopiers. Also covers the examination of incidental marks, the functions of photography in document examination, and the role of the document examiner as an expert presenting evidence in a court of law.

Herbertson, Gary. *Document Examination on the Computer: A Guide for Forensic Document Examiners*. Berkeley, Calif.: WideLine, 2002. Focuses on techniques of document examination involving digital image processing, which the author, a former document examiner for the Federal Bureau of Investigation, asserts will almost wholly replace techniques using photography and microscopic analysis in the future. Includes chapters on the restoration of documents and on the analysis of forgeries.

Koppenhaver, Katherine M. *Forensic Document Examination: Principles and Practice*. Totowa, N.J.: Humana Press, 2007. Describes the history of document examination from early work in handwriting analysis through modern techniques for evaluating altered, photocopied, and disguised documents. Includes a helpful final chapter that discusses court cases and provides informative appendixes and glossaries.

Levinson, Jay. *Questioned Documents: A Lawyer's Handbook*. New York: Academic Press, 2001. Explains the basics behind the document analysis process for lawyers who need to address document examination evidence. Chapters cover such topics as handwriting, printers, seals, photography, writing utensils, document alterations, and fingerprints. Helpful appendixes include examples of questions for courtroom testimony and a list of organizations concerned with document examination.

Vastrick, Thomas W. *Forensic Document Examination Techniques*. Altamonte Springs, Fla.: Institute of Internal Auditors Research Foundation, 2004. Following an informative primer on document analysis, individual chapters focus on specific topic areas, such as forgery, alterations, counterfeiting, writing instruments, and anonymous messages. Also discusses the qualifications of forensic document examiners and how document analysts prepare to present their findings in court. Includes a helpful glossary.

Drug Analysis

Cole, M. D., and B. Caddy. *The Analysis of Drugs of Abuse: An Instruction Manual*. New York: Ellis Horwood, 1995. Textbook provides easily understood information on how drugs of abuse affect the human body and how chemists test for the presence of these drugs. Opens with an overview of the use of forensic science in the investigation of drug-related crimes. Each chapter includes student exercises.

Gough, Terry A., ed. *The Analysis of Drugs of Abuse*. New York: John Wiley & Sons, 1991. Chapters in the first part of this collection provide thorough discussion of the techniques that forensic scientists use in drug analysis, including spectrometry, chromatography, and immunoassay tests. Those in the second section emphasize the cooperation of forensic analysts, customs agents, and law-enforcement officers in efforts to address drug-related crime.

Kintz, Pascal, ed. *Analytical and Practical Aspects of Drug Testing in Hair*. Boca Raton, Fla.: CRC Press, 2007. Collection includes an introduction explaining how drug components can infiltrate human hair, followed by chapters written by specialists that describe the testing of hair for evidence of the use of cocaine, opioids, cannabinoids, amphetamine, and pharmaceutical drugs. The techniques of testing are described, and the situations in which evidence from hair analysis may be useful are discussed.

Smith, Frederick P., ed. *Handbook of Forensic Drug Analysis*. Burlington, Mass.: Elsevier Academic Press, 2005. Brief opening chapter presents background on the types of drugs forensic scientists commonly analyze, methods of drug analysis, and the importance of the findings of such analysis to legal cases. The chapters that follow discuss types of analytic methods in great technical detail as well as types of drug groups and their respective detection and testing processes.

Wong, Raphael C., and Harley Y. Tse, eds. *Drugs of Abuse: Body Fluid Testing*. Totowa, N.J.: Humana Press, 2005. Focuses on the different kinds of drug tests conducted with samples of saliva, sweat, urine, and hair. Includes discussion of trends in drug testing and the relationship of drug testing to the criminal justice system in the United States.

Ethics

Barnett, Peter D. *Ethics in Forensic Science: Professional Standards for the Practice of*

Criminalistics. Boca Raton, Fla.: CRC Press, 2001. Addresses the need for the establishment of a code of ethics for forensic science professionals, outlining the kinds of conflicts that inevitably arise within such a profession and identifying key components of what an ideal code of ethics should entail. Presents examples of possible resolutions for conflicts within the field and identifies the strengths and weaknesses of each.

Candilis, Philip J., Robert Weinstock, and Richard Martinez. *Forensic Ethics and the Expert Witness*. New York: Springer, 2007. Thorough discussion first introduces the ethical gray area that is debated among scientists and lawyers and provides examples of legal cases in which these are illuminated. Ethical behavior approaches and theories are then described, and real court cases are used to show the applications of these approaches. Includes an appendix of the ethics codes of organizations related to forensic science.

Resnick, David B. *The Price of Truth: How Money Affects the Norms of Science*. New York: Oxford University Press, 2007. Asserts that scientists' sources of funding can have profound effects on the evidential outcomes of particular studies. After clear discussion of the concepts of objectivity, disclosure, intellectual property, and accountability in science and government, presents an argument for the vital importance of "truth and integrity in research."

Shiffman, Melvin A., ed. *Ethics in Forensic Science and Medicine: Guidelines for the Forensic Expert and the Attorney*. Springfield, Ill.: Charles C Thomas, 1999. Clarifies the expectations of established codes of ethics in fields related to forensic science, including those in areas such as confidentiality, the definition of an expert, attorney preparation for cases involving these professionals, and the validity and use of scientific evidence. Also includes guidelines regarding instances of drug abuse, brain injury, and abuse of forensic sciences.

Impression Evidence

Ashbaugh, David R. *Quantitative-Qualitative Friction Ridge Analysis: An Introduction to Basic and Advanced Ridgeology*. Boca Raton, Fla.: CRC Press, 1999. Offers a brief history of identification using fingerprint analysis and then explains the histology and growth of the skin before describing fingerprint identification techniques and processes. Also includes discussion of reports on the findings of fingerprint analysis.

Bodziak, William J. *Footwear Impression Evidence: Detection, Recovery, and Examination*. 2d ed. Boca Raton, Fla.: CRC Press, 2000. Provides thorough discussion of the process of the examination of footprint evidence. Describes each stage, from detection, photography, and casting at the crime scene to examination of prints in the laboratory. Covers lifting, enhancement, sizing, print comparisons, and wear characteristics, among other topics. Uses examples from real cases to illustrate important points.

Cole, Simon A. *Suspect Identities: A History of Fingerprinting and Criminal Identification*. Cambridge, Mass.: Harvard University Press, 2001. Follows the science of criminal identification through fingerprinting from its earliest stages through the evolution of techniques using photography to the development of modern automated systems. Addresses how the concept of individuality, issues of law-enforcement power, and varying levels of scientific certainty in the use of fingerprints have overlapped throughout history.

McDonald, Peter. *Tire Imprint Evidence*. Boca Raton, Fla.: CRC Press, 1993. Comprehensive text offers a lengthy introduction to tire construction and the basics of tire tread patterns before turning to crime scene investigation. Topics covered include imprint recording, proper measurement techniques, identification systems, and the implications of tire imprint evidence in legal investigations. The types of cases addressed include those in which a suspect's vehicle is not present, those in which a suspect's vehicle is present, and traffic accidents. Real-world case studies are presented to illustrate important points.

Robbins, Louise M. *Footprints: Collection, Analysis, and Interpretation.* Springfield, Ill.: Charles C Thomas, 1985. Focuses on the anatomy and morphology of the human foot, explaining how these apply to the analysis of footprint evidence to identify or rule out suspects in criminal investigations. Discusses the collection of footprints at crime scenes only briefly.

Legal Issues

Brown, Michael F. *Criminal Investigation: Law and Practice.* 2d ed. Boston: Butterworth-Heinemann, 2001. Focuses on the relationship between criminal investigation and the workings of the legal system in the United States in describing the steps taken by investigators. Discusses the processing of crime scenes, the analysis of different kinds of evidence at forensic laboratories, and the procedures law-enforcement investigators follow in interviewing witnesses, interrogating suspects, and following leads. Also addresses how investigators and forensic scientists prepare to present courtroom testimony.

Hanzlick, Randy. *Death Investigation: Systems and Procedures.* Boca Raton, Fla.: CRC Press, 2007. Describes the principles and concepts of death investigations from a legal point of view, discussing the steps that must be taken throughout such cases as established by law. Topics covered include the different types of death investigations, the roles of coroners and medical examiners, the contents of autopsy reports, and the testimony of expert witnesses.

Kiely, Terrence F. *Forensic Evidence: Science and the Criminal Law.* 2d ed. Boca Raton, Fla.: CRC Press, 2006. Provides a brief history of forensic science and its involvement in the criminal justice system and then addresses the presentation in courtrooms of specific kinds of evidence, including hair analysis evidence, evidence concerning ballistics and tool marks, and evidence involving footprints and tire impressions. Each kind of evidence is discussed generally, and then specific examples from legal cases are offered.

Lissitzyn, Christine Beck. *Forensic Evidence in Court: A Case Study Approach.* Durham, N.C.: Carolina Academic Press, 2008. Uses case studies to illuminate the many aspects of forensic science and to show how intricately intertwined the various types of forensic evidence can become and their potential impacts in courtroom trials. Covers a plethora of topics, from DNA evidence to polygraph testimony.

Pyrek, Kelly M. *Forensic Science Under Siege: The Challenges of Forensic Laboratories and the Medico-legal Investigation System.* Burlington, Mass.: Elsevier Academic Press, 2007. Well-organized volume focuses on criticisms that have been directed toward forensic science laboratories, including allegations of incidents of false reporting of test results and failures to preserve and test evidence samples properly. Takes a direct approach in explaining problematic issues and in discussing the causes of quality-related shortcomings at some forensic labs.

Semikhodskii, Andrei. *Dealing with DNA Evidence: A Legal Guide.* New York: Routledge, 2007. Explains for defense attorneys the strategies they can use to try to minimize the role of DNA evidence in legal cases against their clients, given that DNA evidence is often condemning. Asserts that DNA evidence should not be given as much weight as it has come to be given, but instead should be treated as is any other piece of evidence. Describes the methods of DNA testing and points out the weaknesses in each method, suggesting related defense strategies.

Wecht, Cyril H., and John T. Rago, eds. *Forensic Science and Law: Investigative Applications in Criminal, Civil, and Family Justice.* Boca Raton, Fla.: CRC Press, 2006. Presents an extensive introduction to both forensic science and criminal law, then uses this background to explain the application of forensic investigative techniques and conclusions to legal cases. Uses real case examples to illustrate and clarify abstract legal and scientific concepts and procedures.

Postmortem Identification

Fairgrieve, Scott I. *Forensic Cremation: Recovery and Analysis*. Boca Raton, Fla.: CRC Press, 2008. Explains the processes of combustion and the effects of cremation on the human body. Describes the proper procedures for collecting evidence involving cremation, the analysis of such evidence, and the use of the findings to make positive identifications of decedents.

_____, ed. *Forensic Osteological Analysis: A Book of Case Studies*. Springfield, Ill.: Charles C Thomas, 1999. Collection of case studies addresses the identification of deceased persons based solely on skeletal remains. Shows how experts can derive a great deal of information from an individual's bones, such as height, weight, age, and sex; further, skeletal anomalies and pathologies can be compared against medical records of known individuals.

George, Robert M. *Facial Geometry: Graphic Facial Analysis for Forensic Artists*. Springfield, Ill.: Charles C Thomas, 2007. Brief work provides detailed description of the ways in which a person's facial construction can reveal much about that individual's identity. Topics addressed include facial geography, facial geometry, frontal graphic facial analysis, and lateral graphic facial analysis.

Tibbett, Mark, and David O. Carter, eds. *Soil Analysis in Forensic Taphonomy: Chemical and Biological Effects of Buried Human Remains*. Boca Raton, Fla.: CRC Press, 2008. Collection explains the ways in which soils that come into contact with human remains can affect death investigations. Describes how forensic scientists can examine the interactions of surrounding soils with decomposing bodies to determine such information as cause of death, time of death, and some circumstances relating to death.

Trace Evidence

Blackledge, Robert D., ed. *Forensic Analysis on the Cutting Edge: New Methods for Trace Evidence Analysis*. Hoboken, N.J.: John Wiley & Sons, 2007. Collection of essays by leading experts covers advances in the technologies and techniques that forensic scientists use to examine trace evidence. The types of evidence discussed include fingerprints, bloodstains, ink, fibers, glass, tapes, and residues from automotive air bags.

Houck, Max M., ed. *Mute Witnesses: Trace Evidence Analysis*. San Diego, Calif.: Academic Press, 2001. Collection offers a variety of viewpoints on many of the central concerns among experts related to the handling and interpretation of trace evidence.

_____. *Trace Evidence Analysis: More Cases in Mute Witnesses*. Burlington, Mass.: Elsevier Academic Press, 2004. Anthology presents nine real-life cases in which trace evidence played an important role, providing detailed information on the collection and analysis of the evidence in each case.

Robertson, James, ed. *Forensic Examination of Hair*. Philadelphia: Taylor & Francis, 1999. Collection provides comprehensive coverage of the forensic analysis of hair evidence, beginning with a primer on the physiology and growth of human hair. Contributors address topics such as techniques of hair and follicle examination, tests that can be conducted on human hair (including DNA testing and drug testing), and the value of hair analysis findings as evidence.

Robertson, James, and Michael Grieve, eds. *Forensic Examination of Fibres*. 2d ed. Philadelphia: Taylor & Francis, 1999. Provides extremely detailed information on the collection, preservation, and examination of fiber evidence, with in-depth description of the analytical techniques to which fiber samples are subjected in forensic laboratories.

Dwight G. Smith

Glossary

accelerant. Highly flammable chemical used in arson to speed up the burning of property and create maximum destruction from a fire.

acquittal. Decision reached by a judge or jury that a defendant is not guilty of the crime with which he or she has been charged.

actus reus. Act that violates the law; a guilty act.

admissible evidence. Legally adequate evidence that is relevant to proving or disproving a disputed issue in a court of law.

affidavit. Written statement that is taken under an oath and may become part of legal proceedings.

aggravated assault. Purposeful attack on another person that is intended to cause severe bodily harm.

algor mortis. Cooling of the body after death.

alias. Alternative name, often used to conceal the true identity of a person.

alibi. Statement that an individual could not have committed a particular criminal act because he or she was in another location at the time the criminal activity occurred.

alligatoring. Fire pattern in which deep cracking appears on a material surface. Such an indication of prolonged burning in a specific area may help to determine the point of origin of a fire.

alternate light source (ALS) instruments. Light sources employed in crime scene investigations that use filters or special bulbs to emit a narrow range of wavelengths that enable the detection of substances not visible under normal lighting.

amphetamines. Members of a class of drugs that enhance or stimulate the nervous system, increasing energy levels, reducing fatigue, and causing psychological exhilaration.

anabolic steroids. Synthetic chemicals that mimic the action of the hormone testosterone in the body, resulting in muscle growth.

anthropometry. Systematic study of the dimensions of the human body, particularly for purposes of comparison to identify individual persons. See also ***bertillonage***

appeal. Request to retry in a higher court a legal case that has already received a verdict in order to overturn the verdict. An appeal must be based on valid new evidence or novel reconsideration of original evidence.

arch fingerprint. Pattern of fingerprint in which the prominent ridges extend smoothly from one side, rise in the center, and continue through the opposite side of the print.

arrest. Apprehension of a suspected perpetrator of a crime by a law-enforcement officer during or after the commission of the crime.

arson. Illegal, malicious, and deliberate setting of a fire to destroy property.

asphyxia. Sudden or gradual deprivation of the body of a sufficient amount of oxygen to sustain life.

atomic absorption spectrophotometry. Technique used to determine the concentrations of metal elements in a sample based on the absorption of light energy by vaporized atoms.

authentication. Demonstration that an item is genuine.

automated fingerprint identification system. Computerized system that compares images of fingerprints with the images of prints stored in local, state, and federal databases to find potential matches.

autopsy. External and internal medical examination of a dead body to determine cause of death, identify the individual, or study changes caused by disease.

ballistic fingerprint. Distinctive marks etched on a rifle or handgun bullet as it is pushed through the gun's barrel.

ballistics. Field of physics concerned with the physical trajectories and impacts of projectiles (including bullets).

barbiturates. Members of a class of drugs that have sedative or depressing effects on the central nervous system.

bertillonage. System developed in the late nineteenth century by French criminologist Alphonse Bertillon to identify repeat criminal offenders by comparing their anatomical measurements. See also **anthropometry**

biological weapon. Weapon of mass destruction that is based on bacteria, viruses, fungi, and the toxins produced by microorganisms.

biometrics. Science of measuring the physical characteristics of individuals and using them for identification.

bite-mark analysis. Examination and comparison of wounds caused by biting during physical attacks.

blackmail. Attempt to gain money or other reward by the threat of inflicting violence on or exposing some wrongdoing of another; closely related to extortion.

blunt force trauma. Trauma caused to a body part by a blunt instrument or surface through physical impact, injury, or attack.

body farm. Outdoor facility where human remains are allowed to decompose under varying conditions so that forensic anthropologists and other scientists can study the processes that take place.

bribery. Attempt to influence the actions of a person performing a public duty by offering something of value to that person.

burden of proof. Requirement that the prosecution in a court case prove a particular issue for the defendant to be found guilty; in a criminal case, the prosecutor must demonstrate the guilt of the defendant beyond a reasonable doubt.

burglary. Deliberate and illegal entrance into a residence to steal property.

cadaver dog. Dog that is specially trained to find the scents associated with decomposing human remains.

casting. Production of three-dimensional models of impressions left by footwear, tires, or tools at crime scenes.

cause of death. Situation or illness that resulted in the loss of life.

chain of custody. Documentation of the location of physical evidence from the time it is collected until the time it is introduced at trial.

check kiting. Unlawful use of two or more checking accounts to write worthless checks, taking advantage of the time required for checks to clear.

check washing. Use of chemical substances to remove written information from signed checks so that the checks can be altered, enabling the fraudulent collection of funds from bank accounts.

chemical agent. Chemical compound with toxic properties that can be used to cause harm to humans, plants, and animals.

child abuse. Any action by an adult that harms a minor's mental, emotional, or physical state or impairs a minor's normal development.

chromatography. Laboratory technique used to separate chemical mixtures into their individual components and to quantify and identify the isolated components.

circumstantial evidence. Evidence that requires inferences to link it to the material facts of a case; also known as indirect evidence.

cocaine. Powerful drug that stimulates the central nervous system; derived from coca plants. See also **freebase cocaine**

coercion. Intimidation, deception, or physical force used to compel an individual to make a particular choice or take a particular action.

cognitive interview. Interview involving memory recall conducted with an individual who was present at a crime scene; the interviewer asks the subject to relive the event of interest, noting every physical and emotional detail.

cold case. Criminal case that has gone unsolved, often for a long period, and on which active investigation has ceased because the leads or evidence trails have gone cold.

common law. Body of law, going back to early English history, that arises from judicial decisions, rather than from written statutes, and reflects customs, tradition, and precedent.

competency. See **legal competency**

composite drawing. Artistic rendering of the facial features of unknown persons based on eyewitness information for use in narrowing law-enforcement searches.

computed tomography (CT) scanning. Form of radiography in which a three-dimensional image of a scanned object is created by computer from a series of sectional images of the object.

computer crime. Illegal intrusion into computers or computer networks or the use of computers for the perpetration of other crimes.

computer forensics. Examination of computers, computer networks, and communication devices for existing or deleted electronic evidence.

confession. Acknowledgment and admittance of guilt for a crime committed.

consensual crime. Criminal act carried out with the mutual consent of all parties involved.

controlled substance. Drug subject to regulation by law concerning possession and use.

contusion. Injury in which damaged blood vessels leak blood into surrounding tissues; also known as bruise.

conviction. Final determination that a criminal defendant is guilty, made as a result of a trial or a plea bargain.

coroner. Public official who investigates the circumstances of violent or suspicious deaths; a coroner may or may not be a physician. See also **medical examiner**

counterfeiting. Creation of false currency or other items that are intended to be used, sold, or passed off illegally as original or real.

crack cocaine. Form of cocaine that is manufactured through the process of extracting hydrochloride granules through heating; believed to produce a more intense high than powder cocaine.

credit card fraud. Form of identity theft in which a stolen credit card number is used to obtain goods or services fraudulently.

crime laboratories. Public and private facilities at which forensic specialists analyze materials collected from crime scenes for purposes of identification and interpretation.

crime scene. Location where a crime has occurred or where evidence of a crime is collected.

crime scene investigation. Collection and processing of physical evidence at a crime scene by forensic specialists using techniques and procedures designed to protect and preserve all evidence samples for analysis.

crime scene sketch. Representative depiction, annotated and with measurements marked, of the locations and appearances of features and objects found at a crime scene.

criminal investigation. Inquiry into and examination, processing, and evaluation of evidence concerning possible criminal activity based on logic, objectivity, and legal guidelines.

criminal personality profiling. Investigatory technique in which a detailed composite description of an unknown offender is constructed on the basis of crime scene evidence.

criminalistics. Employment of scientific principles in the evaluation of physical evidence to detect, analyze, and solve crimes.

criminology. Scientific study of crime and criminal behavior, including patterns and rates of crime and victimization, etiology of crime, social responses to crime, and crime control.

cross-examination. Attorney's questioning of a witness called by the opposing side in a court proceeding.

cross-projection. Technique used by crime scene investigators to sketch crime scenes in three dimensions.

cryptology. Scientific study of the hiding, disguising, or encryption of messages.

cyanoacrylate fuming. See **superglue fuming**

cybercrime. Crime committed through the use of the Internet and computers.

date rape. Rape committed by a person with whom the victim is voluntarily engaging in a social outing.

***Daubert* standard.** Set of guidelines established by the U.S. Supreme Court concerning the admissibility of expert scientific testimony: Scientific evidence must be based on a testable theory or technique, the theory or technique must be peer-reviewed, the technique must have a known error rate, and the underlying science must be generally accepted by the scientific community.

death certificate. Official document recording the fact of an individual's death.

decomposition. Process by which a cadaver is reduced to a skeleton through the destruction of the body's soft tissue.

defendant. Person accused of having committed a crime in a criminal case.

defense counsel. Attorney who protects the rights and argues the case of the defendant in a legal proceeding.

defensive wound. Injury received by a victim of a physical attack as the result of trying to fend off the attacker.

deoxyribonucleic acid. See **DNA**

direct evidence. Evidence that links directly to material issues in a legal case.

direct examination. Attorney's questioning of a witness called by that attorney to testify in a court proceeding.

DNA. Organic substance found in the chromosomes located in the nucleus of a cell that contains genetic material unique to an individual.

DNA fingerprinting. Procedure in which patterns of sequence variation in DNA samples are analyzed for the purpose of identifying individuals.

DNA profiling. Process of statistically analyzing the output of DNA typing results to determine the probability that another nonrelated individual in the general population might share the same exact DNA fingerprint as the one obtained in an evidence sample.

document examiner. Expert in the examination of questioned documents to establish their authenticity or origin through the analysis and comparison of handwriting, papers, inks, writing instruments, and other elements.

drug abuse. Illegal or improper use of substances that alter normal bodily function.

drug addiction. Physical dependence on a substance characterized by tolerance (need for greater amounts of the substance to achieve the same effect) and withdrawal symptoms accompanying the cessation of use.

drug paraphernalia. Products that have been created, modified, or adopted from their intended uses for the purposes of making, using, or concealing illegal drugs.

drunk driving. Operating or controlling a motor vehicle while under the influence of intoxicants; also known as driving under the influence, or DUI.

electrophoresis. Analytical technique that uses electrical fields to separate and analyze charged molecules.

embezzlement. Unlawful appropriation of money or property held in trust by one person for another.

energy-dispersive spectroscopy. Analytical technique used to construct an elemental profile of a sample of interest.

ethics. Principles of conduct, moral duty, and obligation that guide individuals in their decisions and actions.

evidence. Any form of proof pertaining to an aspect of a legal accusation that can be presented during trial for review by the jury and the judge.

exclusionary rule. Legal principle applied in U.S. courts that holds that evidence obtained in a manner that violates a defendant's constitutional rights is inadmissible in the defendant's prosecution.

exculpatory evidence. Evidence that is favorable for the defendant in a criminal trial; such evidence may clear the defendant or tend to show that the defendant is not guilty.

exhumation. Removal of a body from a grave or tomb, often for further study.

expert witness. Person who possesses specialized knowledge, training, or experience and testifies regarding that expertise in legal proceedings, with the purpose of assisting jurors in understanding an area with which they are unfamiliar.

explosive taggants. Tiny particles or chemicals that are added to explosives by manufacturers to enable authorities to identify the sources of the explosives if they are used in criminal activities.

extortion. Use of illegal threats by one party to obtain money or property from another; closely related to blackmail.

eyewitness testimony. Account given by a person who directly observed the commission of a crime or an action related to a crime.

facial reconstruction. See **forensic sculpture**

Federal Rules of Evidence. Rules governing the admission in U.S. federal courts of the facts that attorneys may use to prove their cases.

felony. Serious crime, usually punishable by a prison sentence (as opposed to a jail sentence) or death.

forensic. Adjective derived from the Latin word for "public," used to describe matters suitable for public discussion and debate, especially in public courts.

forensic accounting. Profession in which accounting, auditing, and investigative skills are applied to assist in legal investigations.

forensic anthropology. Study of human skeletal remains for the purpose of gathering evidence to be used in legal investigations and court proceedings.

forensic archaeology. Profession in which standard archaeological field methods are applied to the recovery of evidence from forensic scenes and archaeological theory and experimental research findings are applied in the interpretation of such scenes.

forensic entomology. Study of insects and their by-products for the purpose of gathering evidence to be used in legal investigations and court proceedings.

forensic geoscience. Scientific field that applies geological information and earth science techniques to investigations related to criminal or other legal proceedings.

forensic nursing. Application of forensic science techniques and nursing practice in proceedings that interface with the law.

forensic odontology. Study of teeth and dentition patterns for the purposes of identifying individuals, living or dead, and gathering evidence to be used in legal investigations and court proceedings.

forensic palynology. Study of pollens and spores for the purpose of gathering evidence to be used in legal investigations and court proceedings.

forensic pathology. Field of medicine in which a variety of techniques are applied to the examination of human remains with the aim of establishing the causes of unnatural deaths.

forensic photography. Photography used to document crime and accident scenes and to provide visual exhibits for legal proceedings.

forensic psychiatry. Field of medical practice that involves the application of medical expertise and research findings concerning mental health in legal contexts.

forensic psychology. Field of psychological practice concerned with assessment, consultation, psychotherapy, and the study of human behavior and thinking within judicial systems.

forensic science. Application of scientific knowledge and techniques to legal matters, particularly to criminal investigations.

forensic sculpture. Process in which sciences such as anthropology, osteology, and anatomy are combined with artistry to approximate, from human remains, parts of individuals in three-dimensional form for purposes of identification.

forensic toxicology. Application of the knowledge of poisons to the identification of cases of homicide, suicide, accidents, and drug abuse for legal purposes.

forgery. Manufacture or alteration of printed or electronic documents, literary works, or works of art with the intention to deceive and defraud.

fraud. Intentional misrepresentation or distortion of facts for some form of gain.

freebase cocaine. Purest form of cocaine, created through the extraction of hydrochloride from powder cocaine.

***Frye* standard.** Legal test that requires the trial court to determine whether a scientific theory or scientific method used to generate evidence is generally accepted as reliable in the scientific community.

gas chromatography. Separation technique used in the qualitative and quantitative analysis of evidence samples.

geographic information system. Computer-based mapping system that can store, retrieve, and analyze relationships among geographically referenced or geospatial data; used by law-enforcement agencies to map crime and carry out strategic planning.

geographic profiling. Use of information about geographic locations and their connections to draw conclusions about the probable characteristics and identity of unknown criminal offenders.

grid search. Search of a crime scene in which investigators methodically follow a grid pattern to maximize the likelihood of finding evidence while minimizing the likelihood that they will fail to discover evidence.

guilty but mentally ill. Legal plea or verdict in which the defendant admits committing the crime but claims to have been mentally incompetent at the time.

gunshot residue. Burned, partially burned, and unburned powder and primer that are released as a firearm is discharged.

habeas corpus. Court order to bring a person being detained before a court or judge to determine whether the person's imprisonment is lawful.

hallucinogen. Synthetic or natural chemical substance that causes alterations of perception, including but not limited to changing what users see, hear, feel, taste, smell, and experience about themselves and their relationship to the world and others.

handwriting analysis. Examination of samples of handwriting, usually to establish validity, fraud, or forgery.

hate crime. Criminal act targeted specifically toward a member of a particular group (whether based on race, ethnicity, sexual orientation, age, gender, or some other characteristic) because of the person's membership in that group.

heroin. Highly addictive opiate drug that is chemically converted from morphine to a solid crystalline form.

hesitation wound. Tentative, superficial injury caused by uncertain movement or pausing in the use of a sharp-edged weapon in an attack or suicide.

high-performance liquid chromatography. Technique used in the separation, detection, and identification of the pure compounds that are present in a mixture.

hit-and-run incident. Situation in which the operator of a motor vehicle causes damage to other persons or property with the vehicle and flees the scene before law-enforcement authorities arrive.

homicide. Death of a human being caused by the act of another. See also **involuntary manslaughter**; **murder**; **voluntary manslaughter**

hypothesis. Tentative assumption that can be tested for validity.

identity theft. Illegal appropriation of another person's personal data for the purpose of gain or profit.

immunity from prosecution. Exemption from being tried in a criminal case in exchange for providing testimony or information that is valuable to the state's prosecution of another.

impression evidence. Evidence that takes the form of an alteration of a surface resulting from contact with a body part or object; includes bite marks, fingerprints, footprints, knife cuts, tire tracks, and tool marks.

inculpatory evidence. Evidence that tends to establish the guilt of a defendant.

indictment. Document that officially charges one or more persons with a criminal offense.

informant. Person who provides information to law-enforcement authorities concerning the parties involved in crimes, often in exchange for some kind of consideration, such as money or immunity from prosecution.

inhalant. Product containing chemicals that emit fumes that, when inhaled, can cause altered mental status.

insanity defense. Legal defense tactic used in the hope of reducing the culpability of criminal defendants by asserting that when they committed their crimes they were incapable of distinguishing between right and wrong, they were unable to resist their impulses, or their criminal actions were products of mental defects or diseases. See also **guilty but mentally ill**

interrogation. Questioning of suspects by law-enforcement personnel to determine their possible involvement in criminal activity under investigation.

involuntary manslaughter. Unintentional killing that results from failure to perform a legal duty to safeguard human life, from the commission of an unlawful act not amounting to a felony, or from the commission of a lawful act involving a risk of injury or death that is done in an unlawful, reckless, or grossly negligent manner.

iodine fuming. Technique used to make latent fingerprints visible.

iris recognition system. Computer-assisted system that identifies individuals based on comparisons of patterns in the irises of the eyes.

judge. Appointed or elected public official who is charged with authoritatively and impartially resolving disputes presented in a court of law.

jurisdiction. Authority of a law-enforcement agency to investigate or a court to decide a given case; also refers to the geographic area within which an agency or court has authority.

jury. Group of persons selected at random who are sworn to consider the facts and evidence in a legal case to arrive at a verdict.

kidnapping. Unlawful detention of a person by force against the person's will.

laceration. Wound with torn or ragged edges.

lands and grooves. Raised and indented characteristics of the rifling in the barrel of a firearm; the marks made by lands and grooves on bullets fired are distinctive to individual weapons.

latent fingerprint. Fingerprint impression that cannot be seen under normal conditions.

legal competency. Individual's capacity to understand the nature and purposes of his or her legal rights and obligations.

less-lethal weapons. Weapons designed to force compliance with the wielders' orders, but not to maim or to kill.

lineup. Law-enforcement investigative tool in which a crime suspect and other people who look similar to the suspect (typically six persons in all) are placed side by side in a room where they can be viewed by an eyewitness for identification purposes.

livor mortis. Discoloration that occurs in the skin of a corpse shortly after death as a result of the gravitational settling of pooled blood; also known as lividity.

Locard's exchange principle. Dictum that holds that whenever two objects come into contact, each leaves some trace or residue on the other that can be detected through careful examination.

loop fingerprint. Pattern of fingerprint in which the ridges enter from either side of the print, recurve, and tend to pass out on the same side where they entered.

luminol. Chemical substance widely used in presumptive or nonspecific tests for blood during crime scene examinations.

M'Naghten rule. First formal test of legal insanity, developed in Great Britain in 1843; focused on whether the defendant's insanity prevented him or her from knowing what he or she was doing or knowing the difference between right and wrong when the crime was committed.

manner of death. Way in which a death was caused, determined by a coroner or medical examiner as falling into one of five classifications: natural, accidental, homicide, suicide, or undetermined.

manslaughter. See **involuntary manslaughter; voluntary manslaughter**

marijuana. Drug derived from the dried leaves and flowering tops of cannabis plants; when smoked or eaten, marijuana alters an individual's mental state.

mass spectrometry. Analytical technique in which ions of a sample are formed and subsequently separated according to their mass-to-charge ratio.

measurement marker. Easily recognizable object of known size that a forensic photographer places next to an item of evidence for comparison purposes before taking a crime scene photograph.

medical examiner. Physician or forensic pathologist responsible for investigating the circumstances of suspicious or violent deaths. See also **coroner**

mens rea. Criminal intent.

methamphetamine. Powerful neurological stimulant drug that influences heart rate, body temperature, blood pressure, appetite, alertness, and mood.

Miranda warnings. Information about certain constitutional rights that law-enforcement personnel in the United States must provide to persons in custody before questioning them; so-called Miranda rights include the right to remain silent and the right to legal counsel.

misdemeanor. Minor crime punishable by a fine or imprisonment for a relatively brief period (less than one year in most U.S. jurisdictions).

Model Penal Code. Code of criminal provisions developed by the American Law Institute and intended to standardize criminal law among the various states.

modus operandi. Method by which a crime is carried out.

morphine. Opiate drug, used medically for pain relief, derived from the principal alkaloid of opium through boiling and filtration techniques.

motive. Reason a person commits a crime.

murder. Intentional unlawful killing of a human being by another.

narcotic. Drug that causes a stuporous effect, used medically in low doses to relieve pain.

narcotic tolerance. Physical need for increasing quantities of a narcotic drug to achieve a given level of effects.

National Crime Information Center. Central U.S. database for crime-related information, maintained by the Federal Bureau of Investigation and available electronically to local, state, and federal law-enforcement agencies.

neighborhood check. Systematic survey conducted by law-enforcement personnel near a crime scene in the search for investigative leads.

neutron activation analysis. Method of determining the presence and composition of trace elements in a substance by bombarding the sample with neutron particles.

oblique lighting analysis. Examination technique that involves lighting an object from different angles to enhance the visibility of its surface features.

offender. Perpetrator of a crime.

opiate. Compound derived from the opium poppy; opiate drugs include codeine, morphine, and opium.

oral autopsy. Examination of the mouth and teeth of a deceased person, usually for the purpose of establishing identity.

organized crime. Criminal activities of highly organized, disciplined associations engaged primarily in illegal operations for monetary gain.

paraffin test. Method formerly used to determine whether a person had recently fired a firearm; the hands were coated with melted paraffin, and then the cooled paraffin casts were examined for the presence nitrates from gunpowder.

paranoia. Mental disorder characterized by fixed delusions, typically involving persecution.

parole. Release of a prisoner, generally subject to conditions, before the individual's sentence has been completed.

partial fingerprint. Fingerprint consisting of only a portion of a pattern area.

PCP. See **phencyclidine**

pedophilia. Sexual attraction to children.

perjury. Deliberate false statement made under oath.

phencyclidine. Powerful synthetic hallucinogen originally developed as an anesthetic.

physical evidence. Any item of a tangible nature that may be of importance during an investigation or may be used to prove facts in a judicial proceeding.

pistol. Handgun that operates on the inertia or blowback principle: When a pistol is fired, the force of the discharge ejects the fired casing, loading and cocking the weapon for the next firing.

plea bargaining. Legal practice in which an agreement is reached between a prosecutor and a defendant that disposes of a criminal matter; generally, the defendant agrees to plead guilty in exchange for a reduction of charges.

police. Officers of municipal law-enforcement agencies whose primary mission is to protect their communities from crime and other threats.

police artist. See **composite drawing**

police detective. Police officer who specializes in criminal investigations.

police lineup. See **lineup**

pollen rain. Release of vast amounts of pollen by male flowering plants within a given ecological landscape.

polygraph. Instrument designed to detect deception on the part of a person being interviewed through the measurement of physiological changes in that individual's body in response to questioning.

pornography. Material depicting erotic behavior that is intended to arouse sexual excitement.

postmortem interval. Length of time since death.

precipitin test. Method used to determine whether a blood sample is of animal or human origin.

predatory criminal. Type of offender who commits crimes that involve confrontation and the selection or stalking of vulnerable victims.

preliminary hearing. Judicial examination of the arrest and charges brought against a person accused of a crime.

preliminary report. First formal report by a law-enforcement investigator concerning a criminal offense, used as the foundation for all subsequent reports.

premeditation. Degree of planning and forethought sufficient to indicate the intention to commit a crime.

presumptive test. Screening test, usually using a chemical reagent, that provides tentative identification of an unidentified substance at a crime scene or in the laboratory.

priority assignment. Method of organization used by law-enforcement agencies in which personnel are assigned to investigations based on the cases' perceived importance.

Privacy Act of 1974. Federal law designed to protect individuals' rights to privacy; prohibits government agencies from reviewing or releasing information on individuals unless certain conditions are met.

private investigator. Non-law-enforcement investigator who is paid by private citizens or organizations to gather information on private matters, generally of a civil rather than criminal nature; also known as a private detective or private eye.

privileged communication. Communication between two individuals whose confidentiality the law protects (such as attorney and client or physician and patient) that takes place in circumstances in which the parties intend for the communication to remain secret. Such communication cannot be admitted into evidence in a judicial proceeding without the permission of the parties involved.

probable cause. Reasonable belief, based on available information, that a person is connected to a crime; the standard of probable cause must be met for police to make an arrest, conduct a search of a person or the person's property, or obtain an arrest warrant.

probation. Conditional sentence that allows a convicted offender to avoid imprisonment as long as the offender abides by the requirements of the court.

profiling. See **criminal personality profiling**

progress report. Report created during a law-enforcement investigation to document formally the progress of investigative efforts.

prosecutor. Attorney who acts on behalf of the government during a criminal proceeding.

psychological profiling. See **criminal personality profiling**

psychopath. Individual with a psychological disorder characterized by egotistical, self-centered, impulsive, and exploitative behaviors, lack of remorse, and emotional callousness.

putrefaction. Stage in the decomposition of animal proteins in which flesh and tissue are broken down by the action of anaerobic microorganisms.

pyromaniac. Individual with a mental illness characterized by a compulsive need to set fires.

racial profiling. Police practice of using race or ethnicity as a primary reason for stopping, questioning, searching, or arresting potential suspects.

radial fracture line. Fracture in a glass surface that results from the bending of the surface toward a striking force, causing jagged lines from the point of impact outward.

rape. Criminal act of engaging in sexual intercourse with a person against that person's will.

rape kit. Package of examination materials used by a doctor or nurse (examiner) for gathering evidence from a victim following a sexual assault.

reagent. Substance that brings about a chemical reaction when added to another particular substance.

reasonable doubt. Absence of moral certainty of a defendant's guilt.

recidivism. Relapse into criminal behavior by persons who have previously been arrested or imprisoned for criminal activity.

rectangular-coordinate method. Crime scene sketching technique in which two right angles are drawn from an evidence item to the nearest permanent object.

response time. Amount of time that elapses between a law-enforcement agency's receipt of a complaint or call for service concerning a crime and the arrival of officers at the crime scene.

revolver. Handgun in which a revolving multichambered cylinder aligns with the barrel prior to discharge.

rigor mortis. Temporary stiffening of the cardiac and skeletal muscles that takes place shortly after death as a result of chemical changes within the muscular tissue.

rip attack. Method of safe burglary in which the exterior metal sheets of the safe are peeled from a weakened corner location.

robbery. Taking of property from a person in the person's presence by the use of force or threat of force.

sadism. Sexual perversion in which pleasure is gained from the infliction of pain on a living thing.

sanity hearing. Judicial procedure in which one or more psychiatric experts testify regarding their evaluations of the defendant's mental status.

search warrant. Court order that authorizes police to search a specific location for certain articles and to seize and produce those articles before the court.

sector search. Search of a crime scene in which investigators divide the location into equal areas to maximize the likelihood of finding evidence while minimizing the likeli-

hood that they will fail to discover evidence.

self-incrimination. Statements or actions of a person that tend to suggest that the individual committed a crime.

semen. Male reproductive fluid; normally contains spermatozoa, reproductive cells carrying male genetic material.

serial offending. Commission by one offender of three or more separate but related crimes with "cooling off" periods between the acts.

sobriety testing. Measures taken by law-enforcement officials to determine whether persons are intoxicated in situations in which being intoxicated is dangerous or unlawful.

spectrophotometer. Instrument used to identify substances through the measurement of light absorption.

spiral search. Search of a crime scene in which investigators move through the scene in an ever-expanding circular fashion from the center to the outer perimeter to maximize the likelihood of finding evidence while minimizing the likelihood that they will fail to discover evidence.

statute. Law enacted by the legislative branch of a government.

statutory rape. Sexual intercourse with an individual under a legally specified age of consent; this act is illegal even if the underage person willingly consents to participate.

sting operation. Law-enforcement tactic in which officers simulate criminal operations in order to catch offenders as they carry out criminal acts.

strip search. Search of a crime scene in which investigators divide the scene into long, narrow sections that are then searched from one end to the other; often multiple searchers walk shoulder to shoulder in a line that moves simultaneously across an area. Also known as a linear search.

subpoena. Writ commanding a person to attend a judicial proceeding.

substance-detection dog. Dog trained to work with a handler to discover, through scent, contraband items and hazardous materials associated with criminal activities or security threats.

suicide. Act of intentionally killing oneself

through one's own effort or with the assistance of another.

summons. Judicial instrument used to initiate a legal proceeding or to command the appearance of a person before a court or other body.

superglue fuming. Use of the fumes of cyanoacrylate esters to develop and preserve fingerprints.

surveillance camera. Video or still camera, often mounted on an elevated location in a public area such as a highway or parking lot, used to monitor activity and record criminal acts for possible use as evidence in prosecutions.

suspect. Person under investigation for possible criminal activity who has not yet been charged.

terrorism. Coercive use of violence or threat of violence to terrorize a community or society to achieve political, economic, or social goals.

testimony. Statement made in a legal proceeding by a witness under oath.

tests of suitability. Three standards used to establish if an item has importance in a legal case: The evidence must be competent, relevant, and material.

tool mark. Impression left on a surface as the result of forceful contact between a tool and the surface.

toxicology. See **forensic toxicology**

trace evidence. Evidence present in very small amounts, requiring careful attention, and often special techniques, to detect.

trajectory. Flight path of a projectile, such as a bullet.

transfer evidence. Evidence that has moved from one person or object to another (such as from an offender to a crime victim) through contact or near contact.

triangulation. Method used in crime scene documentation in which measurements are taken from two fixed points to an item of evidence, forming a triangular frame of location.

ultraviolet light. Radiation in wavelengths beyond the violet, visible end of the light spectrum.

verdict. Formal decision reached by a jury or judge on matters of fact submitted for deliberation and determination in legal proceedings.

vigilantism. Illegal assumption of law-enforcement responsibilities by private citizens.

voiceprint. Visual representation of an individual's voice based on biometric measurements.

voluntary manslaughter. Unintentional killing that results from an intentional act done without malice or premeditation and while in the heat of passion or on sudden provocation.

war crimes. Crimes against humanity committed during armed conflicts that go beyond the acts normally considered permissible in wartime.

white-collar crime. Nonviolent criminal offenses committed by workers of the salaried class.

whorl fingerprint. Pattern of fingerprint in which the ridges encircle a central plain.

withdrawal symptoms. Mental and physical effects produced by the sudden cessation of the ingestion of addictive drugs.

witness. Person who offers testimony in a legal proceeding; also used to refer to a person who was present when a crime took place.

witness interviewing. Questioning of persons who were present when a crime took place (including victims) by law-enforcement personnel to gain information to further the investigation of the crime.

Dwight G. Smith

Indexes

Category Index

ACCIDENT RECONSTRUCTION

Accident investigation and reconstruction, 4
Challenger and *Columbia* accident
    investigations, 214
Driving injuries, 386
Flight data recorders, 478
National Transportation Safety Board, 759
Silkwood/Kerr-McGee case, 926
ValuJet Flight 592 crash investigation, 1010

BIOLOGICAL AGENTS. *See* CHEMICAL AND BIOLOGICAL AGENTS

CHEMICAL AND BIOLOGICAL AGENTS

Accelerants, 1
Air and water purity, 12
Amphetamines, 26
Anthrax, 46
Antianxiety agents, 57
Antibiotics, 59
Antipsychotics, 62
Arsenic, 66
Attention-deficit/hyperactivity disorder
    medications, 90
Bacteria, 102
Bacterial biology, 105
Bacterial resistance and response to
    antibacterial agents, 106
Barbiturates, 113

Biological terrorism, 125
Biological warfare diagnosis, 129
Biological weapon identification, 131
Biological Weapons Convention of 1972, 134
Biotoxins, 144
Blood agents, 150
Botulinum toxin, 174
Brockovich-PG&E case, 179
Bubonic plague, 183
Carbon monoxide poisoning, 198
Chemical agents, 221
Chemical Biological Incident Response Force,
    U.S., 222
Chemical terrorism, 225
Chemical warfare, 228
Chemical Weapons Convention of 1993, 230
Club drugs, 248
Crack cocaine, 299
Decontamination methods, 352
Ebola virus, 404
Escherichia coli, 418
Food poisoning, 481
Halcion, 576
Hallucinogens, 578
Hantavirus, 585
Hemorrhagic fevers, 588
Illicit substances, 616
Lead, 674
Mercury, 722

IDENTIFICATION. *See* **SUBSTANCE
IDENTIFICATION; SUSPECT
IDENTIFICATION; VICTIM
IDENTIFICATION; WEAPON
IDENTIFICATION**

**INJURIES, DISEASES, AND OTHER
MEDICAL CONDITIONS**

INVESTIGATION TYPES

INVESTIGATIVE TECHNIQUES

LAWS AND CONVENTIONS

LEGAL PRINCIPLES AND PROCEDURES

MEDIA DEPICTIONS OF THE FORENSIC SCIENCES

ORGANIZATIONS

SURVEILLANCE

TELEVISION. *See* MEDIA DEPICTIONS OF THE FORENSIC SCIENCES

Subject Index